Toyota RAV4 Automotive Repair Manual

**by Bob Henderson
and John H Haynes**

Member of the Guild of Motoring Writers

Models covered:

All Toyota RAV4 models
1996 through 2005

(92082 - 5L3)

ABCDE
FGHIJ
KLM

Haynes Publishing Group
Sparkford Nr Yeovil
Somerset BA22 7JJ England

Haynes North America, Inc
861 Lawrence Drive
Newbury Park
California 91320 USA

About this manual

Its purpose

The purpose of this manual is to help you get the best value from your vehicle. It can do so in several ways. It can help you decide what work must be done, even if you choose to have it done by a dealer service department or a repair shop; it provides information and procedures for routine maintenance and servicing; and it offers diagnostic and repair procedures to follow when trouble occurs.

We hope you use the manual to tackle the work yourself. For many simpler jobs, doing it yourself may be quicker than arranging an appointment to get the vehicle into a shop and making the trips to leave it and pick it up. More importantly, a lot of money can be saved by avoiding the expense the shop must pass on to you to cover its labor and overhead costs. An added benefit is the sense of satisfaction and accomplishment that you feel after doing the job yourself.

Using the manual

The manual is divided into Chapters. Each Chapter is divided into numbered Sections, which are headed in bold type between horizontal lines. Each Section consists of consecutively numbered paragraphs.

At the beginning of each numbered Section you will be referred to any illustrations which apply to the procedures in that Section. The reference numbers used in illustration captions pinpoint the pertinent Section and the Step within that Section. That is, illustration 3.2 means the illustration refers to Section 3 and Step (or paragraph) 2 within that Section.

Procedures, once described in the text, are not normally repeated. When it's necessary to refer to another Chapter, the reference will be given as Chapter and Section number. Cross references given without use of the word "Chapter" apply to Sections and/or paragraphs in the same Chapter. For example, "see Section 8" means in the same Chapter.

References to the left or right side of the vehicle assume you are sitting in the driver's seat, facing forward.

Even though we have prepared this manual with extreme care, neither the publisher nor the author can accept responsibility for any errors in, or omissions from, the information given.

NOTE

A **Note** provides Information necessary to properly complete a procedure or information which will make the procedure easier to understand.

CAUTION

A **Caution** provides a special procedure or special steps which must be taken while completing the procedure where the Caution is found. Not heeding a Caution can result in damage to the assembly being worked on.

WARNING

A **Warning** provides a special procedure or special steps which must be taken while completing the procedure where the Warning is found. Not heeding a Warning can result in personal injury.

Acknowledgements

We are grateful for the help and cooperation of the Toyota Motor Corporation for their assistance with technical information and certain illustrations. Technical writers who contributed to this project include Jeff Kibler, Rob Maddox, John Wegmann and Jamie Sarté.

© Haynes North America, Inc. 2002, 2007

With permission from J.H. Haynes & Co. Ltd.

A book in the Haynes Automotive Repair Manual Series

Printed in the U.S.A.

ISBN-13: 978-1-56392-695-2
ISBN-10: 1-56392-695-4

Library of Congress Control Number 2007938123

Contents

Introductory pages
About this manual   0-2
Introduction to the Toyota RAV4   0-4
Vehicle identification numbers   0-5
Buying parts   0-6
Maintenance techniques, tools and working facilities   0-6
Jacking and towing   0-12
Booster battery (jump) starting   0-13
Automotive chemicals and lubricants   0-14
Conversion factors   0-15
Fraction/decimal/millimeter equivalents   0-16
Safety first!   0-17
Troubleshooting   0-18

Chapter 1
Tune-up and routine maintenance   1-1

Chapter 2   Part A
Engines - 2000 and earlier   2A-1

Chapter 2   Part B
Engines - 2001 and later   2B-1

Chapter 2   Part C
General engine overhaul procedures   2C-1

Chapter 3
Cooling, heating and air conditioning systems   3-1

Chapter 4
Fuel and exhaust systems   4-1

Chapter 5
Engine electrical systems   5-1

Chapter 6
Emissions and engine control systems   6-1

Chapter 7   Part A
Manual transaxle   7A-1

Chapter 7   Part B
Automatic transaxle   7B-1

Chapter 8
Clutch and driveline   8-1

Chapter 9
Brakes   9-1

Chapter 10
Suspension and steering systems   10-1

Chapter 11
Body   11-1

Chapter 12
Chassis electrical system   12-1

Wiring diagrams   12-25

Index   IND-1

Haynes mechanic, author and photographer with 2002 RAV4

Introduction to the Toyota RAV4

Toyota RAV4 models are available in two- and four-door body styles through model year 2000; 2001 and later models all have four-doors.

The transversely mounted inline four-cylinder engines used in these vehicles are equipped with electronic fuel injection.

The engine drives the front wheels through either a five-speed manual or a four-speed automatic transaxle via independent driveaxles. On 4WD models the rear wheels are also propelled, via a driveshaft, rear differential, and two rear driveaxles.

Suspension is independent at all four wheels, MacPherson struts being used at the front end and trailing arms, control arms, coil springs and telescopic shock absorbers at the rear. The rack-and-pinion steering unit is mounted on the suspension crossmember.

The brakes are disc at the front and drums at the rear, with power assist standard. Some models are equipped with an optional Anti-lock Brake System (ABS). Some 2003 and later models are equiped with rear disc brakes.

Vehicle identification numbers

Modifications are a continuing and unpublicized process in vehicle manufacturing. Since spare parts manuals and lists are compiled on a numerical basis, the individual vehicle numbers are essential to correctly identify the component required.

Vehicle Identification Number (VIN)

This very important identification number is stamped on the firewall in the engine compartment and, on 1997 and later models, on a plate attached to the dashboard inside the windshield on the driver's side of the vehicle

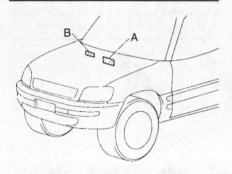

Location of the Manufacturer's Plate (A) and the Vehicle Identification Number (VIN) (B) on 1996 models

(see illustrations). The VIN also appears on the Vehicle Certificate of Title and Registration. It contains information such as where and when the vehicle was manufactured, the model year and the body style.

Manufacturer's Certification Regulation label

The Manufacturer's Certification Regulation label is attached to the driver's side door end or post (see illustration). The label

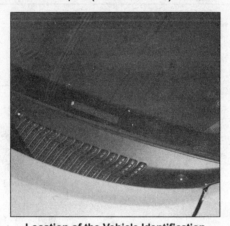

Location of the Vehicle Identification Number (VIN) which is visible through the driver's side of the windshield on 1997 and later models

contains the name of the manufacturer, the month and year of production, the Gross Vehicle Weight Rating (GVWR), the Gross Axle Weight Rating (GAWR) and the certification statement.

VIN model year code

Counting from the left, the model year code letter designation is the 10th character. On all models covered by this manual the model year codes are:

T	1996
V	1997
W	1998
X	1999
Y	2000
1	2001
2	2002
3	2003
4	2004
5	2005
6	2006

Engine number

The engine code number is stamped into a machined pad on the right end (driver's side) of the engine on 2000 and earlier models (see illustration). On 2001 and later models, it can be found on a pad on the front (radiator) side of the cylinder block (see illustration).

Location of the Manufacturer's Certification Regulation label on 1997 and later models

Location of the engine identification number - 2000 and earlier models

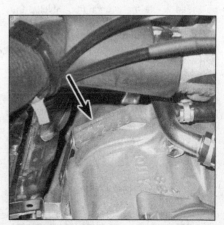

Location of the engine identification number - 2001 and later models

Buying parts

Replacement parts are available from many sources, which generally fall into one of two categories - authorized dealer parts departments and independent retail auto parts stores. Our advice concerning these parts is as follows:

Retail auto parts stores: Good auto parts stores will stock frequently needed components which wear out relatively fast, such as clutch components, exhaust systems, brake parts, tune-up parts, etc. These stores often supply new or reconditioned parts on an exchange basis, which can save a considerable amount of money. Discount auto parts stores are often very good places to buy materials and parts needed for general vehicle maintenance such as oil, grease, filters, spark plugs, belts, touch-up paint, bulbs, etc. They also usually sell tools and general accessories, have convenient hours, charge lower prices and can often be found not far from home.

Authorized dealer parts department: This is the best source for parts which are unique to the vehicle and not generally available elsewhere (such as major engine parts, transmission parts, trim pieces, etc.).

Warranty information: If the vehicle is still covered under warranty, be sure that any replacement parts purchased - regardless of the source - do not invalidate the warranty!

To be sure of obtaining the correct parts, have engine and chassis numbers available and, if possible, take the old parts along for positive identification.

Maintenance techniques, tools and working facilities

Maintenance techniques

There are a number of techniques involved in maintenance and repair that will be referred to throughout this manual. Application of these techniques will enable the home mechanic to be more efficient, better organized and capable of performing the various tasks properly, which will ensure that the repair job is thorough and complete.

Fasteners

Fasteners are nuts, bolts, studs and screws used to hold two or more parts together. There are a few things to keep in mind when working with fasteners. Almost all of them use a locking device of some type, either a lockwasher, locknut, locking tab or thread adhesive. All threaded fasteners should be clean and straight, with undamaged threads and undamaged corners on the hex head where the wrench fits. Develop the habit of replacing all damaged nuts and bolts with new ones. Special locknuts with nylon or fiber inserts can only be used once. If they are removed, they lose their locking ability and must be replaced with new ones.

Rusted nuts and bolts should be treated with a penetrating fluid to ease removal and prevent breakage. Some mechanics use turpentine in a spout-type oil can, which works quite well. After applying the rust penetrant, let it work for a few minutes before trying to loosen the nut or bolt. Badly rusted fasteners may have to be chiseled or sawed off or removed with a special nut breaker, available at tool stores.

If a bolt or stud breaks off in an assembly, it can be drilled and removed with a special tool commonly available for this purpose.

Most automotive machine shops can perform this task, as well as other repair procedures, such as the repair of threaded holes that have been stripped out.

Flat washers and lockwashers, when removed from an assembly, should always be replaced exactly as removed. Replace any damaged washers with new ones. Never use a lockwasher on any soft metal surface (such as aluminum), thin sheet metal or plastic.

Grade 1 or 2   Grade 5   Grade 8

Bolt strength marking (standard/SAE/USS; bottom - metric)

Grade	Identification	Grade	Identification
Hex Nut Grade 5	3 Dots	Hex Nut Property Class 9	Arabic 9
Hex Nut Grade 8	6 Dots	Hex Nut Property Class 10	Arabic 10

Standard hex nut strength markings

Metric hex nut strength markings

Class 10.9   Class 9.8   Class 8.8

Metric stud strength markings

00-1 HAYNES

Fastener sizes

For a number of reasons, automobile manufacturers are making wider and wider use of metric fasteners. Therefore, it is important to be able to tell the difference between standard (sometimes called U.S. or SAE) and metric hardware, since they cannot be interchanged.

All bolts, whether standard or metric, are sized according to diameter, thread pitch and length. For example, a standard 1/2 - 13 x 1 bolt is 1/2 inch in diameter, has 13 threads per inch and is 1 inch long. An M12 - 1.75 x 25 metric bolt is 12 mm in diameter, has a thread pitch of 1.75 mm (the distance between threads) and is 25 mm long. The two bolts are nearly identical, and easily confused, but they are not interchangeable.

In addition to the differences in diameter, thread pitch and length, metric and standard bolts can also be distinguished by examining the bolt heads. To begin with, the distance across the flats on a standard bolt head is measured in inches, while the same dimension on a metric bolt is sized in millimeters (the same is true for nuts). As a result, a standard wrench should not be used on a metric bolt and a metric wrench should not be used on a standard bolt. Also, most standard bolts have slashes radiating out from the center of the head to denote the grade or strength of the bolt, which is an indication of the amount of torque that can be applied to it. The greater the number of slashes, the greater the strength of the bolt. Grades 0 through 5 are commonly used on automobiles. Metric bolts have a property class (grade) number, rather than a slash, molded into their heads to indicate bolt strength. In this case, the higher the number, the stronger the bolt. Property class numbers 8.8, 9.8 and 10.9 are commonly used on automobiles.

Strength markings can also be used to distinguish standard hex nuts from metric hex nuts. Many standard nuts have dots stamped into one side, while metric nuts are marked with a number. The greater the number of dots, or the higher the number, the greater the strength of the nut.

Metric studs are also marked on their ends according to property class (grade). Larger studs are numbered (the same as metric bolts), while smaller studs carry a geometric code to denote grade.

It should be noted that many fasteners, especially Grades 0 through 2, have no distinguishing marks on them. When such is the case, the only way to determine whether it is standard or metric is to measure the thread pitch or compare it to a known fastener of the same size.

Standard fasteners are often referred to as SAE, as opposed to metric. However, it should be noted that SAE technically refers to a non-metric fine thread fastener only. Coarse thread non-metric fasteners are referred to as USS sizes.

Since fasteners of the same size (both standard and metric) may have different strength ratings, be sure to reinstall any bolts,

Metric thread sizes

	Ft-lbs	Nm
M-6	6 to 9	9 to 12
M-8	14 to 21	19 to 28
M-10	28 to 40	38 to 54
M-12	50 to 71	68 to 96
M-14	80 to 140	109 to 154

Pipe thread sizes

1/8	5 to 8	7 to 10
1/4	12 to 18	17 to 24
3/8	22 to 33	30 to 44
1/2	25 to 35	34 to 47

U.S. thread sizes

1/4 - 20	6 to 9	9 to 12
5/16 - 18	12 to 18	17 to 24
5/16 - 24	14 to 20	19 to 27
3/8 - 16	22 to 32	30 to 43
3/8 - 24	27 to 38	37 to 51
7/16 - 14	40 to 55	55 to 74
7/16 - 20	40 to 60	55 to 81
1/2 - 13	55 to 80	75 to 108

Standard (SAE and USS) bolt dimensions/ grade marks

G　Grade marks (bolt strength)
L　Length (in inches)
T　Thread pitch (number of threads per inch)
D　Nominal diameter (in inches)

Metric bolt dimensions/grade marks

P　Property class (bolt strength)
L　Length (in millimeters)
T　Thread pitch (distance between threads in millimeters)
D　Diameter

studs or nuts removed from your vehicle in their original locations. Also, when replacing a fastener with a new one, make sure that the new one has a strength rating equal to or greater than the original.

Tightening sequences and procedures

Most threaded fasteners should be tightened to a specific torque value (torque is the twisting force applied to a threaded component such as a nut or bolt). Overtightening the fastener can weaken it and cause it to break, while undertightening can cause it to eventually come loose. Bolts, screws and studs, depending on the material they are made of and their thread diameters, have specific

torque values, many of which are noted in the Specifications at the beginning of each Chapter. Be sure to follow the torque recommendations closely. For fasteners not assigned a specific torque, a general torque value chart is presented here as a guide. These torque values are for dry (unlubricated) fasteners threaded into steel or cast iron (not aluminum). As was previously mentioned, the size and grade of a fastener determine the amount of torque that can safely be applied to it. The figures listed here are approximate for Grade 2 and Grade 3 fasteners. Higher grades can tolerate higher torque values.

Fasteners laid out in a pattern, su cylinder head bolts, oil pan bolts, diff cover bolts, etc., must be loosened ened in sequence to avoid warpin

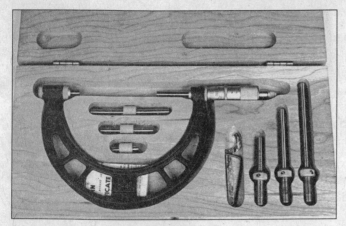

Micrometer set

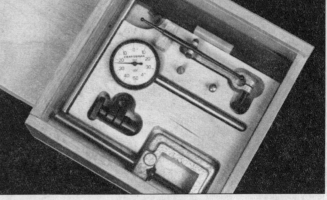

Dial indicator set

ponent. This sequence will normally be shown in the appropriate Chapter. If a specific pattern is not given, the following procedures can be used to prevent warping.

Initially, the bolts or nuts should be assembled finger-tight only. Next, they should be tightened one full turn each, in a criss-cross or diagonal pattern. After each one has been tightened one full turn, return to the first one and tighten them all one-half turn, following the same pattern. Finally, tighten each of them one-quarter turn at a time until each fastener has been tightened to the proper torque. To loosen and remove the fasteners, the procedure would be reversed.

Component disassembly

Component disassembly should be done with care and purpose to help ensure that the parts go back together properly. Always keep track of the sequence in which parts are removed. Make note of special characteristics or marks on parts that can be installed more than one way, such as a grooved thrust washer on a shaft. It is a good idea to lay the disassembled parts out on a clean surface in the order that they were removed. It may also be helpful to make sketches or take instant photos of components before removal.

When removing fasteners from a component, keep track of their locations. Sometimes threading a bolt back in a part, or putting the washers and nut back on a stud, can prevent mix-ups later. If nuts and bolts cannot be returned to their original locations, they should be kept in a compartmented box or a series of small boxes. A cupcake or muffin tin is ideal for this purpose, since each cavity can hold the bolts and nuts from a particular area (i.e. oil pan bolts, valve cover bolts, engine mount bolts, etc.). A pan of this type is especially help-
~~ working on assemblies with very small~~
~~as the carburetor, alternator, valve~~
~~dash and trim pieces. The cavi-~~
~~ked with paint or tape to identify~~

~~wiring looms, harnesses or~~
~~arated, it is a good idea to~~
~~es with numbered pieces~~
~~ey can be easily recon-~~
nected.

Gasket sealing surfaces

Throughout any vehicle, gaskets are used to seal the mating surfaces between two parts and keep lubricants, fluids, vacuum or pressure contained in an assembly.

Many times these gaskets are coated with a liquid or paste-type gasket sealing compound before assembly. Age, heat and pressure can sometimes cause the two parts to stick together so tightly that they are very difficult to separate. Often, the assembly can be loosened by striking it with a soft-face hammer near the mating surfaces. A regular hammer can be used if a block of wood is placed between the hammer and the part. Do not hammer on cast parts or parts that could be easily damaged. With any particularly stubborn part, always recheck to make sure that every fastener has been removed.

Avoid using a screwdriver or bar to pry apart an assembly, as they can easily mar the gasket sealing surfaces of the parts, which must remain smooth. If prying is absolutely necessary, use an old broom handle, but keep in mind that extra clean up will be necessary if the wood splinters.

After the parts are separated, the old gasket must be carefully scraped off and the gasket surfaces cleaned. Stubborn gasket material can be soaked with rust penetrant or treated with a special chemical to soften it so it can be easily scraped off. A scraper can be fashioned from a piece of copper tubing by flattening and sharpening one end. Copper is recommended because it is usually softer than the surfaces to be scraped, which reduces the chance of gouging the part. Some gaskets can be removed with a wire brush, but regardless of the method used, the mating surfaces must be left clean and smooth. If for some reason the gasket surface is gouged, then a gasket sealer thick enough to fill scratches will have to be used during reassembly of the components. For most applications, a non-drying (or semi-drying) gasket sealer should be used.

Hose removal tips

Warning: *If the vehicle is equipped with air*

conditioning, do not disconnect any of the A/C hoses without first having the system depressurized by a dealer service department or a service station.

Hose removal precautions closely parallel gasket removal precautions. Avoid scratching or gouging the surface that the hose mates against or the connection may leak. This is especially true for radiator hoses. Because of various chemical reactions, the rubber in hoses can bond itself to the metal spigot that the hose fits over. To remove a hose, first loosen the hose clamps that secure it to the spigot. Then, with slip-joint pliers, grab the hose at the clamp and rotate it around the spigot. Work it back and forth until it is completely free, then pull it off. Silicone or other lubricants will ease removal if they can be applied between the hose and the outside of the spigot. Apply the same lubricant to the inside of the hose and the outside of the spigot to simplify installation.

As a last resort (and if the hose is to be replaced with a new one anyway), the rubber can be slit with a knife and the hose peeled from the spigot. If this must be done, be careful that the metal connection is not damaged.

If a hose clamp is broken or damaged, do not reuse it. Wire-type clamps usually weaken with age, so it is a good idea to replace them with screw-type clamps whenever a hose is removed.

Tools

A selection of good tools is a basic requirement for anyone who plans to maintain and repair his or her own vehicle. For the owner who has few tools, the initial investment might seem high, but when compared to the spiraling costs of professional auto maintenance and repair, it is a wise one.

To help the owner decide which tools are needed to perform the tasks detailed in this manual, the following tool lists are offered: *Maintenance and minor repair, Repair/overhaul* and *Special*.

The newcomer to practical mechanics should start off with the *maintenance and minor repair* tool kit, which is adequate for the simpler jobs performed on a vehicle. Then, as

Dial caliper

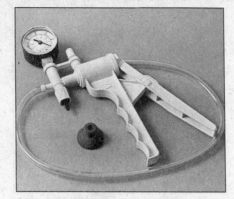

Hand-operated vacuum pump

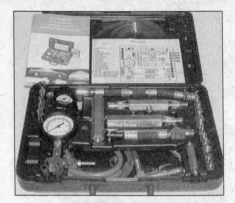

Pressure gauge

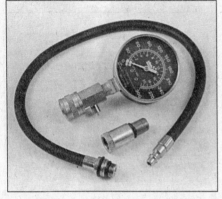

Compression gauge with spark plug hole adapter

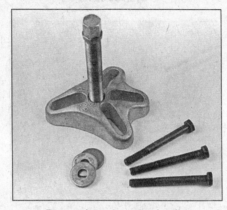

Damper/steering wheel puller

General purpose puller

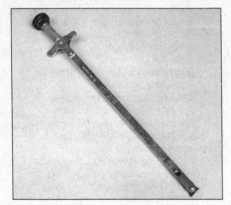

Hydraulic lifter removal tool

Valve spring compressor

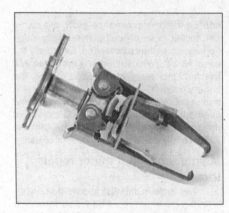

Valve spring compressor

Ridge reamer

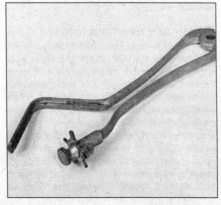

Piston ring groove cleaning tool

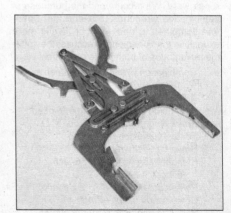

Ring removal/installation tool

Ring compressor

Cylinder hone

Brake hold-down spring tool

Torque angle gauge

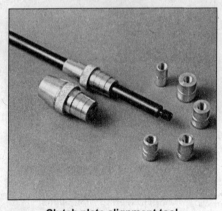

Clutch plate alignment tool

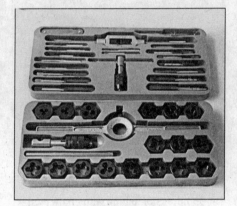

Tap and die set

confidence and experience grow, the owner can tackle more difficult tasks, buying additional tools as they are needed. Eventually the basic kit will be expanded into the *repair and overhaul* tool set. Over a period of time, the experienced do-it-yourselfer will assemble a tool set complete enough for most repair and overhaul procedures and will add tools from the special category when it is felt that the expense is justified by the frequency of use.

Maintenance and minor repair tool kit

The tools in this list should be considered the minimum required for performance of routine maintenance, servicing and minor repair work. We recommend the purchase of combination wrenches (box-end and open-end combined in one wrench). While more expensive than open end wrenches, they offer the advantages of both types of wrench.

> *Combination wrench set (1/4-inch to 1 inch or 6 mm to 19 mm)*
> *Adjustable wrench, 8 inch*
> *Spark plug wrench with rubber insert*
> *Spark plug gap adjusting tool*
> *Feeler gauge set*
> *Brake bleeder wrench*
> *Standard screwdriver (5/16-inch x 6 inch)*
> *Phillips screwdriver (No. 2 x 6 inch)*
> *Combination pliers - 6 inch*
> *Hacksaw and assortment of blades*
> *Tire pressure gauge*

> *Grease gun*
> *Oil can*
> *Fine emery cloth*
> *Wire brush*
> *Battery post and cable cleaning tool*
> *Oil filter wrench*
> *Funnel (medium size)*
> *Safety goggles*
> *Jackstands (2)*
> *Drain pan*

Note: *If basic tune-ups are going to be part of routine maintenance, it will be necessary to purchase a good quality stroboscopic timing light and combination tachometer/dwell meter. Although they are included in the list of special tools, it is mentioned here because they are absolutely necessary for tuning most vehicles properly.*

Repair and overhaul tool set

These tools are essential for anyone who plans to perform major repairs and are in addition to those in the maintenance and minor repair tool kit. Included is a comprehensive set of sockets which, though expensive, are invaluable because of their versatility, especially when various extensions and drives are available. We recommend the 1/2-inch drive over the 3/8-inch drive. Although the larger drive is bulky and more expensive, it has the capacity of accepting a very wide range of large sockets. Ideally, however, the mechanic should have a 3/8-inch drive set and a 1/2-inch drive set.

> *Socket set(s)*
> *Reversible ratchet*
> *Extension - 10 inch*
> *Universal joint*
> *Torque wrench (same size drive as sockets)*
> *Ball peen hammer - 8 ounce*
> *Soft-face hammer (plastic/rubber)*
> *Standard screwdriver (1/4-inch x 6 inch)*
> *Standard screwdriver (stubby - 5/16-inch)*
> *Phillips screwdriver (No. 3 x 8 inch)*
> *Phillips screwdriver (stubby - No. 2)*
> *Pliers - vise grip*
> *Pliers - lineman's*
> *Pliers - needle nose*
> *Pliers - snap-ring (internal and external)*
> *Cold chisel - 1/2-inch*
> *Scribe*
> *Scraper (made from flattened copper tubing)*
> *Centerpunch*
> *Pin punches (1/16, 1/8, 3/16-inch)*
> *Steel rule/straightedge - 12 inch*
> *Allen wrench set (1/8 to 3/8-inch or 4 mm to 10 mm)*
> *A selection of files*
> *Wire brush (large)*
> *Jackstands (second set)*
> *Jack (scissor or hydraulic type)*

Note: *Another tool which is often useful is an electric drill with a chuck capacity of 3/8-inch and a set of good quality drill bits.*

Special tools

The tools in this list include those which are not used regularly, are expensive to buy, or which need to be used in accordance with their manufacturer's instructions. Unless these tools will be used frequently, it is not very economical to purchase many of them. A consideration would be to split the cost and use between yourself and a friend or friends. In addition, most of these tools can be obtained from a tool rental shop on a temporary basis.

This list primarily contains only those tools and instruments widely available to the public, and not those special tools produced by the vehicle manufacturer for distribution to dealer service departments. Occasionally, references to the manufacturer's special tools are included in the text of this manual. Generally, an alternative method of doing the job without the special tool is offered. However, sometimes there is no alternative to their use. Where this is the case, and the tool cannot be purchased or borrowed, the work should be turned over to the dealer service department or an automotive repair shop.

Valve spring compressor
Piston ring groove cleaning tool
Piston ring compressor
Piston ring installation tool
Cylinder compression gauge
Cylinder ridge reamer
Cylinder surfacing hone
Cylinder bore gauge
Micrometers and/or dial calipers
Hydraulic lifter removal tool
Balljoint separator
Universal-type puller
Impact screwdriver
Dial indicator set
Stroboscopic timing light (inductive pick-up)
Hand operated vacuum/pressure pump
Tachometer/dwell meter
Universal electrical multimeter
Cable hoist
Brake spring removal and installation tools
Floor jack

Buying tools

For the do-it-yourselfer who is just starting to get involved in vehicle maintenance and repair, there are a number of options available when purchasing tools. If maintenance and minor repair is the extent of the work to be done, the purchase of individual tools is satisfactory. If, on the other hand, extensive work is planned, it would be a good idea to purchase a modest tool set from one of the large retail chain stores. A set can usually be bought at a substantial savings over the individual tool prices, and they often come with a tool box. As additional tools are needed, add-on sets, individual tools and a larger tool box can be purchased to expand the tool selection. Building a tool set gradually allows the cost of the tools to be spread over a longer period of time and gives the mechanic the freedom to choose only those tools that will actually be used.

Tool stores will often be the only source of some of the special tools that are needed, but regardless of where tools are bought, try to avoid cheap ones, especially when buying screwdrivers and sockets, because they won't last very long. The expense involved in replacing cheap tools will eventually be greater than the initial cost of quality tools.

Care and maintenance of tools

Good tools are expensive, so it makes sense to treat them with respect. Keep them clean and in usable condition and store them properly when not in use. Always wipe off any dirt, grease or metal chips before putting them away. Never leave tools lying around in the work area. Upon completion of a job, always check closely under the hood for tools that may have been left there so they won't get lost during a test drive.

Some tools, such as screwdrivers, pliers, wrenches and sockets, can be hung on a panel mounted on the garage or workshop wall, while others should be kept in a tool box or tray. Measuring instruments, gauges, meters, etc. must be carefully stored where they cannot be damaged by weather or impact from other tools.

When tools are used with care and stored properly, they will last a very long time. Even with the best of care, though, tools will wear out if used frequently. When a tool is damaged or worn out, replace it. Subsequent jobs will be safer and more enjoyable if you do.

How to repair damaged threads

Sometimes, the internal threads of a nut or bolt hole can become stripped, usually from overtightening. Stripping threads is an all-too-common occurrence, especially when working with aluminum parts, because aluminum is so soft that it easily strips out.

Usually, external or internal threads are only partially stripped. After they've been cleaned up with a tap or die, they'll still work. Sometimes, however, threads are badly damaged. When this happens, you've got three choices:

1) *Drill and tap the hole to the next suitable oversize and install a larger diameter bolt, screw or stud.*
2) *Drill and tap the hole to accept a threaded plug, then drill and tap the plug to the original screw size. You can also buy a plug already threaded to the original size. Then you simply drill a hole to the specified size, then run the threaded plug into the hole with a bolt and jam nut. Once the plug is fully seated, remove the jam nut and bolt.*
3) *The third method uses a patented thread repair kit like Heli-Coil or Slimsert. These easy-to-use kits are designed to repair damaged threads in straight-through holes and blind holes. Both are available as kits which can handle a variety of sizes and thread patterns. Drill the hole, then tap it with the special included tap. Install the Heli-Coil and the hole is back to its original diameter and thread pitch.*

Regardless of which method you use, be sure to proceed calmly and carefully. A little impatience or carelessness during one of these relatively simple procedures can ruin your whole day's work and cost you a bundle if you wreck an expensive part.

Working facilities

Not to be overlooked when discussing tools is the workshop. If anything more than routine maintenance is to be carried out, some sort of suitable work area is essential.

It is understood, and appreciated, that many home mechanics do not have a good workshop or garage available, and end up removing an engine or doing major repairs outside. It is recommended, however, that the overhaul or repair be completed under the cover of a roof.

A clean, flat workbench or table of comfortable working height is an absolute necessity. The workbench should be equipped with a vise that has a jaw opening of at least four inches.

As mentioned previously, some clean, dry storage space is also required for tools, as well as the lubricants, fluids, cleaning solvents, etc. which soon become necessary.

Sometimes waste oil and fluids, drained from the engine or cooling system during normal maintenance or repairs, present a disposal problem. To avoid pouring them on the ground or into a sewage system, pour the used fluids into large containers, seal them with caps and take them to an authorized disposal site or recycling center. Plastic jugs, such as old antifreeze containers, are ideal for this purpose.

Always keep a supply of old newspapers and clean rags available. Old towels are excellent for mopping up spills. Many mechanics use rolls of paper towels for most work because they are readily available and disposable. To help keep the area under the vehicle clean, a large cardboard box can be cut open and flattened to protect the garage or shop floor.

Whenever working over a painted surface, such as when leaning over a fender to service something under the hood, always cover it with an old blanket or bedspread to protect the finish. Vinyl covered pads, made especially for this purpose, are available at auto parts stores.

Jacking and towing

Jacking

Warning: *The jack supplied with the vehicle should only be used for changing a tire or placing jackstands under the frame. Never work under the vehicle or start the engine while this jack is being used as the only means of support.*

The vehicle should be on level ground. Place the shift lever in Park, if you have an automatic, or Reverse if you have a manual transaxle. Block the wheel diagonally opposite the wheel being changed. Set the parking brake.

Remove the spare tire and jack from stowage. Remove the wheel cover and trim ring (if so equipped) with the tapered end of the lug nut wrench by inserting and twisting the handle and then prying against the back of the wheel cover. Loosen, but do not remove, the lug nuts (one-half turn is sufficient).

Place the scissors-type jack under the vehicle and adjust the jack height until it engages with the proper jacking point. There is a front and rear jacking point on each side of the vehicle **(see illustrations)**.

Turn the jack handle clockwise until the tire clears the ground. Remove the lug nuts and pull the wheel off. Replace it with the spare.

Install the lug nuts with the beveled edges facing in. Tighten them snugly. Don't attempt to tighten them completely until the vehicle is lowered or it could slip off the jack. Turn the jack handle counterclockwise to lower the vehicle. Remove the jack and tighten the lug nuts in a diagonal pattern.

Install the cover (and trim ring, if used) and be sure it's snapped into place all the way around.

Stow the tire, jack and wrench. Unblock the wheels.

Towing

Two-wheel drive models can be towed from the front with the front wheels off the ground, using a wheel lift type tow truck. If towed from the rear, the front wheels must be placed on a dolly. Four wheel drive models must be towed with all four wheels off the ground. A sling-type tow truck cannot be used, as body damage will result. The best way to tow the vehicle is with a flat-bed car carrier.

In an emergency the vehicle can be towed a short distance with a cable or chain attached to one of the towing eyelets located under the front or rear bumpers. The driver must remain in the vehicle to operate the steering and brakes (remember that power steering and power brakes will not work with the engine off).

Front jacking location (place the jack head under the control arm rear bushing clamp) - 2000 and earlier models

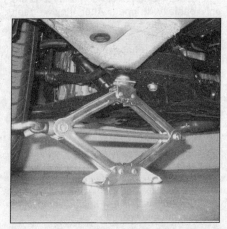

Front jacking location (place the jack head under the control arm rear bushing bolt) - 2001 and later models

Rear jacking location (place the jack head under the protrusion on the trailing arm) - all models

Booster battery (jump) starting

Observe these precautions when using a booster battery to start a vehicle:

a) *Before connecting the booster battery, make sure the ignition switch is in the Off position.*
b) *Turn off the lights, heater and other electrical loads.*
c) *Your eyes should be shielded. Safety goggles are a good idea.*
d) *Make sure the booster battery is the same voltage as the dead one in the vehicle.*
e) *The two vehicles MUST NOT TOUCH each other!*
f) *Make sure the transaxle is in Neutral (manual) or Park (automatic).*
g) *If the booster battery is not a maintenance-free type, remove the vent caps and lay a cloth over the vent holes.*

Connect the red jumper cable to the positive (+) terminals of each battery **(see illustration)**.

Connect one end of the black jumper cable to the negative (-) terminal of the booster battery. The other end of this cable should be connected to a good ground on the vehicle to be started, such as a bolt or bracket on the body.

Start the engine using the booster battery, then, with the engine running at idle speed, disconnect the jumper cables in the reverse order of connection.

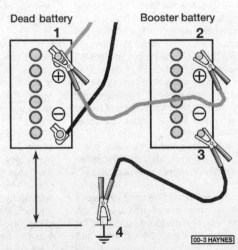

Make the booster battery cable connections in the numerical order shown (note that the negative cable of the booster battery is NOT attached to the negative terminal of the dead battery)

Automotive chemicals and lubricants

A number of automotive chemicals and lubricants are available for use during vehicle maintenance and repair. They include a wide variety of products ranging from cleaning solvents and degreasers to lubricants and protective sprays for rubber, plastic and vinyl.

Cleaners

Carburetor cleaner and choke cleaner is a strong solvent for gum, varnish and carbon. Most carburetor cleaners leave a dry-type lubricant film which will not harden or gum up. Because of this film it is not recommended for use on electrical components.

Brake system cleaner is used to remove brake dust, grease and brake fluid from the brake system, where clean surfaces are absolutely necessary. It leaves no residue and often eliminates brake squeal caused by contaminants.

Electrical cleaner removes oxidation, corrosion and carbon deposits from electrical contacts, restoring full current flow. It can also be used to clean spark plugs, carburetor jets, voltage regulators and other parts where an oil-free surface is desired.

Demoisturants remove water and moisture from electrical components such as alternators, voltage regulators, electrical connectors and fuse blocks. They are non-conductive and non-corrosive.

Degreasers are heavy-duty solvents used to remove grease from the outside of the engine and from chassis components. They can be sprayed or brushed on and, depending on the type, are rinsed off either with water or solvent.

Lubricants

Motor oil is the lubricant formulated for use in engines. It normally contains a wide variety of additives to prevent corrosion and reduce foaming and wear. Motor oil comes in various weights (viscosity ratings) from 0 to 50. The recommended weight of the oil depends on the season, temperature and the demands on the engine. Light oil is used in cold climates and under light load conditions. Heavy oil is used in hot climates and where high loads are encountered. Multi-viscosity oils are designed to have characteristics of both light and heavy oils and are available in a number of weights from 0W-20 to 20W-50.

Gear oil is designed to be used in differentials, manual transmissions and other areas where high-temperature lubrication is required.

Chassis and wheel bearing grease is a heavy grease used where increased loads and friction are encountered, such as for wheel bearings, balljoints, tie-rod ends and universal joints.

High-temperature wheel bearing grease is designed to withstand the extreme temperatures encountered by wheel bearings in disc brake equipped vehicles. It usually contains molybdenum disulfide (moly), which is a dry-type lubricant.

White grease is a heavy grease for metal-to-metal applications where water is a problem. White grease stays soft under both low and high temperatures (usually from -100 to +190-degrees F), and will not wash off or dilute in the presence of water.

Assembly lube is a special extreme pressure lubricant, usually containing moly, used to lubricate high-load parts (such as main and rod bearings and cam lobes) for initial start-up of a new engine. The assembly lube lubricates the parts without being squeezed out or washed away until the engine oiling system begins to function.

Silicone lubricants are used to protect rubber, plastic, vinyl and nylon parts.

Graphite lubricants are used where oils cannot be used due to contamination problems, such as in locks. The dry graphite will lubricate metal parts while remaining uncontaminated by dirt, water, oil or acids. It is electrically conductive and will not foul electrical contacts in locks such as the ignition switch.

Moly penetrants loosen and lubricate frozen, rusted and corroded fasteners and prevent future rusting or freezing.

Heat-sink grease is a special electrically non-conductive grease that is used for mounting electronic ignition modules where it is essential that heat is transferred away from the module.

Sealants

RTV sealant is one of the most widely used gasket compounds. Made from silicone, RTV is air curing, it seals, bonds, waterproofs, fills surface irregularities, remains flexible, doesn't shrink, is relatively easy to remove, and is used as a supplementary sealer with almost all low and medium temperature gaskets.

Anaerobic sealant is much like RTV in that it can be used either to seal gaskets or to form gaskets by itself. It remains flexible, is solvent resistant and fills surface imperfections. The difference between an anaerobic sealant and an RTV-type sealant is in the curing. RTV cures when exposed to air, while an anaerobic sealant cures only in the absence of air. This means that an anaerobic sealant cures only after the assembly of parts, sealing them together.

Thread and pipe sealant is used for sealing hydraulic and pneumatic fittings and vacuum lines. It is usually made from a Teflon compound, and comes in a spray, a paint-on liquid and as a wrap-around tape.

Chemicals

Anti-seize compound prevents seizing, galling, cold welding, rust and corrosion in fasteners. High-temperature ant-seize, usually made with copper and graphite lubricants, is used for exhaust system and exhaust manifold bolts.

Anaerobic locking compounds are used to keep fasteners from vibrating or working loose and cure only after installation, in the absence of air. Medium strength locking compound is used for small nuts, bolts and screws that may be removed later. High-strength locking compound is for large nuts, bolts and studs which aren't removed on a regular basis.

Oil additives range from viscosity index improvers to chemical treatments that claim to reduce internal engine friction. It should be noted that most oil manufacturers caution against using additives with their oils.

Gas additives perform several functions, depending on their chemical makeup. They usually contain solvents that help dissolve gum and varnish that build up on carburetor, fuel injection and intake parts. They also serve to break down carbon deposits that form on the inside surfaces of the combustion chambers. Some additives contain upper cylinder lubricants for valves and piston rings, and others contain chemicals to remove condensation from the gas tank.

Miscellaneous

Brake fluid is specially formulated hydraulic fluid that can withstand the heat and pressure encountered in brake systems. Care must be taken so this fluid does not come in contact with painted surfaces or plastics. An opened container should always be resealed to prevent contamination by water or dirt.

Weatherstrip adhesive is used to bond weatherstripping around doors, windows and trunk lids. It is sometimes used to attach trim pieces.

Undercoating is a petroleum-based, tar-like substance that is designed to protect metal surfaces on the underside of the vehicle from corrosion. It also acts as a sound-deadening agent by insulating the bottom of the vehicle.

Waxes and polishes are used to help protect painted and plated surfaces from the weather. Different types of paint may require the use of different types of wax and polish. Some polishes utilize a chemical or abrasive cleaner to help remove the top layer of oxidized (dull) paint on older vehicles. In recent years many non-wax polishes that contain a wide variety of chemicals such as polymers and silicones have been introduced. These non-wax polishes are usually easier to apply and last longer than conventional waxes and polishes.

Conversion factors

Length (distance)

Inches (in)	X	25.4	= Millimeters (mm)	X 0.0394	= Inches (in)
Feet (ft)	X	0.305	= Meters (m)	X 3.281	= Feet (ft)
Miles	X	1.609	= Kilometers (km)	X 0.621	= Miles

Volume (capacity)

Cubic inches (cu in; in^3)	X 16.387 = Cubic centimeters (cc; cm^3)	X 0.061 = Cubic inches (cu in; in^3)
Imperial pints (Imp pt)	X 0.568 = Liters (l)	X 1.76 = Imperial pints (Imp pt)
Imperial quarts (Imp qt)	X 1.137 = Liters (l)	X 0.88 = Imperial quarts (Imp qt)
Imperial quarts (Imp qt)	X 1.201 = US quarts (US qt)	X 0.833 = Imperial quarts (Imp qt)
US quarts (US qt)	X 0.946 = Liters (l)	X 1.057 = US quarts (US qt)
Imperial gallons (Imp gal)	X 4.546 = Liters (l)	X 0.22 = Imperial gallons (Imp gal)
Imperial gallons (Imp gal)	X 1.201 = US gallons (US gal)	X 0.833 = Imperial gallons (Imp gal)
US gallons (US gal)	X 3.785 = Liters (l)	X 0.264 = US gallons (US gal)

Mass (weight)

Ounces (oz)	X 28.35 = Grams (g)	X 0.035 = Ounces (oz)
Pounds (lb)	X 0.454 = Kilograms (kg)	X 2.205 = Pounds (lb)

Force

Ounces-force (ozf; oz)	X 0.278 = Newtons (N)	X 3.6 = Ounces-force (ozf; oz)
Pounds-force (lbf; lb)	X 4.448 = Newtons (N)	X 0.225 = Pounds-force (lbf; lb)
Newtons (N)	X 0.1 = Kilograms-force (kgf; kg)	X 9.81 = Newtons (N)

Pressure

Pounds-force per square inch (psi; lbf/in^2; lb/in^2)	X 0.070 = Kilograms-force per square centimeter (kgf/cm^2; kg/cm^2)	X 14.223 = Pounds-force per square inch (psi; lbf/in^2; lb/in^2)
Pounds-force per square inch (psi; lbf/in^2; lb/in^2)	X 0.068 = Atmospheres (atm)	X 14.696 = Pounds-force per square inch (psi; lbf/in^2; lb/in^2)
Pounds-force per square inch (psi; lbf/in^2; lb/in^2)	X 0.069 = Bars	X 14.5 = Pounds-force per square inch (psi; lbf/in^2; lb/in^2)
Pounds-force per square inch (psi; lbf/in^2; lb/in^2)	X 6.895 = Kilopascals (kPa)	X 0.145 = Pounds-force per square inch (psi; lbf/in^2; lb/in^2)
Kilopascals (kPa)	X 0.01 = Kilograms-force per square centimeter (kgf/cm^2; kg/cm^2)	X 98.1 = Kilopascals (kPa)

Torque (moment of force)

Pounds-force inches (lbf in; lb in)	X 1.152 = Kilograms-force centimeter (kgf cm; kg cm)	X 0.868 = Pounds-force inches (lbf in; lb in)
Pounds-force inches (lbf in; lb in)	X 0.113 = Newton meters (Nm)	X 8.85 = Pounds-force inches (lbf in; lb in)
Pounds-force inches (lbf in; lb in)	X 0.083 = Pounds-force feet (lbf ft; lb ft)	X 12 = Pounds-force inches (lbf in; lb in)
Pounds-force feet (lbf ft; lb ft)	X 0.138 = Kilograms-force meters (kgf m; kg m)	X 7.233 = Pounds-force feet (lbf ft; lb ft)
Pounds-force feet (lbf ft; lb ft)	X 1.356 = Newton meters (Nm)	X 0.738 = Pounds-force feet (lbf ft; lb ft)
Newton meters (Nm)	X 0.102 = Kilograms-force meters (kgf m; kg m)	X 9.804 = Newton meters (Nm)

Vacuum

Inches mercury (in. Hg)	X 3.377 = Kilopascals (kPa)	X 0.2961 = Inches mercury
Inches mercury (in. Hg)	X 25.4 = Millimeters mercury (mm Hg)	X 0.0394 = Inches mercury

Power

Horsepower (hp)	X 745.7 = Watts (W)	X 0.0013 = Horsepower (hp)

Velocity (speed)

Miles per hour (miles/hr; mph)	X 1.609 = Kilometers per hour (km/hr; kph)	X 0.621 = Miles per hour (miles/hr; mph)

Fuel consumption*

Miles per gallon, Imperial (mpg)	X 0.354 = Kilometers per liter (km/l)	X 2.825 = Miles per gallon, Imperial (mpg)
Miles per gallon, US (mpg)	X 0.425 = Kilometers per liter (km/l)	X 2.352 = Miles per gallon, US (mpg)

Temperature

Degrees Fahrenheit = (°C x 1.8) + 32

Degrees Celsius (Degrees Centigrade; °C) = (°F - 32) x 0.56

*It is common practice to convert from miles per gallon (mpg) to liters/100 kilometers (l/100km), where mpg (Imperial) x l/100 km = 282 and mpg (US) x l/100 km = 235

DECIMALS to MILLIMETERS

Decimal	mm	Decimal	mm
0.001	0.0254	0.500	12.7000
0.002	0.0508	0.510	12.9540
0.003	0.0762	0.520	13.2080
0.004	0.1016	0.530	13.4620
0.005	0.1270	0.540	13.7160
0.006	0.1524	0.550	13.9700
0.007	0.1778	0.560	14.2240
0.008	0.2032	0.570	14.4780
0.009	0.2286	0.580	14.7320
		0.590	14.9860
0.010	0.2540		
0.020	0.5080		
0.030	0.7620		
0.040	1.0160	0.600	15.2400
0.050	1.2700	0.610	15.4940
0.060	1.5240	0.620	15.7480
0.070	1.7780	0.630	16.0020
0.080	2.0320	0.640	16.2560
0.090	2.2860	0.650	16.5100
		0.660	16.7640
0.100	2.5400	0.670	17.0180
0.110	2.7940	0.680	17.2720
0.120	3.0480	0.690	17.5260
0.130	3.3020		
0.140	3.5560		
0.150	3.8100		
0.160	4.0640	0.700	17.7800
0.170	4.3180	0.710	18.0340
0.180	4.5720	0.720	18.2880
0.190	4.8260	0.730	18.5420
		0.740	18.7960
0.200	5.0800	0.750	19.0500
0.210	5.3340	0.760	19.3040
0.220	5.5880	0.770	19.5580
0.230	5.8420	0.780	19.8120
0.240	6.0960	0.790	20.0660
0.250	6.3500		
0.260	6.6040		
0.270	6.8580	0.800	20.3200
0.280	7.1120	0.810	20.5740
0.290	7.3660	0.820	21.8280
		0.830	21.0820
0.300	7.6200	0.840	21.3360
0.310	7.8740	0.850	21.5900
0.320	8.1280	0.860	21.8440
0.330	8.3820	0.870	22.0980
0.340	8.6360	0.880	22.3520
0.350	8.8900	0.890	22.6060
0.360	9.1440		
0.370	9.3980		
0.380	9.6520		
0.390	9.9060		
		0.900	22.8600
0.400	10.1600	0.910	23.1140
0.410	10.4140	0.920	23.3680
0.420	10.6680	0.930	23.6220
0.430	10.9220	0.940	23.8760
0.440	11.1760	0.950	24.1300
0.450	11.4300	0.960	24.3840
0.460	11.6840	0.970	24.6380
0.470	11.9380	0.980	24.8920
0.480	12.1920	0.990	25.1460
0.490	12.4460	1.000	25.4000

FRACTIONS to DECIMALS to MILLIMETERS

Fraction	Decimal	mm	Fraction	Decimal	mm
1/64	0.0156	0.3969	33/64	0.5156	13.0969
1/32	0.0312	0.7938	17/32	0.5312	13.4938
3/64	0.0469	1.1906	35/64	0.5469	13.8906
1/16	0.0625	1.5875	9/16	0.5625	14.2875
5/64	0.0781	1.9844	37/64	0.5781	14.6844
3/32	0.0938	2.3812	19/32	0.5938	15.0812
7/64	0.1094	2.7781	39/64	0.6094	15.4781
1/8	0.1250	3.1750	5/8	0.6250	15.8750
9/64	0.1406	3.5719	41/64	0.6406	16.2719
5/32	0.1562	3.9688	21/32	0.6562	16.6688
11/64	0.1719	4.3656	43/64	0.6719	17.0656
3/16	0.1875	4.7625	11/16	0.6875	17.4625
13/64	0.2031	5.1594	45/64	0.7031	17.8594
7/32	0.2188	5.5562	23/32	0.7188	18.2562
15/64	0.2344	5.9531	47/64	0.7344	18.6531
1/4	0.2500	6.3500	3/4	0.7500	19.0500
17/64	0.2656	6.7469	49/64	0.7656	19.4469
9/32	0.2812	7.1438	25/32	0.7812	19.8438
19/64	0.2969	7.5406	51/64	0.7969	20.2406
5/16	0.3125	7.9375	13/16	0.8125	20.6375
21/64	0.3281	8.3344	53/64	0.8281	21.0344
11/32	0.3438	8.7312	27/32	0.8438	21.4312
23/64	0.3594	9.1281	55/64	0.8594	21.8281
3/8	0.3750	9.5250	7/8	0.8750	22.2250
25/64	0.3906	9.9219	57/64	0.8906	22.6219
13/32	0.4062	10.3188	29/32	0.9062	23.0188
27/64	0.4219	10.7156	59/64	0.9219	23.4156
7/16	0.4375	11.1125	15/16	0.9375	23.8125
29/64	0.4531	11.5094	61/64	0.9531	24.2094
15/32	0.4688	11.9062	31/32	0.9688	24.6062
31/64	0.4844	12.3031	63/64	0.9844	25.0031
1/2	0.5000	12.7000	1	1.0000	25.4000

Safety first!

Regardless of how enthusiastic you may be about getting on with the job at hand, take the time to ensure that your safety is not jeopardized. A moment's lack of attention can result in an accident, as can failure to observe certain simple safety precautions. The possibility of an accident will always exist, and the following points should not be considered a comprehensive list of all dangers. Rather, they are intended to make you aware of the risks and to encourage a safety conscious approach to all work you carry out on your vehicle.

Essential DOs and DON'Ts

DON'T rely on a jack when working under the vehicle. Always use approved jackstands to support the weight of the vehicle and place them under the recommended lift or support points.

DON'T attempt to loosen extremely tight fasteners (i.e. wheel lug nuts) while the vehicle is on a jack - it may fall.

DON'T start the engine without first making sure that the transmission is in Neutral (or Park where applicable) and the parking brake is set.

DON'T remove the radiator cap from a hot cooling system - let it cool or cover it with a cloth and release the pressure gradually.

DON'T attempt to drain the engine oil until you are sure it has cooled to the point that it will not burn you.

DON'T touch any part of the engine or exhaust system until it has cooled sufficiently to avoid burns.

DON'T siphon toxic liquids such as gasoline, antifreeze and brake fluid by mouth, or allow them to remain on your skin.

DON'T inhale brake lining dust - it is potentially hazardous (see Asbestos below).

DON'T allow spilled oil or grease to remain on the floor - wipe it up before someone slips on it.

DON'T use loose fitting wrenches or other tools which may slip and cause injury.

DON'T push on wrenches when loosening or tightening nuts or bolts. Always try to pull the wrench toward you. If the situation calls for pushing the wrench away, push with an open hand to avoid scraped knuckles if the wrench should slip.

DON'T attempt to lift a heavy component alone - get someone to help you.

DON'T rush or take unsafe shortcuts to finish a job.

DON'T allow children or animals in or around the vehicle while you are working on it.

DO wear eye protection when using power tools such as a drill, sander, bench grinder, etc. and when working under a vehicle.

DO keep loose clothing and long hair well out of the way of moving parts.

DO make sure that any hoist used has a safe working load rating adequate for the job.

DO get someone to check on you periodically when working alone on a vehicle.

DO carry out work in a logical sequence and make sure that everything is correctly assembled and tightened.

DO keep chemicals and fluids tightly capped and out of the reach of children and pets.

DO remember that your vehicle's safety affects that of yourself and others. If in doubt on any point, get professional advice.

Asbestos

Certain friction, insulating, sealing, and other products - such as brake linings, brake bands, clutch linings, torque converters, gaskets, etc. - may contain asbestos. Extreme care must be taken to avoid inhalation of dust from such products, since it is hazardous to health. If in doubt, assume that they do contain asbestos.

Fire

Remember at all times that gasoline is highly flammable. Never smoke or have any kind of open flame around when working on a vehicle. But the risk does not end there. A spark caused by an electrical short circuit, by two metal surfaces contacting each other, or even by static electricity built up in your body under certain conditions, can ignite gasoline vapors, which in a confined space are highly explosive. Do not, under any circumstances, use gasoline for cleaning parts. Use an approved safety solvent.

Always disconnect the battery ground (-) cable at the battery before working on any part of the fuel system or electrical system. Never risk spilling fuel on a hot engine or exhaust component. It is strongly recommended that a fire extinguisher suitable for use on fuel and electrical fires be kept handy in the garage or workshop at all times. Never try to extinguish a fuel or electrical fire with water.

Fumes

Certain fumes are highly toxic and can quickly cause unconsciousness and even death if inhaled to any extent. Gasoline vapor falls into this category, as do the vapors from some cleaning solvents. Any draining or pouring of such volatile fluids should be done in a well ventilated area.

When using cleaning fluids and solvents, read the instructions on the container carefully. Never use materials from unmarked containers.

Never run the engine in an enclosed space, such as a garage. Exhaust fumes contain carbon monoxide, which is extremely poisonous. If you need to run the engine, always do so in the open air, or at least have the rear of the vehicle outside the work area.

If you are fortunate enough to have the use of an inspection pit, never drain or pour gasoline and never run the engine while the vehicle is over the pit. The fumes, being heavier than air, will concentrate in the pit with possibly lethal results.

The battery

Never create a spark or allow a bare light bulb near a battery. They normally give off a certain amount of hydrogen gas, which is highly explosive.

Always disconnect the battery ground (-) cable at the battery before working on the fuel or electrical systems.

If possible, loosen the filler caps or cover when charging the battery from an external source (this does not apply to sealed or maintenance-free batteries). Do not charge at an excessive rate or the battery may burst.

Take care when adding water to a non maintenance-free battery and when carrying a battery. The electrolyte, even when diluted, is very corrosive and should not be allowed to contact clothing or skin.

Always wear eye protection when cleaning the battery to prevent the caustic deposits from entering your eyes.

Household current

When using an electric power tool, inspection light, etc., which operates on household current, always make sure that the tool is correctly connected to its plug and that, where necessary, it is properly grounded. Do not use such items in damp conditions and, again, do not create a spark or apply excessive heat in the vicinity of fuel or fuel vapor.

Secondary ignition system voltage

A severe electric shock can result from touching certain parts of the ignition system (such as the spark plug wires) when the engine is running or being cranked, particularly if components are damp or the insulation is defective. In the case of an electronic ignition system, the secondary system voltage is much higher and could prove fatal.

Troubleshooting

Contents

Symptom	Section
Engine	
Engine will not rotate when attempting to start	1
Engine rotates but will not start	2
Engine hard to start when cold	3
Engine hard to start when hot	4
Starter motor noisy or excessively rough in engagement	5
Engine starts but stops immediately	6
Oil puddle under engine	7
Engine lopes while idling or idles erratically	8
Engine misses at idle speed	9
Engine misses throughout driving speed range	10
Engine stumbles on acceleration	11
Engine surges while holding accelerator steady	12
Engine stalls	13
Engine lacks power	14
Engine backfires	15
Pinging or knocking engine sounds during acceleration or uphill	16
Engine runs with oil pressure light on	17
Engine diesels (continues to run) after switching off	18
Engine electrical systems	
Battery will not hold a charge	19
Alternator light fails to go out	20
Alternator light fails to come on when key is turned on	21
Fuel system	
Excessive fuel consumption	22
Fuel leakage and/or fuel odor	23
Cooling system	
Overheating	24
Overcooling	25
External coolant leakage	26
Internal coolant leakage	27
Coolant loss	28
Poor coolant circulation	29
Clutch	
Pedal travels to floor - no pressure or very little resistance	30
Fluid in area of master cylinder dust cover and on pedal	31
Fluid on release cylinder	32
Pedal feels spongy when depressed	33
Unable to select gears	34
Clutch slips (engine speed increases with no increase in vehicle speed	35
Grabbing (chattering) as clutch is engaged	36
Transaxle rattling (clicking)	37
Noise in clutch area	38
Clutch pedal stays on floor	39
High pedal effort	40
Manual transaxle	
Knocking noise at low speeds	41
Noise most pronounced when turning	42
Clunk on acceleration or deceleration	43
Clicking noise in turns	44
Vibration	45
Noisy in neutral with engine running	46
Noisy in one particular gear	47
Noisy in all gears	48
Slips out of gear	49
Leaks lubricant	50
Locked in gear	51
Automatic transaxle	
Fluid leakage	52
Transaxle fluid brown or has burned smell	53
General shift mechanism problems	54
Transaxle will not downshift with accelerator pedal pressed to the floor	55
Engine will start in gears other than Park or Neutral	56
Transaxle slips, shifts roughly, is noisy or has no drive in forward or reverse gears	57
Driveaxles	
Clicking noise in turns	58
Shudder or vibration during acceleration	59
Vibration at highway speeds	60
Brakes	
Vehicle pulls to one side during braking	61
Noise (grinding or high-pitched squeal when the brakes are applied)	62
Brake roughness or chatter (pedal pulsates)	63
Excessive pedal effort required to stop vehicle	64
Excessive brake pedal travel	65
Dragging brakes	66
Grabbing or uneven braking action	67
Brake pedal feels spongy when depressed	68
Brake pedal travels to the floor with little resistance	69
Parking brake does not hold	70
Suspension and steering systems	
Vehicle pulls to one side	71
Abnormal or excessive tire wear	72
Wheel makes a thumping noise	73
Shimmy, shake or vibration	74
Hard steering	75
Poor returnability of steering to center	76
Abnormal noise at the front end	77
Wander or poor steering stability	78
Erratic steering when braking	79
Excessive pitching and/or rolling around corners or during braking	80
Suspension bottoms	81
Cupped tires	82
Excessive tire wear on outside edge	83
Excessive tire wear on inside edge	84
Tire tread worn in one place	85
Excessive play or looseness in steering system	86
Rattling or clicking noise in rack and pinion	87

This section provides an easy reference guide to the more common problems which may occur during the operation of your vehicle. These problems and their possible causes are grouped under headings denoting various components or systems, such as Engine, Cooling system, etc. They also refer you to the chapter and/or section which deals with the problem.

Remember that successful troubleshooting is not a mysterious black art practiced only by professional mechanics. It is simply the result of the right knowledge combined with an intelligent, systematic approach to the problem. Always work by a process of elimination, starting with the simplest solution and working through to the most complex - and never overlook the obvious. Anyone can run the gas tank dry or leave the lights on overnight, so don't assume that you are exempt from such oversights.

Finally, always establish a clear idea of why a problem has occurred and take steps to ensure that it doesn't happen again. If the electrical system fails because of a poor connection, check the other connections in the system to make sure that they don't fail as well. If a particular fuse continues to blow, find out why - don't just replace one fuse after another. Remember, failure of a small component can often be indicative of potential failure or incorrect functioning of a more important component or system.

Engine

1 Engine will not rotate when attempting to start

1   Battery terminal connections loose or corroded (Chapter 1).
2   Battery discharged or faulty (Chapters 1 and 5).
3   Automatic transaxle not completely engaged in Park (Chapter 7) or clutch pedal not completely depressed (Chapter 8).
4   Broken, loose or disconnected wiring in the starting circuit (Chapters 5 and 12).
5   Starter motor pinion jammed in flywheel ring gear (Chapter 5).
6   Starter solenoid faulty (Chapter 5).
7   Starter motor faulty (Chapter 5).
8   Ignition switch faulty (Chapter 12).
9   Starter pinion or flywheel teeth worn or broken (Chapter 5).

2 Engine rotates but will not start

1   Fuel tank empty.
2   Battery discharged (engine rotates slowly) (Chapter 5).
3   Battery terminal connections loose or corroded (Chapter 1).

4   Leaking fuel injector(s), faulty fuel pump, pressure regulator, etc. (Chapter 4).
5   Broken or stripped timing belt (Chapter 2A) or broken timing chain (Chapter 2B).
6   Ignition components damp or damaged (Chapter 5).
7   Worn, faulty or incorrectly gapped spark plugs (Chapter 1).
8   Loose distributor is changing ignition timing (Chapter 5).
9   Broken, loose or disconnected wires at the ignition coil or faulty coil (Chapter 5).
10   Defective crankshaft or camshaft sensor (Chapter 6).

3 Engine hard to start when cold

1   Battery discharged or low (Chapter 1).
2   Malfunctioning fuel system (Chapter 4).
3   Faulty coolant temperature sensor or intake air temperature sensor (Chapter 6).
4   Faulty ignition system (Chapter 5).

4 Engine hard to start when hot

1   Air filter clogged (Chapter 1).
2   Fuel not reaching the fuel injection system (Chapter 4).
3   Corroded battery connections, especially ground (Chapter 1).
4   Faulty coolant temperature sensor or intake air temperature sensor (Chapter 6).

5 Starter motor noisy or excessively rough in engagement

1   Pinion or flywheel gear teeth worn or broken (Chapter 5).
2   Starter motor mounting bolts loose or missing (Chapter 5).

6 Engine starts but stops immediately

1   Loose or faulty electrical connections at distributor, coil or alternator (Chapter 5).
2   Insufficient fuel reaching the fuel injector(s) (Chapters 1 and 4).
3   Vacuum leak at the gasket between the intake manifold/plenum and throttle body (Chapter 4).

7 Oil puddle under engine

1   Oil pan gasket and/or oil pan drain bolt washer leaking (Chapter 2).
2   Oil pressure sending unit leaking (Chapter 2).
3   Valve cover leaking (Chapter 2).

4   Engine oil seals leaking (Chapter 2).
5   Oil pump housing leaking (Chapter 2).

8 Engine lopes while idling or idles erratically

1   Vacuum leakage (Chapters 2 and 4).
2   Leaking EGR valve (2000 and earlier models) (Chapter 6).
3   Air filter clogged (Chapter 1).
4   Malfunction in the fuel injection or engine control system (Chapters 4 and 6).
5   Leaking head gasket (Chapter 2).
6   Timing belt or chain and/or sprockets worn (Chapter 2).
7   Camshaft lobes worn (Chapter 2).

9 Engine misses at idle speed

1   Spark plugs worn or not gapped properly (Chapter 1).
2   Faulty spark plug wires (Chapter 1).
3   Vacuum leaks (Chapter 1).
4   Uneven or low compression (Chapter 2).
5   Problem with the fuel injection system (Chapter 4).

10 Engine misses throughout driving speed range

1   Fuel filter clogged and/or impurities in the fuel system (Chapters 1 and 4).
2   Low fuel pressure (Chapter 4).
3   Faulty or incorrectly gapped spark plugs (Chapter 1).
4   Cracked distributor cap, disconnected distributor wires or damaged distributor components (Chapters 1 and 5).
5   Leaking spark plug wires (Chapters 1 or 5).
6   Faulty emission system components (Chapter 6).
7   Low or uneven cylinder compression pressures (Chapter 2).
8   Weak or faulty ignition system (Chapter 5).
9   Vacuum leak in fuel injection system, intake manifold, air control valve or vacuum hoses (Chapters 4 and 6).

11 Engine stumbles on acceleration

1   Spark plugs fouled (Chapter 1).
2   Problem with fuel injection or engine control system (Chapters 4 and 6).
3   Fuel filter clogged (Chapters 1 and 4).
4   Intake manifold air leak (Chapters 2 and 4).
5   Problem with the emissions control system (Chapter 6).

12 Engine surges while holding accelerator steady

1   Intake air leak (Chapter 4).
2   Fuel pump or fuel pressure regulator faulty (Chapter 4).
3   Problem with fuel injection system (Chapter 4).
4   Problem with the emissions control system (Chapter 6).

13 Engine stalls

1   Idle speed incorrect (Chapter 1).
2   Fuel filter clogged and/or water and impurities in the fuel system (Chapters 1 and 4).
3   Distributor components damp or damaged (Chapter 5).
4   Faulty emissions system components (Chapter 6).
5   Faulty or incorrectly gapped spark plugs (Chapter 1).
6   Faulty spark plug wires (Chapter 1).
7   Vacuum leak in the fuel injection system, intake manifold or vacuum hoses (Chapters 2 and 4).
8   Valve clearances incorrectly set (Chapter 1).

14 Engine lacks power

1   Obstructed exhaust system (Chapter 4).
2   Excessive play in distributor shaft (Chapter 5).
3   Worn rotor, distributor cap, spark plug wires or faulty coil (Chapters 1 and 5).
4   Faulty or incorrectly gapped spark plugs (Chapter 1).
5   Problem with the fuel injection system (Chapter 4).
6   Plugged air filter (Chapter 1).
7   Brakes binding (Chapter 9).
8   Automatic transaxle fluid level incorrect (Chapter 1).
9   Clutch slipping (Chapter 8).
10 Fuel filter clogged and/or impurities in the fuel system (Chapters 1 and 4).
11 Emission control system not functioning properly (Chapter 6).
12 Low or uneven cylinder compression pressures (Chapter 2).

15 Engine backfires

1   Emission control system not functioning properly (Chapter 6).
2   Faulty secondary ignition system (cracked spark plug insulator, faulty plug wires, distributor cap and/or rotor) (Chapters 1 and 5).
3   Problem with the fuel injection system (Chapter 4).
4   Vacuum leak at fuel injector(s), intake manifold, air control valve or vacuum hoses (Chapters 2 and 4).
5   Valve clearances incorrectly set and/or valves sticking (Chapters 1 and 2).

16 Pinging or knocking engine sounds during acceleration or uphill

1   Incorrect grade of fuel.
2   Fuel injection system faulty (Chapter 4).
3   Improper or damaged spark plugs or wires (Chapter 1).
4   Worn or damaged distributor components (Chapter 5).
5   Knock sensor defective (Chapter 6).
5   EGR valve not functioning (Chapter 6).
6   Vacuum leak (Chapters 2 and 4).

17 Engine runs with oil pressure light on

1   Low oil level (Chapter 1).
2   Idle rpm below specification (Chapter 1).
3   Short in wiring circuit (Chapter 12).
4   Faulty oil pressure sender (Chapter 2).
5   Worn engine bearings and/or oil pump (Chapter 2).

18 Engine diesels (continues to run) after switching off

1   Excessive engine operating temperature (Chapter 3).

Engine electrical system

19 Battery will not hold a charge

1   Alternator drivebelt defective or not adjusted properly (Chapter 1).
2   Battery electrolyte level low (Chapter 1).
3   Battery terminals loose or corroded (Chapter 1).
4   Alternator not charging properly (Chapter 5).
5   Loose, broken or faulty wiring in the charging circuit (Chapter 5).
6   Short in vehicle wiring (Chapter 12).
7   Internally defective battery (Chapters 1 and 5).

20 Alternator light fails to go out

1   Faulty alternator or charging circuit (Chapter 5).
2   Alternator drivebelt defective or out of adjustment (Chapter 1).
3   Alternator voltage regulator inoperative (Chapter 5).

21 Alternator light fails to come on when key is turned on

1   Warning light bulb defective (Chapter 12).
2   Fault in the printed circuit, dash wiring or bulb holder (Chapter 12).

Fuel system

22 Excessive fuel consumption

1   Dirty or clogged air filter element (Chapter 1).
2   Emissions system not functioning properly (Chapter 6).
3   Fuel injection system not functioning properly (Chapter 4).
4   Low tire pressure or incorrect tire size (Chapter 1).

23 Fuel leakage and/or fuel odor

1   Leaking fuel feed or return line (Chapters 1 and 4).
2   Tank overfilled.
3   Evaporative canister filter clogged (Chapters 1 and 6).
4   Problem with fuel injection system (Chapter 4).

Cooling system

24 Overheating

1   Insufficient coolant in system (Chapter 1).
2   Water pump drivebelt defective or out of adjustment (Chapter 1).
3   Radiator core blocked or grille restricted (Chapter 3).
4   Thermostat faulty (Chapter 3).
5   Electric coolant fan inoperative or blades broken (Chapter 3).
6   Radiator cap not maintaining proper pressure (Chapter 3).

25 Overcooling

1   Faulty thermostat (Chapter 3).
2   Inaccurate temperature gauge sending unit (Chapter 3).

26 External coolant leakage

1   Deteriorated/damaged hoses; loose clamps (Chapters 1 and 3).
2   Water pump defective (Chapter 3).
3   Leakage from radiator core or coolant reservoir (Chapter 3).
4   Engine drain or water jacket core plugs leaking (Chapter 2).

27   Internal coolant leakage

1   Leaking cylinder head gasket (Chapter 2).
2   Cracked cylinder bore or cylinder head (Chapter 2).

28   Coolant loss

1   Too much coolant in reservoir (Chapter 1).
2   Coolant boiling away because of overheating (Chapter 3).
3   Internal or external leakage (Chapter 3).
4   Faulty radiator cap (Chapter 3).

29   Poor coolant circulation

1   Inoperative water pump (Chapter 3).
2   Restriction in cooling system (Chapters 1 and 3).
3   Water pump drivebelt defective/out of adjustment (Chapter 1).
4   Thermostat sticking (Chapter 3).

Clutch

30   Pedal travels to floor - no pressure or very little resistance

1   Master or release cylinder faulty (Chapter 8).
2   Hose/pipe burst or leaking (Chapter 8).
3   Connections leaking (Chapter 8).
4   No fluid in reservoir (Chapter 8).
5   If fluid level in reservoir rises as pedal is depressed, master cylinder center valve seal is faulty (Chapter 8).
6   If there is fluid on dust seal at master cylinder, piston primary seal is leaking (Chapter 8).
7   Broken release bearing or fork (Chapter 8).
8   Faulty pressure plate diaphragm spring (Chapter 8).

31   Fluid in area of master cylinder dust cover and on pedal

Rear seal failure in master cylinder (Chapter 8).

32   Fluid on release cylinder

Release cylinder plunger seal faulty (Chapter 8).

33   Pedal feels spongy when depressed

Air in system (Chapter 8).

34   Unable to select gears

1   Faulty transaxle (Chapter 7A).
2   Faulty clutch disc or pressure plate (Chapter 8).
3   Faulty release lever or release bearing (Chapter 8).
4   Faulty shift lever assembly or control cables (Chapter 7A).

35   Clutch slips (engine speed increases with no increase in vehicle speed)

1   Clutch plate worn (Chapter 8).
2   Clutch plate is oil soaked by leaking rear main seal (Chapters 2 and 8).
3   Clutch plate not seated (Chapter 8).
4   Warped pressure plate or flywheel (Chapter 8).
5   Weak diaphragm springs (Chapter 8).
6   Clutch plate overheated. Allow to cool.

36   Grabbing (chattering) as clutch is engaged

1   Oil on clutch plate lining, burned or glazed facings (Chapter 8).
2   Worn or loose engine or transaxle mounts (Chapter 2).
3   Worn splines on clutch plate hub (Chapter 8).
4   Warped pressure plate or flywheel (Chapter 8).
5   Burned or smeared resin on flywheel or pressure plate (Chapter 8).

37   Transaxle rattling (clicking)

1   Release lever loose (Chapter 8).
2   Clutch plate damper spring failure (Chapter 8).

38   Noise in clutch area

1   Fork shaft improperly installed (Chapter 8).
2   Faulty bearing (Chapter 8).

39   Clutch pedal stays on floor

1   Clutch master cylinder piston binding in bore (Chapter 8).
2   Broken release bearing or fork (Chapter 8).

40   High pedal effort

1   Piston binding in bore (Chapter 8).
2   Pressure plate faulty (Chapter 8).

3   Incorrect size master or release cylinder (Chapter 8).

Manual transaxle

41   Knocking noise at low speeds

1   Worn driveaxle constant velocity (CV) joints (Chapter 8).
2   Worn side gear shaft counterbore in differential case (Chapter 7A).*

42   Noise most pronounced when turning

Differential gear noise (Chapter 7A).*

43   Clunk on acceleration or deceleration

1   Loose engine or transaxle mounts (Chapter 2).
2   Worn differential pinion shaft in case.*
3   Worn side gear shaft counterbore in differential case (Chapter 7A).*
4   Worn or damaged driveaxle inboard CV joints (Chapter 8).

44   Clicking noise in turns

Worn or damaged outboard CV joint (Chapter 8).

45   Vibration

1   Rough wheel bearing (Chapter 10).
2   Damaged driveaxle (Chapter 8).
3   Out-of-round tires (Chapter 1).
4   Tire out of balance.
5   Worn CV joint (Chapter 8).

46   Noisy in neutral with engine running

1   Damaged input gear bearing (Chapter 7A).*
2   Damaged clutch release bearing (Chapter 8).

47   Noisy in one particular gear

1   Damaged or worn constant mesh gears (Chapter 7A).*
2   Damaged or worn synchronizers (Chapter 7A).*
3   Bent reverse fork (Chapter 7A).*
4   Damaged fourth speed gear or output gear (Chapter 7A).*
5   Worn or damaged reverse idler gear or idler bushing (Chapter 7A).*

48 Noisy in all gears

1   Insufficient lubricant (Chapter 7A).
2   Damaged or worn bearings (Chapter 7A).*
3   Worn or damaged input gear shaft and/or output gear shaft (Chapter 7A).*

49 Slips out of gear

1   Worn or improperly adjusted shift cables (Chapter 7A).
2   Shift linkage does not work freely, binds (Chapter 7A).
3   Input gear bearing retainer broken or loose (Chapter 7A).*
4   Worn shift fork (Chapter 7A).*

50 Leaks lubricant

1   Side gear shaft seals worn (Chapter 7).
2   Excessive amount of lubricant in transaxle (Chapters 1 and 7A).
3   Loose or broken input gear shaft bearing retainer (Chapter 7A).*
4   Input gear bearing retainer O-ring and/or lip seal damaged (Chapter 7A).*

51 Locked in gear

Lock pin or interlock pin missing (Chapter 7A).*
Although the corrective action necessary to remedy the symptoms described is beyond the scope of this manual, the above information should be helpful in isolating the cause of the condition so that the owner can communicate clearly with a professional mechanic.

Automatic transaxle
Note: *Due to the complexity of the automatic transaxle, it is difficult for the home mechanic to properly diagnose and service this component. For problems other than the following, the vehicle should be taken to a dealer or transaxle shop.*

52 Fluid leakage

1   Automatic transaxle fluid is a deep red color. Fluid leaks should not be confused with engine oil, which can easily be blown onto the transaxle by air flow.
2   To pinpoint a leak, first remove all built-up dirt and grime from the transaxle housing with degreasing agents and/or steam cleaning. Then drive the vehicle at low speeds so air flow will not blow the leak far from its source. Raise the vehicle and determine where the leak is coming from. Common areas of leakage are:

a)   *Pan (Chapters 1 and 7)*
b)   *Dipstick tube (Chapters 1 and 7)*
c)   *Transaxle oil lines (Chapter 7)*
d)   *Speed sensor (Chapter 7)*
e)   *Driveaxle oil seals (Chapter 7).*

53 Transaxle fluid brown or has a burned smell

Transaxle fluid overheated (Chapter 1).

54 General shift mechanism problems

1   Chapter 7, Part B, deals with checking and adjusting the shift cable on automatic transaxles. Common problems which may be attributed to poorly adjusted linkage are:
a)   *Engine starting in gears other than Park or Neutral.*
b)   *Indicator on shifter pointing to a gear other than the one actually being used.*
c)   *Vehicle moves when in Park.*
2   Refer to Chapter 7B for the shift cable adjustment procedure.

55 Transaxle will not downshift with accelerator pedal pressed to the floor

Throttle valve cable out of adjustment (Chapter 7B).

56 Engine will start in gears other than Park or Neutral

Park/Neutral Position (PNP) switch malfunctioning (Chapter 7B).

57 Transaxle slips, shifts roughly, is noisy or has no drive in forward or reverse gears

There are many probable causes for the above problems, but the home mechanic should be concerned with only one possibility - fluid level. Before taking the vehicle to a repair shop, check the level and condition of the fluid as described in Chapter 1. Correct the fluid level as necessary or change the fluid and filter if needed. If the problem persists, have a professional diagnose the cause.

Driveaxles

58 Clicking noise in turns

Worn or damaged outboard CV joint (Chapter 8).

59 Shudder or vibration during acceleration

1   Excessive toe-in (Chapter 10).
2   Incorrect spring heights (Chapter 10).
3   Worn or damaged inboard or outboard CV joints (Chapter 8).
4   Sticking inboard CV joint assembly (Chapter 8).

60 Vibration at highway speeds

1   Out-of-balance front wheels and/or tires.
2   Out-of-round front tires (Chapters 1 and 10).
3   Worn CV joint(s) (Chapter 8).

Brakes
Note: *Before assuming that a brake problem exists, make sure that:*
a)   *The tires are in good condition and properly inflated (Chapter 1).*
b)   *The front end alignment is correct.*
c)   *The vehicle is not loaded with weight in an unequal manner.*

61 Vehicle pulls to one side during braking

1   Incorrect tire pressures (Chapter 1).
2   Front end out of alignment (have the front end aligned).
3   Front, or rear, tire sizes not matched to one another.
4   Restricted brake lines or hoses (Chapter 9).
5   Malfunctioning drum brake or caliper assembly (Chapter 9).
6   Loose suspension parts (Chapter 10).
7   Loose calipers (Chapter 9).
8   Excessive wear of brake shoe or pad material or disc/drum on one side (Chapter 9).
9   Contamination (grease or brake fluid) of brake shoe or pad material or disc/drum on one side (Chapter 9) .

62 Noise (grinding or high-pitched squeal when the brakes are applied)

1   Front and/or rear disc brake pads worn out. Replace pads with new ones immediately (Chapter 9).
2   Drum brake shoes worn out (Chapter 9).

63 Brake roughness or chatter (pedal pulsates)

1   Excessive lateral runout (Chapter 9).
2   Uneven pad wear (Chapter 9).
3   Defective disc (Chapter 9).

64 Excessive brake pedal effort required to stop vehicle

1   Malfunctioning power brake booster (Chapter 9).
2   Partial system failure (Chapter 9).
3   Excessively worn pads or shoes (Chapter 9).
4   Piston in caliper or wheel cylinder stuck or sluggish (Chapter 9).
5   Brake pads or shoes contaminated with oil or grease (Chapter 9).
6   Brake disc grooved and/or glazed (Chapter 9).
7   New pads or shoes installed and not yet seated. It will take a while for the new material to seat against the disc or drum.

65 Excessive brake pedal travel

1   Partial brake system failure (Chapter 9).
2   Insufficient fluid in master cylinder (Chapters 1 and 9).
3   Air trapped in system (Chapter 9).

66 Dragging brakes

1   Incorrect adjustment of brake light switch (Chapter 9).
2   Master cylinder pistons not returning correctly (Chapter 9).
3   Restricted brakes lines or hoses (Chapter 9).
4   Incorrect parking brake adjustment (Chapter 9).

67 Grabbing or uneven braking action

1   Malfunction of proportioning valve (Chapter 9).
2   Malfunction of power brake booster unit (Chapter 9).
3   Binding brake pedal mechanism (Chapter 9).

68 Brake pedal feels spongy when depressed

1   Air in hydraulic lines (Chapter 9).
2   Master cylinder mounting bolts loose (Chapter 9).
3   Master cylinder defective (Chapter 9).

69 Brake pedal travels to the floor with little resistance

1   Little or no fluid in the master cylinder reservoir caused by leaking caliper or wheel cylinder piston(s) (Chapter 9).
2   Loose, damaged or disconnected brake lines (Chapter 9).

70 Parking brake does not hold

Parking brake linkage improperly adjusted (Chapter 9).

Suspension and steering systems

Note: *Before attempting to diagnose the suspension and steering systems, perform the following preliminary checks:*

a) Tires for wrong pressure and uneven wear.
b) Steering universal joints from the column to the rack and pinion for loose connectors or wear.
c) Front and rear suspension and the rack and pinion assembly for loose or damaged parts.
d) Out-of-round or out-of-balance tires, bent rims and loose and/or rough wheel bearings.

71 Vehicle pulls to one side

1   Mismatched or uneven tires (Chapter 10).
2   Broken or sagging springs (Chapter 10).
3   Wheel alignment incorrect. Have the wheels professionally aligned.
4   Front brake dragging (Chapter 9).

72 Abnormal or excessive tire wear

1   Wheel alignment out-of-specification. Have the wheels aligned.
2   Sagging or broken springs (Chapter 10).
3   Tire out-of-balance.
4   Worn strut damper (Chapter 10).
5   Overloaded vehicle.
6   Tires not rotated regularly.

73 Wheel makes a thumping noise

1   Blister or bump on tire.
2   Improper strut damper action (Chapter 10).

74 Shimmy, shake or vibration

1   Tire or wheel out-of-balance or out-of-round.
2   Loose or worn wheel bearings (Chapter 10).
3   Worn tie-rod ends (Chapter 10).
4   Worn balljoints (Chapters 1 and 10).
5   Excessive wheel runout (Chapter 10).
6   Blister or bump on tire.

75 Hard steering

1   Lack of lubrication at balljoints, tie-rod

ends and rack and pinion assembly (Chapter 10).
2   Wheel alignment out-of-specifications. Have the wheels professionally aligned.
3   Low tire pressure(s) (Chapter 1).

76 Poor returnability of steering to center

1   Lack of lubrication at balljoints and tie-rod ends (Chapter 10).
2   Binding in balljoints (Chapter 10).
3   Binding in steering column (Chapter 10).
4   Lack of lubricant in steering gear assembly (Chapter 10).
5   Wheel alignment out-of-specifications. Have the wheels professionally aligned.

77 Abnormal noise at the front end

1   Lack of lubrication at balljoints and tie-rod ends (Chapters 1 and 10).
2   Damaged strut mounting (Chapter 10).
3   Worn control arm bushings or tie-rod ends (Chapter 10).
4   Loose stabilizer bar (Chapter 10).
5   Loose wheel nuts (Chapter 1).
6   Loose suspension bolts (Chapter 10).

78 Wander or poor steering stability

1   Mismatched or uneven tires.
2   Lack of lubrication at balljoints and tie-rod ends (Chapters 1 and 10).
3   Worn strut assemblies (Chapter 10).
4   Loose stabilizer bar (Chapter 10).
5   Broken or sagging springs (Chapter 10).
6   Wheels out of alignment. Have the wheels professionally aligned.

79 Erratic steering when braking

1   Wheel bearings worn (Chapter 10).
2   Broken or sagging springs (Chapter 10).
3   Leaking wheel cylinder or caliper (Chapter 10).
4   Warped discs or drums (Chapter 9).

80 Excessive pitching and/or rolling around corners or during braking

1   Loose stabilizer bar (Chapter 10).
2   Worn strut dampers or mountings (Chapter 10).
3   Broken or sagging springs (Chapter 10).
4   Overloaded vehicle.

81 Suspension bottoms

1   Overloaded vehicle.
2   Sagging springs (Chapter 10).

82 Cupped tires

1   Front wheel or rear wheel alignment out-of-specifications. Have the wheels professionally aligned.
2   Worn strut dampers or shock absorbers (Chapter 10).
3   Wheel bearings worn (Chapter 10).
4   Excessive tire or wheel runout.
5   Worn balljoints (Chapter 10).

83 Excessive tire wear on outside edge

1   Inflation pressures incorrect (Chapter 1).
2   Excessive speed in turns.
3   Wheel alignment incorrect (excessive toe-in). Have professionally aligned.

4   Suspension arm bent or twisted (Chapter 10).

84 Excessive tire wear on inside edge

1   Inflation pressures incorrect (Chapter 1).
2   Wheel alignment incorrect (toe-out). Have professionally aligned.
3   Loose or damaged steering components (Chapter 10).

85 Tire tread worn in one place

1   Tires out-of-balance.
2   Damaged or buckled wheel. Inspect and replace if necessary.
3   Defective tire (Chapter 1).

86 Excessive play or looseness in steering system

1   Wheel bearing(s) worn (Chapter 10).
2   Tie-rod end loose (Chapter 10).
3   Steering gear loose (Chapter 10).
4   Worn or loose steering intermediate shaft U-joint (Chapter 10).

87 Rattling or clicking noise in steering gear

1   Steering gear loose (Chapter 10).
2   Steering gear defective.

Chapter 1
Tune-up and routine maintenance

Contents

	Section
Air filter replacement	16
Automatic transaxle fluid and filter change	31
Battery check, maintenance and charging	9
Brake check	15
Brake fluid change	24
Clutch pedal freeplay check and adjustment	8
Cooling system check	12
Cooling system servicing (draining, flushing and refilling)	28
Driveaxle boot check	21
Drivebelt check, adjustment and replacement	10
Engine oil and oil filter change	6
Evaporative emissions control system check	29
Exhaust system check	30
Fluid level checks	4
Fuel filter replacement (2000 and earlier models)	25
Fuel system check	17
Interior ventilation filter replacement (2001 and later models)	23
Introduction	2
Maintenance schedule	1
Manual transaxle lubricant change	32

	Section
Manual transaxle lubricant level check	18
Positive Crankcase Ventilation (PCV) valve and hose check and replacement	35
Rear differential lubricant change (4WD models)	34
Rear differential lubricant level check (4WD models)	22
Seat belt check	14
Spark plug check and replacement	26
Spark plug wire, distributor cap and rotor check and replacement	27
Steering and suspension check	20
Tire and tire pressure checks	5
Tire rotation	13
Transfer case lubricant change (4WD models with automatic transaxle)	33
Transfer case lubricant level check (4WD models with automatic transaxle)	19
Tune-up general information	3
Underhood hose check and replacement	11
Valve clearance check and adjustment	36
Windshield wiper blade inspection and replacement	7

Specifications

Recommended lubricants and fluids

Note: *Listed here are manufacturer recommendations at the time this manual was written. Manufacturers occasionally upgrade their fluid and lubricant specifications, so check with your local auto parts store for current recommendations.*

Engine oil	
Type	API "certified for gasoline engines"
Viscosity	See accompanying chart
Fuel	Unleaded gasoline, 87 octane or higher

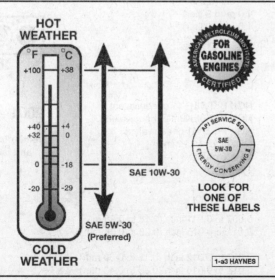

HOT WEATHER

°F   °C
+100 +38

+40 +4
+32 0

0   -18

-20 -29

SAE 10W-30

SAE 5W-30 (Preferred)

COLD WEATHER

FOR GASOLINE ENGINES CERTIFIED

API SERVICE SG
SAE 5W-30
ENERGY CONSERVING II

LOOK FOR ONE OF THESE LABELS

Recommended engine oil viscosity

1-a3 HAYNES

Recommended lubricants and fluids (continued)

Automatic transaxle fluid
  2WD models.. DEXRON III automatic transmission fluid
  4WD models.. Toyota automatic transaxle fluid Type T or T-IV, or equivalent
Manual transaxle lubricant... API GL-5 75W-90 gear oil
Transfer case lubricant (4WD models with automatic transaxle)
  2000 and earlier models... API GL-5 75W-90 gear oil
  2001 and later models
    Below 0-degrees F (-18-degrees C) .... API GL-5 80W or 80W-90 gear oil
    Above 0-degrees F (-18-degrees C)...................... API GL-5 90 gear oil
Rear differential lubricant (4WD models)
  Above 0-degrees F (-18 degrees C) .... API GL-5 SAE 90 hypoid gear oil
  Below 0-degrees F (-18 degrees C)......................... API GL-5 SAE 80W-90 hypoid gear oil
Brake fluid.. DOT 3 brake fluid
Clutch fluid... DOT 3 brake fluid
Engine coolant.. 50/50 mixture of ethylene glycol-based antifreeze and distilled water
Power steering system .... DEXRON III automatic transmission fluid

Capacities*

Engine oil (including filter)
  1996 models... 4.1 qts (3.9 liters)
  1997 through 2000 models .... 4.3 qts (4.1 liters)
  2001 and later models.. 4.4 qts (4.2 liters)
Coolant
  1996 through 2000 models
    Manual transaxle .... 8.5 qts (8.0 liters)
    Automatic transaxle .... 8.1 qts (7.7 liters)
  2001 and later models
    Manual transaxle .... 6.7 qts (6.3 liters)
    Automatic transaxle .... 6.6 qts (6.2 liters)
Transaxle
  Automatic (drain and refill)
    1996 .... Up to 3.5 qts (3.3 liters)
    1997
      2WD .... Up to 3.5 qts (3.3 liters)
      4WD .... Up to 7.4 qts (7.0 liters)
    1998 through 2000... Up to 3.5 qts (3.3 liters)
    2001 and later
      2WD .... Up to 3.5 qts (3.3 liters)
      4WD .... Up to 4.1 qts (3.9 liters)
  Manual
    1996 through 2000
      2WD .... 4.1 qts (3.9 liters)
      4WD .... 5.3 qts (5.0 liters)
    2001 and later
      2WD .... 2.6 qts (2.5 liters)
      4WD .... 3.6 qts (3.4 liters)
Transfer case (4WD models)
  1996 through 2000 .... 0.7 qts (0.7 liters)
  2001 and later .... 1.0 qt (0.9 liter)
Rear differential (4WD models) .... 1.0 qt (0.9 liter)

All capacities approximate. Add as necessary to bring up to appropriate level.

Ignition system

Spark plug type and gap
  Type
    1997 and earlier.. NGK BKR6EP-11 or equivalent
    1998 through 2000... NGK BKR6EKB-11 or equivalent
    2001 and later... NGK IFR6A11 or equivalent
  Gap .... 0.043 inch (1.1 mm)
Spark plug wire resistance (maximum) .... 25,000 ohms
Engine firing order 1-3-4-2

Valve clearances (engine cold)

2000 and earlier
  Intake valve.. 0.007 to 0.011 inch (0.18 to 0.28 mm)
  Exhaust valve... 0.011 to 0.015 inch (0.28 to 0.38 mm)
2001 through 2003
  Intake valve.. 0.007 to 0.012 inch (0.18 to 0.30 mm)
  Exhaust valve... 0.012 to 0.016 inch (0.30 to 0.40 mm)

① ② ③ ④
Front
↓
92082-Specs HAYNES

1996 and 1997

Cylinder location and distributor rotation - 1996 and 1997 models

① ② ③ ④
Front
↓

1998 through 2000

92082-Specs HAYNES

Cylinder and coil terminal locations - 1998 through 2000 models

① ② ③ ④
Front
↓

2001 and later

Cylinder locations - 2001 and later models

2004 and later
  Intake .... 0.008 to 0.0011 inch (0.19 to 0.29 mm)
  Exhaust .... 0.012 to 0.016 inch (0.30 to 0.40 mm)

Cooling system
Thermostat rating
  Starts to open.. 176 to 183-degrees F (80 to 84-degrees C)
  Fully open... 203-degrees F (95-degrees C)

Accessory drivebelt tension - 2000 and earlier models (with Burroughs or Nippondenso tension gauge)
Used belt (a belt which has been used more than 5 minutes)
  Alternator
    With air conditioning .... 110 +/- 10 lbs
    Without air conditioning .... 95 +/- 20 lbs
  Power steering pump .... 60 to 100 lbs
New belt (a belt which has been used less than 5 minutes)
  Alternator.. 170 to 180 lbs
    With air conditioning .... 165 +/- 25 lbs
    Without air conditioning .... 125 +/- 25 lbs
  Power steering pump .... 95 to 145 lbs

Clutch pedal
Freeplay... 3/16 to 5/8 inch (5 to 15 mm)
Height
  2000 and earlier .... 6.38 to 6.77 inches (162 to 172 mm)
  2001 and later .... 6.65 to 7.05 inches (169 to 179 mm)

Brakes
Disc brake pad lining thickness (minimum) .... 3/16 inch (4.7 mm)
Drum brake shoe lining thickness (minimum)............ 1/16 inch (1.6 mm)
Parking brake adjustment.. 6 to 8 clicks

Suspension and steering
Steering wheel freeplay limit...................................... 1-3/16 inch (25.6 mm)
Balljoint allowable movement .... 0 inch (0 mm)

Torque specifications

Note: *One foot-pound (ft-lb) of torque is equivalent to 12 inch-pounds (in-lbs) of torque. Torque values below approximately 15 ft-lbs are expressed in inch-pounds, since most foot-pound torque wrenches are not accurate at these smaller values.*

	Ft-lbs (unless otherwise indicated)	Nm
Engine oil drain plug		
2000 and earlier	27	36.5
2001 and later	18	24.4
Automatic transaxle		
Pan bolts		
1996 and 1997	43 in-lbs	4.8
1998 through 2000		
2WD	48 in-lbs	5.4
4WD	70 in-lbs	8
2001 and later	67 in-lbs	7.5
Filter bolts	84 in-lbs	9.5
Drain plug		
1996 through 2000	156 in-lbs	17.6
2001 and later	35	47.4
Differential case drain plug (2001 and later 2WD models)	40	54
Manual transaxle drain and check/fill plugs	36	48.8
Transfer case drain and check/fill plugs	29	39.3
Rear differential drain and check/fill plugs	36	48.8
Fuel filter banjo bolt (2000 and earlier models only)	21	28.5
Spark plugs		
2000 and earlier	156 in-lbs	17.6
2001 and later	15	20.3
Seat bolts/nuts	27	36.6
Drivebelt tensioner (2001 and later models)		
Nut	44	59.6
Bolt	44	59.6
Wheel lug nuts	76	103

Typical engine compartment components (2000 and earlier models)

1	Brake fluid reservoir	7	Radiator hose	12	Power steering fluid reservoir
2	Fuse/relay block	8	Radiator cap	13	Spark plug
3	Air filter housing	9	Engine oil dipstick	14	PCV valve
4	Relay block	10	Drivebelt	15	Engine oil filler cap
5	Distributor	11	Windshield washer fluid reservoir	16	Battery
6	Coolant reservoir				

Typical engine compartment components (2001 and later models)

1   Brake fluid reservoir
2   Fuse/relay block
3   Coolant reservoir
4   Automatic transaxle fluid dipstick
5   Radiator cap
6   Upper radiator hose
7   Air filter housing
8   Spark plug
9   Engine oil filler cap
10   Engine oil dipstick
11   Drivebelt
12   Windshield washer fluid reservoir
13   Power steering fluid reservoir
14   PCV valve
15   Battery (under cover)

Typical engine compartment underside components

1 Engine oil filter
2 Front suspension strut unit
3 Automatic transaxle drain plug
4 Engine oil drain plug
5 Front disc brake caliper
6 Driveaxle boot
7 Steering gear boot
8 Balljoint

Typical rear underside components

1 Muffler
2 Exhaust system hanger
3 Shock absorber
4 Rear drum brake assembly
5 Driveaxle boot
6 Differential
7 Driveshaft
8 Fuel tank

1 Toyota RAV4 Maintenance schedule

The maintenance intervals in this manual are provided with the assumption that you, not the dealer, will be doing the work. These are the minimum maintenance intervals recommended by the factory for vehicles that are driven daily. If you wish to keep your vehicle in peak condition at all times, you may wish to perform some of these procedures even more often. Because frequent maintenance enhances the efficiency, performance and resale value of your car, we encourage you to do so. If you drive in dusty areas, tow a trailer, idle or drive at low speeds for extended periods or drive for short distances (less than four miles) in below freezing temperatures, shorter intervals are also recommended.

When your vehicle is new, it should be serviced by a factory authorized dealer service department to protect the factory warranty. In many cases, the initial maintenance check is done at no cost to the owner.

Every 250 miles or weekly, whichever comes first

Check the engine oil level (Section 4)
Check the engine coolant level (Section 4)
Check the windshield washer fluid level (Section 4)
Check the brake fluid level (Section 4)
Check the automatic transaxle fluid level (Section 4)
Check the power steering fluid level (Section 4)
Check the tires and tire pressures (Section 5)

Every 3000 miles or 3 months, whichever comes first

All items listed above plus:
Change the engine oil and oil filter (Section 6)
Rotate the tires (4WD models) (Section 13)
Re-torque the driveshaft fasteners (4WD models) (see Chapter 8)

Every 7500 miles or 6 months, whichever comes first

Inspect (and replace, if necessary) the windshield wiper blades (Section 7)
Check the clutch pedal for proper freeplay (Section 8)
Check and service the battery (Section 9)
Check and adjust if necessary the engine drivebelts (Section 10)
Inspect (and replace, if necessary) all underhood hoses (Section 11)
Check the cooling system (Section 12)
Rotate the tires (Section 13)
Check the seat belts (Section 14)

Every 15,000 miles or 12 months, whichever comes first

All items listed above plus:
Inspect the brake system (Section 15)*
Check and replace, if necessary, the air filter (Section 16)*
Inspect the fuel system (Section 17)

Check the manual transaxle lubricant level (Section 18)
Check the transfer case lubricant level (4WD models with automatic transaxle) (Section 19)
Inspect the suspension and steering components (Section 20)*
Check the driveaxle boots (Section 21)
Check the rear differential lubricant level (4WD models) (Section 22)
Replace the interior ventilation filter (2001 and later models) (Section 23)

Every 30,000 miles or 24 months, whichever comes first

All items listed above plus:
Change the brake fluid (Section 24)
Replace the fuel filter (2000 and earlier models) (Section 25)
Check (and replace, if necessary) the spark plugs (conventional, non-platinum or iridium type) (Section 26)
Inspect (and replace, if necessary) the spark plug wires, and, on models so equipped, the distributor cap and rotor (Section 27)
Service the cooling system (drain, flush and refill) (Section 28)
Inspect the evaporative emissions control system (Section 29)
Inspect the exhaust system (Section 30)
Change the automatic transaxle fluid and filter (Section 31)**
Change the manual transaxle lubricant (Section 32)**
Change the rear differential lubricant (4WD models) (Section 34)
Check and replace if necessary the PCV valve (Section 35)

Every 60,000 miles or 48 months, whichever comes first

Change the transfer case lubricant (4WD models with automatic transaxle) (Section 33)*
Replace the spark plugs (platinum or iridium type) (Section 26)
Check and adjust the valve clearances (Section 36)
Replace the timing belt (2000 and earlier models) (Chapter 2A)

This item is affected by "severe" operating conditions as described below. If your vehicle is operated under "severe" conditions, perform all maintenance indicated with an asterisk (*) at 3000 mile/3 month intervals. Severe conditions are indicated if you mainly operate your vehicle under one or more of the following conditions:

Operating in dusty areas
Operating in mud/water
Towing a trailer
Idling for extended periods and/or low speed operation
Operating when outside temperatures remain below freezing and when most trips are less than 4 miles

** If operated under one or more of the following conditions, change the manual or automatic transaxle fluid and differential lubricant every 15,000 miles:*

In heavy city traffic where the outside temperature regularly reaches 90-degrees F (32-degrees C) or higher
In hilly or mountainous terrain
Frequent trailer pulling

2   Introduction

This chapter is designed to help the home mechanic maintain the Toyota RAV4 for peak performance, economy, safety and long life.

Included is a master maintenance schedule, followed by sections dealing specifically with each item on the schedule. Visual checks, adjustments, component replacement and other helpful items are included. Refer to the **accompanying illustrations** of the engine compartment and the underside of the vehicle for the location of various components.

Servicing your vehicle in accordance with the mileage/time maintenance schedule and the following Sections will provide it with a planned maintenance program that should result in a long and reliable service life. This is a comprehensive plan, so maintaining some items but not others at the specified service intervals will not produce the same results.

As you service your RAV4, you will discover that many of the procedures can - and should - be grouped together because of the nature of the particular procedure you're performing or because of the close proximity of two otherwise unrelated components to one another.

For example, if the vehicle is raised for any reason, you should inspect the exhaust, suspension, steering and fuel systems while you're under the vehicle. When you're rotating the tires, it makes good sense to check the brakes and wheel bearings since the wheels are already removed.

Finally, let's suppose you have to borrow or rent a torque wrench. Even if you only need to tighten the spark plugs, you might as well check the torque of as many critical fasteners as time allows.

The first step of this maintenance program is to prepare yourself before the actual work begins. Read through all sections pertinent to the procedures you're planning to do, then make a list of and gather together all the parts and tools you will need to do the job. If it looks as if you might run into problems during a particular segment of some procedure, seek advice from your local parts counterperson or dealer service department.

Owner's Manual and VECI label information

Your vehicle Owner's Manual was written for your year and model and contains very specific information on component locations, specifications, fuse ratings, part numbers, etc. The Owner's Manual is an important resource for the do-it-yourselfer to have; if one was not supplied with your vehicle, it can generally be ordered from a dealer parts department.

Among other important information, the Vehicle Emissions Control Information (VECI) label contains specifications and procedures for tune-up adjustments (if applicable) and, in some instances, spark plugs (see Chapter 6 for more information on the VECI label). The information on this label is the *exact* maintenance data recommended by the manufacturer. This data often varies by intended operating altitude, local emissions regulations, month of manufacture, etc.

This Chapter contains procedural details, safety information and more ambitious maintenance intervals than you might find in the manufacturer's literature. However, you may also find procedures or specifications in your Owner's Manual or VECI label that differ with what's printed here. In these cases, the Owner's Manual or VECI label can be considered correct, since it is specific to your particular vehicle.

3   Tune-up general information

The term *tune-up* is used in this manual to represent a combination of individual operations rather than one specific procedure.

If, from the time the vehicle is new, the routine maintenance schedule is followed closely and frequent checks are made of fluid levels and high wear items, as suggested throughout this manual, the engine will be kept in relatively good running condition and the need for additional work will be minimized.

More likely than not, however, there will be times when the engine is running poorly due to lack of regular maintenance. This is even more likely if a used vehicle, which has not received regular and frequent maintenance checks, is purchased. In such cases, an engine tune-up will be needed outside of the regular routine maintenance intervals.

The first step in any tune-up or engine diagnosis to help correct a poor running engine would be a cylinder compression check. A check of the engine compression (Chapter 2 Part C) will give valuable information regarding the overall performance of many internal components and should be used as a basis for tune-up and repair procedures. If, for instance, a compression check indicates serious internal engine wear, a conventional tune-up will not help the running condition of the engine and would be a waste of time and money.

The following series of operations are those most often needed to bring a generally poor running engine back into a proper state of tune.

Minor tune-up

Check all engine related fluids (Section 4)

Clean, inspect and test the battery (Section 9)

Check and adjust the drivebelts (Section 10)

Check all underhood hoses (Section 11)

Check the cooling system (Section 12)

Check the air filter (Section 16)

Replace the spark plugs (Section 26)

Inspect the distributor cap and rotor (Section 27)

Inspect the spark plug and coil wires (Section 27)

Major tune-up

All items listed under Minor tune-up, plus . . .

Replace the air filter (Section 16)

Check the fuel system (Section 17)

Replace the distributor cap and rotor (Section 27)

Replace the spark plug wires (Section 27)

Check the charging system (Chapter 5)

4   Fluid level checks (every 250 miles or weekly)

1   Fluids are an essential part of the lubrication, cooling, brake, clutch and other systems. Because these fluids gradually become depleted and/or contaminated during normal operation of the vehicle, they must be periodically replenished. See *Recommended lubricants and fluids* and *Capacities* at the beginning of this Chapter before adding fluid to any of the following components. **Note:** *The vehicle must be on level ground before fluid levels can be checked.*

Engine oil

Refer to illustrations 4.2, 4.4a, 4.4b and 4.6

2   The engine oil level is checked with a dipstick located at the front side of the engine **(see illustration)**. The dipstick extends through a metal tube from which it protrudes down into the engine oil pan.

3   The oil level should be checked before the vehicle has been driven, or about five minutes after the engine has been shut off. If the oil is checked immediately after driving the vehicle, some of the oil will remain in the upper engine components, producing an inaccurate reading on the dipstick.

4   Pull the dipstick from the tube and wipe all the oil from the end with a clean rag or paper towel. Insert the clean dipstick all the way back into its metal tube and pull it out again. Observe the oil at the end of the dip-

4.2 The engine oil dipstick is located at the front of the engine

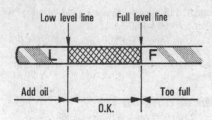

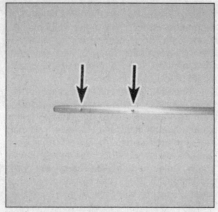

4.4a On 2000 and earlier models, the oil level should be at or near the F mark - if it isn't, add enough oil to bring the level to near the F mark (it takes one full quart to raise the level from the L to the F mark)

4.4b On 2001 and later models, the engine oil dipstick has two dimples - keep the oil level at or near the upper dimple

4.6 The threaded oil filler cap is located on the valve cover - always make sure the area around the opening is clean before unscrewing the cap to prevent dirt from contaminating the engine

stick. At its highest point, the level should be between the L and F marks (2000 and earlier models) or between the two dimples (2001 and later models) **(see illustrations)**.

5   It takes one quart of oil to raise the level from the L mark to the F mark (or the lower dimple and the upper dimple) on the dipstick. Do not allow the level to drop below the L mark (or the lower dimple) or oil starvation may cause engine damage. Conversely, over-filling the engine (adding oil above the F mark or upper dimple) may cause oil fouled spark plugs, oil leaks or oil seal failures.

6   Remove the threaded cap from the valve cover to add oil **(see illustration)**. Use a funnel to prevent spills. After adding the oil, install the filler cap hand tight. Start the engine and look carefully for any small leaks around the oil filter or drain plug. Stop the engine and check the oil level again after it has had sufficient time to drain from the upper block and cylinder head galleys.

7   Checking the oil level is an important preventive maintenance step. A continually dropping oil level indicates oil leakage through damaged seals, from loose connections, or past worn rings or valve guides. If the oil looks milky in color or has water droplets in it, a cylinder head gasket may be blown. The engine should be checked immediately. The condition of the oil should also be checked. Each time you check the oil level, slide your thumb and index finger up the dipstick before wiping off the oil. If you see small dirt or metal particles clinging to the dipstick, the oil should be changed (Section 6).

Engine coolant

Refer to illustrations 4.8a and 4.8b

Warning: *Do not allow antifreeze to come in contact with your skin or painted surfaces of the vehicle. Flush contaminated areas immediately with plenty of water. Don't store new coolant or leave old coolant lying around where it's accessible to children or pets - they're attracted by its sweet smell and may drink it. Ingestion of even a small amount of coolant can be fatal! Wipe up garage floor and drip pan spills immediately. Keep antifreeze containers covered and repair cooling system leaks as soon as they're noticed.*

8   All vehicles covered by this manual are equipped with a coolant recovery system. A white coolant reservoir located in the left front corner of the engine compartment is connected by a hose to the base of the radiator filler neck **(see illustrations)**. If the coolant heats up during engine operation, coolant can escape through a pressurized filler cap, then through a connecting hose into the reservoir. As the engine cools, the coolant is automatically drawn back into the cooling system to maintain the correct level.

9   The coolant level should be checked regularly. It must be between the Full and Low lines on the tank. The level will vary with the temperature of the engine. When the engine is cold, the coolant level should be at or slightly above the Low mark on the tank. Once the engine has warmed up, the level should be at or near the Full mark. If it isn't, allow the fluid in the tank to cool, then remove the cap from the reservoir and add coolant to bring the level up to the Full line. Use only ethylene/glycol type coolant and water in the mixture ratio recommended by your owner's manual. Do not use supplemental inhibitor additives. If only a small amount of coolant is required to bring the system up to the proper level, water can be used. However, repeated additions of water will dilute the recommended anti-freeze and water solution. In order to maintain the proper ratio of antifreeze and water, it is advisable to top up the coolant level with the correct mixture. Refer to your owner's manual for the recommended ratio.

10   If the coolant level drops within a short time after replenishment, there may be a leak in the system. Inspect the radiator, hoses, engine coolant filler cap, drain plugs, air bleeder plugs and water pump. If no leak is evident, have the radiator cap pressure tested by a service station. **Warning:** *Never remove the radiator cap or the coolant recovery reservoir cap when the engine is running or has just been shut down, because the cooling system is hot. Escaping steam and scalding liquid could cause serious injury.*

11   If it is necessary to open the radiator cap, wait until the system has cooled completely, then wrap a thick cloth around the cap and turn it to the first stop. If any steam escapes, wait until the system has cooled further, then remove the cap.

4.8a The coolant reservoir is located in the left front corner of the engine compartment - make sure the level is between Low and Full marks on the reservoir - 2000 and earlier models shown here . . .

4.8b . . . 2001 and later models look like this

12   When checking the coolant level, always note its condition. It should be relatively clear. If it is brown or rust colored, the system should be drained, flushed and refilled. Even if the coolant appears to be normal, the corrosion inhibitors wear out with use, so it must be replaced at the specified intervals.

13   Do not allow antifreeze to come in contact with your skin or painted surfaces of the vehicle. Flush contacted areas immediately with plenty of water.

Windshield washer fluid

Refer to illustration 4.14

14   Fluid for the windshield (and rear window) washer system is stored in a plastic reservoir which is located on the right side of the engine compartment **(see illustration)**. In milder climates, plain water can be used to top up the reservoir, but the reservoir should be kept no more than two-thirds full to allow for expansion should the water freeze. **Note:** *On 2000 and earlier models the fluid level is checked with a small dipstick, located next to the reservoir filler neck.* In colder climates, the use of a specially designed windshield washer fluid, available at your dealer and any auto parts store, will help lower the freezing point of the fluid. Mix the solution with water in accordance with the manufacturer's directions on the container. Do not use regular antifreeze. It will damage the vehicle's paint.

Battery electrolyte

15   On models not equipped with a sealed battery, unscrew the filler/vent cap and check the electrolyte level. It must be between the upper and lower levels. If the level is low, add distilled water. Install and securely retighten the cap. **Caution:** *Overfilling the cells may cause electrolyte to spill over during periods of heavy charging, causing corrosion or damage.*

Brake and clutch fluid

Refer to illustration 4.17

16   The brake master cylinder is mounted on the front of the power booster unit in the engine compartment. The clutch master cylinder used on vehicles with manual transaxles is located next to the brake master cylinder.

17   The brake master cylinder and the clutch master cylinder share a common reservoir. To check the fluid level of either system, simply look at the MAX and MIN marks on the brake fluid reservoir **(see illustration)**. The level should be at or near the maximum fill line.

18   If the level is low, wipe the top of the reservoir cover with a clean rag to prevent contamination of the brake or clutch system before lifting the cover.

19   Add only the specified brake fluid to the reservoir (refer to *Recommended lubricants and fluids* at the front of this chapter or to your owner's manual). Mixing different types of brake fluid can damage the system. Fill the brake master cylinder reservoir only to the dotted line - this brings the fluid to the correct

4.14 The windshield/rear window washer fluid reservoir is located in the right front corner of the engine compartment

level when you put the cover back on. **Warning:** *Use caution when filling the reservoir - brake fluid can harm your eyes and damage painted surfaces. Do not use brake fluid that has been opened for more than one year (even if the cap has been on) or has been left open. Brake fluid absorbs moisture from the air. Excess moisture can cause a dangerous loss of braking.*

20   While the reservoir cap is removed, inspect the master cylinder reservoir for contamination. If deposits, dirt particles or water droplets are present, the fluid in the brake system should be changed (see Section 24 for the brake fluid replacement procedure or Chapter 8 for the clutch hydraulic system bleeding procedure).

21   After filling the reservoir to the proper level, make sure the lid is properly seated to prevent fluid leakage and/or system pressure loss.

22   The brake fluid in the master cylinder will drop slightly as the brake pads at each wheel wear down during normal operation. If the master cylinder requires repeated replenishing to keep it at the proper level, this is an indication of leakage in the brake or clutch release system, which should be corrected immediately. Check all brake and clutch release lines and connections, along with the brake and clutch master cylinders, brake calipers, wheel cylinders and clutch release cylinder (see Section 15 for more information).

23   If, upon checking the master cylinder fluid level, you discover the reservoir empty or nearly empty, the brake system or clutch release system must be diagnosed immediately (see Chapters 8 and 9).

Power steering fluid

Refer to illustration 4.25

24   Unlike manual steering, the power steering system relies on fluid which may, over a period of time, require replenishing.

25   The fluid reservoir for the power steering pump is mounted on the passenger's side

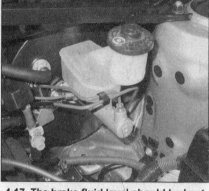

4.17 The brake fluid level should be kept between the MIN and MAX marks on the translucent plastic reservoir

strut tower **(see illustration)**.

26   For the check, the front wheels should be pointed straight ahead and the engine should be off.

27   Use a clean rag to wipe off the reservoir cap and the area around the cap. This will help prevent any foreign matter from entering the reservoir during the check.

28   Twist off the cap and check the temperature of the fluid at the end of the dipstick with your finger.

29   View the level of power steering fluid through the translucent reservoir. At no time should the fluid level drop below the upper mark for each heat range.

30   If additional fluid is required, pour the specified type directly into the reservoir, using a funnel to prevent spills.

31   If the reservoir requires frequent fluid additions, all power steering hoses, hose connections, the power steering pump and the rack-and-pinion assembly should be carefully checked for leaks.

4.25 The power steering fluid reservoir is located on the right side of the engine compartment, mounted to the strut tower - the fluid level is checked by looking through the plastic reservoir

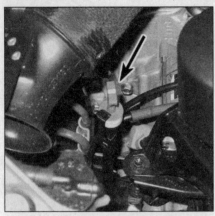

4.35a The automatic transaxle dipstick (arrow) is located in a tube which extends forward from the transaxle toward the radiator

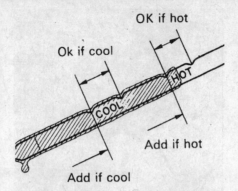

OK if hot

Ok if cool

HOT

COOL

Add if hot

Add if cool

4.35b If the automatic transaxle fluid is cold, the level should be between the two lower notches; if it's at operating temperature, the level should be between the two upper notches

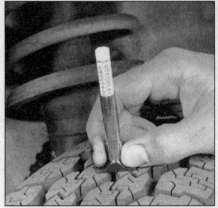

5.2 A tire tread depth indicator should be used to monitor tire wear - they are available at auto parts stores and service stations and cost very little

Automatic transaxle fluid

Refer to illustrations 4.35a and 4.35b

32   The level of the automatic transaxle fluid should be carefully maintained. Low fluid level can lead to slipping or loss of drive, while overfilling can cause foaming, loss of fluid and transaxle damage.

33   The transaxle fluid level should only be checked when the transaxle is hot (at its normal operating temperature). If the vehicle has just been driven over 10 miles (15 miles in a frigid climate), and the fluid temperature is 160 to 175-degrees F, the transaxle is hot. **Caution:** *If the vehicle has just been driven for a long time at high speed or in city traffic in hot weather, or if it has been pulling a trailer, an accurate fluid level reading cannot*

be obtained. Allow the fluid to cool down for about 30 minutes.

34   If the vehicle has not just been driven, park the vehicle on level ground, set the parking brake and start the engine. While the engine is idling, depress the brake pedal and move the selector lever through all the gear ranges, beginning and ending in Park.

35   With the engine still idling, remove the dipstick from its tube **(see illustration)**. Check the level of the fluid on the dipstick **(see illustration)** and note its condition.

36   Wipe the fluid from the dipstick with a clean rag and reinsert it back into the filler tube until the cap seats.

37   Pull the dipstick out again and note the fluid level. If the transaxle is cold, the level should be in the COLD or COOL range on the dipstick. If it is hot, the fluid level should be in

the HOT range. If the level is at the low side of either range, add the specified automatic transmission fluid through the dipstick tube with a funnel.

38   Add just enough of the recommended fluid to fill the transaxle to the proper level. It takes about one pint to raise the level from the low mark to the high mark when the fluid is hot, so add the fluid a little at a time and keep checking the level until it is correct.

39   The condition of the fluid should also be checked along with the level. If the fluid at the end of the dipstick is black or a dark reddish brown color, or if it emits a burned smell, the fluid should be changed (see Section 31). If you are in doubt about the condition of the fluid, purchase some new fluid and compare the two for color and smell.

5   Tire and tire pressure checks (every 250 miles or weekly)

Refer to illustrations 5.2, 5.3, 5.4a, 5.4b and 5.8

1   Periodic inspection of the tires may spare you from the inconvenience of being stranded with a flat tire. It can also provide you with vital information regarding possible problems in the steering and suspension systems before major damage occurs.

2   Normal tread wear can be monitored with a simple, inexpensive device known as a tread depth indicator **(see illustration)**. When the tread depth reaches the specified minimum, replace the tire(s).

3   Note any abnormal tread wear **(see illustration)**. Tread pattern irregularities such as cupping, flat spots and more wear on one side than the other are indications of front end alignment and/or balance problems. If any of these conditions are noted, take the vehicle to a tire shop or service station to correct the problem.

4   Look closely for cuts, punctures and embedded nails or tacks. Sometimes a tire will hold its air pressure for a short time or leak

UNDERINFLATION

CUPPING

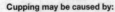

Cupping may be caused by:

• Underinflation and/or mechanical irregularities such as out-of-balance condition of wheel and/or tire, and bent or damaged wheel.
• Loose or worn steering tie-rod or steering idler arm.
• Loose, damaged or worn front suspension parts.

OVERINFLATION

FEATHERING DUE TO MISALIGNMENT

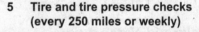

INCORRECT TOE-IN OR EXTREME CAMBER

5.3 This chart will help you determine the condition of your tires, the probable cause(s) of abnormal wear and the corrective action necessary

5.4a If a tire loses air on a steady basis, check the valve core first to make sure it's snug (special inexpensive wrenches are commonly available at auto parts stores)

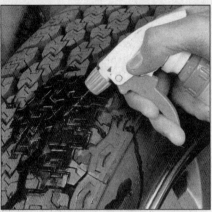

5.4b If the valve core is tight, raise the corner of the vehicle with the low tire and spray a soapy water solution onto the tread as the tire is turned slowly - slow leaks will cause small bubbles to appear

5.8 To extend the life of your tires, check the air pressure at least once a week with an accurate gauge (don't forget the spare!)

down very slowly even after a nail has embedded itself into the tread. If a slow leak persists, check the valve stem core to make sure it is tight **(see illustration)**. Examine the tread for an object that may have embedded itself into the tire or for a "plug" that may have begun to leak (radial tire punctures are repaired with a plug that is installed in a puncture). If a puncture is suspected, it can be easily verified by spraying a solution of soapy water onto the puncture area **(see illustration)**. The soapy solution will bubble if there is a leak. Unless the puncture is inordinately large, a tire shop or gas station can usually repair the punctured tire.

5   Carefully inspect the inner sidewall of each tire for evidence of brake fluid leakage. If you see any, inspect the brakes immediately.

6   Correct tire air pressure adds miles to the lifespan of the tires, improves mileage and enhances overall ride quality. Tire pressure cannot be accurately estimated by looking at a tire, particularly if it is a radial. A tire pressure gauge is therefore essential. Keep an accurate gauge in the glovebox. The pressure gauges fitted to the nozzles of air hoses at gas stations are often inaccurate.

7   Always check tire pressure when the tires are cold. "Cold," in this case, means the vehicle has not been driven over a mile in the three hours preceding a tire pressure check. A pressure rise of four to eight pounds is not uncommon once the tires are warm.

8   Unscrew the valve cap protruding from the wheel or hubcap and push the gauge firmly onto the valve **(see illustration)**. Note the reading on the gauge and compare this figure to the recommended tire pressure shown on the tire placard on the left door. Be sure to reinstall the valve cap to keep dirt and moisture out of the valve stem mechanism. Check all four tires and, if necessary, add enough air to bring them up to the recommended pressure levels.

9   Don't forget to keep the spare tire inflated to the specified pressure (consult your

owner's manual). Note that the air pressure specified for the compact spare is significantly higher than the pressure of the regular tires.

---

6   Engine oil and oil filter change (every 3000 miles or 3 months)

Refer to illustrations 6.2, 6.7, 6.13a, 6.13b and 6.15

1   Frequent oil changes are the best preventive maintenance the home mechanic can give the engine, because aging oil becomes diluted and contaminated, which leads to premature engine wear.

2   Make sure that you have all the necessary tools before you begin this procedure **(see illustration)**. You should also have plenty of rags or newspapers handy for mopping up any spills.

3   Access to the underside of the vehicle is greatly improved if the vehicle can be lifted on a hoist, driven onto ramps or supported by jackstands. **Warning:** *Do not work under a vehicle which is supported only by a bumper, hydraulic or scissors-type jack.*

4   If this is your first oil change, get under the vehicle and familiarize yourself with the location of the oil drain plug. The engine and exhaust components will be warm during the actual work, so try to anticipate any potential problems before the engine and accessories are hot.

5   Park the vehicle on a level spot. Start the engine and allow it to reach its normal operating temperature (the needle on the temperature gauge should be at least above the bottom mark). Warm oil and sludge will flow out more easily. Turn off the engine when it's warmed up. Remove the filler cap in the rear cam cover.

6   Raise the vehicle and support it on jackstands. **Warning:** *To avoid personal injury, never get beneath the vehicle when it is supported by only by a jack. The jack provided with your vehicle is designed solely for raising*

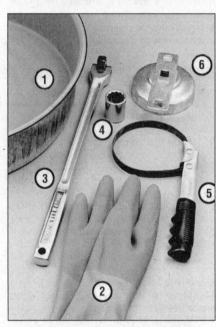

6.2 These tools are required when changing the engine oil and filter

1   **Drain pan -** *It should be fairly shallow in depth, but wide in order to prevent spills*

2   **Rubber gloves -** *When removing the drain plug and filter, it is inevitable that you will get oil on your hands (the gloves will prevent burns)*

3   **Breaker bar -** *Sometimes the oil drain plug is pretty tight and a long breaker bar is needed to loosen it*

4   **Socket -** *To be used with the breaker bar or a ratchet (must be the correct size to fit the drain plug)*

5   **Filter wrench -** *This is a metal band-type wrench, which requires clearance around the filter to be effective*

6   **Filter wrench -** *This type fits on the bottom of the filter and can be turned with a ratchet or beaker bar (different size wrenches are available for different types of filters)*

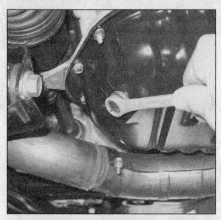

6.7 Use a proper size box-end wrench or socket to remove the oil drain plug and avoid rounding it off

6.13a Oil filter location - 2000 and earlier models (accessed from above)

6.13b Oil filter location - 2001 and later models (accessed from below)

the vehicle to remove and replace the wheels. Always use jackstands to support the vehicle when it becomes necessary to place your body underneath the vehicle.

7   Being careful not to touch the hot exhaust components, place the drain pan under the drain plug in the bottom of the pan and remove the plug **(see illustration)**. You may want to wear gloves while unscrewing the plug the final few turns if the engine is really hot.

8   Allow the old oil to drain into the pan. It may be necessary to move the pan farther under the engine as the oil flow slows to a trickle. Inspect the old oil for the presence of metal shavings and chips.

9   After all the oil has drained, wipe off the drain plug with a clean rag. Even minute metal particles clinging to the plug would immediately contaminate the new oil.

10   Clean the area around the drain plug opening, reinstall the plug and tighten it securely, but do not strip the threads.

11   Move the drain pan into position under the oil filter.

12   If you're working on a 2000 or earlier model, remove all tools, rags, etc. from under the vehicle, being careful not to spill the oil in the drain pan, then lower the vehicle. On 2001 and later models the filter is accessed from underneath.

13   Loosen the oil filter **(see illustrations)** by turning it counterclockwise with the filter wrench. Any standard filter wrench should work. Once the filter is loose, use your hands to unscrew it from the block. Just as the filter is detached from the block, immediately tilt the open end up to prevent the oil inside the filter from spilling out. **Warning:** *The engine exhaust manifold may still be hot, so be careful.*

14   With a clean rag, wipe off the mounting surface on the block. If a residue of old oil is allowed to remain, it will smoke when the block is heated up. It will also prevent the new filter from seating properly. Also make sure that the none of the old gasket remains stuck to the mounting surface. It can be removed with a scraper if necessary.

15   Compare the old filter with the new one

to make sure they are the same type. Smear some engine oil on the rubber gasket of the new filter and screw it into place **(see illustration)**. Because overtightening the filter will damage the gasket, do not use a filter wrench to tighten the filter. Tighten it by hand until the gasket contacts the seating surface. Then seat the filter by giving it an additional 3/4-turn. If you're working on a 2001 or later model, lower the vehicle now.

16   Add new oil to the engine through the oil filler cap in the valve cover. Use a spout or funnel to prevent oil from spilling onto the top of the engine. Pour three quarts of fresh oil into the engine. Wait a few minutes to allow the oil to drain into the pan, then check the level on the oil dipstick (see Section 4 if necessary). If the oil level is at or near the F mark, install the filler cap hand tight, start the engine and allow the new oil to circulate.

17   Allow the engine to run for about a minute. While the engine is running, look under the vehicle and check for leaks at the oil pan drain plug and around the oil filter. If either is leaking, stop the engine and tighten the plug or filter slightly.

18   Wait a few minutes to allow the oil to trickle down into the pan, then recheck the level on the dipstick and, if necessary, add enough oil to bring the level to the F mark.

6.15 Lubricate the oil filter gasket with clean engine oil before installing the filter on the engine

19   During the first few trips after an oil change, make it a point to check frequently for leaks and proper oil level.

20   The old oil drained from the engine cannot be reused in its present state and should be discarded. Check with your local refuse disposal company, disposal facility or environmental agency to see if they will accept the oil for recycling. Don't pour used oil into drains or onto the ground. After the oil has cooled, it can be drained into a suitable container (capped plastic jugs, topped bottles, milk cartons, etc.) for transport to one of these disposal sites.

7   Windshield wiper blade inspection and replacement (every 7500 miles or 6 months)

Refer to illustrations 7.5, 7.6 and 7.7

1   The windshield wiper and blade assembly should be inspected periodically for damage, loose components and cracked or worn blade elements.

2   Road film can build up on the wiper blades and affect their efficiency, so they should be washed regularly with a mild detergent solution.

3   The action of the wiping mechanism can loosen bolts, nuts and fasteners, so they should be checked and tightened, as necessary, at the same time the wiper blades are checked.

4   If the wiper blade elements are cracked, worn or warped, or no longer clean adequately, they should be replaced with new ones.

5   Remove the wiper blade assembly from the arm by pushing on the release lever, then sliding the assembly down and out of the hook in the end of the arm **(see illustration)**.

6   Detach the blade insert element and pull it out of the right end of the wiper frame **(see illustration)**.

7   Insert the new element end with the small protrusions into the right side of the wiper frame **(see illustration)**. Slide the element fully into place, then seat the protrusions in the end of the frames to secure it.

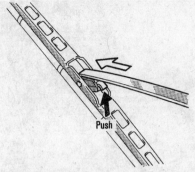

7.5 Push on the release lever and slide the wiper assembly down out of the hook in the end of the wiper arm

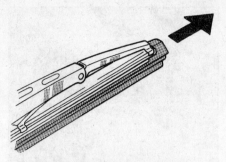

7.6 After detaching the end of the element, slide it out of the end of the frame

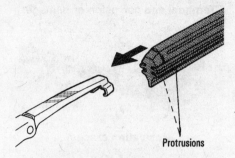

7.7 Insert the end of the element with the protrusions in first

8   Clutch pedal freeplay check and adjustment (every 7500 miles or 6 months)

Refer to illustrations 8.1 and 8.2

1   Press down lightly on the clutch pedal and, with a ruler, measure the distance that it moves freely before the clutch resistance is felt **(see illustration)**. The freeplay should be within the specified limits. If it isn't, it must be adjusted.
2   Loosen the locknut on the pedal end of the clutch pushrod **(see illustration)**.
3   Turn the pushrod until pedal freeplay and pushrod freeplay are correct.
4   Tighten the locknut.
5   After adjusting the pedal freeplay, check the pedal height.
6   If pedal height is incorrect, loosen the locknut and turn the stopper bolt until the height is correct. Tighten the locknut.

9   Battery check, maintenance and charging (every 7500 miles or 6 months)

Refer to illustrations 9.1, 9.5, 9.6a, 9.6b, 9.7a, 9.7b and 9.8
Warning: *Certain precautions must be followed when checking and servicing the battery. Hydrogen gas, which is highly flammable,*

is always present in the battery cells, so keep lighted tobacco and all other open flames and sparks away from the battery. The electrolyte inside the battery is actually dilute sulfuric acid, which will cause injury if splashed on your skin or in your eyes. It will also ruin clothes and painted surfaces. When removing the battery cables, always detach the negative cable first and hook it up last!*

1   A routine preventive maintenance program for the battery in your vehicle is the only way to ensure quick and reliable starts. But before performing any battery maintenance, make sure that you have the proper equipment necessary to work safely around the battery **(see illustration)**.
2   There are also several precautions that should be taken whenever battery maintenance is performed. Before servicing the battery, always turn the engine and all accessories off and disconnect the cable from the negative terminal of the battery. **Note:** *If you're working on a 2001 or later model, remove the cowl cover for access to the battery (see Chapter 11, if necessary).*
3   The battery produces hydrogen gas, which is both flammable and explosive. Never

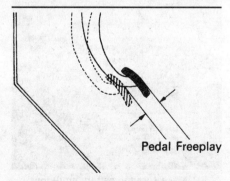

8.1 To check clutch pedal freeplay, measure the distance between the natural resting place of the pedal and the point at which you encounter resistance

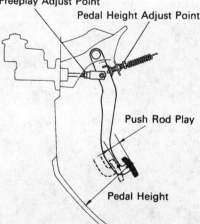

8.2 The clutch pedal pushrod play, pedal height and freeplay adjustments are made by loosening the locknut and turning the appropriate threaded adjuster

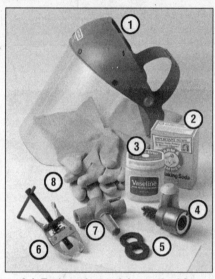

9.1 Tools and materials required for battery maintenance

1   **Face shield/safety goggles** - *When removing corrosion with a brush, the acidic particles can easily fly up into your eyes*
2   **Baking soda** - *A solution of baking soda and water can be used to neutralize corrosion*
3   **Petroleum jelly** - *A layer of this on the battery posts will help prevent corrosion*
4   **Battery post/cable cleaner** - *This wire brush cleaning tool will remove all traces of corrosion from the battery posts and cable clamps*
5   **Treated felt washers** - *Placing one of these on each post, directly under the cable clamps, will help prevent corrosion*
6   **Puller** - *Sometimes the cable clamps are very difficult to pull off the posts, even after the nut/bolt has been completely loosened. This tool pulls the clamp straight up and off the post without damage*
7   **Battery post/cable cleaner** - *Here is another cleaning tool which is a slightly different version of number 4 above, but it does the same thing*
8   **Rubber gloves** - *Another safety item to consider when servicing the battery; remember that's acid inside the battery*

Terminal end corrosion or damage.

Insulation cracks.

Chafed insulation
or exposed wires.

Burned or melted insulation.

9.5 Typical battery cable problems

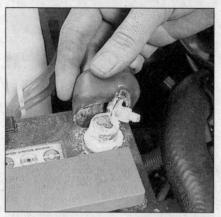

**9.6a Battery terminal corrosion usually
appears as light, fluffy powder**

**9.6b Removing a cable from the battery
post with a wrench - sometimes a pair
of special battery pliers are required for
this procedure if corrosion has caused
deterioration of the nut hex (always
remove the ground (-) cable first
and hook it up last!)**

create a spark, smoke or light a match around the battery. Always charge the battery in a ventilated area.

4   Electrolyte contains poisonous and corrosive sulfuric acid. Do not allow it to get in your eyes, on your skin on your clothes. Never ingest it. Wear protective safety glasses when working near the battery. Keep children away

from the battery.

5   Note the external condition of the battery. If the positive terminal and cable clamp on your vehicle's battery is equipped with a rubber protector, make sure that it's not torn or damaged. It should completely cover the terminal. Look for any corroded or loose connections, cracks in the case or cover or loose hold-down clamps. Also check the entire length of each cable for cracks and frayed conductors **(see illustration)**.

6   If corrosion, which looks like white, fluffy deposits **(see illustration)** is evident, particularly around the terminals, the battery should be removed for cleaning. Loosen the cable clamp bolts with a wrench, being careful to remove the ground cable first, and slide them off the terminals **(see illustration)**. Then disconnect the hold-down clamp bolt and nut, remove the clamp and lift the battery from the engine compartment.

7   Clean the cable clamps thoroughly with a battery brush or a terminal cleaner and a solution of warm water and baking soda **(see illustration)**. Wash the terminals and the top of the battery case with the same solution but make sure that the solution doesn't get into the battery. When cleaning the cables, termi-

nals and battery top, wear safety goggles and rubber gloves to prevent any solution from coming in contact with your eyes or hands. Wear old clothes too - even diluted, sulfuric acid splashed onto clothes will burn holes in them. If the terminals have been extensively corroded, clean them up with a terminal cleaner **(see illustration)**. Thoroughly wash all cleaned areas with plain water.

8   Make sure that the battery tray is in good condition and the hold-down nut and bolt are tight **(see illustration)**. If the battery is removed from the tray, make sure no parts remain in the bottom of the tray when the battery is reinstalled. When reinstalling the hold-down clamp bolt or nut, do not overtighten it.

9   Information on removing and installing the battery can be found in Chapter 5. Information on jump starting can be found at the front of this manual. For more detailed battery checking procedures, refer to the *Haynes Automotive Electrical Manual*.

**9.7a When cleaning the cable clamps, all
corrosion must be removed (the inside of
the clamp is tapered to match the taper on
the post, so don't remove too
much material)**

**9.7b Regardless of the type of tool used
to clean the battery posts, a clean, shiny
surface should be the result**

**9.8 Make sure the battery hold-down
fasteners are tight**

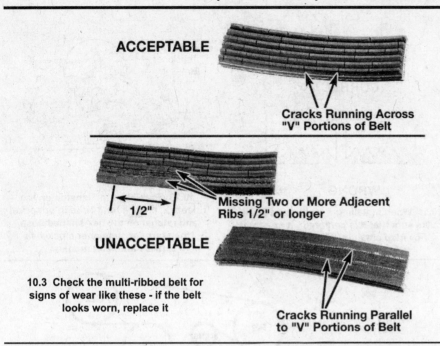

ACCEPTABLE

Cracks Running Across
"V" Portions of Belt

1/2"

Missing Two or More Adjacent
Ribs 1/2" or longer

UNACCEPTABLE

10.3 Check the multi-ribbed belt for
signs of wear like these - if the belt
looks worn, replace it

Cracks Running Parallel
to "V" Portions of Belt

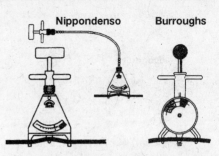

Nippondenso   Burroughs

10.4 If you are able to borrow either a
Nippondenso or Burroughs belt tension
gauge, this is how it's installed on the belt
- compare the reading on the scale with
the specified drivebelt tension

10.5 Firmly push on the drivebelt and
check how much it deflects (2000
and earlier models only)

Cleaning

10   Corrosion on the hold-down components, battery case and surrounding areas can be removed with a solution of water and baking soda. Thoroughly rinse all cleaned areas with plain water.

11   Any metal parts of the vehicle damaged by corrosion should be covered with a zinc-based primer, then painted.

Charging

Warning: *When batteries are being charged, hydrogen gas, which is very explosive and flammable, is produced. Do not smoke or allow open flames near a charging or a recently charged battery. Wear eye protection when near the battery during charging. Also, make sure the charger is unplugged before connecting or disconnecting the battery from the charger.*

12   Slow-rate charging is the best way to restore a battery that's discharged to the point where it will not start the engine. It's also a good way to maintain the battery charge in a vehicle that's only driven a few miles between starts. Maintaining the battery charge is particularly important in the winter when the battery must work harder to start the engine and electrical accessories that drain the battery are in greater use.

13   It's best to use a one or two-amp battery charger (sometimes called a "trickle" charger). They are the safest and put the least strain on the battery. They are also the least expensive. For a faster charge, you can use a higher amperage charger, but don't use one rated more than 1/10th the amp/hour rating of the battery. Rapid boost charges that claim to restore the power of the battery in one to two hours are hardest on the battery and can damage batteries not in good condition. This type of charging should only be used in emergency situations.

14   The average time necessary to charge a battery should be listed in the instructions that come with the charger. As a general rule, a trickle charger will charge a battery in 12 to 16 hours.

10   Drivebelt check, adjustment and replacement (every 7500 miles or 6 months)

Check

Refer to illustrations 10.3, 10.4 and 10.5

1   The alternator, power steering pump and air conditioning compressor drivebelts, also referred to as simply "fan" belts, are located at the right end of the engine. The good condition and proper adjustment of the alternator belt is critical to the operation of the engine. Because of their composition and the high stresses to which they are subjected, drivebelts stretch and deteriorate as they get older. They must therefore be periodically inspected.

2   On 2000 and earlier models, multiple belts are used; one belt transmits power from the crankshaft to the alternator, one drives the air conditioning compressor (if equipped), and one drives the power steering pump. On 2001 and later models, a single "serpentine" drivebelt is used.

3   With the engine off, open the hood and locate the drivebelt(s). With a flashlight, check each belt for separation of the adhesive rubber on both sides of the core, core separation from the belt side, a severed core, separation of the ribs from the adhesive rubber, cracking or separation of the ribs, and torn or worn ribs or cracks in the inner ridges of the ribs **(see illustration)**. Also check for fraying and glazing, which gives the belt a shiny appearance. Both sides of the belt should be inspected, which means you will have to twist the belt to

check the underside. Use your fingers to feel the belt where you can't see it. If any of the above conditions are evident, replace the belt (go to Step 8).

4   Belt tension on 2000 and earlier models must be manually adjusted, while on 2001 and later models the tension is adjusted automatically. To check the tension of each belt in accordance with factory specifications, install either a Nippondenso or Burroughs belt tension gauge on the belt **(see illustration)**. Measure the tension in accordance with the manufacturer's instructions and compare your measurement to the specified drivebelt tension for either a used or new belt. **Note:** *A "used" belt is defined as any belt which has been operated more than five minutes on the engine; a "new" belt is one that has been used for less than five minutes.*

5   If you don't have either of the above tools, and cannot borrow one, the following rule of thumb method is recommended: Push firmly on the belt with your thumb at a distance halfway between the pulleys and note how far the belt can be pushed (deflected) **(see illustration)**. The belt should deflect approximately 1/4-inch if the distance from pulley center to pulley center is between 7 and 11 inches; the belt should deflect about 1/2-inch if the distance from pulley center to pulley center is between 12 and 16 inches.

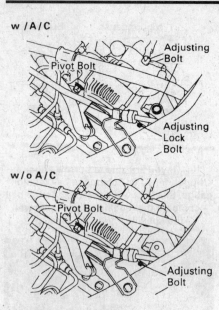

w /A/C

w/o A/C

10.6 After loosening the lock bolt, turn the adjusting bolt to tension the alternator/air conditioning compressor drivebelt

CORRECT

WRONG

10.11 When installing a multi-ribbed belt, make sure that it is centered - it must not overlap either edge of the pulley

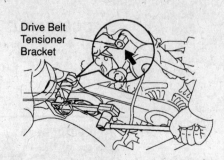

10.13 To release the tension on the drivebelt, place a long wrench or socket and ratchet on the hex-shaped boss, then turn the tensioner clockwise (2001 and later models)

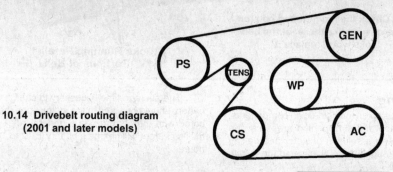

10.14 Drivebelt routing diagram (2001 and later models)

92082 1 10.14 HAYNES

Adjustment

2000 and earlier models

Refer to illustration 10.6

6   To adjust the alternator, air conditioning compressor belt, loosen the alternator pivot bolt and the adjusting lock bolt (models with air conditioning) or the adjusting bolt (models without air conditioning) at the alternator bracket. On models with air conditioning, turn the adjusting bolt and measure the belt tension in accordance with one of the above methods. On models without air conditioning, pry the alternator up in its bracket. When the proper tension is achieved, tighten the lock bolt and pivot bolt securely.

7   Adjust the power steering pump belt by loosening the pivot bolt and the lock bolt that secures the pump to the slotted bracket, then pivot the pump (away from the engine to tighten the belt, toward it to loosen it) until the proper tension is reached. When the proper tension is achieved, tighten the lock bolt and pivot bolt securely.

2001 and later models

8   Drivebelt tension on 2001 and later models is adjusted automatically by a spring-loaded tensioner.

Replacement

Warning: *Disconnect the cable from the negative terminal of the battery before performing this procedure.*

2000 and earlier models

Refer to illustration 10.11

9   To replace a belt, follow the above procedures for drivebelt adjustment but slip the belt off the crankshaft pulley and remove it. If you are replacing the power steering pump belt, you will have to remove the air condi-

tioning compressor belt first because of the way they are arranged on the crankshaft pulley. Because of this and because belts tend to wear out more or less together, it is a good idea to replace both belts at the same time. Mark each belt and its appropriate pulley groove so the replacement belts can be installed in their proper positions.

10   Take the old belts to the parts store in order to make a direct comparison for length, width and design.

11   After replacing the drivebelt, make sure that it fits properly in the ribbed grooves in the pulleys **(see illustration)**. It is essential that the belt be properly centered.

10.16 The drivebelt tensioner on 2001 and later models is retained by a nut and a bolt

12   Adjust the belt(s) in accordance with the procedure outlined above.

2001 and later models

Refer to illustrations 10.13 and 10.14

13   Rotate the belt tensioner clockwise to release the tension, then slip the belt off the pulleys **(see illustration)**. Slowly release the tensioner.

14   Route the new belt over the pulleys **(see illustration)**, again rotating the tensioner to allow the belt to be installed, then release the belt tensioner.

15   Make sure the belt is properly centered in the pulleys **(see illustration 10.11)**.

Drivebelt tensioner replacement (2001 and later models)

Refer to illustration 10.16

Warning: *Disconnect the cable from the negative terminal of the battery before performing this procedure.*

16   To replace a tensioner that can't properly tension the belt, or one that exhibits binding or a worn-out bearing/pulley, remove the drivebelt (see Step 13) then unscrew the mounting bolt and nut **(see illustration)**.

17   Installation is the reverse of the removal procedure. Tighten the fasteners to the torque values listed in this Chapter's Specifications.

18   Install the drivebelt (see Steps 14 and 15).

11 Underhood hose check and replacement (every 7500 miles or 6 months)

Caution: *Replacement of air conditioning hoses must be left to a dealer service department or air conditioning shop that has the equipment to depressurize the system safely. Never remove air conditioning components or hoses until the system has been depressurized.*

General

1   High temperatures in the engine compartment can cause the deterioration of the rubber and plastic hoses used for engine, accessory and emission systems operation. Periodic inspection should be made for cracks, loose clamps, material hardening and leaks.

2   Information specific to the cooling system hoses can be found in Section 12.

3   Some, but not all, hoses are secured to the fittings with clamps. Where clamps are used, check to be sure they haven't lost their tension, allowing the hose to leak. If clamps aren't used, make sure the hose has not expanded and/or hardened where it slips over the fitting, allowing it to leak.

Vacuum hoses

4   It's quite common for vacuum hoses, especially those in the emissions system, to be color coded or identified by colored stripes molded into them. Various systems require hoses with different wall thickness, collapse resistance and temperature resistance. When replacing hoses, be sure the new ones are made of the same material.

5   Often the only effective way to check a hose is to remove it completely from the vehicle. If more than one hose is removed, be sure to label the hoses and fittings to ensure correct installation.

6   When checking vacuum hoses, be sure to include any plastic T-fittings in the check. Inspect the fittings for cracks and the hose where it fits over the fitting for distortion, which could cause leakage.

7   A small piece of vacuum hose (1/4-inch inside diameter) can be used as a stethoscope to detect vacuum leaks. Hold one end of the hose to your ear and probe around vacuum hoses and fittings, listening for the "hissing" sound characteristic of a vacuum leak. **Warning:** *When probing with the vacuum hose stethoscope, be very careful not to come into contact with moving engine components such as the drivebelts, cooling fan, etc.*

Fuel hose

Warning: *Gasoline is extremely flammable, so take extra precautions when you work on any part of the fuel system. Don't smoke or allow open flames or bare light bulbs near the work area, and don't work in a garage where a gas-type appliance (such as a water heater or a clothes dryer) is present. Since gasoline is*

carcinogenic, wear fuel-resistant gloves when there's a possibility of being exposed to fuel, and, if you spill any fuel on your skin, rinse it off immediately with soap and water. Mop up any spills immediately and do not store fuel-soaked rags where they could ignite. The fuel system is under constant pressure, so, if any fuel lines are to be disconnected, the fuel pressure in the system must be relieved first. When you perform any kind of work on the fuel system, wear safety glasses and have a Class B type fire extinguisher on hand.

8   Check all rubber fuel lines for deterioration and chafing. Check especially for cracks in areas where the hose bends and just before fittings, such as where a hose attaches to the fuel filter.

9   High quality fuel line, specifically designed for fuel injection systems, must be used for fuel line replacement. **Warning:** *Never use anything other than the proper fuel line for fuel line replacement.*

10   Spring-type clamps are commonly used on fuel lines. These clamps often lose their tension over a period of time, and can be "sprung" during removal. Replace all spring-type clamps with screw clamps whenever a hose is replaced.

Metal lines

11   Sections of metal line are often used for fuel line between the fuel pump and fuel injection unit. Check carefully to be sure the line has not been bent or crimped and that cracks have not started in the line.

12   If a section of metal fuel line must be replaced, only seamless steel tubing should be used, since copper and aluminum tubing don't have the strength necessary to withstand normal engine vibration.

13   Check the metal brake lines where they enter the master cylinder and brake proportioning unit (if used) for cracks in the lines or loose fittings. Any sign of brake fluid leakage calls for an immediate thorough inspection of the brake system.

12 Cooling system check (every 7500 miles or 6 months)

Refer to illustration 12.4

1   Many major engine failures can be attributed to a faulty cooling system. If the vehicle is equipped with an automatic transaxle, the cooling system also cools the transaxle fluid and thus plays an important role in prolonging transaxle life.

2   The cooling system should be checked with the engine cold. Do this before the vehicle is driven for the day or after the engine has been shut off for at least three hours.

3   Remove the radiator cap by turning it to the left until it reaches a stop. If you hear a hissing sound (indicating there is still pressure in the system), wait until it stops. Now press down on the cap with the palm of your hand and continue turning to the left until the cap

Check for a chafed area that could fail prematurely.

Check for a soft area indicating the hose has deteriorated inside.

Overtightening the clamp on a hardened hose will damage the hose and cause a leak.

Check each hose for swelling and oil-soaked ends. Cracks and breaks can be located by squeezing the hose.

12.4 Hoses, like drivebelts, have a habit of failing at the worst possible time - to prevent the inconvenience of a blown radiator or heater hose, inspect them carefully as shown here

can be removed. Thoroughly clean the cap, inside and out, with clean water. Also clean the filler neck on the radiator. All traces of corrosion should be removed. The coolant inside the radiator should be relatively transparent. If it's rust colored, the system should be drained and refilled (see Section 26). If the coolant level isn't up to the top, add additional antifreeze/coolant mixture (see Section 4).

4   Carefully check the large upper and lower radiator hoses along with the smaller diameter heater hoses which run from the engine to the firewall. Inspect each hose along its entire length, replacing any hose which is cracked, swollen or shows signs of deterioration. Cracks may become more apparent if the hose is squeezed (**see illustration**). Regardless of condition, it's a good idea to replace hoses with new ones every two years.

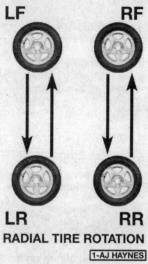

RADIAL TIRE ROTATION

1-AJ HAYNES

13.2a Four-tire rotation pattern

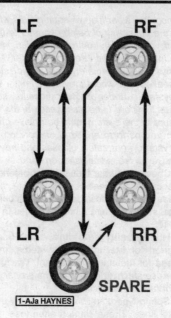

1-AJa HAYNES

13.2b Five-tire rotation pattern (to be used only if the spare tire is the same as the other four)

15.6 You will find an inspection hole like this in each caliper through which you can view the thickness of remaining friction material for the inner pad

5   Make sure that all hose connections are tight. A leak in the cooling system will usually show up as white or rust colored deposits on the areas adjoining the leak. If wire-type clamps are used at the ends of the hoses, it may be a good idea to replace them with more secure screw-type clamps.

6   Use compressed air or a soft brush to remove bugs, leaves, etc. from the front of the radiator or air conditioning condenser. Be careful not to damage the delicate cooling fins or cut yourself on them.

7   Every other inspection, or at the first indication of cooling system problems, have the cap and system pressure tested. If you don't have a pressure tester, most gas stations and repair shops will do this for a minimal charge.

13   Tire rotation (see Maintenance Schedule for service intervals)

Refer to illustrations 13.2a and 13.2b

1   The tires should be rotated at the specified intervals and whenever uneven wear is noticed. Since the vehicle will be raised and the tires removed anyway, check the brakes (see Section 16) at this time.

2   Radial tires must be rotated in a specific pattern (**see illustrations**).

3   Refer to the information in *Jacking and towing* at the front of this manual for the proper procedures to follow when raising the vehicle and changing a tire. If the brakes are to be checked, do not apply the parking brake as stated. Make sure the tires are blocked to prevent the vehicle from rolling.

4   Preferably, the entire vehicle should be raised at the same time. This can be done on a hoist or by jacking up each corner and then lowering the vehicle onto jackstands placed under the frame rails. Always use four jackstands and make sure the vehicle is firmly supported.

5   After rotation, check and adjust the tire

pressures as necessary and be sure to check the lug nut tightness.

6   For further information on the wheels and tires, refer to Chapter 10.

14   Seat belt check (every 7500 miles or 6 months)

1   Check the seat belts, buckles, latch plates and guide loops for obvious damage and signs of wear. Seat belts that exhibit fraying along the edges should be replaced.

2   Where the seat belt receptacle bolts to the floor of the vehicle, check that the bolts are secure.

3   See if the seat belt reminder light comes on when the key is turned to the Run or Start position. A chime should also sound.

15   Brake check (every 15,000 miles or 12 months)

Warning: *Dust created by the brake system is harmful to your health. Never blow it out with compressed air and don't inhale any of it. An approved filtering mask should be worn when working on the brakes. Do not, under any circumstances, use petroleum-based solvents to clean brake parts. Use brake system cleaner only!*

Note: *For detailed photographs of the brake system, refer to Chapter 9.*

1   In addition to the specified intervals, the brakes should be inspected every time the wheels are removed or whenever a defect is suspected. Any of the following symptoms could indicate a potential brake system defect: The vehicle pulls to one side when the brake

pedal is depressed; the brakes make squealing or dragging noises when applied; brake travel is excessive; the pedal pulsates; brake fluid leaks, usually onto the inside of the tire or wheel.

2   The disc brake pads have built-in wear indicators which should make a high-pitched squealing or scraping noise when they are worn to the replacement point. When you hear this noise, replace the pads immediately or expensive damage to the discs can result.

3   Loosen the wheel lug nuts.

4   Raise the vehicle and place it securely on jackstands.

5   Remove the wheels (see *Jacking and towing* at the front of this book, or your owner's manual, if necessary).

Disc brakes

Refer to illustration 15.6

6   There are two pads - an outer and an inner - in each caliper. The inner pads are visible through small inspection holes in each caliper **(see illustration)**. The outerpads are more easily viewed a the edge of the caliper.

7   Check the pad thickness by looking at each end of the caliper and through the inspection hole in the caliper body. If the lining material is less than the thickness listed in this Chapter's Specifications, replace the pads. **Note:** *Keep in mind that the lining material is riveted or bonded to a metal backing plate and the metal portion is not included in this measurement.*

8   If it is difficult to determine the exact thickness of the remaining pad material by the above method, or if you are at all concerned about the condition of the pads, then remove the caliper(s) and remove the pads for further inspection (see Chapter 9).

9   Once the pads are removed from the calipers, clean them with brake cleaner and re-measure them.

10   Measure the disc thickness with a micrometer to make sure that it still has service life remaining. If any disc is thinner than the specified minimum thickness, replace it

15.13 A quick check of the remaining drum brake shoe lining material can be made by removing the rubber plug in the backing plate and looking through the inspection hole

(refer to Chapter 9). Even if the disc has service life remaining, check its condition. Look for scoring, gouging and burned spots. If these conditions exist, remove the disc and have it resurfaced (see Chapter 9).

11   Before installing the wheels, check all brake lines and hoses for damage, wear, deformation, cracks, corrosion, leakage, bends and twists, particularly in the vicinity of the rubber hoses at the calipers.

12   Check the clamps for tightness and the connections for leakage. Make sure that all hoses and lines are clear of sharp edges, moving parts and the exhaust system. If any of the above conditions are noted, repair, reroute or replace the lines and/or fittings as necessary (see Chapter 9).

Rear drum brakes

Refer to illustrations 15.13, 15.15 and 15.17

13   To check the brake shoe lining thickness without removing the brake drums, remove the rubber plug from the backing plate and use a

flashlight to inspect the linings **(see illustration)**. For a more thorough brake inspection, follow the procedure below.

14   Refer to Chapter 9 and remove the rear brake drums.

15   Note the thickness of the lining material on the rear brake shoes **(see illustration)** and look for signs of contamination by brake fluid and grease. If the lining material is within 1/16-inch of the recessed rivets or metal shoes, replace the brake shoes with new ones. The shoes should also be replaced if they are cracked, glazed (shiny lining surfaces) or contaminated with brake fluid or grease. See Chapter 9 for the replacement procedure.

16   Check the shoe return and hold-down springs and the adjusting mechanism to make sure they're installed correctly and in good condition. Deteriorated or distorted springs, if not replaced, could allow the linings to drag and wear prematurely.

17   Check the wheel cylinders for leakage by carefully peeling back the rubber boots **(see illustration)**. If brake fluid is noted behind the boots, the wheel cylinders must be replaced (see Chapter 9).

18   Check the drums for cracks, score marks, deep scratches and hard spots, which will appear as small discolored areas. If imperfections cannot be removed with emery cloth, the drums must be resurfaced by an automotive machine shop (see Chapter 9 for more detailed information).

19   Install the brake drums.

20   Install the wheels and lug nuts.

21   Remove the jackstands and lower the vehicle.

22   Tighten the wheel lug nuts to the torque listed in this Chapter's Specifications.

Brake booster check

23   Sit in the driver's seat and perform the following sequence of tests.

24   With the brake fully depressed, start the engine - the pedal should move down a little

when the engine starts.

25   With the engine running, depress the brake pedal several times - the travel distance should not change.

26   Depress the brake, stop the engine and hold the pedal in for about 30 seconds - the pedal should neither sink nor rise.

27   Restart the engine, run it for about a minute and turn it off. Then firmly depress the brake several times - the pedal travel should decrease with each application.

28   If your brakes do not operate as described above when the preceding tests are performed, the brake booster has failed. Refer to Chapter 9 for the replacement procedure.

Parking brake

29   Slowly pull up on the parking brake and count the number of clicks you hear until the handle is up as far as it will go. The adjustment is correct if you hear the specified number of clicks. If you hear more or fewer clicks, it's time to adjust the parking brake (refer to Chapter 9).

30   An alternative method of checking the parking brake is to park the vehicle on a steep hill with the parking brake set and the transaxle in Neutral (be sure to stay in the vehicle for this procedure). If the parking brake cannot prevent the vehicle from rolling, it is in need of adjustment (see Chapter 9).

16 Air filter replacement (every 15,000 miles or 12 months)

Refer to illustrations 16.2a, 16.2b and 16.2c

1   The air filter is located inside a housing at the left (driver's) side of the engine compartment (2000 and earlier models) or directly on top of the engine (2001 and later models).

2   To remove the air filter, release the spring clips that keep the two halves of the air filter housing together, then pull the cover away

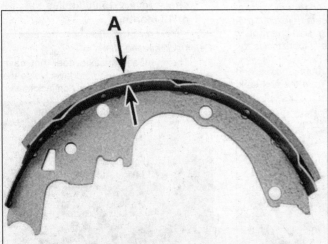

15.15 If the lining is bonded to the brake shoe, measure the lining thickness from the outer surface to the metal shoe, as shown here; if the lining is riveted to the shoe, measure from the lining outer surface to the rivet head

15.17 Carefully peel back the wheel cylinder boot and check for leaking fluid indicating that the cylinder must be replaced or rebuilt

16.2a On 2000 and earlier models, unlatch these clips to lift off
the top of the air filter housing

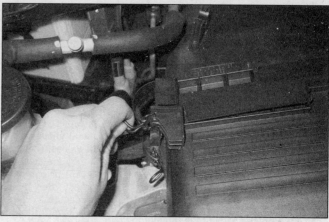

16.2b On 2001 and later models, unlatch these clips . . .

and, noting how the filter is installed, remove the air filter element **(see illustrations)**.

3   Inspect the outer surface of the filter element. If it is dirty, replace it. If it is only moderately dusty, it can be reused by blowing it clean from the back to the front surface with compressed air. Because it is a pleated paper type filter, it cannot be washed or oiled. If it cannot be cleaned satisfactorily with compressed air, discard and replace it. While the cover is off, be careful not to drop anything down into the housing. **Caution:** *Never drive the vehicle with the air cleaner removed. Excessive engine wear could result and backfiring could even cause a fire under the hood.*

4   Wipe out the inside of the air filter housing.

5   Place the new filter into the air cleaner housing, making sure it seats properly.

6   Installation of the cover is the reverse of removal.

17 Fuel system check (every 15,000 miles or 12 months)

Refer to illustrations 17.2 and 17.5
Warning: *Gasoline is extremely flammable, so take extra precautions when you work on any part of the fuel system. Don't smoke or allow open flames or bare light bulbs near the work area, and don't work in a garage where a gas-type appliance (such as a water heater or a clothes dryer) is present. Since gasoline is carcinogenic, wear fuel-resistant gloves when there's a possibility of being exposed to fuel, and, if you spill any fuel on your skin, rinse it off immediately with soap and water. Mop up any spills immediately and do not store fuel-soaked rags where they could ignite. The fuel system is under constant pressure, so, if any fuel lines are to be disconnected, the fuel pressure in the system must be relieved first. When you perform any kind of work on the fuel system, wear safety glasses and have a Class B type fire extinguisher on hand.*

1   If you smell gasoline while driving or after the vehicle has been sitting in the sun, inspect the fuel system immediately.

2   Remove the fuel filler cap and inspect it for damage and corrosion. The gasket should have an unbroken sealing imprint. If the gasket is damaged or corroded, remove it and install a new one **(see illustration)**.

3   Inspect the fuel feed and return lines for cracks. Make sure that the threaded flare-nut type connectors which secure the metal fuel lines to the fuel rail and, on 2000 and earlier models, the banjo bolt that secures the banjo fitting to the in-line fuel filter are tight.

4   Since some components of the fuel system - the fuel tank and part of the fuel feed and return lines, for example - are underneath the vehicle, they can be inspected more easily with the vehicle raised on a hoist. If that's not possible, raise the vehicle and support it securely on jackstands.

5   With the vehicle raised and safely supported, inspect the fuel tank and filler neck for punctures, cracks and other damage. The connection between the filler neck and the tank is particularly critical. Sometimes a rubber filler neck will leak because of loose clamps or deteriorated rubber **(see illustration)**. These are problems a home mechanic can usually rectify. **Warning:** *Do not, under any circumstances, try to repair a fuel tank (except rubber components). A welding torch or any open flame can easily cause fuel vapors inside the tank to explode.*

6   Carefully check all rubber hoses and metal lines leading away from the fuel tank.

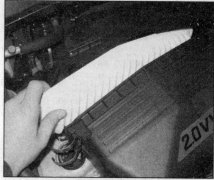

16.2c . . . pull the cover out of the way
and lift the element out

Check for loose connections, deteriorated hoses, crimped lines and other damage. Carefully inspect the lines from the tank to the fuel injection system. Repair or replace damaged sections as necessary (see Chapter 4).

18 Manual transaxle lubricant level check (every 15,000 miles or 12 months)

Refer to illustration 18.1
1   The manual transaxle does not have a dipstick. To check the fluid level, raise the vehicle and support it securely on jackstands,

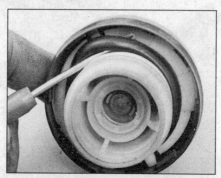

17.2 Use a small screwdriver to carefully
pry out the old gasket - take care not to
damage the cap

17.5 Inspect the filler hose for cracks and
make sure the clamps are tight

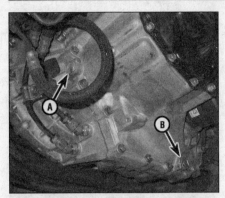

18.1 Remove the check/fill plug and use your finger as a dipstick to check the manual transaxle lubricant level

A   *Check/fill plug*
B   *Drain plug*

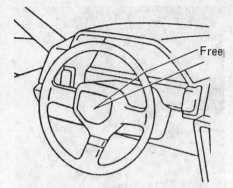

20.1 Steering wheel freeplay is the amount of travel between an initial steering input and the point at which the front wheels begin to turn (indicated by a slight resistance)

20.7 To check a balljoint for wear, try to pry the control arm up and down to make sure there is no play in the balljoint (if there is, replace it)

then remove the undervehicle splash shield. On the front side of the transaxle housing, you will see a plug **(see illustration)**. Remove it. If the lubricant level is correct, it should be up to the lower edge of the hole.

2   If the transaxle needs more lubricant (if the level is not up to the hole), use a syringe or a gear oil pump to add more. Stop filling the transaxle when the lubricant begins to run out the hole.

3   Install the plug and tighten it securely. Drive the vehicle a short distance, then check for leaks.

19   Transfer case lubricant level check (4WD models with automatic transaxle) (every 15,000 miles or 12 months)

2000 and earlier models

1   Loosen the right front wheel lug nuts, raise the front of the vehicle and support it securely on jackstands. Remove the wheel.

2   Working through the wheelwell, remove the transfer case dipstick, wipe it off, reinsert it, then pull it out and check the lubricant level on the dipstick. It should be between the LOW and HIGH marks on the dipstick.

3   If the lubricant level is below the LOW mark, add the specified fluid through the dipstick tube until the level is between the marks. **Caution:** *Be careful not to overfill the transfer case. Reinsert the dipstick.*

4   Install the wheel and lug nuts, then lower the vehicle and tighten the lug nuts to the torque listed in this Chapter's Specifications.

2001 and later models

5   Raise the vehicle and support it securely on jackstands.

6   Using the appropriate wrench, unscrew the check/fill plug from the transfer case.

7   Use your little finger to reach inside the housing to feel the lubricant level. The level should be at or near the bottom of the plug hole. If it isn't, add the recommended lubri-

cant through the plug hole with a syringe or squeeze bottle.

8   Install and tighten the plug. Check for leaks after the first few miles of driving.

20   Steering and suspension check (every 15,000 miles or 12 months)

Refer to illustrations 20.1, 20.7 and 20.8
Note: *For detailed illustrations of the steering and suspension components, refer to Chapter 10.*

With the wheels on the ground

1   With the vehicle stopped and the front wheels pointed straight ahead, rock the steering wheel gently back and forth. If freeplay **(see illustration)** is excessive , a front wheel bearing, steering shaft universal joint or lower arm balljoint is worn or the steering gear is out of adjustment or broken. Refer to Chapter 10 for the appropriate repair procedure.

2   Other symptoms, such as excessive vehicle body movement over rough roads, swaying (leaning) around corners and binding as the steering wheel is turned, may indicate faulty steering and/or suspension components.

3   Check the shock absorbers by pushing down and releasing the vehicle several times at each corner. If the vehicle does not come back to a level position within one or two bounces, the shocks/struts are worn and must be replaced. When bouncing the vehicle up and down, listen for squeaks and noises from the suspension components. Additional information on suspension components can be found in Chapter 10.

Under the vehicle

4   Raise the vehicle with a floor jack and support it securely on jackstands. See *Jacking and towing* at the front of this book for the proper jacking points.

5   Check the tires for irregular wear patterns and proper inflation. See Section 5 in this Chapter for information regarding tire

20.8 Push on the balljoint boot to check for damage

wear and Chapter 10 for the wheel bearing replacement procedures.

6   Inspect the universal joint between the steering shaft and the steering gear housing. Check the steering gear housing for grease leakage or oozing. Make sure that the dust seals and boots are not damaged and that the boot clamps are not loose. Check the steering linkage for looseness or damage. Check the tie-rod ends for excessive play. Look for loose bolts, broken or disconnected parts and deteriorated rubber bushings on all suspension and steering components. While an assistant turns the steering wheel from side to side, check the steering components for free movement, chafing and binding. If the steering components do not seem to be reacting with the movement of the steering wheel, try to determine where the slack is located.

7   Check the balljoints for wear by trying to move each control arm up and down with a pry bar **(see illustration)** to ensure that its balljoint has no play. If any balljoint does have play, replace it. See Chapter 10 for the balljoint replacement procedure.

8   Inspect the balljoint boots for damage and leaking grease **(see illustration)**. Replace the balljoints with new ones if they are damaged (see Chapter 10).

9   At the rear of the vehicle, inspect the suspension arm bushings for deterioration.

21   Driveaxle boot check (every 15,000 miles or 12 months)

Refer to illustration 21.2

1   The driveaxle boots are very important because they prevent dirt, water and foreign material from entering and damaging the constant velocity (CV) joints. Oil and grease can cause the boot material to deteriorate prematurely, so it's a good idea to wash the boots with soap and water. Because it constantly pivots back and forth following the steering action of the front hub, the outer CV boot wears out sooner and should be inspected regularly.

2   Inspect the boots for tears and cracks as well as loose clamps **(see illustration)**. If there is any evidence of cracks or leaking lubricant, they must be replaced as described in Chapter 8.

22   Rear differential lubricant level check (4WD models) (every 15,000 miles or 12 months)

Refer to illustration 22.2

1   Raise the vehicle and support it securely on jackstands.

2   Using the appropriate wrench, unscrew the plug from the rear differential **(see illustration)**.

3   Use your little finger to reach inside the housing to feel the lubricant level. The level should be at or near the bottom of the plug hole. If it isn't, add the recommended lubricant through the plug hole with a syringe or squeeze bottle.

4   Install and tighten the plug. Check for leaks after the first few miles of driving.

23   Interior ventilation filter replacement (2001 and later models) (every 15,000 miles or 12 months)

Refer to illustration 23.2

1   Open the glove box door, push in on the sides and allow the door to hang down (see Chapter 11, if necessary).

2   Pull the filter element straight out of the case **(see illustration)**.

3   Installation is the reverse of removal.

24   Brake fluid change (every 30,000 miles or 24 months)

Warning: *Brake fluid can harm your eyes and damage painted surfaces, so use extreme caution when handling or pouring it. Do not use brake fluid that has been standing open or is more than one year old. Brake fluid absorbs moisture from the air. Excess moisture can cause a dangerous loss of braking effectiveness.*

21.2   Flex the driveaxle boots by hand to check for cracks and/or leaking grease

1   At the specified intervals, the brake fluid should be drained and replaced. Since the brake fluid may drip or splash when pouring it, place plenty of rags around the master cylinder to protect any surrounding painted surfaces.

2   Before beginning work, purchase the specified brake fluid (see *Recommended lubricants and fluids* at the beginning of this Chapter).

3   Remove the cap from the master cylinder reservoir.

4   Using a hand-held suction pump or similar device, withdraw the fluid from the master cylinder reservoir.

5   Add new fluid to the master cylinder until it rises to the line indicated on the reservoir.

6   Bleed the brake system as described in Chapter 9 at all four brakes until new and uncontaminated fluid is expelled from the bleeder screw. Be sure to maintain the fluid level in the master cylinder as you perform the bleeding process. If you allow the master cylinder to run dry, air will enter the system.

7   Refill the master cylinder with fluid and check the operation of the brakes. The pedal should feel solid when depressed, with no sponginess. **Warning:** *Do not operate the vehicle if you are in doubt about the effectiveness of the brake system.*

23.2   The interior ventilation filter is retained in the blower case by clips on each side

22.2   Location of the rear differential check/fill plug (A) - B is the drain plug (4WD models)

25   Fuel filter replacement (2000 and earlier models) (every 30,000 miles or 24 months)

Refer to illustrations 25.4a and 25.4b
Warning: *See the* **Warning** *in Section 17.*
Note: *The fuel filter on 2001 and later models is integral with the fuel pump module in the fuel tank; there is no routine maintenance interval for fuel filter replacement on these models.*

1   Relieve the fuel system pressure (see Chapter 4). Disconnect the negative battery cable.

2   The canister filter is mounted in a bracket on the firewall under the air filter housing and fuse/relay block.

3   Remove the air filter housing and fuse/relay block.

4   Using a backup wrench to steady the filter, remove the banjo bolt at the top and, using a flare-nut wrench, if available, loosen the fitting at the bottom of the fuel filter **(see illustration)**.

5   Remove both bracket bolts from the firewall and remove the old filter and the filter support bracket assembly.

25.4   The fuel filter is mounted to the left strut tower (2000 and earlier models)

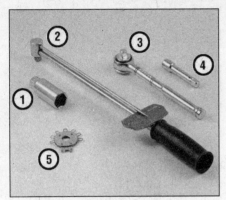

26.1 Tools required for changing spark plugs

1 **Spark plug socket** - This will have special padding inside to protect the spark plug porcelain insulator
2 **Torque wrench** - Although not mandatory, use of this tool is the best way to ensure that the plugs are tightened properly
3 **Ratchet** - Standard hand tool to fit the plug socket
4 **Extension** - Depending on model and accessories, you may need special extensions and universal joints to reach one or more of the plugs
5 **Spark plug gap gauge** - This gauge for checking the gap comes in a variety of styles. Make sure the gap for your engine is included

6   Note that the inlet and outlet pipes are clearly labeled on their respective ends of the filter and that the flanged end of the filter faces down. Make sure the new filter is installed so that it's facing the proper direction as noted above. When correctly installed, the filter should be installed so that the outlet pipe faces up and the inlet pipe faces down.
7   Connect the threaded fitting to the bottom of the filter and tighten it securely. Using new sealing washers, connect the banjo fitting to the top of the filter and tighten the banjo bolt to the torque listed in this Chapter's Specifications.
8   The remainder of installation is the reverse of the removal procedure.

---

26   Spark plug check and replacement (see maintenance schedule for service intervals)

Refer to illustrations 26.1, 26.4a, 26.4b, 26.4c, 26.6, 26.8, 26.10a and 26.10b

1   Spark plug replacement requires a spark plug socket which fits onto a ratchet wrench. This socket is lined with a rubber grommet to protect the porcelain insulator of the spark plug and to hold the plug while you remove it from the spark plug hole. You will also need a wire-type feeler gauge to check and adjust the spark plug gap and a torque wrench to

26.4a Spark plug manufacturers recommend using a wire-type gauge when checking the gap - if the wire does not slide between the electrodes with a slight drag, adjustment is required

tighten the new plugs to the specified torque **(see illustration)**.
2   If you are replacing the plugs, purchase the new plugs, adjust them to the proper gap and then replace each plug one at a time. **Note:** *When buying new spark plugs, it's essential that you obtain the correct plugs for your specific vehicle. This information can be found in the Specifications Section at the beginning of this Chapter.*
3   Inspect each of the new plugs for defects. If there are any signs of cracks in the porcelain insulator of a plug, don't use it.
4   Check the electrode gaps of the new plugs. Check the gap by inserting the wire gauge of the proper thickness between the electrodes at the tip of the plug **(see illustrations)**. The gap between the electrodes should be identical to that listed in this Chapter's Specifications or in your owner's manual. If the gap is incorrect, use the notched adjuster on the feeler gauge body to bend the curved side electrode slightly **(see illustration)**. **Caution:** *The spark plugs on 2001 and*

26.4c To change the gap, bend the side electrode only, as indicated by the arrows, and be very careful not to crack or chip the porcelain insulator surrounding the center electrode

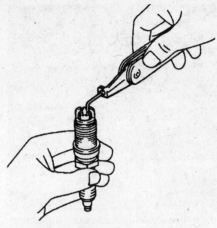

26.4b The spark plugs on 1998 through 2000 models have two ground electrodes - check the gap between each ground electrode and the center electrode

later models use iridium-coated electrodes. Don't attempt to adjust the gap on a used iridium-coated plug.
5   If the side electrode is not exactly over the center electrode, use the notched adjuster to align them. **Caution:** *If the gap of a new plug must be adjusted, bend only the base of the ground electrode - do not touch the tip.*

Removal

6   To prevent the possibility of mixing up spark plug wires, work on one spark plug at a time. Remove the wire and boot from one spark plug (2000 and earlier models only). Grasp the boot - not the cable - as shown, give it a half twisting motion and pull straight up **(see illustration)**. On 2001 and later models, remove the ignition coils (see Chapter 5).
7   If compressed air is available, blow any dirt or foreign material away from the spark plug area before proceeding.
8   Remove the spark plug **(see illustration)**.
9   Whether you are replacing the plugs at

26.6 When removing the spark plug wires on 2000 and earlier models, pull only on the boot and use a twisting/pulling motion

26.8 Use a spark plug socket with a long extension to unscrew the spark plug

26.10a Apply a thin coat of anti-seize compound to the spark plug threads

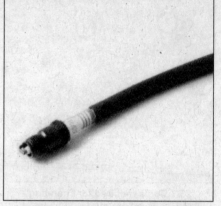

26.10b A length of snug-fitting rubber hose will save time and prevent damaged threads when installing the spark plugs

this time or intend to reuse the old plugs, compare each old spark plug with the chart on the inside back cover of this manual to determine the overall running condition of the engine.

Installation

10   Prior to installation, it's a good idea to coat the spark plug threads with anti-seize compound **(see illustration)**. Also, it's often difficult to insert spark plugs into their holes without cross-threading them. To avoid this possibility, fit a length of snug-fitting rubber hose over the end of the spark plug **(see illustration)**. The flexible hose acts as a universal joint to help align the plug with the plug hole. Should the plug begin to cross-thread, the hose will slip on the spark plug, preventing thread damage. Tighten the plug to the torque listed in this Chapter's Specifications.

11   On 2000 and earlier models, attach the plug wire to the new spark plug, again using a twisting motion on the boot until it is firmly seated on the end of the spark plug. On 2001 and later models, install the ignition coil.

12   Follow the above procedure for the remaining spark plugs, replacing them one at a time to prevent mixing up the spark plug wires.

27   Spark plug wire, distributor cap and rotor check and replacement (every 30,000 miles or 24 months)

Refer to illustrations 27.8, 27.11a, 27.11b, 27.12a, 27.12b and 27.13

Note: *Only 1996 and 1997 models are equipped with distributors. 1998 through 2000 models have a distributorless ignition system. All 2000 and earlier models have spark plug wires, but 2001 and later models have "coil over plug" ignition systems, where the ignition coils fit directly over the spark plugs. Therefore, this procedure does not apply to 2001 and later models.*

1   The spark plug wires should be checked whenever new spark plugs are installed.

2   Begin this procedure by making a visual check of the spark plug wires while the engine is running. In a darkened garage (make sure there is ventilation) start the engine and observe each plug wire. Be careful not to come into contact with any moving engine parts. If there is a break in the wire, you will see arcing or a small spark at the damaged area. If arcing is noticed, make a note to obtain new wires, then allow the engine to cool and check the distributor cap and rotor.

3   The spark plug wires should be inspected one at a time to prevent mixing up the order, which is essential for proper engine operation. Each original plug wire should be numbered to help identify its location. If the number is illegible, a piece of tape can be marked with the correct number and wrapped around the plug wire.

4   Disconnect the plug wire from the spark plug. A removal tool can be used for this purpose or you can grasp the rubber boot, twist the boot half a turn and pull the boot free. Do not pull on the wire itself.

5   Check inside the boot for corrosion, which will look like a white crusty powder.

6   Push the wire and boot back onto the end of the spark plug. It should fit tightly onto the end of the plug. If it doesn't, remove the wire and use pliers to carefully crimp the metal connector inside the wire boot until the fit is snug.

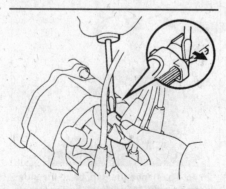

27.8 Use a small screwdriver to lift the lock claw up when detaching the spark plug boot from the distributor

7   Using a clean rag, wipe the entire length of the wire to remove built-up dirt and grease. Once the wire is clean, check for burns, cracks and other damage. Do not bend the wire sharply, because the conductor might break.

8   Disconnect the wire from the distributor cap (1997 and earlier models) or coil pack (1998 through 2000 models), using a small screwdriver to lift up on the lock claw, if equipped **(see illustration)**. Check for corrosion and a tight fit. Reconnect the wire.

9   Inspect the remaining spark plug wires, making sure that each one is securely fastened at the distributor or coil pack and spark plug when the check is complete.

10   If new spark plug wires are required, purchase a set for your specific engine model. Pre-cut wire sets with the boots already installed are available. Remove and replace the wires one at a time to avoid mix-ups in the firing order.

11   On 1997 and earlier models, detach the distributor cap by removing the retaining screws **(see illustration)**. Look inside it for cracks, carbon tracks and worn, burned or loose contacts **(see illustration)**.

12   Remove the screws and pull the rotor off the distributor shaft **(see illustration)**.

27.11a Remove the screws (upper screw shown, lower screw not visible) and detach the distributor cap

Examine it for cracks and carbon tracks **(see illustration)**. Replace the cap and rotor if any damage or defects are noted.

13   It is common practice to install a new cap and rotor whenever new spark plug wires are installed, but if you wish to continue using the old cap, check the resistance between the spark plug wires and the cap first **(see illustration)**. If the indicated resistance is more than the maximum value listed in this Chapter's Specifications, replace the cap and/or wires.

14   When installing a new cap, remove the wires from the old cap one at a time and attach them to the new cap in the exact same location - do not simultaneously remove all the wires from the old cap or firing order mix-ups may occur.

28   Cooling system servicing (draining, flushing and refilling) (every 30,000 miles or 24 months)

Warning: *Do not allow engine coolant (antifreeze) to come in contact with your skin or painted surfaces of the vehicle. Rinse off spills immediately with plenty of water. Antifreeze is highly toxic if ingested. Never leave antifreeze lying around in an open container or in puddles on the floor; children and pets are attracted by it's sweet smell and may drink it. Check with local authorities on disposing of used antifreeze. Many communities have collection centers which will see that antifreeze is disposed of safely. Antifreeze is flammable under certain conditions - be sure to read the precautions on the container.*

Note: *Non-toxic antifreeze is available at most auto parts stores. Although the antifreeze is non-toxic when fresh, proper disposal is still required.*

1   Periodically, the cooling system should be drained, flushed and refilled to replenish the antifreeze mixture and prevent formation

of rust and corrosion, which can impair the performance of the cooling system and cause engine damage. When the cooling system is serviced, all hoses and the radiator cap should be checked and replaced if necessary.

Draining

Refer to illustrations 28.4 and 28.5

2   Apply the parking brake and block the wheels. If the vehicle has just been driven, wait several hours to allow the engine to cool down before beginning this procedure.

3   Once the engine is completely cool, remove the radiator cap.

4   Move a large container under the radiator drain to catch the coolant. Attach a 3/8-inch inner diameter hose to the drain fitting to direct the coolant into the container (some models are already equipped with a hose), then open the drain fitting (a pair of pliers may be required to turn it) **(see illustration)**.

5   After the coolant stops flowing out of the radiator, move the container under the engine

27.11b Inspect the distributor cap for carbon tracks, charred or eroded terminals and other damage (if in doubt about its condition, install a new one)

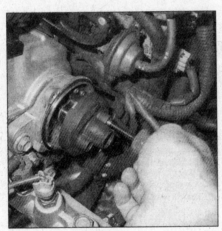

27.12a The rotor is secured by two screws

27.12b Check the rotor for damage, wear and corrosion (if in doubt about its condition, buy a new one)

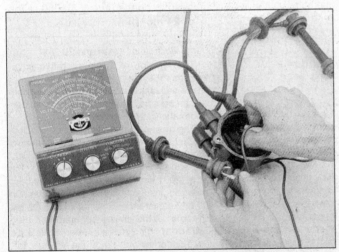

27.13 Measure the resistance value of the distributor cap and the spark plug wires - if it exceeds the specified maximum value, replace either the cap, or the wires, or both

28.4 On most models you will have to remove a cover for access to the radiator drain fitting located at the bottom of the radiator - before opening the valve, push a short section of 3/8-inch ID hose onto the plastic fitting (arrow) to prevent the coolant from splashing

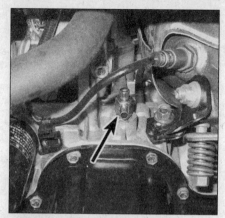

28.5 On 2001 and later models, attach a length of tubing to the spigot on the engine block drain, then loosen the drain bolt and allow the block to drain

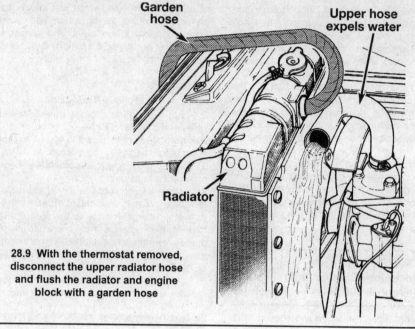

28.9 With the thermostat removed, disconnect the upper radiator hose and flush the radiator and engine block with a garden hose

block drain plug **(see illustration)**. Loosen the plug and allow the coolant in the block to drain.

6   While the coolant is draining, check the condition of the radiator hoses, heater hoses and clamps (refer to Section 12 if necessary). Replace any damaged clamps or hoses.

Flushing

Refer to illustration 28.9

7   Once the system is completely drained, remove the thermostat from the engine (see Chapter 3). Then reinstall the thermostat housing without the thermostat. This will allow the system to be thoroughly flushed.

8   Tighten the radiator drain plug. Turn your heating system controls to Hot, so that the heater core will be flushed at the same time as the rest of the cooling system.

9   Disconnect the upper radiator hose from the radiator, then place a garden hose in the upper radiator inlet and flush the system until the water runs clear at the upper radiator hose **(see illustration)**.

10   In severe cases of contamination or clogging of the radiator, remove the radiator (see

Chapter 3) and have a radiator repair facility clean and repair it if necessary.

11   Many deposits can be removed by the chemical action of a cleaner available at auto parts stores. Follow the procedure outlined in the manufacturer's instructions. **Note:** *When the coolant is regularly drained and the system refilled with the correct antifreeze/water mixture, there should be no need to use chemical cleaners or descalers.*

12   Remove the overflow hose from the coolant recovery reservoir. Drain the reservoir and flush it with clean water, then reconnect the hose.

Refilling

13   Close and tighten the radiator drain. Install and/or tighten the block drain plug. Reinstall the thermostat (see Chapter 3).

14   Place the heater temperature control in the maximum heat position.

15   Slowly add new coolant (a 50/50 mixture

of water and antifreeze) to the radiator until it's full. Add coolant to the reservoir up to the lower mark.

16   Leave the radiator cap off and run the engine in a well-ventilated area until the thermostat opens (coolant will begin flowing through the radiator and the upper radiator hose will become hot).

17   Turn the engine off and let it cool. Add more coolant mixture to bring the level back up to the lip on the radiator filler neck.

18   Squeeze the upper radiator hose to expel air, then add more coolant mixture if necessary. Replace the radiator cap.

19   Start the engine, allow it to reach normal operating temperature and check for leaks.

29   Evaporative emissions control system check (every 30,000 miles or 24 months)

Refer to illustrations 29.2a and 29.2b

1   The function of the evaporative emissions control system is to draw fuel vapors from the gas tank and fuel system, store them in a charcoal canister and then burn them during normal engine operation.

2   The most common symptom of a fault in the evaporative emissions control system is a strong fuel odor in the engine compartment (2000 and earlier models) or from under the vehicle (2001 and later models). If a fuel odor is detected, inspect the charcoal canister. On 2000 and earlier models it's located in the left rear corner of the engine compartment **(see illustration)**. On 2001 and later models it's located under the vehicle on the left side, forward of the fuel tank **(see illustration)**. Check the canister and all hoses for damage and deterioration.

3   The evaporative emissions control system is explained in more detail in Chapter 6.

29.2a Check the evaporative emissions control canister for damage and the hose connections for cracks and damage - 2000 and earlier models shown

29.2b On 2001 and later models, the EVAP canister is located under the vehicle on the left side, forward of the fuel tank (cover removed)

30.4 Be sure to check each exhaust system rubber hanger for damage

31.7a Remove the automatic transaxle drain plug with a hex wrench

30 Exhaust system check (every 30,000 miles or 24 months)

Refer to illustration 30.4

1   With the engine cold (at least three hours after the vehicle has been driven), check the complete exhaust system from its starting point at the engine to the end of the tailpipe. This should be done on a hoist where unrestricted access is available.

2   Check the pipes and connections for evidence of leaks, severe corrosion or damage. Make sure that all brackets and hangers are in good condition and tight.

3   At the same time, inspect the underside of the body for holes, corrosion, open seams, etc. which may allow exhaust gases to enter the passenger compartment. Seal all body openings with silicone or body putty.

4   Rattles and other noises can often be traced to the exhaust system, especially the mounts and hangers. Try to move the pipes, muffler and catalytic converter. If the components can come in contact with the body or suspension parts, secure the exhaust system with new mounts **(see illustration)**.

5   Check the running condition of the engine by inspecting inside the end of the tailpipe. The exhaust deposits here are an indication of engine state-of-tune. If the pipe is black and sooty or coated with white deposits, the engine is in need of a tune-up, including a thorough fuel system inspection.

31 Automatic transaxle fluid and filter change (every 30,000 miles or 24 months)

Refer to illustrations 31.7a, 31.7b, 31.8a, 31.8b, 31.9 and 31.11

Note: *Some filters are not actually "filters," but fine-mesh screens which can be cleaned with solvent instead of being replaced.*

1   At the specified time intervals, the automatic transaxle fluid should be drained and replaced.

2   Before beginning work, purchase the specified transmission fluid (see *Recommended lubricants and fluids* at the front of this chapter).

3   Other tools necessary for this job include jackstands to support the vehicle in a raised position, wrenches, drain pan capable of holding at least four quarts, newspapers and clean rags.

4   The fluid should be drained immediately after the vehicle has been driven. Hot fluid is more effective than cold fluid at removing built up sediment. **Warning:** *Fluid temperature can exceed 350-degrees F in a hot transaxle. Wear protective gloves.*

5   After the vehicle has been driven to warm up the fluid, raise it and support it on jackstands for access to the transaxle and differential drain plugs.

6   Move the necessary equipment under the vehicle, being careful not to touch any of the hot exhaust components.

7   Place the drain pan under the drain plug in the transaxle pan and remove the drain plug with the Allen wrench **(see illustration)**. Be sure the drain pan is in position, as fluid will come out with some force. Once the fluid is drained, reinstall the drain plug securely. On 2001 and later 2WD models there's also a drain plug on the transaxle's differential housing. Remove the plug and allow the fluid to drain **(see illustration)**. After the fluid has drained, reinstall the plug (using a new gasket) and tighten it to the torque listed in this Chapter's Specifications.

8   Remove the front transaxle pan bolts, then loosen the rear bolts and carefully pry the pan loose with a screwdriver and allow the remaining fluid to drain **(see illustrations)**. Once the fluid had drained, remove the bolts

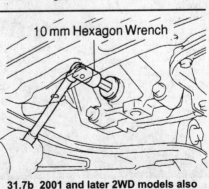

31.7b 2001 and later 2WD models also have a drain plug on the differential case

31.8a After loosening the front bolts, remove the rear transaxle pan bolts and . . .

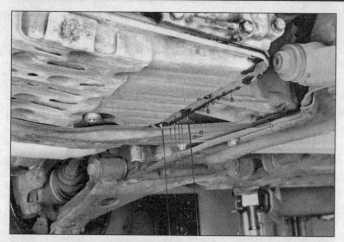

31.8b ... allow the remaining fluid to drain out

31.9 Remove the filter bolts and lower the filter (be careful, there may be some residual fluid)

and lower the pan.

9   Remove the filter retaining bolts, disconnect the clip (some models) and lower the filter from the transaxle **(see illustration)**. Be careful when lowering the filter as it contains residual fluid.

10   Place the new (or cleaned) filter in position, connect the clip (if equipped) and install the bolts. Tighten the bolts to the torque listed in the Specifications Section at the beginning of this Chapter.

11   Carefully clean the gasket surfaces of the fluid pan, removing all traces of old gasket material. Noting their location, remove the magnets, wash the pan in clean solvent and dry it with compressed air. Be sure to clean and reinstall any magnets **(see illustration)**.

12   Install a new gasket, place the fluid pan in position and install the bolts in their original positions. Tighten the bolts to the torque listed in this Chapter's Specifications.

13   Lower the vehicle.

14   With the engine off, add new fluid to the transaxle through the dipstick tube (see *Recommended lubricants and fluids* for the recommended fluid type and capacity). Use a funnel to prevent spills. It is best to add a

little fluid at a time, continually checking the level with the dipstick (see Section 4). Allow the fluid time to drain into the pan.

15   Start the engine and shift the selector into all positions from P through L, then shift into P and apply the parking brake.

16   With the engine idling, check the fluid level. Add fluid up to the Cool level on the dipstick.

32 Manual transaxle lubricant change (every 30,000 miles or 24 months)

1   Raise the rear of the vehicle and support it securely on jackstands.

2   Raise the vehicle and support it securely on jackstands. Remove the drain plug(s) and drain the lubricant **(see illustration 18.1)**.

3   Reinstall the drain plug(s) and tighten to the torque listed in this Chapter's Specifications.

4   Add new lubricant until it is even with the lower edge of the filler hole (see Section 18). See *Recommended lubricants and fluids* for the specified lubricant type.

33 Transfer case lubricant change (4WD models with automatic transaxle) (every 60,000 miles or 48 months)

Refer to illustration 33.2

1   If you're working on a 2000 or earlier model, loosen the right front wheel lug nuts.

2   Remove the drain plug and drain the lubricant **(see illustration)**.

3   Reinstall the drain plug and tighten it to the torque listed in this Chapter's Specifications.

4   2000 and earlier models: Remove the right front wheel and, working through the wheelwell, remove the transfer case dipstick. Add the specified type and amount of fluid through the dipstick tube, then use the dipstick to check the lubricant level (see Section 19, if necessary). After installing the wheel and lug nuts and lowering the vehicle, tighten the lug nuts to the torque listed in this Chapter's Specifications.

5   2001 and later models: Remove the check/fill plug and add the specified type of lubricant until is even with the lower edge

31.11 Noting their locations, remove any magnets and wash them and the pan in solvent before reinstalling them

33.2 Transfer case drain plug

35.1a On 2000 and earlier models the PCV valve is mounted in a rubber grommet in the valve cover (location on the cover may vary)

35.1b On 2001 and later models the PCV valve is threaded into the valve cover

of the hole. Reinstall the check/fill plug and tighten it to the torque listed in this Chapter's Specifications.

34 Rear differential lubricant change (4WD models) (every 30,000 miles or 24 months)

1   Raise the rear of the vehicle and support it securely on jackstands.
2   Remove the drain plug and drain the lubricant (see illustration 22.2).
3   Reinstall the drain plug and tighten it to the torque listed in this Chapter's Specifications.
4   Add new lubricant until it is even with the lower edge of the filler hole (see Section 22). See *Recommended lubricants and fluids* for the specified lubricant type.

35 Positive Crankcase Ventilation (PCV) valve and hose check and replacement (every 30,000 miles or 24 months)

Refer to illustrations 35.1a, 35.1b and 35.4
1   The PCV valve and hose is located in the valve cover. On 2000 and earlier models it's mounted in a grommet on the valve cover (see illustration). On 2001 and later models it's threaded into the left (driver's) end of the valve cover (see illustration).
2   Remove the PCV valve from the cover. On 2000 and earlier models, grasp the valve firmly and pull it out of its grommet. On 2001 and later models, detach the hose, unscrew the valve from the cover, then reattach the hose.
3   With the engine idling at normal operating temperature, place your finger over the end of the valve. If there's no vacuum at the valve, check for a plugged hose or valve. Replace any plugged or deteriorated hoses.
4   Turn off the engine. Remove the PCV valve from the hose. Connect a clean piece

of hose and blow through the valve from the valve cover (cylinder head) end. If air will not pass through the valve in this direction, replace it with a new one (see illustration).
5   When purchasing a replacement PCV valve, make sure it's for your particular vehicle and engine size. Compare the old valve with the new one to make sure they're the same.

36 Valve clearance check and adjustment (every 60,000 miles or 48 months)

Warning: *These models are equipped with airbags. Always disable the airbag system before working in the vicinity of any airbag system component to avoid the possibility of accidental deployment of the airbag(s), which could cause personal injury (see Chapter 12).*
Note: *If you're working on a 1997 or earlier model, the following procedure requires the use of a special valve lifter tool. It is impossible to perform this task without it.*

Check
Refer to illustrations 36.6a, 36.6b and 36.7
1   Disconnect the negative cable from the battery.
2   Disconnect the spark plug wires (2000 and earlier models - see Section 27) or ignition coils (2001 and later models - see Chapter 5) and remove any other components that will interfere with valve cover removal.

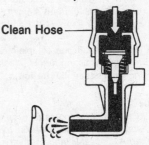

Cylinder Head Side

Clean Hose

35.4 To check the PVC valve, first attach a clean section of hose to the cylinder head side of the valve and blow through it - air should pass through easily - then blow through the intake manifold side of the valve and verify that air passes through with difficulty

3   Blow out the recessed area around the spark plug openings with compressed air, if available, to remove any debris that might fall into the cylinders, then remove the spark plugs (see Section 26).
4   Remove the valve cover (refer to Chapter 2).
5   Refer to Chapter 2 and position the number 1 piston at TDC on the compression stroke.
6   Measure the clearances of the indicated valves with feeler gauges (see illustrations).

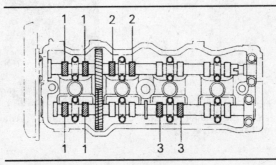

36.6a When the no. 1 piston is at TDC on the compression stroke, the valve clearance for the no. 1 and no. 3 cylinder exhaust valves and the no. 1 and no. 2 cylinder intake valves can be measured (2000 and earlier models shown, later models similar)

36.6b Check the clearance for each valve with a feeler gauge of the specified thickness - if the clearance is correct, you should feel a slight drag on the gauge as you pull it out

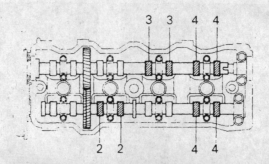

36.7 When the no. 4 piston is at TDC on the compression stroke, the valve clearance for the no. 2 and no. 4 exhaust valves and the no. 3 and no. 4 intake valves can be measured

Record the measurements which are out of specification. They will be used later to determine the required replacement shims (2000 and earlier models) or lifters (2001 and later models).

7   Turn the crankshaft one complete revolution and realign the timing marks. Measure the remaining valves (see illustration).

Adjustment

Note: *2000 and earlier models use replaceable adjustment shims that ride on top of the lifters. 2001 and later models don't have shims; instead, they use lifters of different thickness to provide proper valve clearance.*

2000 and earlier models

Refer to illustrations 36.9a, 36.9b and 36.9c

8   If any of the valve clearances were out of specification, turn the crankshaft pulley until the camshaft lobe above the first valve which you intend to adjust is pointing upward, away from the shim.

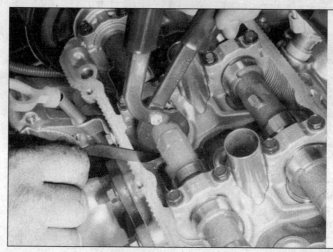

36.9a Install the valve lifter tool as shown and squeeze the handles together to depress the valve lifter, then hold the lifter down with the smaller tool so the shim can be removed

9   Position the notch in the valve lifter toward the spark plug. Then depress the valve lifter with the special valve lifter tools (see illustration). Place the special valve lifter tool in position as shown, with the longer jaw of the tool gripping the lower edge of the cast lifter boss and the upper, shorter jaw gripping the upper edge of the lifter itself. Depress the valve lifter by squeezing the handles of the valve lifter tool together, then hold the lifter down with the smaller tool and remove the larger one. Remove the adjusting shim

with a small screwdriver or a pair of tweezers (see illustrations). Note that the wire hook on the end of some valve lifter tool handles can be used to clamp both handles together to keep the lifter depressed while the shim is removed.

2001 and later models

10   If any of the valve clearances were out of adjustment, remove the camshaft(s) from over the lifter(s) that was/were out of the specified clearance range (see Chapter 2, Part B).

36.9b Keep pressure on the lifter with the smaller tool and remove the shim with a small screwdriver . . .

36.9c . . . a pair of tweezers or a magnet as shown here

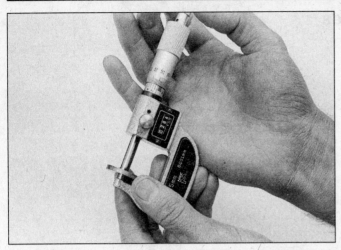

36.11a Measure the shim thickness with a micrometer
(2000 and earlier models)

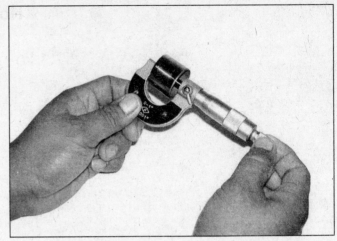

36.11b On 2001 and later models, measure the thickness of the
lifter head with a micrometer

All models

Refer to illustrations 36.11a, 36.11b, 36.12a and 36.12b

11   Measure the thickness of the shim (2000 and earlier models) or lifter (2001 and later models) with a micrometer **(see illustrations)**. To calculate the correct thickness of a replacement shim or lifter that will place the valve clearance within the specified value, use the following formula:

$N = T + (A - V)$

T = *thickness of the old shim or lifter*
A = *valve clearance measured*
N = *thickness of the new shim or lifter*
V = *desired valve clearance* (see this Chapter's Specifications)

12   Select a shim (2000 and earlier models) or lifter (2001 and later models) with a thickness as close as possible to the valve clearance calculated. The shims on 2000 and earlier models, which are available in 17 sizes in increments of 0.0020-inch (0.050 mm), range in size from 1.0984-inch (2.500 mm)

to 0.1299-inch (3.300 mm) **(see illustration)**. The lifters on 2001 and later models are available in 35 sizes in increments of 0.0008-inch (0.020 mm), range in size from 0.1992-inch (5.060 mm) to 0.2260-inch (5.740 mm) **(see illustration)**. **Note:** *Through careful analysis of the shim or lifter sizes needed to bring the out-of-specification valve clearance within specification, it is often possible to simply move a shim or lifter that has to come out anyway to another location requiring a shim or lifter of that particular size, thereby reducing the number of new shims or lifters that must be purchased.*

2000 and earlier models

13   Place the special valve lifter tool in position **as shown in illustration 36.9a**, with the longer jaw of the tool gripping the lower edge of the cast lifter boss and the upper, shorter jaw gripping the upper edge of the lifter itself, press down the valve lifter by squeezing the handles of the valve lifter tool together and install the new adjusting shim (note that the

wire hook on the end of one valve lifter tool handle can be used to clamp the handles together to keep the lifter depressed while the shim is inserted. Measure the clearance with a feeler gauge to make sure that your calculations are correct.

14   Repeat this procedure until all the valves which are out of clearance have been corrected.

2001 and later models

15   Install the proper thickness lifter(s) in position, making sure to lubricate them with camshaft installation lube first. **Note:** *Apply the lubricant to the underside of the lifter where it contacts the valve stem, the walls of the lifter and the face of the lifter.*

16   Install the camshaft(s) (see Chapter 2B).

All models

17   Installation of the spark plugs, valve cover, spark plug wires and boots (or ignition coils), etc. is the reverse of removal.

New shim thickness   mm (in.)

Shim No.	Thickness	Shim No.	Thickness
1	2.500 (0.0984)	10	2.950 (0.1161)
2	2.550 (0.1004)	11	3.000 (0.1181)
3	2.600 (0.1024)	12	3.050 (0.1201)
4	2.650 (0.1043)	13	3.100 (0.1220)
5	2.700 (0.1063)	14	3.150 (0.1240)
6	2.750 (0.1083)	15	3.200 (0.1260)
7	2.800 (0.1102)	16	3.250 (0.1280)
8	2.850 (0.1122)	17	3.300 (0.1299)
9	2.900 (0.1142)		

36.12a Valve adjusting shim thickness chart
(2000 and earlier models)

New lifter thickness   mm (in.)

Lifter No.	Thickness	Lifter No.	Thickness	Lifter No.	Thickness
06	5.060 (0.1992)	30	5.300 (0.2087)	54	5.540 (0.2181)
08	5.080 (0.2000)	32	5.320 (0.2094)	56	5.560 (0.2189)
10	5.100 (0.2008)	34	5.340 (0.2102)	58	5.580 (0.2197)
12	5.120 (0.2016)	36	5.360 (0.2110)	60	5.600 (0.2205)
14	5.140 (0.2024)	38	5.380 (0.2118)	62	5.620 (0.2213)
16	5.160 (0.2031)	40	5.400 (0.2126)	64	5.640 (0.2220)
18	5.180 (0.2039)	42	5.420 (0.2134)	66	5.660 (0.2228)
20	5.200 (0.2047)	44	5.440 (0.2142)	68	5.680 (0.2236)
22	5.220 (0.2055)	46	5.460 (0.2150)	70	5.700 (0.2244)
24	5.240 (0.2063)	48	5.480 (0.2157)	72	5.720 (0.2252)
26	5.260 (0.2071)	50	5.500 (0.2165)	74	5.740 (0.2260)
28	5.280 (0.2079)	52	5.520 (0.2173)		

36.12b Valve lifter thickness chart (2001 and later models)

Notes

Chapter 2 Part A
Engines - 2000 and earlier

Contents

	Section		Section
Camshaft oil seal - replacement	9	General information	1
Camshafts and valve lifters - removal, inspection and installation	10	Intake manifold - removal and installation	5
CHECK ENGINE light on	See Chapter 6	Oil pan - removal and installation	12
Crankshaft front oil seal - replacement	8	Oil pump - removal, inspection and installation	13
Cylinder compression check	See Chapter 2C	Powertrain mounts - check and replacement	16
Cylinder head - removal and installation	11	Rear main oil seal - replacement	15
Drivebelt check, adjustment and replacement	See Chapter 1	Repair operations possible with the engine in the vehicle	2
Engine oil and filter change	See Chapter 1	Spark plug replacement	See Chapter 1
Engine overhaul - general information	See Chapter 2C	Timing belt and sprockets - removal, inspection and installation	7
Engine - removal and installation	See Chapter 2C	Top Dead Center (TDC) for number one piston - locating	3
Exhaust manifold - removal and installation	6	Valve cover - removal and installation	4
Flywheel/driveplate - removal and installation	14	Water pump - removal and installation	See Chapter 3

Specifications

General

Engine designation	3S-FE
Displacement	121.9 cubic inches (2.0 liters)
Cylinder numbers (drivebelt end-to-transaxle end)	1-2-3-4
Firing order	1-3-4-2

Cylinder head
Warpage limits

Cylinder head-to-block surface	0.002 inch (0.05 mm)
Intake and exhaust manifolds	0.0031 inch (0.08 mm)

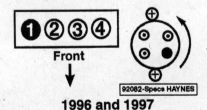

1996 and 1997

Cylinder numbering and distributor rotation

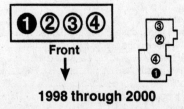

1998 through 2000

Cylinder numbering and coil terminal location

Timing belt

Idler pulley spring free length

1996 and 1997	1.811 inches (46.0 mm)
1998 through 2000	1.653 inches (42.0 mm)

Camshaft

Journal diameter (all)	1.0614 to 1.0620 inches (26.959 to 26.975 mm)
Runout limit	0.0016 inch (0.04 mm)

Bearing oil clearance

Standard	0.0010 to 0.0024 inch (0.025 to 0.062 mm)
Service limit	0.0039 inch (0.10 mm)

Lobe height

Intake camshaft

Standard	1.6539 to 1.6579 inches (42.01 to 42.11 mm)
Service limit	1.6496 inches (41.90 mm)

Exhaust camshaft

Standard	1.5772 to 1.5811 inches (40.06 to 40.16 mm)
Service limit	1.5728 inches (39.95 mm)

Camshaft thrust clearance (endplay)

Intake camshaft

Standard	0.0018 to 0.0039 inch (0.045 to 0.100 mm)
Service limit	0.0047 inch (0.12 mm)

Exhaust camshaft

Standard	0.0012 to 0.0033 inch (0.030 to 0.085 mm)
Service limit	0.0039 inch (0.10 mm)
Camshaft gear spring end gap	0.886 to 0.902 inch (22.5 to 22.9 mm)

Camshaft gear backlash

Standard	0.0008 to 0.0079 inch (0.020 to 0.200 mm)
Service limit	0.0188 inch (0.30 mm)

Valve lifter

Diameter	1.2191 to 1.2195 inches (30.966 to 30.976 mm)
Bore diameter	1.2205 to 1.2211 inches (31.000 to 31.016 mm)

Lifter oil clearance

Standard	0.0009 to 0.0020 inch (0.024 to 0.052 mm)
Service limit	0.0028 inch (0.07 mm)

Oil pump

Driven rotor-to-case clearance

Standard	0.0039 to 0.0063 inch (0.10 to 0.16 mm)
Service limit	0.0079 inch (0.20 mm)

Rotor tip clearance

Standard	0.0016 to 0.0063 inch (0.04 to 0.16 mm)
Service limit	0.0079 inch (0.20 mm)

Torque specifications

	Ft-lbs (unless otherwise indicated)	Nm
Intake manifold nuts/bolts	168 in-lbs	19
Intake manifold brace bolts	31	42
Exhaust manifold nuts/bolts	36	49
Engine balancer assembly mounting bolts	36	49
Crankshaft pulley-to-crankshaft bolt	80	108
Flywheel/driveplate bolts		
Flywheel (manual transaxle)	65	88
Driveplate (automatic transaxle)	61	83
Idler pulley bolts	31	42
Cylinder head bolts (in sequence - **see illustration 11.23**)		
Step 1	36	49
Step 2	Tighten an additional 90-degrees (1/4 turn)	
Camshaft bearing cap bolts	168 in-lbs	19
Camshaft sprocket bolt	40	54
Oil pump body-to-oil pump case	78 in-lbs	8.8
Oil pump-to-engine block bolts	78 in-lbs	8.8
Oil pump sprocket nut	18	24
Oil pick-up (strainer) nuts/bolts	48 in-lbs	5.4
Oil pan-to-block bolts	48 in-lbs	5.4
Oil pan-to-oil pump bolts	48 in-lbs	5.4
Spark plug tube nuts	33	44
Rear main oil seal retainer bolts	108 in-lbs	13

Torque specifications

	Ft-lbs (unless otherwise indicated)	Nm
Engine mounts		
Front mount through-bolt	47	64
Front mount bracket to transaxle bolts	47	64
Front mount-to-crossmember nuts	59	80
Rear mount through-bolt	47	64
Rear mount bracket-to-transaxle bolts	47	64
Rear mount-to-crossmember nuts	82	111
Passenger side mount bracket-to-engine bolts	38	51
Passenger side mount-to-engine bracket bolt	27	36
Passenger side mount-to-engine bracket nuts	38	51
Passenger side mount-to-chassis bolts	47	64
Driver's side mount bracket-to transaxle bolts/nuts		
1996 and 1997	47	64
1998 through 2000	38	51
Driver's side mount through bolt	47	64

1 General information

This Part of Chapter 2 is devoted to in-vehicle repair procedures for the 2000 and earlier four-cylinder engine. All information concerning engine removal, installation and overhaul can be found in Part C of this Chapter.

The following repair procedures are based on the assumption that the engine is installed in the vehicle. If the engine has been removed from the vehicle and mounted on a stand, many of the steps outlined in this Part of Chapter 2 will not apply.

The Specifications included in this Part of Chapter 2 apply only to the in vehicle procedures contained in this Part. Part C of Chapter 2 contains the general Specifications for all the engines covered by this manual.

During the years covered by this manual, the 2000 and earlier four-cylinder engine in the RAV4 is designated the 3S-FE. This engine design includes dual overhead camshafts (DOHC) and four valves per cylinder and a timing belt which drives the camshafts.

2 Repair operations possible with the engine in the vehicle

Many major repair operations can be accomplished without removing the engine from the vehicle.

Clean the engine compartment and the exterior of the engine with some type of degreaser before any work is done. It will make the job easier and help keep dirt out of the internal areas of the engine.

Depending on the components involved, it may be helpful to remove the hood to improve access to the engine as repairs are performed (refer to Chapter 11 if necessary). Cover the fenders to prevent damage to the paint. Special pads are available, but an old bedspread or blanket will also work.

If vacuum, exhaust, oil or coolant leaks develop, indicating a need for gasket or seal replacement, the repairs can generally be made with the engine in the vehicle. The intake and exhaust manifold gaskets, oil pan gasket, crankshaft oil seals and cylinder head gasket are all accessible with the engine in place.

Exterior engine components, such as the intake and exhaust manifolds, the oil pan, the oil pump, the water pump, the starter motor, the alternator and the fuel system components can be removed for repair with the engine in place.

Since the cylinder head can be removed without pulling the engine, camshaft and valve component servicing can also be accomplished with the engine in the vehicle. Replacement of the timing belt and pulleys is also possible with the engine in the vehicle.

3 Top Dead Center (TDC) for number one piston - locating

Refer to illustration 3.6

1 Top Dead Center (TDC) is the highest point in the cylinder that each piston reaches as it travels up-and-down when the crankshaft turns. Each piston reaches TDC on the compression stroke and again on the exhaust stroke, but TDC generally refers to piston position on the compression stroke. The timing marks on the vibration damper installed

3.6 Align the crankshaft drivebelt pulley notch (arrow) with the 0 on the timing plate

on the front of the crankshaft are referenced to the number one piston at TDC on the compression stroke.

2 Positioning the piston(s) at TDC is an essential part of procedures such as valve adjustment and timing belt and sprocket replacement.

3 In order to bring any piston to TDC, the crankshaft must be turned using one of the methods outlined below. When looking at the timing belt end of the engine, normal crankshaft rotation is clockwise. **Warning:** *Before beginning this procedure, be sure to place the transmission in Neutral and remove the ignition key.*

a) *The preferred method is to turn the crankshaft with a large socket and breaker bar attached to the large bolt threaded into the center of the crankshaft pulley.*

b) *A remote starter switch, which may save some time, can also be used. Attach the switch leads to the S (switch) and B (battery) terminals on the starter motor. Once the piston is close to TDC, use a socket and breaker bar as described in the previous paragraph.*

c) *If an assistant is available to turn the ignition switch to the Start position in short bursts, you can get the piston close to TDC without a remote starter switch. Use a socket and breaker bar as described in Paragraph a) to complete the procedure.*

4 Disable the ignition system by disconnecting the primary electrical connectors at the ignition coil pack/modules (see Chapter 5).

5 Remove the spark plugs and install a compression gauge in the number one cylinder. Turn the crankshaft clockwise with a socket and breaker bar as described above.

6 When the piston approaches TDC, compression will be noted on the compression gauge. Continue turning the crankshaft until the notch in the crankshaft damper is aligned with the TDC mark on the front cover **(see illustration)**. At this point number one cylinder is at TDC on the compression stroke. If the marks aligned but there was no compression, the piston was on the exhaust stroke. Continue rotating the crankshaft 360-degrees (1-turn).

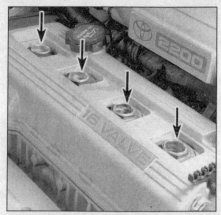

4.5 The valve cover is held in place by the large spark plug tube nuts (arrows)

7   After the number one piston has been positioned at TDC on the compression stroke, TDC for any of the remaining cylinders can be located by turning the crankshaft 180 degrees and following the firing order (refer to the Specifications). Rotating the engine 180 degrees past TDC #1 will put the engine at TDC compression for cylinder #3.

4   Valve cover - removal and installation

Refer to illustrations 4.5 and 4.7

Removal

1   Disconnect the negative cable from the battery.
2   Detach the breather hose from the valve cover.
3   Remove the spark plug wires from the spark plugs, handling them by the boots, not pulling on the wires.
4   Remove the wiring harness bolts at the timing belt cover and move the harness aside. Also remove the accelerator cable bracket from the intake manifold and position it aside to allow access for valve cover removal.
5   Remove the spark plug tube nuts, then detach the cover and gasket from the head.

5.5b Press in on the clips to release the wiring harness retainers

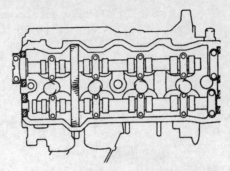

4.7 Apply sealant to the eight points indicated by the shaded areas before installing the valve cover

The spark plug tube nuts are used to hold the cover in place **(see illustration)**. If the cover is stuck to the head, bump the end with a block of wood and a hammer to jar it loose. If that doesn't work, try to slip a flexible putty knife between the head and cover to break the seal. **Caution:** *Don't pry at the cover-to-head joint or damage to the sealing surfaces may occur, leading to oil leaks after the cover is reinstalled.*

Installation

6   The mating surfaces of the housing or cylinder head and cover must be clean when the cover is installed. Use a gasket scraper to remove all traces of sealant and old gasket material, then clean the mating surfaces with lacquer thinner or acetone. If there's residue or oil on the mating surfaces when the cover is installed, oil leaks may develop.
7   Apply RTV sealant to the gasket/seal joints **(see illustration)**. Install the spark plug tube grommets in the valve cover with the index marks facing the timing belt end of the engine.
8   Position a new valve cover gasket on the cylinder head, then install the valve cover and spark plug tube nuts.
9   Tighten the spark plug tube nuts to the torque listed in this Chapter's Specifications in three or four equal steps.
10   Reinstall the remaining parts, run the engine and check for oil leaks.

5.5c Disconnect the two ground straps (arrows) from the firewall side of the intake manifold, then disconnect the knock sensor

5.5a The various hoses should be marked to ensure correct reinstallation

5   Intake manifold - removal and installation

Refer to illustrations 5.5a, 5.5b, 5.5c, 5.6a, 5.6b, 5.7 and 5.8
Warning: *Wait until the engine is completely cool before beginning this procedure.*

Removal

1   Disconnect the negative cable from the battery.
2   Loosen the air cleaner hose clamp at the throttle body and remove the air cleaner top (four clamps), resonator and hose.
3   Disconnect the coolant hoses from the throttle body and plug them to prevent coolant leakage.
4   Remove the EGR valve and the vacuum modulator valve (see Chapter 6) from the intake manifold.
5   Label and detach any wire harness and control cables or hoses connected to the intake manifold and the throttle body **(see illustrations)**. Carefully lift the wire harness over the manifold.
6   Unbolt the intake manifold-to-engine braces **(see illustrations)**.
7   Remove the mounting nuts/bolts **(see illustration)**, then detach the manifold from the engine.

5.6a Remove the bolts (arrows) from the intake manifold-to-block braces (seen from below)

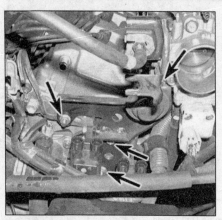

5.6b Disconnect the electrical connectors from the coil pack, then remove the mounting bolts (arrows) and remove the coil pack mount/intake brace

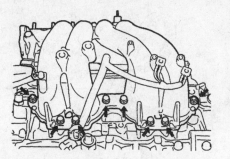

5.7 Locations of the intake manifold bolts/nuts

5.8 Remove all traces of old gasket material and sealant with a scraper - be careful not to gouge the aluminum manifold

Installation

8   Use a scraper to remove all traces of old gasket material and sealant from the manifold and cylinder head **(see illustration)**, then clean the mating surfaces with lacquer thinner or acetone. If the gasket was leaking, have the manifold checked for warpage at an automotive machine shop and resurfaced if necessary.

9   Install a new gasket, then position the manifold on the head and install the nuts/bolts.

10   Tighten the nuts/bolts in three or four equal steps to the torque listed in this Chapter's Specifications. Work from the center out towards the ends to avoid warping the manifold.

11   Install the remaining parts in the reverse order of removal.

12   Before starting the engine, check the throttle linkage for smooth operation.

13   Check the coolant and add some, if necessary, to bring it to the appropriate level. Run the engine and check for coolant and vacuum leaks.

14   Road test the vehicle and check for proper operation of all accessories, including the cruise control system.

6   Exhaust manifold - removal and installation

Refer to illustrations 6.3, 6.6 and 6.7
Warning: *The engine must be completely cool before beginning this procedure.*

Removal

1   Disconnect the negative cable from the battery.

2   Unplug the oxygen sensor wire harness and the clamp over the harness. If you're installing a new exhaust manifold, remove the sensor (see Chapter 6).

3   Remove the upper heat insulator from the manifold **(see illustration)**.

4   Apply penetrating oil to the exhaust manifold mounting nuts/bolts.

5   Disconnect the exhaust pipe from the exhaust manifold (see Chapter 4).

6   Remove the exhaust manifold brace (some models have two braces) and lower heat insulator **(see illustration)**.

7   Remove the nuts/bolts and detach the manifold and gasket **(see illustration)**.

6.6 Unbolt the exhaust manifold flange brace (arrow) near the front engine mount

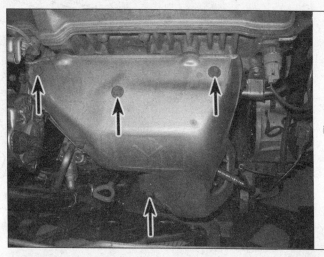

6.3 Remove the exhaust manifold heat insulator bolts (arrows)

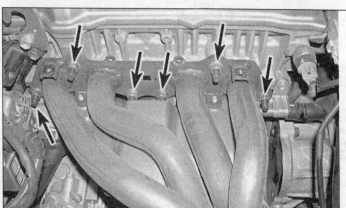

6.7 Remove the exhaust manifold fasteners (arrows) at the cylinder head

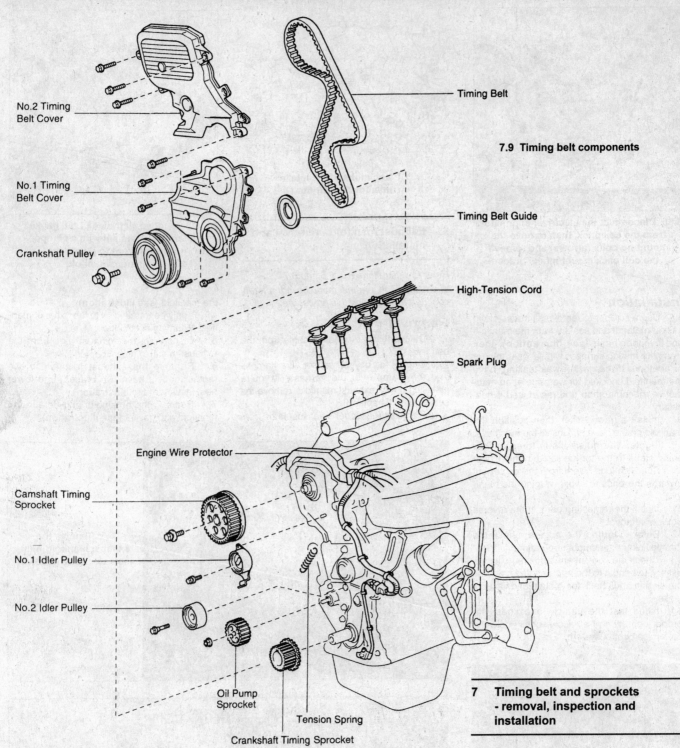

No.2 Timing Belt Cover

No.1 Timing Belt Cover

Crankshaft Pulley

Timing Belt

7.9 Timing belt components

Timing Belt Guide

High-Tension Cord

Spark Plug

Engine Wire Protector

Camshaft Timing Sprocket

No.1 Idler Pulley

No.2 Idler Pulley

Oil Pump Sprocket

Tension Spring

Crankshaft Timing Sprocket

7   Timing belt and sprockets - removal, inspection and installation

Installation

8   Use a scraper to remove all traces of old gasket material and carbon deposits from the manifold and cylinder head mating surfaces. If the gasket was leaking, have the manifold checked for warpage at an automotive machine shop and resurfaced if necessary.
9   Position a new gasket over the cylinder head studs.

10   Install the manifold and thread the mounting nuts/bolts into place.
11   Working from the center out, tighten the nuts/bolts to the torque listed in this Chapter's Specifications in three or four equal steps.
12   Reinstall the remaining parts in the reverse order of removal.
13   Run the engine and check for exhaust leaks.

Removal

Refer to illustrations 7.9, 7.10, 7.11, 7.12, 7.13, 7.14a, 7.14b, 7.15, 7.16, 7.17a and 7.17b

1   Disconnect the negative cable from the battery.
2   Block the rear wheels and set the parking brake.
3   Loosen the lug nuts on the right front wheel and raise the vehicle. Support the front of the vehicle securely on jackstands.

4   Remove the right front wheel and the lower splash shield.

5   Remove the power steering reservoir tank and bracket. (see Chapter 10). If equipped ABS brakes, remove the ABS actuator and bracket (see Chapter 9).

6   Remove the spark plugs and drivebelts (see Chapter 1).

7   Remove the alternator and bracket (see Chapter 5). Also disconnect the wire harness bracket for the Data Link Connector.

8   Support the engine from underneath with a jack (use a wood block on the jack and place the block under the oil pan) and remove the right engine mount and engine support rod (see Section 16)

9   Remove the upper timing belt cover screws, pull up the wiring harness (see Section 4) and remove the upper (no. 2) timing belt cover and gaskets (see illustration).

10   Position the number one piston at TDC on the compression stroke (see Section 3). Make sure the small hole in the camshaft pulley is aligned with the TDC mark on the cam

bearing cap (see illustration).

11   If you plan to re-use the timing belt, apply match marks on the sprocket and belt and an arrow indicating direction of travel on the belt (see illustration).

12   Loosen the upper (no. 1) idler pulley set bolt and unhook the spring (see illustration). Slip the timing belt off the sprocket. If you're removing the upper part of the belt only, for camshaft seal replacement or cylinder head removal, it isn't necessary to detach the belt from the crankshaft sprocket.

13   If the camshaft sprocket is worn or damaged, remove the valve cover, hold the rear (intake) camshaft with a large wrench and remove the bolt, then detach the sprocket (see illustration).

14   Remove the crankshaft pulley bolt. With the flywheel inspection cover removed, wedge a large screwdriver into the flywheel/driveplate ring gear teeth or against a converter bolt to keep the engine from turning. Use a breaker bar and socket to loosen the pulley bolt (see illustration). Remove the bolt and

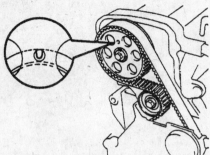

7.10 Align the upper camshaft sprocket timing marks with the number 1 cylinder at TDC

detach the pulley with prybars or a vibration damper puller (see illustration). Do not use an outside-jaw gear puller! Before the pulley is removed completely, double-check that the crankshaft is still at TDC.

7.11 If you intend to re-use the timing belt, apply match marks on the camshaft sprocket and belt (arrow)

7.12 Loosen the upper idler pulley set bolt (arrow) and unhook the spring

7.13 Remove the valve cover and hold the camshaft with a large wrench on the raised hex as the sprocket bolt is loosened - DO NOT use the timing belt tension to keep the sprocket from turning!

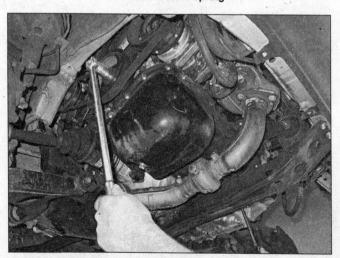

7.14a Remove the flywheel/driveplate cover and use a prybar wedged against the ring gear teeth or a converter bolt to hold the crankshaft while loosening the pulley bolt with a breaker b̶ - the bolt is very tight, so use the appropriate tools

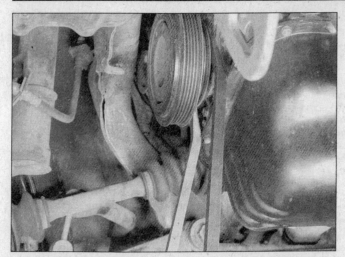

7.14b Often the crankshaft pulley can be removed with even applications of a pry bar - if you use a puller, it must be the type that attaches to the hub only (do not use a jaw-type puller)

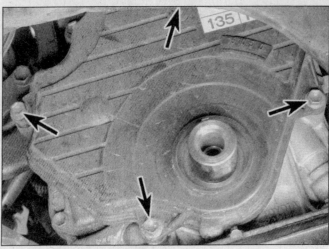

7.15 Remove the lower timing belt cover bolts (arrows) and slip the cover and gaskets off the engine

15   Remove the lower (no. 1) timing belt cover and gaskets **(see illustration)** and slip the belt guide off the crankshaft.

16   If you plan to re-use the timing belt, apply match marks on the crankshaft sprocket and belt **(see illustration)**.

17   Slip the timing belt off the sprocket and remove it. If the sprocket is worn or damaged, or if you need to replace the crankshaft front oil seal, remove the sprocket from the crankshaft **(see illustrations)**.

Inspection

Refer to illustrations 7.18 and 7.20

Caution: *Do not bend, twist or turn the timing belt inside out. Do not allow it to come in contact with oil, coolant or fuel. Do not utilize timing belt tension to keep the camshaft or crankshaft from turning when installing the sprocket bolt(s). Do not turn the crankshaft or camshaft more than a few degrees (if necessary for tooth alignment) while the timing belt is removed.*

18   Remove the idler pulleys and check the bearings for smooth operation and excessive play. Inspect the spring for damage and compare the free length to this Chapter's Specifi-

7.16 If you plan to re-use the timing belt, apply match marks (arrow) on the belt and crankshaft sprocket

cations **(see illustration)**.

19   If the timing belt broke during engine operation, the belt may have been contaminated or overtightened.

20   If the belt teeth are cracked or missing **(see illustration)**, the water pump, oil pump or camshaft(s) may have seized. **Caution:**

7.17a The crankshaft sprocket should slide off the crankshaft easily

If the timing belt broke during engine operation, the valves may have come in contact with the pistons, causing damage. Check the valve clearance (see Chapter 1) - bent valves usually will have excessive clearance, indicating damage that will require head removal to repair.

7.17b If the crankshaft sprocket is stuck, remove it with a puller (you may have to drill and tap two holes in the sprocket to attach the puller)

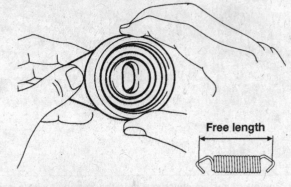

7.18 Check the idler pulley bearing for smooth operation and measure the free length of the tension spring for comparison to this Chapter's Specifications

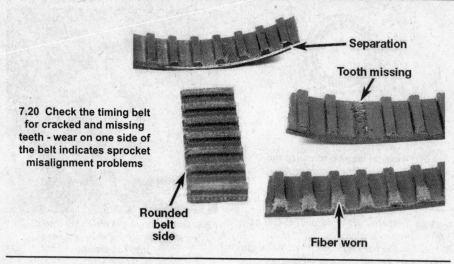

7.20 Check the timing belt for cracked and missing teeth - wear on one side of the belt indicates sprocket misalignment problems

Separation

Tooth missing

Rounded belt side

Fiber worn

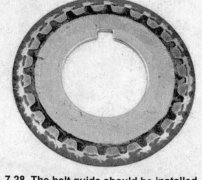

7.28 The belt guide should be installed with the tooth marks in contact with the timing belt and the cupped side facing out

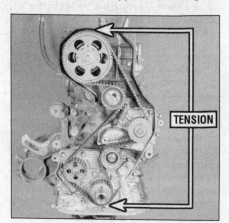

TENSION

7.30 There should be moderate tension on the side of the belt facing the front of the vehicle

21 If there is noticeable wear or cracks on the face of the belt, check to see if there are nicks or burrs on the idler pulleys.

22 If there is wear or damage on only one side of the belt, check the belt guide and the alignment of the sprockets.

23 Replace the timing belt with a new one if obvious wear or damage is noted or if it is the least bit questionable. Correct any problems which contributed to belt failure prior to belt installation. **Note:** *Professionals recommend replacing the belt whenever it is removed, since belt failure can lead to expensive engine damage. The manufacturer recommends changing the belt at 60,000-mile intervals.*

Installation

Refer to illustrations 7.28, 7.30, 7.33 and 7.34

24 Remove all dirt, oil and grease from the timing belt area at the front of the engine.

25 If they were removed, install the idler pulleys and tension spring. The upper (no. 1) idler should be pulled back against spring tension as far as possible and the bolt temporarily tightened. Also install the crankshaft and camshaft sprockets if removed. The crankshaft sprocket must be installed with the crankshaft sensor teeth facing inward toward the oil pump.

26 Recheck the camshaft and crankshaft timing marks to be sure they are properly aligned. The small hole in the camshaft sprocket must be aligned with the mark on the camshaft bearing cap (see Step 10) and the crankshaft sprocket must be aligned with the keyway facing straight up with the No.1 piston at TDC.

27 Install the timing belt on the crankshaft, oil pump, water pump and idler pulleys. If the original belt is being reinstalled, align the marks made during removal (see Steps 11 and 16).

28 Slip the belt guide onto the crankshaft with the cupped side facing out **(see illustration)**.

29 Reinstall the lower timing belt cover and crankshaft pulley and recheck the TDC marks.

30 Slip the timing belt over the camshaft sprocket. Keep tension on the side nearest the front of the vehicle **(see illustration)**. If the original belt is being reinstalled, align the marks made during removal.

31 Loosen the upper (no. 1) idler pulley bolt 1/2-turn, allowing the spring to apply pressure to the idler pulley.

32 Slowly turn the crankshaft clockwise 1-7/8 revolutions until the crank pulley mark lines up with the 45-degree BTDC (before TDC for number one cylinder) mark on the lower belt cover, then tighten the idler pulley bolt to the torque listed in this Chapter's Specifications.

33 Rotate the crankshaft 2-1/8 revolutions to TDC and recheck the timing marks **(see illustration)**. With the crankshaft at TDC for number one cylinder, the camshaft sprocket hole must line up with the timing mark. If the marks are not aligned exactly as shown, repeat the belt installation procedure. **Caution:** *DO NOT start the engine until you're absolutely certain that the timing belt is installed correctly. Serious and costly engine damage could occur if the belt is installed wrong.*

34 Reinstall the remaining parts in the reverse order of removal. **Note:** *When reinstalling the covers, if the sealing material is cut or compressed, clean the covers and apply new self-stick gasket material* **(see illustration)**.

35 Run the engine and check for proper operation.

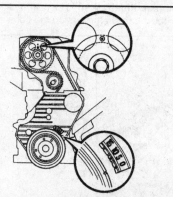

7.33 The marks should align as shown at Top Dead Center

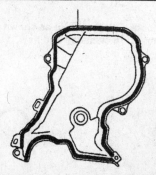

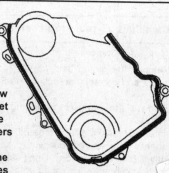

7.34 Install new adhesive gasket material to the timing belt covers in the areas indicated by the thick black lines

8.2a Wrap tape around the screwdriver tip and carefully work the crankshaft front oil seal out of the bore - DO NOT nick or scratch the crankshaft in the process!

8   Crankshaft front oil seal - replacement

Refer to illustrations 8.2a, 8.2b and 4

1   Remove the timing belt and crankshaft sprocket (see Section 7).
2   Note how far the seal is recessed in the bore, then carefully pry it out of the oil pump housing with a screwdriver or seal removal tool **(see illustration)**. Don't scratch the housing bore or damage the crankshaft in the process (if the crankshaft is damaged, the new seal will end up leaking). **Note:** *The seal may be easier to remove if the old seal lip is cut with a sharp utility knife first* **(see illustration).**
3   Clean the bore in the housing and coat the outer edge of the new seal with engine oil or multi-purpose grease. Apply multi-purpose grease to the seal lip.
4   Using a socket with an outside diameter slightly smaller than the outside diameter of the seal, carefully drive the new seal into place with a hammer **(see illustration)**. Make sure it's installed squarely and driven in to the same depth as the original. If a socket isn't available, a short section of large diameter pipe will also work. Check the seal after installation to make sure the spring didn't pop out of place.
5   Reinstall the crankshaft sprocket and timing belt (see Section 7).
6   Run the engine and check for oil leaks at the front seal.

9   Camshaft oil seal - replacement

Refer to illustration 9.3

1   Remove the timing belt, upper (No.1) idler pulley, and camshaft sprocket (see Section 7).
2   Remove the rear (No.3) timing belt cover.
3   Note how far the seal is seated in the bore, then carefully pry it out with a small screwdriver **(see illustration)**. Don't scratch the bore or damage the camshaft in the pro-

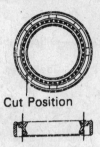

8.2b The seal may be removed more easily by carefully cutting the lip as indicated

cess (if the camshaft is damaged, the new seal will end up leaking).
4   Clean the bore and coat the outer edge of the new seal with engine oil or multi-purpose grease. Apply multi-purpose grease to the seal lip.
5   Using a socket with an outside diameter slightly smaller than the outside diameter of the seal, carefully drive the new seal into place with a hammer. Make sure it's installed squarely and driven in to the same depth as the original. If a socket isn't available, a short section of pipe will also work.
6   Reinstall the timing belt rear cover, camshaft sprocket, and timing belt (see Section 7).
7   Run the engine and check for oil leaks at the camshaft seal.

10   Camshafts and valve lifters - removal, inspection and installation

Note: *Before beginning this procedure, obtain two 6 x 1.0 mm bolts, 16 to 20 mm long. They will be referred to as "service bolts" in the text.*

Removal

Refer to illustrations 10.4, 10.5, 10.6 and 10.15

1   Remove the valve cover as described in Section 4.
2   Remove the distributor (see Chapter 5) if equipped.
3   Remove the timing belt, camshaft

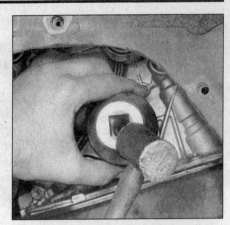

8.4 Gently drive the new seal into place with the spring side installed into the engine

9.3 Carefully pry the camshaft seal out of the bore - DO NOT nick or scratch the camshaft journal

sprocket and rear timing belt cover (see Sections 7 and 9).
4   Measure the camshaft thrust clearance (endplay) with a dial indicator **(see illustration)**. If the clearance is greater than the service limit, replace the camshaft and/or the cylinder head.

Exhaust camshaft

5   Position the knock pin in the INTAKE camshaft at 10 to 45-degrees left of vertical **(see illustration)**. This will position the exhaust camshaft lobes so the camshaft will

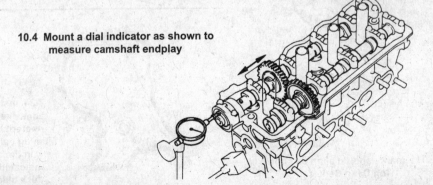

10.4 Mount a dial indicator as shown to measure camshaft endplay

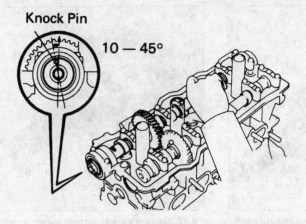

10.5 Turn the INTAKE camshaft until the knock pin is 10 to 45-degrees to the left of 12 o'clock position

10.6 Install a service bolt through the sub-gear, into the main gear (arrow)

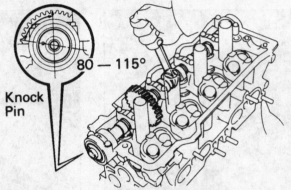

10.15 Turn the intake camshaft until the knock pin is 80 to 115-degrees to the left of the 12 o'clock position

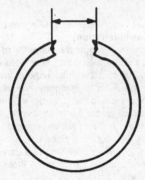

10.20 Measure the distance between the ends of the camshaft gear spring

be pushed out evenly by the valve spring pressure.

6   Secure the exhaust camshaft sub-gear to the main gear by installing one of the service bolts into a threaded hole (see illustration).

7   Remove the rear (transaxle end) exhaust camshaft bearing cap bolts and detach the bearing cap.

8   Loosen the number 1, 2 and 4 exhaust camshaft bearing cap bolts in 1/4-turn increments until the bolts can be removed by hand. Lift off the first, second and fourth bearing caps.

9   Finally, loosen the number 3 bearing cap bolts in 1/4-turn increments until they can be removed by hand, then detach the no. 3 cap. Caution: As the bearing cap bolts are being loosened, make sure the camshaft is moving up evenly. If one end or the other stops moving and the cam gets cocked, start over by reinstalling the bearing caps and resetting the knock pin. DO NOT try to pry or force the camshaft out.

10   Lift the camshaft straight up and out of the head.

11   To disassemble the exhaust camshaft gear, mount it in a vise with the jaws gripping the large hex on the shaft.

12   Install a second service bolt in the unthreaded hole in the camshaft sub-gear. Using a screwdriver positioned against the service bolt just installed, rotate the sub-gear

clockwise and remove the first service bolt from the threaded hole.

13   Remove the sub-gear snap-ring.

14   The wave washer, sub-gear and camshaft gear spring can now be removed from the camshaft.

Intake camshaft

15   Position the knock pin in the intake camshaft at 80 to 115-degrees left of vertical (see illustration).

16   Remove the front (timing belt end) intake camshaft bearing cap bolts and detach the bearing cap and oil seal. Caution: Do not pry the cap off. If it doesn't come loose easily, leave it in place without bolts.

17   Loosen the number 1, 3 and 4 intake camshaft bearing cap bolts in 1/4-turn increments until the bolts can be removed by hand. Lift off the first, third and fourth bearing caps.

18   Finally, loosen the number 2 bearing cap bolts in 1/4-turn increments until they can be removed by hand, then detach the no. 2 bearing cap. Caution: As the bearing cap bolts are being loosened, make sure the camshaft is moving up evenly. If one end or the other stops moving and the cam gets cocked, start over by reinstalling the bearing caps and resetting the knock pin. DO NOT try to pry or force the camshaft out.

19   Lift the camshaft straight up and out of the head.

10.21 Wipe the oil off the valve shims and mark the intakes I and the exhausts E - a magnetic tool works well for removing lifters

Inspection

Refer to illustrations 10.20, 10.21, 10.22, 10.26, 10.27, 10.28a, 10.28b and 10.30

20   Measure the end gap (distance between the ends) of the camshaft gear spring (see illustration) and compare it to this Chapter's Specifications. If not as specified, replace the spring.

21   Carefully label, then remove the valve lifters and shims (see illustration).

10.22 Wipe off the oil and inspect each lifter for wear and scuffing

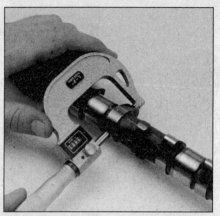

10.26 Measure the lobe heights on each camshaft - if any lobe height is less than the specified allowable minimum, replace that camshaft

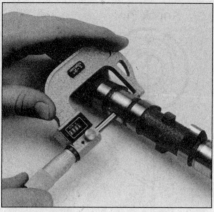

10.27 Measure each journal diameter with a micrometer (if any journal measures less than the specified limit, replace the camshaft)

22   Inspect each lifter for scuffing and score marks (see illustration).

23   Measure the outside diameter of each lifter and the corresponding lifter bore inside diameter. Subtract the lifter diameter from the lifter bore diameter to determine the oil clearance. Compare it to this Chapter's Specifications. If the oil clearance is excessive, a new head and/or new lifters will be required.

24   Store the lifters in a clean box, separated from each other, so they won't be damaged. Make sure the shims stay with the lifters (don't mix them up).

25   Visually examine the cam lobes and bearing journals for score marks, pitting, galling and evidence of overheating (blue, discolored areas). Look for flaking away of the hardened surface layer of each lobe.

26   Using a micrometer, measure the height of each camshaft lobe (see illustration). Compare your measurements with this Chapter's Specifications. If the height for any one lobe is less than the specified minimum, replace the camshaft.

27   Using a micrometer, measure the diameter of each journal at several points (see illustration). Compare your measurements with this Chapter's Specifications. If the diameter of any one journal is less than specified, replace the camshaft.

28   Check the oil clearance for each camshaft journal as follows:

a) Clean the bearing caps and the camshaft journals with lacquer thinner or acetone.

b) Carefully lay the camshaft(s) in place in the head. Don't install the lifters and don't use any lubrication.

c) Lay a strip of Plastigage on each journal (see illustration).

d) Install the bearing caps with the arrows pointing toward the front (timing belt end) of the engine.

e) Tighten the bolts to the specified torque in 1/4-turn increments. Note: Don't turn the camshaft while the Plastigage is in place.

f) Remove the bolts and detach the caps.

g) Compare the width of the crushed Plasti-

10.28a Lay a strip of Plastigage on each camshaft journal

gage (at its widest point) to the scale on the Plastigage envelope (see illustration).

h) If the clearance is greater than specified, replace the camshaft and/or cylinder head.

i) Scrape off the Plastigage with your fingernail or the edge of a credit card - don't scratch or nick the journals or bearing caps.

29   Temporarily install the camshafts without installing the lifters or exhaust camshaft subgear.

30   Measure the gear backlash (the free play between the gear teeth) with a dial indicator (see illustration) and compare it to this Chapter's Specifications.

Installation

Refer to illustrations 10.34, 10.35, 10.36, 10.43, 10.45 and 10.46

Intake camshaft

31   Apply moly-base grease or engine assembly lube to the lifters, then install them in their original locations. Make sure the valve adjustment shims are in place in the lifters.

10.28b Compare the width of the crushed Plastigage to the scale on the envelope to determine the oil clearance

32   Apply moly-base grease or engine assembly lube to the camshaft lobes and bearing journals.

33   Position the intake camshaft in the cylinder head with the knock pin 80-degrees to the left of vertical (see illustration 10.15).

34   Apply a thin coat of RTV sealant to the

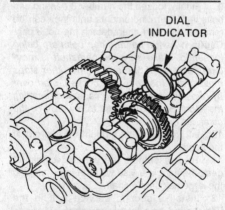

10.30 Position a dial indicator as shown here to measure gear backlash

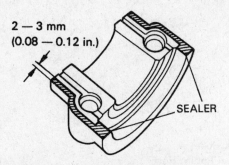

2 — 3 mm
(0.08 — 0.12 in.)

SEALER

10.34 Apply sealant to the shaded areas of the front intake camshaft bearing cap

outer edge of the front bearing cap-to-cylinder head mating surface (see illustration). Note: *The cap must be installed immediately or the sealer will dry prematurely.*

35 Install the bearing caps in numerical order with the arrows pointing toward the timing belt end of the engine (see illustration).

36 Following the recommended tightening sequence (see illustration), tighten the bearing cap bolts in 1/4-turn increments to the torque listed in this Chapter's Specifications.

37 Refer to Section 9 and install a new camshaft oil seal.

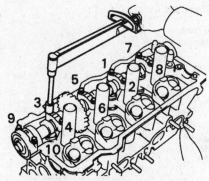

10.36 INTAKE camshaft bearing cap bolt tightening sequence

10.43 Align the camshaft timing gears as shown here

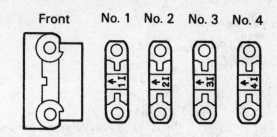

Front   No. 1   No. 2   No. 3   No. 4

10.35 Intake camshaft bearing cap arrangement - the arrows point toward the front or timing belt end of the engine

Exhaust camshaft

38 Reassemble the exhaust camshaft gear. Install the cam gear spring, sub-gear and wave washer in the gear. Secure them with the snap-ring.

39 Reinstall the service bolt in the unthreaded hole, turn the sub-gear with a screwdriver and install the second service bolt in the threaded hole. Tighten it to clamp the sub-gear to the camshaft gear, then remove the first bolt.

40 Apply moly-base grease or engine assembly lube to the lifters, then install them in their original locations. Make sure the valve adjustment shims are in place in the lifters.

41 Apply moly-base grease or engine assembly lube to the camshaft lobes and bearing journals.

42 Rotate the INTAKE camshaft until the knock pin is positioned 10-degrees to the left of vertical (see illustration 10.5).

43 Align the exhaust camshaft gear with the intake camshaft gear by matching up the timing marks on the gears (see illustration). Caution: *There are also assembly reference marks on each gear, above the timing marks - do not mistake them for the timing marks.*

44 Roll the exhaust camshaft down into position. Turn the intake camshaft back and forth a little until the exhaust camshaft sits in the bearings evenly.

45 Install the bearing caps in numerical order with the arrows pointing toward the timing belt end of the engine (see illustration).

46 Following the recommended sequence (see illustration), tighten the bearing cap bolts in 1/4-turn increments to the torque listed in this Chapter's Specifications.

47 Remove the service bolt from the camshaft gear.

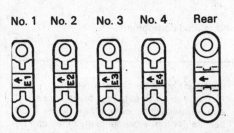

No. 1   No. 2   No. 3   No. 4   Rear

10.45 Exhaust camshaft bearing cap arrangement - the arrows point toward the front (timing belt end) of the engine

48 Remove and reinstall the semi-circular plugs into the cylinder head with new packing material. Install the rear timing belt cover on the cylinder head and the timing belt pulley on the intake camshaft and tighten the bolt to the torque listed in this Chapter's Specifications. Prevent the camshaft from turning by holding it with a wrench on the large hex (see illustration 7.13).

49 Install the timing belt (see Section 7).

50 The remainder of installation is the reverse of the removal procedure.

11   Cylinder head - removal and installation

Note: *The engine must be completely cool before beginning this procedure.*

Removal

Refer to illustrations 11.8 and 11.12

1 Relieve the fuel system pressure (see Chapter 4) then, disconnect the negative cable from the battery.

2 Drain the coolant from the engine block and radiator (see Chapter 1).

3 Drain the engine oil and remove the oil filter (see Chapter 1).

4 Remove the air cleaner housing. Also remove the fuel rail and fuel injectors (see Chapter 4).

5 Remove the intake manifold (see Section 5).

6 Remove the exhaust manifold (see Section 6).

7 Remove the timing belt, camshaft sprocket and upper idler pulley (see Section 7).

Service Bolt

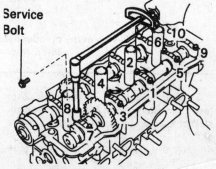

10.46 EXHAUST camshaft be bolt tightening sequen

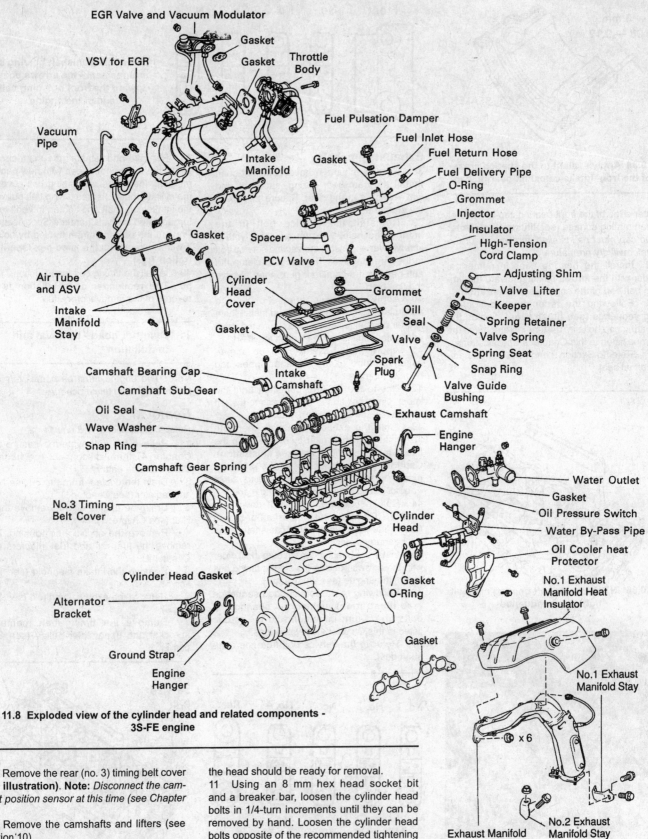

EGR Valve and Vacuum Modulator

Gasket

VSV for EGR

Gasket

Throttle Body

Vacuum Pipe

Fuel Pulsation Damper

Fuel Inlet Hose

Fuel Return Hose

Gasket

Fuel Delivery Pipe

O-Ring

Grommet

Injector

Intake Manifold

Insulator

High-Tension Cord Clamp

Spacer

PCV Valve

Air Tube and ASV

Gasket

Adjusting Shim

Valve Lifter

Grommet

Keeper

Oil Seal

Spring Retainer

Intake Manifold Stay

Cylinder Head Cover

Valve Spring

Valve

Spring Seat

Gasket

Spark Plug

Snap Ring

Valve Guide Bushing

Camshaft Bearing Cap

Intake Camshaft

Camshaft Sub-Gear

Exhaust Camshaft

Oil Seal

Engine Hanger

Wave Washer

Snap Ring

Camshaft Gear Spring

Water Outlet

Gasket

No.3 Timing Belt Cover

Oil Pressure Switch

Cylinder Head

Water By-Pass Pipe

Oil Cooler heat Protector

Cylinder Head Gasket

Alternator Bracket

Gasket

O-Ring

No.1 Exhaust Manifold Heat Insulator

Ground Strap

Gasket

Engine Hanger

No.1 Exhaust Manifold Stay

x 6

No.2 Exhaust Manifold Stay

Exhaust Manifold

11.8 Exploded view of the cylinder head and related components - 3S-FE engine

8   Remove the rear (no. 3) timing belt cover **(see illustration)**. **Note:** *Disconnect the camshaft position sensor at this time (see Chapter 6).*
9   Remove the camshafts and lifters (see Section 10).
10   Label and remove any remaining items, such as coolant fittings, tubes, cables, hoses or wires **(see illustration 5.5a)**. At this point

the head should be ready for removal.
11   Using an 8 mm hex head socket bit and a breaker bar, loosen the cylinder head bolts in 1/4-turn increments until they can be removed by hand. Loosen the cylinder head bolts opposite of the recommended tightening sequence **(see illustration 11.23)** to avoid warping or cracking the head.
12   Lift the cylinder head off the engine

11.12 If the head is stuck, pry only at the overhang, not between the mating surfaces

11.15 Remove all traces of old gasket material - the cylinder head and block mating surfaces must be perfectly clean to ensure a good gasket seal

block. If it's stuck, very carefully pry up at the transaxle end, beyond the gasket surface **(see illustration)**.

13   Remove all external components from the head to allow for thorough cleaning.

Installation

Refer to illustrations 11.15 and 11.23

14   The mating surfaces of the cylinder head and block must be perfectly clean when the head is installed.

15   Use a gasket scraper to remove all traces of carbon and old gasket material **(see illustration)**, then clean the mating surfaces with lacquer thinner or acetone. If there's oil on the mating surfaces when the head is installed, the gasket may not seal correctly and leaks could develop. When working on the block, stuff the cylinders with clean shop rags to keep out debris. Use a vacuum cleaner to remove material that falls into the cylinders.

16   Check the block and head mating surfaces for nicks, deep scratches and other damage. If damage is slight, it can be removed with a file; if it's excessive, machining may be the only alternative.

17   Use a tap of the correct size to chase the threads in the cylinder head bolt holes, then clean the holes with compressed air - make sure that nothing remains in the holes. **Warning:** *Wear eye protection when using compressed air!*

18   Use a wire wheel on the bolt threads to remove corrosion and restore the threads. Dirt, corrosion, sealant and damaged threads will affect torque readings.

19   Install the components that were removed from the head.

20   Position the new gasket over the dowel pins in the block.

21   Carefully set the head on the block without disturbing the gasket.

22   Before installing the head bolts, apply a small amount of clean engine oil to the threads.

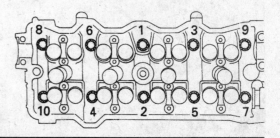

11.23 Cylinder head bolt TIGHTENING sequence

23   Install the bolts in their original locations and tighten them finger tight. Following the recommended sequence, tighten the bolts to the torque listed in this Chapter's Specifications **(see illustration)**. **Note:** *The bolts should be lightly oiled on the threads and under the heads, and washers must be used.*

24   The remaining installation steps are the reverse of removal.

25   Check and adjust the valves as necessary (see Chapter 1).

26   Refill the cooling system, install a new oil filter and add oil to the engine (see Chapter 1).

27   Run the engine and check for leaks. Set the ignition timing (see Chapter 5) and road test the vehicle.

12   Oil pan - removal and installation

Refer to illustrations 12.8, 12.9 and 12.14

Removal

1   Disconnect the negative cable from the battery.

2   Set the parking brake and block the rear wheels.

3   Raise the front of the vehicle and support it securely on jackstands.

4   Remove the splash shields under the engine, if equipped.

5   Drain the engine oil and remove the oil filter (see Chapter 1). Remove the oil dipstick.

6   Disconnect the three nuts holding the front exhaust pipe to the exhaust manifold, then the two bolts/nuts where the converter attaches to the rest of the exhaust system (see Chapter 4).

7   Unbolt the two bolts and remove the support bracket, then remove the front exhaust pipe. Remove the brace from the exhaust manifold (see Section 6).

8   Remove the front (radiator side) block-to-transaxle brace **(see illustration)**.

9   Remove the bolts and detach the oil pan. If it's stuck, pry it loose very carefully with a

12.8 Remove the bolts (arrows) on the front (radiator side) block-to-transaxle brace

12.9 Carefully pry the oil pan away from the block - if the mating surfaces are damaged, oil leaks could develop

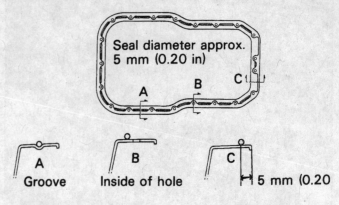

12.14 Apply a bead of RTV sealant to the oil pan flange

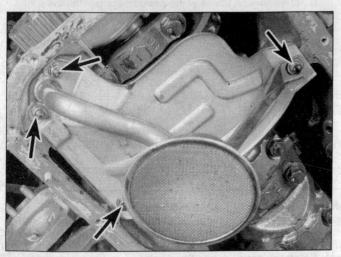

13.2 The oil pick-up assembly and baffle plate are held in place with two nuts and two bolts (arrows)

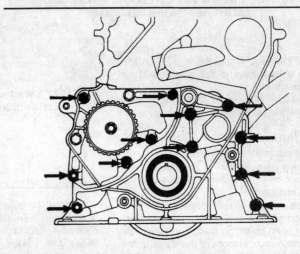

13.4 Remove the oil pump case-to-block bolts (arrows)

small screwdriver or putty knife **(see illustration)**. Don't damage the mating surfaces of the pan and block or oil leaks could develop.

Installation

10   Use a scraper to remove all traces of old gasket material and sealant from the block and oil pan. Clean the mating surfaces with lacquer thinner or acetone.

11   Make sure the threaded bolt holes in the block are clean.

12   Check the oil pan flange for distortion, particularly around the bolt holes. If necessary, place the pan on a block of wood and use a hammer to flatten and restore the gasket surface.

13   Inspect the oil pump pick-up tube assembly for cracks and a blocked strainer. If the pick-up was removed, clean it thoroughly and install it now, using a new O-ring or gasket. Tighten the nuts/bolts to the torque listed in this Chapter's Specifications.

14   Apply a 5 mm wide bead of RTV sealant to the oil pan flange **(see illustration)**. **Note:** *The oil pan must be installed within 5 minutes once the sealant has been applied.*

15   Carefully position the oil pan on the

engine block and install the bolts. Working from the center out, tighten them to the torque listed in this Chapter's Specifications in three or four steps.

16   The remainder of installation is the reverse of removal. Be sure to add oil and install a new oil filter. Use new "doughnut" gaskets on each end of the front exhaust pipe.

17   Run the engine and check for oil pressure and leaks.

13 Oil pump - removal, inspection and installation

Removal

Refer to illustrations 13.2, 13.4, 13.5a, 13.5b, 13.6 and 13.8

1   Remove the oil pan (see Section 12).

2   Remove the nuts/bolts and detach the oil pick-up tube assembly **(see illustration)**.

3   Support the engine securely from above and remove the lower idler pulley, crankshaft pulley, timing belt, and crankshaft sprocket (see Section 7).

4   Remove the 12 bolts and detach the oil pump housing from the engine **(see illustration)**. You may have to pry carefully between the front main bearing cap and the pump housing with a screwdriver.

5   Remove the two remaining bolts **(see illustration)** and separate the pump body from the case. Lift out the driven rotor and remove the O-ring **(see illustration)**.

Bolt Length 16 mm (0.63 in.)

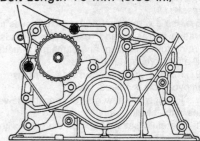

13.5a Remove the oil pump body-to-oil pump case bolts

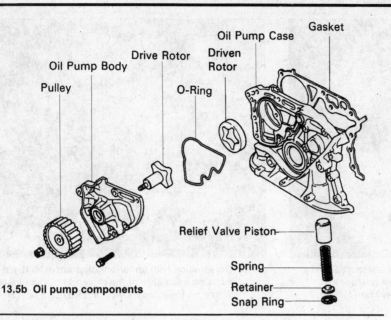

Pulley · Oil Pump Body · Drive Rotor · O-Ring · Driven Rotor · Oil Pump Case · Gasket

Relief Valve Piston
Spring
Retainer
Snap Ring

13.5b Oil pump components

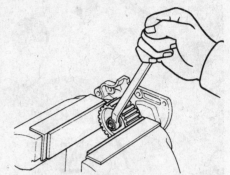

13.6 Hold the oil pump sprocket in a well-padded vise while the retaining nut is removed

13.8 Remove the snap-ring to disassemble the oil pressure relief valve

6   Clamp the pump sprocket in a well-padded vise **(see illustration)** and remove the sprocket nut and sprocket. Remove the drive rotor.

7   Use a scraper to remove all traces of sealant and old gasket material from the pump case and engine block, then clean the mating surfaces with lacquer thinner or acetone.

8   Remove the oil pressure relief valve snap-ring **(see illustration)**, retainer, spring and piston. **Warning:** *The spring is tightly compressed - be careful and wear eye protection.*

Inspection

Refer to illustrations 13.11a and 13.11b

9   Clean all components with solvent, then inspect them for wear and damage.

10   Check the oil pressure relief valve piston sliding surface and valve spring. If either the spring or the valve is damaged, they must be replaced as a set.

11   Check the driven rotor-to-case and drive rotor tip clearance with feeler gauges **(see illustrations)** and compare the results to this

Chapter's Specifications. If the clearance is excessive, replace the rotors as a set. If necessary, replace the oil pump case and body.

Installation

Refer to illustration 13.14

12   Pry the old drive rotor shaft seal out with a screwdriver. Using a deep socket and a hammer, carefully drive a new seal into place. Apply multi-purpose grease to the seal lip.

13   Install a new crankshaft seal using the same procedure as outlined in the previous step. Apply multi-purpose grease to the seal lip.

14   Install a new O-ring, then lubricate the driven rotor with clean engine oil and place it in the pump case with the mark facing out **(see illustration)**.

15   Lubricate the shaft and install the drive rotor in the pump body, then reinstall the pulley and tighten the nut to the torque listed in this Chapter's Specifications.

16   Pack the pump cavity with petroleum jelly and attach the pump body to the case with the 16 mm-long bolts **(see illustration 13.5a)**.

17   Lubricate the oil pressure relief valve piston with clean engine oil and reinstall the valve components in the pump case.

18   Place a new gasket on the engine block (the dowel pins should hold it in place).

19   Position the pump case against the block and install the mounting bolts.

20   Tighten the bolts to the torque listed in this Chapter's Specifications in three or four steps. Follow a criss-cross pattern to avoid warping the case.

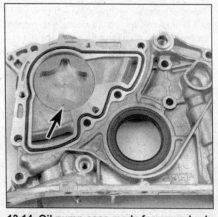

13.14 Oil pump case ready for pump body installation; note that the seal is in place, the O-ring is in place and the mark on the driven rotor is facing out (arrow)

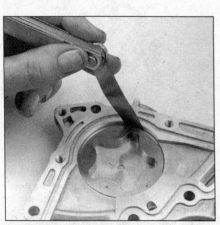

13.11a Measure the driven rotor-to-case clearance . . .

13.11b . . . and the rotor tip clearance with a feeler gauge

14.3 Mark the flywheel/driveplate and the crankshaft so they can be reassembled in the same relative positions - most models will have eight flywheel bolts

14.5 On vehicles with an automatic transaxle, there is a spacer plate on each side of the driveplate; when installing, line up the spacers with the locating pin (arrow)

21   Using a new gasket, install the oil pick-up tube assembly and baffle plate. Tighten the fasteners to the torque listed in this Chapter's Specifications.

22   Reinstall the remaining parts in the reverse order of removal.

23   Add oil, start the engine and check for oil pressure and leaks.

24   Recheck the engine oil level.

14   Flywheel/driveplate - removal and installation

Refer to illustrations 14.3 and 14.5

Removal

1   Refer to Chapter 7 and remove the transaxle. If it's leaking, now would be a very good time to replace the front pump seal/O-ring (automatic transaxle only).

2   Remove the pressure plate and clutch disc (Chapter 8) (manual transaxle equipped vehicles). Now is a good time to check/replace the clutch components.

3   Use a center punch or paint to make alignment marks on the flywheel/driveplate and crankshaft to ensure correct alignment during reinstallation **(see illustration)**.

4   Remove the bolts that secure the fly-wheel/driveplate to the crankshaft. If the crankshaft turns, wedge a screwdriver in the ring gear teeth to jam the flywheel.

5   Remove the flywheel/driveplate from the crankshaft. Since the flywheel is fairly heavy, be sure to support it while removing the last bolt. Automatic transaxle equipped vehicles have spacers on both sides of the driveplate **(see illustration)**. Keep them with the drive-plate.

Installation

6   Clean the flywheel to remove grease and oil. Inspect the surface for cracks, rivet grooves, burned areas and score marks. Light scoring can be removed with emery cloth.

Check for cracked and broken ring gear teeth. Lay the flywheel on a flat surface and use a straightedge to check for warpage.

7   Clean and inspect the mating surfaces of the flywheel/driveplate and the crankshaft. If the crankshaft rear seal is leaking, replace it before reinstalling the flywheel/driveplate.

8   Position the flywheel/driveplate against the crankshaft. Be sure to align the marks made during removal. Note that some engines have an alignment dowel or staggered bolt holes to ensure correct installation. Before installing the bolts, apply thread locking compound to the threads.

9   Wedge a screwdriver in the ring gear teeth to keep the flywheel/driveplate from turning and tighten the bolts to the torque listed in this Chapter's Specifications. Follow a criss-cross pattern and work up to the final torque in three or four steps.

10   The remainder of installation is the reverse of the removal procedure.

15   Rear main oil seal - replacement

Refer to illustrations 15.2, 15.5 and 15.6

1   The transaxle must be removed from the vehicle for this procedure (see Chapter 7).

2   The seal can be replaced without removing the oil pan or removing the seal retainer. However, this method is not recommended because the lip of the seal is quite stiff and it's possible to cock the seal in the retainer bore or damage it during installation. If you want to take the chance, pry out the old seal with a screwdriver **(see illustration)**. Apply multi-purpose grease to the crankshaft seal journal and the lip of the new seal and carefully push the new seal into place. The lip is stiff so carefully work it onto the seal journal of the crank-shaft with a smooth object like the end of an extension as you tap the seal into place. Don't rush it or you may damage the seal.

3   The following method is recommended

but requires removal of the oil pan (see Section 12) and the seal retainer.

4   After the oil pan has been removed, remove the bolts, detach the seal retainer and remove all the old gasket material.

5   Position the seal and retainer assembly between two wood blocks on a workbench and drive the old seal out from the back side with a screwdriver **(see illustration)**.

6   Drive the new seal into the retainer with a block of wood **(see illustration)** or a section of pipe slightly smaller in diameter than the outside diameter of the seal.

7   Lubricate the crankshaft seal journal and the lip of the new seal with multi-purpose grease. Position a new gasket on the engine block.

8   Slowly and carefully push the seal onto the crankshaft. The seal lip is stiff, so work it onto the crankshaft with a smooth object such as the end of an extension as you push the retainer against the block.

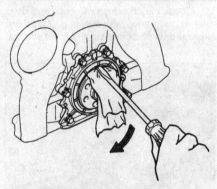

15.2 The quick way to replace the rear main oil seal is to simply pry the old one out with a screwdriver, lubricate the crankshaft journal and the lip of the new seal with multi-purpose grease and push the new seal into place - the seal lip is very stiff and can be easily damaged during installation if you're not careful

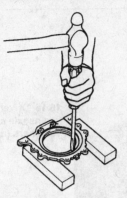

15.5 After removing the retainer assembly from the block, support it between two wood blocks and drive out the old seal with a screwdriver and hammer

15.6 Drive the new seal into the retainer with a block of wood or a section of pipe, if you have one large enough - make sure that you don't cock the seal in the retainer bore

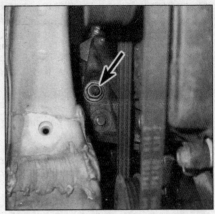

16.8 Working from below, remove the passenger side engine mount-to-engine bracket retaining nut (arrow)

9   Install and tighten the retainer bolts to the torque listed in this Chapter's Specifications. The bottom sealing flange of the retainer must not extend below the bottom sealing flange (oil pan rail) of the block.
10   The remaining steps are the reverse of removal.

16   Powertrain mounts - check and replacement

Refer to illustrations 16.8, 16.9, 16.12 and 16.16
1   The powertrain mounts seldom require attention, but broken or deteriorated mounts should be replaced immediately or the added strain placed on the driveline components may cause damage or wear.

Check

2   During the check, the engine must be raised slightly to remove the weight from the mounts.
3   Raise the vehicle and support it securely on jackstands, then remove the splash shields under the engine (if equipped) and position a jack under the engine oil pan. Place a large

block of wood between the jack head and the oil pan, then carefully raise the engine just enough to take the weight off the mounts. Do not position the wood block under the drain plug. **Warning:** *DO NOT place any part of your body under the engine when it's supported only by a jack!*
4   Check the mounts **(see illustration)** to see if the rubber is cracked, hardened or separated from the bushing in the center of the mount.
5   Check for relative movement between the mount plates and the engine or frame (use a large screwdriver or pry bar to attempt to move the mounts). If movement is noted, lower the engine and tighten the mount fasteners.
6   Rubber preservative should be applied to the mounts to slow deterioration.

Replacement

7   Disconnect the negative battery cable from the battery, then raise the vehicle and support it securely on jackstands (if not already done). Support the engine as described in Step 3.

Passenger side engine mount

8   Working below the vehicle, remove the nut securing the right side mount to the engine bracket **(see illustration)**.
9   Working above in the engine compartment, remove the remaining nut and bolts securing the right side mount to the engine bracket **(see illustration)**. If the vehicle is equipped with ABS brakes it will be necessary to remove the ABS actuator and bracket first to allow access to the mount (see Chapter 9).
10   Detach the mount from the vehicle.
11   Installation is the reverse of removal. Use thread locking compound on the mount bolts/ nuts and be sure to tighten them securely. **Caution:** *Be sure to bleed the brakes properly if the vehicle is equipped with an Antilock Brake System (see Chapter 9).*

Front and rear transaxle mounts

12   Working up through the holes in the center suspension crossmember detach the mount-to-crossmember retaining bolts **(see illustration)**.
13   Remove the through-bolt securing the mount to the transaxle bracket and detach the mount from the vehicle.

16.9 Working from above, remove the passenger side engine mount fasteners (arrows)

16.12 Transaxle mount fasteners (arrows) - front mount shown, rear mount similar

14   Installation is the reverse of removal. Use thread locking compound on the mount bolts/nuts and be sure to tighten them securely.

Driver's side transaxle mount

15   Remove the air filter housing (see Chapter 4).

16   Remove the nuts and bolts securing the mount to the transaxle **(see illustration)**.

17   Remove the though-bolt securing the mount to the chassis and remove the mount from the vehicle

18   Installation is the reverse of removal. Use thread locking compound on the mount bolts/nuts and be sure to tighten them securely.

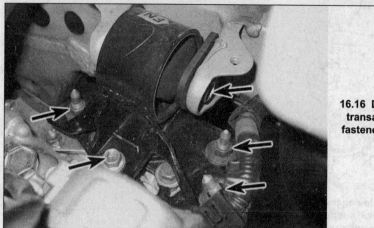

16.16 Driver's side transaxle mount fasteners (arrows)

Chapter 2 Part B
Engines - 2001 and later

Contents

	Section
Camshafts and lifters - removal, inspection and installation	7
CHECK ENGINE light	See Chapter 6
Crankshaft front oil seal - replacement	12
Crankshaft pulley/vibration damper - removal and installation	11
Cylinder compression check	See Chapter 2C
Cylinder head - removal and installation	10
Drivebelt - check, adjustment and replacement	See Chapter 1
Engine - removal and installation	See Chapter 2C
Engine oil and filter change	See Chapter 1
Engine overhaul - general information	See Chapter 2C
Exhaust manifold - removal and installation	9
Flywheel/driveplate - removal and installation	15
General information	1
Intake manifold - removal and installation	8
Oil pan - removal and installation	13
Oil pump - removal and installation	14
Powertrain mounts - check and replacement	17
Rear main oil seal - replacement	16
Repair operations possible with the engine in the vehicle	2
Spark plug replacement	See Chapter 1
Timing chain and sprockets - removal, inspection and installation	6
Top Dead Center (TDC) for number one piston - locating	3
Valve cover - removal and installation	4
Variable Valve Timing (VVT) system - description	5
Water pump - removal and installation	See Chapter 3

Specifications

General

Engine designation
- 2001 through 2003 ... 1AZ-FE
- 2004 and later ... 2AZ-FE

Displacement
- 2001 through 2003 ... 122 cubic inches (2.0 liters)
- 2004 and later ... 144.2 cubic inches (2.4 liters)

Cylinder numbers (drivebelt end-to-transaxle end) ... 1-2-3-4
Firing order ... 1-3-4-2

2001 and later
Cylinder numbering and coil terminal identification diagram

Cylinder head
Warpage limit ... 0.0031 inch (0.08 mm)

Timing chain
Timing chain sprocket wear limit (see illustration 6.20b)
- Camshaft sprocket(s) (w/chain) ... 3.831 inches (97.3 mm)
- Crankshaft sprocket (w/chain) ... 2.031 inches (51.6 mm)

Timing chain stretch limit (see illustration 6.20a)
- 8 links (16 pins) ... 4.827 inches (122.6 mm)

Timing chain guide wear limit ... 0.039 inch (1.0 mm)

Camshaft and lifters
Journal diameter
- No. 1 journal ... 1.4162 to 1.4167 inches (35.971 to 35.985 mm)
- All others ... 0.9040 to 0.9045 inch (22.959 to 22.975 mm)

Bearing oil clearance
- No.1 journal
  - Intake ... 0.0003 to 0.0015 inch (0.007 to 0.038 mm)
  - Exhaust
    - 2001 through 2003 ... 0.0006 to 0.0021 inch (0.015 to 0.054 mm)
    - 2004 and later ... 0.0015 to 0.0031 inch (0.040 to 0.079 mm)
- All others ... 0.0010 to 0.0024 inch (0.025 to 0.062 mm)

Runout limit ... 0.0012 inch (0.03 mm)

Thrust clearance (endplay)
- Intake ... 0.0016 to 0.0037 inch (0.040 to 0.095 mm)
- Exhaust ... 0.0032 to 0.0053 inch (0.080 to 0.135 mm)

Camshaft and lifters (continued)

Lobe height
  Intake camshaft
    Standard .... 1.8305 to 1.8345 inches (46.495 to 46.595 mm)
    Service limit (minimum) .... 1.8262 inches (46.385 mm)
  Exhaust camshaft
    Standard .... 1.8106 to 1.8143 inches (45.983 to 46.083 mm)
    Service limit (minimum) .... 1.8060 inches (45.873)
Valve lifter
  Diameter... 1.2191 to 1.2195 inches (30.966 to 30.976 mm)
  Bore diameter... 1.2208 to 1.2215 inches (31.009 to 31.025 mm)
Lifter oil clearance
  Standard... 0.0013 to 0.0023 inch (0.033 to 0.059 mm)
  Service limit... 0.0031 inch (0.079 mm)

Oil pump

Drive chain sprocket wear limit (w/chain) .... 1.898 inches (48.2 mm)
Drive chain stretch limit
  4 links (8 pins) .... 2.063 inches (52.4 mm)
Drive chain guide wear limit.. 0.020 inch (0.5 mm)

Torque specifications

	Ft-lbs (unless otherwise indicated)	Nm
Camshaft bearing cap bolts		
Journal No.1 (intake and exhaust)	22	29.5
All others	80 in-lbs	9
Camshaft sprocket bolts	40	54
Crankshaft pulley/vibration damper bolt		
2001 through 2003	125	170
2004 and later	132	180
Cylinder head bolts (in sequence - **see illustration 10.24**)		
Step 1	58	79
Step 2	Tighten an additional 90-degrees	
Drivebelt tensioner	44	60
Engine mounts		
Passenger's side mount		
Mount-to-frame bolts	38	52
Mount-to engine mount bracket nuts/bolts	38	52
Driver's side mount		
Mount-to-frame bolts	41	56
Mount through-bolt	41	56
Front mount		
Mount-to-frame bolts	41	56
Mount through-bolt	41	56
Rear mount		
Mount-to-frame bolts	41	56
Mount through-bolt	65	88
Exhaust manifold nuts/bolts	25	37
Exhaust manifold brace bolts	33	44
Exhaust manifold heat shield bolts	108 in-lbs	12
Exhaust pipe-to-exhaust manifold bolts	32	43
Flywheel/driveplate bolts		
Manual transaxle	96	130
Automatic transaxle	72	98
Intake manifold nuts/bolts	22	30
Lower crankcase-to-engine block bolts	25	33
Oil pump bolts	15	19
Oil pump drive chain tensioner	108 in-lbs	12
Oil pump sprocket bolt	20	30
Oil pan bolts	80 in-lbs	9
Timing chain guide bolts (stationary)	80 in-lbs	9
Timing chain tensioner pivot arm bolt	168 in-lbs	19
Timing chain cover bolts (see illustrations 7.14a and 7.14b)		
10 mm head	80 in-lbs	9
12 mm head	15	21
14 mm head	32	43
Timing chain cover nuts	80 in-lbs	9
Timing chain tensioner nuts	80 in-lbs	9
Valve cover	96 in-lbs	11

1 General information

This Part of Chapter 2 is devoted to in-vehicle repair procedures for the 2001 and later four-cylinder engine. All information concerning engine removal, installation and overhaul can be found in Part C of this Chapter.

The following repair procedures are based on the assumption that the engine is installed in the vehicle. If the engine has been removed from the vehicle and mounted on a stand, many of the steps outlined in this Part of Chapter 2 will not apply.

The Specifications included in this Part of Chapter 2 apply only to the in-vehicle procedures contained in this Part. Part C of Chapter 2 contains the general Specifications for all the engines covered by this manual.

2001 through 2003 four-cylinder engines in the RAV4 are designated 1AZ-FE (2.0L). 2004 and later four-cylinder engines are designated 2AZ-FE (2.4L). These engines incorporate an aluminum cylinder block with a lower crankcase to strengthen the lower half of the block. Although the cylinder head utilizes the usual dual overhead camshafts (DOHC) with four valves per cylinder as in previous model years, it is of new design also. The camshafts are driven from a single timing chain off the crankshaft, and a Variable Valve Timing (VVT) system is incorporated on the intake camshaft to increase horsepower and decrease emissions.

2 Repair operations possible with the engine in the vehicle

Many major repair operations can be accomplished without removing the engine from the vehicle.

Clean the engine compartment and the exterior of the engine with some type of degreaser before any work is done. It will make the job easier and help keep dirt out of the internal areas of the engine.

Depending on the components involved, it may be helpful to remove the hood to improve access to the engine as repairs are performed (refer to Chapter 11 if necessary). Cover the fenders to prevent damage to the paint. Special pads are available, but an old bedspread or blanket will also work.

If vacuum, exhaust, oil or coolant leaks develop, indicating a need for gasket or seal replacement, the repairs can generally be made with the engine in the vehicle. The intake and exhaust manifold gaskets, oil pan gasket, crankshaft oil seals and cylinder head gasket are all accessible with the engine in place.

Exterior engine components, such as the intake and exhaust manifolds, the oil pan, the oil pump, the water pump, the starter motor, the alternator and the fuel system components can be removed for repair with the engine in place.

Since the cylinder head can be removed without pulling the engine, camshaft and valve component servicing can also be accomplished with the engine in the vehicle. Replacement of the timing chain and sprockets is also possible with the engine in the vehicle.

3 Top Dead Center (TDC) for number one piston - locating

Refer to illustrations 3.5 and 3.8

1   Top Dead Center (TDC) is the highest point in the cylinder that each piston reaches as it travels up the cylinder bore. Each piston reaches TDC on the compression stroke and again on the exhaust stroke, but TDC generally refers to piston position on the compression stroke.

2   Positioning the piston(s) at TDC is an essential part of many procedures such as valve adjustment and camshaft and timing chain/sprocket removal.

3   Before beginning this procedure, be sure to place the transmission in Neutral and apply the parking brake or block the rear wheels. Disable the ignition system by disconnecting the primary electrical connectors at the ignition coils (see Chapter 5). Also disable the fuel system (see Chapter 4, Section 2).

4   In order to bring any piston to TDC, the crankshaft must be turned using one of the methods outlined below. When looking at the front of the engine, normal crankshaft rotation is clockwise.

a) *The preferred method is to turn the crankshaft with a socket and ratchet attached to the bolt threaded into the front of the crankshaft. Turn the bolt in a clockwise direction only.*

c) *If an assistant is available to turn the ignition switch to the Start position in short bursts, you can get the piston close to TDC without a remote starter switch. Make sure your assistant is out of the vehicle, away from the ignition switch, then use a socket and ratchet as described in Paragraph (a) to complete the procedure.*

5   Remove the spark plugs (see Chapter 1) and install a compression gauge in the number one spark plug hole **(see illustration)**. It should be a gauge with a screw-in fitting and a hose at least six inches long.

6   Rotate the crankshaft using one of the methods described above while observing for pressure on the compression gauge. The moment the gauge shows pressure indicates that the number one cylinder has begun the compression stroke.

7   Once the compression stroke has begun, TDC for the compression stroke is reached by bringing the piston to the top of the cylinder.

8   Continue turning the crankshaft until the notch in the crankshaft damper is aligned with the "TDC" or the "0" mark on the timing chain cover **(see illustration)**. At this point, the number one cylinder is at TDC on the compression stroke. If the marks are aligned but there was no compression, the piston was on the exhaust stroke; continue rotating the crankshaft 360-degrees (1-turn). **Note:** *If a compression gauge is not available, you can simply place a blunt object over the spark plug hole and listen for compression as the engine is rotated. Once compression at the No.1 spark plug hole is noted the remainder of the Step is the same.*

9   After the number one piston has been positioned at TDC on the compression stroke, TDC for any of the remaining cylinders can be located by turning the crankshaft 180 degrees and following the firing order (refer to the Specifications). Rotating the engine 180 degrees past TDC #1 will put the engine at TDC compression for cylinder #3.

4 Valve cover - removal and installation

Removal

Refer to illustration 4.4

1   Disconnect the cable from the negative terminal of the battery.

2   Disconnect the electrical connectors

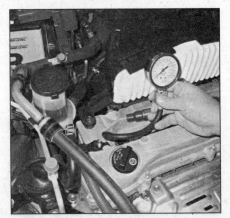

3.5 A compression gauge can be used in the number one plug hole to assist in finding TDC

3.8 Align the groove in the damper with the "0" mark on the timing chain cover

4.4 Valve cover fastener locations

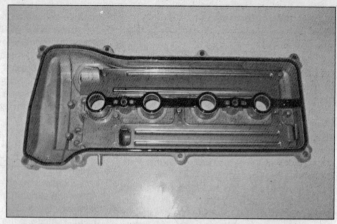

4.5 The valve cover gasket and the spark plug tube seals are incorporated into a single rubber O-ring-like seal (arrow) - press the gasket evenly into the grooves around the underside of the valve cover and the spark plug openings

from the ignition coils, remove the nuts securing the wiring harness to the valve cover and position the ignition coil wiring harness aside. Then remove the ignition coil pack from each of the spark plugs (see Chapter 5).

3   Detach the PCV hoses from the valve cover.

4   Remove the valve cover mounting nuts, then detach the valve cover and gasket from the cylinder head (see illustration). If the valve cover is stuck to the cylinder head, bump the end with a wood block and a hammer to jar it loose. If that doesn't work, try to slip a flexible putty knife between the cylinder head and valve cover to break the seal. Caution: Don't pry at the valve cover-to-cylinder head joint or damage to the sealing surfaces may occur, leading to oil leaks after the valve cover is reinstalled.

Installation

Refer to illustrations 4.5 and 4.6

5   Remove the valve cover gasket from the valve cover and clean the mating surfaces with lacquer thinner or acetone. Install a new rubber gasket, pressing it evenly into the grooves around the underside of the valve cover. **Note**: *Make sure the spark plug tube*

seals are in place on the underside of the valve cover before reinstalling it (see illustration). The mating surfaces of the timing chain cover, the cylinder head and valve cover must be perfectly clean when the valve cover is installed. If there's residue or oil on the mating surfaces when the valve cover is installed, oil leaks may develop.

6   Apply RTV sealant at the timing chain cover-to-cylinder head joint, then install the valve cover and fasteners (see illustration).

7   Tighten the nuts/bolts to the torque listed in this Chapter's Specifications in three or four equal steps.

8   Reinstall the remaining parts, run the engine and check for oil leaks.

5   Variable Valve Timing (VVT) system - description

Refer to illustrations 5.2a and 5.2b

1   The VVT system varies intake camshaft timing by directing oil pressure to advance or retard the intake camshaft sprocket/actuator assembly. Changing the intake camshaft timing during certain engine conditions increases

engine power output, fuel economy and reduces emissions.

2   System components include the Powertrain Control Module (PCM), the VVT oil control valve (OCV) and the intake camshaft sprocket/actuator assembly (see illustrations).

3   The PCM uses inputs from the following sensors to turn the oil control valve ON or OFF:

a) *Vehicle Speed Sensor (VSS)*
b) *Throttle Position Sensor (TPS)*
c) *Mass Airflow (MAF) sensor*
d) *Engine Coolant Temperature (ECT) sensor*

4   Once the VVT oil control valve is actuated by the PCM it directs the specified amount of oil pressure from the engine to advance or retard the intake camshaft sprocket/actuator assembly.

5   The intake camshaft sprocket/actuator assembly is equipped with an inner hub that is attached to the camshaft. The inner hub consists of a series of fixed vanes that use oil pressure as a wedge against the vanes to rotate the camshaft. The higher the oil pressure (or flow) the more the actuator assembly

4.6 Apply sealant at the timing chain cover-to-cylinder head joint before installing the valve cover

5.2a The Variable Valve Timing (VVT) oil control valve is located at the rear of the cylinder head

5.2b The intake camshaft actuator assembly (arrow) is only visible with the valve cover removed

6.7 Verify the engine is at TDC by observing the position of the camshaft sprocket marks (lower arrows) - they must be aligned with the marks on the camshaft bearing caps (upper arrows)

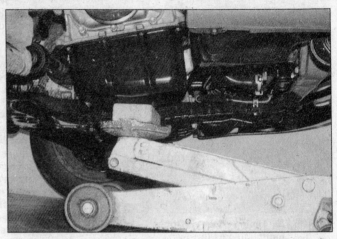

6.9 If an engine support fixture is not available, the engine can be supported from below using a floor jack and a block of wood

will rotate, thereby advancing or retarding the camshaft.

6   When oil is applied to the advance side of the vanes, the actuator can advance the camshaft up to 21 degrees in a clockwise direction. When oil is applied to the retard side of the vanes, the actuator will start to rotate the camshaft counterclockwise back to 0 degrees which is the normal position of the actuator during engine operation under no load or at idle. The PCM can also send a signal to the oil control valve to stop oil flow to both (advance and retard) passages to hold camshaft advance in its current position.

7   Under light engine loads, the VVT system will retard the camshaft timing to decrease valve overlap and stabilize engine output. Under medium engine loads, the VVT system will advance the camshaft timing to increase valve overlap, thereby increasing fuel economy and decreasing exhaust emissions. Under heavy engine loads at low RPM, the VVT system will advance the camshaft timing to help close the intake valve faster, which improves low to midrange torque. Under heavy engine loads at high RPM, the VVT system will retard the camshaft timing to slow the closing of the intake valve to improve engine horsepower.

6.11 Drivebelt tensioner mounting bolts

6   Timing chain and sprockets - removal, inspection and installation

Warning: *Wait until the engine is completely cool before beginning this procedure.*
Note: *Special tools are required for this procedure. Read through the entire procedure and acquire the necessary tools and equipment before beginning work.*

Removal

Refer to illustrations 6.7, 6.9, 6.11, 6.13a, 6.13b, 6.14a, 6.14b, 6.14c, 6.14d, 6.15, 6.16 and 6.19

1   Detach the cable from the negative terminal of the battery.
2   Remove the drivebelt (see Chapter 1) and the alternator (see Chapter 5).
3   Remove and the valve cover (see Section 4) and the ABS actuator if equipped (see Chapter 9).
4   With the parking brake applied and the rear wheels blocked, loosen the right front wheel lug nuts, then raise the front of the vehicle and support it securely on jackstands. Remove the right front wheel and the right splash shield from the wheelwell.
5   Drain the cooling system (see Chapter 1).
6   While the coolant is draining, refer to Chapter 10 and remove the power steering pump from the engine without disconnecting the fluid lines. Tie the power steering pump to the body with a piece of wire and position it out of the way.
7   Position the number one piston at TDC on the compression stroke (see Section 3). Visually confirm the engine is at TDC on the compression stroke by verifying that the timing mark on the crankshaft pulley/vibration damper is aligned with the "0" mark on the timing chain cover and the camshaft sprocket marks are aligned and parallel with the top of the timing chain cover **(see illustration 3.8 and the accompanying illustration). Note:**

There are two sets of marks on the camshaft sprockets. The marks that align at TDC are for TDC reference only; the other two marks are used to align the sprockets with the timing chain during installation.
8   Remove the crankshaft pulley/vibration damper, being careful not to rotate the engine from TDC (see Section 11). If the engine rotates off TDC during this step, reposition the engine back to TDC before proceeding. The engine should be left at TDC for the No. 1 piston during this entire procedure.
9   Support the engine from above, using an engine support fixture (available at rental yards), or from below using a floor jack. Use a wood block between the floor jack and the engine to prevent damage **(see illustration)**.
10   Remove the passenger side engine mount (see Section 17).
11   Remove the drivebelt tensioner and the crankshaft position sensor from the timing chain cover **(see illustration)**. Also remove the bolt securing the crankshaft position sensor wiring harness to the timing chain cover.
12   Remove the oil pan (see Section 13).
13   Detach the main wiring harness junction and remove the timing chain tensioner from the rear side of the timing chain cover **(see illustrations)**.

6.13a Remove the two bolts securing the main harness to the timing chain cover and position the harness aside

**6.13b Timing chain tensioner
mounting nuts (arrows)**

14   Remove the timing chain cover fasteners and pry the cover off the engine (see illustrations).
15   Slide the crankshaft position sensor reluctor ring off the crankshaft (see illustration).

16   Remove the timing chain tensioner pivot arm/chain guide and the lower chain guide (see illustration).
17   Lift the timing chain off the camshaft sprockets and remove the timing chain and the crankshaft sprocket as an assembly from the engine. The crankshaft sprocket should slip off the crankshaft by hand. If not, use several flat bladed screwdrivers to evenly pry the sprocket off the crankshaft. **Note:** *If you intend to reuse the timing chain, use white paint or chalk to make a mark indicating the front of the chain. If a used timing chain is reinstalled with the wear pattern in the opposite direction, noise and increased wear may occur.*
18   Remove the stationary timing chain guide (see illustration 6.16).
19   To remove the camshaft sprockets, loosen the bolts while holding the lug on the camshaft with a wrench (see illustration). Note the identification marks on the camshaft sprockets before removal, then remove the bolts. Pull on the sprockets by hand until they slip off the dowels. If necessary, use a small puller, with the legs inserted in the relief holes,

to pull the sprockets off. **Note:** *These models are equipped with variable valve timing, which consists of an actuator assembly attached to the intake camshaft sprocket. When removing the intake camshaft sprocket on these models only loosen and remove the center bolt, which fastens the sprocket to the camshaft. Do not loosen the outer four bolts that secure the actuator to the sprocket.*

Inspection

Refer to illustrations 6.20a, 6.20b and 6.21
20   Visually inspect all parts for wear and damage. Check the timing chain for loose pins, cracks, worn rollers and side plates. Check the sprockets for hook-shaped, chipped and broken teeth. Also check the timing chain for stretching and the diameter of the timing sprockets for wear with the chain assembled on the sprockets (see illustrations). Be sure to measure across the chain rollers when checking the sprocket diameter and to measure chain stretch at three or more places around the chain. Maximum chain elongation and minimum sprocket diameter (with chain)

6.14a Timing chain cover upper fasteners

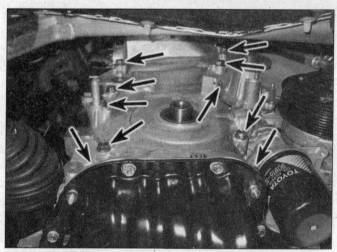

**6.14b Timing chain cover lower fasteners - make a note of the
fastener sizes, locations and lengths as your removing them as
they must be installed back in the original position**

**6.14c It will be necessary to remove the
timing chain cover studs . . .**

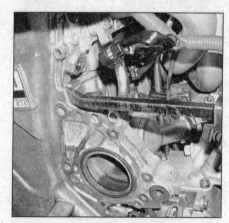

**6.14d . . . before prying the timing chain
cover off the engine**

**6.15 Slide the crankshaft position sensor
reluctor ring off the crankshaft - note the
"F" mark (arrow) on the front (it must be
facing outward upon installation)**

6.16 Timing chain guide mounting details

A Pivot bolt
B Tensioner pivot arm/chain guide
C Stationary chain guide mounting bolts
D Stationary chain guide
E Lower timing chain guide

cated, it will also be necessary to inspect the chain guide oil hole on the front of the block for clogging **(see illustration 14.5d)**.

Installation

Refer to illustrations 6.27, 6.28, 6.29, 6.32a, 6.32b, 6.34, 6.35 and 6.37

22   Remove all traces of old sealant from the timing chain cover and the mating surfaces of the engine block and cylinder head.

23   Make sure the camshafts are positioned with the dowel pins at the top in the 12 o'clock position, then install both camshaft sprockets in their original locations by aligning the dowel pin hole on the rear of the sprockets with dowel pin on the camshaft. Apply medium strength thread locking compound to the camshaft sprocket bolt threads and make sure the washers are in place. Hold the camshaft from turning as described in Step 19 and tighten the bolts to the torque listed in this Chapter's Specifications.

24   Rotate the camshafts as necessary to align the TDC marks on the camshaft sprockets **(see illustration 6.7)**.

should not exceed the amount listed in this Chapter's Specifications. Replace the timing chain and sprockets as a set if the engine has high mileage or fails inspection.

21   Check the chain guides for excessive wear **(see illustration)**. Replace the chain guides if scoring or wear exceeds the amount listed in this Chapter's Specifications. Note that some scoring of the timing chain guide shoes is normal. If excessive wear is indi-

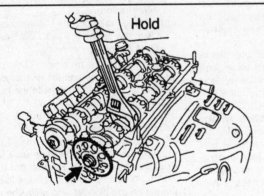

6.19 Hold the lug on the camshaft with a wrench to keep it from rotating as the sprocket bolts are loosened - - when loosening the intake camshaft sprocket, loosen the center bolt only which secures the sprocket to the camshaft

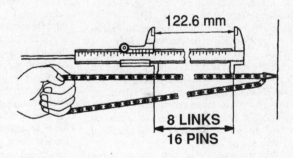

6.20a Timing chain stretch is measured by checking the length of the chain between 8 links (16 pins) at 3 or more places (selected randomly) around the chain - if chain stretch exceeds the specifications between any 8 links, the chain must be replaced

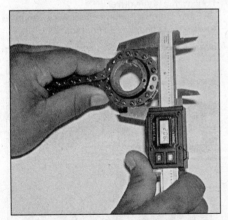

6.20b Wrap the chain around each of the timing sprockets and measure the diameter of the sprockets across the chain rollers - if the measurement exceeds the minimum sprocket diameter, the chain and the timing sprockets must be replaced

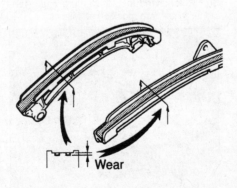

6.21 Timing chain guide wear is measured from the top of the chain contact surface to the bottom of the wear grooves

6.27 Loop the timing chain around the crankshaft sprocket and align the No.1 colored link with the mark on the crankshaft sprocket, then install the chain and crankshaft sprocket as an assembly on the engine and install the lower chain guide

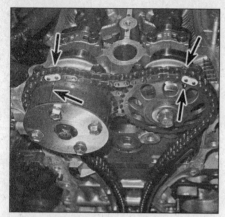

6.28 Loop the timing chain up over the exhaust camshaft and around the intake camshaft, while aligning the remaining two colored links with the marks on the camshaft sprockets

6.29 After the tensioner pivot arm is installed, make sure the tab (arrow) on the pivot arm can't move past the stopper on the cylinder head

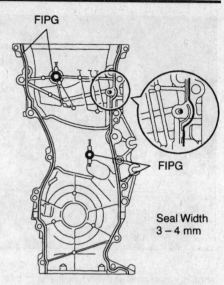

6.32a Timing chain cover sealant installation details

25 If the crankshaft has been rotated off TDC during this procedure, it will be necessary to rotate the crankshaft until the keyway is pointing straight up in the 12 o'clock position with the centerline of the cylinder bores.

26 Install the stationary timing chain guide **(see illustration 6.16)**.

27 Loop the timing chain around the crankshaft sprocket and align the No.1 colored link with the mark on the crankshaft sprocket. Install the chain and crankshaft sprocket as an assembly on the engine, then install the lower timing chain guide **(see illustration)** **Note:** *There are three colored links on the timing chain. The No.1 colored link is the link farthest away from the two colored links that are closest together.*

28 Slip the timing chain into the lip of the stationary timing chain guide and over the exhaust camshaft sprocket, then around the intake camshaft sprocket making sure to align the remaining two colored links with the marks on the camshaft sprockets **(see illustration)**. Make sure to remove all slack from the right side of the chain when doing so.

29 Use one hand to remove the slack from the left side of the chain and install the timing chain tensioner pivot arm/chain guide. Tighten the pivot bolt to torque listed in this Chapter's Specifications. After installation, make sure the tab on the pivot arm can't move past the stopper on the cylinder head **(see illustration)**.

30 Reconfirm that the number one piston is still at TDC on the compression stroke and that the timing marks on the crankshaft and camshaft sprockets are aligned with the colored links on the chain.

31 Install the crankshaft position sensor reluctor ring with the "F" mark facing outward.

32 Apply a bead of RTV sealant to the timing chain cover sealing surfaces **(see illustrations)**. Place the timing chain cover in position on the engine and install the bolts in their original locations.

33 Tighten the bolts evenly in several steps to the torque listed in this Chapter's Specifications **(see illustration)**. Be sure to follow the sealant manufacturer's recommendations for assembly and sealant curing times.

34 Reload and lock the timing chain tensioner to its "zero" position as follows:

Seal Width
3 – 4 mm

a) *Raise the ratchet pawl and push the plunger inward until it bottoms out* **(see illustration)**.

b) *Engage the hook on the tensioner body with the pin on the tensioner plunger to lock the plunger in place.*

35 Lubricate the tensioner O-ring with a small amount of oil and install the tensioner into the timing chain cover with the hook facing up **(see illustration)**.

36 Install the crankshaft pulley/vibration damper (see Section 11).

37 Rotate the engine counterclockwise slightly to set the chain tension **(see illustration)**. As the engine is rotated, the hook on the tensioner body should release itself from the pin on the plunger and allow the plunger to spring out and apply tension to the timing chain. If the plunger does not spring outward and apply tension to the timing chain, press downward on the pivot arm and release the hook with a screwdriver.

38 Rotate the engine clockwise several turns and reposition the number one piston

6.32b Also apply a bead of sealant on each side of the parting line between the cylinder head and the engine block

6.34 Raise the ratchet pawl and push the plunger inward until the hook on the tensioner body can be engaged with pin on the plunger to lock the plunger in place

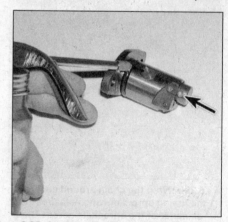

6.35 Apply a small amount of oil to the tensioner O-ring and insert the tensioner into the timing chain cover with the hook facing upward

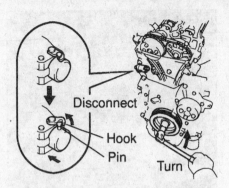

6.37 Rotate the engine counterclockwise to disengage the hook from the plunger pin on the tensioner, then rotate it clockwise and confirm that the plunger has extended outward against the pivot arm/chain guide

7.4 With the TDC marks aligned, apply a dab of paint to the timing chain links where they meet the upper timing marks on the camshaft sprockets

at TDC on the compression stroke (see Section 3). Visually confirm that the timing mark on the crankshaft pulley/vibration damper is aligned with the "0" mark on the timing chain cover and the camshaft sprocket marks are aligned and parallel with the top of the timing chain cover as shown in **illustration 6.7**.

39 The remainder of the installation is the reverse of removal.

7 Camshafts and lifters - removal, inspection and installation

Note: *The camshafts should always be thoroughly inspected before installation and camshaft endplay should always be checked prior to camshaft removal (see Step 13).*

Removal
Refer to illustrations 7.4, 7.7, 7.8, 7.11a and 7.11b

1 Disconnect the cable from the negative terminal of the battery.

2 Remove the valve cover (see Section 4).

3 Refer to Section 3 and place the engine on TDC for number 1 cylinder. Visually confirm the engine is at TDC on the compression stroke by verifying that the timing mark on the crankshaft pulley/vibration damper is aligned with the "0" mark on the timing chain cover and the camshaft sprocket TDC marks are aligned and parallel with the top of the timing chain cover **(see illustrations 3.8 and 6.7)**.

4 With the TDC marks aligned, apply a dab of paint to the timing chain links where they meet the upper timing marks on the camshaft sprockets **(see illustration)**. **Note:** *There are two sets of marks on the camshaft sprockets. The marks that align at TDC are for TDC reference only, the other two marks are used to align the sprockets with the timing chain during installation.*

5 Using a wrench to hold the camshaft sprockets from turning, loosen the camshaft sprocket bolts several turns **(see illustration 6.19)**. If the camshaft sprockets have rotated during the bolt loosening process, rotate the

engine clockwise until the "TDC" marks on the cam sprockets are realigned.

6 Remove the timing chain tensioner from the timing cover **(see illustrations 6.13a and 6.13b)** and the camshaft position sensor from the cylinder head (see Chapter 6).

7 Remove the camshaft sprocket retaining bolts. Disengage the timing chain from the sprockets and remove the camshaft sprockets from the engine. Make sure to note that the Variable Valve Timing (VVT) actuator is installed on the intake (rear) camshaft. After removing the sprockets, hang the timing chain up with a piece of wire and attach it to an object on the firewall **(see illustration)**. This will prevent the timing chain from falling into the engine as the remaining steps in this procedure are performed. Also place a rag into the opening of the timing chain cover to prevent any foreign objects from falling into the engine.

8 Verify the markings on the camshaft bearing caps. The caps should be marked from 1 to 5 with an "I" or an "E" mark on the cap indicating whether they're for the intake or exhaust camshaft **(see illustration)**.

7.7 With the camshaft sprockets removed, hang the timing chain out of the way with a piece of wire and place a shop rag in the timing chain cover opening to prevent foreign objects from falling into the engine

7.8 The camshaft bearing caps are numbered and have an arrow that should face the timing chain end of the engine

7.11a Mark the lifters (I for intake, E for exhaust, and number their location) and remove them with a magnetic retrieval tool

7.11b Mark up a cardboard box to store the lifters and bearing caps in order

7.13 Mount a dial indicator as shown to measure camshaft endplay - pry the camshaft forward and back and read the endplay on the dial

9   Loosen the camshaft bearing caps in two or three steps, in the reverse order of the tightening sequence **(see illustration 7.22)**. **Caution:** *Keep the caps in order. They must go back in the same location they were removed from.*

10   Detach the bearing caps, then remove the camshaft(s) from the cylinder head. Mark the camshaft(s) "Intake" or "Exhaust" to avoid mixing them up. **Note:** *When looking at the engine from the front of the vehicle, the for-*

7.14a Inspect the No.2 through No.5 cam bearing surfaces in the cylinder head for pits, score marks and abnormal wear - if wear or damage is noted, the cylinder head must be replaced

ward facing cam is the exhaust camshaft and the cam nearest the firewall is the intake camshaft. It is very important that the camshafts are returned to their original locations during installation.

11   Remove the lifters from the cylinder head, keeping them in order with their respective valve and cylinder **(see illustrations)**. **Caution:** *Keep the lifters in order. They must go back in the position from which they were removed.*

12   Inspect the camshafts, camshaft bearings and lifters as described below. Also inspect the camshaft sprockets for wear on the teeth. Inspect the chains for cracks or excessive wear of the rollers, and for stretching (see Section 7). If any of the components show signs of excessive wear they must be replaced.

Inspection

Refer to illustrations 7.13, 7.14a, 7.14b, 7.15, 7.16, 7.18 and 7.19

13   Before the camshafts are removed from the engine, check the camshaft endplay by placing a dial indicator with the stem in line with the camshaft and touching the snout **(see illustration)**. Push the camshaft all the way to the rear and zero the dial indicator. Next, pry the camshaft to the front as far as possible and check the reading on the dial indicator. The distance it moves is the endplay. If the endplay for the intake camshaft is greater than the Specifications listed in this Chapter,

check the thrust surfaces of the No.1 journal bearing for wear. If the thrust surface is worn, the bearings must be replaced. If the endplay for the exhaust camshaft is greater than the Specifications listed in this Chapter, the camshaft or the cylinder head (or both) may need to be replaced.

14   With the camshafts removed, visually check the camshaft bearing surfaces in the cylinder head for pitting, score marks, galling and abnormal wear. If the bearing surfaces are damaged, the cylinder head or the No.1 journal bearings of the intake camshaft may have to be replaced **(see illustration)**.

15   Measure the outside diameter of each camshaft bearing journal and record your measurements **(see illustration)**. Compare them to the journal outside diameter specified in this Chapter, then measure the inside diameter of each corresponding camshaft bearing and record the measurements. Subtract each cam journal outside diameter from its respective cam bearing bore inside diameter to determine the oil clearance for each bearing. Compare the results to the specified journal-to-bearing clearance. If any of the measurements fall outside the standard specified wear limits in this Chapter, either the camshaft or the cylinder head, or both, must be replaced. **Note:** *If precision measuring tools are not available, Plastigage may be used to determine the bearing journal oil clearance.*

16   Using a micrometer, measure the height of each camshaft lobe **(see illustra-**

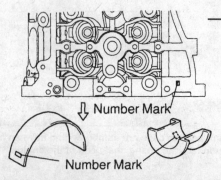

⇩ **Number Mark**

Number Mark

Cylinder head journal bore diameter:

Mark 1	40.000 – 40.008 mm (1.5748 – 1.5751 in.)
Mark 2	40.009 – 40.017 mm (1.5752 – 1.5755 in.)
Mark 3	40.018 – 40.025 mm (1.5755 – 1.5758 in.)

7.14b If the No.1 journal bearings are worn or damaged - it will be necessary to replace them with the same size as originally installed

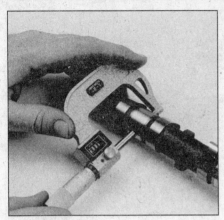

7.15 Measure each journal diameter with a micrometer - if any journal measures less than the specified limit, replace the camshaft

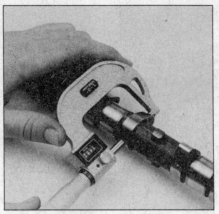

7.16 Measure the lobe heights on each camshaft - if any lobe height is less than the specified allowable minimum, replace that camshaft

7.18 Wipe off the oil and inspect each lifter for wear and scuffing

tion). Compare your measurements with this Chapter's Specifications. If the height for any one lobe is less than the specified minimum, replace the camshaft.

17   Check the camshaft runout by placing the camshaft back into the cylinder head and set up a dial indicator on the center journal. Zero the dial indicator. Turn the camshaft slowly and note the dial indicator readings. Runout should not exceed 0.0012 inch (0.03 mm). If the measured runout exceeds the specified runout, replace the camshaft.

18   Inspect each lifter for scuffing and score marks (see illustration).

19   Measure the outside diameter of each lifter (see illustration) and the corresponding lifter bore inside diameter. Subtract the lifter diameter from the lifter bore diameter to determine the oil clearance. Compare it to this Chapter's Specifications. If the oil clearance is excessive, a new cylinder head and/or new lifters will be required.

them into the cylinder head and the bearing cap now (see illustrations). Apply moly-based engine assembly lubricant to the camshaft lobes and journals and install the camshaft into the cylinder head with the No.1 cylinder camshaft lobes pointing outward away from each other, and the dowel pins facing upward (see illustration). If the old camshafts are being used, make sure they're installed in the exact location from which they came.

21   Install the bearing caps and bolts and tighten them hand tight.

22   Tighten the bearing cap bolts in several equal steps, to the torque listed in this Chapter's Specifications, using the proper tightening sequence (see illustration).

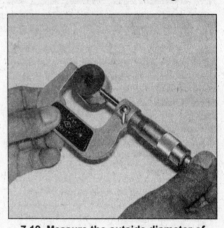

7.19 Measure the outside diameter of each lifter and the inside diameter of each lifter bore to determine the oil clearance measurement

Installation

Refer to illustrations 7.20a, 7.20b, 7.20c and 7.22

20   If the No.1 journal bearings for intake camshaft were removed or replaced, install

7.20a Place the thrust bearing for the intake camshaft in the No.1 journal on the cylinder head . . .

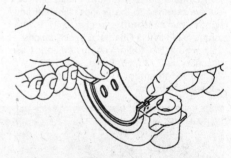

7.20b . . . and the upper bearing in the intake camshaft No.1 journal bearing cap

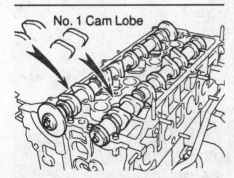

7.20c Place the camshafts in the cylinder head with the No.1 cylinder lobes pointing outward at approximately a 30-degree angle

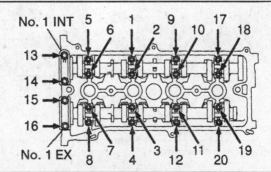

7.22 Camshaft bearing cap bolt TIGHTENING sequence

8.4 Label and disconnect the vacuum hoses (A) and the wire harness retainers (B) from the intake manifold

8.5 Intake manifold lower fastener locations (arrows)

23   Engage the camshaft sprocket teeth with the timing chain links so that the match marks made during removal align with the upper timing marks on the sprockets, then position the sprockets over the dowels on the camshaft hubs and install the camshaft sprocket bolts finger tight. At this point the mark on the crankshaft pulley should be aligned with the "0" mark on the timing chain cover, the camshaft sprocket TDC marks should be aligned and parallel with the top of the timing chain cover and the timing chain match marks should be aligned with the upper timing sprocket marks with all of the slack in the chain positioned towards the tensioner side of the engine (see illustration 7.4).
24   Double check that the timing sprockets are returned to the proper camshaft and tighten the camshaft sprocket bolts to the torque listed in this Chapter's Specifications.
25   Install the timing chain tensioner as described in Section 6, Steps 34 and 35.
26   The remainder of installation is the reverse of removal.

8   Intake manifold - removal and installation

Warning: *Wait until the engine is completely cool before beginning this procedure.*

Removal
Refer to illustrations 8.4, 8.5 and 8.6
1   Relieve the fuel system pressure (see Chapter 4), then disconnect the negative cable from the battery.
2   Remove the air intake duct and resonator (see Chapter 4). Then remove the cowl cover and vent tray (see Chapter 11).
3   Remove the fuel rail and injectors as an assembly. Also remove the throttle linkage and the throttle body from the intake manifold (see Chapter 4).
4   Label and detach the PCV and vacuum hoses connected to the rear of the intake manifold (see illustration).
5   Raise the vehicle and support it securely on jackstands. Working below the vehicle,

remove the manifold lower mounting bolts (see illustration).
6   Working from above, remove the intake manifold upper mounting nuts and bolts. Remove the manifold, the gasket and the manifold insulator from the engine (see illustration).

Installation
Refer to illustration 8.8
7   Clean the mating surfaces of the intake manifold and the cylinder head mounting surface with lacquer thinner or acetone. If the gasket shows signs of leaking, check the manifold for warpage with a straight edge. If the manifold is warped it must be replaced.
8   Press a new gasket into the grooves on the intake manifold (see illustration). Install the manifold and gasket over the studs on the cylinder head.
9   Tighten the manifold-to-cylinder head nuts/bolts in three or four equal steps to the torque listed in this Chapter's Specifications. Work from the center out towards the ends to avoid warping the manifold.

8.6 Intake manifold upper fastener locations (arrows)

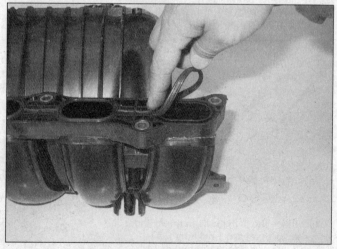

8.8 Press the gasket into the groove on the intake manifold

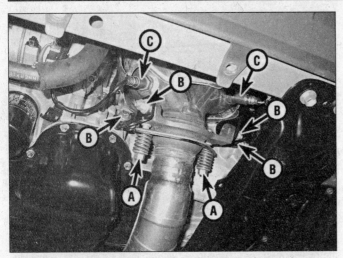

9.3 Working below the vehicle, remove the exhaust pipe-to-manifold mounting bolts (A) and lower the front exhaust pipe. Be careful not to damage the oxygen sensor (C) - (B) indicates the mounting bolts for the exhaust manifold lower brace

9.5 Working from the engine compartment, remove the upper heat shield mounting bolts (arrows) . . .

10   Install the remaining parts in the reverse order of removal. Check the coolant level, adding as necessary (see Chapter 1).

11   Before starting the engine, check the throttle linkage for smooth operation.

12   Run the engine and check for coolant and vacuum leaks.

13   Road test the vehicle and check for proper operation of all accessories, including the cruise control system, if equipped.

9   Exhaust manifold - removal and installation

Warning: *The engine must be completely cool before beginning this procedure.*

Removal
Refer to illustrations 9.3, 9.5 and 9.6

1   Disconnect the negative cable from the battery.

2   Raise the front of the vehicle and support it securely on jackstands. Working below the vehicle, remove the lower splash shields.

3   Apply penetrating oil to the bolts and springs retaining the exhaust pipe to the manifold. After the bolts have soaked, remove the bolts retaining the exhaust pipe to the manifold. Separate the front exhaust pipe from the manifold, being careful not to damage the oxygen sensor **(see illustration)**.

4   Unbolt the lower exhaust manifold braces and remove them from the engine. Also disconnect the oxygen sensor connectors.

5   Working in the engine compartment, remove the upper heat shield from the manifold **(see illustration)**. **Note:** *There is also a lower heat shield, but it is attached to the manifold from underneath and does not need to be removed.*

6   Remove the nuts/bolts and detach the manifold and gasket **(see illustration)**.

Installation

7   Use a scraper to remove all traces of old gasket material and carbon deposits from the manifold and cylinder head mating surfaces. If the gasket shows signs of leaking, check the manifold for warpage with a straight edge. If

the manifold is warped it must be replaced. **Note:** *If the manifold is being replaced with a new one it will be necessary to remove the lower heat shield and fasten it to the new manifold.*

8   Position a new gasket over the cylinder head studs, noting any directional marks or arrows on the gasket which may be present.

9   Install the manifold and thread the mounting nuts into place.

10   Working from the center out, tighten the nuts/bolts to the torque listed in this Chapter's Specifications in three or four equal steps.

11   Reinstall the remaining parts in the reverse order of removal.

12   Run the engine and check for exhaust leaks.

10   Cylinder head - removal and installation

Warning: *The engine must be completely cool before beginning this procedure.*

Removal
Refer to illustrations 10.11 and 10.13

1   Relieve the fuel system pressure (see Chapter 4), then disconnect the cable from the negative terminal of the battery.

2   Drain the engine coolant (see Chapter 1).

3   Remove the drivebelt and the alternator (see Chapter 5).

4   Remove the valve cover (see Section 4).

5   Remove the throttle body, fuel injectors and fuel rail (see Chapter 4).

6   Remove the intake manifold (see Section 8).

7   Remove the exhaust manifold (see Section 9).

8   Remove the timing chain and camshaft sprockets (see Section 6).

9.6 . . . and the exhaust manifold retaining nuts, then pull the manifold off the studs on the cylinder head and remove from above

9 Remove the camshafts and lifters (see Section 7).
10 Remove the variable valve timing control valve **(see illustration 5.2a)**.
11 Label and remove the coolant hoses and electrical connections from the cylinder head **(see illustration)**.
12 Using a 10 mm hex-head socket bit and a breaker bar, loosen the cylinder head bolts in 1/4-turn increments until they can be removed by hand. Loosen the cylinder head bolts in the reverse order of the recommended tightening sequence **(see illustration 10.24)** to avoid warping or cracking the cylinder head.
13 Lift the cylinder head off the engine block. If it's stuck, very carefully pry up at the transaxle end, beyond the gasket surface **(see illustration)**.
14 Remove any remaining external components from the cylinder head to allow for thorough cleaning and inspection.

Installation

Refer to illustrations 10.16, 10.21a, 10.21b and 10.24

15 The mating surfaces of the cylinder head and block must be perfectly clean when the cylinder head is installed.
16 Use a gasket scraper to remove all traces of carbon and old gasket material **(see**

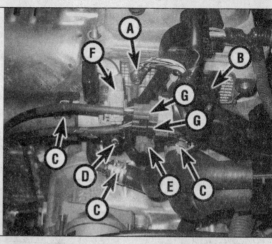

10.11 Disconnect the following components from the driver's side of the cylinder head and position the electrical wiring harness aside

A   Ground straps
B   Camshaft position sensor
C   Coolant hoses
D   Oil pressure sending unit
E   Coolant temperature sensor
F   Radio noise suppressor
G   Oxygen sensor connector

illustration), then clean the mating surfaces with lacquer thinner or acetone. If there's oil on the mating surfaces when the cylinder head is installed, the gasket may not seal correctly and leaks could develop. When working on the block, stuff the cylinders with clean shop rags to keep out debris. Use a vacuum cleaner to remove material that falls into the cylinders.
17 Check the block and cylinder head mating surfaces for nicks, deep scratches and other damage. If damage is slight, it can be

removed with a file; if it's excessive, machining may be the only alternative.
18 Use a tap of the correct size to chase the threads in the cylinder head bolt holes, then clean the holes with compressed air - make sure that nothing remains in the holes. **Warning:** *Wear eye protection when using compressed air!*
19 Using a wire brush, clean the threads on each bolt to remove corrosion and restore the threads. Dirt, corrosion, sealant and damaged threads will affect torque readings.

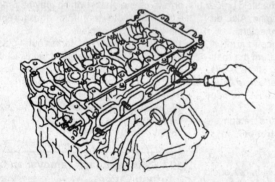

10.13 Pry the cylinder head off the engine block at the casting protrusion - be careful not to damage the mating surfaces

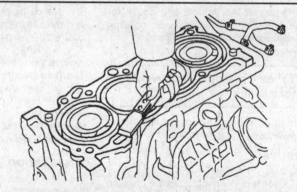

10.16 Remove all traces of old gasket material - the cylinder head and block mating surfaces must be perfectly clean to ensure a good gasket seal

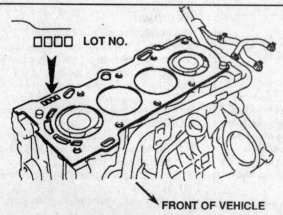

10.21a Place the head gasket over the dowels in the block with the marks facing UP

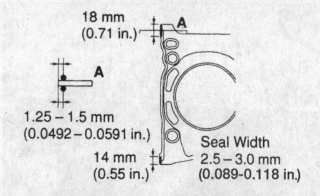

10.21b Apply RTV sealant to the areas on the cylinder head gasket as shown

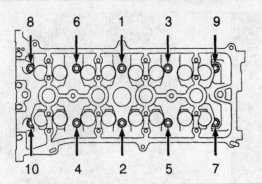

10.24 Cylinder head bolt TIGHTENING sequence

20   Install the components that were removed from the cylinder head.
21   Position the new gasket over the dowel pins in the block (see illustration). Then apply RTV sealant to the end of the cylinder head gasket as shown (see illustration).
22   Carefully set the cylinder head on the block without disturbing the gasket.
23   Before installing the cylinder head bolts,

apply a small amount of clean engine oil to the threads and under the bolt heads.
24   Install the bolts in their original locations and tighten them finger tight. Following the recommended sequence, tighten the bolts to the torque listed in this Chapter's Specifications (see illustration). Step 2 of the tightening sequence requires each bolt to be tightened an additional 90-degrees. If you don't have an angle-torque attachment for your torque wrench, simply apply a paint mark at one edge of each cylinder head bolt and tighten the bolt until that mark is 90-degrees (1/4-turn) from where you started.
25   The remaining installation steps are the reverse of removal.
26   Check and adjust the valves as necessary (see Chapter 1).
27   Change the engine oil and filter (see Chapter 1.
28   Refill the cooling system (see Chapter 1), run the engine and check for leaks.

11   Crankshaft pulley/vibration damper - removal and installation

Refer to illustrations 11.4, 11.5 and 11.6
1   Detach the cable from the negative terminal of the battery.
2   Remove the drivebelt (see Chapter 1).
3   With the parking brake applied and the shifter in Park (automatic) or in gear (manual),

loosen the lug nuts from the right front wheel, then raise the front of the vehicle and support it securely on jackstands. Remove the right front wheel and the right splash shield from the wheelwell.
4   Remove the bolt from the front of the crankshaft. A breaker bar will probably be necessary, since the bolt is very tight (see illustration).
5   Using a puller that bolts to the crankshaft hub, remove the crankshaft pulley from the crankshaft (see illustration). Note: *Depending on the type of puller you have it may be necessary to support the engine from above, remove the right side engine mount and lower to engine to gain sufficient clearance to use the puller.* Caution: *Do not use a jaw-type puller - it will damage the pulley/damper assembly.*
6   To install the crankshaft pulley, slide the pulley onto the crankshaft as far as it will slide on, then use a vibration damper installation tool to press the pulley onto the crankshaft. Note that the slot (keyway) in the hub must be aligned with the Woodruff key in the end of the crankshaft (see illustration) and that the crankshaft bolt can also be used to press the crankshaft pulley into position.
7   Tighten the crankshaft bolt to the torque and angle of rotation listed in this Chapter's Specifications.
8   The remaining installation steps are the reverse of removal.

12   Crankshaft front oil seal - replacement

Refer to illustrations 12.2, 12.3 and 12.4
1   Remove the crankshaft pulley (see Section 11).
2   Note how the seal is installed - the new one must be installed to the same depth and facing the same way. Carefully pry the oil seal out of the cover with a seal puller or a large screwdriver (see illustration). Be very careful not to distort the cover or scratch the crankshaft! Wrap electrician's tape around the tip of the screwdriver to avoid damage to the crankshaft.

11.4 A puller base and several spacers can be mounted to the center hub of the pulley to keep the crankshaft from turning as the pulley retaining bolt is loosened - install the socket over the crankshaft bolt head before installing the puller, then insert the extension through the center hole of the puller

11.5 Reinstall the puller back onto the crankshaft pulley with the center bolt attached and remove the crankshaft pulley

11.6 Align the keyway in the crankshaft pulley hub with the Woodruff key in the crankshaft (arrow)

12.2 Carefully pry the old seal out of the timing chain cover - don't damage the crankshaft in the process

3   Apply clean engine oil or multi-purpose grease to the outer edge of the new seal, then install it in the cover with the lip (spring side) facing IN. Drive the seal into place with a seal driver or a large socket and a hammer **(see illustration)**. Make sure the seal enters the bore squarely and stop when the front face is at the proper depth.

4   Check the surface on the pulley hub that the oil seal rides on. If the surface has been grooved from long-time contact with the seal, a press-on sleeve may be available to renew the sealing surface **(see illustration)**. This sleeve is pressed into place with a hammer and a block of wood and is commonly available at auto parts stores for various applications.

5   Lubricate the pulley hub with clean engine oil and reinstall the crankshaft pulley (see Section 11).

6   Install the crankshaft pulley retaining bolt and tighten it to the torque listed in this Chapter's Specifications.

7   The remainder of installation is the reverse of the removal.

13   Oil pan - removal and installation

Removal

Refer to illustrations 13.6a and 13.6b

1   Disconnect the cable from the negative terminal of the battery.

2   Set the parking brake and block the rear wheels.

3   Raise the front of the vehicle and support it securely on jackstands.

4   Remove the two plastic splash shields under the engine, if equipped.

5   Drain the engine oil and remove the oil filter (see Chapter 1). Remove the oil dipstick.

6   Remove the bolts and detach the oil pan. If it's stuck, pry it loose very carefully with a small screwdriver or putty knife **(see illustrations)**. Don't damage the mating surfaces of the pan and block or oil leaks could develop.

Installation

Refer to illustration 13.11

7   Use a scraper to remove all traces of old sealant from the block and oil pan. Clean the mating surfaces with lacquer thinner or acetone.

8   Make sure the threaded bolt holes in the block are clean.

9   Check the oil pan flange for distortion, particularly around the bolt holes. Remove any nicks or burrs as necessary.

10   Inspect the oil pump pick-up tube assembly for cracks and a blocked strainer. If the pick-up was removed, clean it thoroughly and install it now, using a new gasket. Tighten the nuts/bolts to the torque listed in this Chapter's Specifications.

11   Apply a 3/16-inch wide bead of RTV sealant to the mating surface of the oil pan **(see illustration)**. **Note:** *Be sure follow the sealant manufacturers recommendations for*

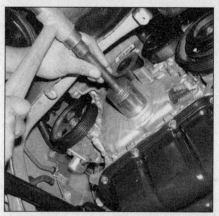

12.3 Drive the new seal into place with a large socket and hammer

12.4 If the sealing surface of the pulley hub has a wear groove from contact with the seal, repair sleeves are available at most auto parts stores

13.6a Oil pan mounting bolts

assembly and sealant curing times.

12   Carefully position the oil pan on the engine block and install the oil pan-to-engine block bolts loosely.

13   Working from the center out, tighten the oil pan-to-engine block bolts to the torque listed in this Chapter's Specifications in three or four steps.

14   The remainder of installation is the reverse of removal. Be sure to wait at least one hour before adding oil to allow the sealant to properly cure.

15   Run the engine and check for oil pressure and leaks.

14   Oil pump - removal and installation

Removal

Refer to illustrations 14.2a, 14.2b, 14.3, 14.5a, 14.5b, 14.5c and 14.5d

1   Refer to Section 6, Steps 1 through 17 and remove the timing chain and the crankshaft sprocket.

2   Remove the oil pump drive chain and sprockets **(see illustrations)**.

13.6b Pry the oil pan loose with a screwdriver or putty knife - be careful not to damage the mating surfaces of the pan and block or oil leaks may develop

3   Remove the three bolts and detach the oil pump body from the engine **(see illustration)**. You may have to pry carefully between the front of the block and the pump body with a screwdriver to remove it.

4   Use a scraper to remove all traces of sealant and old gasket material from the pump body and engine block, then clean the mating surfaces with lacquer thinner or acetone.

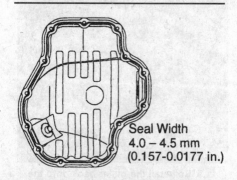

Seal Width
4.0 – 4.5 mm
(0.157-0.0177 in.)

13.11 Oil pan sealant installation details

14.2a Rotate the engine 90-degrees counterclockwise (from TDC) and set the crankshaft key to the left horizontal position (A), then remove the oil pump drive chain tensioner and bolt (B)

14.2b Using a screwdriver to lock the lower gear in place, loosen the retaining bolt and remove the drive chain and lower gear and from the engine

14.3 Oil pump mounting bolts (arrows)

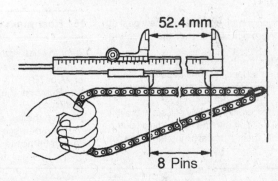

14.5a Oil pump drive chain stretch is measured by checking the length of the chain between 4 links (8 pins) at 3 or more places (selected randomly) around the chain - if chain stretch exceeds the specifications between any 4 links, the chain must be replaced

5   Inspect the oil pump and chain for wear and damage. If the oil pump shows signs of wear or you're in doubt about its condition it is simply best to replace it. The oil pump drive chain and tensioner, however, can be inspected as follows (see illustrations). Also check the the oil jet for blockage (see illustration).

Installation

Refer to illustration 14.9

6   Lubricate the pump cavity by pouring a small amount of clean engine oil into the inlet side of the oil pump and turning the drive gear shaft.

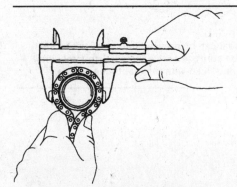

14.5b Wrap the chain around each of the oil pump drive sprockets and measure the diameter of the sprockets across the chain rollers - if the measurement exceeds the minimum sprocket diameter, the chain and the sprockets must be replaced

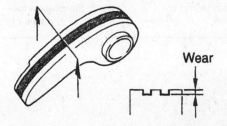

14.5c Oil pump chain guide wear is measured from the top of the chain contact surface to the bottom of the wear grooves

14.5d Check that the oil jet is free of debris - a blockage here will lead to an excessively worn timing chain, oil pump drive chain and guides

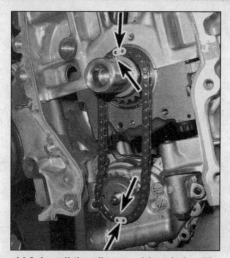

14.9 Install the oil pump drive chain with the colored links aligned with the marks on the sprockets

7   Position the oil pump and a new gasket against the block and install the mounting bolts.

8   Tighten the bolts to the torque listed in this Chapter's Specifications in several steps. Follow a criss-cross pattern to avoid warping the body.

9   With the crankshaft key still set in the left horizontal position and the flat on the oil pump drive shaft facing upward, install the drive chain and sprockets so that the colored links on the chain align with the alignment marks on the drive gears **(see illustration)**.

10   Tighten the lower drive sprocket retaining bolt to the torque listed in this Chapter's Specifications.

11   Reinstall the remaining parts in the reverse order of removal.

12   Add oil to the proper level, start the engine and check for oil pressure and leaks.

15   Flywheel/driveplate - removal and installation

The flywheel/driveplate replacement for 2001 and later engines is identical to the flywheel/driveplate replacement procedure for the 2000 and earlier engines. Refer to Chapter 2 Part A for the procedure and use the torque figures in this Chapter's Specifications.

16   Rear main oil seal - replacement

Refer to illustrations 16.3 and 16.4

1   Remove the transmission (see Chapter 7A or 7B).

2   Remove the flywheel/driveplate (see Section 15).

3   Pry the oil seal from the rear of the engine with a screwdriver **(see illustration)**. Be careful not to nick or scratch the crankshaft or the seal bore. Be sure to note how far it's recessed into the bore before removal so the new seal can be installed to the same depth. Thoroughly clean the seal bore in the block with a shop towel. Remove all traces of oil and dirt.

4   Lubricate the outside diameter of the seal and install the seal over the end of the crankshaft. Make sure the lip of the seal points toward the engine. Preferably, a seal installation tool (available at most auto parts store) is needed to press the new seal back into place. If the proper seal installation tool is unavailable, use a large socket, section of pipe or a blunt tool and carefully drive the new seal squarely into the seal bore and flush with the edge of the engine block **(see illustration)**.

5   Install the flywheel/driveplate (see Section 15).

6   Install the transmission (see Chapter 7A or 7B).

17   Powertrain mounts - check and replacement

The powertrain mount replacement for 2001 and later engines is identical to the powertrain mount replacement procedure for the 2000 and earlier engines. Refer to Chapter 2 Part A for the procedure and use the torque figures in this Chapter's Specifications.

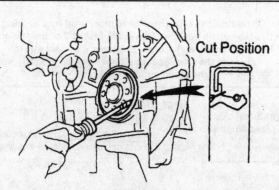

16.3 Carefully pry out the old seal with a screwdriver - it may be helpful to cut the seal lip with a razor blade first to make removal of the seal easier

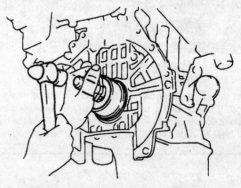

16.4 The rear oil seal can be pressed into place with a seal installation tool - be sure the seal is installed squarely into the seal bore and flush with the rear of the engine

Chapter 2 Part C
General engine overhaul procedures

Contents

	Section
CHECK ENGINE light	See Chapter 6
Cylinder compression check	3
Engine - removal and installation	7
Engine external components - disassembly sequence	8
Engine external components - reassembly sequence	9
Engine rebuilding alternatives	5

	Section
Engine removal - methods and precautions	6
General information - engine overhaul	1
Initial start-up and break-in after installation	10
Oil pressure check	2
Vacuum gauge diagnostic checks	4

Specifications

General

Engine designation
2000 and earlier 3S-FE
2001 through 2003 .... 1AZ-FE
2004 and later 2AZ-FE
Displacement
3S-FE .... 121.9 cubic inches (2.0 liters)
1AZ-FE .... 121.9 cubic inches (2.0 liters)
2AZ-FE .... 144.2 cubic inches (2.4 liters)
Bore and stroke
3S-FE .... 3.39 x 3.39 inches (86.0 x 86.0 mm)
1AZ-FE .... 3.39 x 3.39 inches (86.0 x 86.0 mm)
2AZ-FE .... 3.48 x 3.78 inches (88.5 x 96.0 mm)
Cylinder compression pressure @ 250 rpm
1996 and 1997
Standard .... 185 psi (13.0 kg/cm^2) or more
Minimum .... 135 psi (9.5 kg/cm^2)
Difference between cylinders .... 14 psi (1.0 kg/cm^2) or less
1998 through 2000
Standard .... 178 psi (12.5 kg/cm^2) or more
Minimum .... 128 psi (9.0 kg/cm^2)
Difference between cylinders .... 14 psi (1.0 kg/cm^2) or less
2001 and later
Standard .... 184 psi (13.0 kg/cm^2) or more
Minimum .... 145 psi (10.2 kg/cm^2)
Difference between cylinders .... 15 psi (1.0 kg/cm^2) or less
Oil pressure (engine warm)
2000 and earlier
At idle .... 4.3 psi (0.3 kg/cm^2) minimum
At 3000 rpm .... 36 to 71 psi (2.5 to 5.0 kg/cm^2)
2001 and later
At idle .... 4.3 psi (0.3 kg/cm^2) minimum
At 3000 rpm .... 36 to 78 psi (2.2 to 5.5 kg/cm^2)

Torque specifications

	Ft-lbs	Nm
Connecting rod bearing cap nuts		
Step 1	18	25
Step 2	Tighten an additional 90-degrees	
Main bearing cap bolts		
2000 and earlier models	43	59
2001 and later models		
Step 1	15	20
Step 2	30	40
Step 3	Tighten an additional 90-degrees	
Lower crankcase-to-cylinder block bolts	25	33

2.2a The oil pressure sending unit (arrow) is located at the end of the cylinder head on the driver's side of the vehicle - 2001 and later shown, 2000 and earlier similar

2.2b The oil pressure can be checked by removing the sending unit and installing a pressure gauge in its place

1   General information - engine overhaul

Included in this portion of Chapter 2 are general information and diagnostic testing procedures for determining the overall mechanical condition of your engine.

The information ranges from advice concerning preparation for an overhaul and the purchase of replacement parts and/or components to detailed, step-by-step procedures covering removal and installation.

The following Sections have been written to help you determine whether your engine needs to be overhauled and how to remove and install it once you've determined it needs to be rebuilt. For information concerning in-vehicle engine repair, see Chapter 2 Part A or Part B.

The Specifications included in this Part are general in nature and include only those necessary for testing the oil pressure and checking the engine compression. Refer to Part A or Part B for additional engine Specifications.

It's not always easy to determine when, or if, an engine should be completely overhauled, as a number of factors must be considered.

High mileage is not necessarily an indication that an overhaul is needed, while low mileage doesn't preclude the need for an overhaul. Frequency of servicing is probably the most important consideration. An engine that's had regular and frequent oil and filter changes, as well as other required maintenance, will most likely give many thousands of miles of reliable service. Conversely, a neglected engine may require an overhaul very early in its life.

Excessive oil consumption is an indication that piston rings, valve seals and/or valve guides are in need of attention. Make sure that oil leaks aren't responsible before deciding that the rings and/or guides are bad. Per-

form a cylinder compression check to determine the extent of the work required (see Section 3). Also check the vacuum readings under various conditions (see Section 4).

Check the oil pressure with a gauge installed in place of the oil pressure sending unit and compare it to this Chapter's Specifications (see Section 2). If it's extremely low, the bearings and/or oil pump are probably worn out.

Loss of power, rough running, knocking or metallic engine noises, excessive valve train noise and high fuel consumption rates may also point to the need for an overhaul, especially if they're all present at the same time. If a complete tune-up doesn't remedy the situation, major mechanical work is the only solution.

An engine overhaul involves restoring the internal parts to the specifications of a new engine. During an overhaul, the piston rings are replaced and the cylinder walls are reconditioned (rebored and/or honed). If a rebore is done by an automotive machine shop, new oversize pistons will also be installed. The main bearings, connecting rod bearings and camshaft bearings are generally replaced with new ones and, if necessary, the crankshaft may be reground to restore the journals. Generally, the valves are serviced as well, since they're usually in less-than-perfect condition at this point. While the engine is being overhauled, other components, such as the distributor, starter and alternator, can be rebuilt as well. The end result should be a like new engine that will give many trouble free miles. **Note:** *Critical cooling system components such as the hoses, drivebelts, thermostat and water pump should be replaced with new parts when an engine is overhauled. The radiator should be checked carefully to ensure that it isn't clogged or leaking (see Chapter 3). If you purchase a rebuilt engine or short block, some rebuilders will not warranty their engines unless the radiator has been professionally flushed. Also, we don't*

recommend overhauling the oil pump - always install a new one when an engine is rebuilt.

Overhauling the internal components on today's engines is a difficult and time-consuming task which requires a significant amount of specialty tools and is best left to a professional engine rebuilder. A competent engine rebuilder will handle the inspection of your old parts and offer advice concerning the reconditioning or replacement of the original engine. Never purchase parts or have machine work done on other components until the block has been thoroughly inspected by a professional machine shop. As a general rule, time is the primary cost of an overhaul, especially since the vehicle may be tied up for a minimum of two weeks or more. Be aware that some engine builders only have the capability to rebuild the engine you bring them, while other rebuilders have a large inventory of rebuilt exchange engines in stock. Also be aware that many machine shops could take as much as two weeks time to completely rebuild your engine depending on shop workload. Sometimes it makes more sense to simply exchange your engine for another engine that's already rebuilt to save time.

2   Oil pressure check

Refer to illustrations 2.2a and 2.2b

1   Low engine oil pressure can be a sign of an engine in need of rebuilding. A "low oil pressure" indicator (often called an "idiot light") is not a test of the oiling system. Such indicators only come on when the oil pressure is dangerously low. Even a factory oil pressure gauge in the instrument panel is only a relative indication, although much better for driver information than a warning light. A better test is with a mechanical (not electrical) oil pressure gauge.

2   Find the oil pressure indicator sending unit **(see illustrations)**.

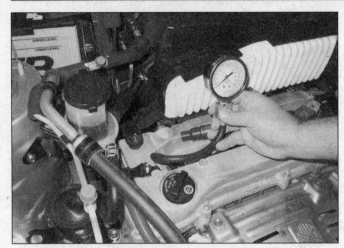

3.6 A compression gauge with a threaded fitting for the spark plug hole is preferred over the type that requires hand pressure to maintain the seal - be sure to block open the throttle valve as far as possible during the compression check!

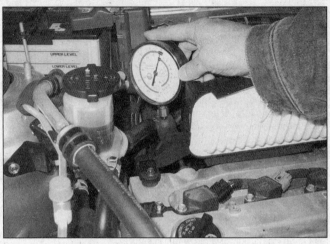

4.4 A simple vacuum gauge can be handy in diagnosing engine condition and performance

3   Remove the oil pressure sending unit and install a fitting which will allow you to directly connect your hand-held, mechanical oil pressure gauge. Use Teflon tape or sealant on the threads of the adapter and the fitting on the end of your gauge's hose.

4   Connect an accurate tachometer to the engine, according to the tachometer manufacturer's instructions.

5   Check the oil pressure with the engine running (normal operating temperature) at the specified engine speed, and compare it to this Chapter's Specifications. If it's extremely low, the bearings and/or oil pump are probably worn out.

3   Cylinder compression check

Refer to illustration 3.6

1   A compression check will tell you what mechanical condition the upper end of your engine (pistons, rings, valves, head gaskets) is in. Specifically, it can tell you if the compression is down due to leakage caused by worn piston rings, defective valves and seats or a blown head gasket. **Note:** *The engine must be at normal operating temperature and the battery must be fully charged for this check.*

2   Begin by cleaning the area around the spark plugs before you remove them (compressed air should be used, if available). The idea is to prevent dirt from getting into the cylinders as the compression check is being done.

3   Remove all of the spark plugs from the engine (see Chapter 1).

4   Block the throttle wide open.

5   Disable the ignition system by disconnecting the primary (low voltage) electrical connectors from the coil packs (see Chapter 5). The fuel pump circuit must also be disabled (see Chapter 4, Section 2).

6   Install the compression gauge in the spark plug hole **(see illustration)**.

7   Crank the engine over at least seven

compression strokes and watch the gauge. The compression should build up quickly in a healthy engine. Low compression on the first stroke, followed by gradually increasing pressure on successive strokes, indicates worn piston rings. A low compression reading on the first stroke, which doesn't build up during successive strokes, indicates leaking valves or a blown head gasket (a cracked head could also be the cause). Deposits on the undersides of the valve heads can also cause low compression. Record the highest gauge reading obtained.

8   Repeat the procedure for the remaining cylinders and compare the results to this Chapter's Specifications.

9   Add some engine oil (about three squirts from a plunger-type oil can) to each cylinder, through the spark plug hole, and repeat the test.

10   If the compression increases after the oil is added, the piston rings are definitely worn. If the compression doesn't increase significantly, the leakage is occurring at the valves or head gasket. Leakage past the valves may be caused by burned valve seats and/or faces or warped, cracked or bent valves.

11   If two adjacent cylinders have equally low compression, there's a strong possibility that the head gasket between them is blown. The appearance of coolant in the combustion chambers or the crankcase would verify this condition.

12   If one cylinder is slightly lower than the others, and the engine has a slightly rough idle, a worn lobe on the camshaft could be the cause.

13   If the compression is unusually high, the combustion chambers are probably coated with carbon deposits. If that's the case, the cylinder head(s) should be removed and decarbonized.

14   If compression is way down or varies greatly between cylinders, it would be a good idea to have a leak-down test performed by an automotive repair shop. This test will pin-

point exactly where the leakage is occurring and how severe it is.

15   After all of the cylinders have been checked, unblock the throttle and restore the ignition and fuel system functions.

4   Vacuum gauge diagnostic checks

Refer to illustrations 4.4 and 4.6

A vacuum gauge provides valuable information about what is going on in the engine at a low-cost. You can check for worn rings or cylinder walls, leaking head or intake manifold gaskets, incorrect carburetor adjustments, restricted exhaust, stuck or burned valves, weak valve springs, improper ignition or valve timing and ignition problems.

Unfortunately, vacuum gauge readings are easy to misinterpret, so they should be used in conjunction with other tests to confirm the diagnosis.

Both the absolute readings and the rate of needle movement are important for accurate interpretation. Most gauges measure vacuum in inches of mercury (in-Hg). The following references to vacuum assume the diagnosis is being performed at sea level. As elevation increases (or atmospheric pressure decreases), the reading will decrease. For every 1,000 foot increase in elevation above approximately 2000 feet, the gauge readings will decrease about one inch of mercury.

Connect the vacuum gauge directly to intake manifold vacuum, not to ported (throttle body) vacuum **(see illustration)**. Be sure no hoses are left disconnected during the test or false readings will result.

Before you begin the test, allow the engine to warm up completely. Block the wheels and set the parking brake. With the transmission in Park, start the engine and allow it to run at normal idle speed. **Warning:** *Keep your hands and the vacuum gauge clear of the fans.*

Read the vacuum gauge; an average, healthy engine should normally produce about 17 to 22 in-Hg with a fairly steady needle **(see illustration)**. Refer to the following vacuum gauge readings and what they indicate about the engine's condition:

1   A low steady reading usually indicates a leaking gasket between the intake manifold and cylinder head(s) or throttle body, a leaky vacuum hose, late ignition timing or incorrect camshaft timing. Check ignition timing with a timing light and eliminate all other possible causes, utilizing the tests provided in this Chapter before you remove the timing chain cover to check the timing marks.

2   If the reading is three to eight inches below normal and it fluctuates at that low reading, suspect an intake manifold gasket leak at an intake port or a faulty fuel injector.

3   If the needle has regular drops of about two-to-four inches at a steady rate, the valves are probably leaking. Perform a compression check or leak-down test to confirm this.

4   An irregular drop or down-flick of the needle can be caused by a sticking valve or an ignition misfire. Perform a compression check or leak-down test and read the spark plugs.

5   A rapid vibration of about four in-Hg vibration at idle combined with exhaust smoke indicates worn valve guides. Perform a leak-down test to confirm this. If the rapid vibration occurs with an increase in engine speed, check for a leaking intake manifold gasket or head gasket, weak valve springs, burned valves or ignition misfire.

6   A slight fluctuation, say one inch up and down, may mean ignition problems. Check all the usual tune-up items and, if necessary, run the engine on an ignition analyzer.

7   If there is a large fluctuation, perform a compression or leak-down test to look for a weak or dead cylinder or a blown head gasket.

8   If the needle moves slowly through a wide range, check for a clogged PCV system, incorrect idle fuel mixture, carburetor/throttle body or intake manifold gasket leaks.

9   Check for a slow return after revving the engine by quickly snapping the throttle open until the engine reaches about 2,500 rpm and let it shut. Normally the reading should drop to near zero, rise above normal idle reading (about 5 in-Hg over) and then return to the previous idle reading. If the vacuum returns slowly and doesn't peak when the throttle is snapped shut, the rings may be worn. If there is a long delay, look for a restricted exhaust system (often the muffler or catalytic converter). An easy way to check this is to temporarily disconnect the exhaust ahead of the suspected part and redo the test.

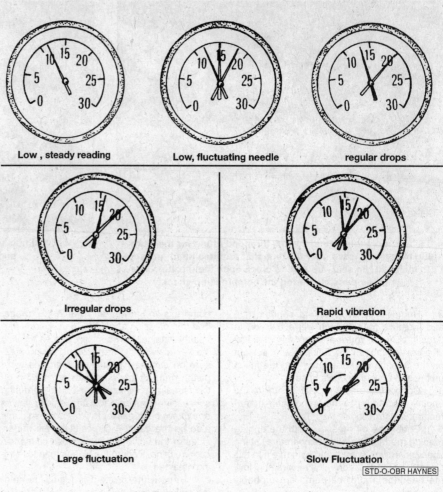

Low , steady reading   Low, fluctuating needle   regular drops

Irregular drops   Rapid vibration

Large fluctuation   Slow Fluctuation

STD-O-OBR HAYNES

4.6 Typical vacuum gauge readings

5   Engine rebuilding alternatives

The do-it-yourselfer is faced with a number of options when purchasing a rebuilt engine. The major considerations are cost, warranty, parts availability and the time required for the rebuilder to complete the project. The decision to replace the engine block, piston/connecting rod assemblies and crankshaft depends on the final inspection results of your engine. Only then can you make a cost-effective decision whether to have your engine overhauled or simply purchase an exchange engine for your vehicle.

Some of the rebuilding alternatives include:

Individual parts - If the inspection procedures reveal that the engine block and most engine components are in reusable condition, purchasing individual parts and having a rebuilder rebuild your engine may be the most economical alternative. The block, crankshaft and piston/connecting rod assemblies should all be inspected carefully by a machine shop first.

Short block - A short block consists of an engine block with a crankshaft and piston/connecting rod assemblies already installed. All new bearings are incorporated and all clearances will be correct. The existing camshafts, valve train components, cylinder head and external parts can be bolted to the short block with little or no machine shop work necessary.

Long block - A long block consists of a short block plus an oil pump, oil pan, cylinder head, valve cover, camshaft and valve train components, timing sprockets and chain/belt or gears and timing cover. All components are installed with new bearings, seals and gaskets incorporated throughout. The installation of manifolds and external parts is all that's necessary.

Low mileage used engines - Some companies now offer low-mileage used engines which is a very cost effective way to get your vehicle up and running again. These engines often come from vehicles which have been totaled in accidents or come from other countries which have a higher vehicle turnover rate. A low-mileage used engine also usually has a similar warranty like the newly remanufactured engines.

Give careful thought to which alternative is best for you and discuss the situation with local automotive machine shops, auto parts dealers and experienced rebuilders before ordering or purchasing replacement parts.

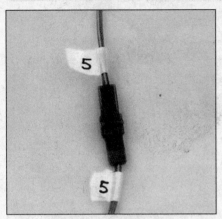

7.9 Label both ends of each wire and hose before disconnecting it

6 Engine removal - methods and precautions

If you've decided that an engine must be removed for overhaul or major repair work, several preliminary steps should be taken.

Locating a suitable place to work is extremely important. Adequate work space, along with storage space for the vehicle, will be needed. If a shop or garage isn't available, at the very least a flat, level, clean work surface made of concrete or asphalt is required.

Cleaning the engine compartment and engine before beginning the removal procedure will help keep tools clean and organized.

An engine hoist or A-frame will also be necessary. Make sure the equipment is rated in excess of the combined weight of the engine and transaxle. Safety is of primary importance, considering the potential hazards involved in lifting the engine out of the vehicle.

If the engine is being removed by a novice, a helper should be available. Advice and aid from someone more experienced would also be helpful. There are many instances when one person cannot simultaneously perform all of the operations required when lifting the engine out of the vehicle.

Plan the operation ahead of time. Arrange for or obtain all of the tools and equipment you'll need prior to beginning the job. Some of the equipment necessary to perform engine removal and installation safely and with relative ease are (in addition to an engine hoist) a heavy duty floor jack, complete sets of wrenches and sockets as described in the front of this manual, wooden blocks and plenty of rags and cleaning solvent for mopping up spilled oil, coolant and gasoline. If the hoist must be rented, make sure that you arrange for it in advance and perform all of the operations possible without it beforehand. This will save you money and time.

· Plan for the vehicle to be out of use for quite a while. A machine shop will be required to perform all of the work which is beyond the scope of the home mechanic. These shops often have a busy schedule, so it would be a good idea to consult them before removing the engine in order to accurately estimate the amount of time required to rebuild or repair components that may need work.

Always be extremely careful when removing and installing the engine. Serious injury can result from careless actions. Plan ahead, take your time and a job of this nature, although major, can be accomplished successfully.

7 Engine - removal and installation

Warning 1: *The models covered by this manual are equipped with Supplemental Restraint systems (SRS), more commonly known as airbags. Always disable the airbag system before working in the vicinity of airbag system components to avoid the possibility of accidental deployment of the airbag, which could cause personal injury (see Chapter 12).*

Warning 2: *Gasoline is extremely flammable, so take extra precautions when you work on any part of the fuel system. Don't smoke or allow open flames or bare light bulbs near the work area, and don't work in a garage where a gas-type appliance (such as a water heater or a clothes dryer) is present. Since gasoline is carcinogenic, wear latex gloves when there's a possibility of being exposed to fuel, and, if you spill any fuel on your skin, rinse it off immediately with soap and water. Mop up any spills immediately and do not store fuel-soaked rags where they could ignite. The fuel system is under constant pressure, so, if any fuel lines are to be disconnected, the fuel pressure in the system must be relieved first (see Chapter 4 for more information). When you perform any kind of work on the fuel system, wear safety glasses and have a Class B type fire extinguisher on hand.*

Note: *Engine removal on these models is a difficult job, especially for the do-it-yourself mechanic working at home. Because of the vehicle's design, the manufacturer states that the engine and transaxle have to be removed as a unit from the bottom of the vehicle, not the top. With a floor jack and jackstands the vehicle can't be raised high enough and supported safely enough for the engine/transaxle assembly to slide out from underneath. The manufacturer recommends that removal of the engine/transaxle assembly only be performed on a vehicle hoist.*

Removal
Refer to illustrations 7.9, 7.20 and 7.23

1   Park the vehicle on a frame-contact type vehicle hoist. The pads of the hoist arms must contact the body welt along each side of the vehicle (see *Jacking and towing* at the front of this manual).

2   Relieve the fuel system pressure (see Chapter 4), then disconnect the negative cable from the battery.

3   Place protective covers on the fenders and cowl and remove the hood (see Chapter 11).

4   Remove the air cleaner assembly (see Chapter 4). Also disconnect the accelerator cable and bracket from the engine and position them aside.

5   Remove the cowl cover and the vent tray (see Chapter 11).

6   Remove the battery. On 2001 and later models also remove the battery tray (see Chapter 5).

7   On 2000 and earlier models, remove the charcoal canister (see Chapter 6). On 2001 and later models, remove the coolant reservoir (see Chapter 3).

8   Loosen the front wheel lug nuts and the driveaxle/hub nuts, then raise the vehicle on the hoist. Drain the cooling system and engine oil and remove the drivebelts (see Chapter 1).

9   Clearly label, then disconnect all vacuum lines, coolant and emissions hoses, wiring harness connectors, ground straps and fuel lines. Masking tape and/or a touch up paint applicator work well for marking items **(see illustration)**. Take instant photos or sketch the locations of components and brackets.

10   Remove the engine wiring harness connectors from the engine compartment junction box. Also detach the wiring harness connectors from the PCM in the passenger compartment (see Chapter 6) and pull the wiring harness from the passenger compartment into the engine compartment.

11   Remove the alternator and the starter (see Chapter 5).

12   Remove the power steering pump (see Chapter 10).

13   Remove the cooling fan(s), shroud(s) and radiator (see Chapter 3). **Note:** *This step is not absolutely necessary, but it will help avoid damage to the cooling fans and radiator as the engine is lowered out of the vehicle. If the radiator is not taken out it will still be necessary to detach the transaxle oil cooler lines from the bottom of the radiator on automatic transaxle equipped vehicles.*

14   On air-conditioned models, unbolt the air conditioning compressor and set it aside. Do not disconnect the refrigerant hoses.

15   Detach the front exhaust pipe from the exhaust manifold (see Chapter 4).

16   Disconnect the shift linkage from the transaxle, then detach the cables from the front crossmember (see Chapter 7A or 7B). Also disconnect any wiring harness connectors from the transaxle.

17   If equipped with a manual transaxle disconnect the clutch release cylinder from the transaxle (see Chapter 8).

18   Remove the front driveaxles (see Chapter 8). On 4WD vehicles remove the rear driveshaft.

19   On 2001 and later models, detach the stabilizer bar links from the bar (see Chapter 10). Also remove the two bolts securing the steering gear to the front crossmember and the bolts securing the lower ball joints to the lower control arms referring the Chapter 10.

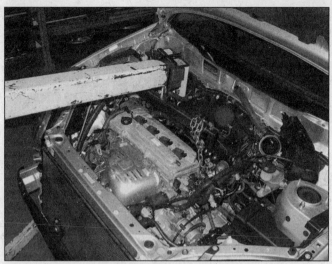

7.20 With the chain or sling attached securely to the engine, take up the slack until there is slight tension on the chain

7.23 Front (and center) crossmember-to-chassis bolts (arrows)

20   Attach a lifting sling or chain to the engine **(see illustration)**. Position an engine hoist and connect the sling to it. Take up the slack until there is slight tension on the sling or chain. Remember that the transaxle end of the engine will be heavier, so position the chain on the hoist so it balances the engine and the transaxle level with the vehicle.

21   Recheck to be sure nothing except the mounts are still connecting the engine to the vehicle or to the transaxle. Disconnect and label anything still remaining.

22   Remove the through-bolt on the driver's side transaxle mount and the passenger side engine mount (see Chapter 2A or 2B).

23   Remove the front crossmember and the center crossmember mounting bolts **(see illustration)**.

24   Slowly lower the engine/transaxle from the vehicle. **Note:** *Placing a sheet of hardboard or paneling between the engine and the floor makes moving the powertrain easier.*

25   Once the powertrain is on the floor, disconnect the engine lifting hoist and raise the vehicle hoist until the powertrain can be slid out from underneath. **Note:** *A helper will be needed to move the powertrain.*

26   Reconnect the chain or sling and raise the engine with the hoist several inches off the ground. Remove the through-bolts on the front and rear mounts and slide the front crossmember out from under the engine. Lower the engine back to the ground and separate the engine from the transaxle (see Chapter 7). Disregard the steps that do not apply since the transaxle is already removed from the vehicle.

27   Remove the driveplate/flywheel and mount the engine on a stand.

Installation

28   Check the engine/transaxle mounts. If they're worn or damaged, replace them.

29   On manual transaxle equipped models,

inspect the clutch components (see Chapter 8) and on automatic models inspect the converter seal and bushing.

30   On manual transaxle equipped vehicles, apply a dab of high temperature grease to the splines of the input shaft. On automatic transaxle equipped models, apply a dab of grease to the nose of the torque converter.

31   Carefully guide the transaxle into place, following the procedure outlined in Chapter 7. **Caution:** *Do not use the bolts to force the engine and transaxle into alignment. It may crack or damage major components.*

32   Install the engine-to-transaxle bolts and tighten them securely.

33   Slide the engine/transaxle over a sheet of hardboard or paneling until it is in the appropriate position under the vehicle, then lower the vehicle over the engine.

34   Roll the engine hoist into position, attach the chain or sling in a position that will allow a good balance and slowly raise the powertrain until the mount at the transaxle end can be attached.

35   Support the transaxle with a floor jack for extra security, then reinstall the front crossmember and attach the passenger side engine mount.

36   Reinstall the remaining components and fasteners in the reverse order of removal.

37   Add coolant, oil, power steering and transmission fluids as needed (see Chapter 1).

38   Run the engine and check for proper operation and leaks. Shut off the engine and recheck the fluid levels.

8   Engine external components - disassembly sequence

1   It's much easier to remove the external components if the engine is mounted on a portable engine stand. A stand can often

be rented quite cheaply from an equipment rental yard. Before the engine is mounted on a stand, the flywheel/driveplate should be removed from the engine.

2   If a stand isn't available, it's possible to remove the external engine components with it blocked up on the floor. Be extra careful not to tip or drop the engine when working without a stand.

3   If you're going to obtain a rebuilt engine, all external components must come off first, to be transferred to the replacement engine. These components include:

   Emissions control components
   Distributor (1997 and earlier)
   Spark plug wires and spark plugs
   Ignition coils (1998 and later)
   Thermostat and housing cover
   Water pump (2001 and later)
   Water bypass tube
   EFI components
   Intake/exhaust manifolds
   Oil filter
   Engine mount brackets
   Clutch and flywheel/driveplate
   Engine rear plate (2000 and earlier)

Note: *When removing the external components from the engine, pay close attention to details that may be helpful or important during installation. Note the installed position of gaskets, seals, spacers, pins, brackets, washers, bolts and other small items.*

4   If you're obtaining a short block, which consists of the engine block, crankshaft, pistons and connecting rods all assembled, then the timing belt or chain, the cylinder head, the oil pan, the oil pump, the lower crankcase (2001 and later) and the water pump (2000 and earlier) will have to be removed as well from your engine so that your short block can be turned in to the rebuilder as a core (see Chapter 2A or 2B). See *Engine rebuilding alternatives* for additional information regarding the different possibilities to be considered.

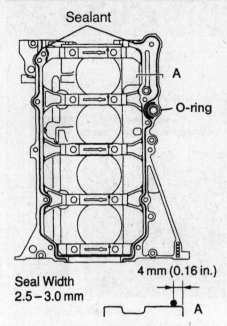

Seal Width
2.5 – 3.0 mm

4 mm (0.16 in.)

9.2a Cylinder block-to-lower crankcase
sealant installation details -
2001 and later models

9 Engine external components - reassembly sequence

Refer to illustrations 9.2a and 9.2b

1   Before beginning engine reassembly, make sure you have all the necessary new parts, gaskets and seals as well as the following items on hand:

Common hand tools
A 1/2-inch drive torque wrench
New engine oil
Gasket sealant
Thread locking compound

2   If you obtained a short block it will be necessary to install the cylinder head, the oil pump, the water pump (2000 and earlier models), the timing belt or chain, the lower crankcase (see illustrations), the front covers, the oil pan and the valve cover (see Chapter 2A or 2B). In order to save time and avoid problems, the external components must be installed in the following general order:

Thermostat and housing cover
Water pump (2001 and later)
Water by pass tube
Intake/exhaust manifolds
EFI components
Emissions control components
Distributor (1997 and earlier)
Spark plug wires and spark plugs
Ignition coils (1998 and later)
Oil filter
Engine mount brackets
Engine rear plate (2000 and earlier)
Clutch and flywheel/driveplate

10 Initial start-up and break-in after installation

Warning: *Have a fire extinguisher handy when starting the engine for the first time.*

1   Once the engine has been installed in the vehicle, double-check the engine oil and coolant levels.

2   With the spark plugs out of the engine and the ignition system and fuel pump disabled (see Section 4), crank the engine until oil pressure registers on the gauge or the light goes out.

3   Install the spark plugs, hook up the plug wires and restore the ignition system and fuel pump functions.

4   Start the engine. It may take a few moments for the fuel system to build up pressure, but the engine should start without a great deal of effort.

5   After the engine starts, it should be allowed to warm up to normal operating tem-

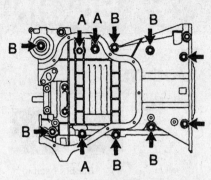

9.2b Lower crankcase bolt locations - (A)
indicates the location of the long bolts
and (B) indicates the location of
the short bolts

perature. While the engine is warming up, make a thorough check for fuel, oil and coolant leaks.

6   Shut the engine off and recheck the engine oil and coolant levels.

7   Drive the vehicle to an area with minimum traffic, accelerate from 30 to 50 mph, then allow the vehicle to slow to 30 mph with the throttle closed. Repeat the procedure 10 or 12 times. This will load the piston rings and cause them to seat properly against the cylinder walls. Check again for oil and coolant leaks.

8   Drive the vehicle gently for the first 500 miles (no sustained high speeds) and keep a constant check on the oil level. It is not unusual for an engine to use oil during the break-in period.

9   At approximately 500 to 600 miles, change the oil and filter.

10   For the next few hundred miles, drive the vehicle normally. Do not pamper it or abuse it.

11   After 2000 miles, change the oil and filter again and consider the engine broken in.

ENGINE BEARING ANALYSIS

Debris

Babbitt bearing embedded with debris from machinings

Microscopic detail of debris

Microscopic detail of gouges

Overplated copper alloy bearing gouged by cast iron debris

Aluminum bearing embedded with glass beads

Microscopic detail of glass beads

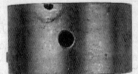

Damaged lining caused by dirt left on the bearing back

Misassembly

Result of a lower half assembled as an upper - blocking the oil flow

Excessive oil clearance is indicated by a short contact arc

Polished and oil-stained backs are a result of a poor fit in the housing bore

Result of a wrong, reversed, or shifted cap

Overloading

Damage from excessive idling which resulted in an oil film unable to support the load imposed

Damaged upper connecting rod bearings caused by engine lugging; the lower main bearings (not shown) were similarly affected

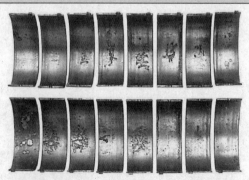

The damage shown in these upper and lower connecting rod bearings was caused by engine operation at a higher-than-rated speed under load

Misalignment

A warped crankshaft caused this pattern of severe wear in the center, diminishing toward the ends

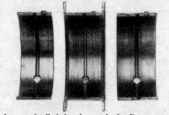

A poorly finished crankshaft caused the equally spaced scoring shown

A tapered housing bore caused the damage along one edge of this pair

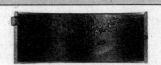

A bent connecting rod led to the damage in the "V" pattern

Lubrication

Result of dry start: The bearings on the left, farthest from the oil pump, show more damage

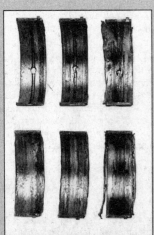

Result of a low oil supply or oil starvation

Severe wear as a result of inadequate oil clearance

Corrosion

Microscopic detail of corrosion

Corrosion is an acid attack on the bearing lining generally caused by inadequate maintenance, extremely hot or cold operation, or inferior oils or fuels

Microscopic detail of cavitation

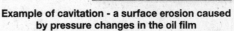

Example of cavitation - a surface erosion caused by pressure changes in the oil film

Damage from excessive thrust or insufficient axial clearance

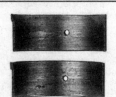

Bearing affected by oil dilution caused by excessive blow-by or a rich mixture

COMMON ENGINE OVERHAUL TERMS

B

Backlash - The amount of play between two parts. Usually refers to how much one gear can be moved back and forth without moving gear with which it's meshed.

Bearing Caps - The caps held in place by nuts or bolts which, in turn, hold the bearing surface. This space is for lubricating oil to enter.

Bearing clearance - The amount of space left between shaft and bearing surface. This space is for lubricating oil to enter.

Bearing crush - The additional height which is purposely manufactured into each bearing half to ensure complete contact of the bearing back with the housing bore when the engine is assembled.

Bearing knock - The noise created by movement of a part in a loose or worn bearing.

Blueprinting - Dismantling an engine and reassembling it to EXACT specifications.

Bore - An engine cylinder, or any cylindrical hole; also used to describe the process of enlarging or accurately refinishing a hole with a cutting tool, as to bore an engine cylinder. The bore size is the diameter of the hole.

Boring - Renewing the cylinders by cutting them out to a specified size. A boring bar is used to make the cut.

Bottom end - A term which refers collectively to the engine block, crankshaft, main bearings and the big ends of the connecting rods.

Break-in - The period of operation between installation of new or rebuilt parts and time in which parts are worn to the correct fit. Driving at reduced and varying speed for a specified mileage to permit parts to wear to the correct fit.

Bushing - A one-piece sleeve placed in a bore to serve as a bearing surface for shaft, piston pin, etc. Usually replaceable.

C

Camshaft - The shaft in the engine, on which a series of lobes are located for operating the valve mechanisms. The camshaft is driven by gears or sprockets and a timing chain. Usually referred to simply as the cam.

Carbon - Hard, or soft, black deposits found in combustion chamber, on plugs, under rings, on and under valve heads.

Cast iron - An alloy of iron and more than two percent carbon, used for engine blocks and heads because it's relatively inexpensive and easy to mold into complex shapes.

Chamfer - To bevel across (or a bevel on) the sharp edge of an object.

Chase - To repair damaged threads with a tap or die.

Combustion chamber - The space between the piston and the cylinder head, with the piston at top dead center, in which air-fuel mixture is burned.

Compression ratio - The relationship between cylinder volume (clearance volume) when the piston is at top dead center and cylinder volume when the piston is at bottom dead center.

Connecting rod - The rod that connects the crank on the crankshaft with the piston. Sometimes called a con rod.

Connecting rod cap - The part of the connecting rod assembly that attaches the rod to the crankpin.

Core plug - Soft metal plug used to plug the casting holes for the coolant passages in the block.

Crankcase - The lower part of the engine in which the crankshaft rotates; includes the lower section of the cylinder block and the oil pan.

Crank kit - A reground or reconditioned crankshaft and new main and connecting rod bearings.

Crankpin - The part of a crankshaft to which a connecting rod is attached.

Crankshaft - The main rotating member, or shaft, running the length of the crankcase, with offset throws to which the connecting rods are attached; changes the reciprocating motion of the pistons into rotating motion.

Cylinder sleeve - A replaceable sleeve, or liner, pressed into the cylinder block to form the cylinder bore.

D

Deburring - Removing the burrs (rough edges or areas) from a bearing.

Deglazer - A tool, rotated by an electric motor, used to remove glaze from cylinder walls so a new set of rings will seat.

E

Endplay - The amount of lengthwise movement between two parts. As applied to a crankshaft, the distance that the crankshaft can move forward and back in the cylinder block.

F

Face - A machinist's term that refers to removing metal from the end of a shaft or the face of a larger part, such as a flywheel.

Fatigue - A breakdown of material through a large number of loading and unloading cycles. The first signs are cracks followed shortly by breaks.

Feeler gauge - A thin strip of hardened steel, ground to an exact thickness, used to check clearances between parts.

Free height - The unloaded length or height of a spring.

Freeplay - The looseness in a linkage, or an assembly of parts, between the initial application of force and actual movement. Usually perceived as slop or slight delay.

Freeze plug - See Core plug.

G

Gallery - A large passage in the block that forms a reservoir for engine oil pressure.

Glaze - The very smooth, glassy finish that develops on cylinder walls while an engine is in service.

H

Heli-Coil - A rethreading device used when threads are worn or damaged. The device is installed in a retapped hole to reduce the thread size to the original size.

I

Installed height - The spring's measured length or height, as installed on the cylinder head. Installed height is measured from the spring seat to the underside of the spring retainer.

J

Journal - The surface of a rotating shaft which turns in a bearing.

K

Keeper - The split lock that holds the valve spring retainer in position on the valve stem.

Key - A small piece of metal inserted into matching grooves machined into two parts fitted together - such as a gear pressed onto a shaft - which prevents slippage between the two parts.

Knock - The heavy metallic engine sound, produced in the combustion chamber as a result of abnormal combustion - usually detonation. Knock is usually caused by a loose or worn bearing. Also referred to as detonation, pinging and spark knock. Connecting rod or main bearing knocks are created by too much oil clearance or insufficient lubrication.

L

Lands - The portions of metal between the piston ring grooves.

Lapping the valves - Grinding a valve face and its seat together with lapping compound.

Lash - The amount of free motion in a gear train, between gears, or in a mechanical assembly, that occurs before movement can begin. Usually refers to the lash in a valve train.

Lifter - The part that rides against the cam to transfer motion to the rest of the valve train.

M

Machining - The process of using a machine to remove metal from a metal part.

Main bearings - The plain, or babbit, bearings that support the crankshaft.

Main bearing caps - The cast iron caps, bolted to the bottom of the block, that support the main bearings.

O

O.D. - Outside diameter.

Oil gallery - A pipe or drilled passageway in the engine used to carry engine oil from one area to another.

Oil ring - The lower ring, or rings, of a piston; designed to prevent excessive amounts of oil from working up the cylinder walls and into the combustion chamber. Also called an oil-control ring.

Oil seal - A seal which keeps oil from leaking out of a compartment. Usually refers to a dynamic seal around a rotating shaft or other moving part.

O-ring - A type of sealing ring made of a special rubberlike material; in use, the O-ring is compressed into a groove to provide the sealing action.

Overhaul - To completely disassemble a unit, clean and inspect all parts, reassemble it with the original or new parts and make all adjustments necessary for proper operation.

P

Pilot bearing - A small bearing installed in the center of the flywheel (or the rear end of the crankshaft) to support the front end of the input shaft of the transmission.

Pip mark - A little dot or indentation which indicates the top side of a compression ring.

Piston - The cylindrical part, attached to the connecting rod, that moves up and down in the cylinder as the crankshaft rotates. When the fuel charge is fired, the piston transfers the force of the explosion to the connecting rod, then to the crankshaft.

Piston pin (or wrist pin) - The cylindrical and usually hollow steel pin that passes through the piston. The piston pin fastens the piston to the upper end of the connecting rod.

Piston ring - The split ring fitted to the groove in a piston. The ring contacts the sides of the ring groove and also rubs against the cylinder wall, thus sealing space between piston and wall. There are two types of rings: Compression rings seal the compression pressure in the combustion chamber; oil rings scrape excessive oil off the cylinder wall.

Piston ring groove - The slots or grooves cut in piston heads to hold piston rings in position.

Piston skirt - The portion of the piston below the rings and the piston pin hole.

Plastigage - A thin strip of plastic thread, available in different sizes, used for measuring clearances. For example, a strip of plastigage is laid across a bearing journal and mashed as parts are assembled. Then parts are disassembled and the width of the strip is measured to determine clearance between journal and bearing. Commonly used to measure crankshaft main-bearing and connecting rod bearing clearances.

Press-fit - A tight fit between two parts that requires pressure to force the parts together. Also referred to as drive, or force, fit.

Prussian blue - A blue pigment; in solution, useful in determining the area of contact between two surfaces. Prussian blue is commonly used to determine the width and location of the contact area between the valve face and the valve seat.

R

Race (bearing) - The inner or outer ring that provides a contact surface for balls or rollers in bearing.

Ream - To size, enlarge or smooth a hole by using a round cutting tool with fluted edges.

Ring job - The process of reconditioning the cylinders and installing new rings.

Runout - Wobble. The amount a shaft rotates out-of-true.

S

Saddle - The upper main bearing seat.

Scored - Scratched or grooved, as a cylinder wall may be scored by abrasive particles moved up and down by the piston rings.

Scuffing - A type of wear in which there's a transfer of material between parts moving against each other; shows up as pits or grooves in the mating surfaces.

Seat - The surface upon which another part rests or seats. For example, the valve seat is the matched surface upon which the valve face rests. Also used to refer to wearing into a good fit; for example, piston rings seat after a few miles of driving.

Short block - An engine block complete with crankshaft and piston and, usually, camshaft assemblies.

Static balance - The balance of an object while it's stationary.

Step - The wear on the lower portion of a ring land caused by excessive side and back-clearance. The height of the step indicates the ring's extra side clearance and the length of the step projecting from the back wall of the groove represents the ring's back clearance.

Stroke - The distance the piston moves when traveling from top dead center to bottom dead center, or from bottom dead center to top dead center.

Stud - A metal rod with threads on both ends.

T

Tang - A lip on the end of a plain bearing used to align the bearing during assembly.

Tap - To cut threads in a hole. Also refers to the fluted tool used to cut threads.

Taper - A gradual reduction in the width of a shaft or hole; in an engine cylinder, taper usually takes the form of uneven wear, more pronounced at the top than at the bottom.

Throws - The offset portions of the crankshaft to which the connecting rods are affixed.

Thrust bearing - The main bearing that has thrust faces to prevent excessive endplay, or forward and backward movement of the crankshaft.

Thrust washer - A bronze or hardened steel washer placed between two moving parts. The washer prevents longitudinal movement and provides a bearing surface for thrust surfaces of parts.

Tolerance - The amount of variation permitted from an exact size of measurement. Actual amount from smallest acceptable dimension to largest acceptable dimension.

U

Umbrella - An oil deflector placed near the valve tip to throw oil from the valve stem area.

Undercut - A machined groove below the normal surface.

Undersize bearings - Smaller diameter bearings used with re-ground crankshaft journals.

V

Valve grinding - Refacing a valve in a valve-refacing machine.

Valve train - The valve-operating mechanism of an engine; includes all components from the camshaft to the valve.

Vibration damper - A cylindrical weight attached to the front of the crankshaft to minimize torsional vibration (the twist-untwist actions of the crankshaft caused by the cylinder firing impulses). Also called a harmonic balancer.

W

Water jacket - The spaces around the cylinders, between the inner and outer shells of the cylinder block or head, through which coolant circulates.

Web - A supporting structure across a cavity.

Woodruff key - A key with a radiused backside (viewed from the side).

Notes

Chapter 3
Cooling, heating and air conditioning systems

Contents

	Section
Air conditioning and heating system - check and maintenance.....	11
Air conditioning compressor - removal and installation	13
Air conditioning condenser - removal and installation	14
Air conditioning receiver/drier - removal and installation	12
Antifreeze - general information	2
Blower motor - removal and installation	8
CHECK ENGINE light.. See Chapter 6
Coolant level check .... See Chapter 1
Coolant temperature sending unit and radiator fan switch - replacement	7
Cooling system check.. See Chapter 1

	Section
Cooling system servicing (draining, flushing and refilling)... See Chapter 1
Drivebelt check, adjustment and replacement................ See Chapter 1
Engine cooling fans - replacement	4
General information	1
Heater and air conditioning control assembly - removal and installation and cable adjustment......................................	9
Heater core - removal and installation................................	10
Radiator and coolant reservoir - removal and installation	5
Thermostat - check and replacement.................................	3
Underhood hose check and replacement....................... See Chapter 1
Water pump - check and replacement..................................	6

Specifications

General

Radiator cap pressure rating	
1996 and 1997	10.7 to 14.9 psi (73.7 to 102.7 kPa)
1998 and later	13.5 to 17.8 psi 93 to 122.7 kPa)
Thermostat rating	
Opens	176 to 183-degrees F (80 to 84-degrees C)
Fully open	203-degrees F (95-degrees C)
Refrigerant type	R-134a
Refrigerant capacity	
2000 and earlier models	24.7 +/- 1.7 ounces (700 +/- 50 grams)
2001 and later models	17.6 +/- 1.7 ounces (500 +/- 50 grams)

Torque specifications

	Ft-lbs (unless otherwise indicated)	Nm
Thermostat housing bolts		
2000 and earlier	78 in-lbs	8.8
2001 and later	80 in-lbs	9
Water pump-to-block bolts		
2000 and earlier	78 in-lbs	8.8
2001 and later	80 in-lbs	9
Receiver/drier end plug (2001 and later models)	108 in-lbs	12.3

1.1 Typical cooling system component locations (2000 and earlier shown, 2001 and later similar)

1	Condenser	3	Water pump	5	Radiator
2	Thermostat	4	Cooling fans	6	Coolant reservoir

1   General information

Engine cooling system

Refer to illustrations 1.1 and 1.2

All vehicles covered by this manual employ a pressurized engine cooling system with thermostatically controlled coolant circulation **(see illustration)**. An impeller type water pump mounted on the front of the block pumps coolant through the engine. The coolant flows around each cylinder and toward the rear of the engine. Cast-in coolant passages direct coolant around the intake and exhaust ports, near the spark plug areas and in proximity to the exhaust valve guides.

A wax pellet-type thermostat is located in the thermostat housing near the front of the vehicle **(see illustration)**. During warm up, the closed thermostat prevents coolant from circulating through the radiator. When the engine reaches normal operating temperature, the thermostat opens and allows hot coolant to travel through the radiator, where it is cooled before returning to the engine.

The cooling system is sealed by a pressure-type radiator cap. This raises the boiling point of the coolant, and the higher boiling point of the coolant increases the cooling efficiency of the radiator. If the system pressure exceeds the cap pressure relief value, the excess pressure in the system forces the spring-loaded valve inside the cap off its seat and allows the coolant to escape through the overflow tube into a coolant reservoir. When the system cools, the excess coolant is automatically drawn from the reservoir back into the radiator.

The coolant reservoir serves as both the point at which fresh coolant is added to the cooling system to maintain the proper fluid level and as a holding tank for overheated coolant.

This type of cooling system is known as a closed design because coolant that escapes past the pressure cap is saved and reused.

Heating system

The heating system consists of a blower fan and heater core located within the heater box, the inlet and outlet hoses connecting the heater core to the engine cooling system and the heater/air conditioning control head on the dashboard. Hot engine coolant is circulated through the heater core. When the heater mode is activated, a flap door opens to expose the heater box to the passenger compartment. A fan switch on the control head activates the blower motor, which forces air through the core, heating the air.

Air conditioning system

The air conditioning system consists of a condenser mounted in front of the radiator, an evaporator mounted adjacent to the heater core under the dashboard, a compressor mounted on the engine, a filter-drier (accumulator) which contains a high pressure relief valve and the plumbing connecting all of the above.

A blower fan forces the warmer air of the passenger compartment through the evaporator core (sort of a radiator-in-reverse), transferring the heat from the air to the refrigerant. The liquid refrigerant boils off into low pressure vapor, taking the heat with it when it leaves the evaporator. The compressor keeps refrigerant circulating through the system, pumping the warmed coolant through the condenser where it is cooled and then circulated back to the evaporator.

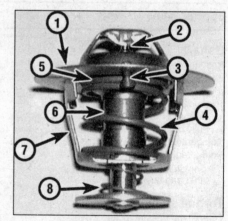

1.2 A typical thermostat

1	Flange	5	Valve seat
2	Piston	6	Valve
3	Jiggle valve	7	Frame
4	Main coil spring	8	Secondary coil spring

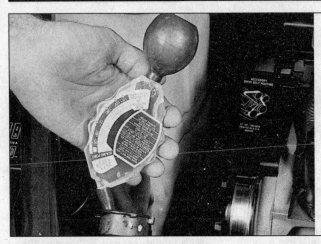

2.4 An inexpensive hydrometer can be used to test the condition of your coolant

2   Antifreeze - general information

Refer to illustration 2.4

Warning: *Do not allow antifreeze to come in contact with your skin or painted surfaces of the vehicle. Rinse off spills immediately with plenty of water. Antifreeze is highly toxic if ingested. Never leave antifreeze lying around in an open container or in puddles on the floor; children and pets are attracted by it's sweet smell and may drink it. Check with local authorities about disposing of used antifreeze. Many communities have collection centers which will see that antifreeze is disposed of safely. Never dump used antifreeze on the ground or into drains.*

Note: *Non-toxic coolant is available at local auto parts stores. Although the coolant is non-toxic when fresh, proper disposal of used coolant is still required.*

The cooling system should be filled with a water/ethylene-glycol based antifreeze solution, which will prevent freezing down to at least -20 degrees F, or lower if local climate requires it. It also provides protection against corrosion and increases the coolant boiling point.

The cooling system should be drained, flushed and refilled at least every other year (see Chapter 1). The use of antifreeze solutions for periods of longer than two years is likely to cause damage and encourage the formation of rust and scale in the system. If your tap water is "hard", i.e. contains a lot of dissolved minerals, use distilled water with the antifreeze.

Before adding antifreeze to the system, check all hose connections, because antifreeze tends to leak through very minute openings. Engines do not normally consume coolant. Therefore, if the level goes down find the cause and correct it.

The exact mixture of antifreeze-to-water which you should use depends on the relative weather conditions. The mixture should contain at least 50 percent antifreeze, but should never contain more than 70 percent antifreeze. Consult the mixture ratio chart on the antifreeze container before adding coolant. Hydrometers are available at most auto parts stores to test the ratio of antifreeze to water **(see illustration)**. Use antifreeze which meets the vehicle manufacturer's specifications.

3   Thermostat - check and replacement

Warning: *Do not attempt to remove the radiator cap, coolant or thermostat until the engine has cooled completely.*

General check

1   Before assuming the thermostat is responsible for a cooling system problem, check the coolant level (Chapter 1), drivebelt tension (Chapter 1) and temperature gauge (or light) operation.

2   If the engine takes a long time to warm up (as indicated by the temperature gauge or heater operation), the thermostat is probably stuck open. Replace the thermostat with a new one.

3   If the engine runs hot, use your hand to check the temperature of the lower radiator hose. If the hose is not hot, but the engine is, the thermostat is probably stuck in the closed position, preventing the coolant inside the

3.7 A thermostat can be accurately checked by heating it in a container of water with a thermometer and observing the opening and fully-open temperature

radiator from being drawn into the engine. Replace the thermostat. **Caution:** *Do not drive the vehicle without a thermostat. The computer may stay in open loop and emissions and fuel economy will suffer.*

4   If the lower radiator hose is hot, it means that the coolant is flowing and the thermostat is open. Consult the Troubleshooting Section at the front of this manual for further diagnosis.

Thermostat test

Refer to illustration 3.7

5   A more thorough test of the thermostat can only be made when it is removed from the vehicle (see below). If the thermostat remains in the open position at room temperature, it is faulty and must be replaced.

6   To test it fully, suspend the (closed) thermostat on a length of string or wire in a container of cold water, with a thermometer (cooking type that reads beyond 212 de-grees F). A clear Pyrex cooking container is easiest to use.

7   Heat the water on a stove while observing the temperature and the thermostat. Neither should contact the sides of the container **(see illustration)**.

8   Note the temperature when the thermostat begins to open and when it is fully open. Compare the temperatures to the Specifications in this Chapter. The number stamped into the thermostat is generally the fully-open temperature. Some manufacturers provide Specifications for the beginning-to-open temperature, the fully-open temperature, and sometimes the amount the valve should open.

9   If the thermostat doesn't open and close as specified, or sticks in any position, replace it.

Replacement

Refer to illustrations 3.12, 3.13, 3.15 and 3.17

10   Disconnect the negative cable from the battery.

11   Drain the coolant from the radiator (see Chapter 1). Disconnect the radiator hose from the thermostat housing or water inlet pipe.

12   On 2000 and earlier models, remove the thermostat housing from the back of the water pump housing **(see illustration)**. **Note:** *For easier access to the lower bolt, remove the oil filter.*

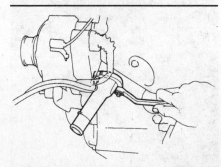

3.12 The thermostat housing on 2000 and earlier models is located behind the water pump - access to the nuts is easier with the oil filter removed

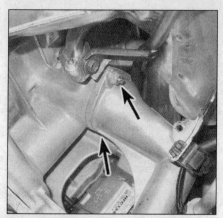

3.13 With the alternator removed, remove the nuts (arrows) securing the thermostat housing to the side of the engine block - 2001 and later

3.15 The thermostat gasket fits around the edge of the thermostat like a grooved sealing ring

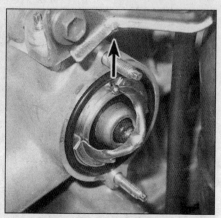

3.17 Position the jiggle valve straight up - 2001 models shown, 2000 and earlier models similar except for the fact that the thermostat is installed in the thermostat housing and not in the engine block

13   On 2001 and later models, remove the alternator (see Chapter 5) then unbolt the thermostat housing from the engine block **(see illustration)**.

14   Remove the thermostat, noting the direction in which it was installed in the housing, and thoroughly clean the sealing surfaces.

15   Fit a new rubber gasket onto the thermostat **(see illustration)**. Make sure it is evenly fitted all the way around.

16   On 2000 and earlier models, install the thermostat into the thermostat housing, then install the housing and thermostat into the back of the water pump housing. Be sure to position the jiggle pin upward at the highest point.

17   On 2001 and later models, install the thermostat into the engine block, then install the thermostat housing. Be sure to position the jiggle valve upward at the highest point **(see illustration)**.

18   Tighten the housing fasteners to the torque listed in this Chapter's Specifications and reinstall the remaining components in the reverse order of removal.

19   Refill the cooling system (see Chapter 1). Run the engine and check for leaks and proper operation.

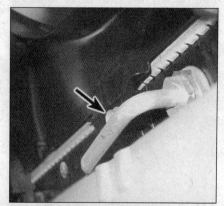

4.4a Condenser fan lower retaining bolt (arrow) - 2001 and later model shown, 2000 and earlier models have two lower retaining bolts

4   Engine cooling fans - replacement

Refer to illustrations 4.4a, 4.4b, 4.4c, 4.5 and 4.6

Warning: *To avoid possible injury, keep clear of the fan blades, as they may start turning at any time!*

1   Disconnect the negative battery cable.

2   Disconnect the wiring connector at the fan motors.

3   On 2000 and earlier models, The condenser fan has one bolt on the top and two on the bottom securing the fan to the radiator and the main cooling fan has two bolts at the top and two at the bottom securing the fan to the radiator. On 2001 and later models, the condenser fan has two bolts at the top and one bolt at the bottom, while the main cooling fan has two bolts at the top and two retaining tabs at the bottom.

4   Jack up the front of the vehicle and support it securely on jackstands. Remove the splash shields from below the engine and the lower bolt from the condenser fan **(see illustration)**. Working above in the engine compartment unbolt the fan/shrouds from the radiator and lift them from the vehicle **(see illustrations)**.

5   Hold the fan blades and remove the fan retaining screws or nut **(see illustration)**. **Note:** *The main cooling fan blade is attached with a nut and the condenser fan blade is retained by three screws.*

6   Unbolt the fan motor from the shroud **(see illustration)**.

7   Installation is the reverse of removal.

5   Radiator and coolant reservoir - removal and installation

Refer to illustrations 5.8 5.9a and 5.9b

Warning: *Do not start this procedure until the engine is completely cool. Do not allow antifreeze to come in contact with your skin or painted surfaces of the vehicle. Rinse off spills*

immediately with plenty of water. Antifreeze is highly toxic if ingested. Never leave antifreeze lying around in an open container or in puddles on the floor; children and pets are attracted by it's sweet smell and may drink it. Check with local authorities about disposing of used antifreeze. Many communities have collection centers which will see that antifreeze is disposed of safely. Never dump used antifreeze on the ground or into drains.

Note: *Non-toxic coolant is available at local auto parts stores. Although the coolant is non-toxic when fresh, proper disposal of used coolant is still required.*

Radiator

1   Disconnect the negative battery cable.

2   Drain the coolant into a container (see Chapter 1).

3   On 2000 and earlier models, unbolts the air conditioning condenser from the radiator and position it back away from the radiator.

4   On 2001 and later models, remove the radiator grille, the headlight filler panel and the hood latch (see Chapter 11).

5   Remove both the upper and lower radiator hoses.

6   Disconnect the reservoir hose from the radiator filler neck.

7   Remove the cooling fans (see Section 4). Also disconnect the connector from the radiator fan cooling switch.

8   If equipped with an automatic transaxle, disconnect the cooler lines from the radiator **(see illustration)**. Place a drip pan to catch the fluid and cap the fittings.

9   Remove the bolts that attach the radiator to its support **(see illustrations)**.

10   Lift out the radiator. Be aware of dripping fluids and the sharp fins.

11   With the radiator removed, it can be inspected for leaks, damage and internal blockage. If in need of repairs, have a professional radiator shop or dealer service department perform the work, as special techniques are required.

12   Bugs and dirt can be cleaned from the

4.4b Upper retaining bolts for the main cooling fan - On 2001 and later models simply pull the fan upward from the retaining tabs at the bottom - On 2000 and earlier models there are two bolts securing the bottom of the fan to the radiator

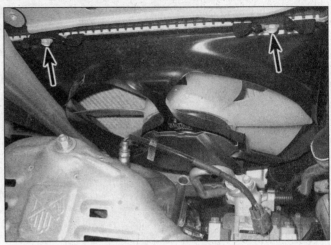

4.4c Upper retaining bolts for the condenser fan - 2001 and later model shown, 2000 and earlier models only have one bolt securing the top of the condenser fan

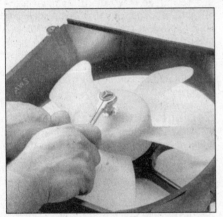

4.5 Remove the fan from the motor - main cooling fan shown, condenser fan has three screws securing it to the fan motor

4.6 Remove the screws (arrows) and separate the motor from the shroud

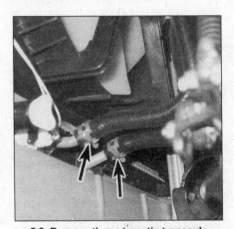

5.8 Remove the automatic transaxle cooler lines (arrows)

radiator with compressed air and a soft brush. Don't bend the cooling fins as this is done. **Warning:** *Wear eye protection.*

13   Installation is the reverse of the removal procedure. Be sure the rubber mounts are in place.

14   After installation, fill the cooling system with the proper mixture of antifreeze and water. Refer to Chapter 1 if necessary.

15   Start the engine and check for leaks. Allow the engine to reach normal operating temperature, indicated by the upper radiator hose becoming hot. Recheck the coolant level and add more if required.

16   On automatic transmission equipped models, check and add transmission fluid as needed (see Chapter 1).

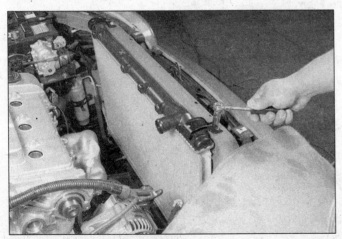

5.9a Remove the hold-down clamps from each end of the radiator - 2000 and earlier models

5.9b Radiator support panel retaining bolts (arrows) - 2001 and later models

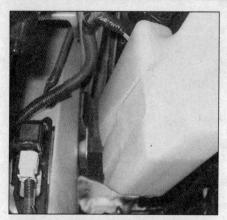

**5.17 Typical coolant reservoir removal -
pull the reservoir off the bracket**

**6.3 Water pump weep hole location - 2001
and later shown**

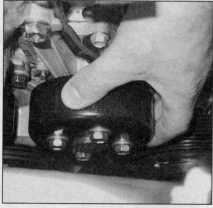

**6.4 Rock the water pump pulley back and
forth - any noticeable movement indicates
the need for replacement**

Coolant reservoir

Refer to illustration 5.17

17   On most models, the coolant reservoir simply pulls up and out of the bracket on the fenderwell **(see illustration)**.

18   Pour the coolant into a container. Wash out and inspect the reservoir for cracks and chafing. Replace it if damaged.

19   Installation is the reverse of removal.

6   Water pump - check and replacement

Warning: *Do not start this procedure until the engine is completely cool. Do not allow antifreeze to come in contact with your skin or painted surfaces of the vehicle. Rinse off spills immediately with plenty of water. Antifreeze is highly toxic if ingested. Never leave antifreeze lying around in an open container or in puddles on the floor; children and pets are attracted by it's sweet smell and may drink it. Check with local authorities about disposing of used antifreeze. Many communities have collection centers which will see that antifreeze is disposed of safely. Never dump used antifreeze on the ground or into drains.*
Note: *Non-toxic coolant is available at local auto parts stores. Although the coolant is non-toxic when fresh, proper disposal of used coolant is still required.*

Check

Refer to illustrations 6.3 and 6.4

1   A failure in the water pump can cause serious engine damage due to overheating.

2   With the engine running and warmed to normal operating temperature, squeeze the upper radiator hose. If the water pump is working properly, a pressure surge should be felt as the hose is released. **Warning:** *Keep hands away from fan blades!*

3   Water pumps are equipped with weep or vent holes. If a failure occurs in the pump seal, coolant will leak from this hole **(see illustration)**. In most cases it will be necessary to use a flashlight to find the hole on the water pump by looking through the space behind the pulley just below the water pump shaft. A slight gray discoloration around the weep hole is normal, while dark brown stains indicate a problem.

4   If the water pump shaft bearings fail there may be a howling sound at the front of the engine while it is running. Bearing wear can be felt if the water pump pulley is rocked up and down **(see illustration)**. Do not mistake drivebelt slippage, which causes a squealing sound, for water pump failure. Spray automotive drivebelt dressing on the belts to eliminate the belt as a possible cause of the noise (2001 and later models only; the water pump on 2000 and earlier models is turned by the timing belt).

Replacement

5   Disconnect the negative battery cable and drain the cooling system.

2000 and earlier models

Refer to illustrations 6.7, 6.8, 6.10, 6.13a and 6.13b

6   Remove the timing belt and the, number 1 and number 2 idler pulleys (see Chapter 2A).

**6.7 Remove the alternator
adjusting bar (arrow)**

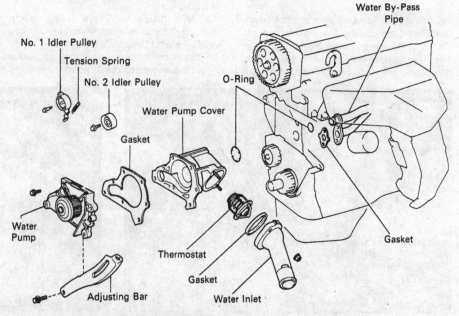

6.8 Water pump components - 2000 and earlier models

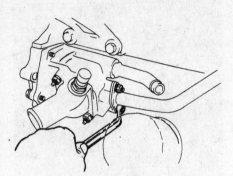

6.10 Disconnect the coolant bypass hose from the water neck - the heater pipe is attached with two nuts

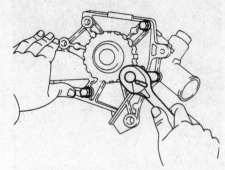

6.13a Install these bolts first . . .

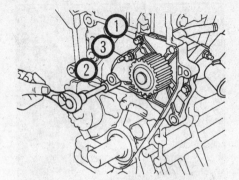

6.13b . . . then tighten these bolts in the order shown

6.16 Loosen the water pump pulley bolts while applying pressure to the engine drivebelt tensioner

6.18a Water pump retaining bolts - 2001 and later models

6.18b Pry the water pump from the housing by the casting protrusion at the top

7   Remove the alternator adjusting bar **(see illustration)**. On models with an engine oil cooler, unbolt the air conditioning compressor and set it aside without disconnecting the refrigerant lines (see Section 13). Disconnect the lower radiator hose.

8   Remove the bolts from the water pump **(see illustration)**, noting the locations of the different length bolts and the sequence of removal. Remove the pump and gasket. If necessary, tap the pump loose with a soft-face hammer.

9   It isn't necessary to remove the pump cover (housing), but a thorough job would include removing it to replace the gaskets and O-rings.

10   Disconnect the coolant bypass hose from the water neck, then remove the two nuts and heater pipe **(see illustration)** and lift out the pump cover (housing).

11   Thoroughly clean all sealing surfaces, removing all traces of old gaskets, sealer and O-rings.

12   Be sure to use new O-rings between the pump cover and engine block and also a new gasket between the heater pipe and cover.

13   Using a new gasket, install the pump and bolts **(see illustrations)** and tighten them to the torque listed in this Chapter's Specifications.

14   Install the remaining parts in the reverse order of removal.

15   Refill the cooling system (see Chapter 1), run the engine and check for leaks and proper operation.

2001 and later models

Refer to illustrations 6.16, 6.18a, 6.18b and 6.20

16   Loosen the water pump pulley bolts **(see illustration)**, then remove the engine drivebelt (see Chapter 1).

17   Remove the wiring harness from the clamp on the water pump.

18   Remove the water pump retaining bolts and pry the water pump from the housing on the engine block **(see illustrations)**.

19   Thoroughly clean all sealing surfaces, removing all traces of old gasket sealer.

20   Apply a 1/8 inch bead of RTV sealant to the outside of the groove on the water pump **(see illustration)**.

21   Install the water pump and tighten the bolts and nuts to the torque listed in this Chapter's Specifications.

22   Install the remaining parts in the reverse order of removal.

23   Refill the cooling system (see Chapter 1), run the engine and check for leaks and proper operation.

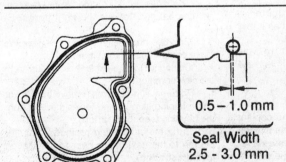

0.5 – 1.0 mm

Seal Width
2.5 - 3.0 mm

6.20 Water pump sealant application details - 2001 and later models

7.2 Coolant temperature gauge sending unit location - 2000 and earlier models

7.9 Radiator fan switch location

8.5 Blower motor location

A   *Blower motor*
B   *Blower motor connector*

7   Coolant temperature sending unit and radiator fan switch - replacement

Warning: *Do not start this procedure until the engine is completely cool. Do not allow antifreeze to come in contact with your skin or painted surfaces of the vehicle. Rinse off spills immediately with plenty of water. Anti-freeze is highly toxic if ingested. Never leave antifreeze lying around in an open container or in puddles on the floor; children and pets are attracted by it's sweet smell and may drink it. Check with local authorities about disposing of used antifreeze. Many communities have collection centers which will see that anti-freeze is disposed of safely. Never dump used antifreeze on the ground or into drains.*
Note: *Non-toxic coolant is available at local auto parts stores. Although the coolant is non-toxic when fresh, proper disposal of used coolant is still required.*

Coolant temperature gauge sending unit

2000 and earlier models
Refer to illustration 7.2
1   Drain the coolant (see Chapter 1).
2   Disconnect the wiring connector from the sending unit **(see illustration)**.
3   Using a deep socket or a wrench, remove the sending unit.
4   Install the new unit and tighten it securely. Do not use thread sealant as it may electrically insulate the sending unit.
5   Reconnect the wiring connector, refill the cooling system and check for coolant leakage and proper gauge function.

2001 and later models
6   On 2001 and later models, the coolant temperature gauge sending unit is an integral part of the engine coolant temperature sensor. Refer to Chapter 6 for the engine coolant temperature sensor replacement procedure.

Radiator fan switch
Refer to illustration 7.9
7   Raise the front of the vehicle and support it securely on jackstands.
8   Remove the lower splash shields from the vehicle. Drain the coolant (see Chapter 1)
9   Disconnect the wiring connector from the radiator fan switch **(see illustration)**.
10 Using a deep socket or a wrench, remove the switch.
11 Install the new switch and tighten it securely. Do not use thread sealer as it may electrically insulate the sending unit.
12 Reconnect the wiring connector, refill the cooling system and check for coolant leakage and proper operation of the cooling fans.

8   Blower motor - removal and installation

Refer to illustrations 8.5 and 8.6
Warning: *The models covered by this manual are equipped with Supplemental Restraint systems (SRS), more commonly known as airbags. Always disconnect the negative battery cable, then the positive battery cable and wait two minutes before working in the vicinity of the impact sensors, steering column or instrument panel to avoid the possibility of accidental deployment of the airbag, which could cause personal injury (see Chapter 12).*
1   Disconnect the negative cable from the battery.
2   The blower unit is located in the passenger compartment above the right front footwell.
3   On 2000 and earlier models, remove the glove compartment (see Chapter 11).
4   Disconnect the electrical connector from the blower motor.
5   To remove the blower, remove the blower unit retaining screws and lower the unit from the housing **(see illustration)**.
6   If the motor is being replaced, transfer the fan to the new motor prior to installation **(see illustration)**.
7   Installation is the reverse of removal. Check for proper operation.

9   Heater and air conditioning control assembly - removal and installation and cable adjustment

Refer to illustrations 9.5, 9.6a and 9.6b
Warning: *The models covered by this manual are equipped with Supplemental Restraint systems (SRS), more commonly known as airbags. Always disable the airbag system before working in the vicinity of any airbag system components to avoid the possibility of accidental deployment of the airbag, which could cause personal injury (see Chapter 12).*

Removal and installation
1   Disconnect the negative cable from the battery.
2   Remove the center instrument trim panel (see Chapter 11).
3   On 2000 and earlier models, remove the glove box and the lower center trim panel also referring to Chapter 11. Then pull off the control knobs and remove the heater control assembly trim panel.
4   On 2001 and later models, remove the radio (see Chapter 12). Then remove the lower left finish panel from the front of the floor console.

8.6 Use pliers to release and remove the clip, then lift the blower fan off the motor shaft

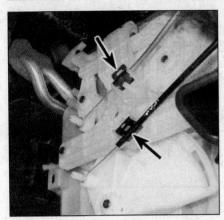

9.5 Disconnect the control cables from the clamps (arrows) on the heater /air conditioning unit then remove the ends of the cable from the levers - 2001 and later models shown, 2000 and earlier models have three cables to disconnect

5　Disconnect the heater control cables from the levers on the heater/air conditioning unit **(see illustration)**.
6　Remove the mounting screws located on the front of the control assembly **(see illustrations)**.

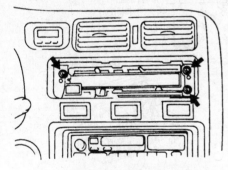

9.6a Heater/air conditioning control assembly mounting screws - 2000 and earlier models

7　Pull the control assembly out of the instrument panel with the control cables attached.
8　Installation is the reverse of the removal procedure.
9　Run the engine and check for proper functioning of the heater (and air conditioning, if equipped).

Cable adjustment
2000 and earlier models
10　To adjust the air inlet control cable set the control lever to RECIRC, install the cable and clamp it in place.
11　To adjust the air mix control cable, set the air mix to COOL, install the cable and lock the clamp while applying slight pressure (away from the firewall) on the outer cable.
12　To adjust the mode control cable, set the mode damper to the DEF position, install the cable and clamp it in place.

2001 and later models
13　To adjust the air mix control cable, set the air mix to MAX COOL, install the cable and clamp it in place.
14　To adjust the mode control cable, position the mode control lever so it faces the rear of the vehicle. Install the cable and lock the clamp while applying slight pressure (away from the firewall) on the outer cable outer cable.

10 Heater core - removal and installation

Refer to illustrations 10.4, 10.6, 10.8, 10.10, 10.14, 10.18, 10.19 and 10.20
Warning 1: *The models covered by this manual are equipped with Supplemental Restraint systems (SRS), more commonly known as airbags. Always disable the airbag system before working in the vicinity of any airbag system components to avoid the possibility of accidental deployment of the airbag, which could cause personal injury (see Chapter 12).*
Warning 2: *Do not allow antifreeze to come in*

contact with your skin or painted surfaces of the vehicle. Rinse off spills immediately with plenty of water. Antifreeze is highly toxic if ingested. Never leave antifreeze lying around in an open container or in puddles on the floor; children and pets are attracted by it's sweet smell and may drink it. Check with local authorities about disposing of used antifreeze. Many communities have collection centers which will see that antifreeze is disposed of safely. Never dump used antifreeze on the ground or into drains.
Warning 3: *The air conditioning system is under high pressure. DO NOT loosen any fittings or remove any components until after the system has been discharged. Air conditioning refrigerant should be properly discharged into an EPA-approved container at a dealer service department or an automotive air conditioning repair facility. Always wear eye protection when disconnecting air conditioning system fittings.*
Warning 4: *Wait until the engine is completely cool before beginning this procedure.*
Note: *Replacement of the heater core on 2001 and later models is a difficult procedure for the home mechanic, involving removal of the entire dashboard, floor console and many wiring connectors. If you attempt this procedure at home, keep track of the assemblies by taking notes and keeping screws and other hardware in small, marked plastic bags for reassembly.*
1　If the vehicle is equipped with air conditioning, have the air conditioning system discharged at a dealer service department or service station.
2　Turn the heater control setting to HOT. Drain the cooling system (see Chapter 1). If the coolant is relatively new, or tests in good condition (see Section 2), save it and re-use it.
3　Disconnect the cable from the negative terminal of the battery.
4　Working in the engine compartment, disconnect the heater hoses where they enter the firewall **(see illustration)**. **Caution:** *If the heater hoses are stuck, it is better to cut off the hoses than to twist them with pliers and risk breaking the heater core tubes.*

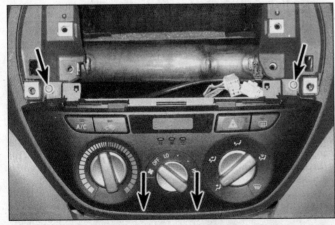

9.6b Heater/air conditioning control assembly mounting screws - 2001 and later models - lower arrows indicate the area of two plastic retaining clips - be careful not to break them

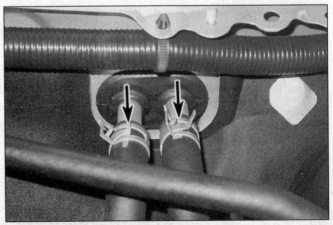

10.4 Squeeze the clamps and disconnect the heater hoses (arrows) at the firewall

10.6 Using a spring lock coupling tool remove the refrigerant lines (arrows) from the evaporator core

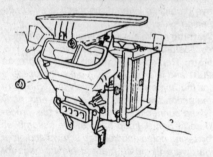

10.10 Heater core housing mounting nuts - 2000 and earlier models

5   Remove the rubber grommets where the heater core tubes go through the firewall.

6   Disconnect the air conditioning refrigerant lines and rubber grommet from the evaporator core if the vehicle is so equipped **(see illustration). Warning:** *Always wear eye protection when disconnecting air conditioning system fittings and always cap the fitting ends to prevent moisture from entering the refrigerant lines.*

2000 and earlier models

7   Remove the instrument panel glove box (see Chapter 12).

8   Remove the evaporator housing **(see illustration).**

9   Detach the rear floor duct from the heater core housing.

10   Remove the two nuts and slide the heater unit to the right and out through the glove box opening **(see illustration).**

11   Remove the screws securing the defroster duct to the top of the heater unit, then remove the heater core retaining clamp and remove it from the heater core housing.

12   Installation is the reverse of removal.

2001 and later models

13   Remove the entire instrument panel and the reinforcement beam (see Chapter 11).

14   Disconnect the electrical connectors from the blower motor and the blower resistor, then remove the blower unit **(see illustration).**

10.8 Evaporator housing mounting screws and nuts - 2000 and earlier models

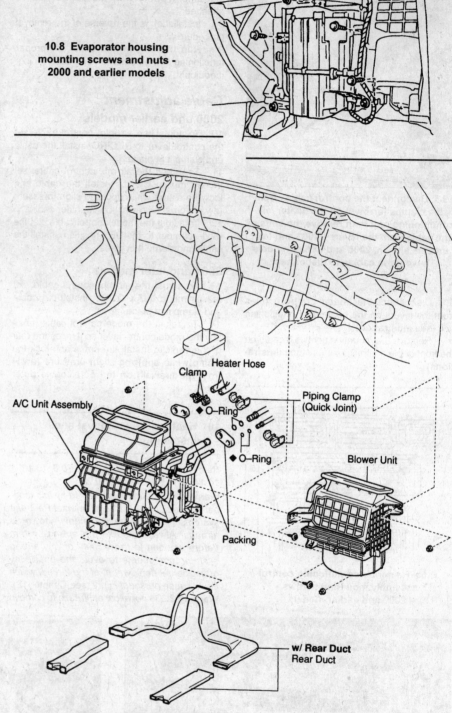

10.14 Heating and air conditioning unit installation details

15   Remove the rear floor duct.

16   Remove the two nuts and the A/C unit.

17   Pry open the claws and remove the thermistor and the wiring harness from the A/C unit.

18   Remove the evaporator from the A/C unit **(see illustration).**

19   Detach the retaining screws and remove the heater core from the A/C housing **(see illustration).**

20   Reinstall the remaining parts in the reverse order of removal. Be sure to install the thermistor in the bracket plate with the correct amount protruding as shown **(see illustration).**

21   Refill the cooling system (see Chapter 1), reconnect the battery and run the engine. Check for leaks and proper operation of the system. Have the air conditioning system recharged if equipped.

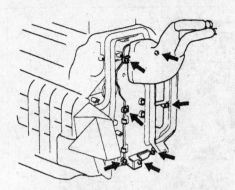

10.18 Evaporator core mounting screws - 2001 and later models

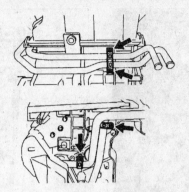

10.19 Heater core retaining screws - 2001 and later models

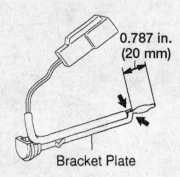

0.787 in. (20 mm)

Bracket Plate

10.20 Install the thermistor in the bracket plate with the end of the thermistor protruding out of the bracket the specified amount

11   Air conditioning and heating system - check and maintenance

Air conditioning system

Refer to illustration 11.1

Warning: *The air conditioning system is under high pressure. Do not loosen any hose fittings or remove any components until after the system has been discharged. Air conditioning refrigerant should be properly discharged into an EPA-approved recovery/recycling unit at a dealer service department or an automotive air conditioning repair facility. Always wear eye protection when disconnecting air conditioning system fittings.*

Caution 1: *All models covered by this manual use environmentally friendly R-134a. This refrigerant (and its appropriate refrigerant oils) is not compatible R-12 refrigerant system components and must never be mixed or the components will be damaged.*

Caution 2: *When replacing entire components, additional refrigerant oil should be added equal to the amount that is removed with the component being replaced. Be sure to read the can before adding any oil to the system, to make sure it is compatible with the R-134a system.*

1   The following maintenance checks should be performed on a regular basis to ensure that the air conditioning continues to operate at peak efficiency.

a) *Inspect the condition of the compressor drivebelt. If it is worn or deteriorated, replace it (see Chapter 1).*
b) *Check the drivebelt tension and, if necessary, adjust it (see Chapter 1).*
c) *Inspect the system hoses. Look for cracks, bubbles, hardening and deterioration. Inspect the hoses and all fittings for oil bubbles or seepage. If there is any evidence of wear, damage or leakage, replace the hose(s).*
d) *Inspect the condenser fins for leaves, bugs and any other foreign material that may have embedded itself in the fins. Use a "fin comb" or compressed air to remove debris from the condenser.*
e) *Make sure the system has the correct refrigerant charge.*
f) *If you hear water sloshing around in the dash area or have water dripping on the carpet, check the evaporator housing drain tube* **(see illustration)** *and insert a piece of wire into the opening to check for blockage.*

2   It's a good idea to operate the system for about ten minutes at least once a month. This is particularly important during the winter months because long term non-use can cause hardening, and subsequent failure, of the seals. Note that using the Defrost function operates the compressor.

3   If the air conditioning system is not working properly, proceed to Step 6.

4   Because of the complexity of the air conditioning system and the special equipment necessary to service it, in-depth troubleshooting and repairs beyond checking the refrigerant charge and the compressor clutch operation are not included in this manual. However, simple checks and component replacement procedures are provided in this Chapter. For more complete information on the air conditioning system, refer to the *Haynes Automotive Heating and Air Conditioning Manual*.

5   The most common cause of poor cooling is simply a low system refrigerant charge. If a noticeable drop in system cooling ability occurs, one of the following quick checks will help you determine whether the refrigerant level is low. Should the system lose its cooling ability, the following procedure will help you pinpoint the cause.

Check

Refer to illustration 11.9

6   Warm the engine up to normal operating temperature.

7   Place the air conditioning temperature selector at the coldest setting and put the blower at the highest setting. Open the doors (to make sure the air conditioning system doesn't cycle off as soon as it cools the passenger compartment).

8   After the system reaches operating temperature, feel the two pipes connected to the evaporator at the firewall.

9   The pipe (thinner tubing) leading from the condenser outlet to the evaporator should be cold, and the evaporator outlet line (the thicker tubing that leads back to the compressor) should be slightly colder (3 to 10 degrees F colder). If the evaporator outlet is considerably warmer than the inlet, the system needs a charge. Insert a thermometer in the center

11.1 Check that the evaporator housing drain tube (arrow) at the firewall is clear of any blockage - the view here is from below the engine

11.9 Insert a thermometer in the center duct while operating the air conditioning system - the output air should be 35-40 degrees F less than the ambient temperature, depending on humidity

11.18 A basic charging kit for 134a systems is available at most auto parts stores - it must say 134a (not R-12) and so must the can of refrigerant

air distribution duct **(see illustration)** while operating the air conditioning system at its maximum setting - the temperature of the output air should be 35 to 40 degrees F below the ambient air temperature (down to approximately 40 degrees F). If the ambient (outside) air temperature is very high, say 110 degrees F, the duct air temperature may be as high as 60 degrees F, but generally the air conditioning is 35 to 40 degrees F cooler than the ambient air.

10   If the air isn't as cold as it used to be, the system probably needs a charge.

11   If the air is warm and the system doesn't seem to be operating properly check the operation of the compressor clutch.

12   Have an assistant switch the air conditioning On while you observe the front of the compressor. The clutch will make an audible click and the center of the clutch should rotate.

13   If the clutch didn't operate, check the appropriate fuses. Inspect the fuses in the interior fuse panel.

14   If the fuses are OK, refer to the wiring diagrams at the end of Chapter 12 and check

the compressor clutch circuit and pressure switch for proper operation.

15   If the compressor clutch circuit and pressure switch are OK, the compressor clutch is probably faulty.

16   If the compressor clutch, relay and related circuits are known to be in good working order and the system is fully charged with refrigerant and the compressor does not operate under normal conditions, have the PCM and related circuits checked by a dealer service department or other properly equipped repair facility.

17   Further inspection or testing of the system is beyond the scope of the home mechanic and should be left to a professional.

Adding refrigerant

Refer to illustration 11.18

Caution: *Make sure any refrigerant, refrigerant oil or replacement component your purchase is designated as compatible with environmentally friendly R-134a systems.*

18   Purchase an R-134a automotive charging kit at an auto parts store **(see illustra-**

tion). A charging kit includes a 12-ounce can of refrigerant, a tap valve and a short section of hose that can be attached between the tap valve and the system low side service valve. Because one can of refrigerant may not be sufficient to bring the system charge up to the proper level, it's a good idea to buy an additional can. **Warning:** *Never add more than two cans of refrigerant to the system.*

19   Hook up the charging kit by following the manufacturer's instructions. **Warning:** *DO NOT hook the charging kit hose to the system high side!* The fittings on the charging kit are designed to fit **only** on the low side of the system.

20   Back off the valve handle on the charging kit and screw the kit onto the refrigerant can, making sure first that the O-ring or rubber seal inside the threaded portion of the kit is in place. **Warning:** *Wear protective eyewear when dealing with pressurized refrigerant cans.*

21   Remove the dust cap from the low-side charging and attach the quick-connect fitting on the kit hose.

22   Warm up the engine and turn on the air conditioning. Keep the charging kit hose away from the fan and other moving parts. **Note:** *The charging process requires the compressor to be running. If the clutch cycles off, you can put the air conditioning switch on High and leave the car doors open to keep the clutch on and compressor working.*

23   Turn the valve handle on the kit until the stem pierces the can, then back the handle out to release the refrigerant. You should be able to hear the rush of gas. Add refrigerant to the low side of the system, keeping the can upright at all times, but shaking it occasionally. Allow stabilization time between each addition. **Note:** *The charging process will go faster if you wrap the can with a hot-water-soaked shop rag to keep the can from freezing up.*

24   If you have an accurate thermometer,

11.32 With the glove box removed, spray the disinfectant through the interior air filter opening

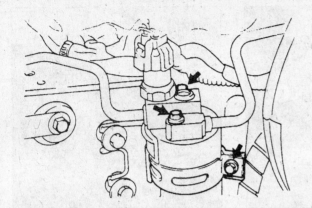

12.3 Receiver/drier mounting details - 2000 and earlier models

you can place it in the center air conditioning duct inside the vehicle and keep track of the output air temperature **(see illustration 11.9)**. A charged system that is working properly should cool down to approximately 40-degrees F. If the ambient (outside) air temperature is very high, say 110 degrees F, the duct air temperature may be as high as 60 degrees F, but generally the air conditioning is 30-40 degrees F cooler than the ambient air.

25 When the can is empty, turn the valve handle to the closed position and release the connection from the low-side port. Replace the dust cap.

26 Remove the charging kit from the can and store the kit for future use with the piercing valve in the UP position, to prevent inadvertently piercing the can on the next use.

Heating systems

27 If the carpet under the heater core is damp, or if antifreeze vapor or steam is coming through the vents, the heater core is leaking. Remove it (see Section 10) and install a new unit (most radiator shops will not repair a leaking heater core).

28 If the air coming out of the heater vents isn't hot, the problem could stem from any of the following causes:

12.4 The receiver/drier on 2001 and later models is located in a tube on the side of the condenser - arrow shows location of the end plug

a) The thermostat is stuck open, preventing the engine coolant from warming up enough to carry heat to the heater core. Replace the thermostat (see Section 3).

b) There is a blockage in the system, preventing the flow of coolant through the heater core. Feel both heater hoses at the firewall. They should be hot. If one of them is cold, there is an obstruction in one of the hoses or in the heater core, or the heater control valve is shut. Detach the hoses and back flush the heater core with a water hose. If the heater core is clear but circulation is impeded, remove the two hoses and flush them out with a water hose.

c) If flushing fails to remove the blockage from the heater core, the core must be replaced (see Section 10).

Eliminating air conditioning odors

Refer to illustration 11.32

29 Unpleasant odors that often develop in air conditioning systems are caused by the growth of a fungus, usually on the surface of the evaporator core. The warm, humid environment there is a perfect breeding ground for mildew to develop.

30 The evaporator core on most vehicles is difficult to access, and factory dealerships have a lengthy, expensive process for eliminating the fungus by opening up the evaporator case and using a powerful disinfectant and rinse on the core until the fungus is gone. You can service your own system at home, but it takes something much stronger than basic household germ-killers or deodorizers.

31 Aerosol disinfectants for automotive air conditioning systems are available in most auto parts stores, but remember when shopping for them that the most effective treatments are also the most expensive. The basic procedure for using these sprays is to start by running the system in the RECIRC mode for ten minutes with the blower on its highest speed. Use the highest heat mode to dry out the system and keep the compressor from engaging by disconnecting the wiring connector at the compressor (see Section 13).

32 The disinfectant can usually comes with a long spray hose. Remove the interior air

filter (see Chapter 1), point the nozzle inside the hole and to the left towards the evaporator core, and spray according to the manufacturer's recommendations **(see illustration)**. Try to cover the whole surface of the evaporator core, by aiming the spray up, down and sideways. Follow the manufacturer's recommendations for the length of spray and waiting time between applications.

33 Once the evaporator has been cleaned, the best way to prevent the mildew from coming back again is to make sure your evaporator housing drain tube is clear **(see illustration 11.1)**.

12 Air conditioning receiver/drier - removal and installation

Refer to illustrations 12.3 and 12.4
Warning: *The air conditioning system is under high pressure. Do not loosen any hose fittings or remove any components until the system has been discharged. Air conditioning refrigerant should be properly discharged into an EPA-approved recovery/recycling unit by a dealer service department or an automotive air conditioning repair facility. Always wear eye protection when disconnecting air conditioning system fittings.*

1 Have the refrigerant discharged by an air conditioning technician.

2 Disconnect the negative battery cable.

3 On 2000 and earlier models, disconnect the refrigerant lines **(see illustration)** from the receiver/drier and cap the open fittings to prevent entry of moisture. Loosen the clamp bolt and slip the receiver/drier out of the bracket.

4 On 2001 and later models, remove the condenser (see Section 14). Using an Allen wrench, detach the end plug **(see illustration)** and remove the dryer from the condenser.

5 Installation is the reverse of removal. Be sure to tighten the end plug on 2001 and later models to the torque listed in this Chapter's Specifications.

6 Have the system evacuated, charged and leak tested by the shop that discharged it. If the receiver was replaced, have them add the proper amount of refrigeration oil to the compressor. Use only compressor oil compatible with R-134a refrigerant.

13 Air conditioning compressor - removal and installation

Refer to illustrations 13.4a and 13.4b
Warning: *The air conditioning system is under high pressure. Do not loosen any hose fittings or remove any components until the system has been discharged. Air conditioning refrigerant should be properly discharged into an EPA-approved recovery/recycling unit by a dealer service department or an automotive air conditioning repair facility. Always wear eye protection when disconnecting air conditioning system fittings.*

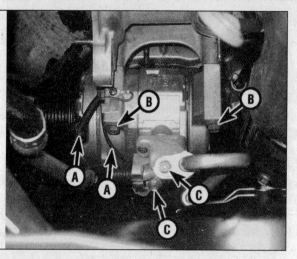

13.4a Compressor mounting details (alternator and thermostat housing removed for clarity) - 2001 and later models shown

A　Electrical connector
B　Upper mounting bolts
C　Refrigerant lines

13.4b A/C compressor lower mounting bolts (arrows)

1   Have the refrigerant discharged by an automotive air conditioning technician.
2   Disconnect the negative cable from the battery. Raise the front of the vehicle and support it securely on jackstands, then remove the lower splash shield from the right side of the vehicle.
3   Remove the drivebelt from the compressor (see Chapter 1).
4   Detach the wiring connector and the refrigerant lines **(see illustrations)**.
5   Unbolt the compressor and lower it from the vehicle.
6   If a new or rebuilt compressor is being installed, follow the directions which come with it regarding the proper level of oil prior to installation.
7   Installation is the reverse of removal. Replace any O-rings with new ones specifically made for the purpose and lubricate them

with refrigerant oil.
8   Have the system evacuated, recharged and leak tested by the shop that discharged it.

14   Air conditioning condenser - removal and installation

Refer to illustrations 14.3 and 14.4
Warning: *The air conditioning system is under high pressure. Do not loosen any hose fittings or remove any components until the system has been discharged. Air conditioning refrigerant should be properly discharged into an EPA-approved recovery/recycling unit by a dealer service department or an automotive air conditioning repair facility. Always wear eye protection when disconnecting air conditioning system fittings.*

1   Have the refrigerant discharged by an air conditioning technician.
2   On 2001 and later models, remove the front bumper (see Chapter 11).
3   Disconnect the inlet and outlet fittings **(see illustration)**. Cap the open fittings immediately to keep moisture and dirt out of the system.
4   Remove the mounting bolts and pull the condenser up and out of the vehicle **(see illustration)**.
5   Install the condenser, brackets and bolts, making sure the rubber cushions fit on the mounting points properly.
6   Reconnect the refrigerant lines, using new O-rings where needed.
7   Reinstall the remaining parts in the reverse order of removal. Have the system evacuated, charged and leak tested by the shop that discharged it.

14.3 Disconnect the refrigerant lines (arrows) from the condenser - 2001 and later model shown

14.4 Condenser mounting bolts - 2001 and later model shown

Chapter 4
Fuel and exhaust systems

Contents

	Section
Accelerator cable - removal, installation and adjustment	11
Air filter housing - removal and installation	10
Air filter replacement	See Chapter 1
CHECK ENGINE light	See Chapter 6
Electronic fuel injection system - check	13
Electronic fuel injection system - general information	12
Exhaust system check	See Chapter 1
Exhaust system servicing - general information	17
Fuel level sending unit - replacement	7
Fuel lines and fittings - general information	4
Fuel pressure regulator - removal and installation	6

	Section
Fuel pressure relief	2
Fuel pulsation damper (2001 and later models) - replacement	15
Fuel pump/fuel pressure - check	3
Fuel pump - removal and installation	5
Fuel rail and injectors - removal and installation	16
Fuel system check	See Chapter 1
Fuel tank cleaning and repair - general information	9
Fuel tank - removal and installation	8
General information	1
Throttle body - check, removal and installation	14
Underhood hose check and replacement	See Chapter 1

Specifications

Fuel system

Fuel system pressure	44 to 50 psi (304 to 345 kPa)
Fuel system hold pressure (after five minutes)	21 psi minimum (145 kPa)
Injector resistance (approximate)	13.4 to 14.2 ohms

Torque specifications

	Ft-lbs (unless otherwise indicated)	Nm
Fuel rail mounting bolts		
2000 and earlier models	108 in-lbs	13
2001 and later models	15	20
Throttle body mounting bolts		
2000 and earlier models	14	19
2001 and later models	22	30
Fuel pulsation damper bolts	80 in-lbs	9
Fuel tank strap bolts	29	40

1   General information

Refer to illustrations 1.1a and 1.1b

The fuel system consists of a fuel tank, an electric fuel pump (located in the fuel tank), a fuel pressure regulator located next to the fuel pump in the tank, an EFI main relay, a fuel pump relay (circuit opening relay), the fuel rail and fuel injectors, an air filter housing and a throttle body unit. All models are equipped with a Sequential Electronic Fuel Injection system **(see illustrations)**.

Sequential Electronic Fuel Injection system

Sequential Electronic Fuel Injection uses timed impulses to inject the fuel directly into the intake port of each cylinder according to its firing order. The injectors are controlled by the Powertrain Control Module (PCM). The PCM monitors various engine parameters and delivers the exact amount of fuel required into the intake ports. The throttle body serves only to control the amount of air passing into the system. Because each cylinder is equipped with its own injector, much better control of the fuel/air mixture ratio is possible.

Fuel pump and lines

Fuel is circulated from the fuel tank to the fuel injection system through a metal line running along the underside of the vehicle. An electric fuel pump and fuel level sending unit is located inside the fuel tank.

The fuel pump relay is equipped with a primary and secondary circuit. The primary circuit is controlled by the PCM and the secondary circuit is linked directly to the EFI main relay from the ignition switch. With the ignition switch ON (engine not running), the PCM will ground the relay for two seconds. During cranking, the PCM grounds the fuel pump relay as long as the camshaft position sensor sends its position signal (see Chapter 6). If there are no reference pulses, the fuel pump will shut off after two seconds.

Exhaust system

The exhaust system consists of an exhaust manifold, exhaust pipes, a catalytic converter, a muffler and a tail pipe.

The catalytic converter is an emission control device added to the exhaust system to reduce pollutants. Refer to Chapter 6 for more information regarding the catalytic converter.

2   Fuel pressure relief

Refer to illustration 2.2
Warning: *Gasoline is extremely flammable, so take extra precautions when you work on any part of the fuel system. Don't smoke or allow open flames or bare light bulbs near the work area, and don't work in a garage where a gas-type appliance (such as a water heater or a clothes dryer) is present. Since gasoline is carcinogenic, wear latex gloves when*

1.1a Fuel system components - 2000 and earlier models

1   Fusible link box
2   Intake manifold
3   Throttle body

4   Air filter housing
5   Fuel rail (mounted on top of intake manifold runners)

there's a possibility of being exposed to fuel, and, if you spill any fuel on your skin, rinse it off immediately with soap and water. Mop up any spills immediately and do not store fuel-soaked rags where they could ignite. The fuel system is under constant pressure, so, if any fuel lines are to be disconnected, the fuel pressure in the system must be relieved first. When you perform any kind of work on the fuel system, wear safety glasses and have a Class B type fire extinguisher on hand.

1   Remove the fuel filler cap - this will relieve any pressure built up in the tank.
2   Remove the rear seat and liner to access the fuel pump/sending unit access cover (see Section 5). Disconnect the harness connector **(see illustration)**.
3   Start the engine and allow it to run until

1.1b Fuel system components - 2001 and later models

1   Air filter housing
2   Throttle body (under air filter housing)

3   Relay and fuse box
4   Air intake duct

2.2 Disconnect the fuel pump directly at the fuel pump harness connector (arrow)

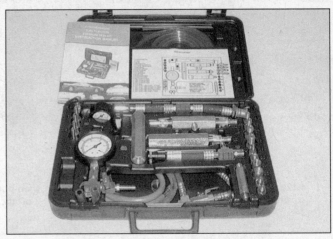

3.3a This aftermarket fuel pressure testing kit contains all the necessary fittings and adapters, along with the fuel pressure gauge, to test most automotive fuel systems

it stops. Turn the ignition switch OFF and disconnect the cable from the negative terminal of the battery before working on the fuel system.

4   The fuel system pressure is now relieved. Place a shop rag around any fitting to be disconnected to catch the residual fuel as it bleeds off. Dispose of the fuel soaked rag in an approved safety container.

5   When you're finished working on the fuel system, reconnect the fuel pump/sending unit harness connector and connect the negative cable to the battery.

3   Fuel pump/fuel pressure - check

Warning: *Gasoline is extremely flammable, so take extra precautions when you work on any part of the fuel system. See the* **Warning** *in Section 2.*

General checks

1   If you suspect insufficient fuel delivery check the following items first:

a) *Check the battery and make sure it's fully charged (see Chapter 5).*
b) *Check the fuel pump fuse.*
c) *Inspect all fuel lines to ensure that the problem is not simply a leak in a line.*

2   Verify the fuel pump actually runs. Have an assistant turn the ignition switch to ON - you should hear a brief whirring noise (for approximately two seconds) as the pump comes on and pressurizes the system. **Note:** *The fuel pump is easily heard through the gas tank filler neck. If there is no response from the fuel pump (makes no sound), check the fuel pump electrical circuit. If the fuel pump runs, but a fuel system problem is suspected, continue with the fuel pump pressure check.*

Fuel pump pressure check

Refer to illustrations 3.3a, 3.3b and 3.3c
Note 1: *In order to perform the fuel pressure test, you will need to obtain a fuel pressure gauge capable of measuring high fuel pressure and the proper adapter set for the specific fuel injection system.*
Note 2: *2000 and earlier models are equipped*

with a bolt-and-washer type fuel line connection at the fuel filter, while 2001 and later models are equipped with an in-line quick-connect fuel fitting. Each type will require a different kind of adapter to enable you to connect a fuel pressure gauge.
Note 3: *2000 and earlier models are equipped with a fuel filter mounted on the left strut tower in the engine compartment, with an additional fuel strainer mounted integral with the fuel pump assembly in the tank. 2001 and later models are equipped with one fuel filter mounted in the fuel pump assembly.*

3   Relieve the fuel system pressure (see Section 2). Connect the fuel pressure gauge.

a) *On 2000 and earlier models, remove the fuse/relay box from the left strut tower, disconnect the fuel filter outlet line and connect an adapter and fuel pressure gauge to the fuel filter and fuel line* **(see illustrations)**.
b) *On 2001 and later models, disconnect the fuel tube connector near the fuel rail* **(see illustration)** *and connect the fuel pressure gauge using the proper adapters.*

3.3b On 2000 and earlier models attach the fuel pressure gauge to the fuel filter (arrow) and fuel line; turn the ignition key ON and check the fuel pressure

3.3c Location of the fuel tube connector (arrow) on 2001 and later models

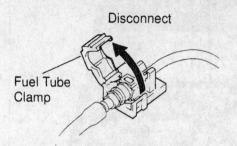

4.12a On quick-connect fuel line fittings, pinch the tabs . . .

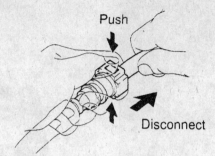

4.12b . . . then push and pull the fitting off the fuel line

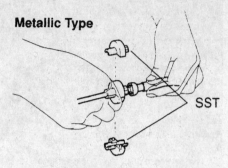

4.12c On metal tube type fuel line fittings, install the upper and lower sections of the special fuel line disconnect tool . . .

4   Turn all the accessories Off and switch the ignition key On. The fuel pump should run for about two seconds; note the reading on the gauge. If the fuel pressure is higher than specified, replace the fuel pressure regulator. If the pressure is too low, the fuel filter (or in-tank strainer) could be clogged, the lines could be restricted or leaking, a fuel injector could be leaking, or the fuel pressure regulator and/or the fuel pump could be defective.

5   Start the engine and let it idle at normal operating temperature. The pressure should fall within the range listed in this Chapter's Specifications. If the pressure is lower than specified check the items listed in Step 4. **Note:** *If no obvious problems are found, most likely the fuel pressure regulator and/or the fuel pump is defective. In this situation, it is recommended that both the fuel pressure regulator and fuel pump are replaced to prevent any future fuel pressure problems.*

6   Turn the engine off and check the gauge - the pressure should hold steady. After five minutes it should not drop below the minimum listed in this Chapter's Specifications. If it does drop, the fuel pump or pressure regulator could be defective, or a fuel injector could be leaking.

7   After the testing is done, relieve the fuel pressure (see Section 2) and remove the fuel pressure gauge.

Fuel pump electrical circuit check

8   If the pump does not turn on (makes no sound) with the ignition switch in the ON position, check the IGN fuse and the EFI fuse located in the engine compartment fuse center. Also, check the EFI main relay and circuit opening relay. **Note:** *These models are equipped with an EFI main relay and a fuel pump relay (circuit opening relay). On 2000 and earlier models, the EFI main relay is located in the engine compartment fuse/relay box and the fuel pump relay (circuit opening relay) is located behind the driver's side kick panel under the dash. On 2001 and later models, the EFI main relay and fuel pump relay (circuit opening relay) are located in the engine compartment fuse/relay box.*

9   If the relays are good and the fuel pump does not operate, check the fuel pump circuit. Refer to the wiring diagrams at the end of Chapter 12.

4   Fuel lines and fittings - general information

Warning: *Gasoline is extremely flammable, so take extra precautions when you work on any part of the fuel system. See the* **Warning** *in Section 2.*

1   Always relieve the fuel pressure before servicing fuel lines or fittings (see Section 2).

2   The fuel line extends from the fuel tank to the engine compartment. The line is secured to the underbody with clip and screw assemblies. This line must be occasionally inspected for leaks, kinks and dents.

3   If evidence of dirt is found in the system or fuel filter during disassembly, the line should be disconnected and blown out. Check the fuel strainer on the fuel gauge sending unit (see Section 5) for damage and deterioration.

Steel tubing

4   If replacement of a fuel line or emission line is called for, use welded steel tubing meeting the manufacturer's specifications or its equivalent.

5   Don't use copper or aluminum tubing to replace steel tubing. These materials cannot withstand normal vehicle vibration.

6   Because fuel lines used on fuel-injected vehicles are under high pressure, they require special consideration.

7   Some fuel lines have threaded fittings with O-rings. Any time the fittings are loosened to service or replace components:

a)   *Use a flare-nut wrench while loosening and tightening fittings, and hold the stationary portion of the line (or component) with another wrench.*

b)   *Check all O-rings for cuts, cracks and deterioration. Replace any that appear hardened, worn or damaged.*

c)   *If the lines are replaced, always use original equipment parts, or parts that meet the original equipment standards.*

Flexible hose

Warning: *Use only original equipment replacement hoses or their equivalent. Others may fail from the high pressures of this system.*

8   Don't route fuel hose within four inches of any part of the exhaust system or within ten inches of the catalytic converter. Metal lines and rubber hoses must never be allowed to chafe against the frame. A minimum of 1/4-inch clearance must be maintained around a line or hose to prevent contact with the frame.

9   Some models may be equipped with nylon fuel line and quick-connect fittings at the fuel filter and/or fuel pump. The quick-connect fittings cannot be serviced separately. Do not attempt to service these types of fuel lines in the event the retainer tabs or the line becomes damaged. Replace the entire fuel line as an assembly.

Replacement

Refer to illustrations 4.12a, 4.12b, 4.12c, 4.12d and 4.13

10   In the event of any fuel line damage (metal or flexible lines) it is necessary to replace the damaged lines with factory replacement parts. Others may fail from the high pressures of this system.

11   Relieve the fuel pressure.

12   Remove all fasteners attaching the lines to the vehicle body. On fuel lines so equipped, detach the clamp(s) that attach the fuel hoses to the metal lines, then pull the hose off the fitting. Twisting the hoses back and forth will allow them to separate more easily. If equipped with quick-connect fittings, hold the connector with one hand and depress the retaining tabs with the other hand, then separate the connector from the pipe **(see illustrations)**.

13   Installation is the reverse of removal. Be sure to use new O-rings at the threaded fittings (if equipped). On quick-connect fittings, align the retainer locking pawls with the connector grooves. Push the connector onto the pipe until both retaining pawls lock with a clicking sound. When connecting rubber hose to a metal line, make sure it's completely pushed onto the metal line and secured with a hose clamp **(see illustration)**.

5 Fuel pump - removal and installation

Warning: *Gasoline is extremely flammable, so take extra precautions when you work on any part of the fuel system. See the* **Warning** *in Section 2.*

Removal

Refer to illustrations 5.4a, 5.4b, 5.5, 5.7, 5.8, 5.9a, 5.9b, 5.9c, 5.10a and 5.10b

1   Relieve the fuel system pressure (see Section 2) and remove the fuel tank cap.
2   Disconnect the cable from the negative terminal of the battery.
3   Remove the left rear seat from inside the passenger compartment (see Chapter 11).
4   Remove the fuel pump/sending unit floor service hole cover **(see illustrations)**.

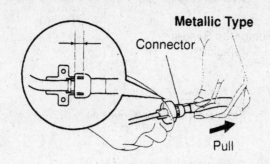

4.12d ... then insert the tool into the coupler to release the connection

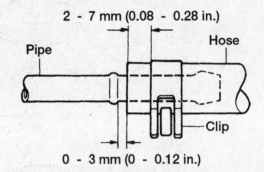

4.13 When attaching a section of rubber hose to a metal fuel line, be sure to overlap the hose as shown, secure it to the line with a new hose clamp of the proper type

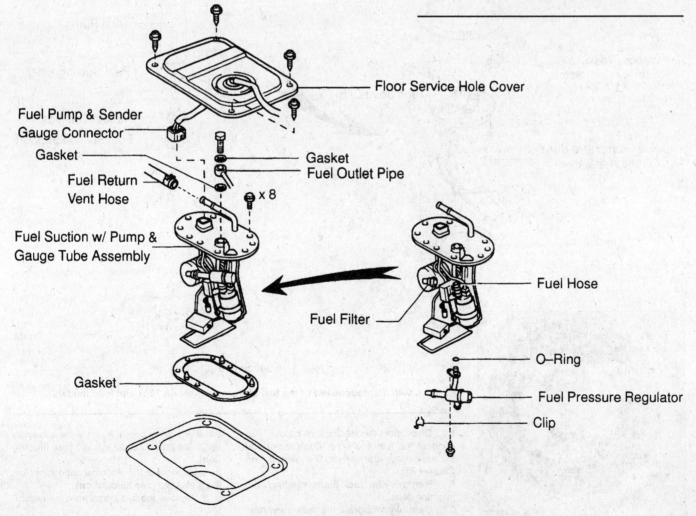

5.4a Exploded view of the fuel pump assembly on 2000 and earlier models

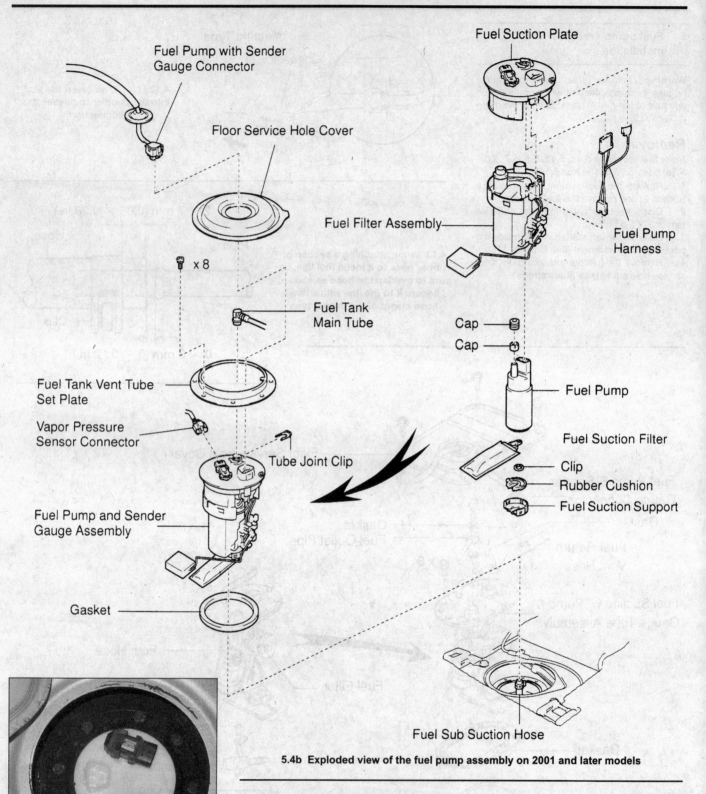

Fuel Pump with Sender Gauge Connector

Floor Service Hole Cover

Fuel Suction Plate

Fuel Filter Assembly

Fuel Pump Harness

x 8

Fuel Tank Main Tube

Cap

Cap

Fuel Pump

Fuel Tank Vent Tube Set Plate

Vapor Pressure Sensor Connector

Tube Joint Clip

Fuel Suction Filter

Clip

Rubber Cushion

Fuel Suction Support

Fuel Pump and Sender Gauge Assembly

Gasket

Fuel Sub Suction Hose

5.4b Exploded view of the fuel pump assembly on 2001 and later models

5.5 First remove the floor service hole cover to gain access to the fuel line

5   Disconnect the electrical connector. Disconnect the fuel line (see illustration) and the vapor pressure sensor, if equipped (see Chapter 6).
6   Remove the fuel pump/sending unit retaining bolts.
7   Carefully withdraw the fuel pump/fuel level sending unit assembly from the fuel tank. Note: On 2001 and later models, disconnect

the fuel sub-suction hose once the assembly has been pulled out far enough (see illustration).
8   Disconnect the electrical connector from the fuel pump (see illustration).
9   Remove the fuel pump from the assembly.

a) On 2000 and earlier models, slide the hose clamp up the hose, loosen the

5.7 On 2001 and later models, disconnect the fuel sub-suction hose (arrow)

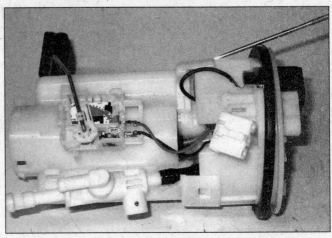

5.8 Disconnect the sending unit connector and the fuel pump connector from the main body

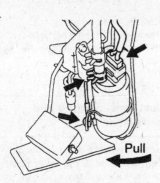

5.9a Pull the lower end of the fuel pump from the bracket (2000 and earlier models)

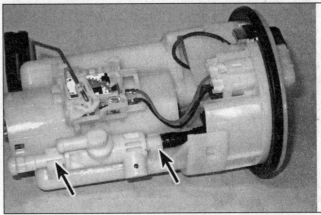

5.9b Disconnect the jet tube from the main body of the fuel pump (arrows) (2001 and later models)

fuel pump clamp and pull the lower end of the fuel pump loose from the bracket **(see illustration).** *Withdraw the pump from the hose.*

b) *On 2001 and later models, disconnect the fuel level sending unit from the fuel suction plate. Remove the fuel filter. Remove the fuel suction plate by prying up on the housing snap-retainers. Disconnect the*

fuel pump electrical connector. Remove the upper bracket by prying on the snap-retainers in the sequence shown and separating the fuel pump from the housing **(see illustrations).**

10 Remove the clip securing the inlet strainer to the pump **(see illustrations).**

11 Remove the strainer and inspect it for contamination. If it is dirty, replace it.

Installation

12 Reassemble the fuel pump/sending unit in the reverse order of disassembly.

13 Install the fuel pump/sending unit assembly in the fuel tank. Connect the fuel line and electrical connector. If equipped with a quick-connect fitting, see Section 4.

14 The remainder of installation is the reverse of removal.

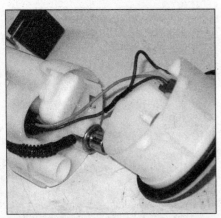

5.9c Disconnect the pump harness from the fuel suction plate and separate the two assemblies (2001 and later models)

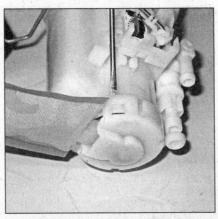

5.10a Pry the fuel suction support and rubber cushion from the fuel pump using a small screwdriver

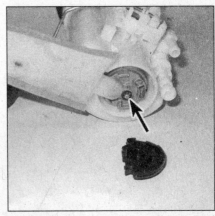

5.10b Remove the clip (arrow) and the strainer from the fuel pump

6.3 Clamp, clip and mounting screw locations (arrows) on 2000 and earlier models

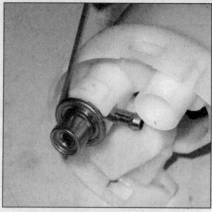

6.8 Carefully pry the fuel pressure regulator from the pump housing (2001 and later models)

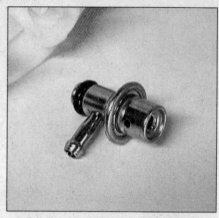

6.9 Be sure to install a new O-ring onto the fuel pressure regulator before installing it back into the fuel pump assembly

6 Fuel pressure regulator - removal and installation

Refer to illustrations 6.3, 6.8 and 6.9
Warning: *Gasoline is extremely flammable, so take extra precautions when you work on any part of the fuel system. See the* **Warning** *in Section 2.*
1   Relieve the fuel system pressure (see Section 2). Disconnect the negative battery cable.
2   Remove the fuel pump/fuel level sending unit from the fuel tank (see Section 5).

2000 and earlier models
3   Remove the clip securing the pressure regulator to the filter, then loosen the hose-to-regulator clamp and detach the hose from the regulator **(see illustration).**
4   Remove the regulator mounting screw and separate the regulator from the assembly.
5   Installation is the reverse of removal. Be sure to install new O-rings.

2001 and later models
6   Remove the fuel suction plate from the fuel pump assembly (see Section 5).
7   Disconnect the fuel return jet tube from

the clamp on the fuel pressure regulator.
8   Separate the fuel pressure regulator from the fuel pump assembly **(see illustration).**
9   Installation is the reverse of removal. Be sure to install a new O-ring **(see illustration)** on the fuel pressure regulator.

7 Fuel level sending unit - replacement

Refer to illustrations 7.1 and 7.4
Warning: *Gasoline is extremely flammable, so take extra precautions when you work on any part of the fuel system. See the* **Warning** *in Section 2.*
Note: *These models are equipped with an additional fuel level sending unit located in the right side of the tank, and can be accessed by removing the right-rear seat.*
1   Remove the fuel pump/fuel level sending unit assembly **(see illustration)** from the fuel tank (see Section 5).
2   Carefully angle the sending unit out of the opening without damaging the fuel level float located at the bottom of the assembly.
3   Disconnect the electrical connectors

from the sending unit.
4   Remove the mounting screws or clips **(see illustration)** and separate the sending unit from the assembly.
5   Installation is the reverse of removal.

8 Fuel tank - removal and installation

Refer to illustrations 8.8, 8.10a and 8.10b
Warning: *Gasoline is extremely flammable, so take extra precautions when you work on any part of the fuel system. See the* **Warning** *in Section 2.*
1   Relieve the fuel system pressure (see Section 2).
2   Remove the fuel filler cap to relieve fuel tank pressure.
3   Detach the cable from the negative terminal of the battery.
4   If the tank is full or nearly full, siphon the fuel into an approved container using a siphoning kit (available at most auto parts stores). **Warning:** *Do not start the siphoning action by mouth!*
5   Raise the vehicle and place it securely

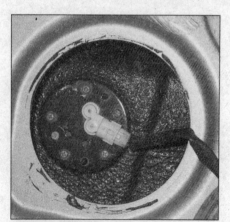

7.1 An additional fuel level sending unit mounted on the opposite side of the tank monitors the fuel level within the other section of the fuel tank

7.4 Location of the fuel level sending unit (arrow)

8.8 Locations of the fuel vapor and fuel return lines (arrows) - be sure to remove the inner fender covers to access the fuel tank components

on jackstands.

6   Remove the exhaust system from the center exhaust pipe, completely to the rear of the vehicle.

7   On 4WD models, remove the driveshaft (see Chapter 8).

8   Disconnect the fuel lines, the vapor return line and the fuel inlet pipe from the fuel tank fittings **(see illustration)**. **Note:** *Be sure to plug the hoses to prevent leakage and contamination of the fuel system.*

9   Support the fuel tank with a floor jack. Place a sturdy plank between the jack head and the fuel tank to protect the tank.

10   Remove the bolts from the fuel tank retaining straps **(see illustrations)**.

11   Lower the tank enough to disconnect the electrical connector from the fuel pump/fuel gauge sending unit.

12   Remove the tank from the vehicle.

13   Installation is the reverse of removal.

8.10a Remove the fuel tank strap mounting bolts (arrows) from the body

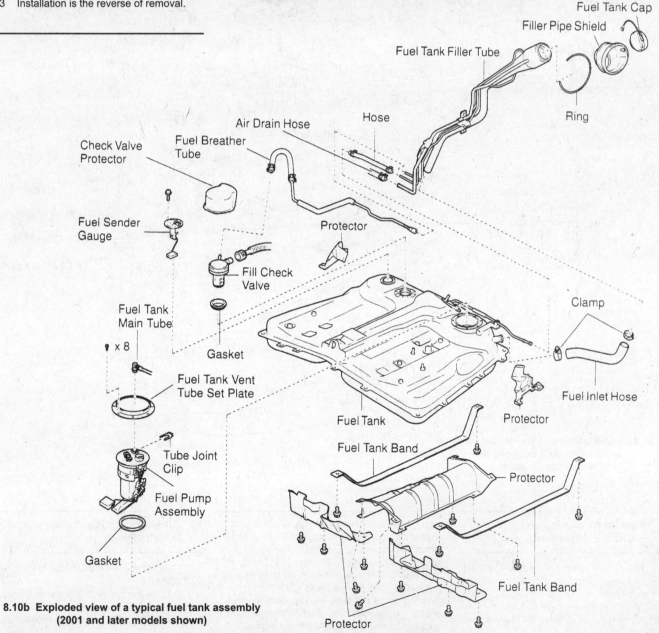

8.10b Exploded view of a typical fuel tank assembly (2001 and later models shown)

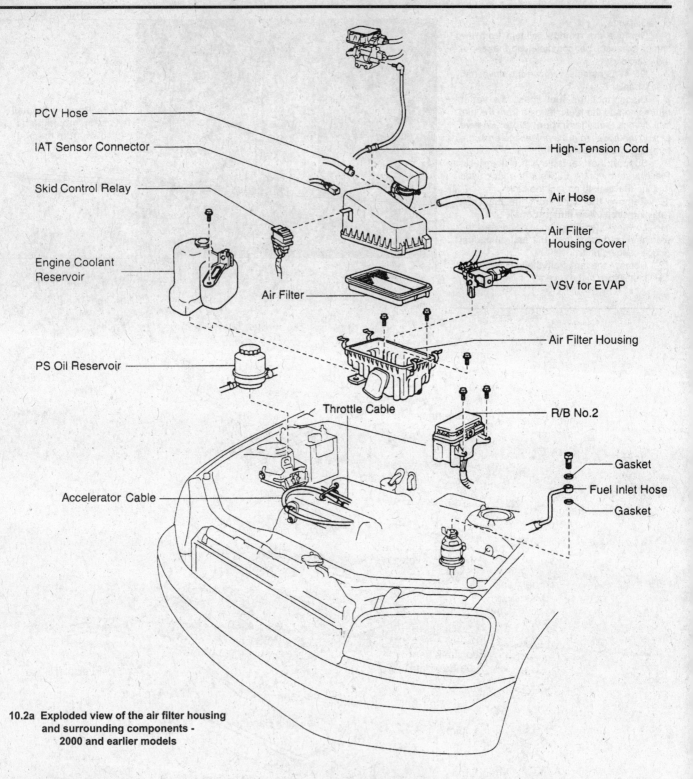

PCV Hose

IAT Sensor Connector

Skid Control Relay

Engine Coolant Reservoir

Air Filter

PS Oil Reservoir

Throttle Cable

Accelerator Cable

High-Tension Cord

Air Hose

Air Filter Housing Cover

VSV for EVAP

Air Filter Housing

R/B No.2

Gasket

Fuel Inlet Hose

Gasket

10.2a Exploded view of the air filter housing and surrounding components - 2000 and earlier models

---

9 Fuel tank cleaning and repair - general information

1   Any repairs to the fuel tank or filler neck should be carried out by a professional who has experience in this critical and potentially dangerous work. Even after cleaning and flushing of the fuel system, explosive fumes can remain and ignite during repair of the tank. **Note:** *Later models are equipped with plastic tanks which can't be repaired.*

2   If the fuel tank is removed from the vehicle, it should not be placed in an area where sparks or open flames could ignite the fumes coming out of the tank. Be especially careful inside garages where a gas-type appliance is located, because it could cause an explosion.

10 Air filter housing - removal and installation

Refer to illustrations 10.2a, 10.2b, 10.3, 10.4, 10.5 and 10.6

1   Detach the clips, lift up the air cleaner cover and remove the filter element (see Chapter 1). On 2000 and earlier models, dis-

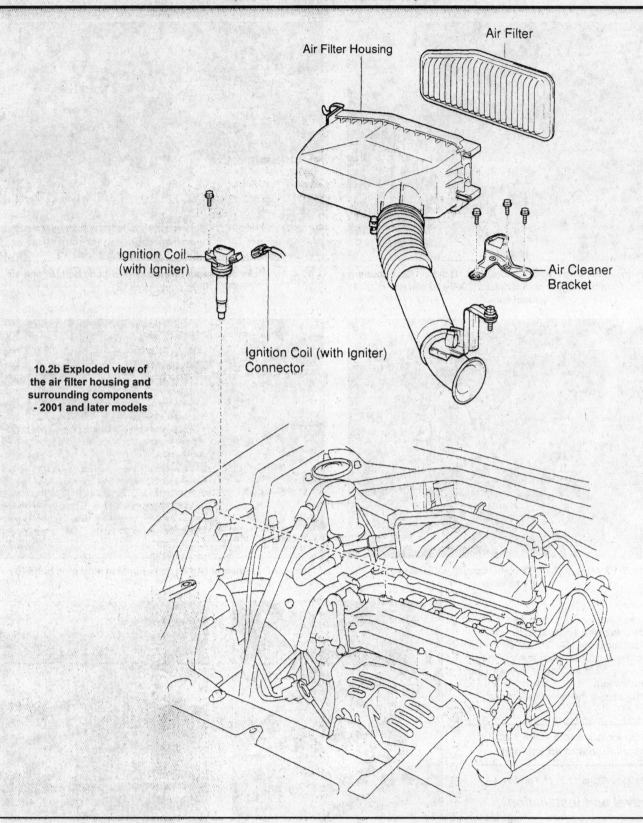

Air Filter Housing

Air Filter

Ignition Coil
(with Igniter)

Ignition Coil (with Igniter)
Connector

Air Cleaner
Bracket

10.2b Exploded view of the air filter housing and surrounding components - 2001 and later models

connect the harness connector from the Skid Control relays on the side of the air filter housing.

2   On 2000 and earlier models, disconnect the air intake hose from the cover **(see illustrations)**.

3   Remove the three bolts and remove the air cleaner assembly from the engine compartment **(see illustration)**.

4   On 2001 and later models, unsnap the two retainer clips and remove the body-to-intake duct mounting bracket bolt **(see illus-

tration)**. Remove the air filter cover and duct as an assembly.

5   Disconnect the EVAP hoses from the VSV **(see illustration)**, unplug the VSV connector, detach the CCV hose from the air filter housing and the PCV hose from the valve

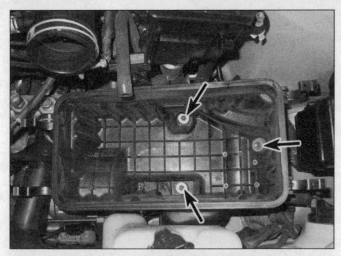

10.3 Remove the three bolts (arrows) and lift the air filter housing from the engine compartment (2000 and earlier model shown)

10.4 Air intake duct mounting bracket-to-body bolt (A) and air filter cover clips (B)

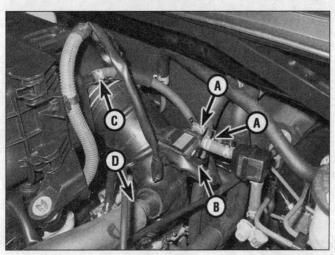

10.5 VSV hoses (A), VSV connector (B), CCV hose (C), PCV hose (D)

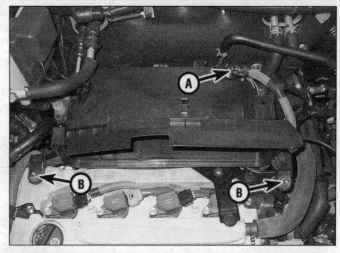

10.6 MAF connector (A); air filter housing mounting bolts (B)

cover (see Chapter 6). Loosen the air intake duct clamp from the throttle body.

6   Disconnect the MAF sensor connector, remove the two bolts, then remove the air filter housing from the engine compartment **(see illustration)**.

7   Installation is the reverse of removal.

---

11   Accelerator cable - removal, installation and adjustment

Refer to illustrations 11.2, 11.3 and 11.4

Removal and installation

1   Detach the cable from the negative terminal of the battery.

2   Loosen the locknut on the threaded portion of the accelerator cable at the throttle body **(see illustration)**.

3   Rotate the throttle lever, then slip the accelerator cable end out of the slot in the lever **(see illustration)**.

11.2 Loosen the locknuts on the accelerator cable using two wrenches

4   Detach the accelerator cable from the accelerator pedal **(see illustration)**.

5   Pull the cable and casing out of the firewall into the engine compartment.

11.3 Rotate the throttle lever and remove the cable end from the slot using needle-nose pliers

6   Installation is the reverse of removal. Make sure the cable grommet seats completely in the firewall.

11.4 Pull the cable end (arrow) away from the accelerator pedal arm, then pass the cable through the slot in the arm

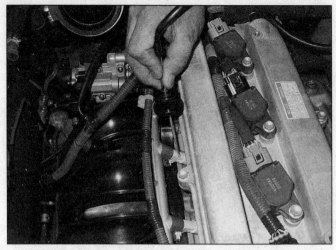

13.7 Use a stethoscope or a screwdriver to determine if the injectors are working properly - they should make a steady clicking sound that rises and falls with engine speed changes

Adjustment

7   To adjust the cable:

a)   *Lift up on the cable to remove any slack.*

b)   *Turn the adjusting nut until it is 1/8-inch (3 mm) away from the cable bracket.*

c)   *Tighten the locknut and check cable deflection between the throttle lever and the cable casing. Deflection should be 3/8 to 1/2-inch. If deflection is not within specifications, loosen the locknut and turn the adjusting nut until the deflection is as specified.*

d)   *After you have adjusted the accelerator cable, have an assistant help you verify that the throttle valve opens all the way when you depress the accelerator pedal to the floor and that it returns to the idle position when you release the accelerator. Verify the cable operates smoothly. It must not bind or stick.*

12   Electronic fuel injection system - general information

The Electronic Fuel Injection (EFI) system consists of three sub-systems: air intake, electronic control and fuel delivery. The system uses a Powertrain Control Module (PCM) along with several sensors to determine the proper air/fuel ratio under all operating conditions. **Refer to illustrations 1.1a and 1.1b** for component locations.

The fuel injection system and the emissions control system are closely linked in function and design. For additional information, refer to Chapter 6.

Air intake system

The air intake system consists of the air cleaner, the air intake ducts, the throttle body, the idle control system and the intake manifold. 2000 and earlier models are equipped with an intake manifold and plenum as one component. 2001 and later models

are equipped with a special designed intake manifold with intake manifold tuning. Refer to Chapters 2A or 2B for the manifold replacement procedures.

The throttle body is a single barrel, side-draft design. The lower portion of the throttle body is heated by engine coolant to prevent icing in cold weather. The idle adjusting screw is located on top of the throttle body. A throttle position sensor is attached to the throttle shaft to monitor changes in the throttle opening.

When the engine is idling, the air/fuel ratio is controlled by the idle air control system, which consists of the Powertrain Control Module (PCM), the Idle Air Control (IAC) valve and the various other sensors (ECT, IAT, TPS, MAP, MAF etc.) working in conjunction with the EFI system. The IAC valve is activated by the PCM depending upon the running conditions of the engine (air conditioning on, power steering demand, cold or warm temperature etc.). This valve regulates the amount of airflow bypassing the throttle plate and into the intake manifold. The PCM receives information from the sensors and adjusts the idle according to the demands of the engine and driver. Finally, to prevent rough running after the engine starts, the starting valve is opened during cranking and immediately after starting to provide additional air into the intake manifold.

Electronic control system

The electronic control system, Powertrain Control Module and sensors are described in Chapter 6.

Fuel delivery system

The fuel delivery system consists of these components: The fuel pump, fuel pressure regulator, fuel filter, fuel lines, fuel rail and the fuel injectors. 2000 and earlier models are equipped with a fuel filter mounted on the left strut tower in the engine compartment, with an additional fuel filter mounted in the fuel pump assembly in the tank. 2001 and

later models are equipped with one fuel filter mounted in the fuel pump assembly.

The fuel pump is an electric in-line type. Fuel is drawn through an inlet strainer into the pump, flows through the fuel pressure regulator, passes through the fuel filter and is delivered to the injectors. The fuel pressure regulator maintains a constant fuel pressure to the injectors.

The injectors are solenoid-actuated, constant stroke, pintle types consisting of a solenoid, plunger, needle valve and housing. When current is applied to the solenoid coil, the needle valve raises and pressurized fuel fills the injector housing and squirts out the nozzle. The injection quantity is determined by the length of time the valve is open (the length of time during which current is supplied to the solenoid coils). Because it determines opening and closing intervals - which in turn determines the air-fuel mixture ratio - injector timing must be quite accurate.

The EFI main relay, located in the engine compartment relay/fuse box, supplies power to the fuel pump relay (circuit opening relay) from the ignition key. The PCM controls the grounding signal to the fuel pump in response to the starting and camshaft position signals at start-up.

13   Electronic fuel injection system - check

Refer to illustrations 13.7 and 13.8
Warning: *Gasoline is extremely flammable, so take extra precautions when you work on any part of the fuel system. See the* **Warning** *in Section 2.*

1   Check all electrical connectors, especially ground connections, for the system. Loose connectors and poor grounds can cause many engine control system problems.

2   Verify that the battery is fully charged because the Powertrain Control Module (PCM) and sensors cannot operate properly

13.8 Using an ohmmeter, measure the resistance across both terminals of the injector

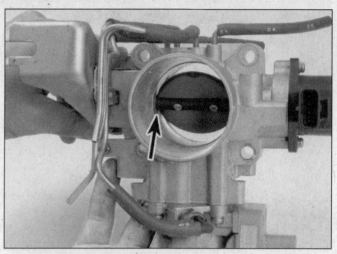

14.2a The area inside the throttle body near the throttle plate (arrow) suffers from sludge build-up because the PCV hose vents vapor from the crankcase here

without adequate supply voltage.

3   Refer to Chapter 1 and check the air filter element. A dirty or partially blocked filter will reduce performance and economy.

4   Check fuel pump operation (Section 3). If the fuel pump fuse is blown, replace it and see if it blows again. If it does, refer to Chapter 12 and the wiring diagrams and look for a short in the wiring harness to the fuel pump.

5   Inspect the vacuum hoses connected to the intake manifold for damage, deterioration and leakage.

6   Remove the air intake duct from the throttle body and check for dirt, carbon, varnish, or other residue in the throttle body, particularly around the throttle plate. If it's dirty, refer to Chapter 6 and troubleshoot the PCV and EGR systems for the cause of excessive varnish/carbon buildup.

7   With the engine running, place an automotive stethoscope against each injector, one at a time, and listen for a clicking sound,

indicating operation **(see illustration)**. If you don't have a stethoscope, place the tip of a screwdriver against the injector and listen through the handle. If you hear the injectors operating but there is a misfire condition present, the electrical circuits are functioning, but the injectors may be dirty or fouled from carbon deposits - commercial cleaning products may help, or the injectors may require replacement.

8   If you can't hear an injector operating, disconnect the injector electrical connector and measure the resistance of the injector **(see illustration)**. Compare the measurement with the resistance value listed in this Chapter's Specifications. Replace any injector whose resistance value does not fall within specifications.

9   If the injector wasn't operating but the resistance reading was within specifications, the PCM or the circuit to the injector may be faulty.

14   Throttle body - check, removal and installation

Warning: *Gasoline is extremely flammable, so take extra precautions when you work on any part of the fuel system. See the* **Warning** *in Section 2.*

Check

Refer to illustrations 14.2a and 14.2b

1   Verify that the throttle linkage operates smoothly.

2   Remove the air intake duct from the throttle body and check for carbon and residue build-up. If it is dirty, clean it with aerosol carburetor cleaner and a tooth brush. Make sure the can specifically states that it is safe with oxygen sensor systems and catalytic converters **(see illustrations)**. **Caution:** *Do not clean the throttle position sensor (TPS) or Idle Air Control (IAC) valve with the solvent.*

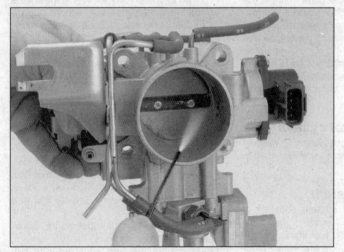

14.2b With the engine off, use aerosol carburetor cleaner (make sure it is safe for use with catalytic converters and oxygen sensors), a toothbrush and a rag to clean the throttle body - open the throttle plate so you can clean behind it

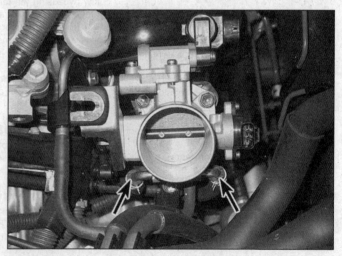

14.7 Remove the coolant hoses from the base of the throttle body (arrows)

14.9a Location of the throttle body mounting bolts (arrows) on 2000 and earlier models (fourth bolt hidden from view)

14.9b Location of the throttle body mounting bolts (arrows) on 2001 through 2003 models

Removal and installation

2003 and earlier models

Refer to illustrations 14.7, 14.9a and 14.9b

Warning: *Wait until the engine is completely cool before beginning this procedure.*

3   Detach the cable from the negative terminal of the battery.

4   Loosen the hose clamps and remove the air intake duct.

5   Detach the accelerator cable from the throttle lever (see Section 11).

6   If you are working on a 2000 or earlier model with an automatic transmission, detach the throttle valve (TV) cable from the throttle lever (see Chapter 7B).

7   Clearly label, then detach, all vacuum and coolant hoses from the throttle body **(see illustration)**. Plug the coolant hoses to prevent coolant leakage.

8   Disconnect the electrical connector from the Throttle Position Sensor (TPS).

9   Remove the throttle body mounting nuts/bolts **(see illustrations)**.

10   Detach the throttle body and gasket from the intake manifold.

11   Installation of the throttle body is the reverse of removal. Be sure to use a new gasket between the throttle body and the intake manifold.

12   Be sure to tighten the throttle body mounting nuts/bolts to the torque listed in this Chapter's Specifications.

13   Check the coolant level and add some, if necessary, to bring it to the appropriate level (see Chapter 1).

2004 and later models

Refer to illustration 14.19 and 14.21

Warning: *Wait until the engine is completely cool before beginning this procedure.*

14   Disconnect the cable from the negative battery terminal (see Chapter 5, Section 1).

15   Remove the strut brace (see Chapter 10).

16   Remove the intake duct and air filter cover.

17   Remove the air filter housing with the MAF sensor and bracket (see Section 10).

18   Clamp off the coolant hoses to the throttle body to minimize coolant loss.

19   Disconnect the electrical connecter from the throttle body and disengage the electrical harness from the clip on the fuel pipe bracket **(see illustration)**.

20   Disengage the fuel hose from the fuel pipe bracket, then clearly label and disconnect the vacuum and coolant hoses from the throttle body. Plug the coolant hoses to prevent coolant leakage.

21   Remove the throttle body mounting bolts **(see illustration)** and remove the throttle body.

22   Remove and discard the old throttle body gasket.

23   Installation is the reverse of removal. Be sure to use a new gasket and tighten the throttle body mounting bolts to the torque listed in this Chapter's Specifications. Check the coolant level, adding as necessary (see Chapter 1).

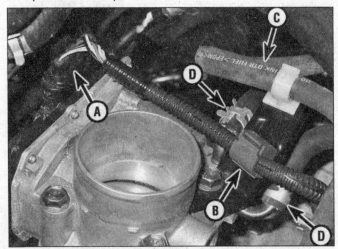

14.19 Before detaching the throttle body, disconnect the electrical connector (A), disconnect the electrical harness from this clip (B), disengage the fuel hose (C) from the clip on the fuel pipe bracket and detach both coolant hoses (D)

14.21 To detach the throttle body from the intake manifold, remove these mounting bolts

15   Fuel pulsation damper (2001 and later models) - replacement

Refer to illustration 15.6

Warning: *Gasoline is extremely flammable, so take extra precautions when you work on any part of the fuel system. See the* **Warning** *in Section 2.*

1   Relieve the fuel system pressure (see Section 2).

2   Disconnect the negative battery cable.

3   Remove the air filter housing (see Section 10).

4   Remove the accelerator cable from the throttle valve (see Section 11).

5   Remove the fuel tube clamp from the fuel line and disconnect the line using a special tool (see Section 4).

6   Remove the mounting bolts from the fuel pulsation damper **(see illustration)**.

7   Separate the fuel pulsation damper from the fuel rail.

8   Installation is the reverse of removal. Be sure to install a new o-ring onto the fuel pulsation damper. Tighten the bolts to the torque listed in this Chapter's Specifications.

16   Fuel rail and injectors - removal and installation

Warning: *Gasoline is extremely flammable, so take extra precautions when you work on any part of the fuel system. See the* **Warning** *in Section 2.*

Removal

1   Relieve the fuel pressure (see Section 2).

2   Detach the cable from the negative terminal of the battery.

2000 and earlier models

Refer to illustrations 16.5, 16.10, 16.11, 16.12 and 16.13

3   Remove the valve cover (see Chapter 2A).

4   Remove the throttle body (see Section 14).

5   Remove the two clamps and disconnect the wiring harness from the intake manifold **(see illustration)**. Disconnect the four injector connectors from the injectors.

15.6 Location of the fuel pulsation damper mounting bolts (arrow) (other bolt hidden from view)

6   Remove the engine wire protector from the right side of the intake manifold.

7   Remove the EGR valve and the EGR pipe (see Chapter 6).

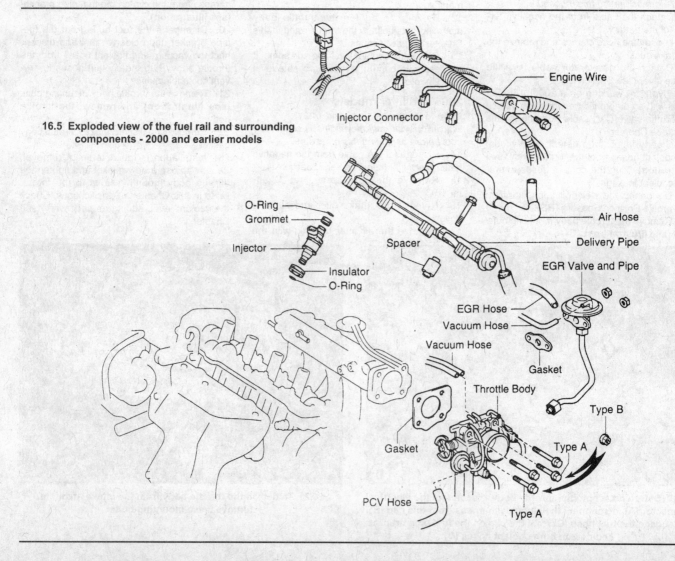

16.5 Exploded view of the fuel rail and surrounding components - 2000 and earlier models

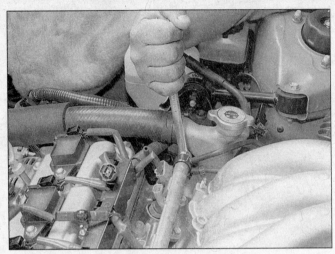

16.10 Disconnect the fuel lines from the fuel rail

16.11 Remove the fuel rail mounting bolts (arrows)

8   Remove the top fitting on the fuel filter (see Chapter 1) and separate the fuel line from the fuel filter.

9   Disconnect the brake booster vacuum hose at the intake manifold.

10   Disconnect the fuel lines from the fuel rail (see illustration).

11   Remove the fuel rail bolts (see illustration) and separate the fuel rail from the fuel injectors.

12   Remove the fuel injector(s) from the fuel rail (see illustration) and set them aside in a clearly labeled storage container.

13   If you intend to re-use the same injectors, replace the grommets and O-rings (see illustration).

2001 and later models

Refer to illustrations 16.16a, 16.16b, 16.17 and 16.19

14   Remove the air filter housing (see Section 10).

15   Disconnect the PCV hose (see Chapter 6).

16   Disconnect the fuel lines from the fuel rail (see illustrations).

17   Remove the fuel rail mounting bolts (see illustration).

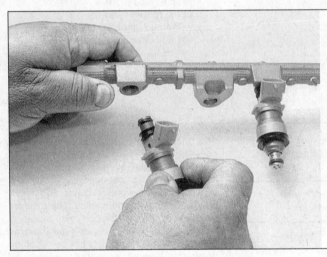

16.12 Simultaneously twist and pull the injector to remove it from the fuel rail

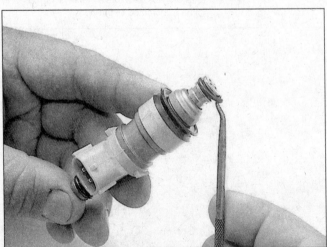

16.13 If you plan to reinstall the original injectors, remove and discard the O-rings and grommets and replace them with new ones

16.16a Disconnect the harness clamps from the intake manifold

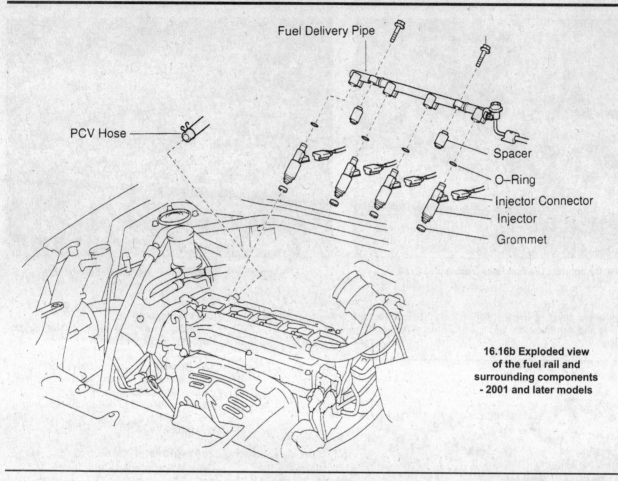

Fuel Delivery Pipe

PCV Hose

Spacer
O-Ring
Injector Connector
Injector
Grommet

16.16b Exploded view of the fuel rail and surrounding components - 2001 and later models

18   Remove the fuel rail with the fuel injectors attached.
19   Remove the fuel injector(s) from the fuel rail (see illustration) and set them aside in a clearly labeled storage container.
20   If you intend to re-use the same injectors, replace the grommets and O-rings.

Installation
21   Installation of the fuel injectors is the reverse of removal.

22   Tighten the fuel rail mounting bolts to the torque listed in this Chapter's Specifications.

17   Exhaust system servicing - general information

Refer to illustrations 17.1a, 17.1b and 17.4
Warning: *Inspection and repair of exhaust system components should be done only*

after the system components have cooled completely.
1   The exhaust system consists of the exhaust manifold, catalytic converter, the muffler, the tailpipe and all connecting pipes, brackets, hangers and clamps. The exhaust system is attached to the body with mounting brackets and rubber hangers (see illustrations). If any of these parts are damaged or deteriorated, excessive noise and vibration will be transmitted to the body.

16.17 Remove the fuel rail mounting bolts (arrows)

16.19 Be sure to install new O-rings on the injectors and the fuel pressure regulator

17.1a The exhaust pipe and the catalytic converter is fastened to the underbody using rubber hangers (arrows)

17.1b Inspect the exhaust system hangers (arrows) for cracks

2   Conducting regular inspections of the exhaust system will keep it safe and quiet. Look for any damaged or bent parts, open seams, holes, loose connections, excessive corrosion or other defects which could allow exhaust fumes to enter the vehicle. Deteriorated exhaust system components should not be repaired - they should be replaced with new parts.

3   If the exhaust system components are extremely corroded or rusted together, they will probably have to be cut from the exhaust system. The convenient way to accomplish this is to have a muffler repair shop remove the corroded sections with a cutting torch. If, however, you want to save money by doing it yourself and you don't have an oxy/acetylene welding outfit with a cutting torch, simply cut off the old components with a hack-saw. If you have compressed air, special pneumatic cutting chisels can also be used. If you do decide to tackle the job at home, be sure to wear eye protection to protect your eyes from metal chips and work gloves to protect your hands.

4   Here are some simple guidelines to apply when repairing the exhaust system:

a) *Work from the back to the front when removing exhaust system components.*

b) *Apply penetrating oil to the exhaust system component fasteners to make them easier to remove* **(see illustration)**.

c) *Use new gaskets, hangers and clamps when installing exhaust system components.*

d) *Apply anti-seize compound to the threads of all exhaust system fasteners during reassembly. Be sure to allow sufficient clearance between newly installed parts and all points on the underbody to avoid overheating the floor pan and pos-*

sibly damaging the interior carpet and insulation. Pay particularly close attention to the catalytic converter and its heat shield. **Warning:** *The catalytic converter operates at very high temperatures and takes a long time to cool. Wait until it's completely cool before attempting to remove the converter. Failure to do so could result in serious burns.*

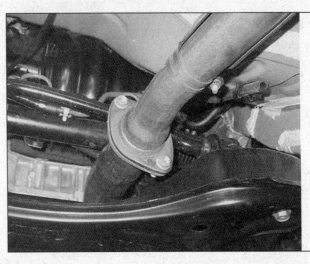

17.4 Lubricate the exhaust system fasteners with penetrating oil before attempting to loosen them

Notes

Chapter 5
Engine electrical systems

Contents

	Section
Alternator - removal and installation	12
Battery cables - replacement	4
Battery - check and replacement	3
Battery check, maintenance and charging	See Chapter 1
Battery - emergency jump starting	2
Charging system - check	11
Charging system - general information and precautions	10
CHECK ENGINE light	See Chapter 6
Distributor (1996 and 1997 models) - removal and installation	9
Drivebelt check, adjustment and replacement	See Chapter 1

	Section
General information, precautions and battery disconnection	1
Igniter (1996 and 1997 models) - replacement	8
Ignition coil(s) - check and replacement	7
Ignition system - check	6
Ignition system - general information and precautions	5
Spark plug replacement	See Chapter 1
Spark plug wire check and replacement	See Chapter 1
Starter motor and circuit - check	14
Starter motor - removal and installation	15
Starting system - general information and precautions	13

Specifications

Ignition coil

1996 and 1997 models
Primary resistance	0.35 to 0.55 ohms
Secondary resistance	
Cold	9.0 to 15.4 k-ohms
Hot	11.4 to 18.1 k-ohms

1998 through 2000 models
Primary resistance	not available
Secondary resistance	
Cold	9.7 to 16.7 k-ohms
Hot	12.4 to 19.6 k-ohms
2001 and later	not available

Charging system

Charging voltage	13.5 to 15.0 volts
Standard amperage	
No load	10 amps or less
With load	30 amps or more

1 General information, precautions and battery disconnection

Refer to illustrations 1.1a and 1.1b

The engine electrical systems include all ignition, charging and starting components **(see Illustrations)**. Because of their engine-related functions, these components are discussed separately from body electrical devices such as the lights, the instruments, etc. (which are included in Chapter 12).

Precautions

Always observe the following precautions when working on the electrical system:

a) *Be extremely careful when servicing engine electrical components. They are easily damaged if checked, connected or handled improperly.*

b) *Never leave the ignition switched on for long periods of time when the engine is not running.*

c) *Never disconnect the battery cables while the engine is running.*

d) *Maintain correct polarity when connecting battery cables from another vehicle during jump starting - see the "Booster battery (jump) starting" section at the front of this manual.*

1.1a Charging and ignition system components - 1996 and 1997 models

1	Battery	3	Ignition coil	5	Spark plug wires
2	Igniter	4	Distributor	6	Alternator

1.1b Charging and ignition system components - 2001 and later models

1	Battery (under cowl cover)	3	Relay and fuse box	5	Alternator
2	Igniter/coil/spark plug assembly	4	Starter		

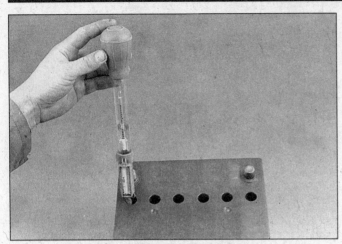

3.1a Use a battery hydrometer to draw electrolyte from the battery cell - this hydrometer is equipped with a thermometer to make temperature corrections

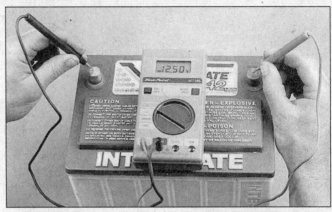

3.1b To test the open circuit voltage of the battery, connect the black probe of the voltmeter to the negative terminal and the red probe to the positive terminal of the battery - a fully charged battery should indicate approximately 12.5 volts depending on the outside air temperature

e) *Always disconnect the negative battery cable from the battery before working on the electrical system, but read the following battery disconnection procedure first.*

It's also a good idea to review the safety-related information regarding the engine electrical systems located in the *"Safety first!"* section at the front of this manual, before beginning any operation included in this Chapter.

Battery disconnection

Several systems on the vehicle require battery power to be available at all times, either to ensure their continued operation (such as the radio, alarm system, power door locks, windows, etc.) or to maintain control unit memories (such as that in the engine management system's Engine Control Module [ECM]) which would be lost if the battery were to be disconnected. Therefore, whenever the battery is to be disconnected, first note the following to ensure that there are no unforeseen consequences of this action:

a) *The engine management system's ECM will lose the information stored in its memory when the battery is disconnected. This includes idling and operating values, any fault codes detected and system monitors required for emissions testing. Whenever the battery is disconnected, the computer will require a certain period of time to "re-learn" the operating values (see Chapter 6).*

b) *On any vehicle with power door locks, it is a wise precaution to remove the key from the ignition and to keep it with you, so that it does not get locked inside if the power door locks should engage accidentally when the battery is reconnected!*

Devices known as "memory-savers" can be used to avoid some of the above problems. Precise details vary according to the device used. Typically, it is plugged into the cigarette lighter and is connected by its own wires to a spare battery; the vehicle's own battery is then disconnected from the electrical system,

leaving the "memory-saver" to pass sufficient current to maintain audio unit security codes and ECM memory values, and also to run permanently live circuits such as the clock and radio memory, all the while isolating the battery in the event of a short-circuit occurring while work is carried out.

Warning 1: *Some of these devices allow a considerable amount of current to pass, which can mean that many of the vehicle's systems are still operational when the main battery is disconnected. If a "memory-saver" is used, ensure that the circuit concerned is actually "dead" before carrying out any work on it!*

Warning 2: *If work is to be performed around any of the airbag system components, the battery must be disconnected. If a memory-saver device is used, power will be supplied to the airbag and personal injury may result if the airbag is accidentally deployed.*

The battery on these vehicles is located in the corner of the engine compartment (see Section 3). If you're working on a 2001 or later model, remove the cowl cover for access (see Chapter 11). To disconnect the battery for service procedures requiring power to be cut from the vehicle, peel back the insulator (if equipped), loosen the negative cable clamp nut and detach the negative cable from the negative battery post (see Section 3). Isolate the cable end to prevent it from accidentally coming into contact with the battery post.

2 Battery - emergency jump starting

Refer to the *Booster battery (jump) starting* procedure at the front of this manual.

3 Battery - check and replacement

Warning: *Hydrogen gas is produced by the battery, so keep open flames and lighted cigarettes away from it at all times. Always wear*

eye protection when working around a battery. Rinse off spilled electrolyte immediately with large amounts of water.

Check

Refer to illustrations 3.1a, 3.1b and 3.1c

1 A battery cannot be accurately tested until it is at or near a fully charged state. Disconnect the negative battery cable from the battery and perform the following tests:

a) **Battery state of charge test** - *Visually inspect the indicator eye (if equipped) on the top of the battery. If the indicator eye is dark in color, charge the battery as described in Chapter 1. If the battery is equipped with removable caps, check the battery electrolyte. The electrolyte level should be above the upper edge of the plates. If the level is low, add distilled water. DO NOT OVERFILL. The excess electrolyte may spill over during periods of heavy charging. Test the specific gravity of the electrolyte using a hydrometer* **(see illustration).** *Remove the caps and extract a sample of the electrolyte and observe the float inside the barrel of the hydrometer. Follow the instructions from the tool manufacturer and determine the specific gravity of the electrolyte for each cell. A fully charged battery will indicate approximately 1.270 (green zone) at 68-degrees F (20-degrees C). If the specific gravity of the electrolyte is low (red zone), charge the battery as described in Chapter 1.*

b) **Open circuit voltage test** - *Using a digital voltmeter, perform an open circuit voltage test* **(see illustration).** *Connect the negative probe of the voltmeter to the negative battery post and the positive probe to the positive battery post. The battery voltage should be greater than 12.5 volts. If the battery is less than the specified voltage, charge the battery before proceeding to the next test. Do not proceed with the battery load test until the battery is fully charged.*

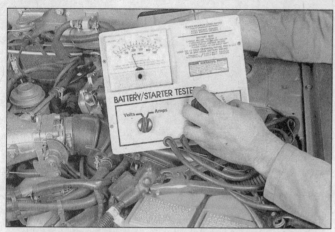

3.1c Some battery load testers are equipped with an ammeter which enables the battery load to be precisely dialed in, as shown - less expensive testers have a load switch and a voltmeter only

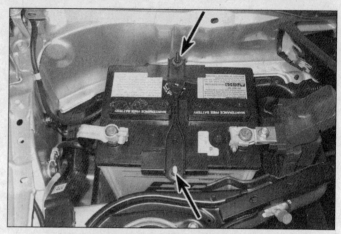

3.4 Remove the two nuts (arrows) and detach the hold-down clamps

c) **Battery load test** - *An accurate check of the battery condition can only be performed with a load tester (available at most auto parts stores). This test evaluates the ability of the battery to operate the starter and other accessories during periods of heavy amperage draw (load). Connect a battery load testing tool to the battery terminals* **(see illustration)**. *Load test the battery according to the tool manufacturer's instructions. Maintain the load on the battery for 15 seconds and observe that the battery voltage does not drop below 9.6 volts. If the battery condition is weak or defective, the tool will indicate this condition immediately.* **Note:** *Cold temperatures will cause the voltage reading to drop slightly. Follow the chart given in the tool manufacturer's instructions to compensate for cold climates. Minimum load voltage for freezing temperatures (32 degrees F/0-degrees C) should be approximately 9.1 volts.*

d) **Battery drain test** - *This test will indicate whether there's a constant drain on the vehicle's electrical system that can cause the battery to discharge. Make sure all accessories are turned Off. If the vehicle has an underhood light, verify it's working properly, then disconnect it. Connect one lead of a digital ammeter to the disconnected negative battery cable clamp and the other lead to the negative battery post. A drain of approximately 100 milliamps or less is considered normal (due to the engine control computer clocks, digital radios and other components which normally cause a key-off battery drain). An excessive drain (approximately 500 milliamps or more) will cause the battery to discharge. The problem circuit or component can be located by removing the fuses, one at a time, until the excessive drain stops and normal drain is indicated on the meter.*

Replacement

Refer to illustration 3.4

Caution: *Always disconnect the negative cable first and hook it up last or the battery may be shorted by the tool being used to loosen the cable clamps.*

Note: *If you're working on a 2001 or later model, remove the cowl cover for access (see Chapter 11).*

2   Loosen the cable clamp nut and remove the negative battery cable from the negative battery post. Isolate the cable end to prevent it from accidentally coming into contact with the battery post.

3   Loosen the cable clamp nut and remove the positive battery cable from the positive battery post.

4   Remove the battery hold-down clamp **(see illustration)**.

5   Lift out the battery. Be careful - it's heavy. **Note:** *Battery straps and handlers are available at most auto parts stores for a reasonable price. They make it easier to remove and carry the battery.*

6   While the battery is out, inspect the battery tray for corrosion. If corrosion exists, clean the deposits with a mixture of baking soda and water to prevent further corrosion.

4.4a The negative battery cable is attached to the chassis (arrow) as well as the engine to ensure a proper ground

Flush the area with plenty of clean water and dry thoroughly.

7   If you are replacing the battery, make sure you replace it with a battery with the identical dimensions, amperage rating, cold cranking rating, etc.

8   When installing the battery, make sure the center notch in the battery foot is aligned with the hold-down clamp hole in the battery tray. Install the hold-down clamp and tighten the bolt to the torque listed in this Chapter's Specifications. Do not over-tighten the bolt.

9   The remainder of installation is the reverse of removal.

4   Battery cables - replacement

Refer to illustrations 4.4a, 4.4b and 4.4c

1   Periodically inspect the entire length of each battery cable for damage, cracked or burned insulation and corrosion. Poor battery cable connections can cause starting problems and decreased engine performance.

2   Check the cable-to-terminal connections at the ends of the cables for cracks, loose wire strands and corrosion. The presence of white, fluffy deposits under the insulation at the cable terminal connection is a sign that the cable is corroded and should be replaced. Check the terminals for distortion, missing mounting bolts and corrosion.

3   When removing the cables, always disconnect the negative cable from the negative battery post first and hook it up last or the battery may be shorted by the tool used to loosen the cable clamps. Even if only the positive cable is being replaced, be sure to disconnect the negative cable from the negative battery post first (see Chapter 1 for further information regarding battery cable maintenance).

4   Disconnect the old cables from the battery, then disconnect them from the opposite end. Detach the cables from the starter solenoid, underhood fuse box and ground terminals, as necessary **(see illustrations)**. Note

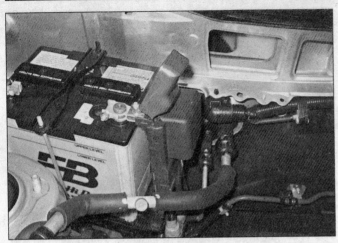

4.4b Note the routing of the positive cable and replace it as originally installed

4.4c Disconnect the positive battery cable from the starter

the routing of each cable to ensure correct installation.

5   If you are replacing either or both of the battery cables, take them with you when buying new cables. It is vitally important that you replace the cables with identical parts. Cables have characteristics that make them easy to identify: Positive cables are usually red and larger in cross-section; ground cables are usually black and smaller in cross-section.

6   Clean the threads of the starter solenoid or ground connection with a wire brush to remove rust and corrosion. Apply a light coat of battery terminal corrosion inhibitor or petroleum jelly to the threads to prevent future corrosion.

7   Attach the cable to the terminal and tighten the mounting nut/bolt securely.

8   Before connecting a new cable to the battery, make sure that it reaches the battery post without having to be stretched.

9   After installing the cables, connect the negative cable to the negative battery post.

5   Ignition system - general information and precautions

Conventional electronic ignition system (1996 and 1997 models)

1   1996 and 1997 models are equipped with a conventional electronic ignition system. This system includes the ignition switch, the battery, the pick-up coil (distributor), the ignition coil, the igniter (module), the crankshaft position sensor, the spark plugs and the primary (low voltage) and secondary (high voltage) wiring circuits.

2   The Electronic Control Module (ECM) controls the ignition timing using the data provided by the information sensors which monitors various engine functions (such as rpm, intake air volume, engine temperature, etc.). The ECM ensures perfect spark timing under all operating conditions. The igniter is

a separate component from the distributor and is mounted on the right side of the engine compartment.

3   This electronic ignition system incorporates the pick-up coil inside the distributor, the external coil mounted near the distributor on the intake manifold and the igniter mounted in the engine compartment for cooling purposes.

Distributorless Ignition System (DIS) (1998 and later models)

4   1998 and later models are equipped with a Distributorless Ignition System (DIS). There are two different versions of the DIS on these models. 1998 through 2000 models incorporate the igniter with the coil packs as a single assembly. The ignition coil/igniter assembly is mounted on the intake manifold on a large bracket. 2001 and later models use a separate coil/igniter assembly for each cylinder, mounted directly over each spark plug. There are no secondary ignition wires with this system.

DIS with a coil/igniter assembly (1998 through 2000 models)

5   1998 through 2000 models are equipped with an early version of DIS. The DIS system includes the camshaft position sensor, the crankshaft position sensor, coils (one coil for a pair of cylinders), the igniter and the PCM (computer). The coil and igniter are built into one unit and mounted near the front of the engine. The camshaft and crankshaft sensors send cylinder identification signals to the PCM, which causes the igniter to trigger the correct coil. The igniter distributes the signal to the proper coil driver circuit and determines dwell period based on coil primary current flow. This DIS system uses a "waste spark" method of spark distribution. Each cylinder is paired with its companion cylinder in the firing order, 1-4, 3-2; the cylinder under compression fires simultaneously with its companion cylinder, which is on the exhaust stroke. Since

the cylinder on the exhaust stroke requires very little of the available voltage to fire its spark plug, most of the voltage is used to fire the plug of the cylinder on the compression stroke.

6   The coil/igniter assembly is mounted onto a bracket on the intake manifold. Secondary ignition wires run to each spark plug from the coil packs.

DIS with coil/igniter/spark plug assemblies (2001 and later models)

7   2001 and later models are equipped with the latest version of DIS. This DIS system includes the camshaft position sensor, the crankshaft position sensor, a coil/igniter/spark plug assembly for each cylinder and the PCM (computer). The coil and igniter are built into one unit and mounted over each cylinder's spark plug. The camshaft and crankshaft sensors generate cylinder identification signals which allow the PCM to trigger the correct igniter/coil assembly. The igniter distributes the signal to the coil driver circuit and determines dwell period based on coil primary current flow. The spark is direct (cylinder specific) and sequenced to the engine's firing order. There is no "waste spark" effect with this system.

All models

8   When working on the ignition system, take the following precautions:

a) *Do not keep the ignition switch on for more than 10 seconds if the engine will not start.*

b) *Always connect a tachometer in accordance with the manufacturer's instructions. Some tachometers may be incompatible with this ignition system. Consult an auto parts counterperson before buying a tachometer for use with this vehicle.*

c) *Never allow the ignition coil terminals to touch ground. Grounding the coil could result in damage to the igniter and/or the ignition coil.*

d) *Do not disconnect the battery when the engine is running.*

6.1a On 2001 and later models, first remove the front half of the air filter housing for access to the coil/igniter assemblies, then remove a mounting bolt and lift one of the units from the cylinder head

6.1b Next, install a calibrated ignition tester - simply connect it to the coil/igniter assembly, clip the tester to a convenient ground and operate the starter with the ignition ON – if there is enough power to fire the plug, sparks will be visible between the electrode tip and the tester body

6   Ignition system - check

Refer to illustrations 6.1a and 6.1b

Warning: *Because of the high voltage generated by the ignition system, extreme care should be taken whenever an operation is performed involving ignition components. This not only includes the igniter, coil and spark plug wires, but related components such as plug connectors, tachometer and other test equipment as well.*

1   If the engine turns over but won't start, disconnect the spark plug wire from any spark plug and attach it to a calibrated ignition tester (available at most auto parts stores) **(see illustrations).**

2   Connect the clip on the tester to a bolt or metal bracket on the engine.

3   Relieve the fuel pressure (see Chapter 4). Keep the fuel system disabled while performing the ignition system checks.

4   Crank the engine and watch the end of the tester to see if bright blue, well-defined sparks occur.

5   If sparks occur, sufficient voltage is reaching the spark plug to fire it (repeat the

check at the remaining spark plug wires to verify that all the ignition coils are functioning). However, the plugs themselves may be fouled, so remove and check them as described in Chapter 1 or install new ones.

6   If no sparks or intermittent sparks occur, check for battery voltage to the ignition coils. Refer to the wiring diagrams at the end of Chapter 12. If battery voltage is present, check the coil resistance (see Section 7).

7   Also, if no sparks or intermittent sparks occur, check the ignition wires to each spark plug (see Chapter 1).

8   If the checks are all correct, there may be a defective pick-up coil (1996 and 1997 models), camshaft position sensor (1998 and later models) and/or crankshaft position sensor.

7   Ignition coil(s) - check and replacement

Check

Refer to illustrations 7.1, 7.2a and 7.2b

Note 1: *There are no specifications available for the primary resistance check on 1998 through 2000 models, or either check for the coil/igniter assemblies on 2001 and later ignition systems.*

Note 2: *The following checks should be made with the engine cold. If the engine is hot, the resistance will be greater.*

1   Check the primary resistance of the ignition coil. With the ignition key OFF, disconnect the electrical harness connector(s) from each coil. Connect an ohmmeter across the coil primary terminals **(see illustration).** The resistance should be as listed in this Chapter's Specifications. If not, replace the coil.

2   Check the secondary resistance of each ignition coil. With the ignition key OFF, label and detach the spark plug wires from each coil. Connect an ohmmeter across the two secondary terminals of each coil **(see illustrations).** The resistance should be as listed in this Chapter's Specifications. If not, replace the coil.

Replacement

3   Disconnect the negative cable from the battery.

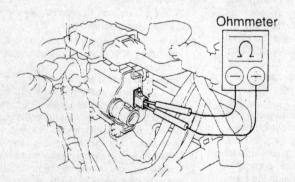

7.1 Checking the primary resistance on a 1996 and 1997 model

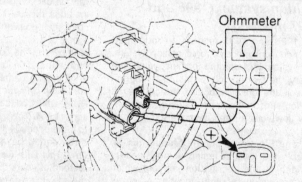

7.2a Checking the secondary resistance on a 1996 and 1997 model

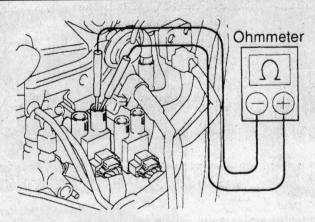

7.2b Checking the secondary resistance on a 1998 through 2000 model

7.5 The ignition coil on 1996 and 1997 models is mounted on a bracket on the engine compartment firewall

1996 and 1997 models

Refer to illustration 7.5

4   Disconnect the ignition coil electrical connector. Detach the coil wire.

5   Remove the bolts from the mounting bracket and separate the bracket/coil assembly from the engine **(see illustration)**.

6   Remove the bolts securing the ignition coil to the mounting bracket and remove the coil.

7   Installation is the reverse of the removal procedure.

1998 through 2000 models

Refer to illustration 7.11

8   Remove the throttle body from the intake manifold (see Chapter 4).

9   Remove the air filter housing cover (see Chapter 1).

10   Disconnect the ignition coil electrical connector(s) from each individual coil pack. Label each connector so they don't get mixed up. Label and detach the spark plug wires.

11   Remove the bolts securing the ignition coil bracket to the engine **(see illustration)** and remove the bracket coil.

12   Separate the coil from the bracket.

13   Installation is the reverse of the removal procedure.

2001 and later models

14   Remove the front half of the air filter housing (see Chapter 1, if necessary).

15   Each ignition coil/igniter assembly is secured by one bolt. Unscrew the bolt, disconnect the electrical connector and pull the coil/igniter assembly straight up, using a twisting motion.

16   Installation is the reverse of removal.

8   Igniter (1996 and 1997 models) - replacement

Refer to illustration 8.3

Note: *On 1998 and later models the igniters are integral with the ignition coils.*

1   Disconnect the negative cable from the battery.

2   Disconnect the electrical connector from the igniter.

3   Remove the igniter mounting screws **(see illustration)**.

4   Remove the igniter from the engine compartment.

5   Installation is the reverse of removal.

9   Distributor (1996 and 1997 models) - removal and installation

Removal

Refer to illustration 9.5

1   Detach the cable from the negative battery terminal.

2   Disconnect the electrical connectors from the distributor.

3   Look for a raised "1" on the distributor cap. This marks the location for the number one cylinder spark plug wire terminal. If the cap does not have a mark for the number one terminal, locate the number one spark plug and trace the wire back to the terminal on the cap. Refer to the firing order schematics in the Specifications in Chapter 1.

4   Remove the distributor cap (see Chapter 1) and turn the engine over until the rotor is pointing toward the number one spark plug terminal (see locating TDC procedure in Chapter 2A).

5   Mark the distributor base and the engine block to ensure that the distributor is installed correctly **(see illustration)**. Also, remove the distributor cap and make a mark on the edge

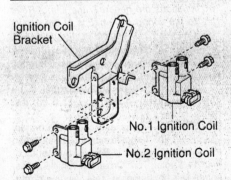

7.11 The ignition coil on 1998 through 2000 models is mounted on a bracket at the left end of the cylinder head

8.3 The igniter on 1996 and 1997 models is located near the master cylinder on the engine compartment firewall

9.5 Make an alignment mark on the base of the distributor and the cylinder head (arrow)

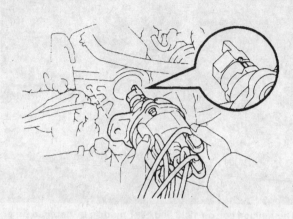

9.8 Align the cut-out portion of the coupling with the groove in the housing

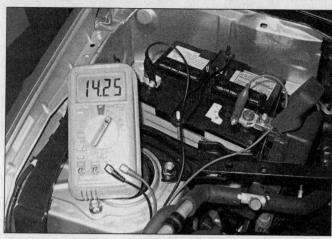

11.2 Connect a voltmeter to the battery terminals and check the battery voltage with the engine Off and again with the engine running

of the distributor housing directly below the rotor tip and in line with it.

6   Remove the distributor hold-down bolt, then pull the distributor straight out to remove it. **Caution:** *DO NOT turn the crankshaft while the distributor is out of the engine, or the alignment marks will be useless.*

Installation

Refer to illustration 9.8

Note: *If the crankshaft has been moved while the distributor is out, locate Top Dead Center (TDC) for the number one piston (see Chapter 2A) and position the distributor and the rotor accordingly.*

7   Install a new distributor O-ring.

8   Align the cut-out portion of the coupling with the groove in the housing **(see illustration)**.

9   Insert the distributor into the engine in exactly the same relationship to the block that it was in when removed.

10   If the distributor does not seat completely, recheck the alignment marks between the distributor base and the block to verify that the distributor is in the same position it was in before removal. Also, check the rotor to see if it's aligned with the mark you made on the edge of the distributor.

11   The remainder of installation is the reverse of removal.

12   Tighten the distributor hold-down bolt securely.

10   Charging system - general information and precautions

The charging system includes the alternator, an internal voltage regulator, a charge indicator, the battery, a fusible link and the wiring between all the components. The charging system supplies electrical power for the ignition system, the lights, the radio, etc. The alternator is driven by a drivebelt at the front of the engine.

The purpose of the voltage regulator is to limit the alternator's voltage to a preset value. This prevents power surges, circuit overloads, etc., during peak voltage output.

The charging system doesn't ordinarily require periodic maintenance. However, the drivebelt, battery and wires and connections should be inspected at the intervals outlined in Chapter 1.

The dashboard warning light should come on when the ignition key is turned to Start, then should go off immediately. If it remains on, there is a malfunction in the charging system. Some vehicles are also equipped with a voltage gauge. If the voltage gauge indicates abnormally high or low voltage, check the charging system (see Section 11).

Be very careful when making electrical circuit connections to a vehicle equipped with an alternator and note the following:

a)   *When reconnecting wires to the alternator from the battery, be sure to note the polarity.*

b)   *Before using arc welding equipment to repair any part of the vehicle, disconnect the wires from the alternator and the battery terminals.*

c)   *Never start the engine with a battery charger connected.*

d)   *Always disconnect both battery leads before using a battery charger.*

e)   *The alternator is driven by an engine drivebelt which could cause serious injury if your hand, hair or clothes become entangled in it with the engine running.*

f)   *Because the alternator is connected directly to the battery, it could arc or cause a fire if overloaded or shorted out.*

11   Charging system - check

Refer to illustration 11.2

1   If a malfunction occurs in the charging circuit, do not immediately assume that the

alternator is causing the problem. First, check the following items:

a)   *Make sure the battery cable clamps, where they connect to the battery, are clean and tight.*

b)   *Test the condition of the battery (see Section 3). If it does not pass all the tests, replace it with a new battery.*

c)   *Check the external alternator wiring and connections.*

d)   *Check the drivebelt condition and tension (see Chapter 1).*

e)   *Check the alternator mounting bolts for tightness.*

f)   *Run the engine and check the alternator for abnormal noise.*

g)   *Check the fusible links (if equipped) in the engine compartment fuse box (see Chapter 12). If they're burned, determine the cause and repair the circuit.*

h)   *Check the charge light on the dash. It should illuminate when the ignition key is turned ON (engine not running). If it does not, check the circuit from the alternator to the charge light on the dash.*

i)   *Check all the fuses that are in series with the charging system circuit. The location of these fuses and fusible links may vary from year and model but the designations are generally the same. Refer to the wiring schematics at the end of Chapter 12 for additional information.*

2   With the ignition key off, check the battery voltage with no accessories operating **(see illustration)**. It should be approximately 12.5 volts. It may be slightly higher if the engine had been operating within the last hour.

3   Start the engine and check the battery voltage again. It should now be greater than the voltage recorded in Step 2, but not more than 14.5 volts. Turn On all the vehicle accessories (air conditioning, rear window defogger, blower motor, etc.) and increase the engine speed to 2,000 rpm - the voltage should not drop below the voltage recorded in Step 2.

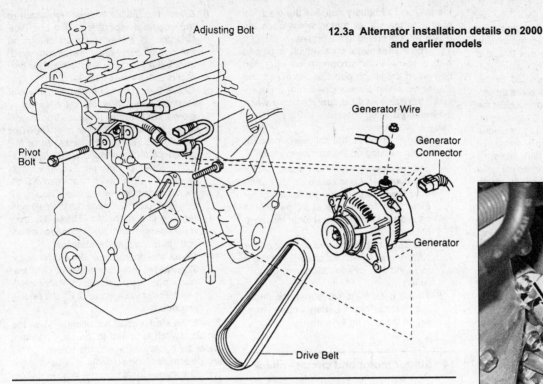

12.3a Alternator installation details on 2000 and earlier models

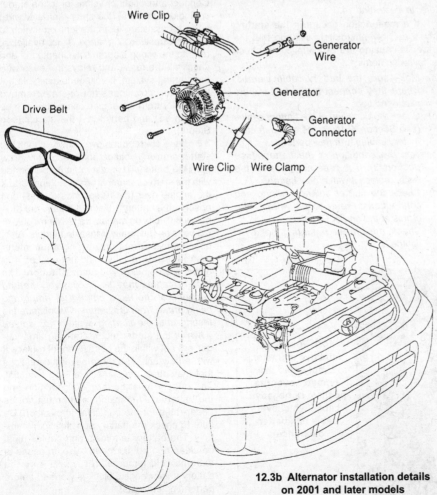

12.3b Alternator installation details on 2001 and later models

12.5 Location of the alternator mounting bolts - 2001 and later models (arrows)

4   If the indicated voltage is greater than the specified charging voltage, replace the voltage regulator. **Note:** *It is recommended to replace the alternator/voltage regulator as a complete unit, using either a rebuilt or new alternator.*

5   If the indicated voltage reading is less than the specified charging voltage, the alternator is probably defective. Have the charging system checked at a dealer service department or other properly equipped repair facility. **Note:** *Many auto parts stores will bench test an alternator off the vehicle. Refer to your local auto parts store regarding their policy (many will perform this service free of charge).*

12   Alternator - removal and installation

Removal

Refer to illustrations 12.3a, 12.3b and 12.5

1   Detach the cable from the negative terminal of the battery.

2   Remove the drivebelt(s) (see Chapter 1).

3   Detach the electrical connectors from the alternator **(see illustrations).**

4   On 2000 and earlier models, remove the alternator adjustment and pivot bolts.

5   On 2001 and later models, remove the alternator mounting bolts **(see illustration).**

6   Remove the alternator from the mounting bracket.

Installation

7   If you are replacing the alternator, take the old alternator with you when purchasing a replacement unit. Make sure that the new/rebuilt unit is identical to the old alternator. Look at the terminals - they should be the same in number, size and locations as the terminals on the old alternator. Finally, look at the identification markings - they will be stamped in the housing or printed on a tag or plaque affixed to the housing. Make sure that these numbers are the same on both alternators.

8   Many new/rebuilt alternators do not have a pulley installed, so you may have to switch the pulley from the old unit to the new/rebuilt one. When buying an alternator, find out the shop's policy regarding installation of pulleys - some shops will perform this service free of charge.

9   Installation is the reverse of removal.

10   Check the charging voltage to verify proper operation of the alternator (see Section 11).

13 Starting system - general information and precautions

The starting system consists of the battery, the starter motor, the starter solenoid and the electrical circuit connecting the components. The solenoid is mounted directly on the starter motor. The starter circuit consists of the ignition switch, the starter relay, the MAIN and AM2 fuses, the harness wiring to the solenoid and the heavy gauge wiring to the starter. The manual transaxle starting systems include the clutch start switch mounted at the clutch pedal while automatic transaxle systems include the Park/Neutral Position (PNP) switch mounted on the transaxle.

The solenoid/starter motor assembly is installed on the upper part of the transaxle bellhousing.

When the ignition key is turned to the START position, the starter solenoid is actuated through the starter control circuit. The starter solenoid then connects the battery to

the starter. The battery supplies the electrical energy to the starter motor, which does the actual work of cranking the engine.

The starter motor on a vehicle equipped with a manual transaxle can be operated only when the clutch pedal is depressed; the starter on a vehicle equipped with an automatic transaxle can be operated only when the transaxle selector lever is in Park or Neutral.

Always observe the following precautions when working on the starting system:

a) Excessive cranking of the starter motor can overheat it and cause serious damage. Never operate the starter motor for more than 15 seconds at a time without pausing to allow it to cool for at least two minutes.

b) The starter is connected directly to the battery and could arc or cause a fire if mishandled, overloaded or short circuited.

c) Always detach the cable from the negative terminal of the battery before working on the starting system.

14 Starter motor and circuit - check

Refer to illustration 14.3

1   If a malfunction occurs in the starting circuit, do not immediately assume that the starter is causing the problem. First, check the following items:

a) Make sure the battery cable clamps, where they connect to the battery, are clean and tight.

b) Check the condition of the battery cables (see Section 4). Replace any defective battery cables with new parts.

c) Test the condition of the battery (see Section 3). If it does not pass all the tests, replace it with a new battery.

d) Check the starter solenoid wiring and connections. Refer to the wiring diagrams at the end of Chapter 12.

e) Check the starter mounting bolts for tightness.

f) Check the fusible links (if equipped) in the engine compartment fuse box (see Chapter 12). If they're burned, determine the cause and repair the circuit. Also, check the ignition switch circuit for correct operation (see Chapter 12).

g) Check the operation of the Park/Neutral Position switch (automatic transaxle) or clutch start switch (manual transaxle). Make sure the shift lever is in PARK or NEUTRAL. (automatic transaxle) or the clutch pedal is pressed (manual transaxle). Refer to Chapter 7 for the Park/Neutral Position switch check and adjustment procedure. Refer to the Chapter 12 wiring diagrams, if necessary, when performing circuit checks. These systems must operate correctly to provide battery voltage to the ignition solenoid.

h) Check the operation of the starter relay. The starter relay is located in the fuse/relay box inside the engine compartment. Refer to Chapter 12 for the testing procedure.

2   If the starter does not actuate when the ignition switch is turned to the start position, check for battery voltage to the solenoid. This will determine if the solenoid is receiving the correct voltage signal from the ignition switch. Connect a test light or voltmeter to the starter solenoid S terminal (the small-diameter wire) while an assistant turns the ignition switch to the start position. If voltage is not available, refer to the wiring diagrams in Chapter 12 and check all the fuses and relays in series with the starting system. If voltage is available but the starter motor does not operate, remove the starter from the engine compartment (see Section 15) and bench test the starter (see Step 4).

3   If the starter turns over slowly, check the starter cranking voltage and the current draw from the battery. This test must be performed with the starter assembly on the engine. Crank the engine over (for 10 seconds or less) and observe the battery voltage. It should not drop below 8.0 volts on manual transaxle models or 8.5 volts on automatic transaxle models. Also, observe the current draw using an ammeter **(see illustration)**. It should not exceed 400 amps or drop below 250 amps. **Caution:** *The battery cables may be excessively heated because of the large amount of amperage being drawn from the battery. Discontinue the testing until the starting system has cooled down.* If the starter motor cranking amp values are not within the correct range, replace it with a new unit. There are several conditions that may affect the starter cranking potential. The battery must be in good condition and the battery cold-cranking rating must not be under-rated for the particular application. Be sure to check the battery specifications carefully. The battery terminals and cables must be clean and not corroded. Also, in cases of extreme cold temperatures, make sure the battery and/or engine block is warmed before performing the tests.

14.3 To use an inductive ammeter, simply hold the ammeter over the positive or negative cable (whichever cable has better clearance)

15.6 The starter motor mounting bolts are accessible from the front and from the back (bolt not visible) of the starter motor assembly (2001 model shown)

4   If the starter is receiving voltage but does not activate, remove and check the starter/solenoid assembly on the bench. Most likely the solenoid is defective. In some rare cases, the engine may be seized so be sure to try and rotate the crankshaft pulley (see Chapter 2A or 2B) before proceeding. With the starter/solenoid assembly mounted in a vise on the bench, install one jumper cable from the negative battery terminal to the body of the starter. Install the other jumper cable from the positive battery terminal to the B+ terminal on the starter. Install a starter switch and apply battery voltage to the solenoid S terminal (for 10 seconds or less) and see if the solenoid plunger, shift lever and overrunning clutch extends and rotates the pinion drive. If the pinion drive extends but does not rotate, the solenoid is operating but the starter motor is defective. If there is no movement but the solenoid clicks, the solenoid and/or the starter motor is defective. If the solenoid plunger extends and rotates the pinion drive, the starter/solenoid assembly is working properly.

15 Starter motor - removal and installation

Refer to illustration 15.6

1   Detach the cable from the negative terminal of the battery.
2   Remove the air filter housing (see Chapter 4).
3   Remove the cruise control actuator from the engine compartment and position the assembly off to the side without disconnecting the cables.
4   Remove the coolant reservoir from the engine compartment (see Chapter 3).
5   Detach the electrical connectors from the starter/solenoid assembly.
6   Remove the starter motor mounting bolts **(see illustration)**. Remove the starter motor assembly from the engine compartment.
7   Installation is the reverse of removal.

Notes

This doesn't mean, however, that emissions control systems are particularly difficult to maintain and repair. You can quickly and easily perform many checks and do most of the regular maintenance at home with common tune-up and hand tools. **Note:** *Because of a Federally mandated warranty which covers the emissions control system components, check with your dealer about warranty coverage before working on any emissions-related systems. Once the warranty has expired, you* *may wish to perform some of the component checks and/or replacement procedures in this Chapter to save money.*

Pay close attention to any special precautions outlined in this Chapter. It should be noted that the illustrations of the various systems may not exactly match the system installed on your vehicle because of changes made by the manufacturer during production or from year-to-year.

A Vehicle Emissions Control Information (VECI) label is attached to the underside of the hood **(see illustration)**. This label contains important emissions specifications and adjustment information. Part of this label, the Vacuum Hose Routing Diagram **(see illustration)**, provides a vacuum hose schematic with emissions components identified. When servicing the engine or emissions systems, the VECI label and the vacuum hose routing diagram in your particular vehicle should always be checked for up-to-date information.

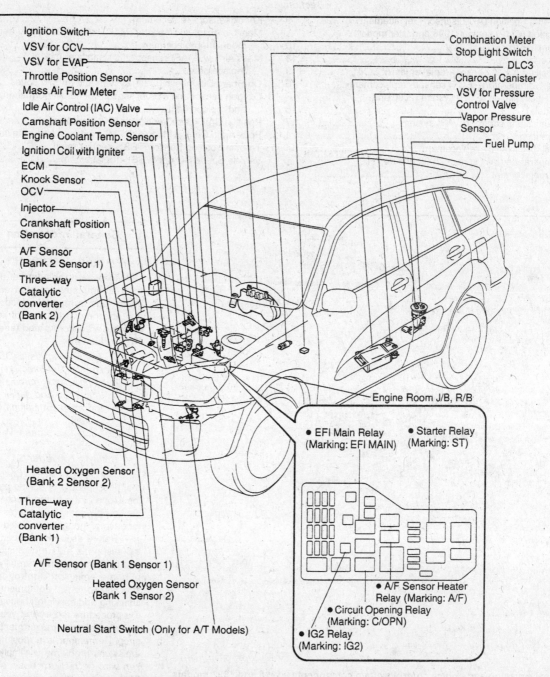

Ignition Switch
VSV for CCV
VSV for EVAP
Throttle Position Sensor
Mass Air Flow Meter
Idle Air Control (IAC) Valve
Camshaft Position Sensor
Engine Coolant Temp. Sensor
Ignition Coil with Igniter
ECM
Knock Sensor
OCV
Injector
Crankshaft Position Sensor
A/F Sensor (Bank 2 Sensor 1)
Three—way Catalytic converter (Bank 2)

Combination Meter
Stop Light Switch
DLC3
Charcoal Canister
VSV for Pressure Control Valve
Vapor Pressure Sensor
Fuel Pump

Heated Oxygen Sensor (Bank 2 Sensor 2)
Three—way Catalytic converter (Bank 1)
A/F Sensor (Bank 1 Sensor 1)
Heated Oxygen Sensor (Bank 1 Sensor 2)
Neutral Start Switch (Only for A/T Models)

Engine Room J/B, R/B

● EFI Main Relay (Marking: EFI MAIN)
● Starter Relay (Marking: ST)
● A/F Sensor Heater Relay (Marking: A/F)
● Circuit Opening Relay (Marking: C/OPN)
● IG2 Relay (Marking: IG2)

1.1b Typical emission and engine control system components - 2001 and later models

Chapter 6
Emissions and engine control systems

Contents

	Section
Accelerator Pedal Position (APP) sensor - replacement	19
Camshaft position (CMP) sensor (1998 and later models) - replacement	10
Catalytic converter	18
Crankshaft position (CKP) sensor - replacement	9
Engine Coolant Temperature (ECT) sensor - replacement	8
Exhaust Gas Recirculation (EGR) system (2000 and earlier models)	16
Evaporative emissions control (EVAP) system	17
General information	1
Idle Air Control (IAC) valve - replacement	14
Intake Air Temperature (IAT) sensor (2000 and earlier models) - replacement	7

	Section
Knock sensor - replacement	1.
Manifold Absolute Pressure (MAP) sensor (2000 and earlier models) - replacement	
Mass Airflow (MAF) sensor (2001 and later models) - replacement	6
On-Board Diagnostic (OBD) system and trouble codes	2
Oxygen sensor and air/fuel sensor - general information and replacement	11
Positive Crankcase Ventilation (PCV) system	15
Powertrain Control Module (PCM) - removal and installation	3
Throttle Position Sensor (TPS) - replacement	4
Vehicle Speed Sensor (VSS) - replacement	13

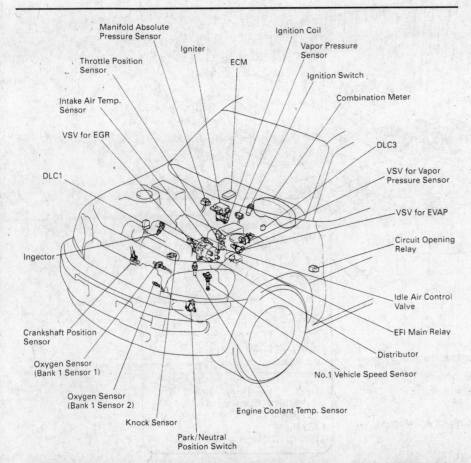

1.1a Typical emission and engine control system components - 1996 and 1997 models (1998 through 2000 similar)

1 General information

Refer to illustrations 1.1a, 1.1b, 1.6a and 1.6b

To prevent pollution of the atmosphere from incompletely burned and evaporating gases, and to maintain good driveability and fuel economy, a number of emission control systems are incorporated **(see illustration)**. They include the:

On-Board Diagnostic (OBD) II system
Electronic Fuel Injection (EFI) system
Exhaust Gas Recirculation (EGR) system (2000 and earlier models)
Evaporative Emissions Control (EVAP) system
Positive Crankcase Ventilation system
Catalytic converter

The Sections in this Chapter include general descriptions, checking procedures within the scope of the home mechanic and component replacement procedures (where possible) for each of the systems listed above.

Before assuming that an emission control system is malfunctioning, check the fuel and ignition systems carefully. The diagnosis of some emission control devices requires specialized tools, equipment and training. If checking and servicing become too difficult, or if a procedure is beyond your ability, consult a dealer service department or other repair shop. Remember, the most frequent cause of emissions problems is simply a loose or broken wire or vacuum hose, so always check the hose and wiring connections

1.6a The Vehicle Emission Control Information (VECI) label contains such essential information as the types of emission control systems installed on the engine and the idle speed and ignition timing specifications

2 On Board Diagnostic (OBD) system and trouble codes

Scan tool information

Refer to illustrations 2.1 and 2.2

1   Hand-held scanners are the most powerful and versatile tools for analyzing engine management systems used on later model vehicles **(see illustration)**. Early model scanners handle codes and some diagnostics for many systems. Each brand scan tool must be examined carefully to match the year, make and model of the vehicle you are working on. Often, interchangeable cartridges are available to access the particular manufacturer (Ford, GM, Chrysler, Toyota etc.). Some manufacturers will specify by continent (Asia, Europe, USA, etc.). **Note:** *An aftermarket generic scanner should work with any model covered by this manual. However, some early OBD-II models, although technically classified as OBD-II compliant by the manufacturer and by the federal government, might not be fully compliant with all SAE standards for OBD-II. Some generic scanners are unable to extract*

2.2 Trouble code readers like the Actron OBD-II diagnostic tester simplify the task of extracting the trouble codes

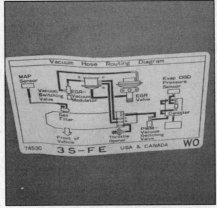

1.6b Vacuum hose routing diagram for a 1996 model

all the codes from these early OBD-II models. Before purchasing a generic scan tool, contact the manufacturer of the scanner you're planning to buy and verify that it will work properly with the OBD-II system you want to scan. If necessary, of course, you can always have the codes extracted by a dealer service department or an independent repair shop with a professional scan tool.

2   With the arrival of the Federally mandated emission control system (OBD-II), a specially designed scanner has been developed. Several tool manufacturers have released OBD-II scan tools for the home mechanic **(see illustration)**.

OBD system general description

3   All models are equipped with the second generation OBD-II system. This system consists of an on-board computer known as the Powertrain Control Module (PCM), and information sensors, which monitor various functions of the engine and send data to the PCM. This system incorporates a series of diagnostic monitors that detect and identify fuel injection and emissions control systems faults and store the information in the computer memory. This updated system also tests sensors and output actuators, diagnoses drive cycles, freezes data and clears codes.

4   This powerful diagnostic computer must be accessed using the new OBD-II scan tool and 16 pin Data Link Connector (DLC) located under the driver's dash area. The PCM is the "brain" of the electronically controlled fuel and emissions system. It receives data from a number of sensors and other electronic components (switches, relays, etc.). Based on the information it receives, the PCM generates output signals to control various relays, solenoids (i.e. fuel injectors) and other actuators. The PCM is specifically calibrated to optimize the emissions, fuel economy and driveability of the vehicle.

5   It isn't a good idea to attempt diagnosis or replacement of the PCM or emission control components at home while the vehicle is under warranty. Because of a Federally mandated warranty which covers the emis-

2.1 Scanners like these from Actron and the AutoXray are powerful diagnostic aids - they can tell you just about anything you want to know about your engine management system

sions system components and because any owner-induced damage to the PCM, the sensors and/or the control devices may void this warranty, take the vehicle to a dealer service department if the PCM or a system component malfunctions.

Information sensors

6   **Oxygen sensors (O2S)** - The O2S generates a voltage signal that varies with the difference between the oxygen content of the exhaust and the oxygen in the surrounding air.

7   **Crankshaft Position (CKP) sensor** - The crankshaft sensor provides information on crankshaft position and the engine speed signal to the PCM.

8   **Camshaft Position (CMP) sensor (1998 and later models)** - The camshaft sensor produces a signal which the PCM uses to identify number 1 cylinder and to time the sequential fuel injection.

9   **Air/Fuel Sensor (1998 and later California models and all 2001 and later models)** - Some vehicles are equipped with an air/fuel ratio sensor mounted upstream of the catalytic converter. These sensors work similar to the O2 sensors.

10   **Engine Coolant Temperature (ECT) sensor** - The coolant temperature (ECT) sensor monitors engine coolant temperature and sends the PCM a voltage signal that affects PCM control of the fuel mixture, ignition timing, and EGR operation.

11   **Intake Air Temperature (IAT) sensor (2000 and earlier models)** - The IAT sensor provides the PCM with intake air temperature information. The PCM uses this information to control fuel flow, ignition timing, and EGR system operation. 2001 and later models are equipped with an IAT sensor built into the MAF sensor.

12   **Throttle Position Sensor (TPS)** - The TPS senses throttle movement and position, then transmits a voltage signal to the PCM. This signal enables the PCM to determine when the throttle is closed, in a cruise position, or wide open.

13   **Manifold Absolute Pressure (MAP) sensor (2000 and earlier models)** - The MAP sensor measures the amount (volume) of the intake airflow entering the engine. The MAP sensor (along with the IAT sensor) provides airflow volume and air temperature information for the most precise fuel metering.

14   **Mass Airflow Sensor (MAF) (2001 and later models)** - The MAF sensor measures the mass of the intake air by detecting volume and weight of the air from samples passing over the hot wire element.

15   **Vehicle Speed Sensor (VSS)** - The vehicle speed sensor provides information to the PCM to indicate vehicle speed.

16   **Vapor pressure sensor** - The vapor pressure sensor is part of the evaporative emission control system and is used to monitor vapor pressure in the EVAP system. The PCM uses this information to turn on and off the vacuum switching valves (VSV) of the evaporative emission system.

17   **Power Steering Pressure (PSP) switch** - The PSP switch is used to increase engine idle speed during low-speed vehicle maneuvers.

18   **Transaxle sensors** - In addition to the vehicle speed sensor, the PCM receives input signals from the following sensors inside the transaxle or connected to it: (a) the direct clutch speed sensor (b) the vehicle speed sensor.

Output actuators

19   **EFI main relay** - The EFI main relay activates power to the fuel pump relay (circuit opening relay). It is activated by the ignition

2.25 16-pin Data Link Connector (DLC) (arrow)

switch and supplies battery power to the PCM and the EFI system when the switch is in the Start or Run position.

20   **Fuel injectors** - The PCM opens the fuel injectors individually in firing order sequence. The PCM also controls the time the injector is open, called the "pulse width." The pulse width of the injector (measured in milliseconds) determines the amount of fuel delivered. For more information on the fuel delivery system and the fuel injectors, including injector replacement, refer to Chapter 4.

21   **Igniter (1996 and 1997 models)** - The igniter triggers the ignition coil and determines proper spark advance based on inputs from the PCM. The igniter is mounted on the fenderwell near the corner of the engine compart-

ment. Refer to Chapter 5 for more information on the igniter.

22   **Idle Air Control (IAC) valve** - The IAC valve controls the amount of air to bypass the throttle plate when the throttle valve is closed or at idle position. The IAC valve opening and the resulting airflow is controlled by the PCM. Refer to Chapter 4 for more information on the IAC valve.

23   **EVAP vacuum switching valve (VSV)** - The EVAP vacuum switching valve is a solenoid valve, operated by the PCM to purge the fuel vapor canister and route fuel vapor to the intake manifold for combustion. This valve is also called the purge control valve.

Obtaining OBD-II system trouble codes

Refer to illustration 2.25

24   The PCM will illuminate the CHECK ENGINE light (also called the Malfunction Indicator Light) on the dash if it recognizes a component fault for two consecutive drive cycles. It will continue to set the light until the PCM does not detect any malfunction for three or more consecutive drive cycles.

25   The diagnostic codes for the OBD-II system can be extracted from the PCM by plugging a generic OBD-II scan tool (see illustrations 2.1 and 2.2) into the PCM's data link connector (see illustration), which is located under the left end of the dash.

26   Plug the scan tool into the 16-pin data link connector (DLC), and then follow the instructions included with the scan tool to extract any stored diagnostic codes.

Diagnostic Trouble Codes

Trouble code	Code identification
P0100	Mass airflow sensor or circuit fault
P0101	Mass airflow sensor range or performance problem
P0105	Manifold absolute pressure sensor or circuit fault
P0106	Manifold absolute pressure range or performance problem
P0110	Intake air temperature sensor or circuit fault
P0115	Engine coolant temperature sensor or circuit fault
P0116	Engine coolant temperature sensor range or performance problem
P0120	Throttle position sensor or circuit fault
P0121	Throttle Position sensor range or performance problem
P0125	Insufficient coolant temperature for closed loop; oxygen sensor heater malfunction
P0128	Thermostat malfunction
P0130	Pre-converter oxygen sensor or circuit fault
P0133	Pre-converter oxygen sensor circuit slow response fault

Trouble code	Code identification
P0135	Pre-converter oxygen sensor heater fault
P0136	Post-converter oxygen sensor or circuit fault
P0141	Post-converter oxygen sensor heater or circuit fault
P0158	Post-converter oxygen sensor heater or circuit fault
P0161	Post-converter oxygen sensor heater or circuit fault
P0171	Fuel injection system lean
P0172	Fuel injection system rich
P0174	Fuel injection system lean
P0175	Fuel injection system rich
P0300	Multiple cylinder misfire detected
P0301	Cylinder no. 1 misfire detected
P0302	Cylinder no. 2 misfire detected
P0303	Cylinder no. 3 misfire detected
P0304	Cylinder no. 4 misfire detected
P0325	Knock sensor or circuit fault
P0335	Crankshaft position sensor or circuit fault
P0336	Camshaft position sensor or range performance fault
P0340	Camshaft position sensor or circuit fault
P0401	EGR insufficient flow detected
P0402	EGR excessive flow detected
P0420	Catalytic converter system fault
P0430	Catalytic converter system fault
P0440	EVAP system malfunction
P0441	EVAP system incorrect purge flow detected
P0442	EVAP system leak detected
P0446	EVAP canister vent control valve circuit fault
P0450	EVAP system pressure sensor or circuit fault
P0451	EVAP system pressure sensor range or performance problem
P0500	Vehicle speed sensor or circuit fault
P0505	Idle air control valve or circuit fault
P0710	Automatic transaxle fluid temperature sensor or circuit fault
P0711	Automatic transaxle fluid temperature sensor range performance or circuit fault
P0750	Automatic transaxle shift solenoid A stuck open or closed
P0753	Automatic transaxle shift solenoid A circuit fault
P0755	Automatic transaxle shift solenoid B stuck open or closed
P0758	Automatic transaxle shift solenoid B circuit fault
P0765	Automatic transaxle shift solenoid D stuck open or closed

Diagnostic Trouble Codes (continued)

Trouble code	Code identification
P0768	Automatic transaxle shift solenoid D circuit fault
P0770	Automatic transaxle shift solenoid E stuck open or closed
P0773	Automatic transaxle shift solenoid E circuit fault
P1130	Air/fuel ratio sensor or range performance fault
P1133	Air/fuel ratio sensor or circuit fault
P1135	Air/fuel ratio sensor heater or circuit fault
P1153	Air/fuel ratio sensor or circuit fault
P1155	Air/fuel ratio sensor heater or circuit fault
P1300 (2000 and earlier)	Ignition system malfunction (#1 igniter circuit fault)
P1300 (2001 and later)	Ignition system malfunction (#1 coil/igniter circuit fault)
P1305 (2001 and later)	Ignition system malfunction (#2 coil/igniter circuit fault)
P1310 (2000 and earlier)	Ignition system malfunction (#2 igniter circuit fault)
P1310 (2001 and later)	Ignition system malfunction (#3 coil/igniter circuit fault)
P1315 (2001 and later)	Ignition system malfunction (#4 coil/igniter circuit fault)
P1335	Crankshaft position sensor or circuit fault
P1346	VVT (variable valve timing) sensor circuit fault
P1349	VVT (variable valve timing) system malfunction
P1500	Starter signal circuit malfunction
P1520	Brake light signal malfunction
P1600	ECM battery supply malfunction
P1656	OCV (oil control valve) circuit malfunction
P1725	Automatic transaxle input turbine speed sensor circuit fault
P1730	Automatic transaxle counter gear speed sensor circuit fault
P1780	Park/Neutral position switch or circuit fault

3 Powertrain Control Module (PCM) - removal and installation

Refer to illustrations 3.1a and 3.1b

Warning: *The models covered by this manual are equipped with Supplemental Restraint systems (SRS), more commonly known as airbags. Always disable the airbag system before working in the vicinity of any airbag system components to avoid the possibility of accidental deployment of the airbag, which could cause personal injury (see Chapter 12).* **Caution:** *To avoid electrostatic discharge damage to the PCM, handle the PCM only by its case. Do not touch the electrical terminals during removal and installation. If available, ground yourself to the vehicle with an anti-static ground strap, available at computer supply stores.*

1   The Powertrain Control Module (PCM) is located under the dash near the center console on the driver's side of the vehicle on 2000 and earlier models **(see illustration)**. On 2001 and later models, the PCM is located inside the passenger compartment to the right of the glovebox, behind the cowl side trim panel **(see illustration)**.

2   Disconnect the cable from the negative battery terminal.

2000 and earlier models

3   Working inside the driver's compartment, remove the carpet and the under-dash trim (see Chapter 11).

4   Unplug the electrical connectors from the PCM. **Caution:** *The ignition switch must be turned OFF when pulling out or plugging in the electrical connectors to prevent damage to the PCM.*

5   Remove the retaining bolts from the PCM bracket.

6   Carefully remove the PCM. **Caution:** *Avoid any static electricity damage to the computer by grounding yourself to the body before touching the PCM and using a special anti-static pad to store the PCM on once it is removed.*

7   Installation is the reverse of removal.

2001 and later models

Refer to illustration 3.10

8   Remove the glovebox (see Chapter 11).

9   Remove the right scuff plate and cowl side trim (see Chapter 11).

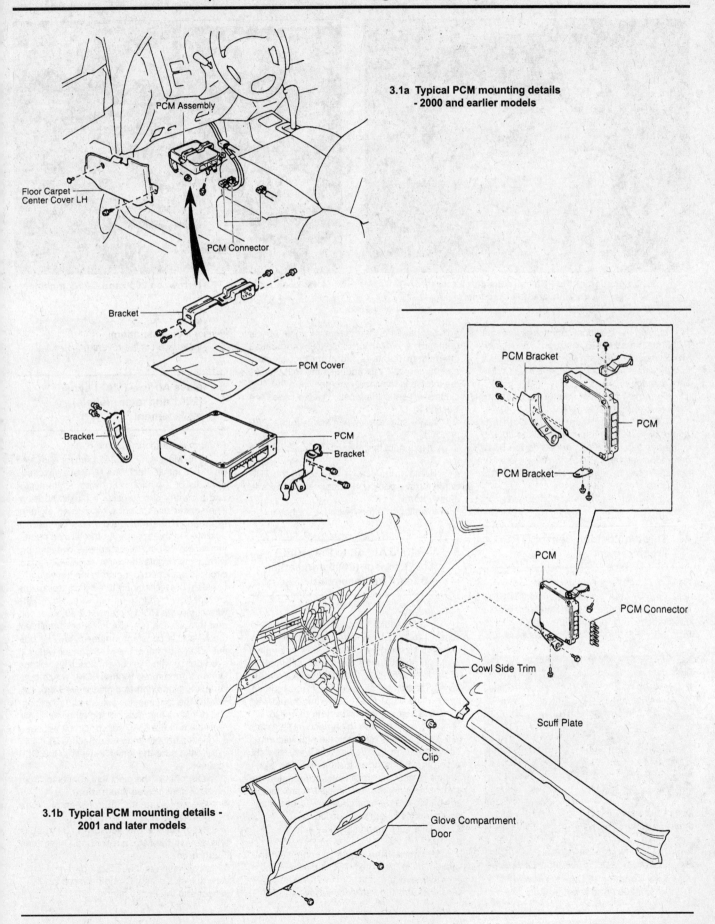

3.1a Typical PCM mounting details - 2000 and earlier models

PCM Assembly

Floor Carpet Center Cover LH

PCM Connector

Bracket

PCM Cover

Bracket

PCM

Bracket

PCM Bracket

PCM

PCM Bracket

PCM

PCM Connector

Cowl Side Trim

Scuff Plate

Clip

Glove Compartment Door

3.1b Typical PCM mounting details - 2001 and later models

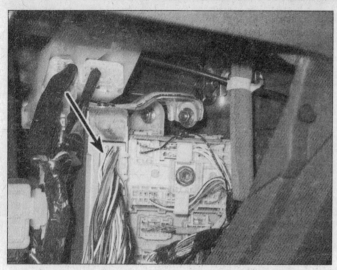

3.10 Location of the PCM harness connector (arrow) on 2001 and later models

4.4a Location of the TPS (arrow) on 2000 and earlier models

10   Unplug the electrical connectors from the PCM **(see illustration)**. **Caution:** *The ignition switch must be turned OFF when pulling out or plugging in the electrical connectors to prevent damage to the PCM.*
11   Remove the retaining bolts from the PCM bracket.
12   Carefully remove the PCM. **Caution:** *Avoid any static electricity damage to the computer by grounding yourself to the body before touching the PCM and using a special anti-static pad to store the PCM on once it is removed.*
13   Installation is the reverse of removal.

---

4   Throttle Position Sensor (TPS) - replacement

Refer to illustrations 4.4a and 4.4b
1   The Throttle Position Sensor (TPS) is located on the end of the throttle shaft on the throttle body. By monitoring the output voltage from the TPS, the PCM can determine fuel

4.4b Location of the TPS (arrow) on 2001 and later models

delivery based on throttle valve angle (driver demand). A broken or loose TPS can cause intermittent bursts of fuel from the injectors and an unstable idle because the PCM thinks the throttle is moving. A problem with the TPS circuits will set a diagnostic trouble code (see Section 2).
2   Make sure the ignition key is in the OFF position.
3   Disconnect the electrical connector from the TPS.
4   Remove the screws that retain the TPS to the throttle body and remove the TPS **(see illustrations)**.
5   Installation is the reverse of removal.

---

5   Manifold Absolute Pressure (MAP) sensor (2000 and earlier models) - replacement

---

Refer to illustration 5.4
1   The Manifold Absolute Pressure (MAP) sensor monitors the intake manifold pressure changes resulting from changes in engine load and speed and converts the information into a voltage output. The PCM uses the MAP sensor to control fuel delivery and ignition timing. The PCM will receive information as a voltage signal that will vary from 1.9 to 2.1 volts at closed throttle (high vacuum) and 0.3 to 0.5 volt at wide open throttle (low vacuum). The voltage range values will vary slightly according to changes in altitude. The MAP sensor is attached to a bracket mounted on the engine compartment firewall. A problem in any of the MAP sensor circuits will set a diagnostic trouble code (see Section 2).
2   Make sure the ignition key is in the OFF position.
3   Disconnect the electrical connector and vacuum hose from the MAP sensor.
4   Remove the bolt that retains the MAP sensor to the firewall and remove the MAP

sensor **(see illustration)**.
5   Installation is the reverse of removal.

---

6   Mass Airflow (MAF) sensor (2001 and later models) - replacement

---

Refer to illustrations 6.3 and 6.4
1   The Mass Airflow (MAF) sensor is located on the air intake duct. The MAF system circuit consists of a platinum hot wire, a thermistor and a control circuit inside a plastic housing. The sensor uses a hot wire sensing element to measure the molecular mass (weight) of air entering the engine. As the throttle opens, increasing volume of air passes over the hot wire, which cools the wire. The MAF sensor circuit is designed to maintain the hot wire at a constant preset temperature by controlling the current flow through the hot wire. So, as the wire cools, the PCM increases the flow of current through the hot wire in order to maintain the wire at a constant temperature. The output voltage signal of the MAF sensor varies in accordance with this current flow. This voltage signal is measured by the PCM, which converts this signal into a digital wave form, calculates the fuel injector pulse width (duration) and turns the injectors on and off accordingly. A problem in the MAF sensor circuit will set a diagnostic trouble code (see Section 2).
2   Make sure the ignition key is in the OFF position.
3   Disconnect the electrical connector from the MAF sensor **(see illustration)**.
4   Remove the air filter assembly (see Chapter 4).
5   Remove the two sensor retaining bolts and remove the MAF sensor and O-ring **(see illustration)**.
6   Installation is the reverse of removal. Be sure to install a new O-ring between the MAF sensor and the intake duct.

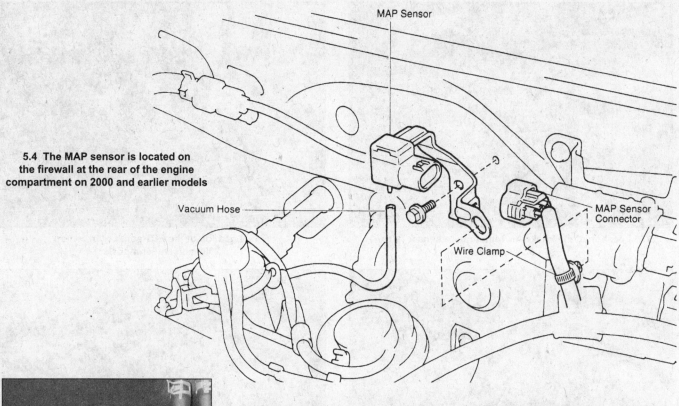

MAP Sensor

Vacuum Hose

MAP Sensor Connector

Wire Clamp

5.4 The MAP sensor is located on the firewall at the rear of the engine compartment on 2000 and earlier models

6.3 Location of the MAF sensor (arrow)

6.5 Location of the MAF sensor mounting bolts (arrows)

7   Intake Air Temperature (IAT) sensor (2000 and earlier models) - replacement

Refer to illustrations 7.1 and 7.3

Note: *2001 and later models are equipped with an IAT sensor that is built into the MAF sensor (see Section 6).*

1   The intake air temperature (IAT) sensor is a thermistor (a resistor which varies the value of its resistance in accordance with temperature changes). The change in the resistance values will directly affect the voltage signal from the sensor to the PCM. As the sensor temperature DECREASES, the resistance values will INCREASE. As the sensor temperature INCREASES, the resistance values will DECREASE **(see illustration)**. A problem in any of the IAT sensor circuits will set a diagnostic trouble code.

2   Make sure the ignition key is in the OFF position.

3   Disconnect the electrical connector from the IAT sensor **(see illustration)**.

4   Remove the IAT sensor from the air filter housing.

5   Installation is the reverse of removal.

Temperature (degrees - F)	Resistance (ohms)
212	125
194	250
176	300
158	400
140	500
122	625
112	750
104	875
95	1000
86	1500
76	2000
68	2500
58	3000
50	3500
40	4000
32	4500

7.1 Coolant temperature and intake air temperature sensors approximate temperature vs. resistance values

7.3 Location of the Intake Air Temperature sensor (arrow) on a 1996 model

8.4a Location of the ECT sensor (arrow) on 2000 and earlier models

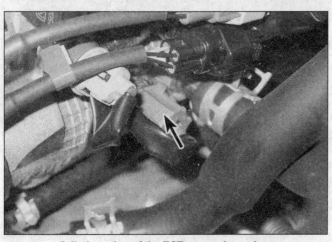

8.4b Location of the ECT sensor (arrow) on 2001 and later models

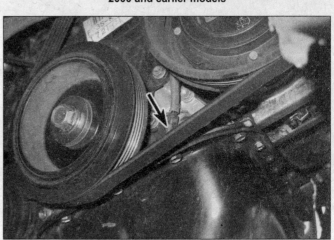

9.4a The crankshaft sensor harness location (arrow) on a 1996 model

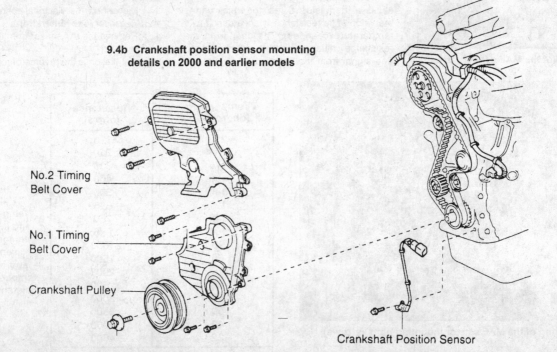

9.4b Crankshaft position sensor mounting details on 2000 and earlier models

No.2 Timing Belt Cover

No.1 Timing Belt Cover

Crankshaft Pulley

Crankshaft Position Sensor

9.5 Location of the crankshaft position sensor harness connector (arrow) on 2001 and later models

8 Engine Coolant Temperature (ECT) sensor - replacement

Refer to illustrations 8.4a and 8.4b
Warning: *Wait until the engine has cooled completely before beginning this procedure.*
1   The engine coolant temperature (ECT) sensor is a thermistor (a resistor which varies the value of its resistance in accordance with temperature changes). The change in the resistance values will directly affect the voltage signal from the sensor to the PCM. As the sensor temperature DECREASES, the resistance values will INCREASE. As the sensor temperature INCREASES, the resistance values will DECREASE. A problem in any of the ECT sensor circuits will set a diagnostic trouble code.

2   Make sure the ignition key is in the OFF position.
3   Drain approximately one gallon from the cooling system.
4   Disconnect the electrical connector and carefully unscrew the sensor (**see illustrations**).
5   Wrap the threads of the new sensor with Teflon sealing tape to prevent leakage and thread corrosion.
6   Installation is the reverse of removal.
Caution: *Handle the coolant sensor with care. Damage to this sensor will affect the operation of the entire fuel injection system.*

9 Crankshaft Position (CKP) sensor - replacement

Refer to illustrations 9.4a, 9.4b, 9.5 and 9.6
1   The crankshaft position sensor (CKP) determines the timing for the fuel injection and ignition on each cylinder. On 2000 and earlier models, the crankshaft position sensor is mounted under the timing belt cover, next to the crankshaft gear. On 2001 and later models, the sensor is mounted on the timing chain cover next to the crankshaft pulley. A problem in the crankshaft position sensor circuit will set a diagnostic trouble code (see Section 2).
2   Disconnect the cable from the negative battery terminal.
3   Working under the vehicle, remove the inner fender shield (see Chapter 11).
4   The timing belt cover must be removed to access the sensor on 2000 and earlier models (**see illustrations**). Refer to Chapter 2A for the timing belt cover removal procedure.

9.6 Location of the crankshaft position sensor (arrow) on 2001 and later models

5   Disconnect the crankshaft position sensor electrical connector (**see illustration**).
6   Remove the bolt and detach the sensor (**see illustration**).
7   Installation is the reverse of removal.

10 Camshaft position (CMP) sensor (1998 and later models) - replacement

Refer to illustrations 10.1a, 10.1b and 10.4
1   The camshaft position sensor determines the position of the no. 1 piston in its cylinder for sequential fuel injection signals to each cylinder. The sensor is mounted on the cylinder head near the camshaft sprocket (**see illustrations**). A problem in the camshaft position sensor circuit will set a diagnostic trouble code (see Section 2).

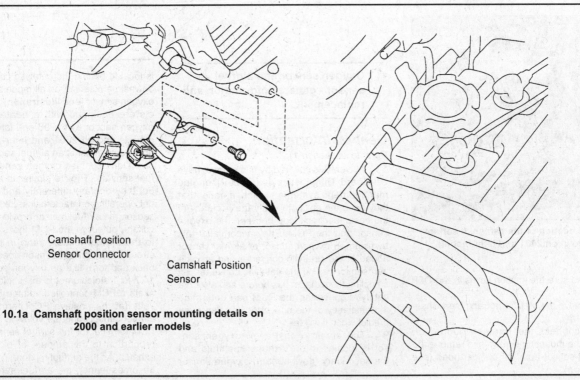

Camshaft Position Sensor Connector

Camshaft Position Sensor

10.1a Camshaft position sensor mounting details on 2000 and earlier models

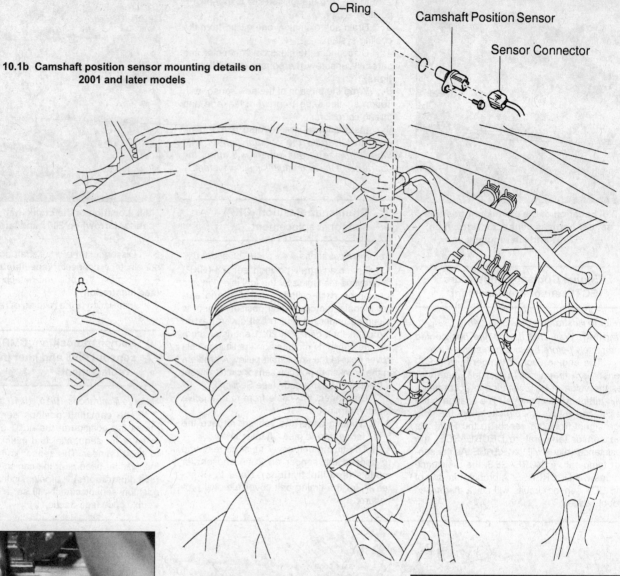

O–Ring

Camshaft Position Sensor

Sensor Connector

10.1b Camshaft position sensor mounting details on 2001 and later models

10.4 Location of the camshaft sensor (arrow) on 2001 and later models

2   Make sure the ignition key is in the OFF position.
3   Remove the air filter housing (see Chapter 4).
4   Disconnect the harness connector, remove the mounting screws and remove the camshaft sensor from the cylinder head (see illustration).

11   Oxygen sensor and air/fuel sensor - general information and replacement

General information

Refer to illustration 11.2

1   All vehicles covered by this manual have On-Board Diagnostics II (OBD-II) engine management systems, which means that they have the ability to verify the accuracy of the basic feedback loop between the oxygen sensor and the PCM. They accomplish this by using an oxygen sensor or air/fuel sensor ahead of the catalytic converter and an oxygen sensor behind the catalytic converter. By sampling the exhaust gas before and after the catalytic converter, the PCM can determine the efficiency of the converter and can even predict when it will fail.

2   The primary (upstream) oxygen sensor is located in the exhaust manifold and the secondary (downstream) oxygen sensor

is located behind the catalytic converter. The downstream sensor on all models is a heated oxygen sensor **(see illustration)**. Some models are equipped with a heated upstream oxygen sensor. On 1998 and later California models and all 2001 and later models, the upstream sensor is an air/fuel sensor.

3   Don't confuse oxygen sensors and air/fuel sensors. They're similar in appearance, but they operate differently and have different operating characteristics. Like an oxygen sensor, the air/fuel sensor provides a variable voltage output to the PCM that's proportional to the air/fuel mixture ratio in the exhaust stream. The air/fuel sensor doesn't "switch" back and forth like an oxygen sensor at the 14.7 to 1 stoichiometric threshold. Instead, it alters a PCM-controlled voltage between 3.3 volts (at the positive PCM terminal for the air/fuel sensor) and 3.0 volts (at the negative PCM terminal for the air/fuel sensor) in direct proportion to the amount of oxygen in the exhaust. As the air/fuel mixture in the exhaust becomes leaner, the air/fuel sensor voltage

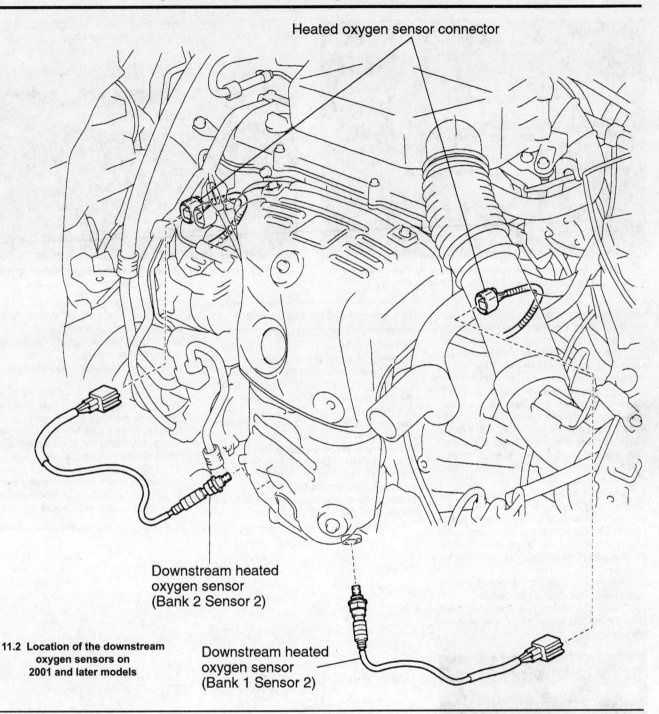

Heated oxygen sensor connector

Downstream heated
oxygen sensor
(Bank 2 Sensor 2)

Downstream heated
oxygen sensor
(Bank 1 Sensor 2)

**11.2 Location of the downstream
oxygen sensors on
2001 and later models**

increases (within its operating range of 3.0
to 3.3 volts). Like an oxygen sensor, the air/
fuel sensor doesn't operate correctly until it's
warmed up. Also, like an oxygen sensor, the
air/fuel sensor has a heating element which
enables it to warm up quickly.

4   Special care must be taken whenever a
sensor is serviced.

a) *Oxygen sensors and air/fuel sensors
have a permanently attached pigtail and
electrical connector which should not be
removed from the sensor. Damage or
removal of the pigtail or electrical connector can adversely affect operation of*

the sensor.

b) *Grease, dirt and other contaminants
should be kept away from the electrical
connector and the louvered end of the
sensor.*

c) *Do not use cleaning solvents of any kind
on an oxygen sensor or air/fuel ratio sensor.*

d) *Do not drop or roughly handle an oxygen
sensor or air/fuel ratio sensor.*

e) *The silicone boot must be installed in the
correct position to prevent the boot from
being melted and to allow the sensor to
operate properly.*

Replacement

Refer to illustrations 11.7, 11.8a and 11.8b

Note: *Because it is installed in the exhaust
manifold or pipe, which contracts when cool,
the oxygen sensor may be very difficult to
loosen when the engine is cold. Rather than
risk damage to the sensor (assuming you are
planning to reuse it in another manifold or
pipe), start and run the engine for a minute
or two, then shut it off. Be careful not to burn
yourself during the following procedure.*

5   Disconnect the cable from the negative
terminal of the battery.

6   If you're replacing the downstream sen-

11.7 Location of the upstream oxygen sensor (arrow) on bank number 2 on 2001 and later models

11.8a Location of the downstream oxygen sensor (arrow) on bank number 1 on 2001 and later models

sor, raise the vehicle and secure it on jack-stands. Access the oxygen sensor harness and then unplug the electrical connector.

7   The upstream sensor can be replaced without raising the vehicle **(see illustration)**. Unplug the sensor electrical connector.

8   Unscrew the sensor from the exhaust manifold or exhaust pipe **(see illustrations)**. **Note:** *The best tool for removing an oxygen sensor is a special slotted socket, especially if you're planning to reuse a sensor. If you don't have this tool, and you plan to reuse the sensor, be extremely careful when unscrewing the sensor.*

9   Apply anti-seize compound to the threads of the sensor to facilitate future removal. The threads of new sensors should already be coated with this compound, but if you're planning to reuse an old sensor, recoat the threads. Install the sensor and tighten it securely.

10   Reconnect the electrical connector of the pigtail lead to the main wiring harness.

11   Lower the vehicle (if it was raised), test drive the car and verify that no trouble codes have been set.

12   Knock sensor - replacement

Refer to illustrations 12.5a and 12.5b
Warning: *Wait for the engine to cool completely before performing this procedure.*

1   The knock control system is designed to reduce spark knock during periods of heavy detonation. This allows the engine to use optimal spark advance to improve driveability. The knock sensor detects abnormal vibration in the engine and produces a voltage output which increases with the severity of the knock. The voltage signal is monitored by the PCM, which retards ignition timing until the detonation ceases. The knock sensor is located on the backside of the engine block, directly

below the cylinder head (facing toward the rear of the engine compartment).

2   Disconnect the cable from the negative terminal of the battery.

3   Drain the cooling system (see Chapter 1).

4   If you're working on a 2000 or earlier 4WD model or any 2001 or later model remove the intake manifold (see Chapter 2A or 2B). If you're working on a 2000 or earlier 2WD model, raise the front of the vehicle and support it securely on jackstands.

5   Disconnect the electrical connector and remove the knock sensor **(see illustrations)**.

6   If you're going to reuse the old sensor, coat the threads with thread sealant. New

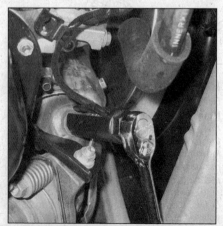

11.8b Use a slotted socket to remove the oxygen sensor from the exhaust manifold

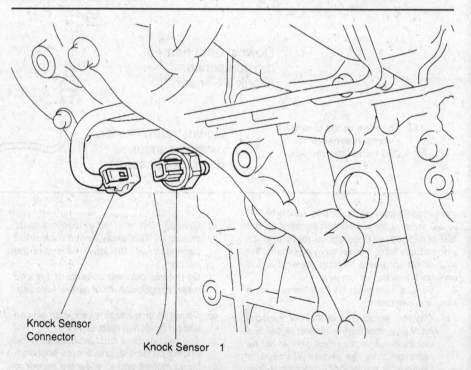

Knock Sensor Connector

Knock Sensor 1

12.5a Knock sensor details on 2000 and earlier models

sensors are pre-coated with thread sealant, do not apply any additional sealant or the operation of the sensor may be affected.

7   Install the knock sensor and tighten it securely (approximately 30 ft-lbs). Don't overtighten the sensor or damage may occur. The remainder of installation is the reverse of removal. Refill the cooling system and check for leaks.

13 Vehicle Speed Sensor (VSS) - replacement

Check

Refer to illustrations 13.1a and 13.1b

1   The Vehicle Speed Sensor (VSS) **(see illustrations)** is located on top of the trans-axle. This sensor is an electronic component that produces a pulsing voltage signal whenever the sensor shaft is rotated. These voltage pulses are monitored by the PCM, which uses this information to help control the fuel and ignition systems and transaxle shifting.

2   Disconnect the electrical connector from the VSS.

3   Unscrew the VSS from the transaxle.

4   Replace the O-ring.

5   Installation is the reverse of removal.

14 Idle Air Control (IAC) valve - replacement

Refer to illustrations 14.1a and 14.1b

Note: *The minimum idle speed is pre-set at the factory and should not require adjustment under normal operating conditions. However if the throttle body has been replaced or you suspect the minimum idle speed has been tampered with (for example, if the idle speed screw was removed from the throttle body), have the vehicle checked by a dealer service department or other qualified automotive repair shop.*

1   The engine idle speed is controlled by

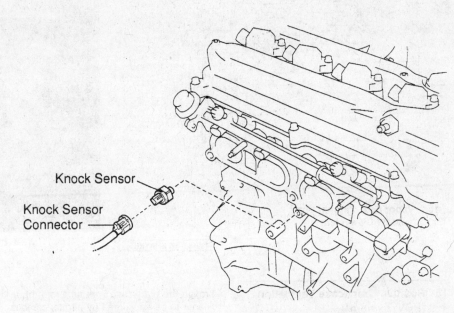

12.5b Knock sensor details on 2001 and later models

the Idle Air Control (IAC) valve **(see illustrations)**. The IAC valve controls the amount of air that bypasses the throttle plate into the intake manifold. The IAC valve is controlled by the PCM in accordance with the demands on the engine (air conditioning, power steering) and the operating conditions (cold or warmed up).

2   Remove the throttle body (see Chapter 4).

3   Remove the mounting screws and detach the IAC valve and gasket.

4   Installation is the reverse of removal. Be sure to use a new gasket when installing the IAC valve.

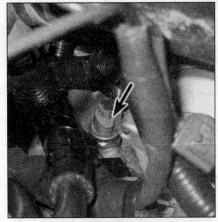

13.1a The VSS (arrow) is located on top of the transaxle - 2000 and earlier model shown

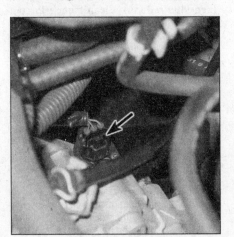

13.1b The VSS (arrow) is located on top of the transaxle - 2001 and later model shown

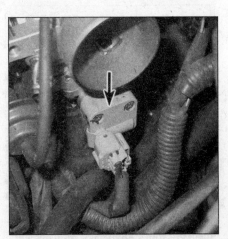

14.1a Location of the IAC valve (arrow) on 2000 and earlier models

14.1b Location of the IAC valve (arrow) on 2001 and later models

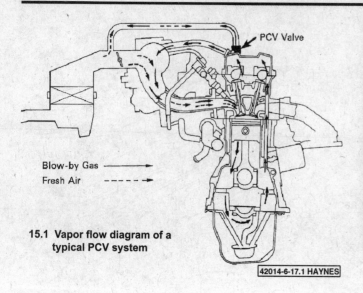

Blow-by Gas ———→
Fresh Air ----- →

15.1 Vapor flow diagram of a typical PCV system

42014-6-17.1 HAYNES

16.4 Location of the EGR valve (arrow)

15 Positive Crankcase Ventilation (PCV) system

Refer to illustration 15.1

1   The Positive Crankcase Ventilation (PCV) system **(see illustration)** reduces hydrocarbon emissions by scavenging crankcase vapors. It does this by circulating fresh air from the air cleaner through the crankcase, where it mixes with blow-by gases and is then rerouted through a PCV valve to the intake manifold.

2   The main components of the PCV system are the PCV valve, a blow-by filter and the vacuum hoses connecting these two components with the engine. Refer to illustrations 17.1a and 17.1b for locations of the PCV valve.

3   To maintain idle quality, the PCV valve restricts the flow when the intake manifold vacuum is high. If abnormal operating conditions (such as piston ring problems) arise, the system is designed to allow excessive amounts of blow-by gases to flow back through the crankcase vent tube into the air cleaner to be consumed by normal combustion.

4   Checking and replacement of the PCV valve is covered in Chapter 1.

16 Exhaust Gas Recirculation (EGR) system (2000 and earlier models)

General description

1   To reduce oxides of nitrogen (NOx) emissions, some of the exhaust gases are recirculated through the EGR valve to the intake manifold to lower combustion temperatures.

2   The EGR system consists of an EGR valve, an EGR modulator, a vacuum switching valve (VSV) and the vacuum lines to the throttle body. The position of the EGR valve is controlled by vacuum which is controlled by the Powertrain Control Module (PCM). Refer to illustration 17.1a for the EGR component locations.

Replacement
EGR valve

Refer to illustration 16.4

3   Remove the throttle body (see Chapter 4).

4   Detach the vacuum hose from the EGR valve. Disconnect the EGR pipe, remove the EGR valve mounting bolts and remove the EGR valve from the intake manifold **(see illustration)**. Check the valve for sticking and heavy carbon deposits. If the valve is sticking or clogged with deposits, clean or replace it. **Caution:** *Don't immerse the valve in solvent.*

5   Installation is the reverse of removal. Be sure to use new gaskets.

EGR vacuum modulator and modulator filter

Refer to illustrations 16.7a and 16.7b

6   Clearly label and disconnect the vacuum hoses to the EGR vacuum modulator. Remove the EGR vacuum modulator from its bracket.

7   If you're planning to reuse the old modulator, pull the cover off and check the filters **(see illustrations)**. Clean them with compressed air and then reinstall the cover. If the filters cannot be cleaned, replace them or replace the modulator.

8   Installation is the reverse of removal.

Vacuum switching valve (VSV)

9   Locate the VSV near the exhaust manifold **(see illustration 17.1a)**. Unplug the electrical connector from the VSV. Clearly label and disconnect the vacuum hoses attached to the VSV.

10   Remove the VSV from its mounting bracket. If you have difficulty removing the VSV from the bracket, remove the bracket bolt, remove the entire assembly and separate the VSV from the bracket off the vehicle.

11   Installation is the reverse of removal.

16.7a To remove the EGR vacuum modulator filters for cleaning, remove the cap . . .

16.7b . . . pull out the two filters and blow them out with compressed air; make sure the coarse side of the outer filter faces out when reinstalling the filters

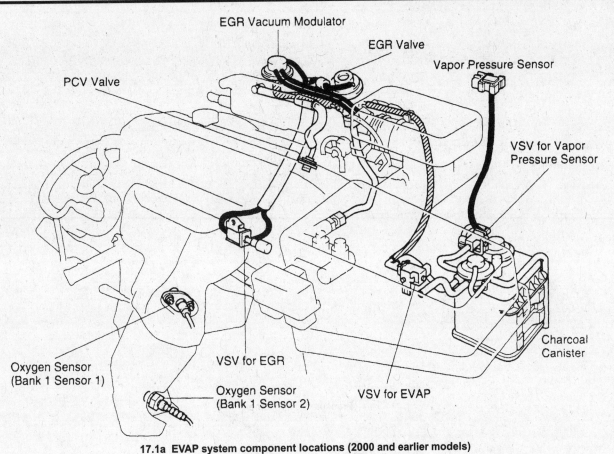

17.1a EVAP system component locations (2000 and earlier models)

17 Evaporative emissions control (EVAP) system

General description

Refer to illustrations 17.1a, 17.1b, 17.6a and 17.6b

1   The fuel evaporative emissions control (EVAP) system absorbs fuel vapors and, during engine operation, releases them into the engine intake where they mix with the incoming air-fuel mixture. On 2000 and earlier models, the charcoal canister is mounted in the engine compartment **(see illustration)**. On 2001 and later models, the charcoal canister is mounted behind the fuel tank under the vehicle **(see illustration)**.

2   When the engine is not operating, fuel vapors are transferred from the fuel tank, throttle body and intake manifold to the charcoal canister where they are stored. When the engine is running, the fuel vapors are purged from the canister by the purge control valve. The gasses are consumed in the normal combustion process. The electronic purge control valve is directly controlled by the PCM.

3   The fuel filler cap is fitted with a two-way valve as a safety device. The valve vents fuel vapors to the atmosphere if the EVAP system fails.

4   The EVAP system also incorporates a vapor pressure sensor. This sensor detects abnormal vapor pressure in the system. On

2000 and earlier models, the vapor pressure sensor is mounted on the engine compartment firewall. On 2001 and later models, the vapor pressure sensor is mounted in the fuel pump/ sending unit assembly on top of the fuel tank.

5   After the engine has been running and warmed up to a pre-set temperature, the vacuum switching valve (VSV) opens. The vacuum switching valve (purge control valve) allows intake manifold vacuum to draw the fuel vapors from the canister to the intake manifold, where they are mixed with intake air before being burned with the air/fuel mixture inside the combustion chambers.

6   The fuel tank vapor pressure sensor monitors changes in pressure inside the tank and, when the pressure exceeds a preset threshold, opens a vacuum switching valve (VSV) **(see illustrations)**, which allows a purge port in the canister to admit fuel tank vapors into the canister.

Replacement

Charcoal canister

7   Disconnect the cable from the negative battery terminal.

8   On 2001 and later models, raise the rear of the vehicle and support it securely on jackstands.

9   Unplug all electrical connectors and clearly label and disconnect the vent hoses to the charcoal canister, remove the bolts

and separate the canister from the engine compartment or the underside of the vehicle. Refer to the illustrations at the beginning of this section if necessary.

10   Installation is the reverse of removal.

18 Catalytic converter

Note1: *Because of a Federally mandated extended warranty which covers emissions-related components such as the catalytic converter, check with a dealer service department before replacing the converter at your own expense.*

Note 2: *On 2001 and later models, the front catalytic converter is incorporated into the exhaust manifold. Refer to Chapter 2B for the exhaust manifold replacement procedure.*

General description

1   The catalytic converter is an emission control device added to the exhaust system to reduce pollutants from the exhaust gas stream. There are two types of converters. The conventional oxidation catalyst reduces the levels of hydrocarbon (HC) and carbon monoxide (CO). The three-way catalyst lowers the levels of oxides of nitrogen (NOx) as well as hydrocarbons (HC) and carbon monoxide (CO). These models are equipped only with three-way catalytic converters.

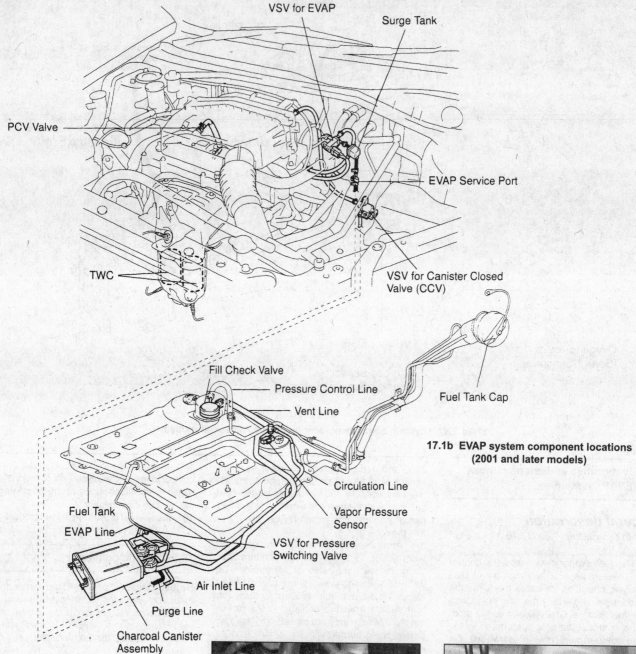

17.1b EVAP system component locations (2001 and later models)

Check

2   The test equipment for a catalytic converter is expensive and highly sophisticated. If you suspect that the converter on your vehicle is malfunctioning, take it to a dealer or authorized emissions inspection facility for diagnosis and repair.

3   Whenever the vehicle is raised for servicing of underbody components, check the converter for leaks, corrosion, dents and other damage. Check the welds/flange bolts that attach the front and rear ends of the converter to the exhaust system. If damage is discovered, the converter should be replaced.

4   Although catalytic converters don't break

17.6a Location of the EVAP vacuum switching valve (VSV) on 2000 and earlier models (arrows)

17.6b Location of the EVAP vacuum switching valve (VSV) on 2001 and later models (arrows)

too often, they can become plugged. The easiest way to check for a restricted converter is to use a vacuum gauge to diagnose the effect of a blocked exhaust on intake vacuum.

a) Connect a vacuum gauge to an intake manifold vacuum source (see Chapter 2C).

b) Warm the engine to operating temperature, place the transaxle in Park (automatic) or Neutral (manual) and apply the parking brake.

c) Note and record the vacuum reading at idle.

d) Quickly open the throttle to near full throttle and release it shut. Note and record the vacuum reading.

e) Perform the test three more times, recording the reading after each test.

f) If the reading after the fourth test is more than one in-Hg lower than the reading recorded at idle, the exhaust system may be restricted (the catalytic converter could be plugged or an exhaust pipe or muffler could be restricted).

Replacement

Refer to illustrations 18.6a and 18.6b

5   Be sure to spray the nuts on the exhaust flange studs before removing them from the catalytic converter.

6   Remove the nuts and separate the catalytic converter from the exhaust system **(see illustrations)**.

7   Installation is the reverse of removal.

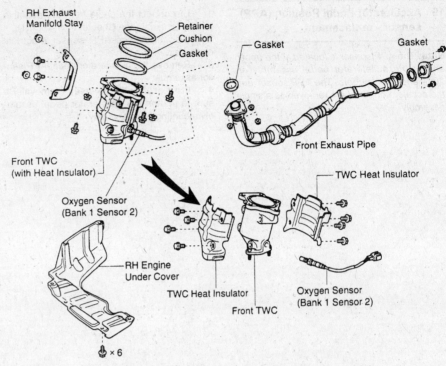

18.6a Catalytic converter details on 2000 and earlier models

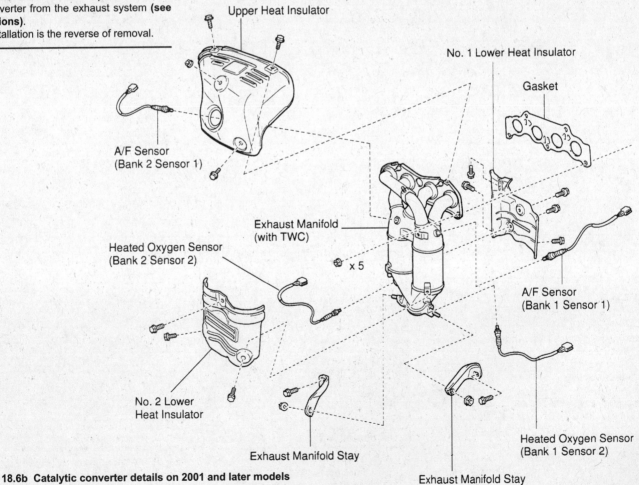

18.6b Catalytic converter details on 2001 and later models

19 Accelerator Pedal Position (APP) sensor - replacement

Note: *The APP sensor is located at the upper end of the accelerator pedal assembly on 2004 and later models. The APP sensor and the accelerator pedal are removed as a single assembly*

1 Disconnect the cable from the negative battery terminal (see Chapter 5, Section 1).
2 Disconnect the APP sensor electrical connector.
3 Remove the accelerator pedal/APP sensor assembly.
4 Installation is the reverse of removal. Be sure to tighten the accelerator pedal assembly mounting bolts securely.

Chapter 7 Part A
Manual transaxle

Contents

	Section			Section
Back-up light switch - check and replacement	4	Oil seal replacement	See Chapter 7B
General information	1	Powertrain mounts - check and replacement	See Chapter 2
Lubricant change	See Chapter 1	Shift cables - removal and installation	2
Lubricant level check	See Chapter 1	Shift lever - removal and installation	3
Manual transaxle - removal and installation	5	Transaxle oil cooler - removal and installation	7
Manual transaxle overhaul - general information	6		

Specifications

Torque specifications

	Ft-lbs (unless otherwise indicated)	Nm
Transaxle-to-engine bolts		
2WD models		
2000 and earlier (see illustrations 5.11a and 5.22a)		
Bolts A	47	64
Bolt B	26	35
Bolts C	22	29
Bolt D	34	46
Bolt E	18	25
Bolts F	78 in-lbs	9
Bolts G	27	37
2001 and later (see illustrations 5.11b and 5.22b)		
Bolts A	47	64
Bolts B	34	46
4WD models		
2000 and earlier (see illustration 5.45a)		
Bolts A	47	64
Bolt B	26	35
Bolts C	22	29
Bolt D	34	46
Bolt E	18	25
Bolt F	78 in-lbs	9
2001 and later (see illustration 5.45b)		
Bolts A	47	64
Bolts B	34	46
Bolts C	32	44

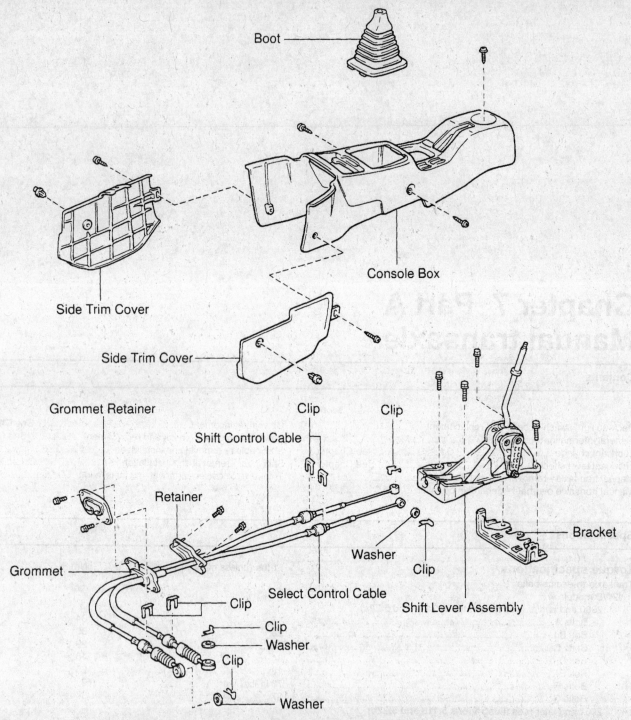

2.1 Shift cable details (2000 and earlier models shown, later models similar)

1   General information

The vehicles covered by this manual are equipped with a 5-speed manual transaxle or a 4-speed automatic transaxle. Information on the manual transaxle is included in this Part of Chapter 7. Service procedures for the automatic transaxle are contained in Chapter 7, Part B.

The manual transaxle is a compact, two-piece, lightweight aluminum alloy housing containing both the transmission and differential assemblies.

Because of the complexity, unavailability of replacement parts and special tools necessary, internal repair procedures for the manual transaxle are beyond the scope of this manual. The bulk of information in this Chapter is devoted to removal and installation procedures.

2   Shift cables - removal and installation

Refer to illustration 2.1
Note: *The shift cables are not adjustable. If they become stretched or worn, causing shifting problems, they must be replaced.*
1   In the engine compartment, remove the retaining clips and washers and disconnect

the shift cables from the selecting bellcrank **(see illustration)**.

2   Remove the cable retainers from the cable bracket. Also, on 2000 and earlier models, follow the cables to the firewall and unbolt the cable grommet retainer.

3   Remove the center console (see Chapter 11).

4   Remove the cable housing clips from the shift lever base.

5   Remove the retaining clips and washers from the cable ends and disconnect the cables from the shift lever assembly.

6   Trace the cables to the firewall and unbolt the interior grommet retainer. Pull the cable assembly through the firewall.

7   Installation is the reverse of removal.

3   Shift lever - removal and installation

1   Remove the center console (see Chapter 11).

2   Remove the shift cable retainers and disconnect both cables from the shift lever (see Section 2).

3   Remove the retaining bolts from the shift lever base **(see illustration 2.1)** and detach the shift lever from the vehicle.

4   Installation is the reverse of removal.

4   Back-up light switch - check and replacement

Refer to illustration 4.1

Check

1   The back-up light switch is located on top of the transaxle **(see illustration)**.

2   Turn the ignition key to the On position and move the shift lever to the Reverse position. The switch should close the back-up light circuit and turn on the back-up lights.

3   If it doesn't, check the back-up light fuse (see Chapter 12).

4   If the fuse is good, unplug the electrical connector from the switch and, using an ohmmeter, check continuity of the switch with the shifter in Neutral and then in Reverse. The meter should indicate continuity when the shifter is in Reverse only. If it doesn't, replace the switch.

5   If the switch is working properly, check the wire between the fuse and the switch; if there is voltage, note whether one or both back-up lights are out.

6   If neither bulb lights up, the bulbs could be the problem, but it's more likely that the wire between the switch and the bulbs has an open somewhere.

Replacement

7   Disconnect the electrical connector from the back-up light switch.

8   Unscrew the switch from the case.

9   To test the new switch before installation, simply check continuity across the switch terminals: with the plunger depressed, there should be continuity; with the plunger free, there should be no continuity.

10   Screw in the new switch and tighten it securely.

11   Connect the electrical connector.

12   Check the operation of the back-up lights.

5   Manual transaxle - removal and installation

2WD models

Refer to illustrations 5.11a, 5.11b, 5.17, 5.22a and 5.22b

Removal

1   Disconnect the negative cable from the battery.

2   Remove the air filter housing (see Chapter 4). Remove the coolant reservoir (see Chapter 3).

3   Loosen the driveaxle/hub nuts (see Chapter 8) and the wheel lug nuts.

4   Remove the clutch release cylinder and the clutch hydraulic line (see Chapter 8). **Caution:** *Do not depress the clutch pedal while the release cylinder is detached from the transaxle.*

5   Unplug the electrical connector from the back-up light switch (see Section 4) and the

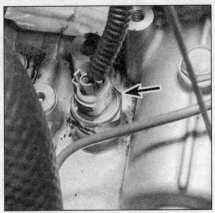

4.1 The back-up light switch is threaded into the top of the transaxle case

speed sensor (see Chapter 6).

6   Remove the ground cable retaining bolt and detach the ground cable from the transaxle.

7   Disconnect the shift cables from the transaxle (see Section 2).

8   Detach any wire harness clamps from the engine and/or transaxle and set the harnesses aside.

9   Remove the starter (see Chapter 5).

10   Attach an engine support fixture to the lifting hook at the transaxle end of the engine. If no hook is provided, use a bolt of the proper size and thread pitch to attach the support fixture chain to a hole at the end of the cylinder head. **Note:** *Engine support fixtures can be obtained at most equipment rental yards and some auto parts stores. The engine must be supported at all times while the transaxle is out of the vehicle.*

11   Remove the upper transaxle-to-engine mounting bolts **(see illustrations)**. Note the location of any ground connectors or brackets, so that they may be installed in their original location.

12   Unbolt the left powertrain mount from the transaxle (see Chapter 2).

13   Raise the vehicle and support it securely on jackstands. Remove the wheels and the under-vehicle splash shields.

14   Drain the transaxle fluid (see Chapter 1). Remove the driveaxles (see Chapter 8).

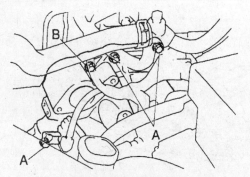

5.11a Upper transaxle-to-engine bolts - 2000 and earlier 2WD models

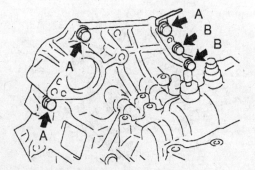

5.11b Upper transaxle-to-engine bolts - 2001 and later 2WD models

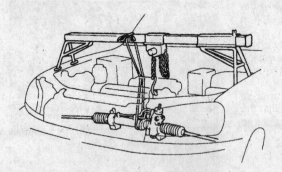

5.17 After unbolting the steering gear from the crossmember, support it with a length of wire or rope from the engine support fixture

15   Remove the front exhaust pipe (see Chapter 4).
16   Disconnect the lubricant cooler hoses from the transaxle, if equipped. Be prepared for spillage, and plug the hoses and the lines on the transaxle.
17   Unbolt the steering gear from the suspension crossmember. Support the steering gear from above with a length of rope or wire. **Note:** *You can tie the rope or wire to the engine support fixture* **(see illustration)**.
18   Remove the front suspension crossmember (see Chapter 10) and the longitudinal crossmember.
19   On 2000 and earlier models, remove the stiffener plate and the engine rear end plate.
20   Support the transaxle with a jack (preferably a special jack made for this purpose; these jacks are available at most equipment rental yards). Safety chains will help steady the transaxle on the jack.
21   Remove the left power train mount and the mount bracket.
22   Remove the rest of the bolts securing the transaxle to the engine **(see illustrations)**.
23   Make a final check that all wires and hoses have been disconnected from the transaxle.
24   Lower the left (driver's) end of the engine while simultaneously lowering the transaxle, then roll the transaxle and jack toward the side of the vehicle. Once the input shaft is clear of the splines in the clutch hub, lower the transaxle and remove it from under the vehicle. Try to keep the transaxle as level as possible.
25   The clutch components can now be inspected (see Chapter 8). In most cases,

new clutch components should be routinely installed whenever the transaxle is removed.

Installation
26   Installation of the transaxle is a reversal of the removal procedure, but note the following points:

a) Apply a little high-temperature grease to the splines on the transaxle input shaft.
b) Tighten the transaxle mounting bolts to the torque values listed in this Chapter's Specifications.
c) Tighten the suspension crossmember mounting bolts and the steering gear fasteners to the torque values listed in the Chapter 10 Specifications.
d) Tighten the driveaxle/hub nuts to the torque value listed in the Chapter 8 Specifications.
e) Tighten the wheel lug nuts to the torque listed in the Chapter 1 Specifications.
f) Fill the transaxle with the correct type and amount of lubricant as described in Chapter 1.

4WD models
Refer to illustrations 5.45a, 5.45b, 5.46a, 5.46b and 5.46c
Warning 1: *Gasoline is extremely flammable so take extra precautions when you work on any part of the fuel system. Don't smoke or allow open flames or bare light bulbs near the work area, and don't work in a garage where a gas-type appliance (such as a water heater or a clothes dryer) is present. Since gasoline is carcinogenic, wear latex gloves when*

there's a possibility of being exposed to fuel, and, if you spill any fuel on your skin, rinse it off immediately with soap and water. Mop up any spills immediately and do not store fuel-soaked rags where they could ignite. The fuel system is under constant pressure, so, if any fuel lines are to be disconnected, the fuel pressure in the system must be relieved first (see Chapter 4). When you perform any kind of work on the fuel system, wear safety glasses and have a Class B type fire extinguisher on hand.
Warning 2: *The air conditioning system is under high pressure - have a licensed air conditioning technician evacuate the system and recover the refrigerant before disconnecting any of the hoses or fittings.*
Note: *Transaxle removal on 4WD models is a difficult job, especially for the do-it-yourself mechanic working at home. Because of the vehicle's design, the manufacturer states that the engine and transaxle have to be removed as a unit from the bottom of the vehicle, not the top. With a floor jack and jackstands the vehicle can't be raised high enough and supported safely enough for the engine/transaxle assembly to slide out from underneath. The manufacturer recommends that removal of the engine/transaxle assembly only be performed on a vehicle hoist.*
27   Disconnect the cable from the negative terminal of the battery. Remove the hood (see Chapter 11).
28   Refer to Chapter 2C, *Engine - removal and installation*, for information on the preliminary engine removal steps, such as disconnecting electrical connectors, control cables and hoses. Make sure no hoses or wires are attached to the engine or transaxle from above.
29   Loosen the driveaxle/hub nuts and the wheel lug nuts. Remove the wheels.
30   Detach the shift cables from the transaxle (see Section 2).
31   Raise the vehicle on the hoist.
32   Remove the under-vehicle splash shield(s).
33   Remove the driveshaft and driveaxles (see Chapter 8).
34   If you're working on a 2000 or earlier model, remove the power steering pump and suspend it out of the way (see Chapter 10).

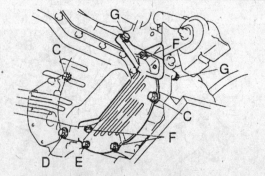

5.22a Lower transaxle-to-engine bolts - 2000 and earlier 2WD models

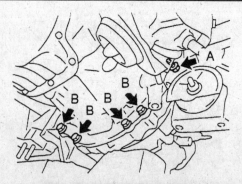

5.22b Lower transaxle-to-engine bolts - 2001 and later 2WD models

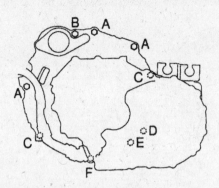

5.45a Transaxle-to-engine bolts - 2000 and earlier 4WD models

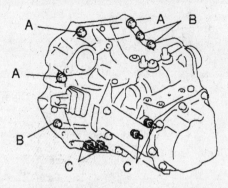

5.45b Transaxle-to-engine bolts - 2001 and later 4WD models

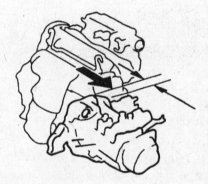

5.46a When removing the transaxle from the engine on 2000 and earlier 4WD models, pull it away from the engine approximately two or three inches . . .

5.46b . . . move the end of the transaxle in the direction of the arrow . . .

5.46c . . . then continue to separate the transaxle from the engine

35 Remove the front section of the exhaust system (see Chapter 4).
36 Remove the suspension crossmember and longitudinal crossmember.
37 Lower the vehicle and attach an engine hoist to the engine/transaxle assembly. Make sure the hoist chain or sling is long enough to allow the engine/transaxle assembly to be lowered to the ground.
38 Unbolt the right and left powertrain mounts from the engine/transaxle assembly (see Chapter 2).
39 Lower the engine/transaxle assembly to the ground, then disconnect the hoist.
40 Raise the vehicle on the hoist and remove the engine/transaxle assembly out from underneath.
41 Remove the starter.
42 Label and disconnect all electrical connectors from the transaxle.
43 Label and disconnect the vacuum hoses from the transfer vacuum actuator, then unbolt and remove the actuator.
44 On 2000 and earlier models, unbolt all three stiffener plates from the transaxle and transfer case. On 2001 and later models, remove the single stiffener plate.
45 Remove the transaxle-to-engine bolts **(see illustrations)**. **Note:** *Note the loca-*

tions of the bolts so they can be returned to their original positions when the transaxle is installed.
46 Separate the transaxle from the engine. On 2000 and earlier models, pull the transaxle approximately two to three inches away from the engine, swing the left end of the transaxle back, then continue to pull the transaxle away from the engine **(see illustrations)**.
47 Installation is the reverse of the removal procedure, noting the points listed in Step 26.

6 Manual transaxle overhaul - general information

1 Overhauling a manual transaxle is a difficult job for the do-it-yourselfer. It involves the disassembly and reassembly of many small parts. Numerous clearances must be precisely measured and, if necessary, changed with select-fit spacers and snap-rings. As a result, if transaxle problems arise, it can be removed and installed by a competent do-it-yourselfer, but overhaul should be left to a transmission repair shop. Rebuilt transaxles may be available - check with your dealer parts department and auto parts stores. At

any rate, the time and money involved in an overhaul is almost sure to exceed the cost of a rebuilt unit.
2 Nevertheless, it's not impossible for an inexperienced mechanic to rebuild a transaxle if the special tools are available and the job is done in a deliberate step-by-step manner so nothing is overlooked.
3 The tools necessary for an overhaul include internal and external snap-ring pliers, a bearing puller, a slide hammer, a set of pin punches, a dial indicator and possibly a hydraulic press. In addition, a large, sturdy workbench and a vise or transaxle stand will be required.
4 During disassembly of the transaxle, make careful notes of how each piece comes off, where it fits in relation to other pieces and what holds it in place.
5 Before taking the transaxle apart for repair, it will help if you have some idea what area of the transaxle is malfunctioning. Certain problems can be closely tied to specific areas in the transaxle, which can make component examination and replacement easier. Refer to the *Troubleshooting* section at the front of this manual for information regarding possible sources of trouble.

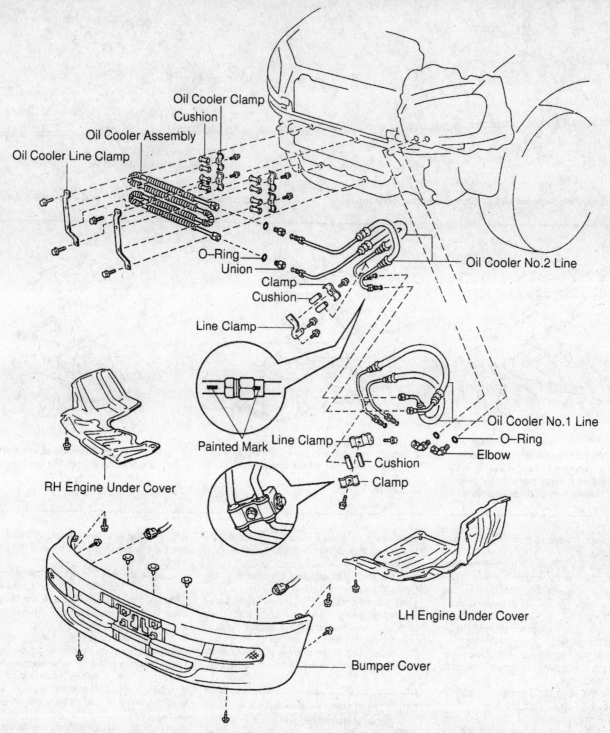

Oil Cooler Clamp
Cushion
Oil Cooler Assembly
Oil Cooler Line Clamp
O-Ring
Union
Clamp
Cushion
Line Clamp
Painted Mark
Line Clamp
Cushion
Clamp
RH Engine Under Cover
Oil Cooler No.2 Line
Oil Cooler No.1 Line
O-Ring
Elbow
LH Engine Under Cover
Bumper Cover

7.3 Transaxle oil cooler installation details (2000 and earlier 4WD models)

7   Transaxle oil cooler - removal and installation

Refer to illustration 7.3
Note: *This procedure applies to 2000 and earlier 4WD models only.*
1   Remove the under-vehicle splash shields.
2   Remove the front bumper cover (see

Chapter 11).
3   Using a flare nut wrench if available, unscrew the line fittings from the oil cooler **(see illustration)**. Hold the stationary fittings on the cooler with an open-end wrench to prevent the cooler tubes from twisting.
4   Unbolt the cooler clamps and detach the cooler from the vehicle.
5   Installation is the reverse of the removal

procedure, noting the following points:
a) *Install new O-rings on the cooler line fittings. Tighten the fittings securely.*
b) *Drive the vehicle a short distance to circulate the transaxle lubricant through the cooler, then park the vehicle and check the transaxle lubricant level as described in Chapter 1. Add the proper type of lubricant as necessary*

Chapter 7 Part B
Automatic transaxle

Contents

	Section		Section
Automatic transaxle - removal and installation	8	General information	1
Automatic transaxle fluid and filter change	See Chapter 1	Oil seal replacement	3
Automatic transaxle fluid level check	See Chapter 1	Park/Neutral Position (PNP) switch - adjustment and	
Automatic transaxle overhaul - general information	9	replacement	6
Automatic transaxle/differential lubricant level		Shift cable - removal, installation and adjustment	5
check/change	See Chapter 1	Shift lock system - description and check	7
Diagnosis - general	2	Throttle Valve (TV) cable - check, adjustment and replacement	4

Specifications

Shift lock system
Shift lock solenoid resistance	26 to 33 ohms
Key interlock solenoid resistance	12.5 to 16.5 ohms

Torque specifications

	Ft-lbs (unless otherwise indicated)	Nm
Park/Neutral Position switch	48 in-lbs	5.5
Torque converter-to-driveplate bolts		
1996 through 2000	20	27
2001 and later		
2WD models	32	43
4WD models	30	40
Transaxle-to-engine bolts		
1996 through 2000		
2WD		
Three upper bolts	47	64
Lower rear bolts		
Small	18	25
Large	34	46
4WD		
14 mm-head bolts	47	64
12 mm-head bolts	34	46
Transfer case-to-transaxle bolts	27	37
2001 and later		
Three upper bolts	47	64
Four lower bolts	32	44
Two rear-side bolts	34	46
Valve body bolts	96 in-lbs	11
Manual valve retaining bolts (4WD models)	96 in-lbs	11

1   General information

All information on the automatic transaxle is included in this Part of Chapter 7. Information for the manual transaxle can be found in Part A of this Chapter.

Because of the complexity of the automatic transaxles and the specialized equipment necessary to perform most service operations, this Chapter contains only those procedures related to general diagnosis, routine maintenance, adjustment and removal and installation.

If the transaxle requires major repair work, it should be left to a dealer service department or an automotive or transmission repair shop. Once properly diagnosed you can, however, remove and install the transaxle yourself and save the expense, even if the repair work is done by a transmission shop.

2   Diagnosis - general

Note: *Automatic transaxle malfunctions may be caused by five general conditions: poor engine performance, improper adjustments, hydraulic malfunctions, mechanical malfunctions or malfunctions in the computer or its signal network. Diagnosis of these problems should always begin with a check of the easily repaired items: fluid level and condition (see Chapter 1), shift linkage adjustment and, on 2000 and earlier models, throttle valve linkage adjustment. Next, perform a road test to determine if the problem has been corrected or if more diagnosis is necessary. Because the transaxle relies on many sensors in the engine control system, and since the transaxle shift points are controlled by the Powertrain Control Module (2001 and later models), you'll also want to check to see if any trouble codes have been stored on the PCM (see Chapter 6 for a list of trouble codes and how to extract them). If the problem persists after the preliminary tests and corrections are completed, additional diagnosis should be done by a dealer service department or transmission repair shop. Refer to the* Troubleshooting *section at the front of this manual for information on symptoms of transaxle problems.*

Preliminary checks

1   Drive the vehicle to warm the transaxle to normal operating temperature.
2   Check the fluid level as described in Chapter 1:

a) *If the fluid level is unusually low, add enough fluid to bring the level within the designated area of the dipstick, then check for external leaks (see below).*

b) *If the fluid level is abnormally high, drain off the excess, then check the drained fluid for contamination by coolant. The presence of engine coolant in the automatic transmission fluid indicates that a failure has occurred in the internal radiator walls that separate the coolant from the transmission fluid (see Chapter 3).*

c) *If the fluid is foaming, drain it and refill the transaxle, then check for coolant in the fluid, or a high fluid level.*

3   Check the engine idle speed. **Note:** *If the engine is malfunctioning, do not proceed with the preliminary checks until it has been repaired and runs normally.*
4   Check the throttle valve cable for freedom of movement (2000 and earlier models only). Adjust it if necessary (see Section 4). **Note:** *The throttle valve cable may function properly when the engine is shut off and cold, but it may malfunction once the engine is hot. Check it cold and at normal engine operating temperature.*
5   Inspect the shift cable (see Section 5). Make sure that it's properly adjusted and that the cable operates smoothly.

Fluid leak diagnosis

6   Most fluid leaks are easy to locate visually. Repair usually consists of replacing a seal or gasket. If a leak is difficult to find, the following procedure may help.
7   Identify the fluid. Make sure it's transmission fluid and not engine oil or brake fluid (automatic transmission fluid is a deep red color).
8   Try to pinpoint the source of the leak. Drive the vehicle several miles, then park it over a large sheet of cardboard. After a minute or two, you should be able to locate the leak by determining the source of the fluid dripping onto the cardboard.
9   Make a careful visual inspection of the suspected component and the area immediately around it. Pay particular attention to gasket mating surfaces. A mirror is often helpful for finding leaks in areas that are hard to see.
10   If the leak still cannot be found, clean the suspected area thoroughly with a degreaser or solvent, then dry it.
11   Drive the vehicle for several miles at normal operating temperature and varying speeds. After driving the vehicle, visually inspect the suspected component again.
12   Once the leak has been located, the cause must be determined before it can be properly repaired. If a gasket is replaced but the sealing flange is bent, the new gasket will not stop the leak. The bent flange must be straightened.
13   Before attempting to repair a leak, check to make sure that the following conditions are corrected or they may cause another leak. **Note:** *Some of the following conditions cannot be fixed without highly specialized tools and expertise. Such problems must be referred to a transmission shop or a dealer service department.*

Gasket leaks

14   Check the pan periodically. Make sure the bolts are tight, no bolts are missing, the gasket is in good condition and the pan is flat (dents in the pan may indicate damage to the valve body inside).
15   If the pan gasket is leaking, the fluid level

or the fluid pressure may be too high, the vent may be plugged, the pan bolts may be too tight, the pan sealing flange may be warped, the sealing surface of the transaxle housing may be damaged, the gasket may be damaged or the transaxle casting may be cracked or porous. If sealant instead of gasket material has been used to form a seal between the pan and the transaxle housing, it may be the wrong sealant.

Seal leaks

16   If a transaxle seal is leaking, the fluid level or pressure may be too high, the vent may be plugged, the seal bore may be damaged, the seal itself may be damaged or improperly installed, the surface of the shaft protruding through the seal may be damaged or a loose bearing may be causing excessive shaft movement.
17   Make sure the dipstick tube seal is in good condition and the tube is properly seated. Periodically check the area around the speedometer gear or sensor for leakage. If transmission fluid is evident, check the O-ring for damage.

Case leaks

18   If the case itself appears to be leaking, the casting is porous and will have to be repaired or replaced.
19   Make sure the oil cooler hose fittings are tight and in good condition.

Fluid comes out vent pipe or fill tube

20   If this condition occurs, the transaxle is overfilled, there is coolant in the fluid, the case is porous, the dipstick is incorrect, the vent is plugged or the drain-back holes are plugged.

3   Oil seal replacement

1   Oil leaks frequently occur due to wear of the driveaxle oil seals and/or the speedometer drive gear oil seal and O-rings. Replacement of these seals is relatively easy, since the repairs can be performed without removing the transaxle from the vehicle.

Driveaxle oil seals

Refer to illustrations 3.4 and 3.6

2   The driveaxle oil seals are located on the sides of the transaxle, where the inner ends of the driveaxles are splined into the differential side gears. If you suspect that a driveaxle oil seal is leaking, raise the vehicle and support it securely on jackstands. If the seal is leaking, you'll see lubricant on the side of the transaxle, below the seal.
3   Remove the driveaxle (see Chapter 8).
4   Using a screwdriver or prybar, carefully pry the oil seal out of the transaxle bore **(see illustration)**.
5   If the oil seal cannot be removed with a screwdriver or prybar, a special oil seal removal tool (available at auto parts stores)

3.4 Carefully pry out the driveaxle oil seal with a seal removal tool
or a large screwdriver; make sure you don't damage the
seal bore or the new seal may leak

3.6 Use a seal installer, a large socket or a piece of
pipe to install the new seal

will be required.

6   Using a seal installer, a large section of pipe or a large deep socket as a drift, install the new oil seal. Drive it into the bore squarely to the proper depth (see illustration):

1996 through 2000 2WD models, right side: 0 (flush with the case) +/- 0.020 inch (0 +/- 0.5 mm)

1996 through 2000 2WD models, left side: 0.205 +/- 0.020 inch (5.2 +/- 0.5 mm)

1996 through 2000 4WD models, either side: 0 (flush with the case) +/- 0.020 inch (0 +/- 0.5 mm)

2001 and later 2WD models, either side: 0 (flush with the case) +/- 0.020 inch (0 +/- 0.5 mm)

2001 and later 4WD models, right side: 0.039 +/- 0.020 inch (1.0 +/- 0.5 mm)

2001 and later 4WD models, left side: 0 (flush with the case) +/- 0.020 inch (0 +/- 0.5 mm)

7   Lubricate the lip of the new seal with multi-purpose grease, then install the driveaxle (see Chapter 8). Be careful not to damage the lip of the new seal.

Speed sensor O-ring

Refer to illustrations 3.9 and 3.10

8   There are two speed sensors mounted on the transaxle; one is an input turbine speed sensor which monitors the rotational speed of the input shaft, the other monitors the rotational speed of the output shaft (driveaxle). They are both mounted in a similar fashion, using a hold-down bolt and sealed by an O-ring. Look for lubricant around the sensor housing to determine if the O-ring is leaking.

9   Unplug the electrical connector and unbolt the vehicle speed sensor from the transaxle (see illustration).

10   Using a scribe or a small screwdriver, remove the O-ring from the sensor (see illustration) and install a new O-ring. Lubricate

the new O-ring with automatic transmission fluid to protect it during installation of the sensor.

11   Installation is the reverse of removal.

Extension housing oil seal (4WD models only)

12   Remove the driveshaft (see Chapter 8).

13   Using a seal removal tool or a large screwdriver, carefully pry the oil seal out of the extension housing. Do not damage the splines on the transfer output shaft.

14   Using a seal driver, a large section of pipe or a very large deep socket as a drift, install the new oil seal. Drive it into the bore squarely to a depth of 0.059 +/- 0.016 inch (1.5 +/- 0.4 mm).

15   Lubricate the splines of the transfer output shaft and the outside of the driveshaft yoke with lightweight grease, then install the driveshaft (see Chapter 8). Be careful not to damage the lip of the new seal.

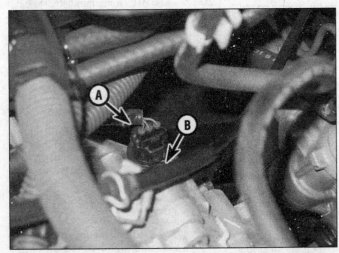

3.9 Unplug the speed sensor electrical connector (A), remove
the bolt (B) and pull the speed sensor unit straight out of the
transaxle (Vehicle Speed Sensor shown, input turbine speed
sensor similar)

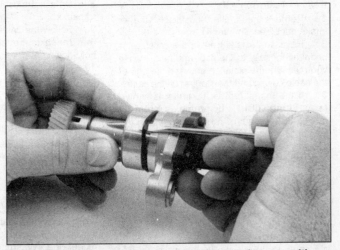

3.10 Remove the oil seal O-ring from the speed sensor with a
small screwdriver; make sure you don't scratch the surface
of the sensor or gouge the O-ring groove

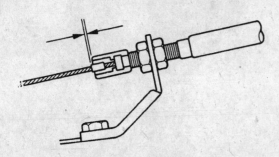

4.3 The distance between the stopper and the cable casing should be 0 to 0.040 inch (0 to 1 mm) when the accelerator pedal is depressed to the floor

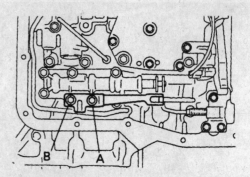

4.12 Remove the manual detent spring (4WD model shown; 2WD models have only one bolt)

A   14 mm bolt   B   37 mm bolt

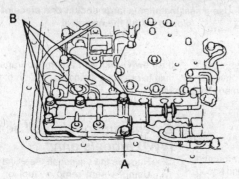

4.13 On 4WD models, remove these bolts and detach the manual valve

A   22 mm bolt   B   37 mm bolt

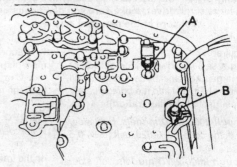

4.16 On 4WD models, remove these two bolts, then pry out the small oil tube, being careful not to damage it

A   39 mm bolt   B   43 mm bolt

4   Throttle Valve (TV) cable - check, adjustment and replacement

Note: *This Section applies to 2000 and earlier models only.*

Check

Refer to illustration 4.3

1   Remove the air filter housing and the air intake duct (see Chapter 4).
2   Have an assistant press the accelerator pedal all the way to the floor and hold it while you measure the distance between the end of the cable casing and the stopper on the cable.
3   If the measurement taken is as shown **(see illustration)**, the cable is properly adjusted. If it's out of range, adjust it as follows.

Adjustment

4   Have your assistant continue to hold the pedal down while you loosen the adjusting nuts and adjust the cable housing so that the distance between the end of the boot and the stopper on the cable is within the range shown.
5   Tighten the adjusting nuts securely, recheck the clearance and make sure the throttle valve opens all the way when the throttle is depressed.

Replacement

Refer to illustrations 4.12, 4.13, 4.16, 4.17a, 4.17b, 4.17c, 4.17d and 4.19

6   Loosen the cable locknut and detach the cable from the bracket at the throttle body.
7   Disconnect the cable from the throttle linkage.
8   Detach the cable from the bracket on the transaxle.
9   Follow the cable down to where it enters the transaxle housing. Remove the cable hold-down bolt.
10   Drain the transaxle fluid, remove the pan and the filter (see Chapter 1).
11   If you're working on a 1996 or 1997 2WD model, remove the two bolts and bracket that secure the oil tubes. Carefully pry the oil tubes out with a large screwdriver.
12   Remove the manual detent spring **(see illustration)**. **Note:** *On 2WD models the spring is secured by one bolt; on 4WD models it's secured by two.*
13   If you're working on a 4WD model, remove the five bolts and detach the manual valve **(see illustration)**.
14   If you're working on a 1996 or 1997 2WD model or a 4WD model, unplug the electrical connectors from the solenoids.
15   4WD models: Remove the bolt and clamp, then carefully pry out all eight oil tubes

with a large screwdriver.
16   4WD models: Remove the bolts securing the electrical connector clamp and the retaining clamp over the small oil tube, then carefully pry out the tube **(see illustration)**.
17   Remove the valve body bolts **(see illustrations)**. Separate the valve body from the transaxle and detach the throttle valve cable from the cam on the valve body **(see illustration)**.

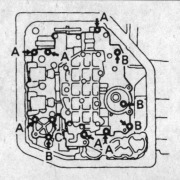

4.17a Valve body mounting bolts - 1996 and 1997 2WD models

A   20 mm bolt
B   30 mm bolt
C   55 mm bolt

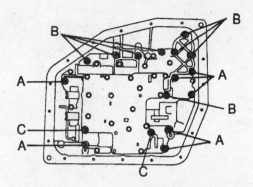

**4.17b Valve body mounting bolts - 1998 through
2000 2WD models**

A   20 mm bolt   C   50 mm bolt
B   28 mm bolt

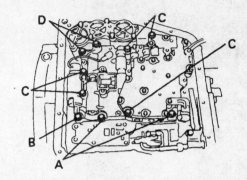

**4.17c Valve body mounting bolts - 1996 through
2000 4WD models**

A   22 mm bolt   C   43 mm bolt
B   32 mm bolt   D   55 mm bolt

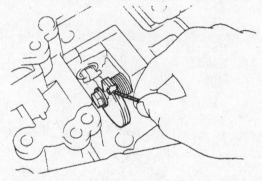

**4.17d Once the valve body has been lowered from the transaxle,
the throttle valve cable can be detached from the cam**

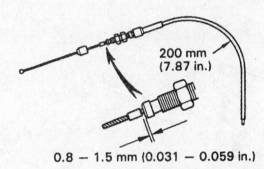

200 mm
(7.87 in.)

0.8 – 1.5 mm (0.031 – 0.059 in.)

4.19 Cable stopper positioning details

18   Installation is the reverse of removal. Be sure to tighten the valve body and related fasteners to the torque listed in this Chapter's Specifications. Refer to Chapter 1 for the torque specifications for the pan bolts and the type and quantity of transaxle fluid required to refill the transaxle.

19   If you are installing a new cable, the stopper on the cable must be crimped to the cable as follows:

a)   *With the upper end of the cable detached from the throttle body, bend the cable to a radius of approximately 8-inches (20 cm).*

b)   *Pull the inner cable out of the cable casing until you feel a slight resistance, position the cable stopper 0.031 to 0.059 inch (0.8 to 1.5 mm) from the end of the cable casing, then crimp the stopper to the cable* **(see illustration)**.

20   Connect the cable to the throttle body and bracket, then adjust the cable as described in Steps 4 and 5.

---

5   Shift cable - removal, installation and adjustment

Warning: *These models are equipped with airbags. Always disable the airbag system before working in the vicinity of any airbag system component to avoid the possibility of accidental deployment of the airbag(s), which could cause personal injury (see Chapter 12).*

Removal and installation

Refer to illustrations 5.2, 5.4a and 5.4b

1   Remove the under-vehicle splash shield. If helpful for access, raise the front of the vehicle and support it securely on jackstands.

2   Disconnect the shift cable from the manual shift lever at the transaxle and detach it from the bracket on the front of the transaxle **(see illustration)**. Also detach the cable from the clip on the top of the transaxle, if equipped.

3   Remove the center console (see Chapter 11).

4   Pry the cable end off the pin on the shifter assembly, then squeeze the tabs on the cable casing and detach the cable from the shifter housing **(see illustrations)**.

**5.2 Remove the nut securing the shift
cable to the manual lever (A), then
remove the clip (B) and detach the
shift cable from the bracket**

**5.4a Pry the end of the shift cable off the
pin on the shifter assembly . . .**

5.4b . . . then squeeze the tabs on the cable casing and detach the cable from the shifter housing

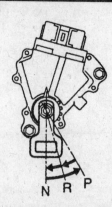

5.9a Manual shift lever Park, Reverse and Neutral positions - 1996 and 1997 2WD models and 1996 through 2000 4WD models

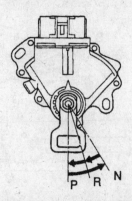

5.9b Manual shift lever Park, Reverse and Neutral positions - 1998 through 2000 2WD models

5.9c Manual shift lever Park, Reverse and Neutral positions - 2001 and later models

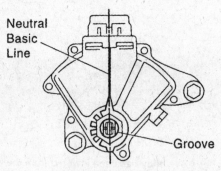

6.5a Park/Neutral Position switch alignment details - 1996 and 1997 2WD models shown, 1998 through 2000 2WD models similar

5   Pull the cable through the grommet in the firewall.
6   Installation is the reverse of removal.
7   When you're done, adjust the shift cable.

Adjustment

Refer to illustrations 5.9a, 5.9b and 5.9c

8   Loosen the nut on the manual shift lever at the transaxle **(see illustration 5.2)**.
9   At the transaxle, place the manual shift lever in the Neutral position **(see illustra-tions)**.
10   Move the shift lever inside the vehicle to the Neutral position.
11   Have an assistant hold the shift lever (inside the vehicle) with a slight pressure toward the Reverse position while you tighten the nut at the manual shift lever securely.
12   Check the operation of the transaxle in each shift lever position (try to start the engine in each gear - the starter should operate in the Park and Neutral positions only).

6   Park/Neutral Position (PNP) switch - adjustment and replacement

Adjustment

Refer to illustrations 6.5a, 6.5b and 6.5c

1   If the engine will start with the shift lever in any position other than Park or Neutral, adjust the Park/Neutral Position switch.
2   Apply the parking brake and block the rear wheels. Raise the front of the vehicle and support it securely on jackstands. Remove the under-vehicle splash shield and shift the transaxle into Neutral.
3   Loosen the switch retaining bolts.
4   Shift the transaxle into Neutral.
5   Align the line on the PNP switch with the groove in the manual lever shaft **(see illustra-tions)**.
6   Tighten the switch retaining bolts securely and check the operation of the switch. If the vehicle still starts in any position other than Park or Neutral, replace the switch.

Replacement

8   Disconnect the negative cable from the battery.

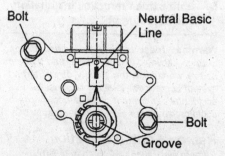

6.5b Park/Neutral Position switch alignment details - 1996 through 2000 4WD models

6.5c Park/Neutral Position switch alignment details - 2001 and later models

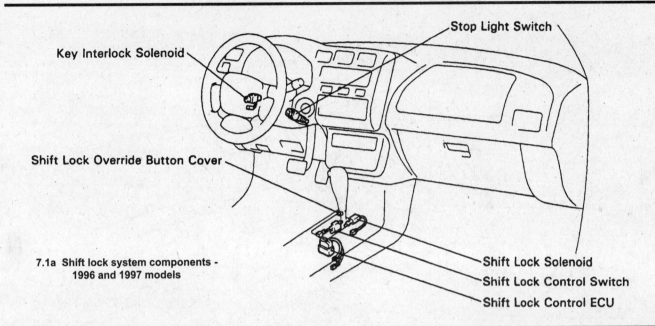

7.1a Shift lock system components - 1996 and 1997 models

9   Apply the parking brake and block the rear wheels. Raise the front of the vehicle and support it securely on jackstands. Remove the under-vehicle splash shield and shift the transaxle into Neutral.
10   Remove the nut and lift off the manual shift lever.
11   Unplug the electrical connector.
12   Remove the retaining bolts and lift the

switch off the shift shaft.
13   To install, line up the flats on the shift shaft with the flats in the switch and push the switch onto the shaft.
14   Rotate the switch until the neutral basic line aligns with the groove **(see illustrations 6.5a, 6.5b and 6.5c)**. Tighten the bolts securely and plug in the electrical connector.
15   Install the shift lever, connect the nega-

tive battery cable and verify the engine will not start with the shift lever in any position other than Park or Neutral.

7   Shift lock system - description and check

Warning: *These models are equipped with airbags. Always disable the airbag system before working in the vicinity of any airbag system component to avoid the possibility of accidental deployment of the airbag(s), which could cause personal injury* (see Chapter 12).

Description

Refer to illustrations 7.1a, 7.1b and 7.1c
1   The shift lock system **(see illustrations)** prevents the shift lever from being shifted out of Park or Neutral until the brake pedal is applied. It also prevents the key from being removed from the ignition lock cylinder until the shift lever is placed in the Park position.

Check

Key interlock solenoid
2   Remove the steering column covers (see Chapter 11).
3   Unplug the electrical connector for the key interlock solenoid.
4   Using an ohmmeter, measure the resistance between the two terminals on the solenoid side of the connector and compare your measurements with the resistance listed in this Chapter's Specifications.
5   Using jumper wires, momentarily apply battery voltage between the same two terminals. Verify that the solenoid makes an audible "click" when energized. **Caution:** *Don't apply battery voltage any longer than necessary for this check, as the solenoid could be damaged.*
6   If the key interlock solenoid fails either of these tests, replace it.

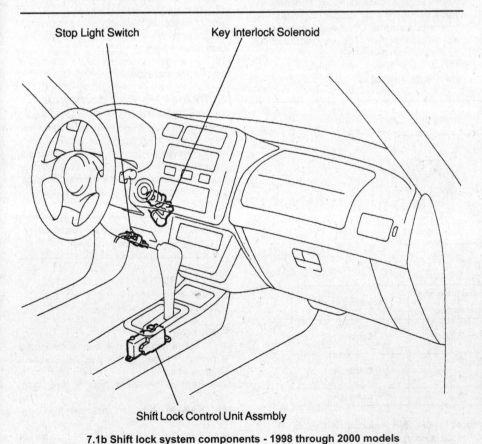

7.1b Shift lock system components - 1998 through 2000 models

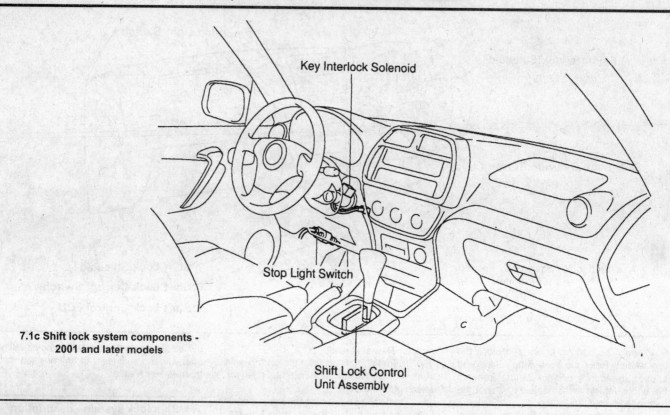

7.1c Shift lock system components - 2001 and later models

Shift lock solenoid (1996 and 1997 models only)

7   Remove the center console (see Chapter 11).

8   Unplug the shift lock solenoid connector.

9   Using an ohmmeter, measure the resistance between the two terminals of the connector (on the solenoid side of the connector), and compare your measurement with the resistance listed in this Chapter's Specifications.

10   Using jumper wires, momentarily apply battery voltage to the same two terminals and verify that there's an audible "click" from the solenoid. **Caution:** *Don't apply battery voltage any longer than necessary for this check, as the solenoid could be damaged.*

11   If the shift lock solenoid fails either of these tests, replace it.

Shift lock control switch (1996 and 1997 models only)

Refer to illustration 7.12

12   Unplug the electrical connector and verify that there's continuity between the indicated terminals in each shift lever position **(see illustration)**.

13   If the shift lock control switch fails any of these tests, replace it.

Shift lock control computer

14   If the above components are functioning properly but the shift lock system still does not, by process of elimination the shift lock control unit is probably defective. Before replacing it, however, check the wiring harnesses between the related components for open or short circuit conditions.

8   Automatic transaxle - removal and installation

2WD models

Refer to illustrations 9.7, 9.8, 9.19a, 9.19b and 9.23

Removal

1   Disconnect the cable from the negative terminal of the battery. Remove the hood (see Chapter 11).

2   Remove the air filter housing (see Chapter 4).

3   Remove the coolant reservoir (see Chapter 3).

4   If you're working on a 2000 or earlier model, disconnect the throttle valve cable

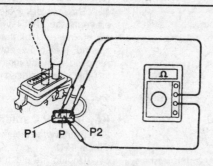

Shift position	Tester condition to terminal number	Specified value
P position (Release button is not pushed)	P – P 1	Continuity
P position (Release button is pushed)	P – P 1 P – P 2	Continuity
R, N, D, 2, L position	P – P 2	Continuity

7.12 Terminal guide and continuity table for the shift lock control switch (1996 and 1997 models only)

9.7 Remove these three transaxle-to-engine bolts before raising the vehicle

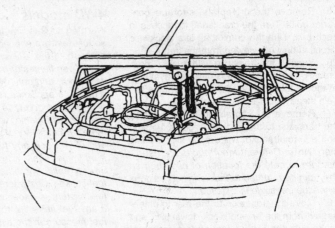

9.8 Attach an engine support fixture to the lifting hook at the transaxle end of the engine

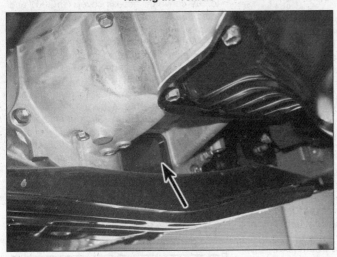

9.19a Pry out this access plug . . .

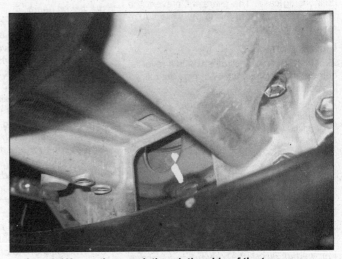

9.19b . . . then mark the relationship of the torque converter to the driveplate

from the throttle body and bracket.
5   Remove the starter (see Chapter 5).
6   Label and disconnect all electrical connectors from the transaxle. Also remove the bolt and detach the ground cable.
7   Remove the transaxle-to-engine bolts that are accessible from above (see illustration).
8   Attach an engine support fixture to the lifting hook at the transaxle end of the engine (see illustration). If no hook is provided, use a bolt of the proper size and thread pitch to attach the support fixture chain to a hole at the end of the cylinder head. Note: Engine support fixtures can be obtained at most equipment rental yards and some auto parts stores.
9   Unbolt the left-side powertrain mount from the transaxle (see Chapter 2).
10   Loosen the driveaxle/hub nuts and the wheel lug nuts, raise the front of the vehicle and support it securely on jackstands. Remove the wheels.
11   Remove the under-vehicle splash shield(s).
12   Disconnect the shift cable from the man-

ual lever on the transaxle, then detach the cable from its bracket and any other securing clips (see Section 5).
13   Drain the transaxle lubricant (see Chapter 1).
14   Remove the driveaxles (see Chapter 8).
15   Remove the front section of the exhaust system (see Chapter 4).
16   Mark and disconnect any electrical connectors accessible from below.
17   Disconnect the fluid cooler hoses from the transaxle. Be prepared for spillage, and plug the hoses and the lines on the transaxle.
18   Unbolt the steering gear from the suspension crossmember. Support the steering gear from above with a length of rope or wire. Note: You can tie the rope or wire to the engine support fixture.
19   On 2001 and later models, remove the torque converter access plug, then mark the relationship of the torque converter to the driveplate (see illustrations).
20   Detach the shift cable from the crossmember (1996 and 1997 models).
21   On 2001 and later models, detach the stabilizer bar links from the stabilizer bar (see

Chapter 10).
22   Remove the front suspension crossmember and the longitudinal crossmember.
23   On 2000 and earlier models, remove the stiffener plate, followed by the torque converter access cover (see illustration).
24   If you're working on a 2000 or earlier model, mark the relationship of the torque converter to the driveplate (see illustration 9.19b).

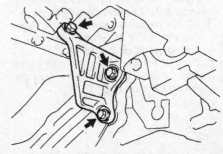

9.23 Unbolt the stiffener plate from the engine and transaxle (2000 and earlier models only)

25   Remove the driveplate-to-torque converter bolts. Turn the crankshaft for access to each bolt. Turn the crankshaft in a clockwise direction only (as viewed from the front).

26   Support the transaxle with a jack - preferably a jack made for this purpose (available at most tool rental yards). Safety chains will help steady the transaxle on the jack.

27   Remove the remaining bolts securing the transaxle to the engine. A long extension and a U-joint socket will greatly simplify this step. **Note:** *Different length bolts are used - be sure to note the location of each bolt so they can be returned to their original positions when the transaxle is installed.*

28   Move the transaxle to the rear to disengage it from the engine block dowel pins and make sure the torque converter is detached from the driveplate. Lower the transaxle with the jack. Clamp a pair of locking pliers on the bellhousing case. The pliers will prevent the torque converter from falling out while you're removing the transaxle.

Installation

29   Installation of the transaxle is a reversal of the removal procedure, but note the following points:

a)   *As the torque converter is reinstalled, ensure that the drive tangs at the center of the torque converter hub engage with the recesses in the automatic transaxle fluid pump inner gear. This can be confirmed by turning the torque converter while pushing it towards the transaxle. If it isn't fully engaged, it will "clunk" into place.*

b)   *When installing the transaxle, make sure the matchmarks you made on the torque converter and driveplate line up.*

c)   *Install all of the driveplate-to-torque converter bolts before tightening any of them.*

d)   *Tighten the driveplate-to-torque converter bolts to the specified torque.*

e)   *Tighten the transaxle mounting bolts to the correct torque.*

f)   *Tighten the suspension crossmember mounting bolts and the steering gear fasteners to the torque values listed in the Chapter 10 Specifications.*

g)   *Tighten the driveaxle/hub nuts to the torque value listed in the Chapter 8 Specifications.*

h)   *Tighten the wheel lug nuts to the torque listed in the Chapter 1 Specifications.*

i)   *Fill the transaxle with the correct type and amount of automatic transmission fluid as described in Chapter 1.*

j)   *On completion, adjust the shift cable and, on 2000 and earlier models, the throttle valve cable.*

4WD models

Warning 1: *Gasoline is extremely flammable so take extra precautions when you work on any part of the fuel system. Don't smoke or allow open flames or bare light bulbs near the work area, and don't work in a garage where a gas-type appliance (such as a water heater or a clothes dryer) is present. Since gasoline is carcinogenic, wear latex gloves when there's a possibility of being exposed to fuel, and, if you spill any fuel on your skin, rinse it off immediately with soap and water. Mop up any spills immediately and do not store fuel-soaked rags where they could ignite. The fuel system is under constant pressure, so, if any fuel lines are to be disconnected, the fuel pressure in the system must be relieved first (see Chapter 4). When you perform any kind of work on the fuel system, wear safety glasses and have a Class B type fire extinguisher on hand.*

Warning 2: *The air conditioning system is under high pressure - have a licensed air conditioning technician evacuate the system and recover the refrigerant before disconnecting any of the hoses or fittings.*

Note: *Transaxle removal on 4WD models is a difficult job, especially for the do-it-yourself mechanic working at home. Because of the vehicle's design, the manufacturer states that the engine and transaxle have to be removed as a unit from the bottom of the vehicle, not the top. With a floor jack and jackstands the vehicle can't be raised high enough and supported safely enough for the engine/transaxle assembly to slide out from underneath. The manufacturer recommends that removal of the engine/transaxle assembly only be performed on a vehicle hoist.*

30   Disconnect the cable from the negative terminal of the battery. Remove the hood (see Chapter 11).

31   Refer to Chapter 2C, *Engine - removal and installation*, for information on the preliminary engine removal steps, such as disconnecting electrical connectors, control cables and hoses. Make sure no hoses or wires are attached to the engine or transaxle from above.

32   Loosen the driveaxle/hub nuts and the wheel lug nuts. Remove the wheels.

33   Raise the vehicle on the hoist.

34   Remove the under-vehicle splash shield(s).

35   Detach the shift cable from the transaxle (see Section 5).

36   Remove the driveshaft and driveaxles (see Chapter 8).

37   If you're working on a 2000 or earlier model, remove the power steering pump and suspend it out of the way (see Chapter 10).

38   Remove the front section of the exhaust system (see Chapter 4).

39   Remove the suspension crossmember and longitudinal crossmember.

40   Lower the vehicle and attach an engine hoist to the engine/transaxle assembly. Make sure the hoist chain or sling is long enough to allow the engine/transaxle assembly to be lowered to the ground.

41   Unbolt the right and left powertrain mounts from the engine/transaxle assembly (see Chapter 2).

42   Lower the engine/transaxle assembly to the ground, then disconnect the hoist.

43   Raise the vehicle on the hoist and remove the engine/transaxle assembly out from underneath.

44   Remove the starter.

45   Remove the stiffener plate (upper and lower) and, on 2000 and earlier models, the torque converter access cover. On 2001 and later models, remove the torque converter access plug.

46   Mark the relationship of the torque converter to the driveplate, then remove the driveplate-to-torque converter bolts as described earlier in this Section.

47   Remove the transaxle/transfer case mounting bolts, then separate the transaxle from the engine. **Note:** *Different length bolts are used - be sure to note the location of each bolt so they can be returned to their original positions when the transaxle is installed.*

48   Installation is the reverse of the removal procedure, noting the points listed in Step 29.

9   Automatic transaxle overhaul - general information

In the event of a problem occurring, it will be necessary to establish whether the fault is electrical, mechanical or hydraulic in nature, before repair work can be contemplated. Diagnosis requires detailed knowledge of the transaxle's operation and construction, as well as access to specialized test equipment, and so is deemed to be beyond the scope of this manual. It is therefore essential that problems with the automatic transaxle are referred to a dealer service department or other qualified repair facility for assessment.

Note that a faulty transaxle should not be removed before the vehicle has been diagnosed by a knowledgeable technician equipped with the proper tools, as troubleshooting must be performed with the transaxle installed in the vehicle.

Chapter 8
Clutch and driveline

Contents

Section

Center support bearing (4WD models) - removal
   and installation 12
Clutch - description and check 2
Clutch components - removal, inspection and installation............ 6
Clutch hydraulic system - bleeding....................................... 5
Clutch master cylinder - removal and installation 3
Clutch release bearing and lever - removal, inspection
   and installation 7
Clutch release cylinder - removal and installation 4
Clutch start switch - replacement 8
Differential lubricant level checks (4WDmodels) .... See Chapter 1

Section

Differential oil seals (rear, 4WD models) - replacement 13
Differential (rear, 4WD models) - removal and installation 14
Driveaxle boot - replacement... 10
Driveaxle oil seal replacement (front)........................... See Chapter 7B
Driveaxles - removal and installation.. 9
Driveshaft (4WD models) - check, removal
   and installation 11
Extension housing oil seal replacement
   (4WD models) .... See Chapter 7B
General information 1

Specifications

Driveaxle standard length (see illustration 10.11)

Front (2000 and earlier)
  Right
    2WD
      M/T .... 33.185 inches (842.9 mm)
      A/T .... 33.252 inches (844.6 mm)
    4WD .... 20.126 inches (511.2 mm)
  Left
    2WD
      M/T .... 21.362 inches (542.6 mm)
      A/T .... 21.594 inches (548.5 mm)
    4WD .... 20.000 inches (508.0 mm)
Front (2001 and later)
  Right
    2WD .... 33.80 inches (858.5 mm)
    4WD .... 36.24 inches (920.5 mm)
  Left
    2WD .... 23.00 inches (585.4 mm)
    4WD .... 20.47 inches (520.5 mm)
Rear (2000 and earlier)
  Right... 23.598 inches (599.4 mm)
  Left.. 21.787 inches (553.4 mm)
Rear (2001 and later)
  Right... 26.059 inches (611.9 mm)
  Left.. 21.787 inches (564.9 mm)

Differential pinion shaft bearing preload

Rear, 4WD models, with used bearing.............................. 5.2 to 6.9 in-lbs (0.6 to 0.8 Nm)

Torque specifications

	Ft-lbs (unless otherwise indicated)	Nm
Clutch pressure plate bolt	14	19
Differential cover mounting bolts (4WD models)	34	47
Differential front mounting bracket bolts (4WD models)	86	117
Differential pinion flange nut (4WD models) (see Section 13)		
Initial	80	108
Maximum	173	235
Differential rear mounting bracket-to-body bolts	48	65
Differential rear mounting bracket-to-differential bolts		
(4WD models)	101	137
Driveaxle/hub nut	159	216
Driveshaft flange-to-rear differential bolts (4WD models)	54	74
Driveshaft center support bearing bolts (4WD models)	27	37
Driveshaft universal joint flange-to-cross groove joint	20	27
Rear drive axle-to-side gear shaft flange	41	56

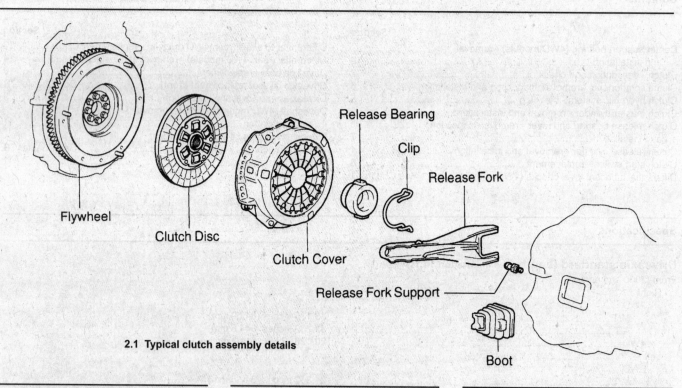

Release Bearing

Clip

Release Fork

Flywheel

Clutch Disc

Clutch Cover

Release Fork Support

Boot

2.1 Typical clutch assembly details

1   General information

The information in this Chapter deals with the components from the rear of the engine to the front wheels, except for the transaxle, which is dealt with in the previous Chapter. For the purposes of this Chapter, these components are grouped into two categories - clutch and driveaxles. Separate Sections within this Chapter offer general descriptions and checking procedures for components in each of the two groups.

Since nearly all the procedures covered in this Chapter involve working under the vehicle, make sure it's securely supported on sturdy jackstands or on a hoist where the vehicle can be easily raised and lowered.

2   Clutch - description and check

Refer to illustration 2.1
1   All vehicles with a manual transaxle use a single dry plate, diaphragm spring type clutch **(see illustration)**. The clutch disc has a splined hub which allows it to slide along the splines of the transaxle input shaft. The clutch and pressure plate are held in contact by spring pressure exerted by the diaphragm in the pressure plate.
2   The clutch release system is operated by hydraulic pressure. The hydraulic release system consists of the clutch pedal, a master cylinder, the hydraulic line, a slave cylinder which actuates the clutch release lever and the clutch release (or throw-out) bearing.

3   When pressure is applied to the clutch pedal to release the clutch, hydraulic pressure is exerted against the outer end of the clutch release lever. As the lever pivots, the shaft fingers push against the release bearing. The bearing pushes against the fingers of the diaphragm spring of the pressure plate assembly, which in turn releases the clutch plate.
4   Terminology can be a problem regarding the clutch components because common names have in some cases changed from that used by the manufacturer. For example, the driven plate is also called the clutch plate or disc, the pressure plate assembly is sometimes referred to as the clutch cover, the clutch release bearing is sometimes called a

3.5 Use a flare-nut wrench when disconnecting the hydraulic line fitting to prevent rounding off the corners of the tubing nut

4.2 Use a flare-nut wrench when disconnecting the hydraulic line fitting, then remove the mounting bolts

throw-out bearing, and the release cylinder is sometimes called the operating or slave cylinder.

5   Other than replacing components that have obvious damage, some preliminary checks should be performed to diagnose a clutch system failure.

a   *The first check should be of the fluid level in the brake master cylinder since it also serves as the reservoir for the clutch release system (see Chapter 1). If the fluid level is low, add fluid as necessary and inspect the hydraulic clutch system for leaks. If the master cylinder reservoir has run dry, bleed the system (see Section 5) and retest the clutch operation.*

b   *To check "clutch spin down time," run the engine at normal idle speed with the transaxle in Neutral (clutch pedal up - engaged). Disengage the clutch (pedal down), wait several seconds and shift the transaxle into Reverse. No grinding noise should be heard. A grinding noise would most likely indicate a problem in the pressure plate or the clutch disc.*

c   *To check for complete clutch release, run the engine (with the parking brake applied to prevent movement) and hold the clutch pedal approximately 1/2-inch from the floor. Shift the transaxle between 1st gear and Reverse several times. If the shift is not smooth, component failure is indicated. Check the release cylinder pushrod travel. With the clutch pedal depressed completely the release cylinder pushrod should extend substantially. If it doesn't, check the fluid level in the clutch master cylinder.*

d   *Visually inspect the clutch pedal bushing at the top of the clutch pedal to make sure there is no sticking or excessive wear.*

e   *Under the vehicle, check that the clutch release lever is solidly mounted on the ball stud.*

3   Clutch master cylinder - removal and installation

Removal

Refer to illustration 3.5

1   Disconnect the negative cable from the battery.

2   Under the dashboard, disconnect the pushrod from the top of the clutch pedal. It's held in place with a clevis pin. To remove the clevis pin, remove the clip.

3   If the vehicle is equipped with cruise control, remove the cruise control actuator cover and the three bolts securing the actuator and place it aside.

4   Clamp a pair of locking pliers onto the fluid feed hose, a couple of inches downstream of the resevoir. The pliers should be just tight enough to prevent fluid flow when the hose is disconnected.

5   Disconnect the hydraulic line at the clutch master cylinder **(see illustration)**. If available, use a flare-nut wrench on the fitting, to protect it from being rounded off. Have rags handy, as some fluid will be lost as the line is removed. **Caution:** *Don't allow brake fluid to come into contact with paint, as it will damage the finish.* Loosen the fluid feed hose clamp and detach the hose from the cylinder.

6   Working under the drivers side dash, unscrew the two clutch master cylinder retaining nuts and remove the cylinder.

Installation

7   Position the master cylinder on the firewall, installing the mounting nuts finger-tight.

8   Connect the hydraulic line to the master cylinder, moving the cylinder slightly as necessary to thread the fitting properly into the bore. Don't cross-thread the fitting as it's installed. Attach the fluid feed hose to the cylinder.

9   Tighten the mounting nuts and the hydraulic line fitting securely and connect the fluid feed hose.

10   Connect the pushrod to the clutch pedal.

11   Remove the locking pliers from fluid feed hose. Fill the master cylinder reservoir with brake fluid conforming to DOT 3 specifications and bleed the clutch system (see Section 5).

4   Clutch release cylinder - removal and installation

Removal

Refer to illustration 4.2

1   Disconnect the negative cable from the battery.

2   Disconnect the hydraulic line at the release cylinder **(see illustration)**. If available, use a flare-nut wrench on the fitting, which will prevent the fitting from being rounded off. Have a small can and rags handy, as some fluid will be spilled as the line is removed.

3   Remove the release cylinder mounting bolts.

4   Remove the release cylinder.

Installation

5   Install the release cylinder on the clutch housing, but don't completely tighten the bolts yet. Make sure the pushrod is seated in the release fork pocket.

6   Connect the hydraulic line to the release cylinder, and then tighten the release cylinder mounting bolts securely. Using a flare-nut wrench, tighten the hydraulic fitting securely.

7   Fill the master cylinder reservoir with brake fluid conforming to DOT 3 specifications and bleed the clutch system as described in Section 5.

5   Clutch hydraulic system - bleeding

1   The hydraulic system should be bled of all air whenever any part of the system has been removed or if the fluid level has been allowed to fall so low that air has been drawn into the master cylinder. The procedure is similar to bleeding a brake system.

2   Fill the master cylinder with new brake fluid conforming to DOT 3 specifications. **Caution:** *Do not re-use any of the fluid coming from the system during the bleeding operation or use fluid which has been inside an open container for an extended period of time.*

3   Locate the bleeder valve on the clutch release cylinder. Remove the dust cap, which fits over the bleeder valve, and push a length of clear tubing over the valve. Place the other end of the hose into a clear container with about two inches of brake fluid in it. The hose end must be submerged in the fluid.

4   Have an assistant depress the clutch pedal and hold it. Open the bleeder valve on the release cylinder, allowing fluid to flow through the hose. Close the bleeder valve when fluid stops flowing from the hose. Once closed, have your assistant release the pedal.

5   Continue this process until all air is evacuated from the system, indicated by a full, solid stream of fluid being ejected from the bleeder valve each time and no air bubbles in the hose or container. Keep a close watch on the fluid level inside the master cylinder reservoir; if the level drops too low, air will be sucked back into the system and the process will have to be started all over again.

7   Install the dust cap. Check carefully for proper operation before placing the vehicle in normal service.

6   Clutch components - removal, inspection and installation

Warning: *Dust produced by clutch wear and deposited on clutch components is hazardous to your health. DO NOT blow it out with compressed air and DO NOT inhale it. DO NOT use gasoline or petroleum based solvents to remove the dust. Brake system cleaner should be used to flush the dust into a drain pan. After the clutch components are wiped clean with a rag, dispose of the contaminated rags and cleaner in a labeled, covered container.*

Removal
Refer to illustration 6.6

1   Access to the clutch components is normally accomplished by removing the transaxle, leaving the engine in the vehicle. If, of course, the engine is being removed for major overhaul, then the opportunity should always be taken to check the clutch for wear and replace worn components as necessary. However, the relatively low cost of the clutch

components compared to the time and labor involved in gaining access to them warrants their replacement any time the engine or transaxle is removed, unless they are new or in near-perfect condition. The following procedures assume that the engine will stay in place.

2   Remove the release cylinder (see Section 4). Hang it out of the way with a piece of wire - it isn't necessary to disconnect the hose.

3   Remove the transaxle from the vehicle (see Chapter 7A).

4   The release fork and release bearing can remain attached to the transaxle for the time being.

5   To support the clutch disc during removal, install a clutch alignment tool through the clutch disc hub.

6   Carefully inspect the flywheel and pressure plate for indexing marks. The marks are usually an X, an O or a white letter. If they cannot be found, scribe marks yourself so the pressure plate and the flywheel will be in the same alignment during installation **(see illustration)**.

7   Slowly loosen the pressure plate-to-flywheel bolts. Work in a diagonal pattern and loosen each bolt a little at a time until all spring pressure is relieved. Then hold the pressure plate securely and completely remove the bolts, followed by the pressure plate and clutch disc.

Inspection
Refer to illustrations 6.10, 6.12a and 6.12b

8   Ordinarily, when a problem occurs in the clutch, it can be attributed to wear of the clutch driven plate assembly (clutch disc). However, all components should be inspected at this time.

9   Inspect the flywheel for cracks, heat checking, score marks and other damage. If the imperfections are slight, a machine shop can resurface it to make it flat and smooth. Refer to Chapter 2 for the flywheel removal procedure.

10   Inspect the lining on the clutch disc. There should be at least 1/32-inch of lining

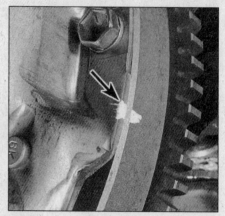

6.6 Mark the relationship of the pressure plate to the flywheel (just in case you're going to re-use the old pressure plate)

above the rivet heads. Check for loose rivets, distortion, cracks, broken springs and other obvious damage **(see illustration)**. As mentioned above, ordinarily the clutch disc is replaced as a matter of course, so if in doubt about the condition, replace it with a new one.

11   The release bearing should be replaced along with the clutch disc (see Section 7).

12   Check the machined surface and the diaphragm spring fingers of the pressure plate **(see illustrations)**. If the surface is grooved or otherwise damaged, replace the pressure plate assembly. Also check for obvious damage, distortion, cracking, etc. Light glazing can be removed with emery cloth or sandpaper. If a new pressure plate is indicated, new or factory rebuilt units are available.

Installation
Refer to illustration 6.14

13   Before installation, carefully wipe the flywheel and pressure plate machined surfaces clean. It's important that no oil or grease is on these surfaces or the lining of the clutch disc. Handle these parts only with clean hands.

14   Position the clutch disc and pressure plate with the clutch held in place with an

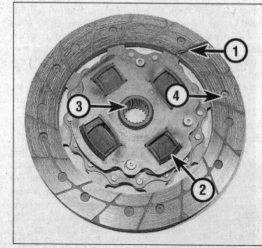

6.10 The clutch disc

1   **Lining** - this will wear down in use

2   **Springs or dampers** - check for cracking and deformation

3   **Splined hub** - the splines must not be worn and should slide smoothly on the transaxle input shaft splines

4   **Rivets** - these secure the lining and will damage the flywheel or pressure plate if allowed to contact the surfaces

NORMAL FINGER WEAR

EXCESSIVE WEAR
EXCESSIVE FINGER WEAR

BROKEN OR BENT FINGERS

6.12a Replace the pressure plate if excessive wear is noted

alignment tool **(see illustration)**. Make sure it's installed properly (most replacement clutch plates will be marked "flywheel side" or something similar - if not marked, install the clutch disc with the damper springs or cushion toward the transaxle).

15   Tighten the pressure plate-to-flywheel bolts only finger tight, working around the pressure plate.

16   Center the clutch disc by ensuring the alignment tool is through the splined hub and

6.12b Inspect the pressure plate friction surface for score marks, cracks and signs of overheating

6.14 Center the clutch disc in the pressure plate with a clutch alignment tool

into the recess in the crankshaft. Wiggle the tool up, down or side-to-side as needed to bottom the tool. Tighten the pressure plate-to-flywheel bolts a little at a time, working in a crisscross pattern to prevent distortion of the cover. After all of the bolts are snug, tighten them to the torque listed in this Chapter's Specifications. Remove the alignment tool.

17   Using high-temperature grease, lubricate the inner groove of the release bearing (see Section 7). Also place a light film of grease on the release lever contact areas and the transaxle input shaft bearing retainer.

18   Install the clutch release bearing (see Section 7).

19   Install the transaxle, release cylinder and all components removed previously, tightening all fasteners to the proper torque specifications.

7   Clutch release bearing and lever - removal, inspection and installation

Warning: *Dust produced by clutch wear and deposited on clutch components is hazardous to your health. DO NOT blow it out with compressed air and DO NOT inhale it. DO NOT use gasoline or petroleum based solvents to remove the dust. Brake system cleaner should be used to flush the dust into a drain*

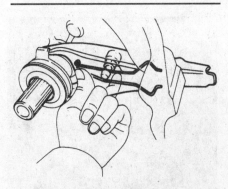
7.3 Reach behind the release lever and disengage the lever from the ball stud by pulling on the retention spring, then remove the lever and bearing

pan. After the clutch components are wiped clean with a rag, dispose of the contaminated rags and cleaner in a labeled, covered container.

Removal
Refer to illustration 7.3

1   Disconnect the negative cable from the battery.

2   Remove the transaxle (see Chapter 7).

3   Remove the clutch release lever from the ball stud, and then remove the bearing from the lever **(see illustration)**.

Inspection
Refer to illustration 7.4

4   Hold the bearing by the outer race and rotate the inner race while applying pressure **(see illustration)**. If the bearing doesn't turn smoothly or if it's noisy, replace the bearing/hub assembly with a new one. Wipe the bearing with a clean rag and inspect it for damage, wear and cracks. Don't immerse the bearing in solvent - it's sealed for life and to do so would ruin it. Also check the release lever for cracks and bends.

Installation
Refer to illustrations 7.5 and 7.6

5   Fill the inner groove of the release bearing with high-temperature grease. Also apply

7.4 To check the operation of the bearing, hold it by the outer race and rotate the inner race while applying pressure - the bearing should turn smoothly - if it doesn't, replace it

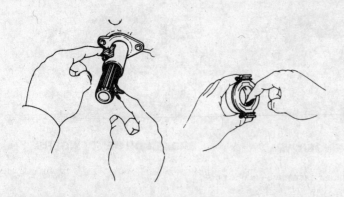
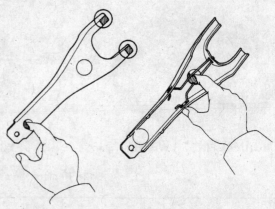

7.5 Apply a thin coat of high-temperature grease to the transaxle bearing retainer and also fill the release bearing groove

7.6 Apply high-temperature grease to the release lever in the areas indicated

a light coat of the same grease to the transaxle input shaft splines and the front bearing retainer **(see illustration)**.

6   Lubricate the release lever ball socket, lever ends and release cylinder pushrod socket with high-temperature grease **(see illustration)**.

7   Attach the release bearing to the release lever. On models that use a retaining clip, make sure it engages properly with the lever.

8   Slide the release bearing onto the transaxle input shaft front bearing retainer while passing the end of the release lever through the opening in the clutch housing. Push the clutch release lever onto the ball stud until it's firmly seated.

9   Apply a light coat of high-temperature grease to the face of the release bearing where it contacts the pressure plate diaphragm fingers.

10   The remainder of installation is the reverse of the removal procedure.

8   Clutch start switch - replacement

Refer to illustration 8.1

1   The clutch start switch is located near the top of the clutch pedal, facing the opposite direction of the cruise control switch (or pedal stopper), shown in illustration.

2   Unplug the electrical connector. Loosen the nut near the body of the switch, and then unscrew the switch.

3   Installation is the reverse of removal.

9   Driveaxles - removal and installation

Front
Removal

Refer to illustrations 9.1, 9.2, 9.6 and 9.7

1   Remove the wheel cover or hub cap. Remove the cotter pin and nut lock (2000 and earlier models). On 2001 and later models, unstake the nut with a punch or chisel **(see illustration)**.

2   Break the hub nut loose with a socket and large breaker bar **(see illustration)**.

3   Loosen the wheel lug nuts, raise the vehicle and support it securely on jackstands. Remove the wheel. Drain the transaxle lubricant (see Chapter 1).

4   Remove the nuts and bolt securing the balljoint to the control arm, then pry the control arm down and separate the lower control arm from the balljoint (see Chapter 10). Now remove the driveaxle/hub nut.

5   Swing the knuckle/hub assembly out (away from the vehicle) until the end of the driveaxle is free of the hub. **Note:** *If the driveaxle splines stick in the hub, tap on the end of the driveaxle with a plastic hammer.* Support the outer end of the driveaxle with a piece of wire to avoid unnecessary strain on the inner CV joint.

6   If you're working on the right-side axle on a 2WD automatic transaxle remove the bolts from the center bearing bracket **(see illustration)**. If you're working on a 2WD manual

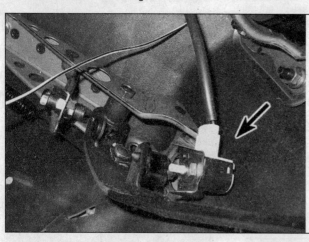

8.1 The clutch start switch is located under the dash on a bracket in front of the clutch pedal

9.1 If the driveaxle nut is "staked", use a center punch to unstake it (wheel removed for clarity)

9.2 Loosen the driveaxle/hub nut with a long breaker bar

9.6 Remove the bolts for the center support bearing (arrows)

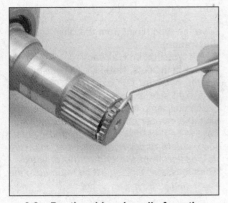

9.8a Pry the old spring clip from the inner end of the driveaxle with a small screwdriver or awl

transaxle remove the snap-ring from the center bearing using a hammer and screwdriver.

7   Carefully pry the inner end of the driveaxle from the transaxle - or, on models so equipped, the intermediate shaft - using a large screwdriver or prybar positioned between the transaxle or bearing support and the CV joint housing **(see illustration)**. Support the CV joints and carefully remove the driveaxle from the vehicle.

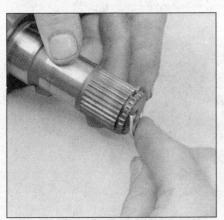

9.8b To install the new spring clip, start one end in the groove and work the clip over the shaft end, into the groove

9.7 To separate the inner end of the driveaxle from the transaxle, pry on the CV joint housing like this with a large screwdriver or prybar - you may need to give the prybar a sharp rap with a brass hammer

Installation

Refer to illustration 9.8a and 9.8b

8   Pry the old spring clip from the inner end of the driveaxle and install a new one **(see illustrations)**. Lubricate the differential or intermediate shaft seal with multi-purpose grease and raise the driveaxle into position while supporting the CV joints.

9   Insert the splined end of the inner CV joint or the intermediate shaft into the differential side gear and make sure the spring clip locks in its groove. If you're installing a driveaxle/intermediate shaft assembly, install the center support bearing bolts or snap-ring, as applicable.

10   Apply a light coat of multi-purpose grease to the outer CV joint splines, pull out on the strut/steering knuckle assembly and install the stub axle into the hub.

11   Reconnect the balljoint to the lower control arm and tighten the nuts (see the torque specifications in Chapter 10).

12   If you're working on a 2001 or later model, install a new driveaxle/hub nut. Tighten the hub nut securely, but don't try to tighten it to the actual torque specification until you've lowered

9.21 Mark the relationship of the driveaxle flange to the differential side gear flange

the vehicle to the ground.

13   Grasp the inner CV joint housing (not the driveaxle) and pull out to make sure the driveaxle has seated securely in the transaxle.

14   Install the wheel and lug nuts, then lower the vehicle.

15   Tighten the lug nuts to the torque listed in the Chapter 1 Specifications. Tighten the hub nut to the torque listed in this Chapter's Specifications. On 2000 and earlier models, install the nut lock and new cotter pin. On 2001 and later models, stake the nut to the groove in the driveaxle, using a hammer and punch.

16   Refill the transaxle with the recommended type and amount of lubricant (see Chapter 1).

Rear (4WD models)
Removal
Refer to illustrations 9.21 and 9.22

17   Remove the wheel cover or hub cap. Remove the cotter pin and nut lock from the driveaxle/hub nut. Break the hub nut loose with a socket and large breaker bar.

18   Block the front wheels to prevent the vehicle from rolling. Loosen the wheel lug nuts, raise the rear of the vehicle and support it securely on jackstands. Remove the wheel.

19   On vehicles with ABS, remove the ABS speed sensor (see Chapter 9).

20   Remove the driveaxle/hub nut.

21   Make reference marks on the driveaxle flange and the differential side gear flange **(see illustration)**.

22   Remove the four nuts and washers **(see illustration)** and detach the axle from the differential side gear flange, then remove the outer end of the driveaxle from the hub.

Installation

23   Installation is the reverse of removal.

24   Install a new driveaxle/hub nut. Tighten the hub nut securely, but don't try to tighten it to the actual torque specification until you've lowered the vehicle.

25   Install the wheel and lug nuts, then lower the vehicle. Tighten the lug nuts to the torque

9.22 Remove the four nuts and washers (fourth nut hidden from view)

10.3 Lift the tabs on the boot clamps with a small screwdriver, then open the clamps

10.4 Remove the boot from the inner CV joint and slide the joint housing from the tripod

10.6 Remove the snap-ring with a pair of snap-ring pliers

listed in the Chapter 1 Specifications.

26 Tighten the driveaxle/hub nut to the torque listed in this Chapter's Specifications, then install the nut lock and a new cotter pin.

10 Driveaxle boot - replacement

Disassembly

Refer to illustrations 10.3, 10.4, 10.6 and 10.7

Note 1: *If the CV joint boots must be replaced, explore all options before beginning the job. Complete rebuilt driveaxles are available on an exchange basis, which eliminates much time and work. Whichever route you choose to take, check on the cost and availability of parts before disassembling the vehicle.*

Note 2: *Some auto parts stores carry "split" type replacement boots, which can be installed without removing the driveaxle from the vehicle. This is a convenient alternative; however, the driveaxle should be removed and the CV joint disassembled and cleaned to ensure the joint is free from contaminants such as moisture and dirt which will acceler-* ate CV joint wear. Do NOT disassemble the outboard CV joint.

1 Remove the driveaxle (see Section 9).

2 Mount the driveaxle in a vise with wood lined jaws (to prevent damage to the axleshaft). Check the CV joint for excessive play in the radial direction, which indicates worn parts. Check for smooth operation throughout the full range of motion for each CV joint. If a boot is torn, disassemble the joint, clean the components and inspect for damage due to loss of lubrication and possible contamination by foreign matter.

3 Using a small screwdriver, pry the retaining tabs of the clamps up to loosen them and slide them off **(see illustration)**.

4 Using a screwdriver, carefully pry up on the edge of the outer boot and push it away from the CV joint. Old and worn boots can be cut off. Pull the inner CV joint boot back from the housing and slide the housing off the tripod **(see illustration)**.

5 Mark the tripod and axleshaft to ensure that they are reassembled properly.

6 Remove the tripod joint snap-ring with a pair of snap-ring pliers **(see illustration)**.

7 Use a hammer and a brass punch to drive the tripod joint from the driveaxle **(see illustration)**.

8 If you haven't already cut them off, remove both boots. **Note:** *Do NOT disassemble the outboard CV joint. If you're working on a right side driveaxle, you'll also have to cut off the clamp for the dynamic damper and slide the damper off.* **Note:** *The damper may have to be pressed off with a hydraulic press. Also, before removing the damper, measure its position from the end of the driveaxle - when reassembling, it must be returned to the same spot.*

Check

9 Thoroughly clean all components, including the outer CV joint assembly, with solvent until the old CV joint grease is completely removed. Inspect the bearing surfaces of the inner tripods and housings for cracks, pitting, scoring and other signs of wear. It's not possible to inspect the bearing surfaces of the inner and outer races of the outer CV joint, but you can at least check the surfaces of the ball bearings themselves. If they're in good shape, so are the races; if they're not, neither are the races. If the inner CV joint is worn, you

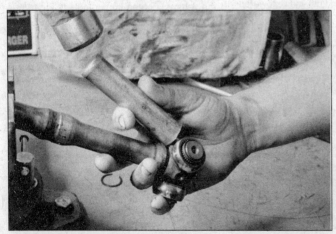

10.7 Drive the tripod joint from the driveaxle with a brass punch and hammer; be careful not to damage the bearing surfaces or the splines on the shaft

10.10a Wrap the splined area of the axleshaft with tape to prevent damage to the boots when removing or installing them

10.10b Install the tripod with the recessed portion of the splines facing the axle shaft

10.10c Place grease at the bottom of the CV joint housing

10.10d Install the boot clamps onto the axleshaft, then insert the tripod into the housing, followed by the rest of the grease

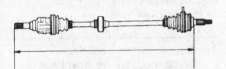

10.11 The driveaxle standard length should be set to the dimension listed in this Chapter's Specifications before the boot clamps are tightened

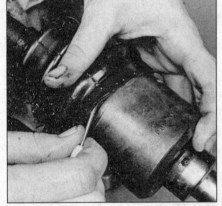

10.12a Equalize the pressure inside the boot by inserting a small, dull screwdriver between the boot and the outer race

10.12b To install the new clamps, bend the tang down . . .

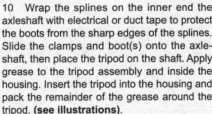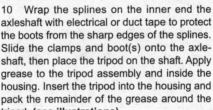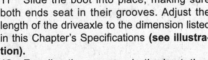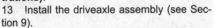

10.12c . . . then tap the tabs over to hold it in place

can buy a new inner CV joint and install it on the old axleshaft; if the outer CV joint is worn, you'll have to purchase a new outer CV joint and axleshaft (they're sold preassembled).

Reassembly

Refer to illustrations 10.10a, 10.10b, 10.10c, 10.10d, 10.11, 10.12a, 10.12b, 10.12c and 10.12d

10   Wrap the splines on the inner end the axleshaft with electrical or duct tape to protect the boots from the sharp edges of the splines. Slide the clamps and boot(s) onto the axleshaft, then place the tripod on the shaft. Apply grease to the tripod assembly and inside the housing. Insert the tripod into the housing and pack the remainder of the grease around the tripod. **(see illustrations)**.

11   Slide the boot into place, making sure both ends seat in their grooves. Adjust the length of the driveaxle to the dimension listed in this Chapter's Specifications **(see illustration)**.

12   Equalize the pressure in the boot, then tighten and secure the boot clamps **(see illustrations)**.

13   Install the driveaxle assembly (see Section 9).

11   Driveshaft (4WD models) - check, removal and installation

Check

1   Raise the rear of the vehicle and support it securely on jackstands. Block the front wheels to keep the vehicle from rolling off the stands. Release the parking brake and place the transmission in Neutral.

2   Crawl under the vehicle and visually inspect the driveshaft. Look for any dents or cracks in the tubing. If any are found, the driveshaft must be replaced.

3   Check for oil leakage at the front and rear of the driveshaft. Leakage where the driveshaft connects to the transfer case indicates a defective transfer case seal. Leakage where the driveshaft connects to the differential indicates a defective pinion seal.

4   While under the vehicle, have an assistant rotate a rear wheel so the driveshaft will rotate. As it does, make sure the universal

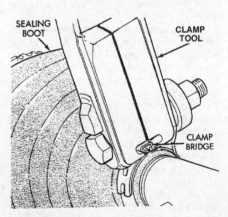

10.12d If your replacement boot came with crimp-type clamps, a special tool such as this one (available at most auto parts stores) will be required to tighten them properly

11.9 Mark the relationship of the driveshaft to the differential pinion flange

11.10 Using a back-up wrench to hold each bolt, break loose all four bolts

joints are operating properly without binding, noise or looseness. Listen for any noise from the center bearing, indicating it's worn or damaged. Also check the rubber portion of the center bearing for cracking or separation.
5   The universal joints can also be checked with the driveshaft motionless, by gripping your hands on either side of the joint and attempting to twist the joint. Any movement at all in the joint is a sign of considerable wear. Lifting up on the shaft will also indicate movement in the universal joints. If the joints are worn, front or rear portion of the driveshaft must be replaced as an assembly.
6   Finally, check the driveshaft mounting bolts at the ends to make sure they're tight.

Removal and installation
Refer to illustrations 11.9, 11.10, 11.11, 11.15a and 11.15b
8   Raise the rear of the vehicle and support it securely on jackstands. Block the front wheels to prevent the vehicle from rolling. Place the transmission in Neutral with the parking brake off.
9   Make reference marks on the driveshaft flange and the differential pinion flange in line with each other **(see illustration)**. This is to make sure the driveshaft is reinstalled in the same position to preserve the balance.
10   Remove the rear universal joint bolts. Turn the driveshaft (or wheels) as necessary to bring the bolts into the most accessible position. Remove the four bolts, nuts and washers **(see illustration)**.
11   Unbolt the center support bearing from the floorpan **(see illustration)**.
12   Pull out the front of the driveshaft from the transaxle and remove the driveshaft assembly.
13   Lubricate the lips of the transfer case seal with multi-purpose grease. Carefully guide the intermediate shaft yoke into the transfer case and then install the mounting bolts through the center support bearing, but don't tighten them yet.

14   Reconnect the driveshaft to the pinion flange. Be sure to align the marks and tighten the fasteners to the torque listed in this Chapter's Specifications.
15   Adjust the position of the center support bearing **(see illustrations)**, then tighten the bolts to the torque listed in this Chapter's Specifiations.

12   Center support bearing (4WD models) - removal and installation

Removal
Refer to illustrations 12.2 and 12.6
1   Remove the driveshaft (see Section 11).
2   Mark the relationship of the universal

11.11 The driveshaft center support bearing is retained by two bolts

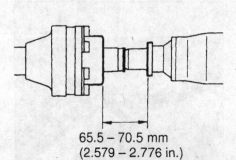

11.15a Adjust the gap between the CV joint cover and the raised part of the rear driveshaft to the dimension shown . . .

65.5 – 70.5 mm
(2.579 – 2.776 in.)

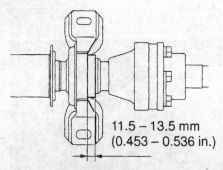

11.5 – 13.5 mm
(0.453 – 0.536 in.)

11.15b . . . then adjust the distance between the rear of the center support bearing and the rear of the rubber insulator to the dimension shown

12.2 Mark the relationship of the universal joint flange to the cross-groove joint flange

joint flange to the cross-groove joint flange on the driveshaft **(see illustration)**.

3   Using a hex bit, remove the six bolts and separate the two halves of the driveshaft.

4   Using a hammer and punch unstake the nut from the universal joint flange.

5   Place the intermediate shaft in a vise lined with wood to hold the front flange and remove the nut and washer. **Caution:** *Don't tighten the vise excessively, as the shaft could be damaged.*

6   Apply matchmarks onto the flange and shaft **(see illustration)**.

7   Using a two-jaw puller, remove the joint flange.

8   Remove the washer and center support bearing.

9   Place the propeller shaft in the vise and check that the cross-groove joint moves smoothly. If there is damage to the joint or grease leakage from the boot, the rear shaft should be replaced.

Installation

Refer to illustration 12.10

10   Place the center bearing and washer on the intermediate shaft **(see illustration)**.

11   Place the flange on the shaft with the marks aligned, followed by a new washer and nut.

12   Use the vise to hold the flange while tightening down the nut. Tighten the nut to the torque value listed in this Chapter's Specifications.

13   Using a hammer and punch, stake the nut into the groove on the shaft.

14   Align the marks on the two halves of the driveshaft, install the washers and bolts and tighten them temporarily.

15   Lubricate the lips of the transfercase seal with multi-purpose grease. Carefully guide the intermediate shaft yoke into the transfer case then install the mounting bolts through the center support bearing. Tighten the bolts temporarily.

16   Reconnect the propeller shaft to the pinion flange. Be sure to align the marks and tighten the fasteners to the torque listed in this Chapter's Specifications.

17   Have an assistant depress and hold the brake pedal and using a hex bit, tighten the two halves of the driveshaft to the torque listed in this Chapter's Specifications.

18   Adjust the position of the center support bearing as described in Section 11.

13   Differential oil seals (4WD models) - replacement

Pinion oil seal

Removal

1   Raise the rear of the vehicle and support it securely on jackstands. Block the front wheels to prevent the vehicle from rolling. Place the transmission in Neutral with the parking brake off.

2   Mark the relationship of the driveshaft to the pinion flange, then unbolt the driveshaft from the flange (see Section 11). Suspend the driveshaft with a piece of wire (don't let it hang by the center support bearing).

3   Using a hammer and a punch, unstake the pinion flange nut.

4   A flange holding tool will be required to keep the companion flange from moving while the self-locking pinion nut is loosened. A chain wrench will also work.

5   Remove the pinion nut.

6   Withdraw the flange. It may be necessary to use a two-jaw puller engaged behind the flange to draw it off. Do not attempt to pry

or hammer behind the flange or hammer on the end of the pinion shaft.

7   Pry out the old seal and discard it.

Installation

8   Lubricate the lips of the new seal and fill the space between the seal lips with wheel bearing grease, then tap it evenly into position with a seal installation tool or a large socket. Make sure it enters the housing squarely and is tapped in to its full depth.

9   Install the pinion flange; if necessary, tighten the pinion nut to draw the flange into place. Do not try to hammer the flange into position. Tighten the nut to the initial torque listed in this Chapter's Specifications.

10   Using an inch-pound torque wrench (dial or beam-type), measure the torque required to rotate the pinion and tighten the nut in small increments (no more than 9 ft-lbs) until it matches the pinion shaft bearing preload listed in this Chapter's Specifications. If the maximum torque listed in this Chapter's Specifications is reached before the specified preload is obtained, the bearing spacer in the differential must be replaced.

11   Once the proper preload is reached, stake the collar of the nut into the slot in the pinion shaft.

12   Reconnect the driveshaft to the pinion flange (see Section 11). Check the differential lubricant level and add some, if necessary, to bring it to the appropriate level (see Chapter 1).

Driveaxle oil seals

Torque-sensing limited slip differential

13   Raise the rear of the vehicle and support it securely on jackstands. Block the front wheels to prevent the vehicle from rolling. Place the transmission in Neutral with the parking brake off.

14   Remove the side gear shaft with a slide hammer or carefully pry between the inner side of the shaft's flange and differential case using prybars positioned on each side. Remove the shaft.

15   Carefully pry out the side gear shaft oil seal with a seal removal tool or a large screwdriver; make sure you don't scratch the seal bore.

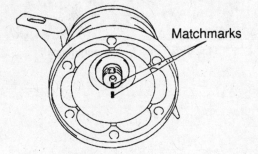

12.6 Mark the relationship of the flange to the shaft

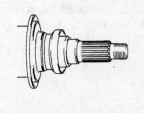
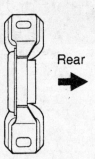

12.10 Install the center support bearing in the direction shown

16   Using a seal installer or a large deep socket as a drift, install the new oil seal. Drive it into the bore squarely and make sure it's completely seated.

17   Lubricate the lip of the new seal with multi-purpose grease, then install the side gear shaft. Be careful not to damage the lip of the new seal.

18   Check the differential lubricant level and add some, if necessary, to bring it to the appropriate level (See Chapter 1).

2 pinion differential

Refer to illustration 13.21

19   If the vehicle is equipped with a 2 pinion differential, remove the differential from the vehicle (see Section 14).

20   Working on a bench, remove the fasteners from the differential cover and separate the cover from the differential.

21   Using needle-nose pliers, remove the snap-ring from the side gear shaft **(see illustration),** and remove the shaft.

22   Carefully pry out the side gear shaft oil seal with a seal removal tool or a large screwdriver; make sure you don't scratch the seal bore.

23   Using a seal installer or a large deep socket as a drift, install the new oil seal. Drive it into the bore squarely and make sure it's completely seated.

24   Lubricate the lip of the new seal with multi-purpose grease, then install the side gear shaft. Be careful not to damage the lip of the new seal.

25   Using the needle-nose pliers, install a new snap-ring to the side gear shaft.

26   Remove all traces of old sealant from the

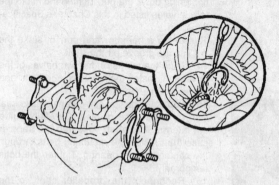

13.21 Use needle nose pliers to remove the snap-rings (2 pinion differential)

cover and mating surface.

27   Apply a small bead of RTV sealant to the differential and carefully install the cover and fasteners. Tighten the fasteners to the torque values listed in this Chapter's Specifications.

28   The remainder of installation is the reverse of removal.

14   Differential (4WD models) - removal and installation

Refer to illustrations 14.5 and 14.6

1   Raise the rear of the vehicle and support it securely on jackstands. Block the front wheels to prevent the vehicle from rolling. Place the transmission in Neutral with the parking brake off.

2   Drain the differential lubricant (see Chapter 1).

3   Detach the driveaxles from the side gear shafts (see Section 9). Support the driveaxles with wire or rope - don't let them hang by the other CV joints.

4   Mark the relationship of the driveshaft to the pinion flange, then unbolt the driveshaft from the flange (see Section 11). Suspend the driveshaft with a piece of wire (don't let it hang by the center support bearing).

5   Support the differential with a floor jack. Remove the two mounting bracket bolts at the rear of the differential **(see illustration)**.

6   Remove the two differential front mounting bolts **(see illustration)**. Slowly lower the jack and remove the differential out from under the vehicle.

7   Installation is the reverse of the removal procedure. Tighten all fasteners to the torque values listed in this Chapter's Specifications. Fill the differential with the proper lubricant (see Chapter 1).

14.5 Differential rear mounting bolts

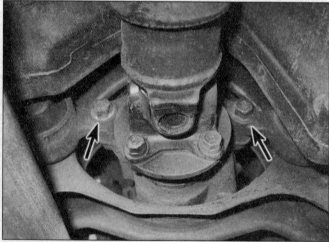

14.6 Differential front mounting bolts

Chapter 9 Brakes

Contents

	Section
Anti-lock Brake System (ABS) - general information, trouble codes and component removal and installation	2
Brake disc - inspection, removal and installation	5
Brake fluid level check	See Chapter 1
Brake hoses and lines - inspection and replacement	9
Brake hydraulic system - bleeding	10
Brake light switch - check and replacement	15
Brake pedal - check and adjustment	14
Brake system check	See Chapter 1
Disc brake caliper - removal and installation	4
Disc brake pads - replacement	3

	Section
Drum brake shoes - replacement	6
General information	1
Master cylinder - removal, installation and reservoir/grommet replacement	8
Parking brake - adjustment	12
Parking brake cables - replacement	13
Parking brake shoes (models with rear disc brakes) - inspection and replacement	16
Power brake booster - check, removal and installation	11
Wheel cylinder - removal and installation	7

Specifications

General

Brake fluid type	See Chapter 1
Brake pedal height (from asphalt sheet)	
2000 and earlier models	6.185 to 6.579 inches (157 to 167 mm)
2001 and later models	6.693 to 7.087 inches (170 to 180 mm)
Brake pedal freeplay	3/64 to 1/4 inch (1.2 to 6.35 mm)
Brake pedal reserve distance (minimum)	
2000 and earlier models	2.95 inches (75 mm)
2001 and later models	4.65 inches (118 mm)
Brake light switch-to-pedal clearance	0.020 to 0.094 inch (0.5 to 2.4 mm)
Power brake booster pushrod-to-master cylinder piston clearance	0.0 inch (0.0 mm)

Disc brakes

Minimum brake pad thickness	See Chapter 1
Disc minimum thickness	Cast or stamped into disc
Disc runout limit	0.002 inch (0.05 mm)

Drum brakes

Drum maximum diameter	Cast or stamped into drum
Shoe friction material minimum thickness	See Chapter 1

Parking brake

Parking brake lever travel	6 to 8 clicks

Torque specifications

	Ft-lbs (unless otherwise indicated)	Nm
Brake hose-to-caliper banjo bolts	22	30
Caliper mounting bolts	20	26
Caliper torque plate-to-steering knuckle bolts	78	106
Deceleration sensor mounting nuts	41	5
Master cylinder-to-brake booster nuts	108 in-lbs	13
Power brake booster mounting nuts	108 in-lbs	13
Wheel cylinder mounting bolts	84 in-lbs	10
Wheel speed sensor bolt (front or rear)	70 in-lbs	8
Wheel lug nuts	See Chapter 1	

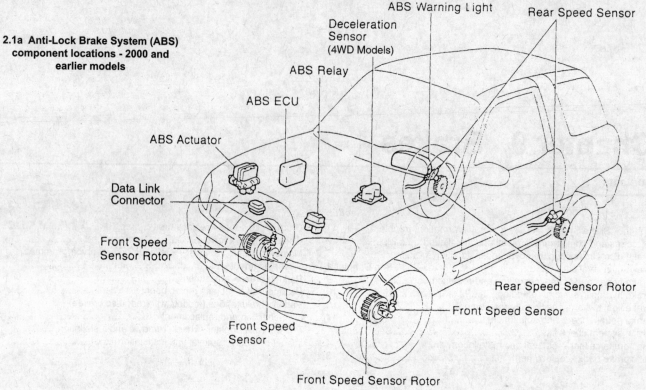

2.1a Anti-Lock Brake System (ABS) component locations - 2000 and earlier models

1   General information

The vehicles covered by this manual are equipped with hydraulically operated front and rear brake systems. The front brakes are disc type and the rear brakes are drum type. Both the front and rear brakes are self adjusting. The disc brakes automatically compensate for pad wear, while the drum brakes incorporate an adjustment mechanism which is activated as the parking brake is applied.

Hydraulic system

The hydraulic system consists of two separate circuits. The master cylinder has separate reservoirs for the two circuits, and, in the event of a leak or failure in one hydraulic circuit, the other circuit will remain operative. A dual proportioning valve on the firewall provides brake balance between the front and rear brakes.

Power brake booster

The power brake booster, utilizing engine manifold vacuum and atmospheric pressure to provide assistance to the hydraulically operated brakes, is mounted on the firewall in the engine compartment.

Parking brake

The parking brake operates the rear brakes only, through cable actuation. It's activated by a lever mounted in the center console.

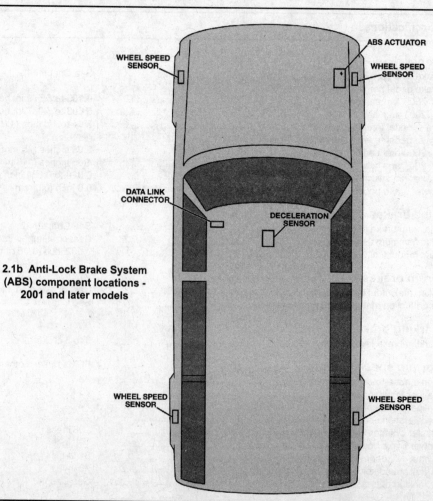

2.1b Anti-Lock Brake System (ABS) component locations - 2001 and later models

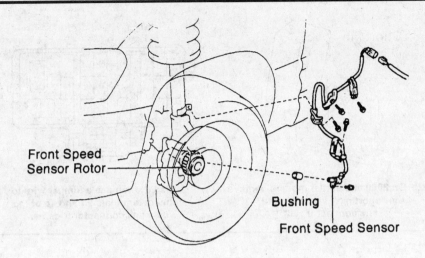

**Front Speed
Sensor Rotor**

Bushing

Front Speed Sensor

2.4 ABS front wheel speed sensor and sensor rotor

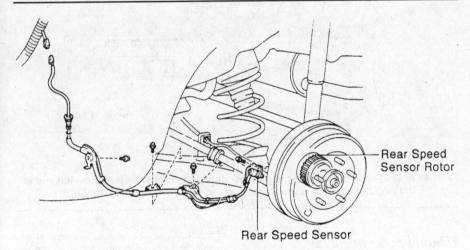

**Rear Speed
Sensor Rotor**

Rear Speed Sensor

**2.5a ABS rear wheel speed sensor and sensor rotor (all 2000 and earlier
models and 2001 and later 4WD models)**

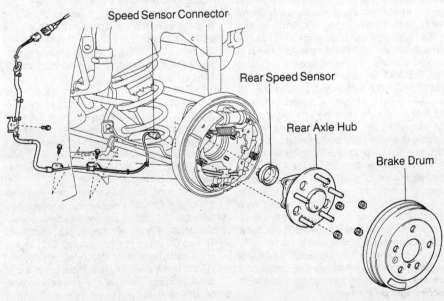

Speed Sensor Connector

Rear Speed Sensor

Rear Axle Hub

Brake Drum

2.5b ABS rear wheel speed sensor (2001 and later 2WD models)

Service

After completing any operation involving disassembly of any part of the brake system, always test drive the vehicle to check for proper braking performance before resuming normal driving. When testing the brakes, perform the tests on a clean, dry, flat surface. Conditions other than these can lead to inaccurate test results.

Test the brakes at various speeds with both light and heavy pedal pressure. The vehicle should stop evenly without pulling to one side or the other. Avoid locking the brakes, because this slides the tires and diminishes braking efficiency and control of the vehicle.

Tires, vehicle load and wheel alignment are factors which also affect braking performance.

2   Anti-lock Brake System (ABS) - general information, trouble codes and component removal and installation

Refer to illustrations 2.1a and 2.1b

1   The Anti-lock Brake System (ABS) **(see illustrations)** is designed to maintain vehicle steerability, directional stability and optimum deceleration under severe braking conditions and on most road surfaces. It does so by monitoring the rotational speed of each wheel and controlling the brake line pressure to each wheel during braking. This prevents the wheel from locking up.

Components
Actuator assembly

2   The actuator assembly consists of an electric hydraulic pump and four solenoid valves. The electric pump provides hydraulic pressure to charge the reservoirs in the actuator, which supplies pressure to the braking system. The pump and reservoirs are housed in the actuator assembly. The solenoid valves modulate brake line pressure during ABS operation.

Speed sensors

Refer to illustrations 2.4, 2.5a and 2.5b

3   The speed sensors, which are located at each wheel, generate small electrical pulsations when the toothed sensor rotors are turning, sending a variable voltage signal to the ABS electronic control unit (ECU) indicating wheel rotational speed.

4   The front speed sensors **(see illustration)** are mounted on the steering knuckles in close relationship to the toothed sensor rotors, which are integral with the outer constant velocity (CV) joints.

5   On all 2000 and earlier models and 2001 and later 4WD models the rear wheel sensors are bolted to the trailing arms **(see illustration)**. On 2001 and later 2WD models the sensors are pressed into the center of the rear hub assemblies **(see illustration)**.

2.12a The data link connector on 2000 and earlier models is located near the power steering fluid reservoir

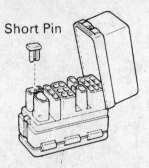

2.12b On 2000 and earlier models, remove the "short pin" from the data link connector . . .

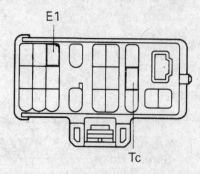

2.12c . . . then use a jumper wire to connect terminals E1 and Tc of the data link connector together

Deceleration sensor

6   2000 and earlier 4WD models and all 2001 and later models are equipped with a deceleration sensor mounted under the center console. This sensor relays negative acceleration data to the ABS computer, which uses this information to determine the forward pitch of the vehicle during panic stops.

ABS computer

7   The ABS electronic control unit (ECU), which is mounted behind the passenger's side kick panel on 2000 and earlier models, or integral with the ABS actuator on 2001 and later models, is the "brain" of the ABS system. The function of the ECU is to accept and process information received from the wheel speed sensors to control the hydraulic line pressure, avoiding wheel lock up. The ECU also constantly monitors the system, even under normal driving conditions, to find faults within the system. If a problem develops within the system, an "ABS" light will glow on the dashboard. A diagnostic code will also be stored in the ECU, which will indicate the problem area or component. These codes can be retrieved without the use of special tools.

Diagnosis and repair

8   If the dashboard warning light comes on and stays on while the vehicle is in operation, the ABS system requires attention and the system should be checked for stored trouble codes. Before checking for trouble codes, however, you should perform a few simple checks.

a) Check the brake fluid level in the reservoir.
b) Check that all electrical connectors are securely connected.
c) Check the fuses.

9   If the above preliminary checks do not rectify the problem, or if any stored trouble codes don't lead you to the problem, the vehicle should be diagnosed and repaired by a dealer service department or other repair shop.

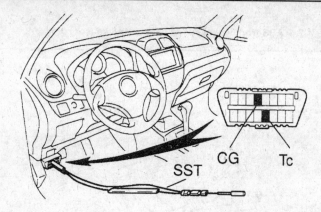

2.12d On 2001 and later models the data link connector is located under the left end of the instrument panel; use a jumper wire to connect terminals CG and Tc

Trouble code retrieval

Refer to illustration 2.12a, 2.12b, 2.12c and 2.12d

10   The ABS system control unit (computer) has a built-in self-diagnosis system which detects malfunctions in the system and alerts the driver by illuminating an ABS warning light in the instrument panel. The computer stores the failure code until the diagnostic system is cleared or malfunction is repaired.

11   The ABS warning light should come on when the ignition switch is placed in the ON position. When the engine is started, the warning light should go out. If the light remains on, the diagnostic system has detected a malfunction or abnormality in the system.

12   The codes for the ABS can be accessed by turning the ignition key to the OFF position (engine not running). On 2000 and earlier models, remove the short pin from the data link connector, then connect a jumper wire to terminals E1 and Tc of the data link connector (see illustrations). On 2001 and later models, connect a jumper wire to terminals Tc and CG of the data link connector (see illustration). Turn the ignition key ON (engine not running) and observe the codes on the ABS warning light on the dash.

13   The diagnostic code is the number of flashes indicated on the ABS light. If any malfunction has been detected, the light will blink the first digit(s) of the code, pause 1.5 seconds, then blink the second digit of the code. For example, a code 34 (left rear wheel sensor) will first blink three flashes, pause 1.5 seconds, then blink four flashes. If there is more than one code stored in the ECM, the ECM will pause 2.5 seconds before flashing the next code. If the system is operating normally (no malfunctions), the warning light will blink once every 0.5 seconds.

14   The accompanying tables explain the code that will be flashed for each of the malfunctions. The accompanying table indicates the diagnostic code - in blinks - along with the system, diagnosis and specific areas. Check the indicated system or component or take the vehicle to a dealer service department to have the malfunction repaired.

15   After the diagnosis check, clear the trouble codes. On 2000 and earlier models, jump terminals E1 and Tc on the data link connector. On 2001 and later models jump terminals Tc and CG. Turn the ignition key ON (engine not running) and clear the codes by depressing the brake pedal eight or more times within three seconds. Remove the jumper wire and, on 2000 and earlier models, reinstall the short pin. Close the cap on the data link connector.

ABS trouble codes

Code number	Trouble area	Action to take
Code 11 (1 flash, pause, 1 flash)	Open circuit in solenoid relay circuit	Check the solenoid relay and the relay circuit
Code 12 (1 flash, pause, 2 flashes)	Short circuit in solenoid relay circuit	Check the solenoid relay and the relay circuit
Code 13 (1 flash, pause, 3 flashes)	Open circuit in ABS motor relay circuit	Check the pump motor relay and circuit
Code 14 (1 flash, pause, 4 flashes)	Short circuit in ABS motor relay circuit	Check the solenoid relay and the relay circuit
Code 21 (2 flashes, pause, 1 flash)	Problem in right front wheel solenoid circuit	Check the actuator solenoid and circuit
Code 22 (2 flashes, pause, 2 flashes)	Problem in left front wheel solenoid circuit	Check the actuator solenoid and circuit
Code 23 (2 flashes, pause, 3 flashes)	Problem in right rear wheel solenoid circuit	Check the actuator solenoid and circuit
Code 24 (2 flashes, pause, 4 flashes)	Problem in left rear wheel solenoid circuit	Check the actuator solenoid and circuit
Code 31 (3 flashes, pause, 1 flash)	Sensor signal problem - right front wheel	Check the speed sensor, sensor rotors, wire harness and connector of the speed sensor
Code 32 (3 flashes, pause, 2 flashes)	Sensor signal problem - left front wheel	Check the speed sensor, sensor rotors, wire harness and connector of the speed sensor
Code 33 (3 flashes, pause, 3 flashes)	Sensor signal problem - right rear wheel	Check the speed sensor, sensor rotors, wire harness and connector of the speed sensor
Code 34 (3 flashes, pause, 4 flashes)	Sensor signal problem - left rear wheel	Check the speed sensor, sensor rotors, wire harness and connector of the speed sensor
Code 35 - 2000 and earlier (3 flashes, pause, 5 flashes)	Open circuit - left front or right rear speed sensor or circuit	Check the speed sensor, wire harness and electrical connector
Code 35 - 2001 and later (3 flashes, pause, 5 flashes)	Debris on right front speed sensor	Check the speed sensor and sensor rotor
Code 36 - 2001 and later (3 flashes, pause, 6 flashes)	Debris on left front speed sensor	Check the speed sensor and sensor rotor
Code 37 (3 flashes, pause, 7 flashes)	Tires not all the same size	Check tire sizes
Code 38 - 2001 and later (3 flashes, pause, 8 flashes)	Debris on right rear speed sensor	Check the speed sensor and sensor rotor
Code 39 - 2001 and later (3 flashes, pause, 9 flashes)	Debris on left rear speed sensor	Check the speed sensor and sensor rotor
Code 41 (4 flashes, pause, 1 flash)	Abnormally low or high battery voltage	Check the charging system (alternator, battery and voltage regulator) for any problems (see Chapter 5)
Code 43 (4 flashes, pause, 3 flashes)	Problem with the deceleration sensor or circuit	Check the wiring to the deceleration sensor. Possible malfunctioning sensor
Code 44 (4 flashes, pause, 4 flashes)	Open or short in the deceleration sensor or circuit	Check the wiring to the deceleration sensor. Possible malfunctioning sensor
Code 45 (4 flashes, pause, 5 flashes)	Problem with the deceleration sensor or circuit	Check the wiring to the deceleration sensor. Possible malfunctioning sensor
Code 49 (4 flashes, pause, 9 flashes)	Open circuit - brake light switch or circuit	Check the brake light switch or circuit
Code 51 (5 flashes, pause, 1 flash)	Pump motor locked	Check the pump motor and relay battery for shorts or abnormalities

Component removal and installation

ABS actuator
Refer to illustrations 2.16a and 2.16b

16   Place some rags under the ABS actuator to catch any brake fluid that spills. Using a flare-nut wrench, unscrew the brake line fittings from the ABS actuator **(see illustrations)**.

17   Remove the power steering fluid reservoir and position it aside (see Chapter 10). On 2000 and earlier models, also unbolt the power steering hose bracket from the ABS actuator bracket.

18   Unplug the electrical connector(s) from the ABS actuator.

19   Unbolt the ABS actuator bracket from the body and remove the actuator from the engine compartment.

20   If necessary, unbolt the actuator from the bracket.

21   Installation is the reverse of removal. Bleed the brake system as described in Section 10.

Front wheel speed sensor

22   Loosen the wheel lug nuts, raise the front of the vehicle and support it securely on jackstands. Block the wheels at the opposite end.

23   Remove the inner fender liner (see Chapter 11).

24   Follow the sensor wiring harness up to the electrical connector, then unplug the connector.

25   Unbolt the wiring harness securing brackets.

26   Remove the sensor mounting bolt and detach the sensor and bushing from the steering knuckle **(see illustration 2.4)**.

27   Installation is the reverse of removal. Be sure to tighten the sensor mounting bolt to the torque listed in this Chapter's Specifications. Tighten the wheel lug nuts to the torque listed in the Chapter 1 Specifications.

Rear wheel speed sensor

All except 2001 and later 2WD models

28   Remove the rear seat cushion and the rear side trim panel (see Chapter 11).

29   Unplug the electrical connector, then push the grommet and wiring harness through the floorpan.

30   Loosen the wheel lug nuts, raise the rear of the vehicle and support it securely on jackstands. Block the wheels at the opposite end.

31   Unbolt the parking brake cable from the suspension arm.

32   Unbolt the wiring harness securing brackets.

33   Remove the sensor mounting bolt and detach the sensor and bushing from the rear axle carrier **(see illustration 2.5a)**.

34   Installation is the reverse of removal. Be sure to tighten the sensor mounting bolt to the torque listed in this Chapter's Specifications. Tighten the wheel lug nuts to the torque listed in the Chapter 1 Specifications.

2001 and later 2WD models

35   Loosen the wheel lug nuts, raise the rear of the vehicle and support it securely on jackstands. Block the wheels at the opposite end.

36   Unplug the electrical connector from the wheel speed sensor **(see illustration 2.5b)**.

37   Remove the rear hub and bearing assembly (see Chapter 10).

38   The speed sensor can be removed from the back of the hub and bearing assembly with a slide hammer and bearing puller attachment. To install the new sensor, it is recommended that a press be used, along with an adapter that bears only on the outer flange of the sensor. Do not tap on the sensor or adapter to install it, as the sensor may be damaged.

39   Installation is the reverse of the removal procedure. Tighten the hub and bearing assembly bolts to the torque listed in the Chapter 10 Specifications. Tighten the wheel lug nuts to the torque listed in the Chapter 1 Specifications.

Deceleration sensor
Refer to illustration 2.41

40   Remove the rear portion of the center console (see Chapter 11).

41   Unplug the electrical connector from the sensor, then remove the two mounting nuts and detach the sensor **(see illustration)**.

42   Installation is the reverse of removal. Be sure to tighten the mounting nuts to the torque listed in this Chapter's Specifications.

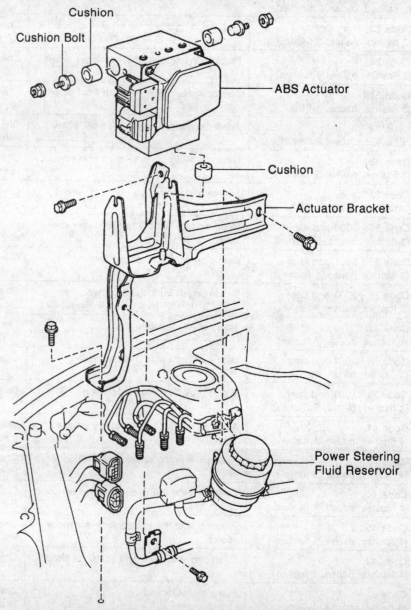

2.16a ABS actuator mounting details - 2000 and earlier models (1996 4WD models are similar, but slightly different)

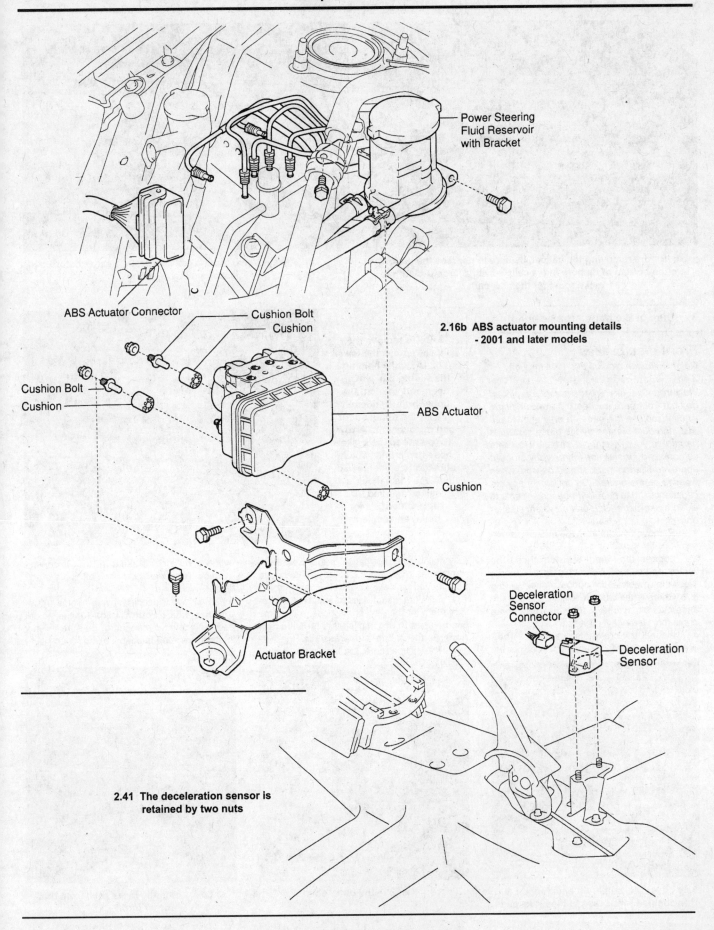

Power Steering
Fluid Reservoir
with Bracket

ABS Actuator Connector

Cushion Bolt

Cushion

**2.16b ABS actuator mounting details
- 2001 and later models**

Cushion Bolt

Cushion

ABS Actuator

Cushion

Actuator Bracket

Deceleration
Sensor
Connector

Deceleration
Sensor

**2.41 The deceleration sensor is
retained by two nuts**

3.5 Before removing the caliper, be sure to depress the piston into the bottom of its bore in the caliper with a large C-clamp to make room for the new pads

3.6a Always wash the brakes with brake cleaner before disassembling anything

3   Disc brake pads - replacement

Front disc brakes

Refer to illustrations 3.5 and 3.6a through 3.6q

Warning: *Disc brake pads must be replaced on both front or rear wheels at the same time - never replace the pads on only one wheel. Also, the dust created by the brake system is harmful to your health. Never blow it out with compressed air and don't inhale any of it. An approved filtering mask should be worn when working on the brakes. Do not, under any circumstances, use petroleum-based solvents to clean brake parts. Use brake system cleaner only!*

1   Remove the cap from the brake fluid reservoir.

2   Loosen the wheel lug nuts, raise the vehicle and support it securely on jackstands. Block the wheels at the opposite end.

3   Remove the wheels. Work on one brake assembly at a time, using the assembled brake for reference if necessary.

4   Inspect the brake disc carefully as outlined in Section 5. If machining is neces-

3.6b To remove the caliper, remove the lower bolt (A) while holding the sliding pin with an open-end wrench; the upper bolt (B) doesn't need to be removed for pad replacement. Arrow (C) points to the brake hose banjo bolt, which shouldn't be unscrewed unless the caliper is being removed for replacement, or for hose replacement

sary, follow the information in that Section to remove the disc, at which time the pads can be removed as well.

5   Push the piston back into its bore to provide room for the new brake pads. A C-clamp can be used to accomplish this **(see illustration)**. As the piston is depressed to the bottom of the caliper bore, the fluid in the master

cylinder will rise. Make sure that it doesn't overflow. If necessary, siphon off some of the fluid.

6   Follow the accompanying photos **(illustrations 3.6a through 3.6q)**, for the actual pad replacement procedure. Be sure to stay in order and read the caption under each illustration.

3.6c Pivot the caliper up and support it in this position for access to the brake pads

3.6d Remove the outer shim . . .

3.6e . . . and the inner shim from the outer brake pad

3.6f Remove the outer brake pad

3.6g Remove the outer shim . . .

3.6h . . . and the inner shim from the inner brake pad

3.6i Remove the inner brake pad

3.6j Remove the pad support plates;
inspect the plates for damage and replace
as necessary (they should fit snugly)

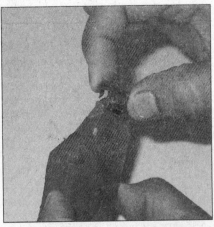

3.6k If equipped, remove the wear
indicator from the old inner brake pad and
transfer it to the new inner pad (if the wear
indicator is worn or bent, replace it)

3.6l Install the pad support plates, the
new inner brake pad and the shims; make
sure the ears on the pad are properly
engaged with the pad support plates
as shown

3.6m Install the outer pad and the shims

3.6n Pull out the lower sliding pin and clean it off (if either boot is damaged, remove it by prying the flange of the metal bushing that retains the boot) . . .

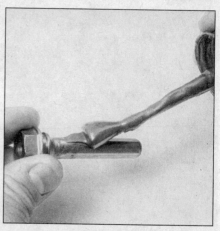

3.6o . . . and apply a coat of high-temperature grease to the pin

3.6p The upper pin can be slid out of its bushing with the caliper attached

3.6q If you have difficulty installing the caliper over the new pads, use a C-clamp to bottom the piston in its bore, then try again - it should now slip over the pads. Install the caliper and tighten the caliper mounting bolt to the torque listed in this Chapter's Specifications

7   When reinstalling the caliper, be sure to tighten the mounting bolts to the torque listed in this Chapter's Specifications. After the job has been completed, firmly depress the brake pedal a few times to bring the pads into contact with the disc. Check the level of the brake fluid, adding some if necessary. Check the operation of the brakes carefully before placing the vehicle into normal service.

Rear disc brakes

Refer to illusration 3.9
Note: On 2003 and later models equipped with rear disc brakes it is not necessary to remove the caliper for brake pad replacement.
8   Wash the brake with brake system cleaner.
9   Carefully pry the brake pad protector from the pad guide pins **(see illustration)**.
Warning: Be careful not to disfigure any components while removing them, Some of these components can be reused.
10   Remove the guide pin retainer clip, then

pull out the pins using a pair of pliers. While pulling out the guide pins, cover the anti-rattle spring with your hand so it doesn't pop out and get lost.
11   Using a large pair of pliers, squeeze the pad against the caliper housing to compress the piston into its bore, making room for the new brake pads. **Note:** Apply force on the brake pad center of the piston; this will keep the piston from binding in its bore, allowing the piston to be more easily compressed.
12   Slide the two pads with the anti-squeal shims out from the caliper.
13   Inspect the brake disc as described in Section 5.
14   Apply a thin coat of disc brake grease to both sides of the inner anti-squeal shims, then attach the inner and outer anti-squeal shims to both inner and outer brake pads.
15   Making sure the guide pin holes on anti-squeal shims are properly aligned with the guide pin holes on the brake pads and the wear indicator tab on the inner pad is facing downward, install the brake pads into

the caliper.
16   Install the anti-rattle spring, guide pins, guide pin retaining clip and the brake pad protector.
17   Pump the brakes several times to bring the brake pads in contact with the brake disc.
18   Check the level of the brake fluid, adding some if necessary. Check the operation of the brakes carefully before placing the vehicle into normal service.

---

4   Disc brake caliper - removal and installation

Warning: Dust created by the brake system is harmful to your health. Never blow it out with compressed air and don't inhale any of it. An approved filtering mask should be worn when working on the brakes. Do not, under any circumstances, use petroleum-based solvents to clean brake parts. Use brake system cleaner only.
Note: If replacement is indicated (usually

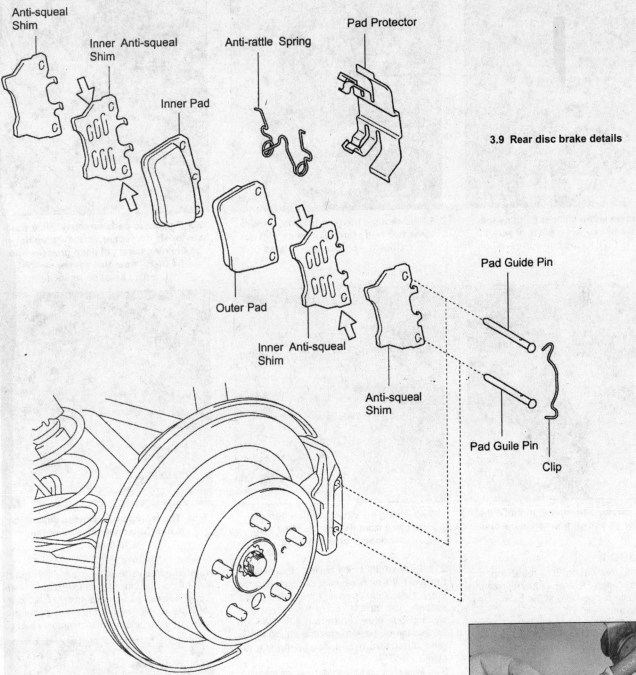

Anti-squeal Shim

Inner Anti-squeal Shim

Inner Pad

Anti-rattle Spring

Pad Protector

3.9 Rear disc brake details

Outer Pad

Inner Anti-squeal Shim

Anti-squeal Shim

Pad Guide Pin

Pad Guile Pin

Clip

because of fluid leakage), it is recommended that the calipers be replaced, not overhauled. New and factory rebuilt units are available on an exchange basis, which makes this job quite easy. Always replace the calipers in pairs - never replace just one of them.

Removal
Refer to illustrations 4.2 and 4.3

1   Loosen the front wheel lug nuts, raise the front of the vehicle and place it securely on jackstands. Remove the wheel.
2   Remove the bolt and disconnect the brake hose from the caliper (**see illustration**

3.6b). Plug the brake hose to keep contaminants out of the brake system and to prevent losing any more brake fluid than is necessary (**see illustration**). Discard the sealing washers - new ones should be used during installation. **Note:** *If the caliper is being removed for access to another component, don't disconnect the hose.*
3   Refer to Section 3 for the caliper removal procedure (it's part of the brake pad replacement procedure). If the caliper is being removed for access to another component, hang it from the coil spring with a piece of wire (**see illustration**).

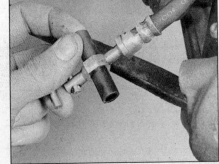

4.2 Using a piece of rubber hose of the appropriate size, plug the brake line; this will prevent brake fluid from leaking out and dirt and moisture from contaminating the system

4.3 Never let the caliper hang by the brake hose - use a piece of wire to tie it to the coil spring

5.2 To remove the torque plate, remove these two bolts (arrows); be careful not to lose the pad support plates

5.3 The brake pads on this vehicle were obviously neglected, as they wore down to the rivets and cut deep grooves into the disc - wear this severe means the disc must be replaced

5.4a To check disc runout, mount a dial indicator as shown and rotate the disc

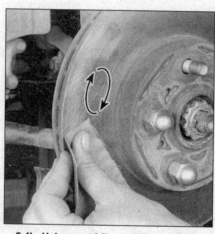

5.4b Using a swirling motion, remove the glaze from the disc surface with sandpaper or emery cloth

5.5a The minimum thickness dimension is cast into the back side of the disc (typical)

Installation

4   Install the caliper by reversing the removal procedure. Remember to replace the sealing washers (gaskets) at the brake hose-to-caliper connection.

5   Bleed the brake circuit according to the procedure in Section 10. Make sure there are no leaks from the hose connections. Test the brakes carefully before returning the vehicle to normal service.

5   Brake disc - inspection, removal and installation

Inspection

Refer to illustrations 5.2, 5.3, 5.4a, 5.4b, 5.5a and 5.5b

1   Loosen the wheel lug nuts, raise the vehicle and support it securely on jackstands. Remove the wheel and install the lug nuts to hold the disc in place against the hub flange. **Note:** *If the lug nuts don't contact the disc when screwed on all the way, install washers under them.*

2   Remove the brake caliper as outlined in Section 4. It isn't necessary to disconnect the brake hose. After removing the caliper bolts, suspend the caliper out of the way with a piece of wire **(see illustration 4.3)**. Remove the two torque plate-to-steering knuckle bolts **(see illustration)** and detach the torque plate.

3   Visually inspect the disc surface for score marks and other damage. Light scratches and shallow grooves are normal after use and may not always be detrimental to brake operation, but deep scoring requires disc removal and refinishing by an automotive machine shop. Be sure to check both sides of the disc **(see illustration)**. If pulsating has been noticed during application of the brakes, suspect disc runout.

4   To check disc runout, place a dial indicator at a point about 1/2-inch from the outer edge of the disc **(see illustration)**. Set the indicator to zero and turn the disc. The indicator reading should not exceed the specified allowable runout limit. If it does, the disc should be refinished by an automotive machine shop.

Note: *The discs should be resurfaced regardless of the dial indicator reading, as this will impart a smooth finish and ensure a perfectly flat surface, eliminating any brake pedal pulsation or other undesirable symptoms related*

5.5b Use a micrometer to measure disc thickness

5.6a If the rear disc is difficult to remove, remove this plug . . .

5.6b . . . insert a screwdriver through the hole (the hole must be at the 6 o'clock position, because that's where the adjuster is located) and rotate the adjuster to back the parking brake shoe away from the drum surface in the disc.

to questionable discs. At the very least, if you elect not to have the discs resurfaced, remove the glaze from the surface with emery cloth or sandpaper, using a swirling motion (see illustration).

5   It's absolutely critical that the disc not be machined to a thickness under the specified minimum thickness. The minimum (or discard) thickness is cast or stamped into the inside of the disc (see illustration). The disc thickness can be checked with a micrometer (see illustration).

Removal

Refer to illustrations 5.6a and 5.6b

6   Remove the lug nuts that were put on to hold the disc in place and slide the disc off the hub. If you're removing a rear disc and it won't come off, it may be interfering with the parking brake shoes; remove the plug (see illustration) and rotate the adjuster to back the parking brake shoes away from the drum surface within the disc (see illustration).

6.4a Mark the relationship of the drum to the hub, so the drum will retain its dynamic balance after reassembly

Installation

7   Place the disc in position over the threaded studs.
8   Install the torque plate and caliper, tightening the bolts to the torque values listed in this Chapter's Specifications.
9   Install the wheel, then lower the vehicle to the ground. Tighten the lug nuts to the torque listed in the Chapter 1 Specifications. Depress the brake pedal a few times to bring the brake pads into contact with the disc. Bleeding won't be necessary unless the brake hose was disconnected from the caliper. Check the operation of the brakes carefully before driving the vehicle.

6   Drum brake shoes - replacement

Refer to illustrations 6.4a through 6.4dd and 6.5

Warning: Drum brake shoes must be replaced on both wheels at the same time - never replace the shoes on only one wheel. Also, the dust created by the brake system is harmful to your health. Never blow it out with compressed air and don't inhale any of it. An approved filtering mask should be worn when working on the brakes. Do not, under any circumstances, use petroleum-based solvents to clean brake parts. Use brake system cleaner only!

Caution: Whenever the brake shoes are replaced, the return and hold-down springs should also be replaced. Due to the continuous heating/cooling cycle the springs are subjected to, they can lose tension over a period of time and may allow the shoes to drag on the drum and wear at a much faster rate than normal.

1   Loosen the wheel lug nuts, raise the rear of the vehicle and support it securely on jackstands. Block the front wheels to keep the vehicle from rolling.

2   Release the parking brake.
3   Remove the wheel. Note: All four rear brake shoes must be replaced at the same time, but to avoid mixing up parts, work on only one brake assembly at a time.
4   Follow the accompanying illustrations for the brake shoe replacement procedure (see illustrations 6.4a through 6.4dd). Be sure to stay in order and read the caption under each illustration. Note: If the brake drum cannot be easily pulled off the axle and shoe assembly, make sure the parking brake is completely released. If the drum still cannot be pulled off, the brake shoes will have to be retracted. This is done by first removing the plug from the brake drum. With the plug removed, pull the lever off the adjuster star wheel with a hooked tool while turning the adjuster wheel with another screwdriver, moving the shoes away from the drum (see illustration 6.4b). The drum should now come off.

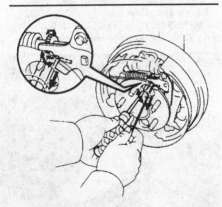

6.4b If the brake drum is hanging up on the shoes because of excessive wear, remove the plug from the drum, pull the adjuster lever away from the star wheel with a hooked tool and turn the star wheel with a screwdriver to retract the brake shoes

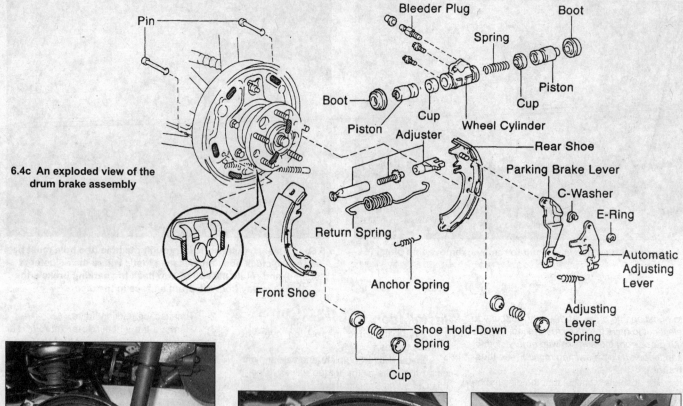

6.4c An exploded view of the drum brake assembly

6.4d Before removing anything, place a drain pan under the brake assembly, clean the brake assembly with brake cleaner and allow it to dry; DO NOT USE COMPRESSED AIR TO BLOW OFF BRAKE DUST! (hub removed for clarity)

6.4e Unhook the return spring from its hole in the front shoe

6.4f Using a hold-down spring tool, remove the hold-down spring by pushing in and rotating it 1/4-turn

6.4g Remove the front shoe and unhook the anchor spring from the rear shoe

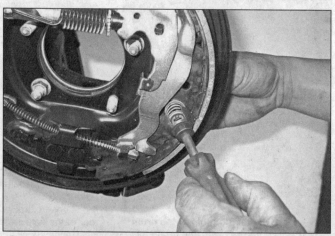

6.4h Remove the rear shoe hold-down spring

6.4i Force the spring back from the parking brake lever and disengage the cable from the lever, then remove the rear shoe assembly

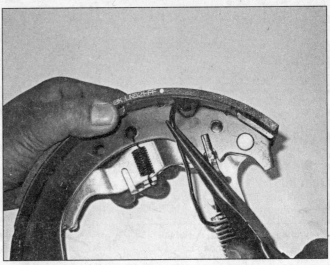

6.4j Unhook the return spring from rear shoe, then remove the spring and adjuster assembly

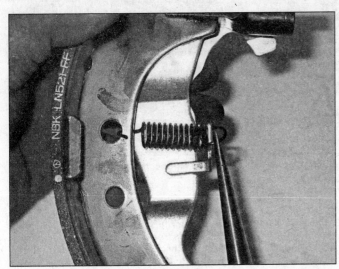

6.4k Unhook the adjusting lever spring from the shoe

6.4l Remove the adjuster end from the rear shoe assembly

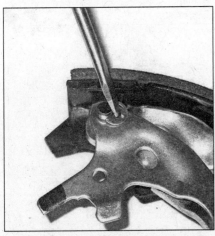

6.4m Pry open the C-clip and detach the adjuster lever from the rear shoe

6.4n Pry off the clip . . .

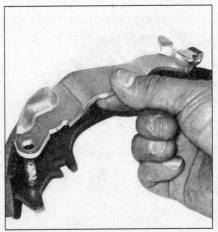

6.4o . . . and detach the parking brake lever from the rear shoe

6.4p Drive the pin out of the old rear shoe . . .

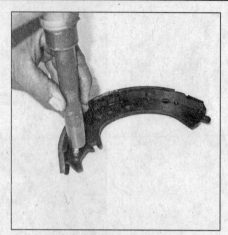

6.4q . . . and install it into the new rear shoe

6.4r Place the parking brake lever on the pin and secure it with a new clip . . .

6.4s . . . then install the adjuster lever on the pin and secure it with a new clip

6.4t Attach the adjuster end to the rear shoe

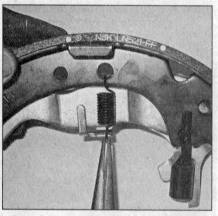

6.4u Connect the adjuster lever spring

5   Before reinstalling the drum, it should be checked for cracks, score marks, deep scratches and hard spots, which will appear as small discolored areas. If the hard spots cannot be removed with fine emery cloth or if any of the other conditions listed above exist, the drum must be taken to an auto-motive machine shop to have it resurfaced. **Note:** *Professionals recommend resurfac-*

ing the drums each time a brake job is done. Resurfacing will eliminate the possibility of out-of-round drums. If the drums are worn so much that they can't be resurfaced without exceeding the maximum allowable diameter (stamped or cast into the drum), then new ones will be required **(see illustration)**. *At the very least, if you elect not to have the drums resurfaced, remove the glaze from the surface*

with emery cloth using a swirling motion.
6   Install the brake drum on the axle flange. Using a screwdriver inserted through the adjusting hole in the brake drum **(see illus-tration 6.4b)**, turn the adjuster star wheel until the brake shoes drag on the drum as the drum is rotated, then back off the star wheel until the shoes don't drag. Reinstall the plug in the drum.

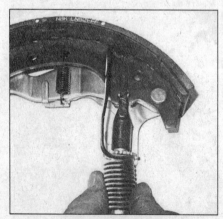

6.4v Insert the adjuster screw into the adjuster end, then connect the return spring to the hole in the shoe

6.4w Front view of the assembled rear shoe/adjuster assembly

6.4x Rear view of the assembled rear shoe/adjuster assembly

6.4y Apply high-temperature grease to the friction points of the backing plate

6.4z Attach the parking brake cable to the parking brake lever . . .

6.4aa . . . then position the rear shoe on the backing plate and install the hold-down spring and retainer

6.4bb Hook both ends of the return spring into their holes in the front and rear shoes

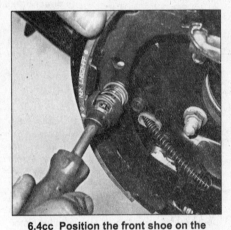

6.4cc Position the front shoe on the backing plate and install the hold-down spring and retainer

6.4dd Connect the return spring to the hole in the front shoe

7   Mount the wheel and install the lug nuts. Lower the vehicle and tighten the lug nuts to the torque listed in the Chapter 1 Specifications.

8   Make a number of forward and reverse stops and operate the parking brake to adjust the brakes until satisfactory pedal action is obtained.

9   Check the operation of the brakes carefully before driving the vehicle.

7   Wheel cylinder - removal and installation

Note: *If replacement is indicated (usually because of fluid leakage or sticky operation), it is recommended that the wheel cylinders be replaced, not overhauled. Always replace the wheel cylinders in pairs - never replace just one of them.*

Removal

Refer to illustration 7.4

1   Raise the rear of the vehicle and support it securely on jackstands. Block the front wheels to keep the vehicle from rolling.

2   Remove the brake shoe assembly (see

Section 6).

3   Remove all dirt and foreign material from around the wheel cylinder.

4   Disconnect the brake line **(see illustration)** with a flare-nut wrench, if available. Don't pull the brake line away from the wheel cylinder.

5   Remove the wheel cylinder mounting bolts.

6.5 The maximum drum diameter is cast into the drum (typical)

6   Detach the wheel cylinder from the brake backing plate. Immediately plug the brake line to prevent fluid loss and contamination.

Installation

7   Place the wheel cylinder in position and install the bolts finger tight. Connect the brake line to the cylinder, being careful not to cross-thread the fitting. Tighten the wheel cylinder

7.4 Disconnect the brake line fitting (1), then remove the two wheel cylinder bolts (2)

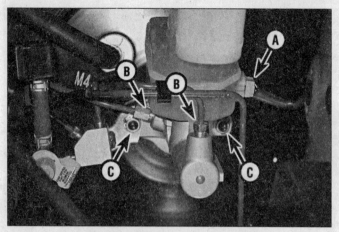

8.2 Master cylinder mounting details

A   *Electrical connector*   C   *Mounting nuts*
B   *Brake line fittings*

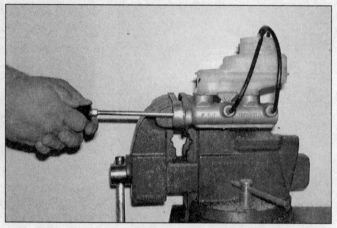

8.8 The best way to bleed air from the master cylinder before installing it on the vehicle is with a pair of bleeder tubes that direct brake fluid into the reservoir during bleeding

bolts to the torque listed in this Chapter's Specifications.
8   Tighten the brake line securely and install the brake shoe assembly (see Section 6).
9   Bleed the brakes (see Section 10).
10   Check the operation of the brakes carefully before driving the vehicle.

---

8   Master cylinder - removal, installation and reservoir/grommet replacement

Removal

Refer to illustrations 8.2

1   If you're working on a 2000 or earlier model, remove the air filter housing cover (See Chapter 4) and the fuse/relay box from the left strut tower.
2   Unplug the electrical connector for the fluid level warning switch **(see illustration)**.
3   Remove as much fluid as possible from the reservoir with a suction gun, large syringe or a poultry baster. **Warning:** *If a poultry baster is used, never again use it for the preparation of food.*
4   Place rags under the fittings and prepare caps or plastic bags to cover the ends of the lines once they're disconnected. **Caution:** *Brake fluid will damage paint. Cover all body parts and be careful not to spill fluid during this procedure.* Loosen the fittings at the ends of the brake lines where they enter the master cylinder. To prevent rounding off the flats, use a flare-nut wrench, which wraps around the fitting hex.
5   Pull the brake lines away from the master cylinder and plug the ends to prevent contamination.
6   Remove the two nuts attaching the master cylinder to the power booster. Pull the master cylinder off the studs to remove it. Again, be careful not to spill the fluid as this is done. Remove and discard the old gasket between the master cylinder and the power

brake booster. Also check the O-ring on the end of the master cylinder, replacing it if it is cracked or hardened.

Installation

Refer to illustrations 8.8 and 8.17

Note: *Before installing a new or rebuilt master cylinder, check the clearance between the booster pushrod and the pocket in the master cylinder piston. If necessary, adjust the length of the power brake booster pushrod (see Section 11).*

7   Bench bleed the master cylinder before installing it. Because it will be necessary to apply pressure to the master cylinder piston and, at the same time, control flow from the brake line outlets, it is recommended that the mater cylinder be mounted in a vise, with the jaws of the vise clamping on the mounting flange.
8   Attach a pair of bleeder tubes (available at most auto parts stores) to the outlet ports of the master cylinder **(see illustration)**.
9   Fill the reservoir with brake fluid of the recommended type (see Chapter 1).
10   Slowly push the pistons into the master cylinder (a large Phillips screwdriver can be used for this) - air will be expelled from the pressure chambers and into the reservoir. Because the tubes are submerged in fluid, air can't be drawn back into the master cylinder when you release the pistons.
11   Repeat the procedure until no more air bubbles are present.
12   Remove the bleed tubes, one at a time, and install plugs in the open ports to prevent fluid leakage and air from entering. Install the reservoir cap.
13   Install the master cylinder over the studs on the power brake booster and tighten the nuts only finger-tight at this time. Don't forget to use a new gasket.
14   Thread the brake line fittings into the master cylinder. Since the master cylinder is still a bit loose, it can be moved slightly so the fittings thread in easily. Don't strip the threads as the fittings are tightened.

15   Tighten the mounting nuts to the torque listed in this Chapter's Specifications. Tighten the brake line fittings securely.
16   Plug in the electrical connector to the fluid level warning switch.
17   Fill the master cylinder reservoir with fluid, then bleed the master cylinder and the brake system (see Section 10). To bleed the master cylinder on the vehicle, have an assistant depress the brake pedal and hold it down. Loosen the fitting to allow air and fluid to escape **(see illustration)**. Tighten the fitting, then allow your assistant to return the pedal to its rest position. Repeat this procedure on both fittings until the fluid is free of air bubbles. Check the operation of the brake system carefully before driving the vehicle.

Reservoir/grommet replacement

Refer to illustration 8.22

Note: *The brake fluid reservoir can be replaced separately from the master cylinder body if it becomes damaged. If there is leak-*

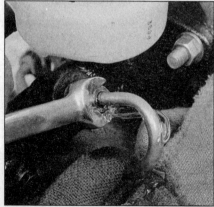

8.17 Have an assistant depress the brake pedal and hold it down, then loosen the fitting nut, allowing the air and fluid to escape; repeat this procedure on both fittings until the fluid is clear of air bubbles

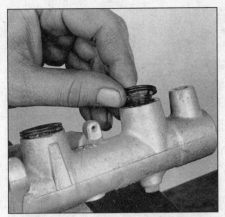

8.22 After the reservoir has been removed, pull the grommets from the master cylinder body; if they're hard, cracked or damaged, or have been leaking, replace them

9.3 Unscrew the brake line threaded fitting with a flare-nut wrench to protect the fitting corners from being rounded off

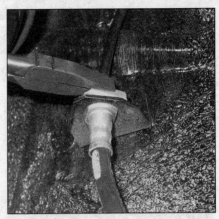

9.4 Pull off the U-clip with a pair of pliers

age between the reservoir and the master cylinder body, the grommets on the reservoir can be replaced.

18   Remove as much fluid as possible from the reservoir with a suction gun, large syringe or a poultry baster. **Warning:** *If a poultry baster is used, never again use it for the preparation of food.*

19   Place rags under the master cylinder to absorb any fluid that may spill out once the reservoir is detached from the master cylinder. **Caution:** *Brake fluid will damage paint. Cover all body parts and be careful not to spill fluid during this procedure.*

20   Remove the screw that retains the reservoir to the master cylinder.

21   Pull the reservoir out of the master cylinder body.

22   Pull the grommets out of the master cylinder **(see illustration)**.

23   Lubricate the new grommets with clean brake fluid, then press them into place.

24   Push the reservoir into the grommets and secure it with the screw.

25   Refill the reservoir with the recommended brake fluid (see Chapter 1) and check for leaks.

26   Bleed the master cylinder **(see illustration 8.17)**, followed by the remainder of the system (see Section 10).

9   Brake hoses and lines - inspection and replacement

Inspection

1   About every six months, with the vehicle raised and supported securely on jackstands, the rubber hoses which connect the steel brake lines with the front and rear brake assemblies should be inspected for cracks, chafing of the outer cover, leaks, blisters and other damage. These are important and vulnerable parts of the brake system and inspection should be complete. A light and mirror

will be helpful for a thorough check. If a hose exhibits any of the above conditions, replace it with a new one.

Replacement

Front brake hose

Refer to illustrations 9.3 and 9.4

2   Loosen the wheel lug nuts, raise the vehicle and support it securely on jackstands. Remove the wheel.

3   At the frame bracket, unscrew the brake line fitting from the hose **(see illustration)**. Use a flare-nut wrench to prevent rounding off the corners. If the bracket begins to bend, hold the hose fitting with an open-end wrench.

4   Remove the U-clip from the female fitting at the bracket with a pair of pliers **(see illustration)**, then pass the hose through the bracket.

5   At the caliper end of the hose, remove the banjo fitting bolt, then separate the hose from the caliper. Note that there are two copper sealing washers on either side of the fitting - they should be replaced with new ones during installation.

6   Unbolt the hose from the bracket on the strut.

7   Installation is the reverse of removal. Make sure the hose isn't twisted between the caliper and the strut bracket. Tighten the banjo bolt to the torque listed in this Chapter's Specifications, and tighten the brake hose-to-brake line fitting securely.

8   Bleed the caliper (see Section 10).

9   Install the wheel and lug nuts, lower the vehicle and tighten the lug nuts to the torque listed in the Chapter 1 Specifications.

Rear brake hose

10   The rear brake hose serves as the flexible connection between two rigid metal lines, one on the body and the other on the trailing arm. Both ends of the hose are attached to these metal lines with threaded fittings and U-clips. Refer to Steps 2, 3 and 4. Be sure to bleed the wheel cylinder when you're done (see Section 10).

Metal brake lines

11   When replacing brake lines, be sure to use the correct parts. Don't use copper tubing for any brake system components. Purchase steel brake lines from a dealer or auto parts store.

12   Prefabricated brake line, with the tube ends already flared and fittings installed, is available at auto parts stores and dealer parts departments. These lines can bent to the proper shape with a tubing bender.

13   When installing the new line, make sure it's securely supported in the brackets and has plenty of clearance between moving or hot components.

14   After installation, check the master cylinder fluid level and add fluid as necessary. Bleed the brake system (see Section 10) and test the brakes carefully before driving the vehicle in traffic.

10   Brake hydraulic system - bleeding

Refer to illustration 10.8

Warning: *Wear eye protection when bleeding the brake system. If the fluid comes in contact with your eyes, immediately rinse them with water and seek medical attention.*

Note: *Bleeding the hydraulic system is necessary to remove any air that manages to find its way into the system when it's been opened during removal and installation of a hose, line, caliper or master cylinder.*

1   You'll probably have to bleed the system at all four brakes if air has entered it due to low fluid level, or if the brake lines have been disconnected at the master cylinder or ABS hydraulic actuator.

2   If a brake line was disconnected only at a wheel, then only that caliper or wheel cylinder must be bled.

3   If a brake line is disconnected at a fitting located between the master cylinder and any of the brakes, the entire system must be bled. And, if the master cylinder has run dry or has been replaced, bleed the master cylinder as

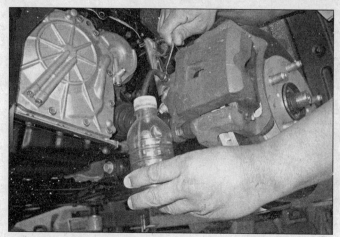

10.8 When bleeding the brakes, a hose is connected to the bleed screw at the caliper or wheel cylinder and then submerged in brake fluid - air will be seen as bubbles in the tube and container (all air must be expelled before moving to the next wheel)

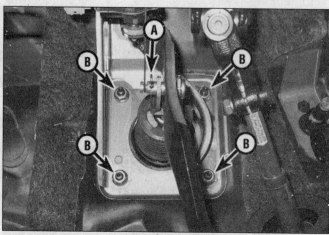

11.10 To disconnect the power brake booster pushrod from the brake pedal, remove the retaining clip (A); to detach the booster from the firewall, remove the four mounting nuts (B)

described in Section 8, Step 17, followed by the remainder of the system.

4 Remove any residual vacuum from the brake power booster by applying the brake several times with the engine off.

5 Remove the master cylinder reservoir cap and fill the reservoir with brake fluid. Reinstall the cap. **Note:** *Check the fluid level often during the bleeding operation and add fluid as necessary to prevent the fluid level from falling low enough to allow air bubbles into the master cylinder.*

6 Have an assistant on hand, as well as a supply of new brake fluid, a clear plastic container partially filled with clean brake fluid, a length of clear tubing to fit over the bleeder valve and a wrench to open and close the bleeder valve.

7 Beginning at the right rear wheel, loosen the bleeder valve slightly, then tighten it to a point where it's snug but can still be loosened quickly and easily.

8 Place one end of the tubing over the bleeder valve and submerge the other end in brake fluid in the container **(see illustration)**.

9 Have the assistant depress the brake pedal slowly and hold the pedal down firmly.

10 While the pedal is held down, open the bleeder valve just enough to allow a flow of fluid to leave the valve. Watch for air bubbles to exit the submerged end of the tube. When the fluid flow slows after a couple of seconds, close the valve and have your assistant release the pedal.

11 Repeat Steps 9 and 10 until no more air is seen leaving the tube, then tighten the bleeder valve and proceed to the left rear wheel, the right front wheel and the left front wheel, in that order, and perform the same procedure. Be sure to check the fluid in the master cylinder reservoir frequently.

12 Never use old brake fluid. It contains moisture which can boil, rendering the brakes inoperative.

13 Refill the master cylinder with fluid at the end of the operation.

14 Check the operation of the brakes. The

pedal should feel solid when depressed, with no sponginess. If necessary, repeat the entire process. **Warning:** *Do not operate the vehicle if the ABS light or BRAKE light fails to go out, if the brakes feel low or spongy, or if you have any doubts as to the effectiveness of the brake system.*

---

11 Power brake booster - check, removal and installation

Operating check

1 Depress the brake pedal several times with the engine off and make sure there's no change in the pedal reserve distance.

2 Depress the pedal and start the engine. If the pedal goes down slightly, operation is normal.

Airtightness check

3 Start the engine and turn it off after one or two minutes. Depress the brake pedal slowly several times. If the pedal depresses less each time, the booster is airtight.

4 Depress the brake pedal while the engine is running, then stop the engine with the pedal depressed. If there's no change in the pedal reserve travel after holding the pedal for 30 seconds, the booster is airtight.

Removal

Refer to illustration 11.10

5 Power brake booster units shouldn't be disassembled. They require special tools not normally found in most automotive repair stations or shops. Because of its critical relationship to brake performance, the booster should be replaced with a new or rebuilt one.

6 Disconnect the hose leading from the engine to the booster. Be careful not to damage the hose when removing it from the booster fitting.

7 Remove the brake master cylinder (see Section 8). If you're working on a 2000 or ear-

lier model, also remove the air intake duct and the fuse/relay block.

8 Remove the left side lower finish panel from the instrument panel (see Chapter 11).

9 Remove the pedal return spring.

10 Locate the pushrod clevis connecting the booster to the brake pedal **(see illustration)**. Remove the clevis pin retaining clip with pliers and pull out the pin.

11 Remove the four nuts holding the brake booster to the firewall **(see illustration 11.10)**; you may need a light to see them.

12 Slide the booster straight out from the firewall until the studs clear the holes.

Installation

Refer to illustrations 11.14a, 11.14b, 11.14c, 11.14d and 11.14e

13 Installation procedures are basically the reverse of removal. Tighten the clevis locknut securely and the booster mounting nuts to the torque listed in this Chapter's Specifications.

14 If a new power brake booster unit is being installed, check the pushrod clearance

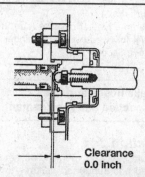

11.14a There should be no clearance between the booster pushrod and the master cylinder pushrod, but no interference either; if there is interference between the two, the brakes may drag; if there is clearance, there will be excessive brake pedal travel

11.14b Measure the distance that the pushrod protrudes from the brake booster at the master cylinder mounting surface (including the gasket)

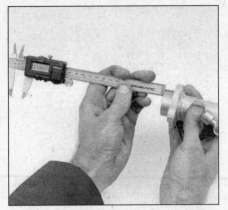

11.14c Measure the distance from the mounting flange to the end of the master cylinder

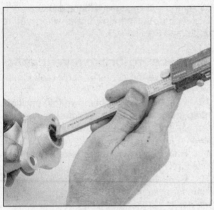

11.14d Measure the distance from the piston pocket to the end of the master cylinder

(see illustration) as follows:

a) *Measure the distance that the pushrod protrudes from the master cylinder mounting surface on the front of the power brake booster, including the gasket. Write down this measurement* **(see illustration)**. *This is "dimension A."*
b) *Measure the distance from the mounting flange to the end of the master cylinder* **(see illustration)**. *Write down this measurement. This is "dimension B."*
c) *Measure the distance from the end of the master cylinder to the bottom of the pocket in the piston* **(see illustration)**. *Write down this measurement. This is "dimension C."*
d) *Subtract measurement B from measurement C, then subtract measurement A from the difference between B and C. This the pushrod clearance.*
e) *Compare your calculated pushrod clearance to the pushrod clearance listed in this Chapter's Specifications. If necessary, adjust the pushrod length to achieve the correct clearance* **(see illustration)**.

15 After the final installation of the master cylinder and brake hoses and lines, the brake pedal height and freeplay must be adjusted and the system must be bled. See the appropriate Sections of this Chapter for the procedures.

12 Parking brake - adjustment

Refer to illustration 12.3

1 The parking brake lever, when properly adjusted, should travel six to eight clicks, when a moderate pulling force is applied. If it travels less than the specified minimum number of clicks, there's a chance the parking brake might not be releasing completely and might be dragging on the drum. If the lever can be pulled up more than the specified maximum number of clicks, the parking brake may not hold adequately on an incline, allowing the car to roll.

2 To gain access to the parking brake cable adjuster, remove the center console (see Chapter 11).

3 Loosen the locknut (the upper nut) while holding the adjusting nut (lower nut) with a wrench **(see illustration)**. Turn the adjusting nut until the desired travel is attained. Tighten the locknut.

4 Install the center console.

13 Parking brake cables - replacement

Equalizer-to-parking brake cable

Refer to illustration 13.4

1 Relieve the fuel system pressure, then disconnect the cable from the negative terminal of the battery (see Chapter 4).

2 Loosen the rear wheel lug nuts, raise the rear of the vehicle and support it securely on jackstands. Block the front wheels. Remove the wheel. Make sure the parking brake is completely released, then remove the brake drum.

3 Remove the brake shoes and disconnect the cable from the parking brake lever (see Section 6).

4 Remove the two cable retaining bolts from the backing plate **(see illustration)** and pull the cable through the backing plate.

5 Remove the fuel tank (see Chapter 4). Also remove the heat shields from above the exhaust system.

6 Unbolt the cable clamps from the trailing arm and floor pan, then disconnect the cable from the equalizer.

7 Installation is the reverse of removal. Apply a light coat of grease to the portion of the

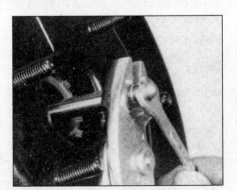

11.14e To adjust the length of the booster pushrod, hold the serrated portion of the rod with a pair of pliers and turn the adjusting screw in or out, as necessary, to achieve the desired setting

12.3 Loosen the locknut, then turn the adjusting nut until the desired handle travel is obtained

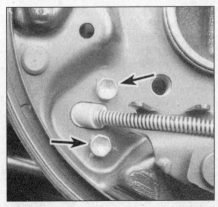

13.4 Unscrew the bolts (arrows) from the backing plate and pass the cable through

cable end that engages with the equalizer.

8   Adjust the parking brake when you're done (see Section 12).

Equalizer-to-brake lever cable

9   Remove the center console (see Chapter 11).

10   With the lever in the down (off) position, remove the locknut and the adjusting nut (see Section 12) and detach the cable from the lever.

11   Raise the rear of the vehicle and support it securely on jackstands.

12 . Remove the heat shields from above the exhaust system, if necessary, for access to the parking brake equalizer.

13   Turn the cable end 90-degrees and disconnect it from the equalizer.

14   Pry out the rubber grommet from the floorpan and pull the cable through the hole in the pan.

15   Installation is the reverse of removal. Apply a light coat of grease to the portion of the cable end that engages with the equalizer. Also, coat the sealing edge of the rubber grommet with silicone sealant to ensure that it remains watertight.

16   Adjust the parking brake lever when you're done (see Section 12).

---

14   Brake pedal - check and adjustment

Pedal height

Refer to illustrations 14.1 and 14.10

1   Measure the pedal height **(see illustration)** and compare your measurement to the pedal height listed in this Chapter's Specifications. If the pedal height is incorrect, adjust it as follows:

2   Remove the steering column lower finish panel and air duct.

3   Unplug the electrical connector from the brake light switch.

4   Loosen the brake light switch locknut and remove the brake light switch.

5   Loosen the pushrod locknut.

6   Adjust the pedal height by turning the pedal pushrod.

7   Tighten the pushrod locknut.

8   Install the brake light switch and turn it until it lightly contacts the pedal stopper.

9   Back off the brake light switch one turn.

10   Measure the distance (clearance "A") between the threaded portion of the brake light switch and the pedal **(see illustration)** and compare your measurement to the clearance listed in this Chapter's Specifications. If the clearance is not as specified, repeat the previous two steps and try again.

11   Tighten the brake light switch locknut.

12   Plug in the brake light switch electrical connector.

13   Verify that brake lights come on when the brake pedal is depressed, and go off when the brake pedal is released.

14   Check the pedal freeplay (see below).

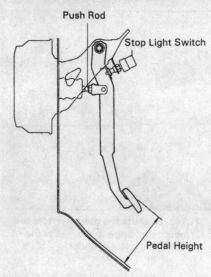

14.1   Brake pedal height is the distance between the pedal and the firewall when the pedal is released

Pedal freeplay

Refer to illustration 14.16

15   Stop the engine, if it's running, and depress the brake pedal several times until there's no more vacuum left in the booster.

16   Push in the pedal until you feel some resistance, then measure the distance between the release pedal and this point at which you can feel resistance **(see illustration)**. Compare your measurement with the pedal freeplay listed in this Chapter's Specifications. If the pedal freeplay is incorrect, adjust it as follows:

17   Check the brake light switch clearance. If the brake light switch clearance is okay, troubleshoot the brake system.

Pedal reserve

18   Start the engine, depress the brake pedal a few times, then press down hard and hold it.

19   Pedal reserve travel is measured from the floor to the top of the pedal while it's being depressed. Compare your measurement to the pedal reserve listed in this Chapter's Specifications.

20   If the pedal reserve is less than specified, check the adjustment of the rear brake shoes and/or the power brake booster pushrod-to-master cylinder piston clearance. If brake pedal feels spongy, bleed the brake system (see Section 10).

---

15   Brake light switch - check and replacement

Check

1   The brake light switch is located on a bracket at the top of the brake pedal **(see illustration 14.1)**. The switch activates the brake lights at the rear of the vehicle when the

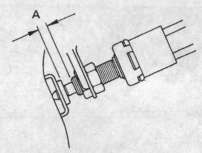

14.10   Clearance "A" is the distance between the brake light switch body and the pedal arm

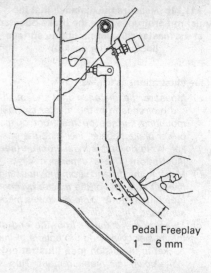

14.16   Brake pedal freeplay is the distance between the pedal when it's released and the point at which some resistance is first felt when the pedal is depressed

pedal is depressed.

2   To check the brake light switch, simply note whether the brake lights come on when the pedal is depressed and go off when the pedal is released. If they don't, check the fuse first (see Chapter 12). If the fuse is good, adjust the switch as described in Section 14 (adjusting the switch is part of brake pedal adjustment).

3   If the lights still don't come on, either the switch is not getting voltage, the switch itself is defective, or the circuit between the switch and the lights is defective. There is always the remote possibility that all of the brake light bulbs are burned out, but this is not very likely.

4   Use a voltmeter or test light to verify that there's voltage present at one side of the switch connector. If no voltage is present, troubleshoot the circuit from the switch to the fuse box. If there is voltage present, check for voltage on the other terminal when the brake pedal is depressed. If no voltage is present, replace the switch. If there is voltage present, troubleshoot the circuit from the switch to the brake lights (see the *Wiring diagrams* at the end of Chapter 12).

16.4 Before disassembling it, be sure to wash the parking brake assembly with brake cleaner

16.5a Remove the rear parking brake shoe return spring from the anchor pin . . .

16.5b . . . and unhook it from the rear shoe

16.5c Remove the front parking brake shoe return spring from the anchor pin . . .

16.5d . . . and unhook it from the front shoe

Replacement

5   Unplug the electrical connector for the brake light switch.

6   Loosen the locknut **(see illustration 14.10)** and unscrew the switch from the pedal bracket.

7   Installation is the reverse of removal.

8   Adjust the brake pedal and brake light switch (see Section 14).

---

16   Parking brake shoes (models with rear disc brakes) - inspection and replacement

Refer to illustrations 16.4 and 16.5a through 16.5u

Warning 1: *Dust created by the brake system is hazardous to your health. Never blow it out with compressed air and don't inhale any of it. An approved filtering mask should be worn when working on the brakes. Do not, under any circumstances, use petroleum-based solvents to clean brake parts. Use brake system cleaner only!*

Warning 2: *Parking brake shoes must be replaced on both wheels at the same time - never replace the shoes on only one wheel.*

16.5e Remove the rear shoe hold-down spring and pull out the pin

1   Remove the brake disc (see Section 5).

2   Inspect the thickness of the lining material on the shoes. If the lining has worn down to 1/32-inch or less, the shoes must be replaced.

3   Remove the hub and bearing assembly (see Chapter 10). **Note:** *It is possible to perform the shoe replacement procedure without removing the hub and bearing assembly,*

10.5f Remove the shoe strut from between the shoes

although working room is limited.

4   Wash off the brake parts with brake system cleaner **(see illustration)**.

5   Follow the accompanying illustrations for the brake shoe replacement procedure **(see illustrations 16.5a through 16.5u)**. Be sure to stay in order and read the caption under each illustration.

6   Install the brake disc. Temporarily thread

16.5g Remove the front shoe hold-down spring and pull out the pin

16.5h Remove the adjuster and the tension spring (the tension spring, which is not visible in this photo, is behind the adjuster and is attached to both shoes)

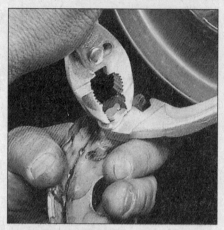

16.5i Pop the C-washer off the pivot pin on the back of the rear shoe . . .

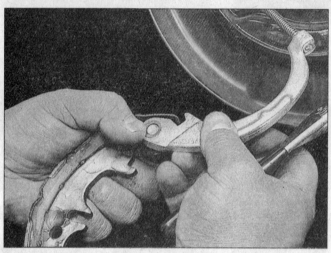

16.5j . . . and pull the parking brake lever off the pivot pin

16.5k Apply a thin coat of high-temperature grease to the contact surfaces of the backing plate

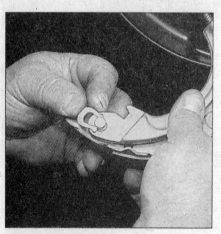

16.5l Slide the parking brake lever onto the pivot pin and install a new C-washer

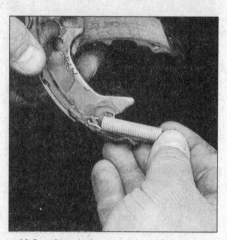

16.5m Attach the tension spring to the back side of the rear shoe . . .

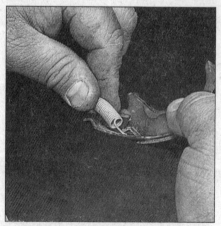

16.5n . . . and to the back side of the front shoe

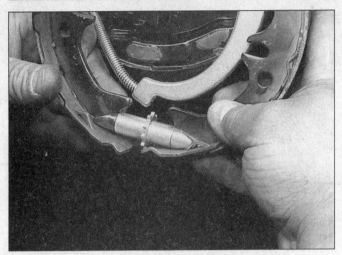

16.5o Flip the shoes around and install the adjuster; make sure both ends of the adjuster are properly engaged with the shoes as shown

16.5p Place the shoes in position and install the strut and spring as shown; make sure the ends of the strut are properly engaged with the shoes as shown

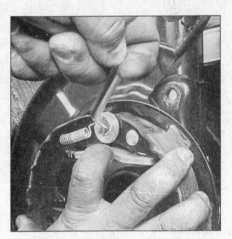

16.5q Install the front shoe return spring . . .

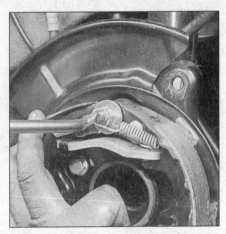

16.5r . . . and the rear shoe return spring

three of the wheel lug nuts onto the studs to hold the disc in place.

7   Remove the hole plug from the brake disc. Adjust the parking brake shoe clearance by turning the adjuster star wheel with a brake adjusting tool or screwdriver until the shoes contact the disc and the disc can't be turned **(see illustrations 5.6a and 5.6b)**. Back off the adjuster eight notches, then install the hole plug.

8   Install the caliper bracket **(see illustration 5.2b)** and brake caliper (see Section 4). Be sure to tighten the bolts to the torque listed in this Chapter's Specifications.

9   Install the wheel and tighten the lug nuts to the torque specified in Chapter 1.

10   Set the parking brake and count the number of clicks that it travels. It should be between about five to seven clicks - if it's not, adjust the parking brake as described in the next Section.

16.5s Install the rear shoe hold-down spring . . .

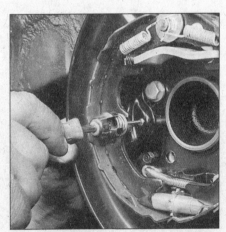

16.5t . . . and the front shoe hold-down spring

16.5u This is how the parking brake assembly should look when you're done!

Notes

Chapter 10
Suspension and steering systems

Contents

	Section		Section
Balljoint - replacement	6	Steering gear - removal and installation	18
Coil spring (rear) - removal and installation	12	Steering gear boots - replacement	17
Control arm - removal, inspection and installation	5	Steering knuckle and hub - removal and installation	7
General information	1	Steering wheel - removal and installation	14
Hub and bearing assembly (front) - removal and installation	8	Strut assembly (front) - removal, inspection and installation	2
Hub and bearing assembly (rear) - removal and installation	13	Strut/spring assembly - replacement	3
Power steering fluid level check	See Chapter 1	Suspension arms (rear) - removal and installation	11
Power steering pump - removal and installation	19	Tie-rod ends - removal and installation	16
Power steering system - bleeding	20	Tire and tire pressure checks	See Chapter 1
Shock absorber (rear) - removal, inspection and installation	10	Tire rotation	See Chapter 1
Stabilizer bar and bushings (front) - removal and installation	4	Wheel alignment - general information	23
Stabilizer bar and bushings (rear) - removal and installation	9	Wheel studs - replacement	21
Steering column - removal and installation	15	Wheels and tires - general information	22

Specifications

Torque specifications

Front suspension

	Ft-lbs (unless otherwise indicated)	Nm
Balljoints		
Balljoint-to-control arm bolt/nuts	94	128
Balljoint-to-steering knuckle nut		
2000 and earlier models	94	128
2001 and later models	98	133
Control arm		
Front pivot bolt		
2000 and earlier models	126	172
2001 and later models	101	137
Rear pivot stud nut (2000 and earlier models)	101	137
Rear bushing bolt (2001 and later models)	101	137
Rear bushing bracket bolts (2000 and earlier models)	101	137
Rear bushing bracket nut (2000 and earlier models)	21	28

Torque specifications

	Ft-lbs (unless otherwise indicated)	Nm
Front suspension (continued)		
Stabilizer bar		
Bracket bolts	22	29
Link nuts		
2000 and earlier models		
2-door models	47	64
4-door models	83	113
2001 and later models	32	44
Struts		
Strut-to-steering knuckle bolts/nuts		
2000 and earlier models	117	158
2001 and later models	105	143
Strut upper mounting nuts..	59	80
Damper shaft nut..	34	47
Suspension crossmember bolts		
2000 and earlier		
Front bolts...	152	206
Rear bolts	101	137
2001 and later		
Front bolts...	82	113
Rear bolts	115	157
Rear suspension		
Suspension arms		
Trailing arm-to-body bolt	98	132
Upper suspension arm-to-body bolt/nut................................	83	113
Upper suspension arm-to-trailing arm		
2000 and earlier models	76	103
2001 and later models	83	113
Lower suspension arm-to-body bolt.......................................	83	113
Lower suspension arm-to-trailing arm		
2000 and earlier models	76	103
2001 and later models	83	113
Hub and bearing assembly-to-trailing arm		
1996 and 1997 models	59	80
1998 through 2000 models		
2WD...	38	51
4WD...	59	80
2001 and later models..	37	50
Stabilizer bar		
Link nuts	32	44
Bracket bolts	168 in-lbs	19
Shock absorber		
Upper mounting nut		
2000 and earlier models	18	25
2001 and later models	132 in-lbs	14.5
Lower mounting bolt..	27	37
Steering		
Airbag module Torx screws	78 in-lbs	8.8
Steering gear mounting bolts		
2000 and earlier models...	83	113
2001 and later models..	101	137
Steering wheel nut		
2000 and earlier models...	25	34
2001 and later models..	35	50
Tie-rod end-to-steering knuckle nut...	36	49
U-joint-to-pinion shaft pinch bolt...	26	35
Power steering pressure line-to-pump union bolt........................	38	52
Power steering pulley nut (2000 and earlier models only)............	32	43
Power steering pump bolts		
Pump mounting bracket-to-engine (2000 and earlier)............	32	43
Pump-to-mounting bracket (2000 and earlier)	32	43
Pump mounting bolts (2001 and later).................................	32	43

1.1a Front suspension and steering components - 2001 and later models shown, earlier models similar

1	Strut/coil spring assembly	3	Balljoint	5	Steering gear
2	Steering knuckle	4	Control arm	6	Suspension crossmember

1   General information

Refer to illustrations 1.1 and 1.2

The front suspension (**see illustration**) is a MacPherson strut design. The upper end of each strut/coil spring assembly is attached to the vehicle's body strut support. The lower end of the strut assembly is connected to the upper end of the steering knuckle. The steering knuckle is attached to a balljoint mounted on the outer end of the suspension control arm. A stabilizer bar reduces body roll.

The rear suspension (**see illustration**) employs a trailing arm, two lateral suspension arms, a coil spring and shock absorber per side, and, on 2001 and later models, a stabilizer bar.

1.2 Typical rear suspension components

1	Shock absorber	3	Upper suspension arm	5	Trailing arm
2	Coil spring	4	Lower suspension arm		

The rack-and-pinion steering gear is located behind the engine/transaxle assembly on the front suspension crossmember and actuates the tie-rods, which are attached to the steering knuckles. The inner ends of the tie-rods are protected by rubber boots which should be inspected periodically for secure attachment, tears and leaking lubricant (which would indicate a failed rack seal).

The power assist system consists of a belt-driven pump and associated lines and hoses. The fluid level in the power steering pump reservoir should be checked periodically (see Chapter 1).

The steering wheel operates the steering shaft, which actuates the steering gear through universal joints. Looseness in the steering can be caused by wear in the steering shaft universal joints, the steering gear, the tie-rod ends and loose retaining bolts.

Precautions

Frequently, when working on the suspension or steering system components, you may come across fasteners which seem impossible to loosen. These fasteners on the underside of the vehicle are continually subjected to water, road grime, mud, etc., and can become rusted or "frozen," making them extremely difficult to remove. In order to unscrew these stubborn fasteners without damaging them (or other components), be sure to use lots of penetrating oil and allow it to soak in for a while. Using a wire brush to clean exposed threads will also ease removal of the nut or bolt and prevent damage to the threads. Sometimes a sharp blow with a hammer and punch will break the bond between a nut and bolt threads, but care must be taken to prevent the punch from slipping off the fastener and ruining the threads. Heating the stuck fastener and surrounding area with a torch sometimes helps too, but isn't recommended because of the obvious dangers associated with fire. Long breaker bars and extension, or "cheater," pipes will increase leverage, but

never use an extension pipe on a ratchet - the ratcheting mechanism could be damaged. Sometimes tightening the nut or bolt first will help to break it loose. Fasteners that require drastic measures to remove should always be replaced with new ones.

Since most of the procedures dealt with in this Chapter involve jacking up the vehicle and working underneath it, a good pair of jackstands will be needed. A hydraulic floor jack is the preferred type of jack to lift the vehicle, and it can also be used to support certain components during various operations. **Warning:** *Never, under any circumstances, rely on a jack to support the vehicle while working on it. Whenever any of the suspension or steering fasteners are loosened or removed they must be inspected and, if necessary, replaced with new ones of the same part number or of original equipment quality and design. Torque specifications must be followed for proper reassembly and component retention. Never attempt to heat or straighten any suspension or steering components. Instead, replace any bent or damaged part with a new one.*

2   Strut assembly (front) - removal, inspection and installation

Removal

Refer to illustrations 2.4a, 2.4b and 2.6

1   Loosen the wheel lug nuts, raise the vehicle and support it securely on jackstands. Remove the wheel.
2   Unbolt the brake hose bracket from the strut. If the vehicle is equipped with ABS, detach the speed sensor wiring harness from the strut by removing the clamp bracket bolt.
3   If you're working on a 2001 or later model, detach the stabilizer bar link from the bracket on the strut (see Section 4).
4   Mark the relationship of the strut to the steering knuckle **(see illustration)**. **Note:** *Also mark the positions of the bolt heads, as*

2.4a Mark the relationship of the strut to the steering knuckle (to preserve the camber setting when reassembling)

special camber adjusting bolts may have been installed at some point. Remove the strut-to-knuckle nuts **(see illustration)** and knock the bolts out with a hammer and punch.
5   Separate the strut from the steering knuckle. Be careful not to overextend the inner CV joint. Also, don't let the steering knuckle fall outward and strain the brake hose.
6   Support the strut and spring assembly with one hand and remove the three strut-to-body nuts **(see illustration)**. Remove the assembly out from the fenderwell.

Inspection

7   Check the strut body for leaking fluid, dents, cracks and other obvious damage which would warrant repair or replacement.
8   Check the coil spring for chips or cracks in the spring coating (this will cause premature spring failure due to corrosion). Inspect the spring seat for cuts, hardness and general deterioration.
9   If any undesirable conditions exist, proceed to the strut disassembly procedure (see Section 3).

2.4b To detach the strut from the steering knuckle, remove the two nuts, then knock out the bolts with a hammer and punch

2.6 To detach the upper end of the strut from the body, remove the upper mounting nuts (arrows)

3.3 Install the spring compressor according to the tool manufacturer's instructions and compress the spring until all pressure is relieved from the upper spring seat

3.4 Remove the damper shaft nut - if the upper spring seat turns while loosening the nut, immobilize it with a chain wrench or strap wrench

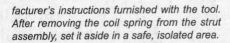

facturer's instructions furnished with the tool. After removing the coil spring from the strut assembly, set it aside in a safe, isolated area.

Installation

10   Guide the strut assembly up into the fenderwell and insert the upper mounting studs through the holes in the body. Once the studs protrude, install the nuts so the strut won't fall back through. This is most easily accomplished with the help of an assistant, as the strut is quite heavy and awkward.

11   Slide the steering knuckle into the strut flange and insert the two bolts. Install the nuts, align the previously made matchmarks and tighten them to the torque listed in this Chapter's Specifications.

12   Connect the brake hose bracket to the strut and tighten the bolt securely. If the vehicle is equipped with ABS, install the speed sensor wiring harness bracket.

13   If you're working on a 2001 or later model, connect the stabilizer bar link to the strut bracket. Tighten the nut to the torque listed in this Chapter's Specifications.

14   Install the wheel and lug nuts, then lower the vehicle and tighten the lug nuts to the torque listed in the Chapter 1 Specifications.

15   Tighten the upper mounting nuts to the torque listed in this Chapter's Specifications.

16   Drive the vehicle to an alignment shop to have the front end alignment checked, and if necessary, adjusted.

3   Strut/spring assembly - replacement

1   If the struts or coil springs exhibit the telltale signs of wear (leaking fluid, loss of damping capability, chipped, sagging or cracked coil springs) explore all options before beginning any work. The strut/shock absorber assemblies are not serviceable and must be replaced if a problem develops. However, strut assemblies complete with springs may be available on an exchange basis, which eliminates much time and work. Whichever route you choose to take, check on the cost and availability of parts before disassembling your vehicle. **Warning:** *Disassembling a strut is potentially dangerous and utmost attention must be directed to the job, or serious injury may result. Use only a high-quality spring compressor and carefully follow the manu-*

Disassembly

Refer to illustrations 3.3, 3.4, 3.5, 3.6 and 3.7

2   Remove the strut assembly following the procedure described in the previous Section. Mount the strut assembly in a vise. Line the vise jaws with wood or rags to prevent damage to the unit and don't tighten the vise excessively.

3   Following the tool manufacturer's instructions, install the spring compressor (which can be obtained at most auto parts stores or equipment yards on a daily rental basis) on the spring and compress it sufficiently to relieve all pressure from the upper spring seat **(see illustration)**. This can be verified by wiggling the spring.

4   Loosen the damper shaft nut with a socket wrench **(see illustration)**.

5   Remove the nut and suspension support **(see illustration)**. Inspect the bearing in the suspension support for smooth operation. If it doesn't turn smoothly, replace the suspension support. Check the rubber portion of the suspension support for cracking and general deterioration. If there is any separation of the rubber, replace it.

6   Lift the spring seat and upper insulator from the damper shaft **(see illustration)**. Check the rubber spring seat for cracking and hardness, replacing it if necessary.

7   Carefully lift the compressed spring from the assembly **(see illustration)** and set it in a safe place. **Warning:** *Never place your head near the end of the spring!*

8   Slide the rubber bumper off the damper shaft.

9   Check the lower insulator (if equipped) for wear, cracking and hardness and replace it if necessary.

Reassembly

Refer to illustrations 3.10, 3.11 and 3.12

10   If the lower insulator is being replaced, set it into position with the dropped portion

3.5 Lift the suspension support off the damper shaft

3.6 Remove the spring seat from the damper shaft

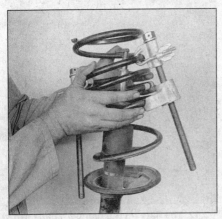

3.7 Remove the compressed spring assembly - keep the ends of the spring pointed away from your body

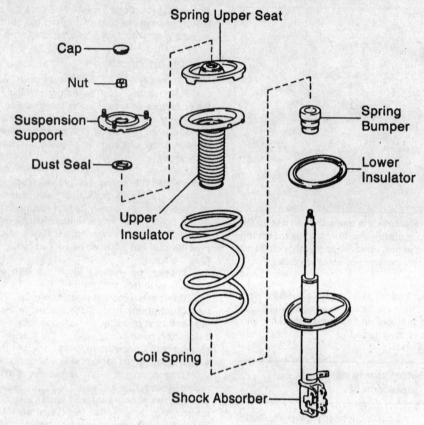

3.10 **Typical strut and coil spring assembly details (2000 and earlier models shown, later models similar)**

3.11 **When installing the spring, make sure the end fits into the recessed portion of the lower seat (arrow)**

4   Stabilizer bar and bushings (front) - removal and installation

Removal

Refer to illustrations 4.2a, 4.2b, 4.3 and 4.4

1   Loosen the front wheel lug nuts. Raise the front of the vehicle and support it securely on jackstands. Apply the parking brake and block the rear wheels to keep the vehicle from rolling off the stands. Remove the front wheels.

2   Detach the stabilizer bar link from the bar **(see illustrations)**. If the ballstud turns with the nut, use an Allen wrench to hold the stud.

3   Unbolt the stabilizer bar bushing clamps **(see illustration)**. Guide the stabilizer bar out from between the crossmember and the body.

4   While the stabilizer bar is off the vehicle, slide off the retainer bushings and inspect them. If they're cracked, worn or deteriorated, replace them. It's also a good idea to inspect the stabilizer bar link. To check it, flip the balljoint stud side to side five or six times

seated in the lowest part of the seat. Extend the damper rod to its full length and install the rubber bumper **(see illustration)**.

11   Carefully place the coil spring onto the lower insulator, with the end of the spring resting in the lowest part of the insulator **(see illustration)**.

12   Install the upper insulator and spring seat, making sure that the flats in the hole in

the seat match up with the flats on the damper shaft **(see illustration)**.

13   Install the dust seal and suspension support to the damper shaft.

14   Install the nut and tighten it to the torque listed in this Chapter's Specifications.

15   Install the strut assembly following the procedure outlined previously (see Section 2).

3.12 **The flats on the damper shaft (arrow) must match up with the flats in the spring seat**

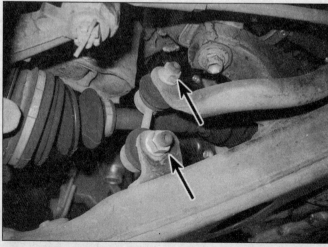

4.2a **2000 and earlier models - if you're removing the stabilizer bar, detach the bar from the link by removing the upper nut; if you're removing the control arm, remove the lower nut and detach the link from the arm**

4.2b 2001 and later models - the stabilizer bar link is connected to a bracket on the strut instead of the control arm (if you're just removing the stabilizer bar, simply disconnect the links from the bar, not the strut)

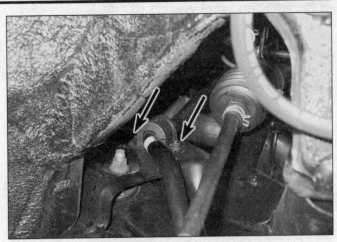

4.3 Stabilizer bar bracket bolts

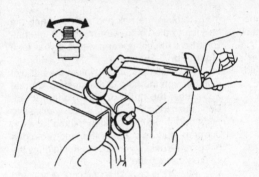

4.4 To check the balljoint in the stabilizer bar link, flip the balljoint stud side to side five or six times as shown, install the nut and, using an inch-pound torque wrench, turn the nut continuously one turn every two to four seconds, then note the torque reading on the fifth turn. It shouldn't be less than about 0.4 in-lbs; if it is, replace the link assembly

paint line (2000 and earlier models) or to the outside of the bushing stop (2001 and later models).

7   Installation is the reverse of removal. Tighten the fasteners to the torque values listed in this Chapter's Specifications.

5   Control arm - removal, inspection and installation

Removal

Refer to illustrations 5.2a, 5.2b, 5.3, 5.4a and 5.4b

1   Loosen the wheel lug nuts on the side to be dismantled, raise the front of the vehicle, support it securely on jackstands and remove the wheel. If you're working on a 2000 or earlier model, disconnect the stabilizer bar link from the control arm (see Section 4).

2   Remove the bolt and two nuts securing the balljoint to the control arm. Use a prybar to disconnect the control arm from the steering knuckle **(see illustrations)**.

as shown **(see illustration)**, then install the nut. Using an inch-pound torque wrench, turn the nut continuously one turn every two to four seconds and note the torque reading on the fifth turn. It should be no less than 0.4 in-lbs. If it is, it's too loose and the link should be replaced.

5   Clean the bushing area of the stabilizer bar with a stiff wire brush to remove any rust or dirt.

Installation

6   Lubricate the inside and outside of the new bushing with vegetable oil (used in cooking) to simplify reassembly. **Caution:** *Don't use petroleum or mineral-based lubricants or brake fluid - they will lead to deterioration of the bushings.* The slits of the bushings must face the rear of the vehicle. Also, the bushings must be positioned to the outside of the

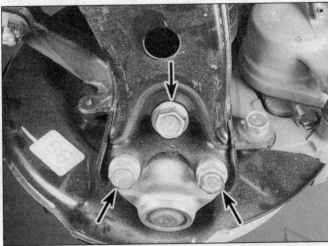

5.2a To detach the control arm from the steering knuckle balljoint, remove this bolt and these two nuts (arrows) . . .

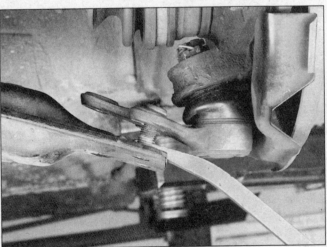

5.2b . . . and pry the control arm and balljoint apart with a large prybar or screwdriver

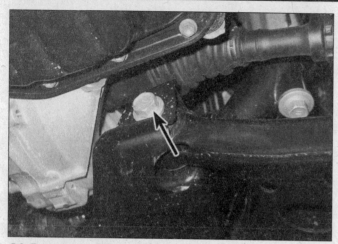

5.3 To detach the front of the control arm from the crossmember, remove this pivot bolt (arrow)

5.4a To detach the rear end of the control arm on a 2000 or earlier model, remove the nut and two bolts

3   Remove the control arm front pivot bolt **(see illustration)**. **Note:** *If you're working on a 2000 or earlier model with an automatic transaxle, and you're removing the left side control arm, the suspension crossmember must be supported, unbolted and then lowered to allow bolt removal.*
4   Remove the rear pivot bushing bracket (2000 and earlier models) **(see illustration)** or the rear bushing bolt (2001 and later models) **(see illustration)**.
5   Remove the control arm.

Inspection

6   Check the control arm for distortion and the bushings for wear, replacing parts as necessary. Do not attempt to straighten a bent control arm.

Installation

7   Installation is the reverse of removal. Tighten all of the fasteners to the torque values listed in this Chapter's Specifications. **Note:** *Before tightening the pivot bolt (and the pivot nut on the rear of the control arm, if you're working on a 2000 or earlier model),*

raise the outer end of the control arm with a floor jack to simulate normal ride height.
8   Install the wheel and lug nuts, lower the vehicle and tighten the lug nuts to the torque listed in the Chapter 1 Specifications.
9   It's a good idea to have the front wheel alignment checked and, if necessary, adjusted after this job has been performed.

6   Balljoint - replacement

Refer to illustration 6.3
1   Loosen the wheel lug nuts, raise the vehicle and support it securely on jackstands. Remove the wheel.
2   Remove the cotter pin from the balljoint stud and loosen the nut (but don't remove it yet).
3   Separate the balljoint from the steering knuckle with a picklefork-type balljoint separator **(see illustration)**. Remove the balljoint stud nut. The clearance between the balljoint stud and the CV joint is very tight. To remove the stud nut, you'll have to alternately back off the nut a turn or two, pull down the stud, turn

the nut another turn or two, etc. until the nut is off.
4   Remove the bolt and nuts securing the balljoint to the control arm. Separate the balljoint from the control arm with a prybar **(see illustration 5.2b)**.
5   To install the balljoint, insert the balljoint stud through the hole in the steering knuckle and install the nut, but don't tighten it yet. Don't push the balljoint stud all the way up into and through the hole; instead, thread the nut onto the stud as soon as the stud protrudes through the hole, then turn the nut to draw the stud up through the hole.
6   Attach the balljoint to the control arm and install the bolt and nuts, tightening them to the torque listed in this Chapter's Specifications.
7   Tighten the balljoint stud nut to the torque listed in this Chapter's Specifications and install a new cotter pin. If the cotter pin hole doesn't line up with the slots on the nut, tighten the nut additionally until it does line up - don't loosen the nut to insert the cotter pin.
8   Install the wheel and lug nuts. Lower the vehicle and tighten the lug nuts to the torque listed in the Chapter 1 Specifications.

5.4b To detach the rear end of the control arm on a 2001 or later model, remove this bolt (arrow)

6.3 Separate the balljoint from the steering knuckle with a picklefork-type balljoint separator

7.8 Use a balljoint removal tool or small puller to force the balljoint stud from the steering knuckle

9.2 To detach a rear stabilizer bar link from the stabilizer bar, remove this nut (arrow) and pivot the link out of the way

9.3 To detach the rear stabilizer bar from the vehicle body, remove the bolts (arrows) from the bushing clamps

7 Steering knuckle and hub - removal and installation

Warning: *Dust created by the brake system is harmful to your health. Never blow it out with compressed air and don't inhale any of it. Do not, under any circumstances, use petroleum-based solvents to clean brake parts. Use brake system cleaner only.*

Removal

Refer to illustration 7.8

1   Remove the wheel cover and loosen, but don't remove, the driveaxle/hub nut. Loosen the wheel lug nuts, raise the vehicle and support it securely on jackstands, then remove the wheel.
2   Remove the brake caliper (don't disconnect the hose) and the brake disc (see Chapter 9), and disconnect the brake hose from the strut. Hang the caliper from the coil spring with a piece of wire - don't let it hang by the brake hose.
3   If the vehicle is equipped with ABS, remove the wheel speed sensor (see Chapter 9).
4   Mark the relationship of the strut to the steering knuckle. Loosen, but don't remove the strut-to-steering knuckle nuts and bolts (see Section 2).
5   Separate the tie-rod end from the steering knuckle arm (see Section 16).
6   Remove the balljoint-to-lower arm bolt and nuts **(see illustrations 5.2a and 5.2b)**.
7   Remove the driveaxle/hub nut and push the driveaxle from the hub as described in Chapter 8. Support the end of the driveaxle with a piece of wire.
8   Using a balljoint removal tool **(see illustration)** or a small puller, remove the balljoint from the steering knuckle. **Note:** *If you're removing the steering knuckle to replace the hub bearings, and the balljoint is in good condition, the balljoint can remain attached.*
9   The strut-to-knuckle bolts can now be removed.
10 Carefully separate the steering knuckle from the strut.

Installation

11 Guide the knuckle and hub assembly into position, inserting the driveaxle into the hub.
12 Push the knuckle into the strut flange and install the bolts and nuts, but don't tighten them yet.
13 If you removed the balljoint from the old knuckle, and are planning to use it with the new knuckle, connect the balljoint to the knuckle and tighten the balljoint stud nut to the torque listed in this Chapter's Specifications. Install a new cotter pin.
14 Attach the balljoint to the control arm, but don't tighten the bolt and nuts yet.
15 Attach the tie-rod to the steering knuckle arm (see Section 16). Tighten the strut bolt nuts, the balljoint-to-control arm bolt and nuts and the tie-rod nut to the torque listed in this Chapter's Specifications.
16 Place the brake disc on the hub and install the caliper as outlined in Chapter 9.
17 Install the driveaxle/hub nut and tighten it securely, but not completely yet.
18 Install the wheel and lug nuts. Lower the vehicle and tighten the lug nuts to the torque listed in the Chapter 1 Specifications.
19 Tighten the driveaxle/hub nut to the torque listed in the Chapter 8 Specifications. Install the wheel cover.
20 Have the front-end alignment checked and, if necessary, adjusted.

8 Hub and bearing assembly (front) - removal and installation

Due to the special tools and expertise required to press the hub and bearing from the steering knuckle, this job should be left to a professional mechanic. However, the steering knuckle and hub may be removed and the assembly taken to an automotive machine shop or other qualified repair facility equipped with the necessary tools. See Section 7 for the steering knuckle and hub removal procedure.

9 Stabilizer bar and bushings (rear) - removal and installation

Refer to illustrations 9.2 and 9.3
Note: *This procedure applies to 2001 and later models only.*

1   Raise the rear of the vehicle and support it securely on jackstands. Block the front wheels to prevent the vehicle from rolling.
2   Remove the stabilizer bar-to-link nut **(see illustration)**. If the ballstud turns with the nut, use a hex wrench to hold the stud.
3   Unbolt the stabilizer bar bushing clamps from the body **(see illustration)**.
4   The stabilizer bar can now be removed from the vehicle. Pull the retainers off the stabilizer bar (if they haven't fallen off already) using a rocking motion.
5   Check the bushings for wear, hardness, distortion, cracking and other signs of deterioration, replacing them if necessary.
6   Check the stabilizer bar links for wear as described in Section 4.
7   Using a wire brush, clean the areas of the bar where the bushings ride. Install the bushings on the bar with the slits facing down. Also, the bushings must be installed to the inside of the paint line on the bar. If necessary, use a light coat of vegetable oil to ease bushing and U-bracket installation (don't use petroleum-based products or brake fluid, as these will damage the rubber).
8   Installation is the reverse of removal. Tighten the fasteners to the torque listed in this Chapter's Specifications.

10 Shock absorber (rear) - removal, inspection and installation

Refer to illustrations 10.3a, 10.3b and 10.4
1   Loosen the wheel lug nuts, raise the vehicle and support it securely on jackstands. Block the front wheels to prevent the vehicle from rolling. Remove the wheel.
2   Support the rear end of the trailing arm with a floor jack. Raise the jack slightly to take the spring pressure off the shock absorber

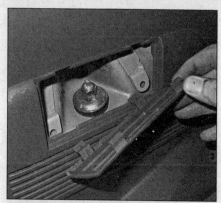

10.3a Remove the trim cover, unscrew the two upper shock mounting nuts, then remove the retainers and bushing; this is a 2000 or earlier model . . .

10.3b . . . and this is a 2001 or later model

10.4 Shock absorber lower mounting bolt

11.2 Suspension arm-to-trailing arm mounting points (2000 and earlier models)

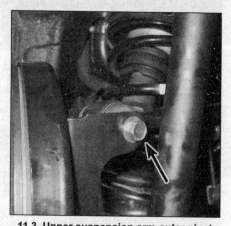

11.3 Upper suspension arm outer pivot bolt (2001 and later models)

lower mount. **Warning:** *The jack must remain in this position throughout the entire procedure.*

3   Working inside the vehicle, remove the trim cover for access to the shock absorber upper mounting nuts. Remove the nuts, upper retainer, bushing and lower retainer **(see illustrations).**

4   Unscrew the shock absorber lower mounting bolt, then pull the shock off the mounting pin **(see illustration)**. Note how the retainers are positioned.

5   Installation is the reverse of the removal procedure. Tighten the mounting fasteners to the torque listed in this Chapter's Specifications.

11   Suspension arms (rear) - removal and installation

1   Loosen the wheel lug nuts, raise the vehicle and support it securely on jackstands. Block the front wheels to prevent the vehicle from rolling. Remove the wheel.

Upper suspension arm
Refer to illustrations 11.2, 11.3 and 11.4

2   If you're working on a 2000 or earlier model, remove the cotter pin and nut from the ballstud at the outer end of the arm **(see illustration)**, then separate the arm from the boss on the trailing arm. If the ballstud sticks in its boss, a two-jaw puller or balljoint removal tool can be used to force it out.

3   If you're working on a 2001 or later model, remove the nut and bolt securing the arm to the bracket on the trailing arm **(see illustration)**.

4   Remove the nut and pivot bolt from the inner end of the arm **(see illustration)**. Remove the arm from the vehicle.

5   Check the arm for bending and cracks, and the bushing for wear, hardness or deterioration. On 2000 and earlier models, also check the ballstud for excessive wear. To check it, flip the balljoint stud side-to-side five or six times, then install the nut. Using an inch-pound torque wrench, turn the nut con-

tinuously one turn every two to four seconds and note the torque reading on the fifth turn (similar to **illustration 4.5**). It should be no less than 7 in-lbs. If it is, it's too loose and the arm should be replaced.

6   Installation is the reverse of removal. Tighten the fasteners to the torque listed in this Chapter's Specifications. **Note:** *Before tightening the pivot bolt nuts, use a floor jack to raise the trailing arm to simulate normal ride height. If you're working on a 2000 or earlier model, install new cotter pins.*

Lower suspension arm
Refer to illustration 11.8

7   If you're working on a 2001 or later model, detach the stabilizer bar link from the lower suspension arm.

8   Refer to Steps 2 through 6 for the removal, check and installation procedures, but note that the camber adjusting cam at the inner end of the arm must be marked to preserve wheel alignment **(see illustration)**.

9   Have the rear wheel alignment checked and, if necessary, adjusted.

11.4 Upper suspension arm inner pivot bolt

11.8 Mark the relationship of the camber adjusting cam to the suspension crossmember

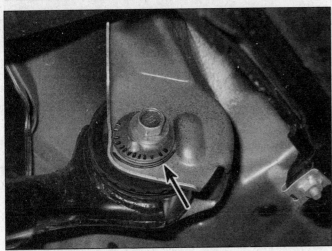

11.14 Mark the relationship of the toe adjusting cam to the trailing arm mounting bracket

12.5 Removing the coil spring out from between the trailing arm and the upper mount

Trailing arm

Refer to illustration 11.14

10   Remove the coil spring (see Section 12).

11   Unbolt the brake hose and brake line brackets from the trailing arm. Unbolt the parking brake cable brackets from the trailing arm.

12   If equipped, remove the ABS wheel speed sensor and unbolt the harness brackets from the trailing arm (see Chapter 9).

13   Remove the hub and bearing assembly (see Section 13). Separate the brake backing plate/brake shoe assembly from the trailing arm and suspend it out of the way with a piece of wire or string.

14   Mark the relationship of the toe adjusting cam to the trailing arm mounting bracket (see **illustration**).

15   Unscrew the pivot bolt and separate the trailing arm from the vehicle.

16   Inspect the trailing arm pivot bushing for signs of deterioration. If it is in need of replacement, take the trailing arm to an automotive machine shop to have the bushing replaced.

17   Installation is the reverse of removal,

13.5 To remove the four bolts or nuts which secure the hub and bearing assembly , rotate the hub flange and align one of the holes in the flange with each of the bolts or nuts

noting the following points:

a) *Align the matchmarks on the toe adjusting cam and the mounting bracket.*

b) *Before fully tightening the trailing arm pivot bolt, raise the rear end of the trailing arm with a floor jack to simulate normal ride height.*

c) *Tighten all fasteners to the proper torque specifications.*

d) *It won't be necessary to bleed the brakes unless a hydraulic fitting was loosened.*

e) *Have the rear wheel alignment checked and, if necessary, adjusted.*

12 Coil spring (rear) - removal and installation

Refer to illustration 12.5

Warning: *Always replace the springs as a set - never replace just one of them.*

1   Loosen the wheel lug nuts, raise the vehicle and support it securely on jackstands. Block the front wheels to prevent the vehicle from rolling. Remove the wheel.

2   If you're working on a 2001 or later model, detach the stabilizer bar link from the lower suspension arm.

3   Support the trailing arm with a floor jack.

4   Detach the lower end of the shock absorber from the trailing arm (see **illustration 10.4**).

5   Slowly lower the floor jack, pull the trailing arm down and remove the coil spring (see **illustration**).

6   Check the spring for cracks and chips, replacing the springs as a set if any defects are found. Also check the upper insulator for damage and deterioration, replacing it if necessary.

7   Installation is the reverse of removal. Be sure to position the lower end of the coil spring in the depressed area of the trailing arm. Tighten all fasteners to the proper torque specifications.

13 Hub and bearing assembly (rear) - removal and installation

Warning: *Dust created by the brake system is harmful to your health. Never blow it out with compressed air and don't inhale any of it. Do not, under any circumstances, use petroleum-based solvents to clean brake parts. Use brake system cleaner only.*

Note: *Due to the special tools required to replace the bearing, the hub and bearing assembly should not be disassembled by the home mechanic. The assembly can be removed, however, and taken to a dealer service department or other repair shop to have the bearing replaced.*

Removal

Refer to illustration 13.5

1   If you're working on a 4WD model, loosen the rear driveaxle/hub nut (see Chapter 8).

2   Loosen the wheel lug nuts, raise the vehicle and support it securely on jackstands. Block the front wheels to prevent the vehicle from rolling. Remove the wheel.

3   Remove the brake drum (see Chapter 9). If you're working on a 1996 or 1997 2WD model or a 2000 or earlier 4WD model, remove the brake shoes, detach the parking brake cable from the brake backing plate and disconnect the brake line from the wheel cylinder (see Chapter 9).

4   If you're working on a 4WD model, remove the rear driveaxle (see Chapter 8).

5   Remove the four hub-to-trailing arm bolts (2000 and earlier models) or nuts (2001 and later models), accessible by turning the hub flange so that the large circular cutout exposes each bolt (see **illustration**).

6   Remove the hub and bearing assembly. If you're working on a 1996 or 1997 2WD model or a 2000 or earlier 4WD model, the brake backing plate is removed along with the hub and bearing. If you're working on a 1998 through 2000 2WD model, reinstall one of the

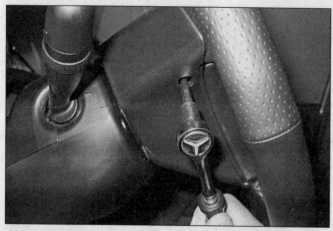

14.2 Back out the Torx screws until the airbag module is free, but don't try to remove them from the screw case

14.3a Lift the airbag module off the steering wheel . . .

bolts to hold the brake backing plate in place.

7   On 1996 or 1997 2WD models or 2000 and earlier 4WD models the rear axle hub can be removed from the bearing to allow replacement of the bearing. Due to the special tools required to do this, you'll have to take the hub and bearing assembly to an automotive machine shop and have the old bearing pulled off the hub and a new bearing pressed on (you can re-use the hub itself, as long as it's in good condition). On all other models, the entire assembly must be replaced as a unit. **Note:** *If you're working on a 2001 or later 2WD model with ABS, remove the wheel speed sensor from the old hub and install it on the new one* (see Chapter 9).

Installation

8   Position the hub and bearing assembly on the trailing arm. Install the bolts or nuts. After all four bolts or nuts have been installed, tighten them to the torque listed in this Chapter's Specifications.

9   If you're working on a 1996 or 1997 2WD model or a 2000 or earlier 4WD model, install the brake shoes and connect the

brake line to the wheel cylinder (see Chapter 9).

10   If you're working on a 4WD model, install the driveaxle (see Chapter 8).

11   Install the brake drum and the wheel.

12   If you're working on a 1996 or 1997 2WD model or a 2000 or earlier 4WD model, bleed the brakes (see Chapter 9).

13   Lower the vehicle and tighten the lug nuts to the torque listed in the Chapter 1 Specifications. If you're working on a 4WD model, tighten the driveaxle/hub nut to the torque listed in the Chapter 8 Specifications, then install a new cotter pin.

14 Steering wheel - removal and installation

Warning 1: *These models are equipped with a Supplemental Restraint System (SRS), more commonly known as airbags. Always disable the airbag system before working in the vicinity of any airbag system component to avoid the possibility of accidental deployment of the airbag(s), which could cause per-*

sonal injury (see Chapter 12).

Warning 2: *Do not use a memory saving device to preserve the PCM or radio memory when working on or near airbag system components.*

Removal

Refer to illustrations 14.2, 14.3a, 14.3b, 14.4, 14.5, 14.6 and 14.7

1   Turn the ignition key to Off, then disconnect the cable from the negative terminal of the battery. Wait at least two minutes before proceeding.

2   Turn the steering wheel so the wheels are pointing straight ahead. If you're working on a 1996 or 1997 model, pry off the covers on either side of the steering wheel. On all models, loosen the Torx screws that attach the airbag module to the steering wheel **(see illustration)**. Loosen each screw until the groove in the circumference of the screw catches on the screw case.

3   Pull the airbag module off the steering wheel **(see illustration)**, disengage the connector lock and disconnect the module electrical connector **(see illustration)**. Set

14.3b . . . then disengage the connector lock and unplug the electrical connector (1998 and later model shown; slide the connector lock in the direction of the arrow. On earlier models the connector lock must be flipped up)

14.4 Unplug the electrical connectors for the horn and cruise control switches

14.5 After removing the steering wheel nut, mark the relationship of the steering wheel to the shaft before removing the wheel

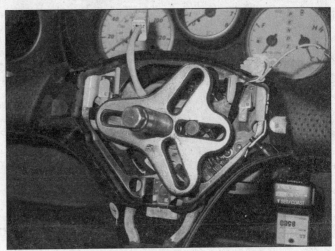

14.6 If the steering wheel is difficult to remove from the shaft, use a steering wheel puller to remove it

the airbag module in a safe, isolated area. **Warning:** *Carry the airbag module with the trim side facing away from you, and set the airbag module down with the trim side facing up. Don't place anything on top of the airbag module.*

4   Unplug the electrical connector for the horn and, if equipped, the cruise control switch **(see illustration)**.

5   Remove the steering wheel retaining nut, then mark the relationship of the steering shaft to the hub (if marks don't already exist or don't line up) to simplify installation and ensure steering wheel alignment **(see illustration)**.

6   Use a puller to disconnect the steering wheel from the shaft **(see illustration)**. **Warning:** *Do not hammer on the shaft or the puller in an attempt to loosen the wheel from the shaft. Also, don't allow the steering shaft to turn with the steering wheel removed. If the shaft turns, the airbag spiral cable will become uncentered, which may cause the wire inside to break when the vehicle is returned to service.*

7   If it is necessary to remove the airbag spiral cable, unplug the electrical connector,

then remove the four screws (2000 and earlier models) or disengage the three claws (2001 and later models) and detach it from the combination switch **(see illustration)**.

Installation

Refer to illustration 14.8

8   Make sure that the front wheels are facing straight ahead, then center the spiral cable. Turn the hub of the spiral cable counterclockwise by hand until it stops (but don't force it, as the cable could break). Rotate the hub clockwise about 2-1/2 turns and align the two pointers **(see illustrations)**.

9   To install the wheel, align the mark on the steering wheel hub with the mark on the shaft and slip the wheel onto the shaft. Install the nut and tighten it to the torque listed in this Chapter's Specifications.

10   Plug in the cruise control and horn connectors.

11   Plug in the electrical connector for the airbag module and close the locking device.

12   Make sure the airbag module electrical connector is positioned correctly and that the wires don't interfere with anything, then install the airbag module and tighten the retaining

screws to the torque listed in this Chapter's Specifications.

13   Connect the negative battery cable.

15   Steering column - removal and installation

Refer to illustrations 15.6, 15.7a and 15.7b

Removal

1   Park the vehicle with the wheels pointing straight ahead. Disconnect the cable from the negative terminal of the battery.

2   Remove the steering wheel (see Section 14), then turn the ignition key to the LOCK position to prevent the steering shaft from turning. **Caution:** *If this is not done, the airbag clockspring could be damaged.*

3   Remove the lower finish panel under the column and the knee bolster behind it (see Chapter 11).

4   Remove the steering column covers (see Chapter 11).

5   Disconnect the electrical connectors for the steering column harness.

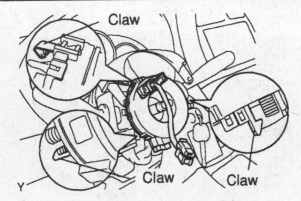

14.7 On 2001 and later models, the airbag spiral cable is retained by three claws

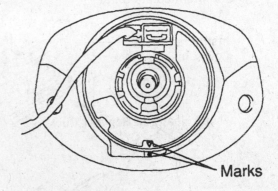

14.8 After properly centering the spiral cable as described in the text, make sure the pointers are aligned - location of pointers may vary

6   Mark the relationship of the U-joint to the steering shaft, then remove the pinch bolt **(see illustration)**.
7   Remove the steering column mounting fasteners **(see illustrations)**, lower the column and pull it to the rear, making sure nothing is still connected. Separate the intermediate shaft from the steering shaft and remove the column.

Installation

8   Guide the steering column into position, connect the intermediate shaft, then install the mounting fasteners, but don't tighten them yet.
9   Tighten the column mounting fasteners to the torque listed in this Chapter's Specifications.

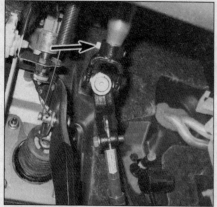

15.6 Mark the U-joint to the steering shaft, then remove the pinch bolt

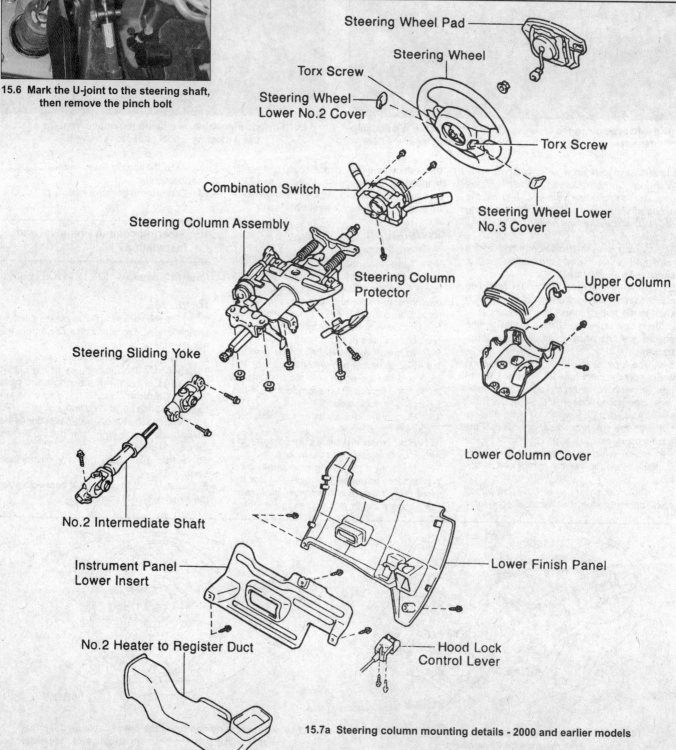

15.7a Steering column mounting details - 2000 and earlier models

15.7b Steering column mounting bolts (bolt indicated by lower right arrow not visible) - 2001 and later models

10   Install the pinch bolt, tightening it to the torque listed in this Chapter's Specifications.
11   The remainder of installation is the reverse of removal.

16   Tie-rod ends - removal and installation

Removal

Refer to illustrations 16.2, 16.3a, 16.3b and 16.4

1   Loosen the wheel lug nuts. Apply the parking brake, raise the front of the vehicle and support it securely on jackstands. Remove the front wheel.
2   Remove the cotter pin (see illustration) and loosen the nut on the tie-rod end stud.
3   Hold the tie-rod with a pair of locking pliers or wrench and loosen the jam nut enough to mark the position of the tie-rod end in relation to the threads (see illustrations).
4   Disconnect the tie-rod from the steering knuckle arm with a puller (see illustration). Remove the nut and detach the tie-rod.
5   Unscrew the tie-rod end from the tie-rod.

Installation

6   Thread the tie-rod end on to the marked position and insert the tie-rod stud into the steering knuckle arm. Tighten the jam nut securely.
7   Install the castle nut on the stud and tighten it to the torque listed in this Chapter's Specifications. Install a new cotter pin. If the hole for the cotter pin doesn't line up with one of the slots in the nut, tighten the nut an additional amount until it does.
8   Install the wheel and lug nuts. Lower the vehicle and tighten the lug nuts to the torque listed in the Chapter 1 Specifications.
9   Have the alignment checked and, if necessary, adjusted.

17   Steering gear boots - replacement

Refer to illustrations 17.3a and 17.3b
1   Loosen the lug nuts, raise the vehicle and support it securely on jackstands. Remove the wheel.

16.2 Remove the cotter pin from the castle nut and loosen - but don't remove - the nut

16.3a Loosen the jam nut . . .

16.3b . . . then mark the position of the tie-rod end in relation to the threads

16.4 Disconnect the tie-rod end from the steering knuckle arm with a puller

17.3a The outer ends of the steering gear boots are secured by band-type clamps; they're easily released with a pair of pliers

17.3b The inner ends of the steering gear boots are retained by boot clamps which must be cut off and discarded

18.4 Disconnect the power steering line fittings (arrows)

18.5a Remove the universal joint cover . . .

2   Remove the tie-rod end and jam nut (see Section 16).

3   Remove the outer steering gear boot clamp with a pair of pliers **(see illustration)**. Cut off the inner boot clamp with a pair of diagonal cutters **(see illustration)**. Slide off the boot.

4   Before installing the new boot, wrap the threads and serrations on the end of the steering rod with a layer of tape so the small end of the new boot isn't damaged.

5   Slide the new boot into position on the steering gear until it seats in the groove in the steering rod and install new clamps.

6   Remove the tape and install the tie-rod end (see Section 16).

7   Install the wheel and lug nuts. Lower the vehicle and tighten the lug nuts to the torque listed in the Chapter 1 Specifications.

18 Steering gear - removal and installation

Warning: *These models are equipped with airbags. Always disable the airbag system before working in the vicinity of any airbag system component to avoid the possibility of*
accidental deployment of the airbag(s), which could cause personal injury (see Chapter 12).

Removal

Refer to illustrations 18.4, 18.5a, 18.5b, 18.9 and 18.10

1   Disconnect the cable from the negative terminal of the battery.

2   Remove the steering wheel (see Section 14). **Note:** *This will prevent the spiral cable from being damaged in the event the steering gear is not centered when it is installed.*

3   Loosen the front wheel lug nuts, raise the front of the vehicle and support it securely on jackstands. Apply the parking brake and remove the wheels. Remove the engine under covers.

4   Place a drain pan under the steering gear. Detach the power steering pressure and return lines **(see illustration)** and cap the ends to prevent excessive fluid loss and contamination.

5   Remove the universal joint cover. Mark the relationship of the lower universal joint to the steering gear input shaft and remove the lower intermediate shaft pinch bolt **(see illustrations)**.

6   Separate the tie-rod ends from the steering knuckle arms (see Section 16).

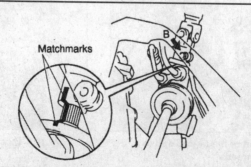

Matchmarks

18.5b . . . then mark the relationship of the universal joint to the steering gear input shaft and remove the U-joint pinch bolt (B)

2000 and earlier models

7   Disconnect the balljoints from the control arms (see illustrations 5.2a and 5.2b).

8   Remove the front section of the exhaust system (see Chapter 4).

9   Support the suspension crossmember with a floor jack. Unbolt the suspension crossmember (see illustration) and lower it along with the control arms (separate the intermediate shaft from the steering gear input shaft as it is being lowered) steering gear and stabilizer bar. The steering gear can now be unbolted from the crossmember

2001 and later models

10   Remove the steering gear mounting bolts (see illustration). Separate the intermediate shaft from the steering gear input shaft, then remove the steering gear.

Installation

11   Installation is the reverse of removal, noting the following points:

a) *When connecting the steering gear input shaft to the intermediate shaft U-joint, be sure to align the matchmarks.*

b) *Tighten all fasteners to the torque values listed in this Chapter's Specifications.*

c) *Tighten the lug nuts to the torque listed in the Chapter 1 Specifications.*

d) *Set the front wheels in the straight-ahead position, then center the spiral cable and install the steering wheel and airbag module (see Section 14).*

e) *Fill the power steering fluid reservoir with the recommended fluid (see Chapter 1). Bleed the steering system (see Section 20).*

---

19   Power steering pump - removal and installation

---

1   Disconnect the cable from the negative battery terminal.

2   Using a large syringe or suction gun, suck as much fluid out of the power steering fluid reservoir as possible. Place a drain pan under the vehicle to catch any fluid that spills out when the hoses are disconnected.

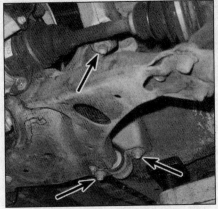

18.9 Suspension crossmember mounting bolts - left side (2000 and earlier models)

18.10 Steering gear mounting bolt - 2001 and later models (left side shown, right side similar)

19.6 Loosen these bolts, push the pump towards the engine, then remove the drivebelt (2000 and earlier models)

2000 and earlier models

Removal

Refer to illustrations 19.6, 19.8 and 19.10

3   Raise the front of the vehicle and support it securely on jackstands. Remove the right-side engine under-cover.

4   Remove the front portion of the exhaust pipe (see Chapter 4).

5   Disconnect the balljoints from the control arms (see Section 5), unbolt the steering gear from the crossmember (see Section 18), then unbolt and remove the suspension crossmember (see illustration 18.9).

6   Loosen the pivot bolt and clamp bolt, then remove the drivebelt (see illustration).

7   Loosen the clamp and disconnect the fluid return hose from the pump.

8   Using a flare-nut wrench, unscrew the pressure line fitting from the pump (see illustration).

9   Detach the two vacuum lines from the pump.

10   Unbolt the pump bracket from the engine block (see illustration) and lower the assembly from the engine compartment.

11   The pump can now be separated from the bracket. If necessary, the pulley can be removed by unscrewing the nut; prevent the pulley from turning by holding the pulley with a pin spanner or by inserting a long punch through one of the holes in the pulley.

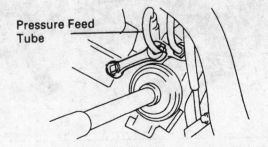

Pressure Feed Tube

19.8 Unscrew the pressure line fitting from the pump (2000 and earlier models)

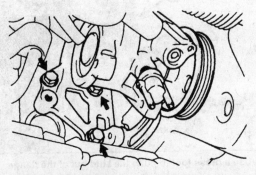

19.10 Power steering pump bracket-to-engine bolts (2000 and earlier models)

19.17 Unscrew the lower mounting bolt (B), loosen the upper mounting bolt (A) and slide the pump out of its mounting bracket (2001 and later models)

Installation

12   Installation is the reverse of removal, noting the following points:

a) *Tighten all fasteners to the torque listed in this Chapter's Specifications.*

b) *Adjust the drivebelt tension following the procedure described in Chapter 1.*

c) *Top up the fluid level in the reservoir (see Chapter 1) and bleed the system (see Section 20).*

2001 and later models

Refer to illustration 19.17

13   Remove the drivebelt (see Chapter 1). Loosen the right front wheel lug nuts, raise the front of the vehicle and support it securely on jackstands. Remove the wheel and the right-side engine under cover

14   Unplug the electrical connector from the power steering fluid pressure switch.

15   Unscrew the pressure line-to-pump union bolt and detach the line from the pump. Discard the sealing washers from either side of the line fitting (they are attached to each other); new ones should be used during installation.

16   Loosen the hose clamp and detach the return hose from the pump.

17   Unscrew the lower mounting bolt, loosen the upper mounting bolt and detach the pump from the engine **(see illustration)**. **Note:** *The upper bolt can't be removed; loosening it will allow the pump to slide from its mounting bracket.*

Installation

18   Installation is the reverse of removal. Be sure to tighten the mounting bolts and the pressure line union bolt to the torque listed in this Chapter's Specifications.

19   Install the engine under cover, wheel and lug nuts. Lower the vehicle and tighten the lug nuts to the torque listed in the Chapter 1 Specifications.

20   Install the drivebelt (see Chapter 1).

21   Top up the fluid level in the reservoir (see Chapter 1) and bleed the system (see Section 20).

20   Power steering system - bleeding

1   Following any operation in which the power steering fluid lines have been disconnected, the power steering system must be bled to remove all air and obtain proper steering performance.

2   With the front wheels in the straight ahead position, check the power steering fluid level and, if low, add fluid until it reaches the Cold mark on the dipstick.

3   Start the engine and allow it to run at fast idle. Recheck the fluid level and add more if necessary to reach the Cold mark on the dipstick.

4   Bleed the system by turning the wheels from side to side, without hitting the stops. This will work the air out of the system. Keep the reservoir full of fluid as this is done.

5   When the air is worked out of the system, return the wheels to the straight ahead position and leave the vehicle running for several more minutes before shutting it off.

6   Road test the vehicle to be sure the steering system is functioning normally and noise free.

7   Recheck the fluid level to be sure it is up to the Hot mark on the dipstick while the engine is at normal operating temperature. Add fluid if necessary (see Chapter 1).

21   Wheel studs - replacement

Refer to illustrations 21.3 and 21.4

Note: *This procedure applies to both the front and rear wheel studs.*

1   Loosen the wheel lug nuts, raise the vehicle and support it securely on jackstands. Remove the wheel.

2   Remove the brake disc or drum (see Chapter 9).

3   Install a lug nut part way onto the stud being replaced. Push the stud out of the hub flange with a press tool **(see illustration)**.

4   Insert the new stud into the hub flange from the back side and install some flat washers and a lug nut on the stud **(see illustration)**.

5   Tighten the lug nut until the stud is seated in the flange.

6   Reinstall the brake drum or disc. Install the wheel and lug nuts. Lower the vehicle and tighten the lug nuts to the torque listed in the Chapter 1 Specifications.

21.3 Use a press tool to push the stud out of the flange

1	Hub flange	3 Press tool
2	Lug nut on stud	

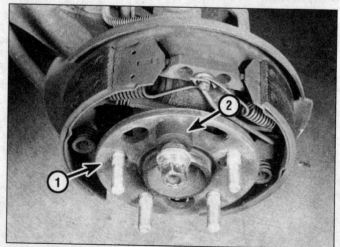

21.4 Install a spacer and a lug nut on the stud, then tighten the nut to draw the stud into place

1 Hub flange	2 Spacer

METRIC TIRE SIZES
P 185 / 80 R 13

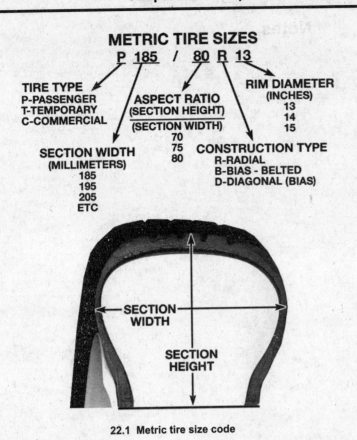

TIRE TYPE
P-PASSENGER
T-TEMPORARY
C-COMMERCIAL

ASPECT RATIO
(SECTION HEIGHT)
——————————
(SECTION WIDTH)
70
75
80

RIM DIAMETER
(INCHES)
13
14
15

SECTION WIDTH
(MILLIMETERS)
185
195
205
ETC

CONSTRUCTION TYPE
R-RADIAL
B-BIAS - BELTED
D-DIAGONAL (BIAS)

SECTION WIDTH

SECTION HEIGHT

22.1 Metric tire size code

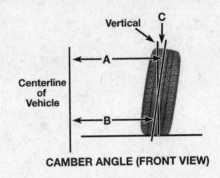

CAMBER ANGLE (FRONT VIEW)

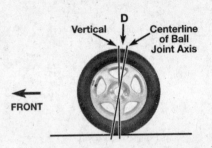

CASTER ANGLE (SIDE VIEW)

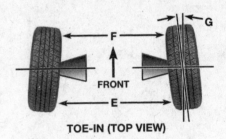

TOE-IN (TOP VIEW)

23.1 Camber, caster and toe-in angles

22 Wheels and tires - general information

Refer to illustration 22.1

1   All vehicles covered by this manual are equipped with metric-sized fiberglass or steel belted radial tires **(see illustration)**. Use of other size or type of tires may affect the ride and handling of the vehicle. Don't mix different types of tires, such as radials and bias belted, on the same vehicle as handling may be seriously affected. It's recommended that tires be replaced in pairs on the same axle, but if only one tire is being replaced, be sure it's the same size, structure and tread design as the other.

2   Because tire pressure has a substantial effect on handling and wear, the pressure on all tires should be checked at least once a month or before any extended trips (see Chapter 1).

3   Wheels must be replaced if they are bent, dented, leak air, have elongated bolt holes, are heavily rusted, out of vertical symmetry or if the lug nuts won't stay tight. Wheel repairs that use welding or peening are not recommended.

4   Tire and wheel balance is important in the overall handling, braking and performance of the vehicle. Unbalanced wheels can adversely affect handling and ride characteristics as well as tire life. Whenever a tire is installed on a wheel, the tire and wheel should be balanced by a shop with the proper equipment.

23 Wheel alignment - general information

Refer to illustration 23.1

A wheel alignment refers to the adjustments made to the wheels so they are in proper angular relationship to the suspension and the ground. Wheels that are out of proper alignment not only affect vehicle control, but also increase tire wear. The front end angles normally measured are camber, caster and toe-in **(see illustration)**. Toe-in and camber are adjustable; if the caster is not correct, check for bent components. Rear camber and toe-in are also adjustable.

Getting the proper wheel alignment is a very exacting process, one in which complicated and expensive machines are necessary to perform the job properly. Because of this, you should have a technician with the proper equipment perform these tasks. We will, however, use this space to give you a basic idea of what is involved with a wheel alignment so you can better understand the process and deal intelligently with the shop that does the work.

Toe-in is the turning in of the wheels. The purpose of a toe specification is to ensure parallel rolling of the wheels. In a vehicle with zero toe-in, the distance between the front edges of the wheels will be the same as the distance between the rear edges of the wheels. The actual amount of toe-in is normally only a fraction of an inch. On the front end, toe-in is controlled by the tie-rod end position on the tie-rod. On the rear end, it's controlled by a cam at the front of the suspension trailing arm. Incorrect toe-in will cause the tires to wear improperly by making them scrub against the road surface.

Camber is the tilting of the wheels from vertical when viewed from one end of the vehicle. When the wheels tilt out at the top, the camber is said to be positive (+). When the wheels tilt in at the top the camber is negative (-). The amount of tilt is measured in degrees from vertical and this measurement is called the camber angle. This angle affects the amount of tire tread which contacts the road and compensates for changes in the suspension geometry when the vehicle is cornering or traveling over an undulating surface. On the front end it is adjusted using special camber adjusting bolts, which alter the relationship between the strut and the steering knuckle. At the rear end camber is adjusted by a cam at the inner end of the lower suspension arm.

Caster is the tilting of the front steering axis from the vertical. A tilt toward the rear is positive caster and a tilt toward the front is negative caster.

Notes

Chapter 11   Body

Contents

	Section
Back door - removal, installation and adjustment	21
Back door latch, lock cylinder and handle - removal and installation	22
Body - maintenance	2
Body repair - major damage	6
Body repair - minor damage	5
Bumpers - removal and installation	11
Center console - removal and installation	23
Cowl cover and vent tray - removal and installation	14
Dashboard trim panels	24
Door - removal, installation and adjustment	16
Door latch, lock cylinder and handles - removal and installation	17
Door trim panels - removal and installation	15
Door window glass - removal and installation	18

	Section
Door window glass regulator - removal and installation	19
Front fender - removal and installation	12
General information	1
Hinges and locks - maintenance	7
Hood - removal, installation and adjustment	9
Hood latch and release cable - removal and installation	10
Instrument panel - removal and installation	26
Mirrors - removal and installation	20
Radiator grille - removal and installation	13
Seats - removal and installation	27
Steering column covers - removal and installation	25
Sunroof - adjustment	28
Upholstery and carpets - maintenance	4
Vinyl trim - maintenance	3
Windshield and fixed glass - replacement	8

1   General information

Warning: *The front seat belts on some models are equipped with pre-tensioners, which are pyrotechnic (explosive) devices designed to retract the seat belts in the event of a collision. On models equipped with pre-tensioners, do not remove the front seat belt retractor assemblies, and do not disconnect the electrical connectors leading to the assemblies. Problems with the pre-tensioners will turn on the SRS (airbag) warning light on the dash. If any pre-tensioner problems are suspected, take the vehicle to a dealer service department.*

These models feature a "unibody" layout, using a floor pan with integral side frame rails which support the body components, front and rear suspension systems and other mechanical components.

Certain components are particularly vulnerable to accident damage and can be unbolted and repaired or replaced. Among these parts are the body moldings, bumpers, front fenders, the hood and trunk lid, doors and all glass.

Only general body maintenance practices and body panel repair procedures within the scope of the do-it-yourselfer are included in this Chapter.

2   Body - maintenance

1   The condition of your vehicle's body is very important, because the resale value depends a great deal on it. It's much more difficult to repair a neglected or damaged body than it is to repair mechanical components. The hidden areas of the body, such as the wheel wells, the frame and the engine compartment, are equally important, although they don't require as frequent attention as the rest of the body.
2   Once a year, or every 12,000 miles, it's a good idea to have the underside of the body steam-cleaned. All traces of dirt and oil will be removed and the area can then be inspected carefully for rust, damaged brake lines, frayed electrical wires, damaged cables and other problems.
3   At the same time, clean the engine and the engine compartment with a steam cleaner or water-soluble degreaser.
4   The wheel wells should be given close attention, since undercoating can peel away and stones and dirt thrown up by the tires can cause the paint to chip and flake, allowing rust to set in. If rust is found, clean down to the bare metal and apply an anti-rust paint.
5   The body should be washed about once a week. Wet the vehicle thoroughly to soften the dirt, then wash it down with a soft sponge and plenty of clean soapy water. If the surplus dirt is not washed off very carefully, it can wear down the paint.
6   Spots of tar or asphalt thrown up from the road should be removed with a cloth soaked in kerosene. Scented lamp oil is available in most hardware stores and the smell is easier to work with than straight kerosene.
7   Once every six months, wax the body and chrome trim. If a chrome cleaner is used to remove rust from any of the vehicle's plated parts, remember that the cleaner also removes part of the chrome, so use it sparingly. On any plated parts where chrome cleaner is used, use a good paste wax over the plating for extra protection.

3 Vinyl trim - maintenance

Don't clean vinyl trim with detergents, caustic soap or petroleum-based cleaners. Plain soap and water works just fine, with a soft brush to clean dirt that may be ingrained. Wash the vinyl as frequently as the rest of the vehicle.

After cleaning, application of a high quality rubber and vinyl protectant will help prevent oxidation and cracks. The protectant can also be applied to weather stripping, vacuum lines and rubber hoses, which often fail as a result of chemical degradation, and to the tires.

4 Upholstery and carpets - maintenance

1   Every three months remove the floormats and clean the interior of the vehicle (more frequently if necessary). Use a stiff whisk broom to brush the carpeting and loosen dirt and dust, then vacuum the upholstery and carpets thoroughly, especially along seams and crevices.

2   Dirt and stains can be removed from carpeting with basic household or automotive carpet shampoos available in spray cans. Follow the directions and vacuum again, then use a stiff brush to bring back the "nap" of the carpet.

3   Most interiors have cloth or vinyl upholstery, either of which can be cleaned and maintained with a number of material-specific cleaners or shampoos available in auto supply stores. Follow the directions on the product for usage, and always spot-test any upholstery cleaner on an inconspicuous area (bottom edge of a backseat cushion) to ensure that it doesn't cause a color shift in the material.

4   After cleaning, vinyl upholstery should be treated with a protectant. **Note:** *Make sure the protectant container indicates the product can be used on seats - some products may make a seat too slippery.* **Caution:** *Do not use protectant on steering wheels.*

5   Leather upholstery requires special care. It should be cleaned regularly with saddle-soap or leather cleaner. Never use alcohol, gasoline, nail polish remover or thinner to clean leather upholstery.

6   After cleaning, regularly treat leather upholstery with a leather conditioner, rubbed in with a soft cotton cloth. Never use car wax on leather upholstery.

7   In areas where the interior of the vehicle is subject to bright sunlight, cover leather seating areas of the seats with a sheet if the vehicle is to be left out for any length of time.

5 Body repair - minor damage

Flexible plastic body panels (front and rear bumper fascia)

The following repair procedures are for minor scratches and gouges. Repair of more serious damage should be left to a dealer service department or qualified auto body shop. Below is a list of the equipment and materials necessary to perform the following repair procedures on plastic body panels. Although a specific brand of material may be mentioned, it should be noted that equivalent products from other manufacturers may be used instead.

>   *Wax, grease and silicone removing solvent*
>   *Cloth-backed body tape*
>   *Sanding discs*
>   *Drill motor with three-inch disc holder*
>   *Hand sanding block*
>   *Rubber squeegees*
>   *Sandpaper*
>   *Non-porous mixing palette*
>   *Wood paddle or putty knife*
>   *Curved-tooth body file*
>   *Flexible parts repair material*

1   Remove the damaged panel, if necessary or desirable. In most cases, repairs can be carried out with the panel installed.

2   Clean the area(s) to be repaired with a wax, grease and silicone removing solvent applied with a water-dampened cloth.

3   If the damage is structural, that is, if it extends through the panel, clean the backside of the panel area to be repaired as well. Wipe dry.

4   Sand the rear surface about 1-1/2 inches beyond the break.

5   Cut two pieces of fiberglass cloth large enough to overlap the break by about 1-1/2 inches. Cut only to the required length.

6   Mix the adhesive from the repair kit according to the instructions included with the kit, and apply a layer of the mixture approximately 1/8-inch thick on the backside of the panel. Overlap the break by at least 1-1/2 inches.

7   Apply one piece of fiberglass cloth to the adhesive and cover the cloth with additional adhesive. Apply a second piece of fiberglass cloth to the adhesive and immediately cover the cloth with additional adhesive in sufficient quantity to fill the weave.

8   Allow the repair to cure for 20 to 30 minutes at 60-degrees to 80-degrees F.

9   If necessary, trim the excess repair material at the edge.

10   Remove all of the paint film over and around the area(s) to be repaired. The repair material should not overlap the painted surface.

11   With a drill motor and a sanding disc (or a rotary file), cut a "V" along the break line approximately 1/2-inch wide. Remove all dust and loose particles from the repair area.

12   Mix and apply the repair material. Apply a light coat first over the damaged area; then continue applying material until it reaches a level slightly higher than the surrounding finish.

13   Cure the mixture for 20 to 30 minutes at 60-degrees to 80-degrees F.

14   Roughly establish the contour of the area being repaired with a body file. If low areas or pits remain, mix and apply additional adhesive.

15   Block sand the damaged area with sandpaper to establish the actual contour of the surrounding surface.

16   If desired, the repaired area can be temporarily protected with several light coats of primer. Because of the special paints and techniques required for flexible body panels, it is recommended that the vehicle be taken to a paint shop for completion of the body repair.

Steel body panels
See photo sequence

Repair of minor scratches

17   If the scratch is superficial and does not penetrate to the metal of the body, repair is very simple. Lightly rub the scratched area with a fine rubbing compound to remove loose paint and built up wax. Rinse the area with clean water.

18   Apply touch-up paint to the scratch, using a small brush. Continue to apply thin layers of paint until the surface of the paint in the scratch is level with the surrounding paint. Allow the new paint at least two weeks to harden, then blend it into the surrounding paint by rubbing with a very fine rubbing compound. Finally, apply a coat of wax to the scratch area.

19   If the scratch has penetrated the paint and exposed the metal of the body, causing the metal to rust, a different repair technique is required. Remove all loose rust from the bottom of the scratch with a pocket knife, then apply rust inhibiting paint to prevent the formation of rust in the future. Using a rubber or nylon applicator, coat the scratched area with glaze-type filler. If required, the filler can be mixed with thinner to provide a very thin paste, which is ideal for filling narrow scratches. Before the glaze filler in the scratch hardens, wrap a piece of smooth cotton cloth around the tip of a finger. Dip the cloth in thinner and then quickly wipe it along the surface of the scratch. This will ensure that the surface of the filler is slightly hollow. The scratch can now be painted over as described earlier in this Section.

Repair of dents

20   When repairing dents, the first job is to pull the dent out until the affected area is as close as possible to its original shape. There is no point in trying to restore the original shape completely as the metal in the damaged area will have stretched on impact and cannot be restored to its original contours. It is better to bring the level of the dent up to a point which is about 1/8-inch below the level of the surrounding metal. In cases where the dent is very shallow, it is not worth trying to pull it out at all.

21   If the back side of the dent is accessible, it can be hammered out gently from behind using a soft-face hammer. While doing this, hold a block of wood firmly against the

opposite side of the metal to absorb the hammer blows and prevent the metal from being stretched.

22   If the dent is in a section of the body which has double layers, or some other factor makes it inaccessible from behind, a different technique is required. Drill several small holes through the metal inside the damaged area, particularly in the deeper sections. Screw long, self tapping screws into the holes just enough for them to get a good grip in the metal. Now the dent can be pulled out by pulling on the protruding heads of the screws with locking pliers.

23   The next stage of repair is the removal of paint from the damaged area and from an inch or so of the surrounding metal. This is easily done with a wire brush or sanding disk in a drill motor, although it can be done just as effectively by hand with sandpaper. To complete the preparation for filling, score the surface of the bare metal with a screwdriver or the tang of a file or drill small holes in the affected area. This will provide a good grip for the filler material. To complete the repair, see the Section on filling and painting.

Repair of rust holes or gashes

24   Remove all paint from the affected area and from an inch or so of the surrounding metal using a sanding disk or wire brush mounted in a drill motor. If these are not available, a few sheets of sandpaper will do the job just as effectively.

25   With the paint removed, you will be able to determine the severity of the corrosion and decide whether to replace the whole panel, if possible, or repair the affected area. New body panels are not as expensive as most people think and it is often quicker to install a new panel than to repair large areas of rust.

26   Remove all trim pieces from the affected area except those which will act as a guide to the original shape of the damaged body, such as headlight shells, etc. Using metal snips or a hacksaw blade, remove all loose metal and any other metal that is badly affected by rust. Hammer the edges of the hole in to create a slight depression for the filler material.

27   Wire brush the affected area to remove the powdery rust from the surface of the metal. If the back of the rusted area is accessible, treat it with rust inhibiting paint.

28   Before filling is done, block the hole in some way. This can be done with sheet metal riveted or screwed into place, or by stuffing the hole with wire mesh.

29   Once the hole is blocked off, the affected area can be filled and painted. See the following subsection on filling and painting.

Filling and painting

30   Many types of body fillers are available, but generally speaking, body repair kits which contain filler paste and a tube of resin hardener are best for this type of repair work. A wide, flexible plastic or nylon applicator will be necessary for imparting a smooth and contoured finish to the surface of the filler mate-

rial. Mix up a small amount of filler on a clean piece of wood or cardboard (use the hardener sparingly). Follow the manufacturer's instructions on the package, otherwise the filler will set incorrectly.

31   Using the applicator, apply the filler paste to the prepared area. Draw the applicator across the surface of the filler to achieve the desired contour and to level the filler surface. As soon as a contour that approximates the original one is achieved, stop working the paste. If you continue, the paste will begin to stick to the applicator. Continue to add thin layers of paste at 20-minute intervals until the level of the filler is just above the surrounding metal.

32   Once the filler has hardened, the excess can be removed with a body file. From then on, progressively finer grades of sandpaper should be used, starting with a 180-grit paper and finishing with 600-grit wet-or-dry paper. Always wrap the sandpaper around a flat rubber or wooden block, otherwise the surface of the filler will not be completely flat. During the sanding of the filler surface, the wet-or-dry paper should be periodically rinsed in water. This will ensure that a very smooth finish is produced in the final stage.

33   At this point, the repair area should be surrounded by a ring of bare metal, which in turn should be encircled by the finely feathered edge of good paint. Rinse the repair area with clean water until all of the dust produced by the sanding operation is gone.

34   Spray the entire area with a light coat of primer. This will reveal any imperfections in the surface of the filler. Repair the imperfections with fresh filler paste or glaze filler and once more smooth the surface with sandpaper. Repeat this spray-and-repair procedure until you are satisfied that the surface of the filler and the feathered edge of the paint are perfect. Rinse the area with clean water and allow it to dry completely.

35   The repair area is now ready for painting. Spray painting must be carried out in a warm, dry, windless and dust free atmosphere. These conditions can be created if you have access to a large indoor work area, but if you are forced to work in the open, you will have to pick the day very carefully. If you are working indoors, dousing the floor in the work area with water will help settle the dust which would otherwise be in the air. If the repair area is confined to one body panel, mask off the surrounding panels. This will help minimize the effects of a slight mismatch in paint color. Trim pieces such as chrome strips, door handles, etc., will also need to be masked off or removed. Use masking tape and several thickness of newspaper for the masking operations.

36   Before spraying, shake the paint can thoroughly, then spray a test area until the spray painting technique is mastered. Cover the repair area with a thick coat of primer. The thickness should be built up using several thin layers of primer rather than one thick one. Using 600-grit wet-or-dry sandpaper,

rub down the surface of the primer until it is very smooth. While doing this, the work area should be thoroughly rinsed with water and the wet-or-dry sandpaper periodically rinsed as well. Allow the primer to dry before spraying additional coats.

37   Spray on the top coat, again building up the thickness by using several thin layers of paint. Begin spraying in the center of the repair area and then, using a circular motion, work out until the whole repair area and about two inches of the surrounding original paint is covered. Remove all masking material 10 to 15 minutes after spraying on the final coat of paint. Allow the new paint at least two weeks to harden, then use a very fine rubbing compound to blend the edges of the new paint into the existing paint. Finally, apply a coat of wax.

6   Body repair - major damage

1   Major damage must be repaired by an auto body shop specifically equipped to perform unibody repairs. These shops have the specialized equipment required to do the job properly.

2   If the damage is extensive, the body must be checked for proper alignment or the vehicle's handling characteristics may be adversely affected and other components may wear at an accelerated rate.

3   Due to the fact that some of the major body components (hood, fenders, doors, etc.) are separate and replaceable units, any seriously damaged components should be replaced rather than repaired. Sometimes the components can be found in a wrecking yard that specializes in used vehicle components, often at considerable savings over the cost of new parts.

7   Hinges and locks - maintenance

Once every 3000 miles, or every three months, the hinges and latch assemblies on the doors, hood and trunk (or liftgate) should be given a few drops of light oil or lock lubricant. The door latch strikers should also be lubricated with a thin coat of grease to reduce wear and ensure free movement. Lubricate the door and trunk (or liftgate) locks with spray-on graphite lubricant.

8   Windshield and fixed glass - replacement

Replacement of the windshield and fixed glass requires the use of special fast-setting adhesive/caulk materials and some specialized tools and techniques. These operations should be left to a dealer service department or a shop specializing in glass work.

These photos illustrate a method of repairing simple dents. They are intended to supplement *Body repair - minor damage* in this Chapter and should not be used as the sole instructions for body repair on these vehicles.

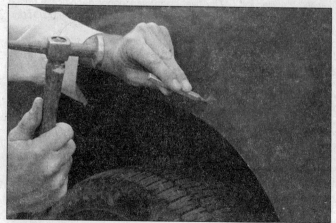

1 If you can't access the backside of the body panel to hammer out the dent, pull it out with a slide-hammer-type dent puller. In the deepest portion of the dent or along the crease line, drill or punch hole(s) at least one inch apart . . .

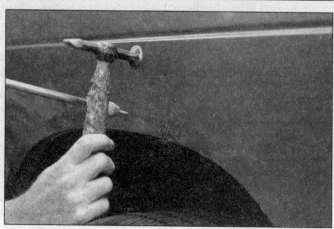

2 . . . then screw the slide-hammer into the hole and operate it. Tap with a hammer near the edge of the dent to help 'pop' the metal back to its original shape. When you're finished, the dent area should be close to its original contour and about 1/8-inch below the surface of the surrounding metal

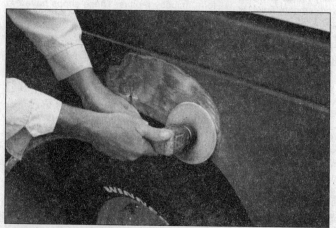

3 Using coarse-grit sandpaper, remove the paint down to the bare metal. Hand sanding works fine, but the disc sander shown here makes the job faster. Use finer (about 320-grit) sandpaper to feather-edge the paint at least one inch around the dent area

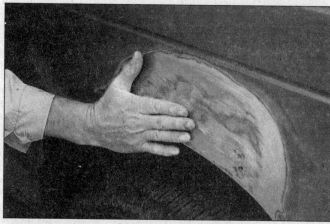

4 When the paint is removed, touch will probably be more helpful than sight for telling if the metal is straight. Hammer down the high spots or raise the low spots as necessary. Clean the repair area with wax/silicone remover

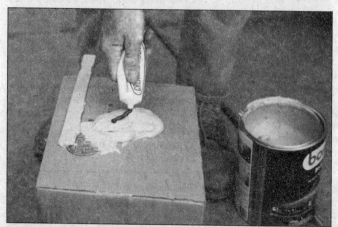

5 Following label instructions, mix up a batch of plastic filler and hardener. The ratio of filler to hardener is critical, and, if you mix it incorrectly, it will either not cure properly or cure too quickly (you won't have time to file and sand it into shape)

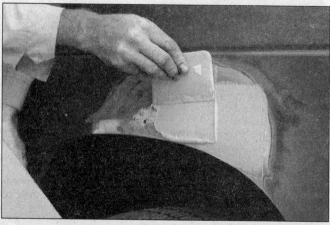

6 Working quickly so the filler doesn't harden, use a plastic applicator to press the body filler firmly into the metal, assuring it bonds completely. Work the filler until it matches the original contour and is slightly above the surrounding metal

7 Let the filler harden until you can just dent it with your fingernail. Use a body file or Surform tool (shown here) to rough-shape the filler

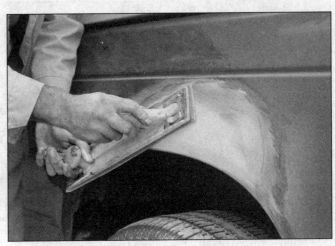

8 Use coarse-grit sandpaper and a sanding board or block to work the filler down until it's smooth and even. Work down to finer grits of sandpaper - always using a board or block - ending up with 360 or 400 grit

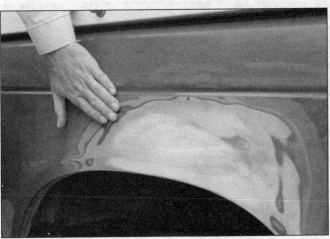

9 You shouldn't be able to feel any ridge at the transition from the filler to the bare metal or from the bare metal to the old paint. As soon as the repair is flat and uniform, remove the dust and mask off the adjacent panels or trim pieces

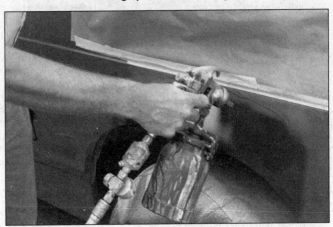

10 Apply several layers of primer to the area. Don't spray the primer on too heavy, so it sags or runs, and make sure each coat is dry before you spray on the next one. A professional-type spray gun is being used here, but aerosol spray primer is available inexpensively from auto parts stores

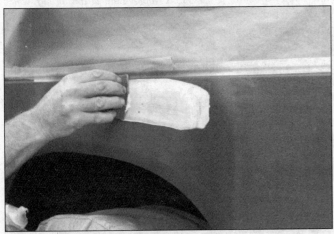

11 The primer will help reveal imperfections or scratches. Fill these with glazing compound. Follow the label instructions and sand it with 360 or 400-grit sandpaper until it's smooth. Repeat the glazing, sanding and respraying until the primer reveals a perfectly smooth surface

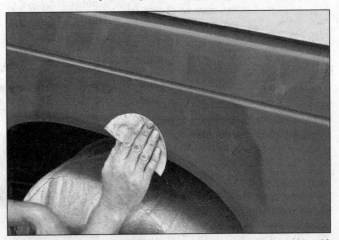

12 Finish sand the primer with very fine sandpaper (400 or 600-grit) to remove the primer overspray. Clean the area with water and allow it to dry. Use a tack rag to remove any dust, then apply the finish coat. Don't attempt to rub out or wax the repair area until the paint has dried completely (at least two weeks)

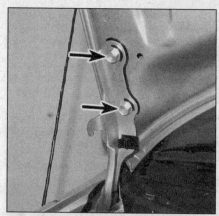

9.3 Draw alignment marks around the hood hinges to ensure proper alignment of the hood when it's reinstalled - arrows indicate the hinge-to-hood retaining bolts

9.9 To adjust the hood latch horizontally or vertically, loosen these bolts (arrows)

9.10a To adjust the vertical height of the leading edge of the hood so that it's flush with the fenders, turn each edge cushion (arrow indicates one) clockwise (to lower the hood) or counterclockwise (to raise the hood)

9 Hood - removal, installation and adjustment

Note: *The hood is somewhat awkward to remove and install, at least two people should perform this procedure.*

Removal and installation

Refer to illustration 9.3

1   Open the hood, then place blankets or pads over the fenders and cowl area of the body. This will protect the body and paint as the hood is lifted off.

2   Disconnect any cables or wires that will interfere with removal. Disconnect the windshield washer tubing from the nozzles on the hood.

3   Make marks around the hood hinge to ensure proper alignment during installation **(see illustration)**.

4   Have an assistant support one side of the hood. Take turns removing the hinge-to-hood bolts and lift off the hood.

5   Installation is the reverse of removal. Align the hinge bolts with the marks made in Step 3.

Adjustment

Refer to illustrations 9.9, 9.10a and 9.10b

6   Fore-and-aft and side-to-side adjustment of the hood is done by moving the hinge plate slot after loosening the bolts or nuts. **Note:** *The factory bolts are "centering" type that will not allow adjustment. To adjust the hood in relation to the hinges, these bolts must be replaced with standard bolts with flat washers and lock washers.*

7   Mark around the entire hinge plate so you can determine the amount of movement.

8   Loosen the bolts and move the hood into correct alignment. Move it only a little at a time. Tighten the hinge bolts and carefully lower the hood to check the position.

9   If necessary after installation, the entire hood latch assembly can be adjusted up-

and-down as well as from side-to-side on the radiator support so the hood closes securely and flush with the fenders. Scribe a line or mark around the hood latch mounting bolts to provide a reference point, then loosen them and reposition the latch assembly, as necessary **(see illustration)**. Following adjustment, retighten the mounting bolts.

10   Finally, adjust the hood bumpers on the radiator support so the hood, when closed, is flush with the fenders **(see illustrations)**.

11   The hood latch assembly, as well as the hinges, should be periodically lubricated with white, lithium-base grease to prevent binding and wear.

10 Hood latch and release cable - removal and installation

Warning: *The models covered by this manual are equipped with Supplemental Restraint systems (SRS), more commonly known as airbags. Always disable the airbag system before working in the vicinity of any airbag*

9.10b On 2001 and later models, there are also hood adjusting bumpers located on the hood

system component to avoid the possibility of accidental deployment of the airbag, which could cause personal injury (see Chapter 12).

10.2 Pry out the cable retainer from the backside of the hood latch assembly, then disengage the cable

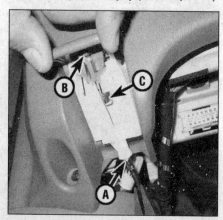

10.5 Lift upward on the handle and pull the cable housing end (A) from the base of the handle, then detach the cable end (B) from the lever - (C) indicates the handle retaining tab

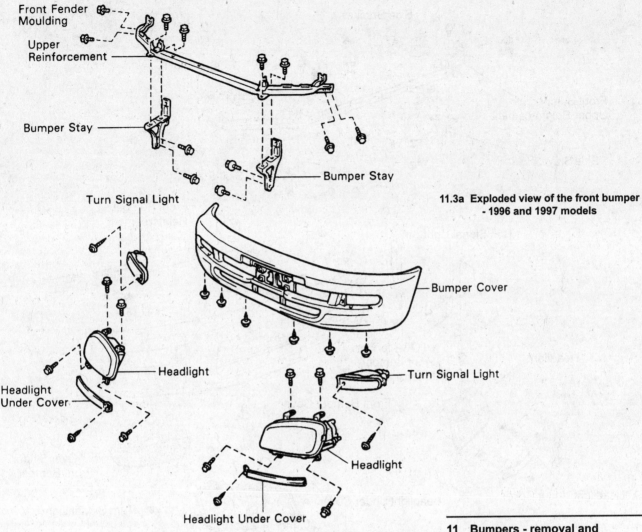

11.3a Exploded view of the front bumper - 1996 and 1997 models

Latch

Refer to illustration 10.2

1   Scribe a line around the latch to aid alignment when installing, then remove the retaining bolts securing the hood latch to the radiator support **(see illustration 9.9)**. Remove the latch.

2   Disconnect the hood release cable by disengaging the cable from the latch assembly **(see illustration)**.

3   Installation is the reverse of removal.
Note: *Adjust the latch so the hood engages securely when closed and the hood bumpers are slightly compressed.*

Cable

Refer to illustration 10.5

4   Working in the passenger compartment, remove the driver's side kick panel.

5   Lift the hood release handle lever upward, then pull down on the cable housing end and disengage the cable from the hood release lever handle. If the handle lever needs to be replaced simply pull outward on the handle retaining tab and push downward to release it from the instrument panel

(see illustration).

6   Attach a piece of thin wire or string to the end of the cable.

7   Working in the engine compartment, disconnect the hood release cable from the latch assembly as described in Steps 1 and 2. Unclip all the cable retaining clips on the radiator support and the inner fenderwell.

8   Pull the cable forward into the engine compartment until you can see the wire or string. then remove the wire or string from the old cable and fasten it to the new cable.

9   With the new cable attached to the wire or string, pull the wire or string back through the firewall until the new cable reaches the inside handle.

10   Working in the passenger compartment, reinstall the new cable into the hood release lever, making sure the cable housing fits snugly into the notch in the handle bracket.
Note: *Pull on the cable with your fingers from the passenger compartment until the cable stop seats in the grommet on the firewall.*

11   The remainder of the installation is the reverse of removal.

11   Bumpers - removal and installation

Warning: *The models covered by this manual are equipped with Supplemental Restraint systems (SRS), more commonly known as airbags. Always disable the airbag system before working in the vicinity of any airbag system component to avoid the possibility of accidental deployment of the airbag, which could cause personal injury (see Chapter 12).*

Front bumper

Refer to illustrations 11.3a, 11.3b, 11.4a, 11.4b, 11.4c, 11.4d and 11.4e

1   Apply the parking brake, raise the vehicle and support it securely on jackstands.

2   Disconnect the negative battery cable, then the positive battery cable and wait two minutes before proceeding any further. Working below the vehicle remove the lower splash shields.

3   On 2000 and earlier models, detach the screws securing the top, bottom and sides of the bumper cover. Pull the cover outward slightly and disconnect the connectors from the front turn signal lights. Remove the cover from the vehicle **(see illustrations)**.

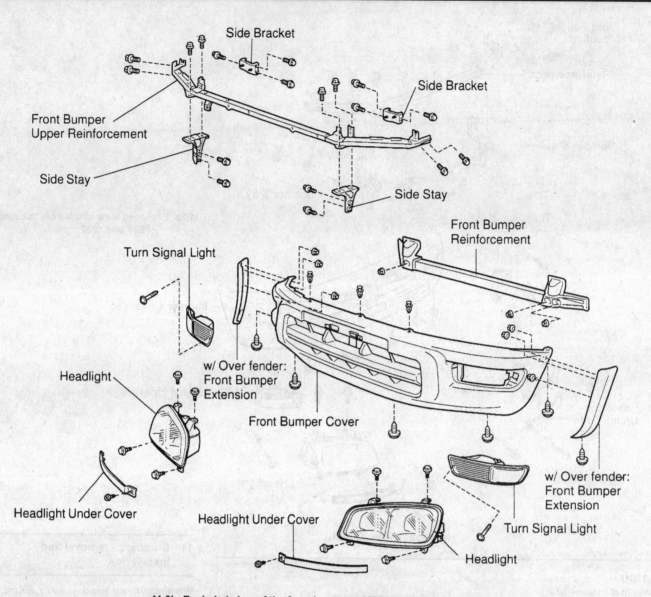

Side Bracket

Side Bracket

Front Bumper
Upper Reinforcement

Side Stay

Side Stay

Front Bumper
Reinforcement

Turn Signal Light

Headlight

w/ Over fender:
Front Bumper
Extension

Front Bumper Cover

w/ Over fender:
Front Bumper
Extension

Headlight Under Cover

Headlight Under Cover

Turn Signal Light

Headlight

11.3b Exploded view of the front bumper - 1998 through 2000 models

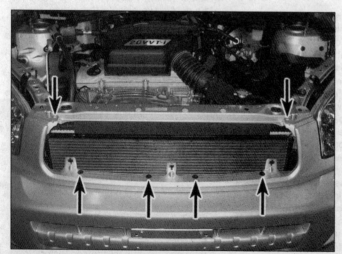

11.4a Remove the two screws at the top (upper arrows) and the push pins at the center of the panel (lower arrows) . . .

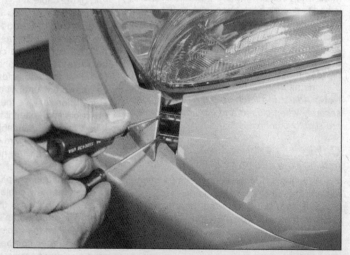

11.4b . . . then depress the tabs securing the ends of the headlight filler panel and remove it from the vehicle

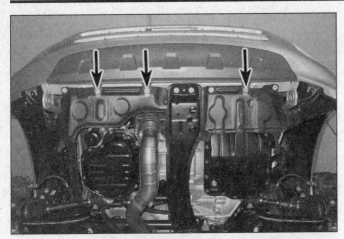

11.4c On 2001 and later models remove the lower retaining bolts (arrows) . . .

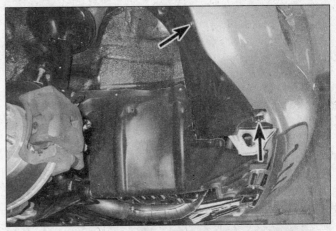

11.4d . . . then remove the lower screws (arrows) securing the front of both inner fenderwells

11.4e Peel back the front of the inner fenderwells and remove the screw (arrow) securing the bumper cover to the fender

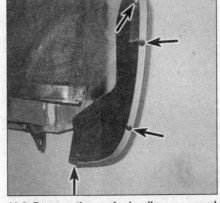

11.6 Remove the push pins (lower arrows) and the upper bolt (upper arrow) from the rear wheelwell

11.7 Inside the back door opening, remove the two bolts securing the inner edge of the rear bumper cover

4   On 2001 and later models, remove the radiator grille (see Section 13) and the headlight filler panel (see illustrations). Remove the bumper cover retaining bolts (see illustrations). Note: Use a small screwdriver to pop the center button up on the plastic fasteners, but do not try to remove the center buttons. They stay in the ferrules. Pull the cover outward slightly and disconnect the connectors from the front turn signal lights. Remove the cover from the vehicle.

5   Installation is the reverse of removal. Make sure the tabs (if equipped) on the back of the bumper cover fit into the corresponding clips on the body before attaching the bolts and screws. An assistant would be helpful at this point. If the bumper reinforcement beam needs to be removed, simply unscrew the bolts, disconnect the horns (if applicable) and remove it from the vehicle.

Rear bumper

Refer to illustrations 11.6 and 11.7

6   Working in the rear wheelwell, detach the plastic clips and the upper bolt securing the edge of the bumper cover (see illustration). Note: *Use a small screwdriver to pop the center button up on the plastic fasteners, but do not try to remove the center buttons.*

They stay in the ferrules.

7   Open the back door and remove the bolts securing the inside edge of the bumper cover (see illustration). Pull the bumper cover out and away from the vehicle.

8   Installation is the reverse of removal.

---

12   Front fender - removal and installation

Refer to illustrations 12.7a, 12.7b, 12.9, 12.10, 12.11a, 12.11b and 12.11c

Warning: *The models covered by this manual are equipped with Supplemental Restraint systems (SRS), more commonly known as airbags. Always disable the airbag system before working in the vicinity of any airbag system component to avoid the possibility of accidental deployment of the airbag, which could cause personal injury (see Chapter 12).*

1   Loosen the front wheel lug nuts. Raise the vehicle, support it securely on jackstands and remove the front wheel.

2   Open the hood.

3   On 2000 and earlier models, remove the finish panel below the headlight housing.

4   On 2001 and later models, remove the

12.7a Remove the bolt and push pins (arrows) at the front lower portion of the inner fenderwell

radiator grille (see Section 13).

5   Remove the front bumper cover (see Section 11).

6   Remove the headlight housing (see Chapter 12).

7   Detach the inner fenderwell push pins, then remove the inner fenderwell and mud shield (see illustrations).

12.7b Detach the main portion of the inner fenderwell, secured by bolts, screws and plastic clips (arrows)

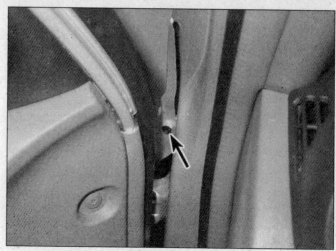

12.9 Remove the upper fender bolt (arrow) with the door open

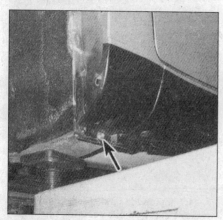

12.10 Remove the bottom bolt (arrow) retaining the fender to the rocker panel area

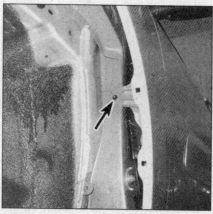

12.11a Remove the bolt in the wheelwell opening (arrow)

10 Remove the lower fender-to-body bolt (see illustration).

11 Remove the remaining fender mounting bolts (see illustrations).

12 Lift off the fender. It's a good idea to have an assistant support the fender while it's being moved away from the vehicle to prevent damage to the surrounding body panels.

13 Installation is the reverse of removal. Check the alignment of the fender to the hood and front edge of the door before final tightening of the fender fasteners.

13   Radiator grille - removal and installation

Refer to illustrations 13.2 and 13.3

1 Open the hood.

2 On 2000 and earlier models, the grille is mounted to the hood. Working from the back of the hood, remove the nuts securing the grille to the hood. Using a pair of pliers squeeze the plastic retaining clips and detach

8 If you're removing the passenger side fender, remove the radio antenna (see Chapter 12). If you're removing the driver side

fender, remove the hood prop rod from the fender and prop the hood open in a safe position.

9 Open the front door, and remove the upper fender-to-body bolt (see illustration).

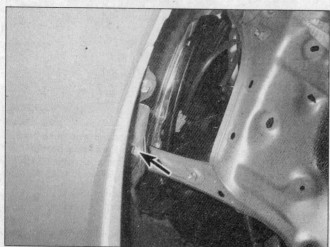

12.11b Remove the front fender-to-brace bolt (arrow) - the upper bolt in this photo is the bumper cover bolt which would already have been removed with the bumper cover

12.11c Remove the three bolts (arrows) along the top of the fender

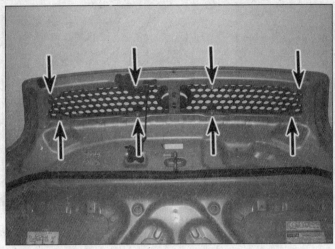

13.2 Radiator grille fasteners - 2000 and earlier models

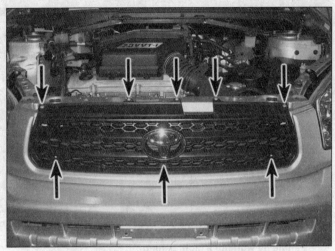

13.3 Remove the screws at the top and disengage the clips at the bottom - 2001 and later models

14.2a Use a small screwdriver to pop the center button up on the plastic fasteners, but do not try to remove the center buttons (they stay in the ferrules) - 2001 and later models shown

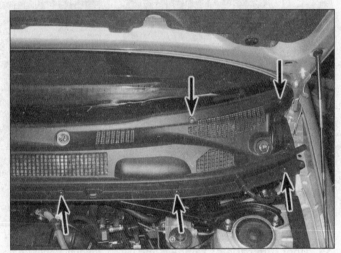

14.2b Driver's side cowl cover fasteners - 2001 and later models

the grille from the hood.
3   On 2001 and later models, remove screws along the top of the grille **(see illustration)**. Pull the top of the grille out slightly

and disengage the retaining clips with a screwdriver. The retaining clips can be disengaged by simply pressing downward on the tabs

4   Once the retaining clips are disengaged, pull the grille out and remove it.
5   Installation is the reverse of removal.

14 Cowl cover and vent tray - removal and installation

Refer to illustrations 14.2a, 14.2b and 14.3
1   Remove the wiper arms (see Chapter 12).
2   Remove the push pin fasteners securing the cowl cover **(see illustrations)**. **Note:** *Use a small screwdriver to pop the center button up on the plastic fasteners, but do not try to remove the center buttons. They stay in the ferrules.*
3   If the vent tray on 2001 and later models needs to be removed, first remove the wiper motor linkage assembly as described in Chapter 12, then remove the vent tray mounting bolts **(see illustration)**.
4   Installation is the reverse of removal.

14.3 Vent tray mounting bolts - 2001 and later models (passenger side shock tower bolts not shown in this photo)

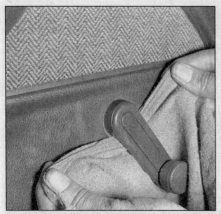

15.1 On models equipped with manual windows, remove the window crank handle by working a cloth behind it to release the clip

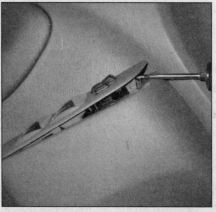

15.2 Pry up the power window switch plate, disconnect the electrical connectors . . .

15.3 Pry off the mirror trim cover

15.4 On 2001 and later models pry out the trim cover on the door grip

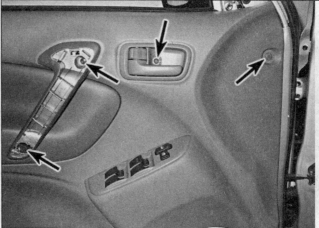

15.5 Door trim panel retaining screws (arrows) - 2001 and later model shown, 2000 and earlier models have two extra screws in the storage compartment area of the front door

15 Door trim panels - removal and installation

Refer to illustrations 15.1, 15.2, 15.3, 15.4, 15.5, 15.7 and 15.9

Removal

Front and rear doors

1   On manual window models, remove the window crank handle **(see illustration)**.

2   On power window models, pry up the window switch plate to access one panel mounting screw underneath **(see illustration)**.

3   Pry out the outside mirror cover **(see illustration)**.

4   On 2001 and later models pry out the door grip trim cover **(see illustration)**.

5   Remove the door trim panel retaining screws and the inside door handle trim cover, then carefully pry the panel out until the clips disengage **(see illustration)**. Work slowly and carefully around the outer edge of the trim panel until it's free. **Note:** *The rear doors only use three screws to secure the door trim panels, two at the door grip and one at the inside handle bezel.*

6   Once all of the clips are disengaged, pull the trim panel up from the door, unplug any wiring harness connectors and remove the panel.

7   For access to the door outside handle or the door window regulator inside the door, raise the window fully, then carefully peel back the plastic watershield **(see illustration)**.

Back door

8   Open the back door.

15.7 Carefully peel back the plastic watershield for access to the inner door

9   Using a screwdriver or trim removal tool pry out the clips and remove the trim panel from the back door **(see illustration)**. On 2000 and earlier models use a small screwdriver to pop the center button up on the plastic fasteners, but do not try to remove the center buttons.

10   For access to other components inside the door, carefully peel back the plastic watershield **(see illustration 15.7)**.

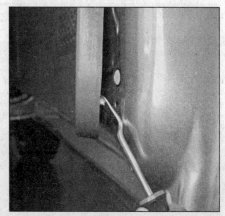

15.9 The trim panel for the back door can be removed by simply prying out the clips

16.6 Remove the bolt(s) retaining the door stop strut (arrows)

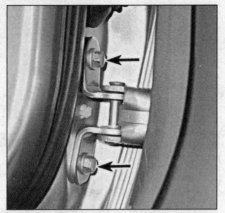

16.8a Remove the door hinge bolts with the door supported (arrows indicate bolts for the bottom hinge, top hinge similar)

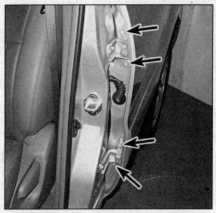

16.8b Open the front door to access the rear door hinge-to-body bolts (arrows)

Installation

11   Prior to installation of the door trim panel, be sure to reinstall any clips in the panel which may have come out when you removed the panel.

12   Position the wire harness connectors for the power door lock switch and the power window switch (if equipped) through the hole in the door trim panel, then place the panel in position in the door. Press the door panel into place until the clips are seated.

13   The remainder of the installation is the reverse of removal.

16   Door - removal, installation and adjustment

Note: *The door is heavy and somewhat awkward to remove and install - at least two people should perform this procedure.*

Removal and installation

Refer to illustrations 16.6, 16.8a and 16.8b

1   Raise the window completely in the door and disconnect the negative cable from the battery.

2   Open the door all the way and support it from the ground on jacks or blocks covered with rags to prevent damaging the paint.

3   Remove the door trim panel and watershield as described in Section 15.

4   Disconnect all electrical connections, ground wires and harness retaining clips from the door. **Note:** *It is a good idea to label all connections to aid the reassembly process.*

5   From the door side, detach the rubber conduit between the body and the door. Then pull the wiring harness through the conduit hole and remove it from the door.

6   Remove the door stop strut bolt(s) **(see illustration)**.

7   Mark around the door hinges with a pen or a scribe to facilitate realignment during reassembly.

8   With an assistant holding the door, remove the hinge-to-door bolts **(see illustrations)** and lift the door off. **Note:** *Draw a reference line around the hinges before removing*

the bolts.

9   Installation is the reverse of removal.

Adjustment

Refer to illustration 16.13

10   Having proper door-to-body alignment is a critical part of a well-functioning door assembly. First check the door hinge pins for excessive play. Fully open the door and lift up and down on the door without lifting the body. If a door has 1/16-inch or more excessive play, the hinges should be replaced.

11   Door-to-body alignment adjustments are made by loosening the hinge-to-body bolts or hinge-to-door bolts and moving the door. Proper body alignment is achieved when the top of the doors are parallel with the roof section, the front door is flush with the fender, the rear door is flush with the rear quarter panel and the bottom of the doors are aligned with the lower rocker panel. If these goals can't be reached by adjusting the hinge-to-body or hinge-to-door bolts, body alignment shims may have to be purchased and inserted behind the hinges to achieve correct alignment.

12   To adjust the door-closed position, scribe

a line or mark around the striker plate to provide a reference point, then check that the door latch is contacting the center of the latch striker. If not adjust the up and down position first.

13   Finally adjust the latch striker sideways position, so that the door panel is flush with the center pillar or rear quarter panel and provides positive engagement with the latch mechanism **(see illustration)**.

17   Door latch, lock cylinder and handles - removal and installation

Caution: *Wear gloves when working inside the door openings to protect against cuts from sharp metal edges.*

Door latch

Refer to illustrations 17.2, 17.4a and 17.4b

1   Raise the window, then remove the door trim panel and watershield (see Section 15).

2   Working through the large access hole, disengage the outside door handle-to-latch rod, outside door lock-to-latch rod, and the inside handle-to-latch rod **(see illustration)**.

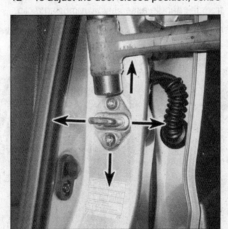

16.13 Adjust the door lock striker by loosening the mounting screws and gently tapping the striker in the desired direction (arrows)

17.2 Detach the plastic clips on the actuating rods leading to the outside handle and the door lock cylinder

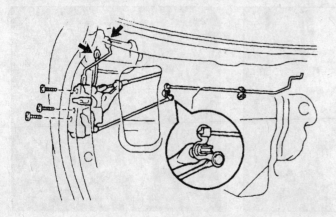

17.4a Door latch mounting details - 2000 and earlier models

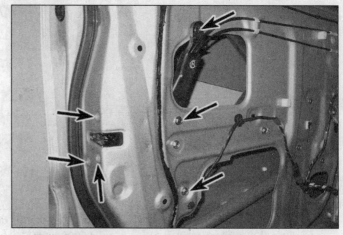

17.4b Door latch mounting details - 2001 and later models

3   All door lock rods are attached by plastic clips. The plastic clips can be removed by unsnapping the portion engaging the connecting rod and then pulling the rod out of its locating hole. On models with power door locks, disconnect the electrical connectors at the latch.

4   Remove the screws securing the latch to the door **(see illustrations)**. Remove the latch assembly through the door opening. On 2001 and later models, it will be necessary to remove the inside handle retaining bolt, then detach the handle from the door and remove the inside handle and the latch as an assembly.

5   Installation is the reverse of removal.

Outside handle and door lock cylinder

Refer to illustrations 17.9a, 17.9b and 17.9c

6   To remove the outside handle and lock cylinder assembly, raise the window and remove the door trim panel and watershield (see Section 15). **Caution:** *Take care not to scratch the paint on the outside of the door. Wide masking tape applied around the handle opening before beginning the procedure can help avoid scratches.*

17.9a Remove the plug from the end of the door to access the door lock cylinder retaining bolt - 2001 and later models

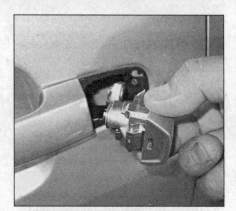

17.9b Removing the door lock cylinder on a 2002 model

7   Working through the access hole, disengage the plastic clips that secure the outside door lock-to-latch rod and the outside door handle-to-latch rod **(see illustration 17.2)**.

8   On 2000 and earlier models, remove the handle retaining bolts and withdraw the handle and lock cylinder as an assembly from the vehicle. The lock cylinder can be removed from the handle assembly by removing a clip.

9   On 2001 and later models, Remove the plug from the end of the door and remove the lock cylinder retaining screw. Withdraw the lock cylinder from the door, and disconnect the electrical connector if equipped. Unbolt the handle from the inside of the door and remove the handle and the handle frame **(see illustrations)**.

10   Installation is the reverse of removal.

17.9c Outside door handle retaining bolts (arrows) - 2001 and later models shown, 2000 and earlier similar except that there is no handle frame

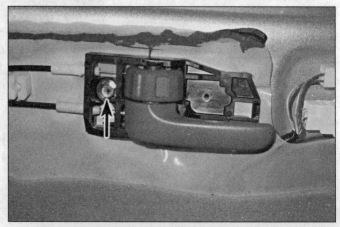

17.12 Inside handle retaining bolt (arrow) - 2001 and later model shown, 2000 and earlier models have two screws securing the handle

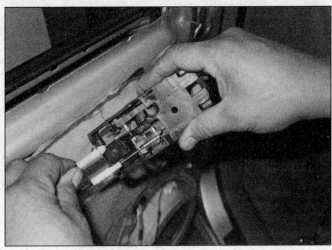

17.13 Removing the cables from the inside handle - 2001 and later models

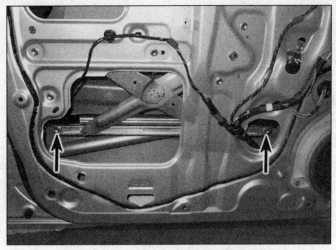

18.3 Raise the window to access the glass retaining bolts (arrows) through the holes in the door frame

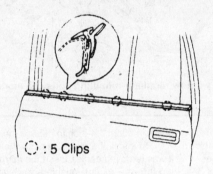

18.9 Outer weatherstrip clip locations - rear door

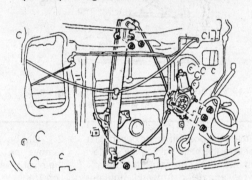

19.4 Front window regulator mounting bolts - 2000 and earlier models

Inside door handle

Refer to illustrations 17.12 and 17.13

11   Remove the door trim panel (see Section 15).

12   Remove the handle retaining screw(s) and disengage the handle from the door **(see illustration)**.

13   Disengage the handle-to-latch rod on 2000 and earlier models or the handle-to-latch cables on 2001 and later models and remove the handle from the door **(see illustration)**.

14   Installation is the reverse of removal.

18 Door window glass - removal and installation

Caution: *Wear gloves when working inside the door openings to protect against cuts from sharp metal edges.*

Front door glass

Refer to illustration 18.3

1   Remove the door trim panel and the plastic watershield (see Section 15).

2   Lower the window glass all the way down into the door.

3   Raise the window just enough to access the window retaining bolts through the holes in the door frame **(see illustration)**.

4   Place a rag over the glass to help prevent scratching the glass and remove the two glass mounting bolts.

5   Remove the glass by pulling it up and out.

6   Installation is the reverse of removal.

Rear door glass (four-door models)

Refer to illustration 18.9

7   Remove the door panel and watershield (see Section 15).

8   Lower the window glass all the way down into the door.

9   Remove the outer weatherstripping. Pry upward on the clips to release it from the door **(see illustration)**.

10   Remove the bolt and screw securing the division bar to the door frame, then remove the division bar and the fixed glass.

11   Raise the window just enough to access the window retaining bolts through the holes in the door frame.

12   Place a rag over the glass to help prevent scratching the glass and remove the two glass mounting bolts.

13   Remove the glass by pulling it up and out.

14   Installation is the reverse of the removal procedure.

Back door glass

15   Replacement of the back door glass requires the use of special fast-setting adhesive/caulk materials and some specialized tools and techniques. These operations should be left to a dealer service department or a shop specializing in glass work.

19 Door window glass regulator - removal and installation

Caution: *Wear gloves when working inside the door openings to protect against cuts from sharp metal edges.*

Front

Refer to illustrations 19.4 and 19.5

1   Remove the door trim panel and the plastic watershield (see Section 15).

2   Remove the window glass (see Section 18).

3   On power-operated windows, disconnect the electrical connector from the window regulator motor.

4   On 2000 and earlier models, remove the regulator/motor assembly mounting bolts **(see illustration)**.

5   On 2001 later models, the regulator assembly is a scissors-type. Before removing

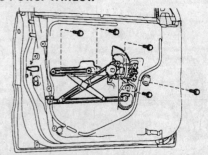

w/o Power Window

w/ Power Window

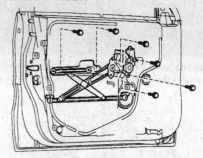

w/ Power Window

**19.5 Front window regulator mounting bolts -
2001 and later models**

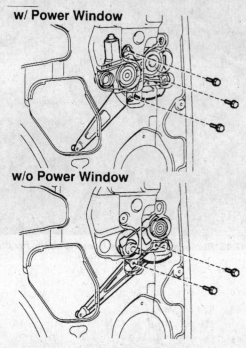

w/ Power Window

w/o Power Window

19.11 Rear window regulator mounting bolts - all models

the bolts, mark the position of the upper roller guide. Remove the bolts holding the window regulator/motor to the door **(see illustration)**.

6   Pull the equalizer arm and regulator assemblies through the service hole in the door frame to remove it.

7   Installation is the reverse of removal. Lubricate the rollers and wear points on the regulator with white grease before installation.

Rear

Refer to illustration 19.11

8   Remove the door trim panel and the plastic watershield (see Section 15).

9   Remove the window glass assembly (see Section 18).

10   On power-operated windows, disconnect the electrical connector from the window regulator motor.

11   Remove the regulator/motor assembly mounting bolts **(see illustration)**.

12   Remove the equalizer bar and raise the regulator assembly through the service hole in the door frame to remove it.

13   Installation is the reverse of removal. Lubricate the rollers and wear points on the regulator with white grease before installation.

20   Mirrors - removal and installation

Outside mirrors

Refer to illustration 20.4

1   Pry off the mirror trim cover on the inside of the door.

2   On power mirror equipped models, remove the door trim panel and peel back the plastic watershield if necessary (see Section 15).

3   Disconnect the electrical connector from the mirror (if equipped).

4   Remove the three mirror retaining bolts and detach the mirror from the vehicle **(see illustration)**.

5   Installation is the reverse of removal.

Inside mirror

Refer to illustration 20.6

6   Pry between the mirror mount and the notch in the base of the mirror stalk with a screwdriver tip covered with tape **(see illustration)**. There is a hairpin-type spring holding the mirror stalk in the base. Push the screw-

driver in about 3/4-inch to release the spring.

7   To install the mirror, reinsert the spring if it was removed earlier. Insert the mirror stalk's lug into the mount, pushing downward until the mirror is secured.

8   If the mount plate itself has come off the windshield, adhesive kits are available at auto parts stores to resecure it. Follow the instructions included with the kit.

21   Back door - removal, installation and adjustment

Note: *The back door is heavy and somewhat awkward to remove and install - at least two people should perform this procedure.*

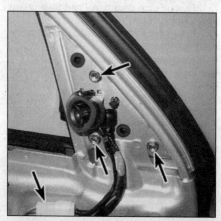

20.4 Remove the three mirror mounting bolts (upper arrows) - on electric mirrors, disconnect the connector (lower arrows)

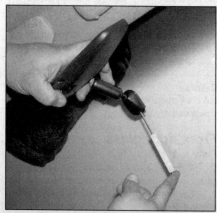

20.6 While pulling up on the inside mirror, push a screwdriver into the slot in the bottom of the base to release it

Removal and installation

Refer to illustration 21.8

1   Disconnect the negative cable from the battery. Remove the spare tire from the back door.

2   Open the door all the way and support it from the ground on jacks or blocks covered with rags to prevent damaging the paint.

3   Remove the door trim panel and watershield as described in Section 15.

4   Disconnect all electrical connections, ground wires and harness retaining clips from the door. **Note:** *It is a good idea to label all connections to aid the reassembly process.*

5   From the door side, detach the rubber conduit between the body and the door. Then pull the wiring harness through the conduit hole and remove it from the door.

6   Remove the door stop strut bolt(s).

7   Mark around the door hinges with a pen or a scribe to facilitate realignment during reassembly.

8   With an assistant holding the door, remove the hinge-to-door bolts **(see illustration)** and lift the door off. **Note:** *Draw a reference line around the hinges before removing the bolts.*

9   Installation is the reverse of removal.

Adjustment

Refer to illustration 21.13

10   Having proper door-to-body alignment is a critical part of a well-functioning door assembly. First check the door hinge pins for excessive play. Fully open the door and lift up and down on the door without lifting the body. If a door has 1/16-inch or more excessive play, the hinges should be replaced.

11   Door-to-body alignment adjustments are made by loosening the hinge-to-body bolts or hinge-to-door bolts and moving the door. Proper body alignment is achieved when the top of the door is parallel with the roof section and the sides of the door are flush with the rear quarter panels and the bottom of the door is aligned with the lower door sill. If these

goals can't be reached by adjusting the hinge-to-body or hinge-to-door bolts, body alignment shims may have to be purchased and inserted behind the hinges to achieve correct alignment.

12   To adjust the door-closed position, scribe a line or mark around the striker plate to provide a reference point, then check that the door latch is contacting the center of the latch striker. If not adjust the up and down position first.

13   Finally adjust the latch striker sideways position, so that the door panel is flush with the rear quarter panel and provides positive engagement with the latch mechanism **(see illustration)**.

22   Back door latch, lock cylinder and handle - removal and installation

Back door latch

Refer to illustration 22.5

1   Disconnect the negative cable from the battery.

2   Open the back door and remove the door trim panel and watershield as described in Section 15.

3   Working through the large access hole, disengage the outside door handle-to-latch rod and the outside door lock-to-latch rod.

4   All door lock rods are attached by plastic clips. The plastic clips can be removed by unsnapping the portion engaging the connecting rod and then pulling the rod out of its locating hole. On models with power door locks, disconnect the electrical connectors at the latch.

5   Remove the screws securing the latch to the door **(see illustration)**. Remove the latch assembly through the door opening. On 2000 and earlier models, pry out the four plastic plugs and remove the screws.

6   Installation is the reverse of removal.

21.8 Back door-to-hinge bolts (upper arrows indicate bolts for the top hinge, bottom hinge similar) - lower arrows are the door stop strut retaining bolts

Backdoor lock cylinder and outside handle

Refer to illustration 22.10

7   Open the back door and remove the door trim panel and watershield as described in Section 15.

8   Working through the large access hole, disengage the outside door handle-to-latch rod and the outside door lock-to-latch rod.

9   All door lock rods are attached by plastic clips. The plastic clips can be removed by unsnapping the portion engaging the connecting rod and then pulling the rod out of its locating hole.

10   Remove the handle retaining bolts through the holes in the door frame and detach the handle and lock assembly from the back door **(see illustration)**.

11   Once the handle is removed the lock cylinder can be removed from the handle by simply removing the retaining screw(s) and detaching it from the handle.

12   The remainder of the installation is the reverse of removal.

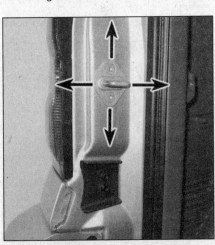

21.13 Adjust the door lock striker by loosening the mounting screws and gently tapping the striker in the desired direction (arrows)

22.5 Back door latch fasteners (arrows)

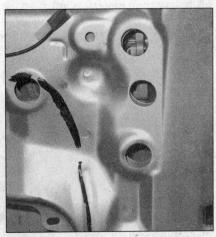

22.10 The outside handle retaining bolts can be accessed through the holes in the door frame

23.4 Removing the shift lever bezel on an automatic transmission vehicle - 2001 and later models shown

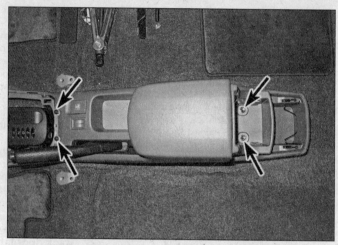

23.7a Rear console mounting screws (arrows) - 2001 and later models

23 Center console - removal and installation

Refer to illustrations 23.4, 23.7a, 23.7b and 23.8

Warning: *The models covered by this manual are equipped with Supplemental Restraint systems (SRS), more commonly known as airbags. Always disable the airbag system before working in the vicinity of any airbag system component to avoid the possibility of accidental deployment of the airbag, which could cause personal injury (see Chapter 12).*
1   Disconnect the negative cable from the battery.
2   Raise the emergency brake handle.
3   If the vehicle is equipped with manual transaxle, unscrew the shift lever knob and remove the shift lever boot (see Chapter 7A).
4   If the vehicle is equipped with an automatic transaxle, remove the shift lever bezel **(see illustration)**.
5   On 2001 and later models, remove the screws then pry the lower center finish panel off the instrument panel (see Section 24). Be sure to tape the tip of the screwdriver tip to

prevent scratching the panels.
6   On 2000 and earlier models, remove the screws at the front and center of the console, then remove the screw at the rear in the cup holder. Pull console up and back to remove it from the vehicle.
7   On 2001 and later models, remove the retaining screws and detach the rear half of the console from the vehicle **(see illustration)**. Also remove the trim covers at the front of the console **(see illustration)**.
8   Remove the front console screws and lift the console up and over the shift lever **(see illustration)**. Disconnect any electrical connections and remove the console from the vehicle.
9   Installation is the reverse of removal.

24 Dashboard trim panels

Warning: *The models covered by this manual are equipped with Supplemental Restraint systems (SRS), more commonly known as airbags. Always disable the airbag system before working in the vicinity of any airbag system component to avoid the possibility of*

accidental deployment of the airbag, which could cause personal injury (see Chapter 12).
1   Disconnect the negative cable from the battery.

Instrument cluster bezel
Refer to illustrations 24.3 and 24.4
2   If equipped with a tilt steering column, tilt the column all the way down.
3   On 2000 and earlier models, remove the screw at the top of the instrument cluster bezel **(see illustration)**. Grasp the bezel with both hands and pull straight out to disengage the bezel from the instrument panel.
4   On 2001 and later models simply grasp the bezel with both hands and pull straight out to disengage the bezel from the instrument panel **(see illustration)**.
5   Installation is the reverse of the removal procedure. Make sure the clips are engaged properly before pushing the bezel firmly into place.

Knee bolster
Refer to illustration 24.8
6   Disengage the cable from the hood-

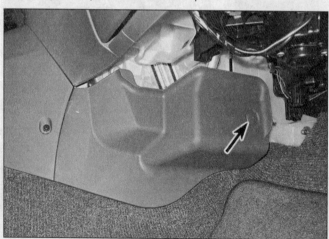

23.7b Console front trim cover - 2001 and later models

23.8 Front console mounting screws - 2001 and later models (the two lower left side screws are not visible in this photo)

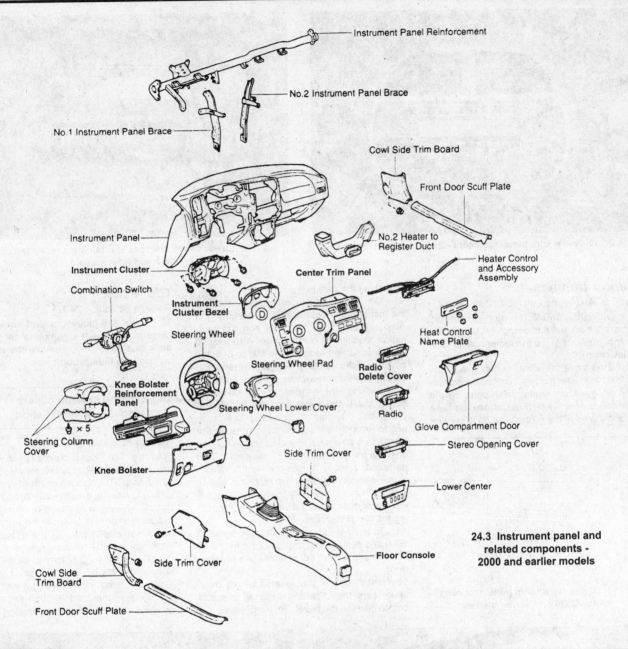

Instrument Panel Reinforcement

No.2 Instrument Panel Brace

No.1 Instrument Panel Brace

Cowl Side Trim Board

Front Door Scuff Plate

Instrument Panel

No.2 Heater to Register Duct

Heater Control and Accessory Assembly

Instrument Cluster

Combination Switch

Center Trim Panel

Instrument Cluster Bezel

Heat Control Name Plate

Steering Wheel

Steering Wheel Pad

Radio Delete Cover

Knee Bolster Reinforcement Panel

Radio

Steering Wheel Lower Cover

Glove Compartment Door

× 5

Steering Column Cover

Stereo Opening Cover

Knee Bolster

Side Trim Cover

Lower Center

24.3 Instrument panel and related components - 2000 and earlier models

Side Trim Cover

Floor Console

Cowl Side Trim Board

Front Door Scuff Plate

24.4 Removing the instrument cluster bezel on a 2001 and later model

24.8 Remove the knee bolster screws (arrows) - 2001 and later shown, 2000 and earlier similar

release lever (see Section 10).

7   On 2001 and later models, remove the dimmer switch bezel (see Chapter 12). On 2000 and earlier models disengage the small fuse panel from the knee bolster by depressing the retaining tab at the top and pushing the fuse panel out of the knee bolster.

8   Remove the screws and pull the knee bolster out to disengage the clips behind it **(see illustration)**.

9   Remove the retaining bolts securing the knee bolster reinforcement, if needed for access to components under the dashboard. Pull outward on the lower edge of the knee bolster reinforcement panel and detach it from the vehicle.

10   Installation is the reverse of removal.

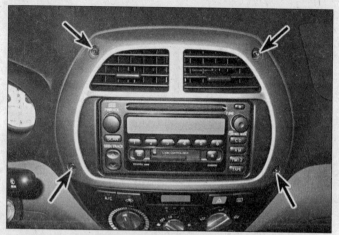

24.11 Center trim panel fasteners - 2001 and later models

24.12 Lower center trim panel retaining screws (arrows) - 2001 and later models

Center trim panels

Refer to illustrations 24.11, 24.12 and 24.14

11   On 2001 and later models, simply remove the screws and detach the upper center trim panel from the instrument panel **(see illustration)**.

12   To remove the lower center trim panel on 2001 and later models, remove the screws then pry the lower center finish panel off the instrument panel **(see illustration)**. Be sure to tape the tip of the screwdriver tip to prevent

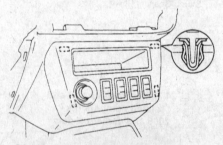

24.14 Lower center trim panel retaining clips - 2000 and earlier models

scratching the panels,

13   On 2000 and earlier models, remove the instrument cluster bezel as described in Step 3. Then pull off the knobs from the heating/air conditioning control panel. Also remove the lower screws securing the stereo opening cover or radio delete cover **(see illustration 24.3)**. Using a screwdriver with the tip taped with masking tape, carefully pry the lower portion of the bezel away from the instrument panel until the clips are released. Take care not to scratch the surrounding trim on the instrument panel. Disconnect any electrical connectors from the rear of the center trim panel and remove it from the vehicle. **Note:** *Some models may have two retaining screws located in the instrument cluster opening which must be removed before disengaging the trim panel clips.*

14   To remove the lower center trim panel on 2000 and earlier models, pry out the four clips and remove it from the vehicle **(see illustration)**.

15   Installation is the reverse of removal. Make sure the clips are engaged properly before pushing the bezel firmly into place.

Glove box

Refer to illustration 24.16

16   Open the glove box and squeeze the sides in to allow the compartment to come back and down, then remove the mounting screws **(see illustration)**.

25   Steering column covers - removal and installation

Refer to illustration 25.2

Warning: *The models covered by this manual are equipped with Supplemental Restraint systems (SRS), more commonly known as airbags. Always disable the airbag system before working in the vicinity of any airbag system component to avoid the possibility of accidental deployment of the airbag, which could cause personal injury (see Chapter 12).*

1   On tilt steering columns, move the column to the lowest position. Refer to Chapter 10 and remove the steering wheel.

2   Remove the screws, then separate the halves and remove the upper and lower steer-

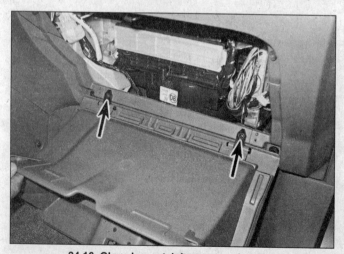

24.16 Glove box retaining screws (arrows)

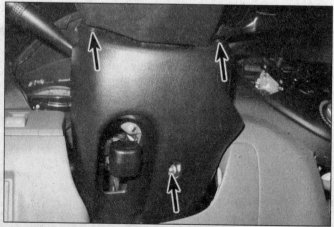

25.2 Remove the screws (arrows), then remove upper and lower covers - 2001 and later shown; on 2000 and earlier models, one more screw secures the upper cover which is accessible after the lower cover is removed

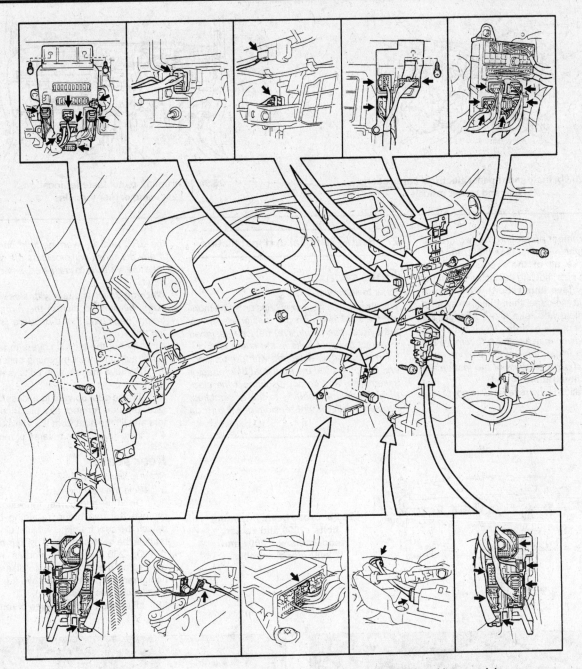

26.8a Instrument panel fastener and electrical connections - 2001 and later models

ing column covers **(see illustration)**.

3   Installation is the reverse of the removal procedure.

26   Instrument panel - removal and installation

Refer to illustrations 26.8a, 26.8b, 26.9a and 26.9b

Warning: *The models covered by this manual are equipped with Supplemental Restraint systems (SRS), more commonly known as airbags. Always disable the airbag system before working in the vicinity of any airbag*

system component to avoid the possibility of accidental deployment of the airbag, which could cause personal injury (see Chapter 12).

1   Disconnect the negative battery cable.

2   Remove the dashboard trim panels (see Section 24) and the center floor console (see Section 23).

3   Remove the instrument cluster (see Chapter 12) .

4   Disconnect the electrical connector from the passenger's side airbag and on 2001 and later models, remove it (see Chapter 12).

5   Remove the audio unit from the center of the dashboard (see Chapter 12).

6   Remove the air conditioning control

panel (see Chapter 3).

7   Remove the driver's knee bolster and reinforcement panel (see Section 24). Then unscrew the bolts securing the steering column and lower it away from the instrument panel (see Chapter 10).

8   A number of electrical connectors must be disconnected in order to remove the instrument panel. Most are designed so that they will only fit on the matching connector (male or female), but if there is any doubt, mark the connectors with masking tape and a marking pen before disconnecting them **(see illustration)**. **Note:** *On 2000 and earlier models, disconnect the main connectors on each side*

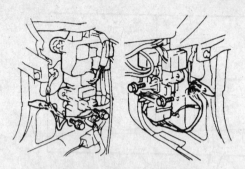

**26.8b Instrument panel electrical connections -
2000 and earlier models**

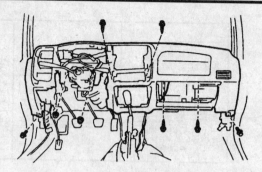

**26.9a Instrument panel fastener locations -
2000 and earlier models**

of the instrument panel and the two ground straps bolts at the center **(see illustration)**.

9   Remove all of the fasteners (bolts, screws and nuts) holding the instrument panel to the body **(see illustration)**. Once all are removed, lift the panel then pull it away from the windshield and take it out through the driver's door opening. **Note:** *This is a two-person job, and you may also have to remove the bolts to the instrument panel reinforcement tube for complete removal of the instrument panel (see illustration).*

10   Installation is the reverse of removal.

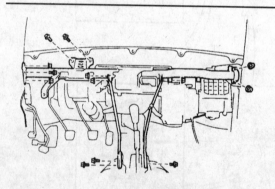

**26.9b Cross beam mounting
bolts - 2000 and earlier
models shown, 2001 and
later models similar**

27   Seats - removal and installation

Front seat

Refer to illustration 27.2

Warning 1: *The front seat belts on some models are equipped with pre-tensioners, which are pyrotechnic (explosive) devices designed to retract the seat belts in the event of a collision. On models equipped with pre-tensioners, do not remove the front seat belt retractor assemblies, and do not disconnect the electrical connectors leading to the assemblies. Problems with the pre-tensioners will turn on* the SRS (airbag) warning light on the dash. *If any pre-tensioner problems are suspected, take the vehicle to a dealer service department.*

Warning 2: *On models with side-impact airbags, be sure to disarm the airbag system before beginning this procedure (see Chapter 12).*

1   Pry out the plastic covers to access the seat tracks and their mounting bolts.

2   Remove the retaining bolts **(see illustration)**.

3   Tilt the seat upward to access the underside, then disconnect any electrical connectors and lift the seat from the vehicle.

4   Installation is the reverse of removal.

Rear seat

Refer to illustration 27.7

5   Fold the seat forward.

6   On 2000 and earlier four-door models, remove the two hinge retaining bolts and detach the seat from the vehicle. On two-door models the seat is retained by four bolts.

7   On 2001 and later models, simply lift upward on the locking bar to disengage the hook from the pivot and remove the seat from the vehicle **(see illustration)**.

8   Installation is the reverse of removal.

27.2 Typical front seat track retaining bolts (arrows indicate the rear bolts; slide the seat to the rear for access to the front bolts

27.7 Lift up on the lock bar to disengage the rear seat from the pivots on the floor

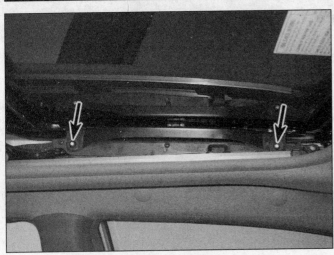

28.4 Sunroof glass retaining bolts (arrows
indicate two of four bolts)

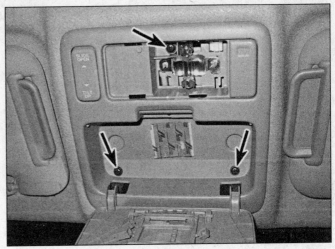

28.5a Pry out the interior light lens, lower the compartment door
and remove the overhead console screws

28 Sunroof - adjustment

*Refer to illustrations 28.4, 28.5a, 28.5b
and 28.5c*

1   The position of the glass panel can be
adjusted in the following manner.

2   Operate the sunroof until it is tilted open.

3   The side-to-side adjustment is achieved
by removing the sunroof drive motor and moving the drive cable until the cable-to-frame
alignment marks are even on both sides.

4   Remove the glass retaining screws and
remove the glass (see illustration).

5   Remove the sunroof drive motor (see
illustrations). Move the drive cable end until
the cable alignment marks are even with the
marks on the frame on each side.

6   When the adjustment is correct, reinstall
the drive motor and the sunroof glass.

7   The final adjustment is the forward and
rearward adjustment. This is achieved by
loosening the glass retaining screws and moving the glass the amount necessary to allow
proper sealing with the front and rear edge.

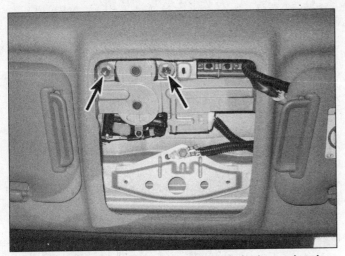

28.5b Remove the drive motor retaining bolts (arrows) and
disengage the drive motor gear from the drive cable

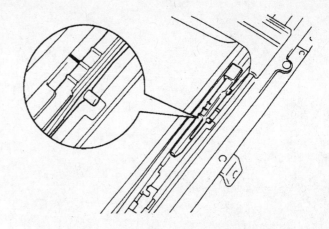

28.5c Working up in the sunroof opening, move the cable end
until the cable-to-frame alignment marks are even on both sides

Notes

Chapter 12
Chassis electrical system

Contents

	Section
Airbag system - general information	26
Antenna - replacement	13
Bulb replacement	19
Circuit breakers - general information	4
Cruise control system - description	21
Daytime Running Lights (DRL) - general information	25
Electric side view mirrors - description	20
Electrical troubleshooting - general information	2
Fuses and fusible links - general information	3
General information	1
Headlight housing - replacement	17
Headlights - adjustment	16
Headlight bulb - replacement	15
Horn - check and replacement	18
Ignition switch and lock cylinder - replacement	8
Instrument cluster - removal and installation	10
Instrument panel switches - replacement	9
Power door lock system - description	23
Power sunroof - description	24
Power window system - description	22
Radio and speakers - removal and installation	12
Rear window defogger - check and repair	14
Relays - general information and testing	5
Steering column switches - replacement	7
Turn signal and hazard flasher - check and replacement	6
Wiper motor - check and replacement	11
Wiring diagrams - general information	27

1 General information

The electrical system is a 12-volt, negative ground type. Power for the lights and all electrical accessories is supplied by a lead/acid-type battery which is charged by the alternator.

This Chapter covers repair and service procedures for the various electrical components not associated with the engine. Information on the battery, alternator, distributor and starter motor can be found in Chapter 5.

It should be noted that when portions of the electrical system are serviced, the cable should be disconnected from the negative battery terminal to prevent electrical shorts and/or fires.

2 Electrical troubleshooting - general information

Refer to illustrations 2.5a, 2.5b, 2.6 and 2.9

A typical electrical circuit consists of an electrical component, any switches, relays, motors, fuses, fusible links or circuit breakers related to that component and the wiring and connectors that link the component to both the battery and the chassis. To help you pinpoint an electrical circuit problem, wiring diagrams are included at the end of this Chapter.

Before tackling any troublesome electrical circuit, first study the appropriate wiring diagrams to get a complete understanding of what makes up that individual circuit.

Trouble spots, for instance, can often be narrowed down by noting if other components related to the circuit are operating properly. If several components or circuits fail at one time, chances are the problem is in a fuse or ground connection, because several circuits are often routed through the same fuse and ground connections.

Electrical problems usually stem from simple causes, such as loose or corroded connections, a blown fuse, a melted fusible link or a failed relay. Visually inspect the condition of all fuses, wires and connections in a problem circuit before troubleshooting the circuit.

If test equipment and instruments are going to be utilized, use the diagrams to plan

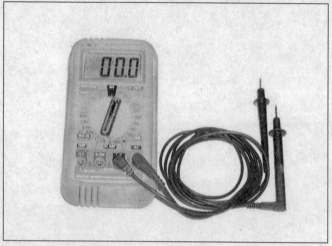

2.5a The most useful tool for electrical troubleshooting is a digital multimeter that can check volts, amps, and test continuity

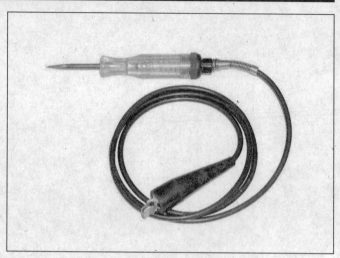

2.5b A simple test light is a very handy tool for testing voltage

ahead of time where you will make the necessary connections in order to accurately pinpoint the trouble spot.

The basic tools needed for electrical troubleshooting include a circuit tester or voltmeter (a 12-volt bulb with a set of test leads can also be used), a continuity tester, which includes a bulb, battery and set of test leads, and a jumper wire, preferably with a circuit breaker incorporated, which can be used to bypass electrical components **(see illustrations)**. Before attempting to locate a problem with test instruments, use the wiring diagram(s) to decide where to make the connections.

Voltage checks

Voltage checks should be performed if a circuit is not functioning properly. Connect one lead of a circuit tester to either the negative battery terminal or a known good ground. Connect the other lead to a connector in the circuit being tested, preferably nearest to the battery or fuse **(see illustration)**. If the bulb of the tester lights, voltage is present, which means that the part of the circuit between the connector and the battery is problem free. Continue checking the rest of the circuit in the same fashion. When you reach a point at which no voltage is present, the problem lies between that point and the last test point with voltage. Most of the time the problem can be traced to a loose connection. **Note:** *Keep in mind that some circuits receive voltage only when the ignition key is in the Accessory or Run position.*

Finding a short

One method of finding shorts in a live circuit is to remove the fuse and connect a test light in place of the fuse terminals (fabricate two jumper wires with small spade terminals, plug the jumper wires into the fuse box and connect the test light). There should be voltage present in the circuit. Move the suspected wiring harness from side-to-side while watch-

ing the test light. If the bulb goes off, there is a short to ground somewhere in that area, probably where the insulation has rubbed through.

Ground check

Perform a ground test to check whether a component is properly grounded. Disconnect the battery and connect one lead of a continuity tester or multimeter (set to the ohms scale), to a known good ground. Connect the other lead to the wire or ground connection being tested. If the resistance is low (less than 5 ohms), the ground is good. If the bulb on a self-powered test light does not go on, the ground is not good.
Continuity check

A continuity check is done to determine if there are any breaks in a circuit - if it is passing electricity properly. With the circuit off (no power in the circuit), a self-powered continuity tester or multimeter can be used to check the circuit. Connect the test leads to both ends of the circuit (or to the "power" end and a good ground), and if the test light comes on the

circuit is passing current properly **(see illustration)**. If the resistance is low (less than 5 ohms), there is continuity; if the reading is 10,000 ohms or higher, there is a break somewhere in the circuit. The same procedure can be used to test a switch, by connecting the continuity tester to the switch terminals. With the switch turned On, the test light should come on (or low resistance should be indicated on a meter).

Finding an open circuit

When diagnosing for possible open circuits, it is often difficult to locate them by sight because the connectors hide oxidation or terminal misalignment. Merely wiggling a connector on a sensor or in the wiring harness may correct the open circuit condition. Remember this when an open circuit is indicated when troubleshooting a circuit. Intermittent problems may also be caused by oxidized or loose connections.

Electrical troubleshooting is simple if you keep in mind that all electrical circuits

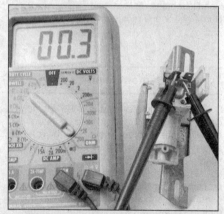

2.6 In use, a basic test light's lead is clipped to a known good ground, then the pointed probe can test connectors, wires or electrical sockets - if the bulb lights, the circuit being tested has battery voltage

2.9 With a multimeter set to the ohms scale, resistance can be checked across two terminals - when checking for continuity, a low reading indicates continuity, a high reading or infinity indicates lack of continuity

3.1a The interior fuse box is located on the dashboard, to the left of the steering column (2001 and later model shown)

are basically electricity running from the battery, through the wires, switches, relays, fuses and fusible links to each electrical component (light bulb, motor, etc.) and to ground, from which it is passed back to the battery. Any electrical problem is an interruption in the flow of electricity to and from the battery.

Connectors

Most electrical connections on these vehicles are made with multiwire plastic connectors. The mating halves of many connectors are secured with locking clips molded into the plastic connector shells. The mating halves of large connectors, such as some of those under the instrument panel, are held together by a bolt through the center of the connector.

To separate a connector with locking clips, use a small screwdriver to pry the clips apart carefully, then separate the connector halves. Pull only on the shell, never pull on the wiring harness as you may damage the individual wires and terminals inside the connectors. Look at the connector closely before trying to separate the halves. Often the

locking clips are engaged in a way that is not immediately clear. Additionally, many connectors have more than one set of clips.

Each pair of connector terminals has a male half and a female half. When you look at the end view of a connector in a diagram, be sure to understand whether the view shows the harness side or the component side of the connector. Connector halves are mirror images of each other, and a terminal shown on the right side end-view of one half will be on the left side end view of the other half.

3   Fuses and fusible links - general information

Fuses

Refer to illustrations 3.1a, 3.1b and 3.3

The electrical circuits of the vehicle are protected by a combination of fuses, circuit breakers and fusible links. Fuse blocks are located under the instrument panel and in the engine compartment depending on the model year of the vehicle **(see illustrations)**.

Each of the fuses is designed to protect a specific circuit, and the various circuits are identified on the fuse panel cover.

Miniaturized fuses are employed in the fuse blocks. These compact fuses, with blade terminal design, allow fingertip removal and replacement. If an electrical component fails, always check the fuse first. The best way to check a fuse is with a test light. Check for power at the exposed terminal tips of each fuse. If power is present on one side of the fuse but not the other, the fuse is blown. A blown fuse can also be confirmed by visually inspecting it **(see illustration)**.

Be sure to replace blown fuses with the correct type. Fuses of different ratings are physically interchangeable, but only fuses of the proper rating should be used. Replacing a fuse with one of a higher or lower value than specified is not recommended. Each electrical circuit needs a specific amount of protection.

The amperage value of each fuse is molded into the fuse body.

If the replacement fuse immediately fails, don't replace it again until the cause of the problem is isolated and corrected. In most cases, this will be a short circuit in the wiring caused by a broken or deteriorated wire.

Fusible links

Some circuits are protected by fusible links. The links are used in circuits which are not ordinarily fused, such as the ignition circuit, or which carry high current.

Cartridge type fusible links are located in the engine compartment fusible link box and are similar to a large fuse. After disconnecting the negative battery cable, simply unplug and replace a fusible link of the same amperage.

2000 and earlier models are equipped with a fusible link box located near the battery. 2001 and later models locate the fusible link box near the right side strut tower in the engine compartment.

4   Circuit breakers - general information

Circuit breakers protect certain circuits, such as the power windows or heated seats. Depending on the vehicle's accessories, there may be one or two circuit breakers, located in the fuse/relay box in the engine compartment **(see illustration 3.1b)**.

Because the circuit breakers reset automatically, an electrical overload in a circuit-breaker-protected system will cause the circuit to fail momentarily, then come back on. If the circuit does not come back on, check it immediately.

For a basic check, pull the circuit breaker up out of its socket on the fuse panel, but just far enough to probe with a voltmeter. The breaker should still contact the sockets.

With the voltmeter negative lead on a good chassis ground, touch each end prong

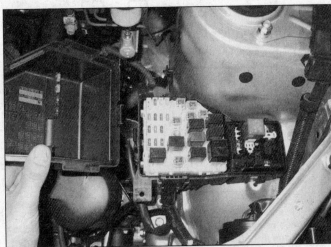

3.1b The main engine compartment fuse/relay box on a 2001 and later model

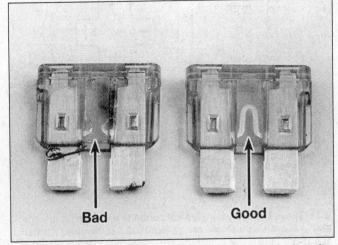

3.3 When a fuse blows, the element between the terminals melts

5.1a The covers of the engine compartment relay boxes have a printed key to identify the relays

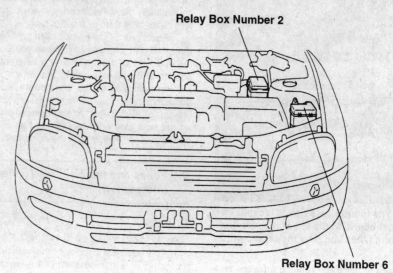

Relay Box Number 2

Relay Box Number 6

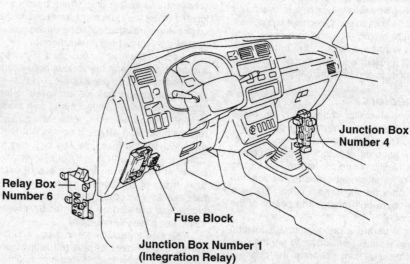

Relay Box Number 6

Junction Box Number 4

Fuse Block

Junction Box Number 1 (Integration Relay)

5.1b Relay box and junction box locations on 2000 and earlier models

of the circuit breaker with the positive meter probe. There should be battery voltage at each end. If there is battery voltage only at one end, the circuit breaker must be replaced.

Some circuit breakers must be reset manually.

5   Relays - general information and testing

General information

Refer to illustrations 5.1a and 5.1b

1   Several electrical accessories in the vehicle, such as the fuel injection system, horns, starter, and fog lamps use relays to transmit the electrical signal to the component. Relays use a low-current circuit (the control circuit) to open and close a high-current circuit (the power circuit). If the relay is defective, that component will not operate properly. Most relays are mounted in the engine compartment fuse/relay boxes, with some special-

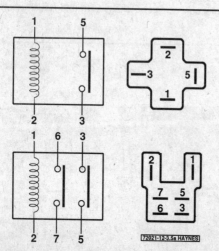

5.3a These two relays are typical normally open types; the one above completes a single circuit (terminal 5 to terminal 3) when energized - the lower relay type completes two circuits (6 and 7, and 3 and 5) when energized

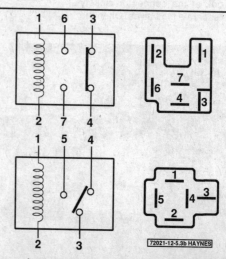

5.3b These relays are normally closed types, where current flows though one circuit until the relay is energized, which interrupts that circuit and completes the second circuit

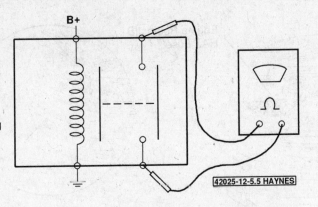

5.6 To test a typical four-terminal normally open relay, connect an ohmmeter to the two terminals of the power circuit - the meter should indicate continuity with the relay energized and no continuity with the relay not energized

ized relays located above the interior fuse box under the dash (see illustrations). If a faulty relay is suspected, it can be removed and tested using the procedure below or by a dealer service department or a repair shop. Defective relays must be replaced as a unit.

Testing

Refer to illustrations 5.3a, 5.3b and 5.6

2   Refer to the wiring diagrams for the circuit to determine the proper connections for the relay you're testing. If you can't determine the correct connection from the wiring diagrams, however, you may be able to determine the test connections from the information that follows.

3   There are four basic types of relays used on these models (see illustrations). Some are normally open type and some normally closed, while others include a circuit of each type.

4   On most relays, two of the terminals are the relay control circuit (they connect to the relay coil which, when energized, closes the large contacts to complete the circuit). The other terminals are the power circuit (they are connected together within the relay when the control-circuit coil is energized).

5   Some relays may be marked as an aid to help you determine which terminals are the control circuit and which are the power circuit. If the relay is not marked, refer to the wiring diagrams at the end of this Chapter to determine the proper hook-ups for the relay you're testing.

6   To test a relay, connect an ohmmeter across the two terminals of the power circuit, continuity should not be indicated (see illustration). Now connect a fused jumper wire between one of the two control circuit terminals and the positive battery terminal. Connect another jumper wire between the other control circuit terminal and ground. When the connections are made, the relay should click and continuity should be indicated on the meter. On some relays, polarity may be critical, so, if the relay doesn't click, try swapping the jumper wires on the control circuit terminals.

7   If the relay fails the above test, replace it.

6   Turn signal and hazard flasher - check and replacement

Refer to illustrations 6.4a and 6.4b

Warning: *The models covered by this manual are equipped with Supplemental Restraint Systems (SRS), more commonly known as airbags. Always disable the airbag system before working in the vicinity of any airbag system components to avoid the possibility of accidental deployment of the airbags, which could cause personal injury (see Section 26).*

1   The turn signal and hazard flasher is a single combination unit.

2   When the flasher unit is functioning properly, an audible click can be heard during its operation. If the turn signals fail on one side or the other and the flasher unit does not make its characteristic clicking sound, or if a bulb on one side of the vehicle flashes much faster than normal but the bulb at the other end of the vehicle (on the same side) doesn't light at all, a faulty turn signal bulb may be indicated.

3   If both turn signals fail to blink, the problem may be due to a blown fuse, a faulty flasher unit, a defective switch or a loose or open connection. If a quick check of the fuse box indicates that the turn signal fuse has blown, check the wiring for a short before installing a new fuse.

4   To replace the flasher, disconnect the electrical connector and remove the flasher unit from its mounting bracket located under the instrument panel to the right of the steering column (see illustrations).

5   Make sure that the replacement unit is identical to the original. Compare the old one to the new one before installing it.

6   Installation is the reverse of removal.

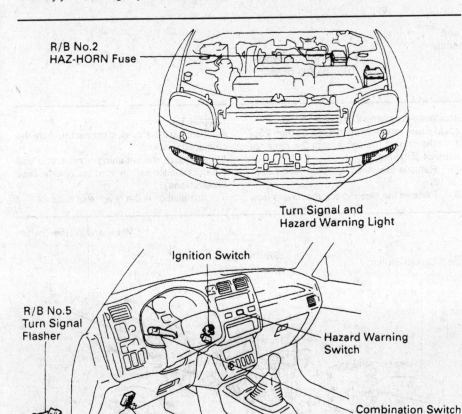

6.4a Location of the turn signal and hazard flasher on 2000 and earlier models

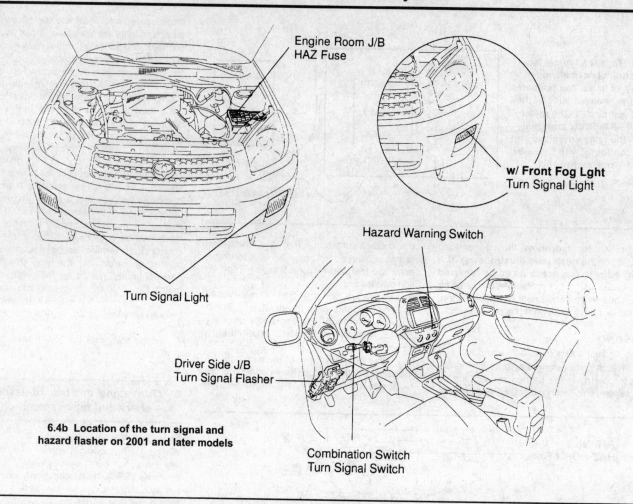

Engine Room J/B
HAZ Fuse

w/ Front Fog Lght
Turn Signal Light

Hazard Warning Switch

Turn Signal Light

Driver Side J/B
Turn Signal Flasher

6.4b Location of the turn signal and hazard flasher on 2001 and later models

Combination Switch
Turn Signal Switch

---

7   Steering column switches - replacement

Refer to illustrations 7.5a and 7.5b
Warning: *The models covered by this manual are equipped with Supplemental Restraint Systems (SRS), more commonly known as airbags. Always disable the airbag system before working in the vicinity of any airbag system components to avoid the possibility of* accidental deployment of the airbag(s), which could cause personal injury (see Section 26).

1   Disconnect the cable from the negative terminal of the battery.
2   Remove the steering wheel (see Chapter 10).
3   Remove the steering column covers (see Chapter 11).
4   Unplug the electrical connectors from the combination switch.
5   Remove the retaining screws and pull the combination switch from the column **(see illustrations)**.
6   Installation is the reverse of removal.

7.5a Combination switch retaining screws (arrows) - turn signal/headlight switch shown, wiper/washer switch similar

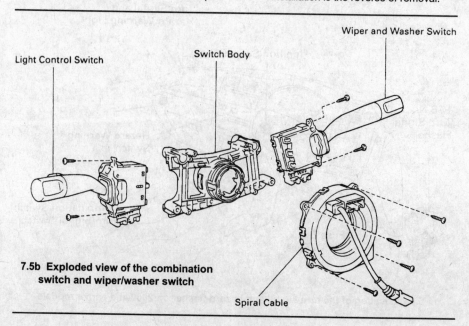

Light Control Switch

Switch Body

Wiper and Washer Switch

7.5b Exploded view of the combination switch and wiper/washer switch

Spiral Cable

8 Ignition switch and key lock cylinder - replacement

Warning: *The models covered by this manual are equipped with Supplemental Restraint Systems (SRS), more commonly known as airbags. Always disable the airbag system before working in the vicinity of any airbag system components to avoid the possibility of accidental deployment of the airbag(s), which could cause personal injury (see Section 26).*
Note: *These models are equipped with an integration relay (see illustration 5.1b). The integration relay works in conjunction with the ignition switch to activate the key unlock warning system and anti-theft system.*

1   Disconnect the cable from the negative terminal of the battery.
2   Place the ignition key in the ACC position.
3   Remove the steering wheel (see Chapter 10).
4   Remove the steering column covers (see Chapter 11).
5   Remove the steering column switches (see Section 7).

Ignition switch

Refer to illustration 8.7
6   Unplug the ignition switch wiring harness connectors.
7   Remove the switch retaining screws **(see illustration)** then pull the switch from the lock cylinder housing.
8   Installation is reverse of the removal.

Lock cylinder

Refer to illustration 8.9
9   Use a small screwdriver or punch to depress the lock cylinder retaining pin **(see illustration).**
10   Pull straight out on the lock cylinder assembly to remove it from the housing.
11   To install the lock cylinder, depress the retaining pin and guide the lock cylinder into the housing until the retaining pin extends itself back into the locating hole in the housing.

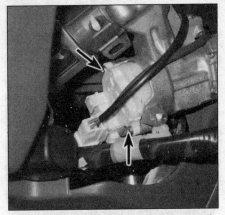

8.7 Detach the retaining screws (arrows) to remove the ignition switch from the steering column housing

12   The remainder of the installation is the reverse of removal.

9 Instrument panel switches - replacement

Warning: *The models covered by this manual are equipped with Supplemental Restraint Systems (SRS), more commonly known as airbags. Always disable the airbag system before working in the vicinity of any airbag system components to avoid the possibility of accidental deployment of the airbag(s), which could cause personal injury (see Section 26).*

Hazard warning switch

2000 and earlier models

Refer to illustrations 9.1 and 9.2
1   Carefully pry the switch **(see illustration)** from the center cluster finish panel (see Chapter 11).
2   Disconnect the electrical connector at the rear of the switch **(see illustration).** Depress the tab and remove the switch from the housing.
3   Installation is the reverse of the removal procedure.

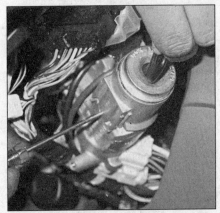

8.9 With the lock cylinder in the ACC position, depress the retaining pin with a small screwdriver, then pull straight out to remove the lock cylinder

9.1 Carefully pry the switch housing out using a flat-bladed screwdriver (arrow)

2001 and later models

Refer to illustration 9.5
4   Carefully remove the center cluster finish panel (see Chapter 11) from the instrument panel.
5   Remove the mounting bolts from the heater control assembly **(see illustration)** and pull the assembly out until you can disconnect the electrical connector at the rear of

9.2 Remove the hazard switch and disconnect the harness connector

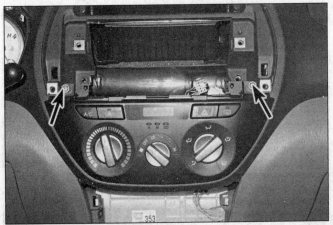

9.5 Remove the mounting bolts (arrows) from the heater control assembly

the switch. Depress the tab and remove the switch from the bezel.

6   Installation is the reverse of the removal procedure.

Power mirror control switch

2000 and earlier models

Refer to illustration 9.8

7   Carefully pry the switch from the instrument panel (see Chapter 11).

8   Disconnect the electrical connector **(see illustration)** and remove the switch.

9   Installation of the is the reverse of the removal procedure.

2001 and later models

Refer to illustration 9.10

10   Carefully pry the number one switch hole base from the instrument panel **(see illustration)**, using tape on the screwdriver tip to prevent scratching the instrument panel.

11   Disconnect the electrical connector and remove the switch.

12   Installation of the is the reverse of the removal procedure.

Defogger control switch

2000 and earlier models

13   Carefully pry the switch from the center cluster finish panel (see Chapter 11).

14   Disconnect the electrical connector at the rear of the switch. Depress the tab and remove the switch from the housing.

15   Installation is the reverse of the removal procedure.

2001 and later models

16   Carefully remove the center cluster finish panel (see Chapter 11) from the instrument panel.

17   Remove the mounting bolts from the heater control assembly **(see illustration 9.5)** and pull the assembly out until you can disconnect the electrical connector at the rear of the switch. Depress the tab and remove the switch from the bezel.

18   Installation is the reverse of the removal procedure.

9.8 Remove the power mirror switch from the instrument panel

Instrument panel light control switch

2000 and earlier models

19   Remove the instrument panel (see Chapter 11).

20   Disconnect the electrical connector and remove the switch.

21   Installation is the reverse of the removal procedure.

2001 and later models

Refer to illustration 9.23

22   Carefully pry the number one switch hole base from the instrument panel **(see illustration 9.10)**, using tape on the screwdriver tip to prevent scratching the instrument panel.

23   Disconnect the electrical connector **(see illustration)** and remove the switch.

24   Installation is the reverse of the removal procedure.

10   Instrument cluster - removal and installation

Refer to illustrations 10.3a and 10.3b
Warning: *The models covered by this manual are equipped with Supplemental Restraint*

9.10 Pry the number one switch hole base from the instrument panel

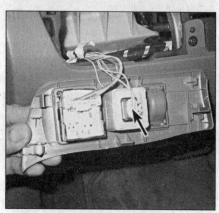

9.23 Disconnect the instrument panel light control switch harness

Systems (SRS), more commonly known as airbags. Always disable the airbag system before working in the vicinity of any airbag system components to avoid the possibility of accidental deployment of the airbag(s), which could cause personal injury (see Section 26).

1   Disconnect the negative battery cable.

2   Remove the instrument cluster trim panel (see Chapter 11).

3   Remove the cluster mounting screws **(see illustrations)** and pull the instrument cluster towards the steering wheel.

10.3a Remove the instrument cluster mounting screws (2000 and earlier models shown) . . .

10.3b . . . then guide the cluster out from between the instrument panel and steering wheel (2001 and later models shown)

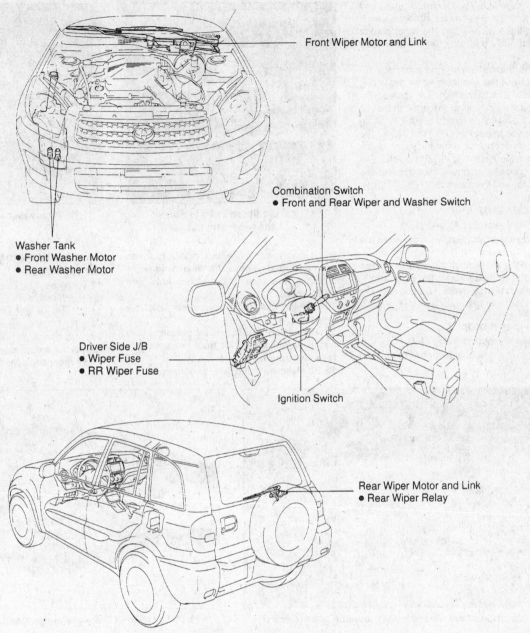

11.2 Details of a typical front and rear wiper motor system

4   Disconnect any electrical connectors that would interfere with removal.
5   Cover the steering column with a cloth to protect the trim covers, then remove the instrument cluster from the vehicle.
6   Installation is the reverse of removal.

11 Wiper motor - check and replacement

Wiper motor circuit check

Refer to illustration 11.2
Note: *Refer to the wiring diagrams for wire colors and locations in the following checks. When checking for voltage, probe a grounded*

12-volt test light to each terminal at a connector until it lights; this verifies voltage (power) at the terminal. If the following checks fail to locate the problem, have the system diagnosed by a dealer service department or other properly equipped repair facility.
1   If the wipers work slowly, make sure the battery is in good condition and has a strong charge (see Chapter 5). If the battery is in good condition, remove the wiper motor (see below) and operate the wiper arms by hand. Check for binding linkage and pivots. Lubricate or repair the linkage or pivots as necessary. Reinstall the wiper motor. If the wipers still operate slowly, check for loose or corroded connections, especially the ground connection. If all connections look OK, replace the motor.

2   If the wipers fail to operate when activated, check the fuse **(see illustration)**. If the fuse is OK, connect a jumper wire between the wiper motor's ground terminal and ground, then retest. If the motor works now, repair the ground connection. If the motor still doesn't work, turn the wiper switch to the HI position and check for voltage at the motor. **Note:** *The cowl cover will have to be removed (see Chapter 11) to access the electrical connector.*
3   If there's voltage at the connector, remove the motor and check it off the vehicle with fused jumper wires from the battery. If the motor now works, check for binding linkage (see Step 1). If the motor still doesn't work, replace it. If there's no voltage to the motor, check for voltage at the wiper control relays. If

there's voltage at the wiper control relays and no voltage at the wiper motor, have the switch tested. If the switch is OK, the wiper control relay is probably bad. See Section 5 for relay testing.

4   If the interval (delay) function is inoperative, check the continuity of all the wiring between the switch and wiper control module.

5   If the wipers stop at the position they're in when the switch is turned off (fail to park), check for voltage at the park feed wire of the wiper motor connector when the wiper switch is OFF but the ignition is ON. If no voltage is present, check for an open circuit between the wiper motor and the fuse panel.

Replacement

Refer to illustrations 11.7a and 11.7b

6   Disconnect the negative cable from the battery.

7   Mark the positions of the wiper arm(s) on the windshield, then remove the wiper arm(s) **(see illustrations)**. **Note:** *Disconnect the washer hose from the wiper arm.*

Front wiper motor

Refer to illustrations 11.9 and 11.11

8   Remove the windshield cowl cover (see Chapter 11).

11.7a Lift the end cap to access the wiper arm nut

11.7b Rear wiper arm mounting details

9   Disconnect the wiper motor harness connector and remove the windshield wiper motor/linkage assembly mounting nuts **(see illustration)**.

10   Lift the windshield wiper motor assembly from the cowl area.

11   Remove the wiper motor mounting nuts and separate the motor from the assembly **(see illustration)**.

12   Installation is the reverse of removal.

Rear wiper motor

Refer to illustration 11.15

13   Remove the back door trim board from the hatch area (see Chapter 11).

14   Remove the service hole cover (see Chapter 11), if equipped.

15   Disconnect the wiper motor harness connector and remove the windshield wiper motor mounting bolts **(see illustration)**.

11.9 Location of the wiper linkage mounting bolts (arrows)

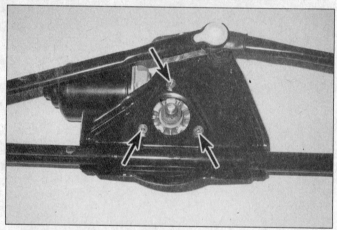

11.11 Location of the wiper motor mounting bolts (arrows)

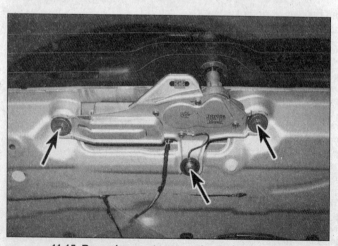

11.15 Rear wiper motor mounting bolts (arrows)

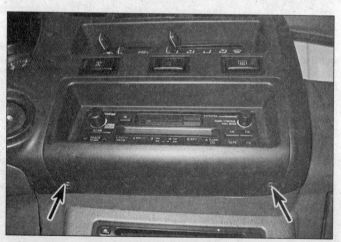

12.2 Remove the center cluster finish panel mounting screws (arrows) (2000 and earlier models)

12.3a Remove the radio mounting screws (arrows)

12.3b Pull the radio forward, then disconnect the antenna lead and the electrical connector

16   Lift the windshield wiper motor assembly from the hatch area.

17   Installation is the reverse of removal.

12   Radio and speakers - removal and installation

Warning: *The models covered by this manual are equipped with Supplemental Restraint Systems (SRS), more commonly known as airbags. Always disable the airbag system before working in the vicinity of any airbag system components to avoid the possibility of accidental deployment of the airbag(s), which could cause personal injury (see Section 26).*

1   Disconnect the negative battery cable.

Radio

Refer to illustrations 12.2, 12.3a and 12.3b

2   Access the radio by removing the dash panel surrounding the radio.

a) *On 2000 and earlier models, remove the center cluster finish panel* (**see illustration**).

b) *On 2001 and later models, remove the instrument cluster trim panel (see Chapter 11).*

3   Remove the retaining screws and pull the radio outward to access the backside, then disconnect the electrical connectors and the antenna lead (**see illustrations**).

4   Installation is the reverse of removal.

Door speakers

Refer to illustration 12.6

5   Remove the door trim panel (see Chapter 11). All models have speakers in both front and rear doors. Rear door speakers are mounted similarly to the front door speakers.

6   Remove the speaker rivets. Drill out the rivets using the correct size drill bit. Disconnect the electrical connector and remove the speaker from the vehicle (**see illustration**).

7   Installation is the reverse of removal.

Tweeters

Refer to illustration 12.8

8   In addition to the standard door and rear speakers, some models are equipped with tweeters for improved high-range sound

(**see illustration**). Mounted in the front doors just ahead of the window glass, they can be removed by drilling out the rivets using the correct size drill bit. Pull the tweeter out and disconnect the electrical connector.

9   Installation is the reverse of removal.

13   Antenna - replacement

Warning: *The models covered by this manual are equipped with Supplemental Restraint Systems (SRS), more commonly known as airbags. Always disable the airbag system before working in the vicinity of any airbag system components to avoid the possibility of accidental deployment of the airbag(s), which could cause personal injury (see Section 26).*

Removal

Fixed antenna

Refer to illustrations 13.1a, 13.1b and 13.1c

1   Separate the antenna from the vehicle body.

a) *On top-mounted antennas, remove the mounting screws* (**see illustration**).

12.6 Remove the speaker rivets (arrows) and disconnect the electrical connector to remove the speaker from the vehicle

12.8 Location of the tweeter (arrow) near front door mirror mount

13.1a Remove the mounting screws (arrows) on top-mounted antennas

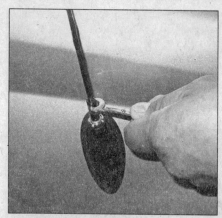

13.1b On fender-mounted antennas, unscrew the antenna rod from the base

13.1c Remove the antenna mount locking nut

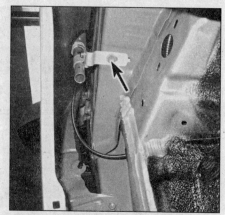

13.7 Remove the antenna bolt (arrow) working in the fenderwell

b) *On fender-mounted antennas, unscrew the antenna rod* (see illustration) *and remove the antenna mount locking nut* (see illustration).

Power antenna

2   With the ignition switch in the LOCK position, loosen the antenna mount locking nut.

3   Press the AM buttons on the radio while simultaneously turning the ignition switch to the ACC position. The antenna will extend fully and be released from the antenna motor.

4   Remove the antenna rod from the motor assembly.

All models

Refer to illustrations 13.7, 13.9 and 13.10

5   On fender-mounted antennas, raise the vehicle and secure it on jackstands.

6   On fender-mounted antennas, remove the front wheel.

7   Remove the antenna assembly from the vehicle body.

a) *On top-mounted antennas, remove the driver's side door pillar trim to access the antenna cable.*

b) *On fender-mounted antennas, working in the fenderwell area, remove the antenna mounting bolt* (see illustration).

8   On fender-mounted antennas, push the

antenna mount into the fender to separate the assembly from the grommet.

9   Remove the radio (see Section 12) and disconnect the antenna cable **(see illustration)**.

10   On fender mounted antennas, remove the glovebox (see Chapter 11) and pull the cable from behind the dash **(see illustration)**.

11   On automatic antennas, disconnect the antenna cable from the motor.

Installation

Fixed antenna

12   On top-mounted antennas, Install the antenna onto the vehicle body and install the mounting bolts.

13   On fender-mounted antennas, install the mounting bolt inside the fenderwell and the antenna mount locking nut.

14   On fender-mounted antennas, install the antenna rod.

Power antenna

Refer to illustration 13.16

15   Install the antenna into the fenderwell area and install the mounting bolt.

16   Install the antenna rod into the mast assembly with the cable teeth facing the front of the vehicle **(see illustration)**.

17   Turn the ignition to the LOCK position to

retract the antenna rod.

18   Install the antenna mount locking nut and carefully tighten the nut until the antenna rod is seated fully inside the mast assembly.

All models

19   Working in the dash area, feed the antenna cable behind the glovebox and into the radio.

20   Install the radio (see Section 12).

21   Install the glovebox (see Chapter 11).

22   Installation is the reverse of removal.

14   Rear window defogger - check and repair

1   The rear window defogger consists of a number of horizontal elements baked onto the glass surface.

2   Small breaks in the element can be repaired without removing the rear window.

Check

Refer to illustrations 14.4, 14.5 and 14.7

3   Turn the ignition switch and defogger system switches to the ON position. Using a voltmeter, place the positive probe against the defogger grid positive terminal and the negative probe against the ground terminal. If battery voltage is not indicated, check the fuse, defogger switch and related wiring. If voltage is indicated, but all or part of the defogger doesn't heat, proceed with the following tests.

13.9 Disconnect the antenna cable from the radio

13.10 Working behind the glovebox, feed the antenna cable through the dash area

13.16 The cable teeth must face toward the front of the vehicle

14.4 When measuring the voltage at the rear window defogger grid, wrap a piece of aluminum foil around the positive probe of the voltmeter and press the foil against the wire with your finger

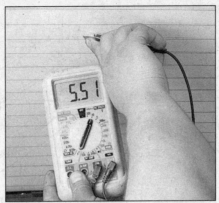

14.5 To determine if a heating element has broken, check the voltage at the center of each element - if the voltage is 5 or 6-volts, the element is unbroken - if the voltage is 10 or 12-volts, the element is broken between the center and the ground side - if there is no voltage, the element is broken between the center and the positive side

14.7 To find the break, place the voltmeter negative lead against the defogger ground terminal, place the voltmeter positive lead with the foil strip against the heating element at the positive terminal end and slide it toward the negative terminal end - the point at which the voltmeter reading changes abruptly is the point at which the element is broken

4   When measuring voltage during the next two tests, wrap a piece of aluminum foil around the tip of the voltmeter positive probe and press the foil against the heating element with your finger **(see illustration)**. Place the negative probe on the defogger grid ground terminal.

5   Check the voltage at the center of each heating element **(see illustration)**. If the voltage is 5 or 6-volts, the element is okay (there is no break). If the voltage is 0-volts, the element is broken between the center of the element and the positive end. If the voltage is 10 to 12-volts the element is broken between the center of the element and ground. Check each heating element.

6   Connect the negative lead to a good body ground. The reading should stay the same. If it doesn't, the ground connection is bad.

7   To find the break, place the voltmeter negative probe against the defogger ground terminal. Place the voltmeter positive probe with the foil strip against the heating element at the positive terminal end and slide it toward the negative terminal end. The point at which the voltmeter deflects from several volts to

zero is the point at which the heating element is broken **(see illustration)**.

Repair

Refer to illustration 14.13

8   Repair the break in the element using a repair kit specifically recommended for this purpose, available at most auto parts stores. Included in this kit is plastic conductive epoxy.

9   Prior to repairing a break, turn off the system and allow it to cool off for a few minutes.

10   Lightly buff the element area with fine steel wool, then clean it thoroughly with rubbing alcohol.

11   Use masking tape to mask off the area being repaired.

12   Thoroughly mix the epoxy, following the instructions provided with the repair kit.

13   Apply the epoxy material to the slit in the masking tape, overlapping the undamaged area about 3/4-inch on either end **(see illustration)**.

14   Allow the repair to cure for 24 hours before removing the tape and using the system.

15 Headlight bulb - replacement

Refer to illustrations 15.2 and 15.3

Warning: *Halogen gas filled bulbs are under pressure and may shatter if the surface is scratched or the bulb is dropped. Wear eye protection and handle the bulbs carefully, grasping only the base whenever possible. Do not touch the surface of the bulb with your fingers because the oil from your skin could cause it to overheat and fail prematurely. If you do touch the bulb surface, clean it with rubbing alcohol.*

1   Reach behind the headlight assembly and unplug the electrical connector.

2   Remove the rubber insulator **(see illustration)**.

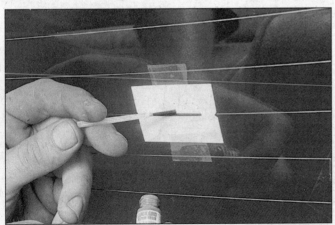

14.13 To use a defogger repair kit, apply masking tape to the inside of the window at the damaged area, then brush on the special conductive coating

15.2 Remove the rubber insulator from the back of the headlight housing

15.3 Rotate bulbholder counterclockwise - remove the bulb from the holder to replace it

3   Grasp the bulb holder securely and rotate it counterclockwise to remove it from the housing **(see illustration)**.
4   Pull straight out on the bulb to remove from it from the bulb holder. Without touching the glass with your bare fingers, insert the new bulb assembly into the headlight housing.
5   Plug in the electrical connector.

16   Headlights - adjustment

Refer to illustrations 16.1, 16.2 and 16.4
Note: *The headlights must be aimed correctly. If adjusted incorrectly they could blind the driver of an oncoming vehicle and cause a serious accident or seriously reduce your ability to see the road. The headlights should be checked for proper aim every 12 months and any time a new headlight is installed or front end body work is performed. It should be emphasized that the following procedure is only an interim step which will provide temporary adjustment until the headlights can be adjusted by a properly equipped shop.*

1996 and 1997 models
1   These models have two adjustment screws located on the back of each headlight housing **(see illustration)**.

16.2 Use a Phillips screwdriver to rotate the gear-drive mechanism on 2001 and later models

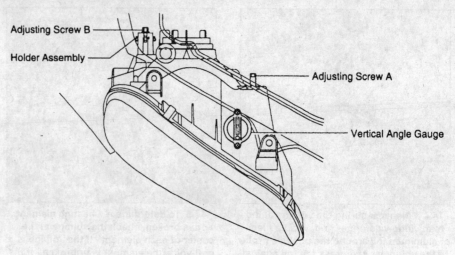

16.1 Location of the headlight adjustment screws on 1996 and 1997 models

1998 and later models
2   These models have one adjustment screw located on the back of each headlight housing. On 1998 through 2000 models a wrench or socket can be used to turn the screw. On 2001 and later models, insert a Phillips screwdriver into the gear-drive mechanism to turn the screw **(see illustration)**.

All models
3   There are several methods of adjusting the headlights. The simplest method requires masking tape, a blank wall and a level floor.
4   Position masking tape vertically on the wall in reference to the vehicle centerline and the centerlines of both headlights **(see illustration)**.
5   Position a horizontal tape line in reference to the centerline of all the headlights.
Note: *It may be easier to position the tape on the wall with the vehicle parked only a few inches away.*
6   Adjustment should be made with the

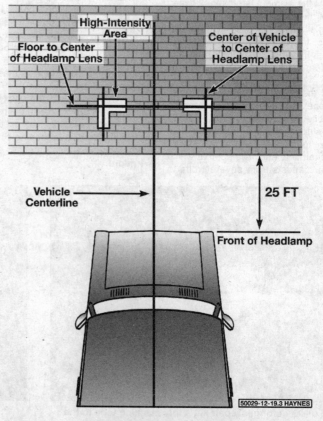

16.4 Headlight adjustment details

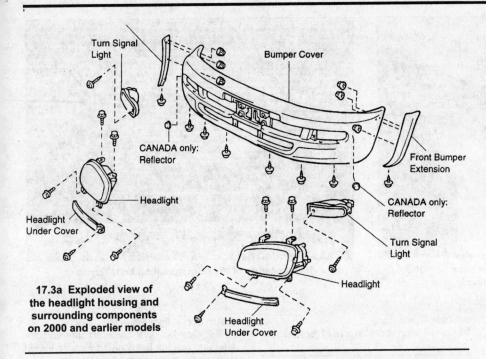

17.3a Exploded view of the headlight housing and surrounding components on 2000 and earlier models

vehicle parked 25 feet from the wall, sitting level, the gas tank half-full and no unusually heavy load in the vehicle.

7   Starting with the low beam adjustment, position the high intensity zone so it is two inches below the horizontal line and two inches to the side of the headlight vertical line, away from oncoming traffic. Adjustment is made by turning the vertical adjusting screw to raise or lower the beam. The horizontal adjusting screw should be used in the same manner to move the beam left or right. **Note:** *1998 and later models are designed to adjust the vertical position only.*

8   With the high beams on, the high intensity zone should be vertically centered with the exact center just below the horizontal line. **Note:** *It may not be possible to position the headlight aim exactly for both high and low beams. If a compromise must be made, keep in mind that the low beams are the most used and have the greatest effect on driver safety.*

9   Have the headlights adjusted by a dealer service department or service station at the earliest opportunity.

17 Headlight housing - replacement

Refer to illustrations 17.3a, 17.3b and 17.3c

Warning: *These vehicles are equipped with halogen gas-filled headlight bulbs which are under pressure and may shatter if the surface is damaged or the bulb is dropped. Wear eye protection and handle the bulbs carefully, grasping only the base whenever possible. Do not touch the surface of the bulb with your fingers because the oil from your skin could cause it to overheat and fail prematurely. If you do touch the bulb surface, clean it with rubbing alcohol.*

1   Remove the headlight bulb (see Section 15).

2   Access the headlight housing lower mounting bolts

a) On 2000 and earlier models, remove the headlight under cover panel.

b) On 2001 and later models, remove the radiator/bumper support panel (see Chapter 11).

3   Remove the retaining bolts, detach the housing and withdraw it from the vehicle **(see illustrations)**.

4   Installation is the reverse of removal. Be sure to check headlight adjustment (see Section 16).

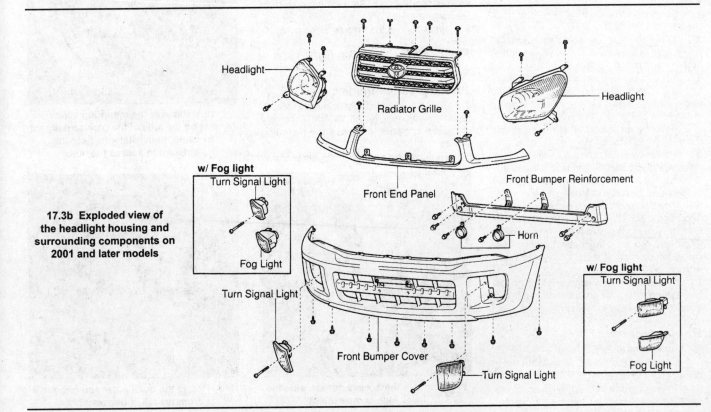

17.3b Exploded view of the headlight housing and surrounding components on 2001 and later models

17.3c Use a screwdriver to separate the clips from the base of the headlight housing

18.9 Location of the horn mounting bolts (arrows)

18 Horn - check and replacement

Warning: *The models covered by this manual are equipped with Supplemental Restraint Systems (SRS), more commonly known as airbags. Always disable the airbag system before working in the vicinity of any airbag system components to avoid the possibility of accidental deployment of the airbag(s), which could cause personal injury (see Section 26).*

Check

Note: *Check the fuses before beginning electrical diagnosis.*
1   Disconnect the electrical connector from the horn.
2   To test the horn, connect battery voltage to the horn terminal with a jumper wire. If the horn doesn't sound, replace it.
3   If the horn does sound, check for voltage at the terminal when the horn button is depressed. If there's voltage at the terminal, check for a bad ground at the horn.
4   If there's no voltage at the horn, check the relay (see Section 5).
5   If the relay is OK, check for voltage to the relay power and control circuits. If either of the circuits is not receiving voltage, inspect the wiring between the relay and the fuse panel.
6   If both relay circuits are receiving voltage, depress the horn button and check the circuit from the relay to the horn button for continuity to ground. If there's no continuity, check the circuit for an open. If there's no open circuit, replace the horn button.
7   If there's continuity to ground through the horn button, check for an open or short in the circuit from the relay to the horn.

Replacement

Refer to illustration 18.9
8   To access the horns, remove the front bumper (see Chapter 11).
9   To replace the horn(s), disconnect the electrical connector and remove the bracket

bolt **(see illustration)**.
10   Installation is the reverse of removal.

19 Bulb replacement

Front park/turn signal lights
Refer to illustration 19.1
1   Remove the screw that secures the side of the park/turn signal light housing **(see illustration)**. Then swing the housing out to access the bulbs located on the backside of the housing.
2   Rotate the bulb holder counterclockwise and pull the bulb out. Remove the bulb from the holder.
3   Installation is the reverse of removal.

Rear tail light/brake light/turn signal

2000 and earlier models
4   To remove the tail light assembly for bulb replacement, remove the taillight assembly under cover panel to access the mounting screws.
5   Remove the two mounting screws and

detach the tail light assembly.
6   Rotate the bulb holders counterclockwise and pull the bulbs out to remove them. Remove the bulb from the holder.
7   Installation is the reverse of removal.

19.1 Remove the mounting screw (arrow) on the side of the park/turn signal housing, then rotate the housing outward to access the bulb

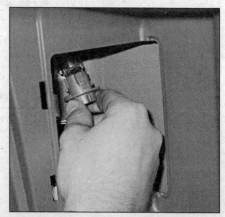

19.8 Remove the access panel inside the trunk side compartment

19.9 Rotate the bulbholder and remove it from the tail light assembly

2001 and later models

Refer to illustrations 19.8 and 19.9

8   To access the tail light bulbs, working in the trunk area, remove the inspection covers **(see illustration)** and remove the access panel.

9   Rotate the bulb holders counterclockwise and pull the bulbs out to remove them **(see illustration)**.

10   Installation is the reverse of removal.

High-mounted brake light

Refer to illustration 19.12

11   Open the trunk and unclip the plastic cover for the high-mounted brake light (see Chapter 11).

12   Twist the bulb holder counterclockwise to remove it, then pull the bulb straight out of the holder **(see illustration)**.

13   Installation is the reverse of removal.

Instrument cluster lights

Refer to illustration 19.14

13   To gain access to the instrument cluster illumination bulbs, the instrument cluster will have to be removed (see Section 10). The bulbs can then be removed and replaced from the rear of the cluster.

14   Rotate the bulb counterclockwise to remove it **(see illustration)**.

15   Installation is the reverse of removal.

Interior light

16   Pry the interior lens off the interior light housing **(see illustration)**.

17   Detach the bulb from the terminals **(see illustration)**. It may be necessary to pry the bulb out - if this is the case, pry only on the ends of the bulb (otherwise the glass may shatter).

18   Installation is the reverse of removal.

License plate light

Refer to illustrations 19.19a and 19.19b

19   Press the two release clips **(see illustration)** and remove the license plate bulb sockets from the trunk lid **(see illustration)**. Replace the bulbs.

20   Installation is the reverse of removal.

Fog light

Refer to illustration 19.22

21   Raise the vehicle and secure it on jackstands.

19.12 Rotate the bulbholder and remove it from the high-mounted brake light assembly

22   Remove the front wheels and remove the inner fender covers to access the fog light assembly **(see illustration)**.

23   Twist the bulbholder from the housing and replace the bulb.

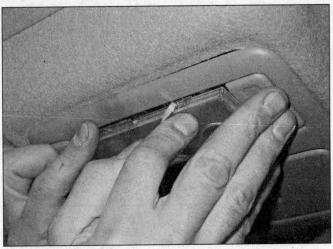

19.16 Carefully pry off the dome light lens using a flat-bladed screwdriver

19.17 Remove the bulb

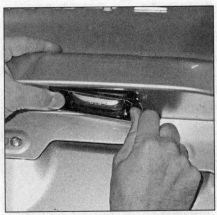

19.19a Press the mounting clips from the side of the license plate bulb sockets

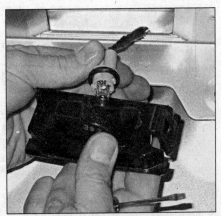

19.19b Rotate the license plate light bulbholder

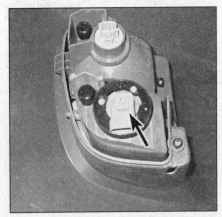

19.22 Location of the fog light bulbholder (arrow)

20 Electric side view mirrors - description

Refer to illustration 20.1

1   Most electric rear view mirrors use two motors to move the glass; one for up and down adjustments and one for left-right adjustments **(see illustration)**.

2   The control switch has a selector portion which sends voltage to the left or right side mirror. With the ignition ON but the engine OFF, roll down the windows and operate the mirror control switch through all functions (left-right and up-down) for both the left and right side mirrors.

3   Listen carefully for the sound of the electric motors running in the mirrors.

4   If the motors can be heard but the mirror glass doesn't move, there's a problem with the drive mechanism inside the mirror. Remove and disassemble the mirror to locate the problem.

5   If the mirrors do not operate and no sound comes from the mirrors, check the fuse (see Chapter 1).

6   If the fuse is OK, remove the mirror control switch from the dashboard. Have the switch continuity checked by a dealership service department or other qualified automobile repair facility.

7   Test the ground connections. Refer to the wiring diagrams at the end of Chapter 12.

8   If the mirror still doesn't work, remove the mirror and check the wires at the mirror for voltage.

9   If there's not voltage in each switch position, check the circuit between the mirror and control switch for opens and shorts.

10   If there's voltage, remove the mirror and test it off the vehicle with jumper wires. Replace the mirror if it fails this test.

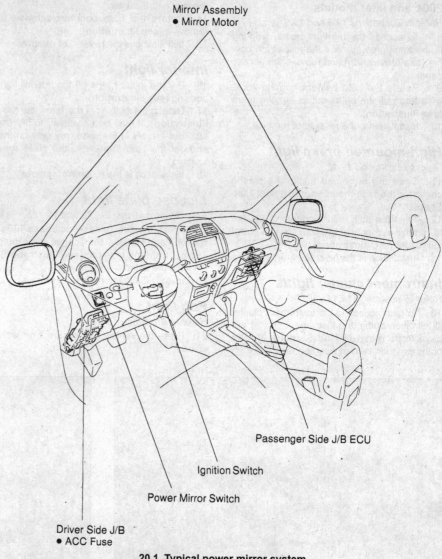

Mirror Assembly
● Mirror Motor

Passenger Side J/B ECU

Ignition Switch

Power Mirror Switch

Driver Side J/B
● ACC Fuse

20.1 Typical power mirror system

21 Cruise control system - description

Refer to illustration 21.5

1   The cruise control system maintains vehicle speed with a electrically-operated motor located in the engine compartment, which is connected to the accelerator pedal by a cable. The system consists of the cruise control unit, brake switch, control switches and vehicle speed sensor. Some features of the system require special testers and diagnostic procedures which are beyond the scope of this manual. Listed below are some general procedures that may be used to locate common problems.

2   Check the fuses (see Section 3).

3   Have an assistant operate the brake lights while you check their operation (voltage from the brake light switch deactivates the cruise control).

4   If the brake lights don't come on or stay on all the time, correct the problem and retest the cruise control.

5   Visually inspect the control cable between cruise control motor and the throttle linkage for free movement **(see illustration)**. Replace it if necessary.

6   The cruise control system uses inputs from the Vehicle Speed Sensor (VSS). Refer to Chapter 6 for more information on the VSS.

7   Test drive the vehicle to determine if the

21.5 Lift the cover from the cruise control actuator to examine the cables

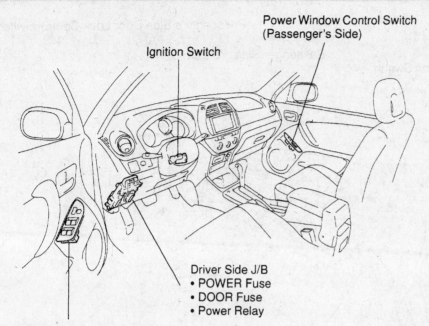

Ignition Switch

Power Window Control Switch (Passenger's Side)

Driver Side J/B
• POWER Fuse
• DOOR Fuse
• Power Relay

Power Window Master Switch

Front Power Window Motor

Rear Power Window Motor

22.1 Typical power window system

addition, many models have a window lock-out switch at the master control switch that, when activated, disables the switches at the rear windows and, sometimes, the switch at the passenger's window also. Always check these items before troubleshooting a window problem.

5   These procedures are general in nature, so if you can't find the problem using them, take the vehicle to a dealer service department or other properly equipped repair facility.

6   If the power windows won't operate, always check the fuse and circuit breaker first.

7   If only the rear windows are inoperative, or if the windows only operate from the master control switch, check the rear window lockout switch for continuity in the unlocked position. Replace it if it doesn't have continuity.

8   Check the wiring between the switches and fuse panel for continuity. Repair the wiring, if necessary.

9   If only one window is inoperative from the master control switch, try the other control switch at the window. **Note:** *This doesn't apply to the driver's door window.*

10   If the same window works from one switch, but not the other, check the switch for continuity. Have the switch checked at a dealer service department or other qualified automobile repair facility.

11   If the switch tests OK, check for a short or open in the circuit between the affected switch and the window motor.

12   If one window is inoperative from both switches, remove the trim panel from the affected door and check for voltage at the switch and at the motor while the switch is operated.

13   If voltage is reaching the motor, disconnect the glass from the regulator (see Chapter 11). Move the window up and down by hand while checking for binding and damage. Also check for binding and damage to the regulator. If the regulator is not damaged and the window moves up and down smoothly, replace the motor. If there's binding or damage, lubricate, repair or replace parts, as necessary.

14   If voltage isn't reaching the motor, check the wiring in the circuit for continuity between the switches and motors. You'll need to consult the wiring diagram for the vehicle. If the circuit is equipped with a relay, check that the relay is grounded properly and receiving voltage.

15   Test the windows after you are done to confirm proper repairs.

cruise control is now working. If it isn't, take it to a dealer service department or an automotive electrical specialist for further diagnosis.

22   Power window system - description

Refer to illustration 22.1

1   The power window system operates electric motors, mounted in the doors, which lower and raise the windows. The system consists of the control switches, relays, the motors, regulators, glass mechanisms and associated wiring **(see illustration)**.

2   The power windows can be lowered and raised from the master control switch by the driver or by remote switches located at the individual windows. Each window has a separate motor that is reversible. The position of the control switch determines the polarity and therefore the direction of operation.

3   The circuit is protected by a fuse and a circuit breaker. Each motor is also equipped with an internal circuit breaker; this prevents one stuck window from disabling the whole system.

4   The power window system will only operate when the ignition switch is ON. In

23   Power door lock system - description

Refer to illustration 23.1

1   A power door lock system operates the door lock actuators mounted in each door **(see illustration)**. The system consists of the switches, actuators, a control unit and associated wiring. Diagnosis can usually be limited to simple checks of the wiring connections

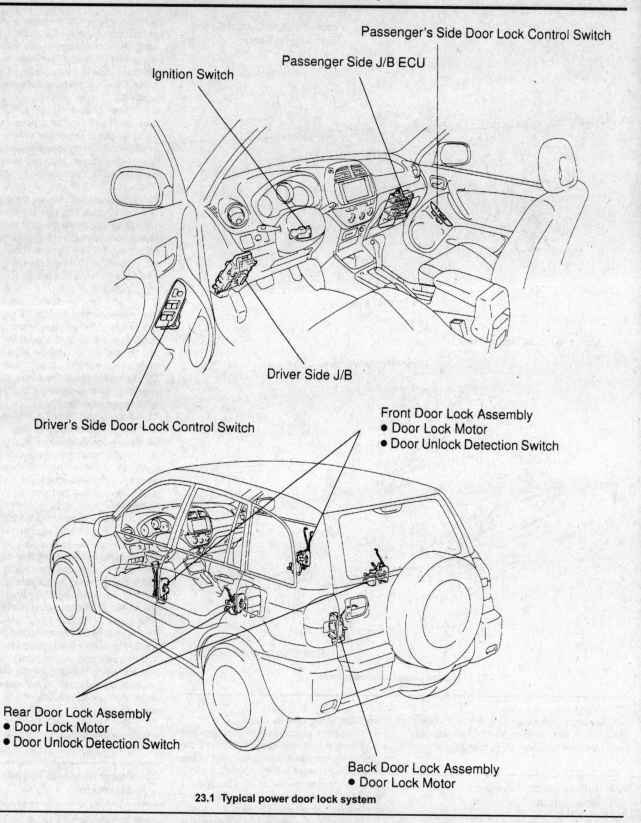

Passenger's Side Door Lock Control Switch

Passenger Side J/B ECU

Ignition Switch

Driver Side J/B

Driver's Side Door Lock Control Switch

Front Door Lock Assembly
● Door Lock Motor
● Door Unlock Detection Switch

Rear Door Lock Assembly
● Door Lock Motor
● Door Unlock Detection Switch

Back Door Lock Assembly
● Door Lock Motor

23.1 Typical power door lock system

and actuators for minor faults that can be easily repaired.

2   Power door lock systems are operated by bi-directional solenoids located in the doors. The lock switches have two operating positions: Lock and Unlock. When activated, the switch sends a ground signal to the door lock control unit to lock or unlock the doors. Depending on which way the switch is activated, the control unit reverses polarity to the solenoids, allowing the two sides of the circuit to be used alternately as the feed (positive) and ground side.

3   Some vehicles may have an anti-theft system incorporated into the power locks. If you are unable to locate the trouble using the following general Steps, consult a dealer service department or other qualified repair shop.

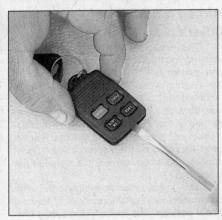

23.14 Use a small screwdriver or coin to separate the transmitter halves

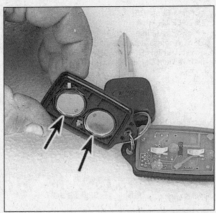

23.15 Replace the lithium batteries with the same type as used originally

4   Always check the circuit protection first. Some vehicles use a combination of circuit breakers and fuses.

5   Operate the door lock switches in both directions (Lock and Unlock) with the engine off. Listen for the click of the solenoids operating.

6   Test the switches for continuity. Remove the switches and have them checked by a dealer service department or other qualified automobile repair facility.

7   Check the wiring between the switches, control unit and solenoids for continuity. Repair the wiring if there's no continuity.

8   Check for a bad ground at the switches or the control unit.

9   If all but one lock solenoids operate, remove the trim panel from the affected door (see Chapter 11) and check for voltage at the solenoid while the lock switch is operated. One of the wires should have voltage in the Lock position; the other should have voltage in the Unlock position.

10   If the inoperative solenoid is receiving voltage, replace the solenoid.

11   If the inoperative solenoid isn't receiving voltage, check the circuit between the lock solenoid and the control unit. **Note:** *It's common for wires to break in the portion of the harness between the body and door (opening and closing the door fatigues and eventually breaks the wires).*

Keyless entry system
Refer to illustrations 23.14 and 23.15

12   The keyless entry system consists of a remote control transmitter that sends a coded infrared signal to a receiver which then operates the door lock system. On models so equipped, the transmitter may also engage the alarm system and provide a "panic" button which flashes the lights and blows the horn for emergencies.

13   Replace the transmitter batteries when the red LED light on the case doesn't light when the button is pushed. As the batteries deteriorate with age, the distance at which the remote transmitter operates will diminish.

14   Use a coin or small screwdriver to carefully separate the case halves for battery replacement **(see illustration)**.

15   Replace the two lithium batteries with the same type as originally installed, observing the polarity diagram on the case **(see illustration)**.

16   Snap the case halves together.

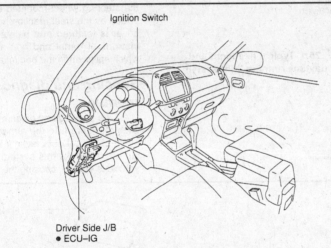

24 Power sunroof - description
Refer to illustration 24.1

1   The power sunroof or sliding roof system consists of the control switch, the module, the roof motor and the glass and track mechanism **(see illustration)**. The sunroof switch is located in a panel in the headliner, above the rear-view mirror. For information on roof panel adjustment details, see Chap-ter 11.

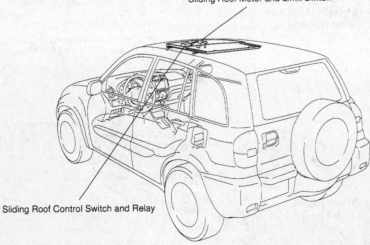

24.1 Typical power roof system

25 Daytime Running Lights (DRL) - general information
Refer to illustration 25.1

The Daytime Running Lights (DRL) system used on Canadian models illuminates the headlights whenever the engine is running **(see illustration)**. The only exception is with the engine running and the parking brake

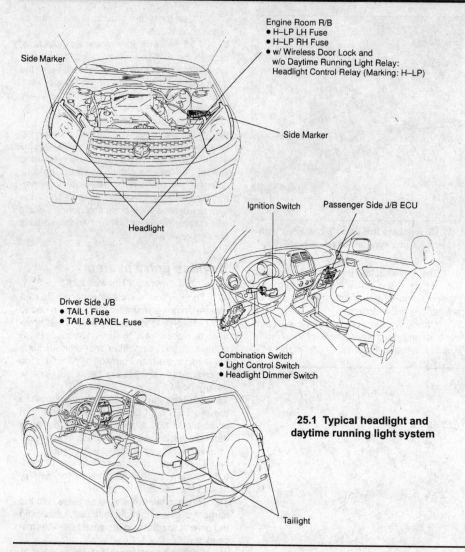

Engine Room R/B
• H–LP LH Fuse
• H–LP RH Fuse
• w/ Wireless Door Lock and
  w/o Daytime Running Light Relay:
  Headlight Control Relay (Marking: H–LP)

Side Marker

Side Marker

Headlight

Ignition Switch   Passenger Side J/B ECU

Driver Side J/B
• TAIL1 Fuse
• TAIL & PANEL Fuse

Combination Switch
• Light Control Switch
• Headlight Dimmer Switch

25.1 Typical headlight and daytime running light system

Taillight

Airbag module

Driver's side

The airbag inflator module contains a housing incorporating the cushion (airbag) and inflator unit, mounted in the center of the steering wheel The inflator assembly is mounted on the back of the housing over a hole through which gas is expelled, inflating the bag almost instantaneously when an electrical signal is sent from the system. A spiral cable assembly on the steering column under the steering wheel carries this signal to the module.

This spiral cable assembly can transmit an electrical signal regardless of steering wheel position. The igniter in the airbag converts the electrical signal to heat and ignites the powder, which inflates the bag.

Passenger's side

The airbag is mounted above the glove compartment and designated by the letters SRS (Supplemental Restraint System). It consists of an inflator containing an igniter, a bag assembly, a reaction housing and a trim cover.

The airbag is considerably larger than the steering wheel-mounted unit and is supported by the steel reaction housing. The trim cover is textured and painted to match the instrument panel and has a molded seam which splits when the bag inflates.

Sensing and diagnostic module

The sensing and diagnostic module supplies the current to the airbag system in the event of the collision, even if battery power is cut off. It checks this system every time the vehicle is started, causing the "AIR BAG" light

engaged. Once the parking brake is released, the lights will remain on as long as the ignition switch is on, even if the parking brake is later applied.

The DRL system supplies reduced power to the headlights so they won't be too bright for daytime use, while prolonging headlight life.

26   Airbag system - general information

All models are equipped with a Supplemental Restraint System (SRS), more commonly known as an airbag. This system is designed to protect the driver, and the front seat passenger, from serious injury in the event of a head-on or frontal collision. It consists of airbag sensors mounted on the front unibody frame members and a sensing/diagnostic module mounted in the center of the vehicle, near the floor console. **Note:** *1996 and 1997 models are not equipped with the airbag sensors mounted up front but instead operate only with the console mounted airbag sensor/diagnostic module.*

26.2 Passenger's side airbag details (2000 and earlier models)

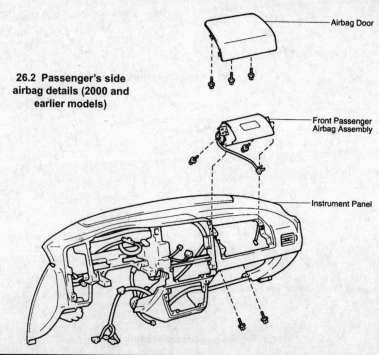

Airbag Door

Front Passenger Airbag Assembly

Instrument Panel

to go on then off, if the system is operating properly. If there is a fault in the system, the light will go on and stay on, flash, or the dash will make a beeping sound. If this happens, the vehicle should be taken to your dealer immediately for service.

Disarming the system and other precautions

Warning: *Failure to follow these precautions could result in accidental deployment of the airbag and personal injury.*

Whenever working in the vicinity of the steering wheel, steering column or any of the other SRS system components, the system must be disarmed. To disarm the system:

a) *Point the wheels straight ahead and turn the key to the Lock position.*

b) *Disconnect the cable from the negative battery terminal, then the positive cable.*

c) *Wait at least two minutes for the back-up power supply to be depleted.*

Whenever handling an airbag module, always keep the airbag opening (the trim side) pointed away from your body. Never place the airbag module on a bench of other surface with the airbag opening facing the surface. Always place the airbag module in a safe location with the airbag opening facing up.

Never measure the resistance of any SRS component. An ohmmeter has a built-in battery supply that could accidentally deploy the airbag.

Never use electrical welding equipment on a vehicle equipped with an airbag without first disconnecting the yellow airbag connector, located under the steering column near the combination switch connector (driver's airbag) and behind the glove box (passenger's airbag).

Never dispose of a live airbag module. Return it to a dealer service department or other qualified repair shop for safe deployment and disposal.

Component removal and installation

Driver's side airbag module and spiral cable

Refer to Chapter 10, Steering wheel - removal and installation, for the driver's side

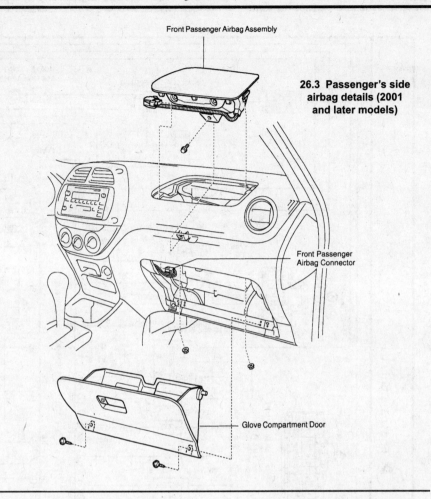

26.3 Passenger's side airbag details (2001 and later models)

Front Passenger Airbag Assembly

Front Passenger Airbag Connector

Glove Compartment Door

---

airbag module and spiral cable removal and installation procedures.

Passenger's side airbag module

Refer to illustrations 26.2 and 26.3

1   Disarm the airbag system as describes previously in this Section.

2   If you're working on a 2000 or earlier model, remove the instrument panel (see Chapter 11). The airbag fasteners are now accessible **(see illustration)**. Remove the fasteners, unplug the electrical connector and detach the airbag module from the instrument panel. Be sure to heed the precautions outlined previously in this Section.

3   If you're working on a 2001 or later model, remove the glove box (see Chapter 11), then unplug the electrical connector and remove the airbag module mounting fasteners **(see illustration)**. Be sure to heed the precautions outlined previously in this Section.

4   Installation is the reverse of the removal procedure. Tighten the airbag module mounting fasteners to 15 ft-lbs (20 Nm).

27 Wiring diagrams - general information

Since it isn't possible to include all wiring diagrams for every year covered by this manual, the following diagrams are those that are typical and most commonly needed.

Prior to troubleshooting any circuits, check the fuse and circuit breakers (if equipped) to make sure they're in good condition. Make sure the battery is properly charged and check the cable connections (see Chapter 1).

When checking a circuit, make sure that all connectors are clean, with no broken or loose terminals. When unplugging a connector, do not pull on the wires. Pull only on the connector housings themselves.

Wire colors are indicated by an alphabetical code.

B	= Black	L	= Blue	R	= Red
BR	= Brown	LG	= Light Green	V	= Violet
G	= Green	O	= Orange	W	= White
GR	= Gray	P	= Pink	Y	= Yellow

The first letter indicates the basic wire color and the second letter indicates the color of the stripe.

Wiring diagram color code chart

Example: L—Y

L
(Blue)

Y
(Yellow)

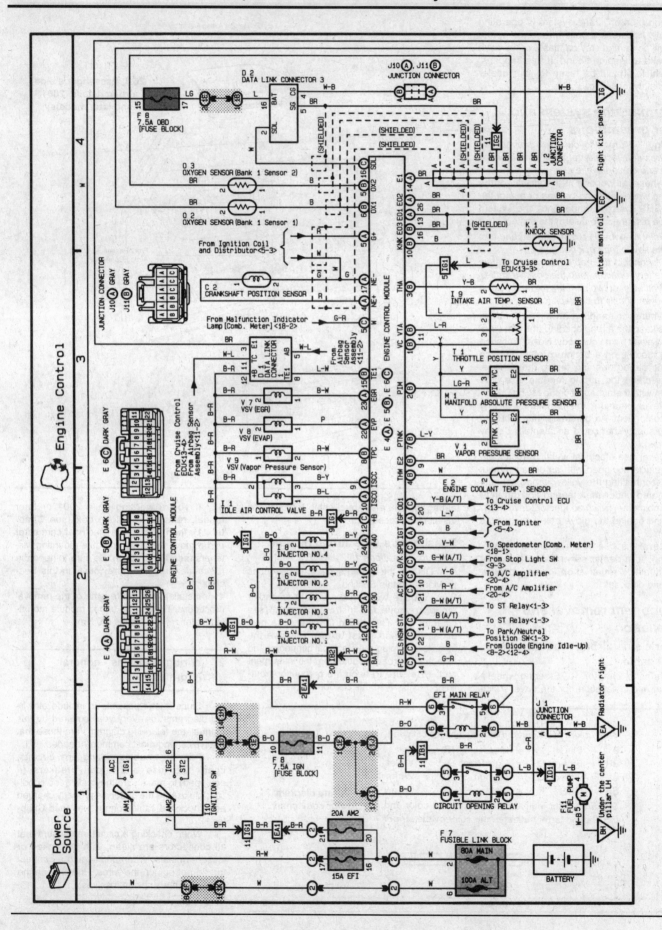

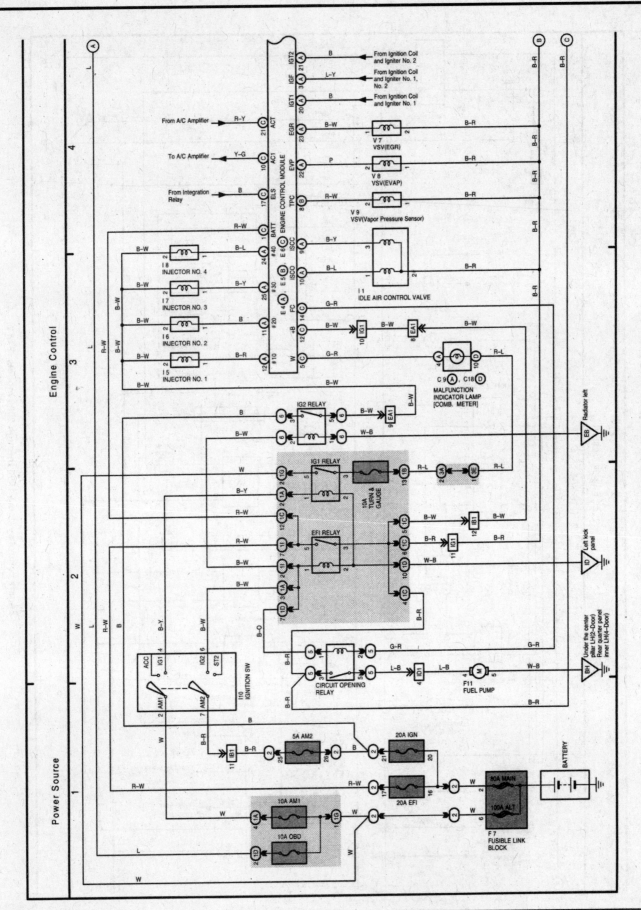

Engine control system - 1998 through 2000 models (1 of 2)

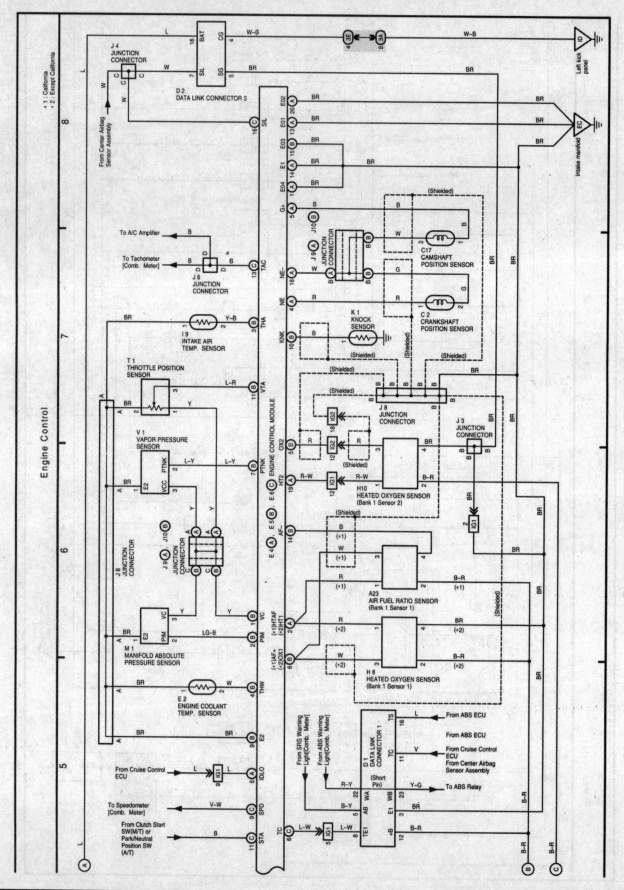

Engine control system - 1998 through 2000 models (2 of 2)

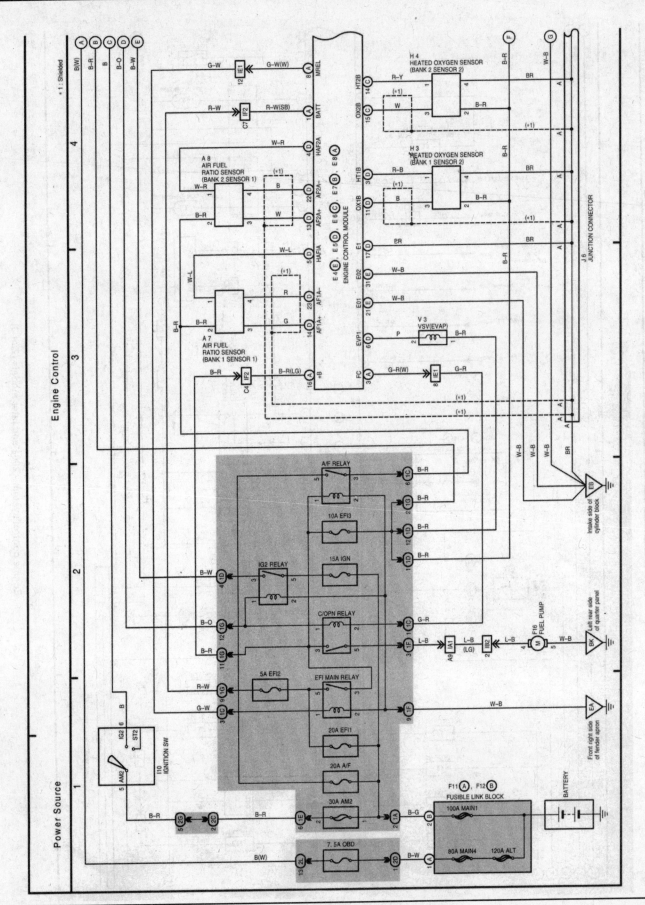

Engine control system - 2001 and later models (1 of 3)

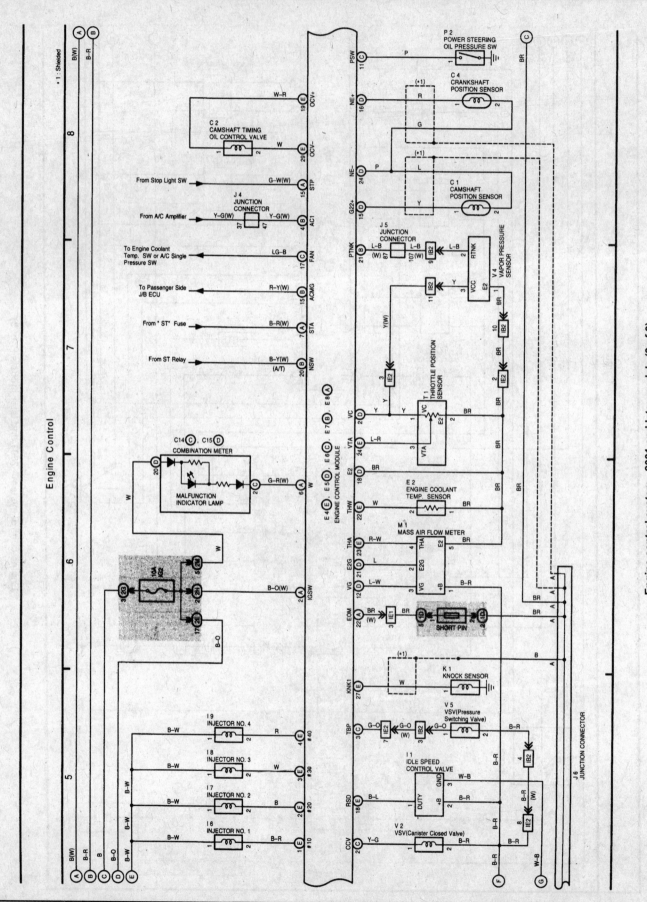

Engine control system - 2001 and later models (2 of 3)

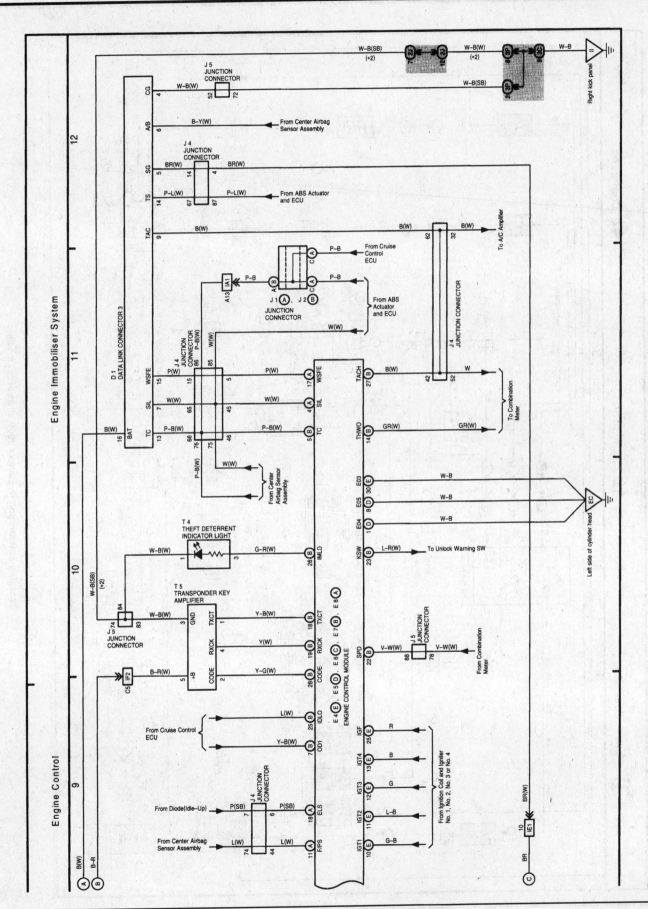

Engine control system - 2001 and later models (3 of 3)

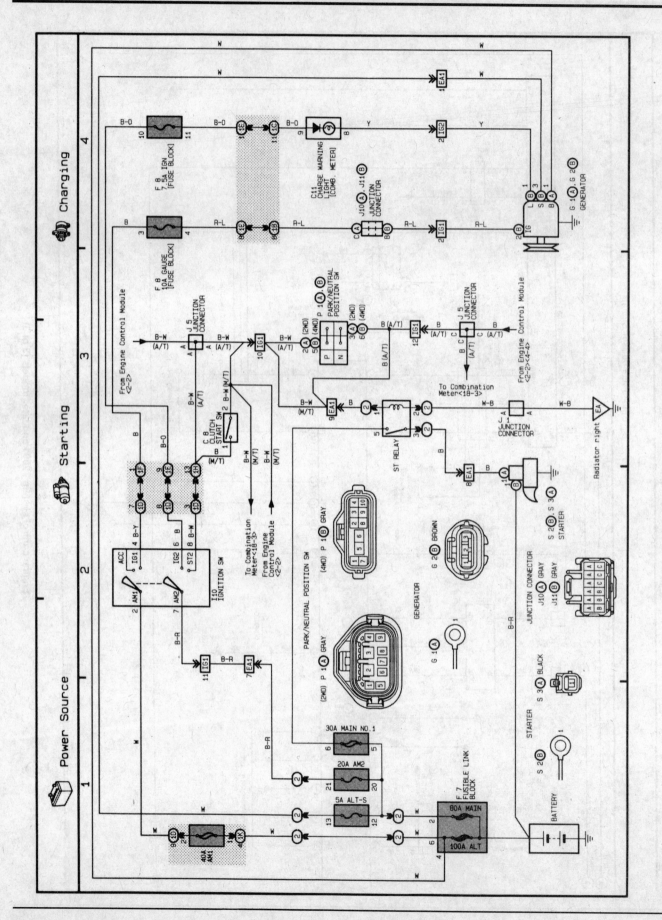

Charging and starting systems - 2000 and earlier models

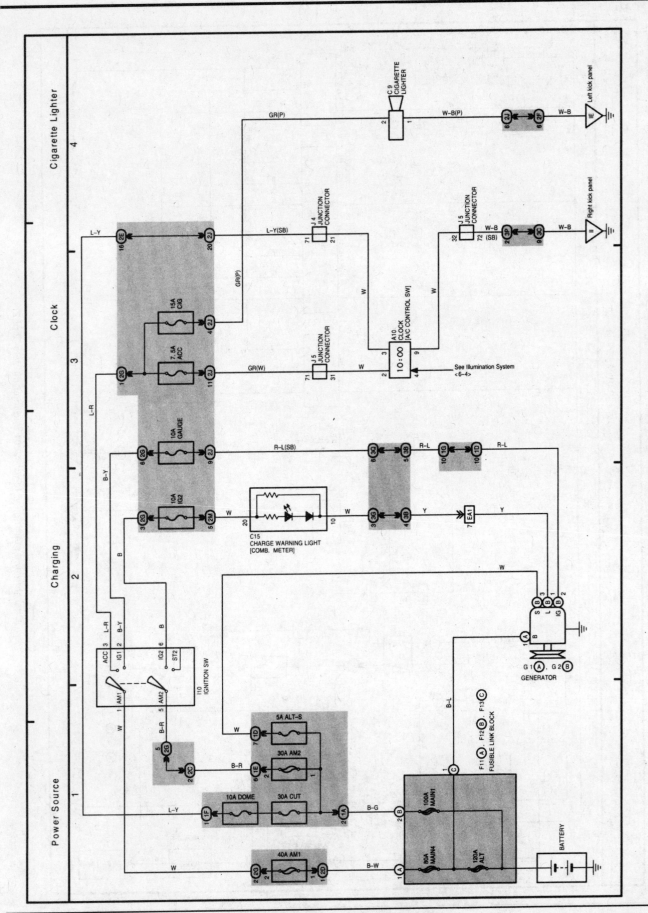

Charging and starting systems - 2001 and later models (1 of 2)

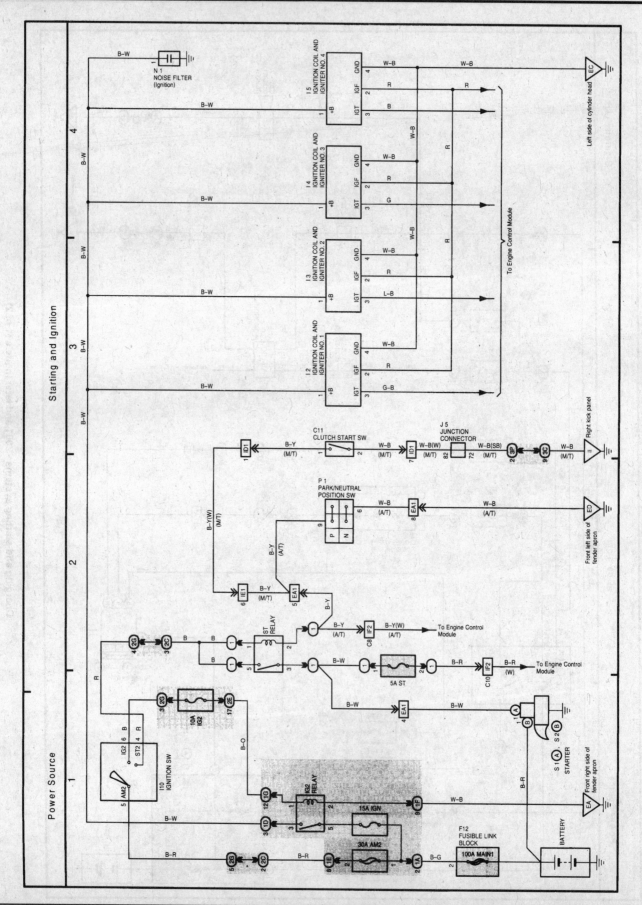

Starting and Ignition

Power Source

Charging and starting systems - 2001 and later models (2 of 2)

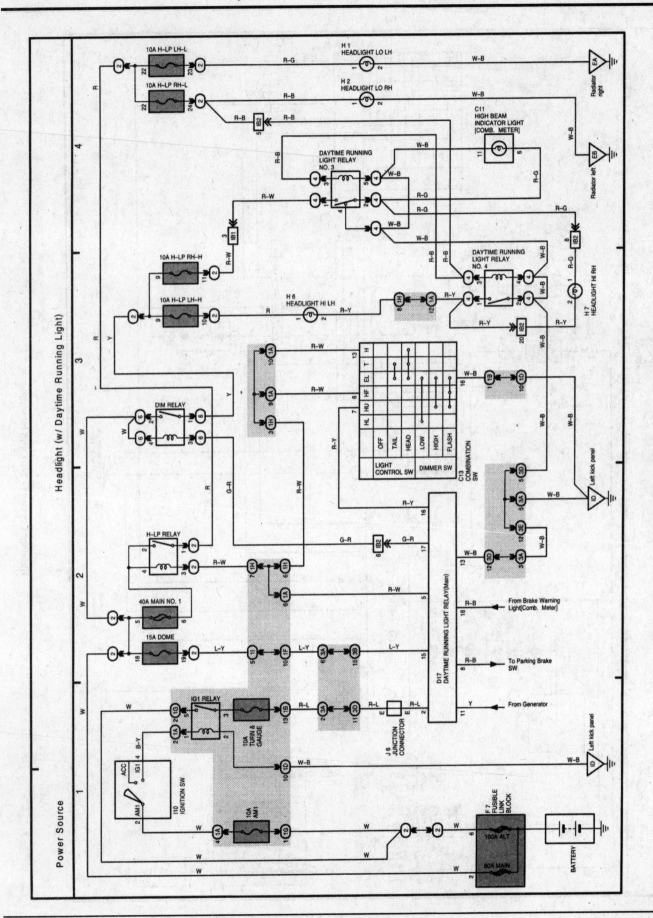

Headlight system - 1998 through 2000 models (1996 and 1997 models similar)

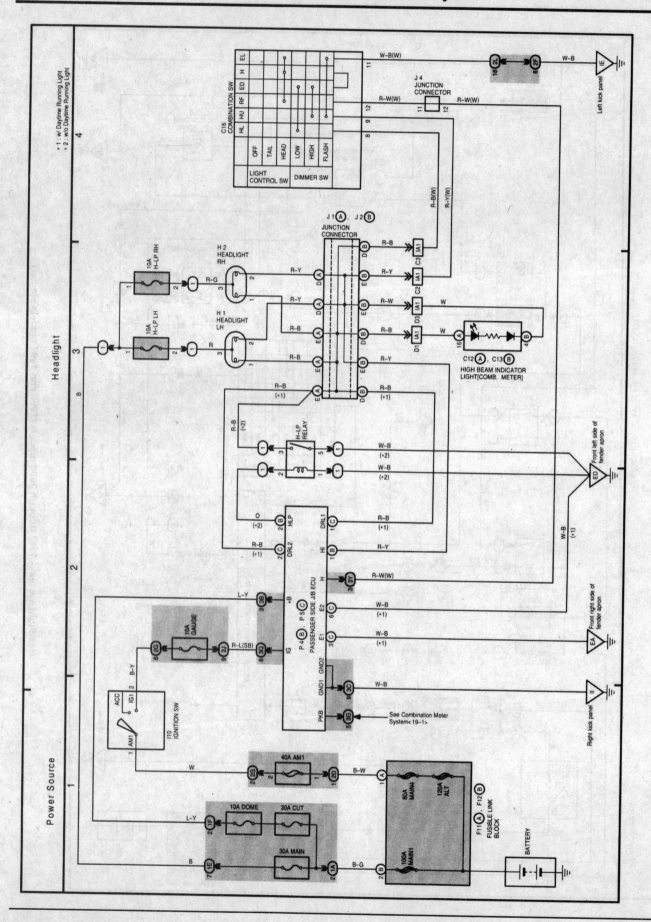

Headlight system - 2001 and later models

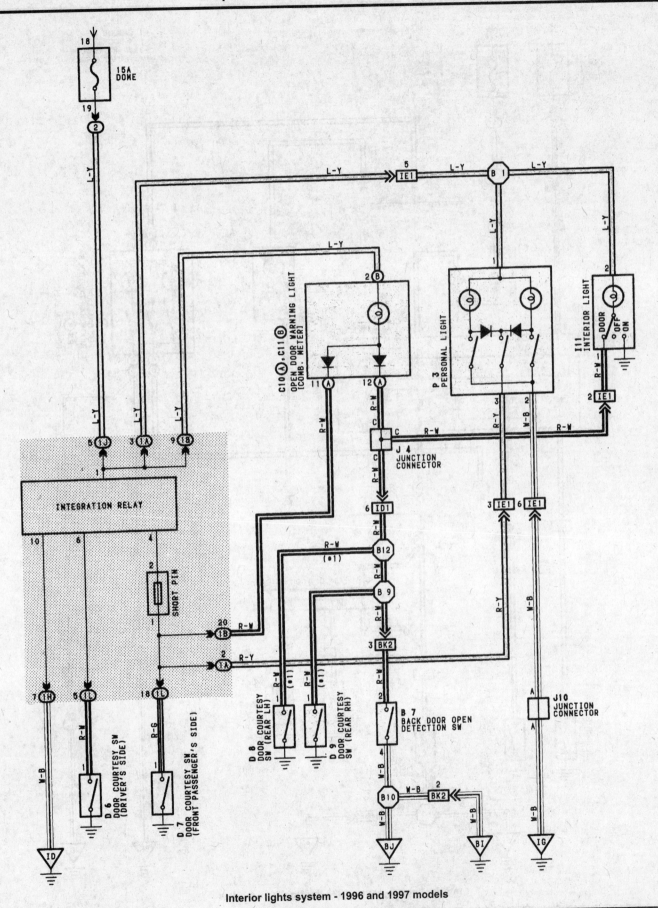

Interior lights system - 1996 and 1997 models

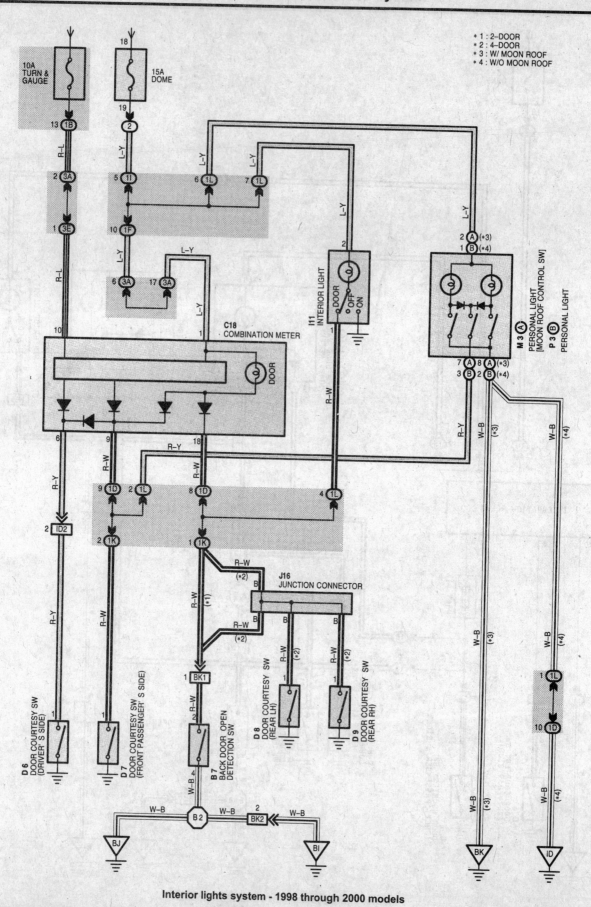

Interior lights system - 1998 through 2000 models

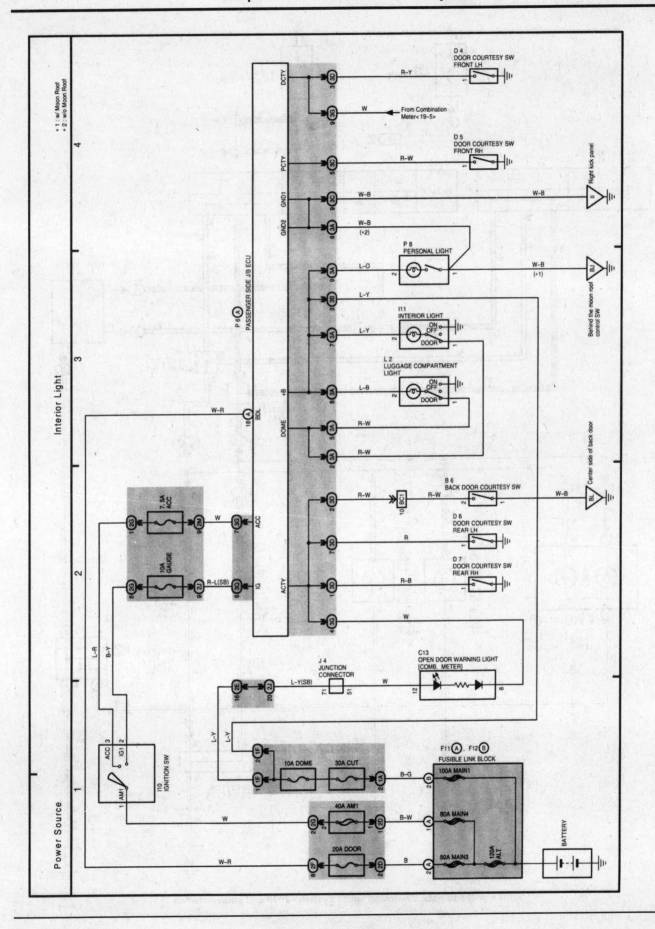

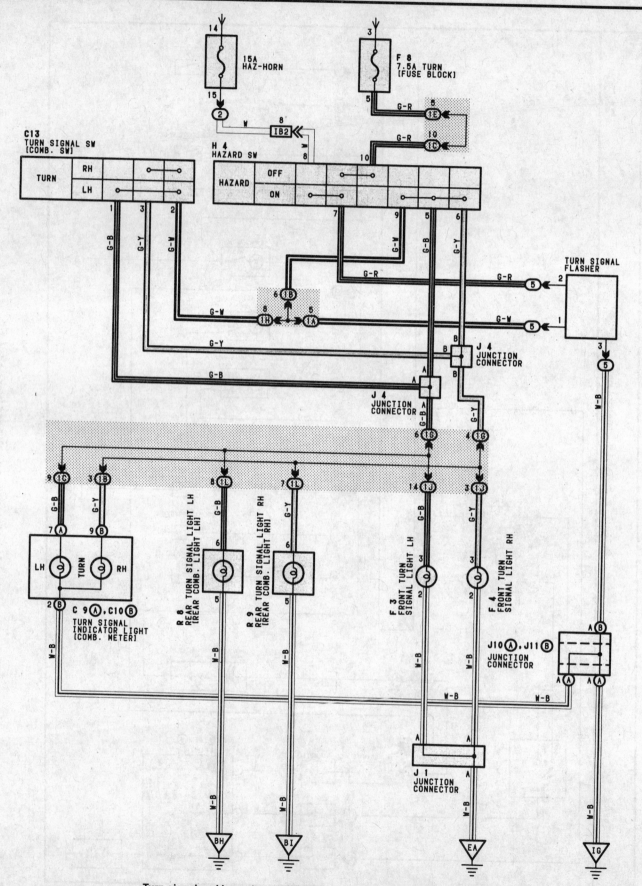

Turn signal and hazard warning lights system - 2000 and earlier models

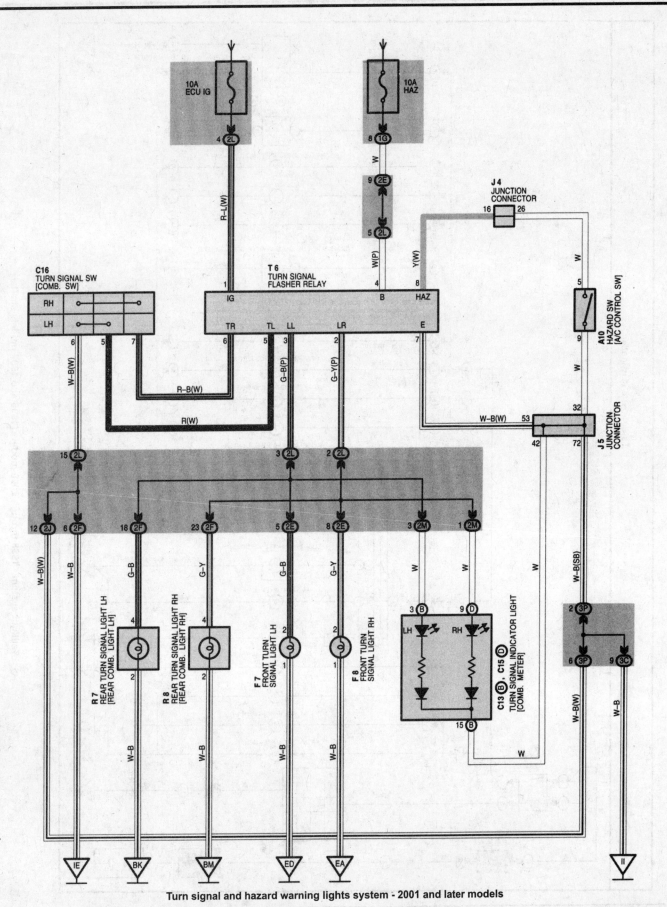

Turn signal and hazard warning lights system - 2001 and later models

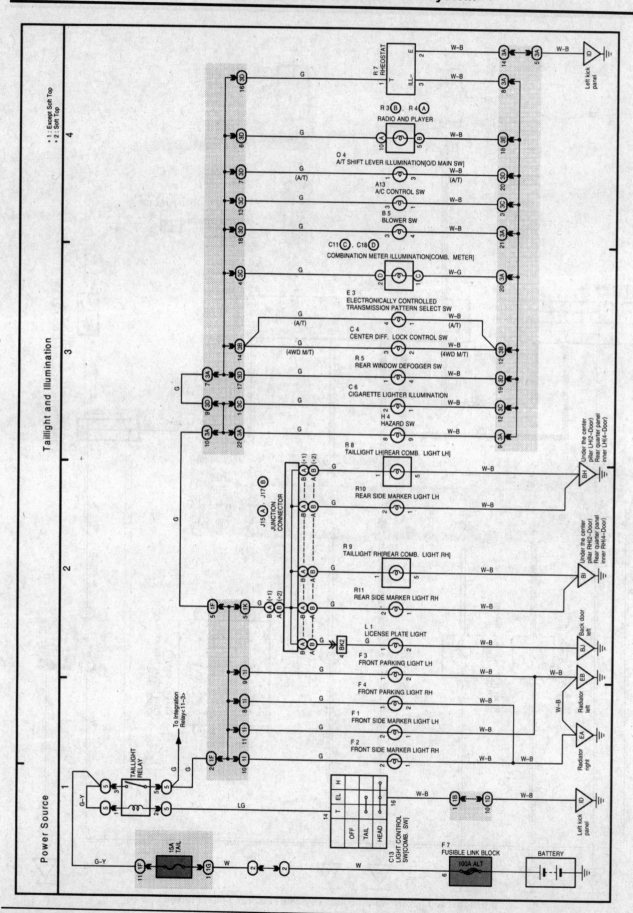

Taillight system - 1998 through 2000 models (1996 and 1997 models similar)

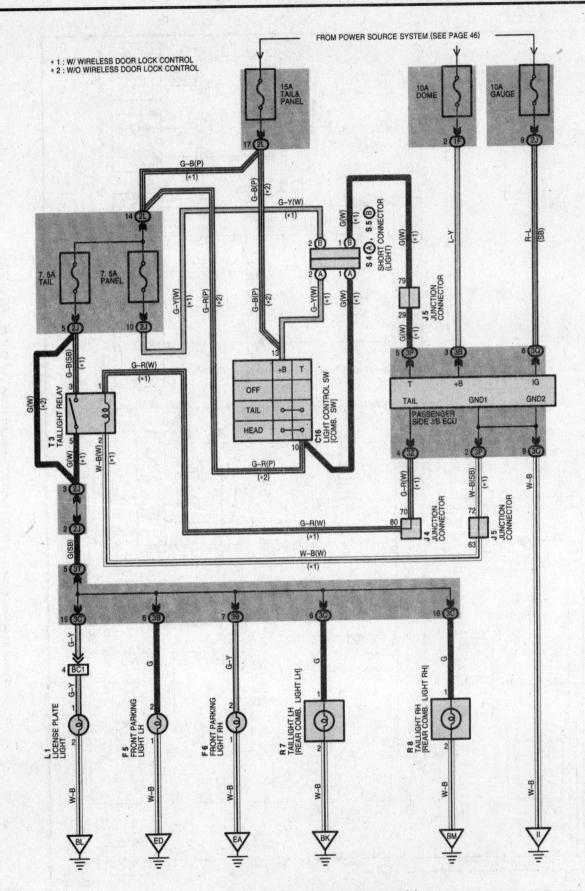

Taillight system - 2001 and later models

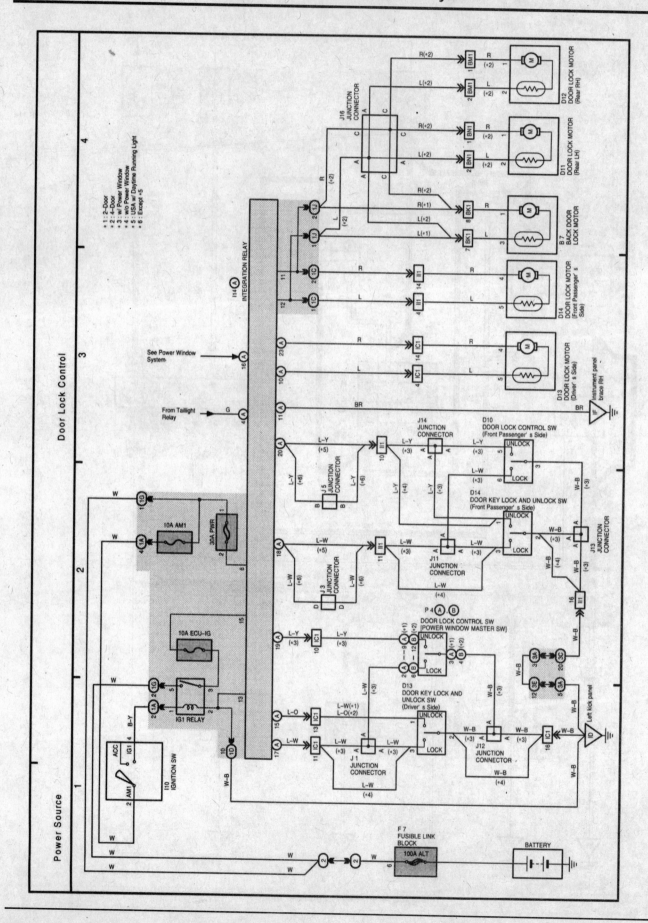

Power door lock system - 1998 through 2000 models (1996 and 1997 models similar)

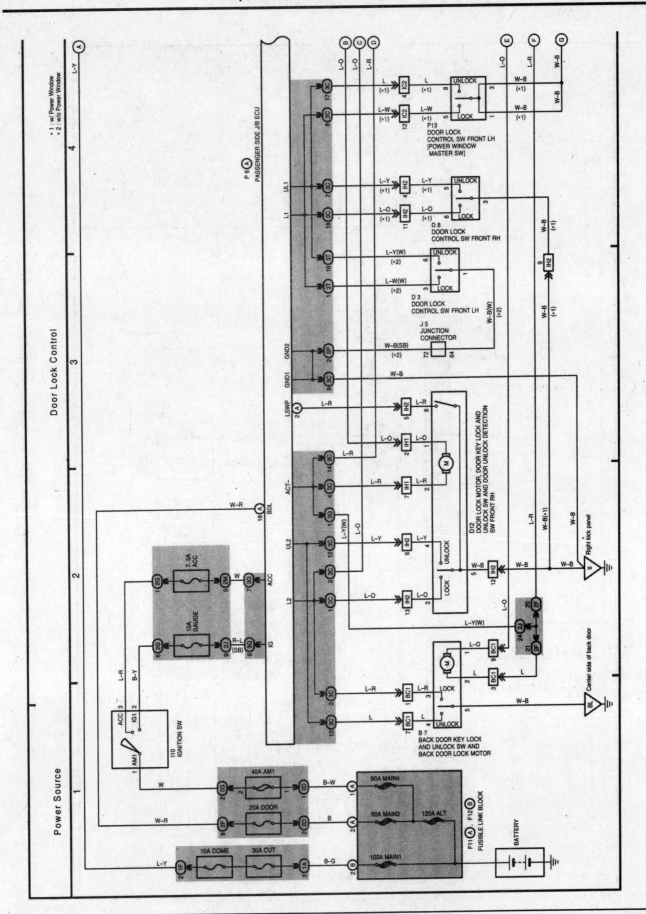

Power door lock system - 2001 and later models (1 of 2)

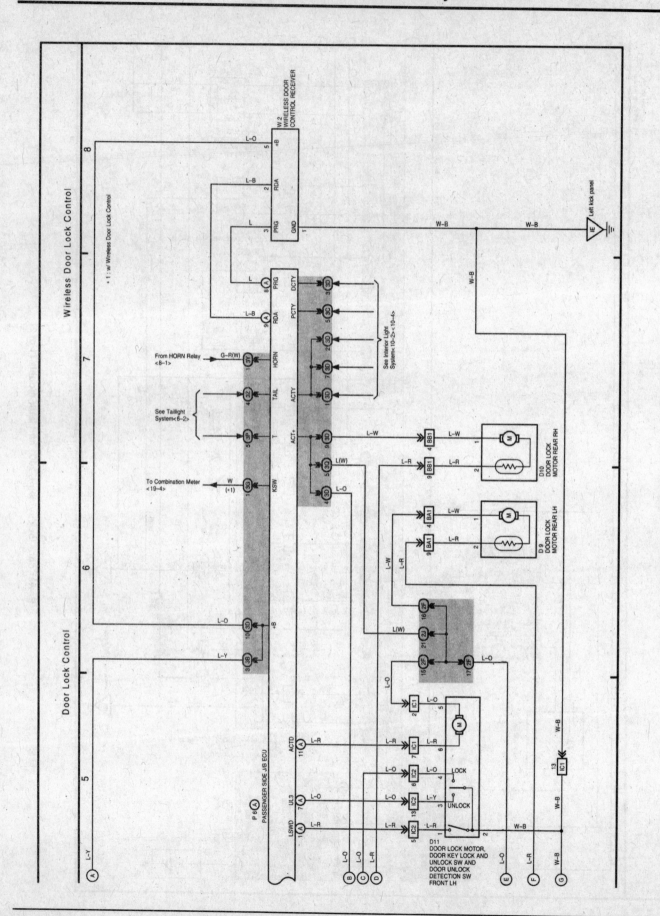

Power door lock system - 2001 and later models (2 of 2)

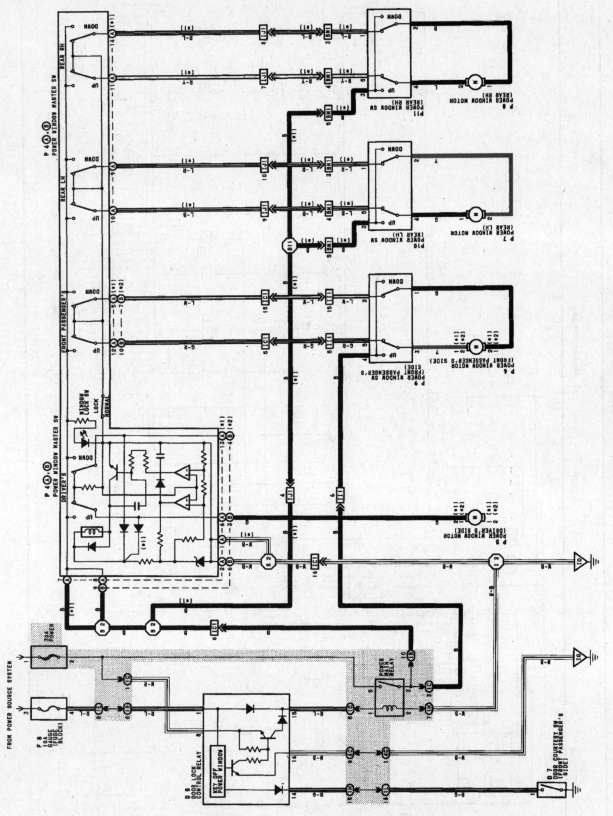

Power window system - 1996 and 1997 models

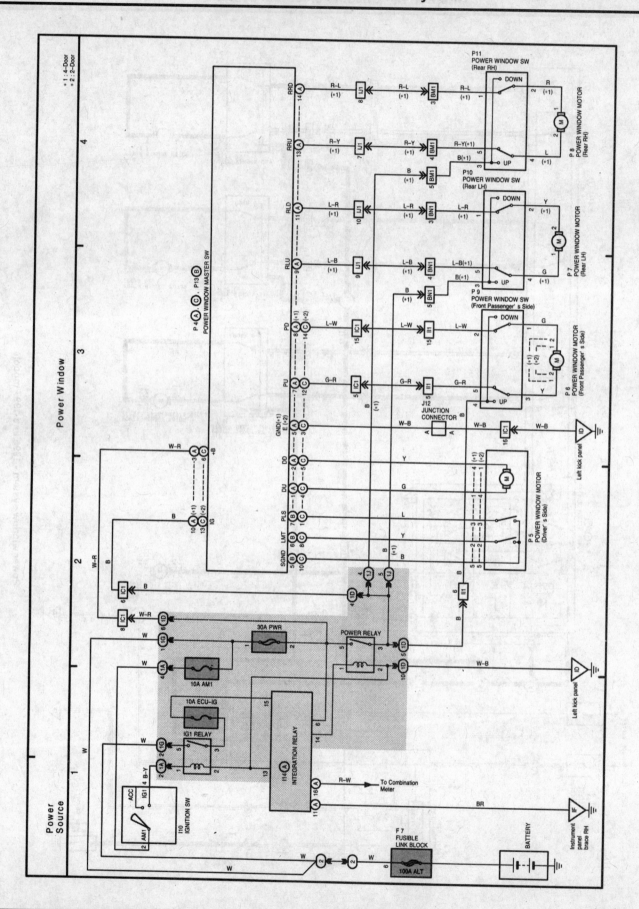

Power window system - 1998 and later models

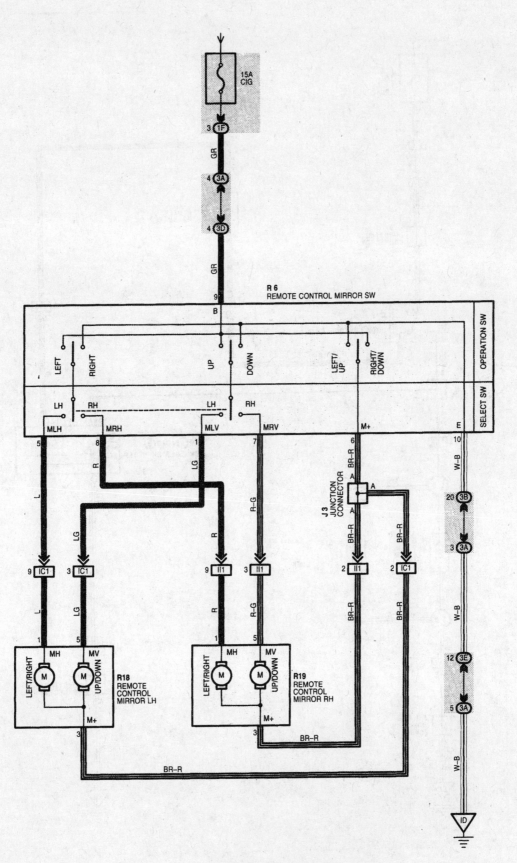

Power mirror system

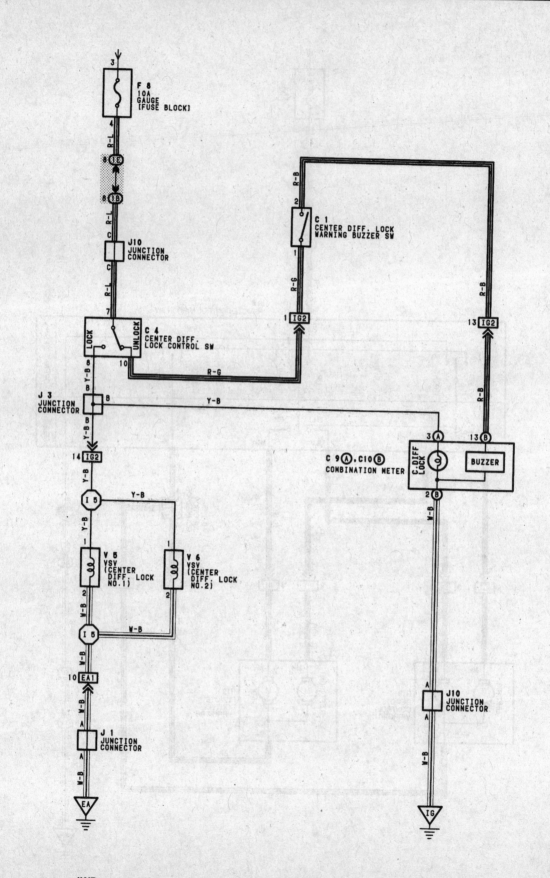

4WD center differential locking system (manual transaxle) - 1996 and 1997 models

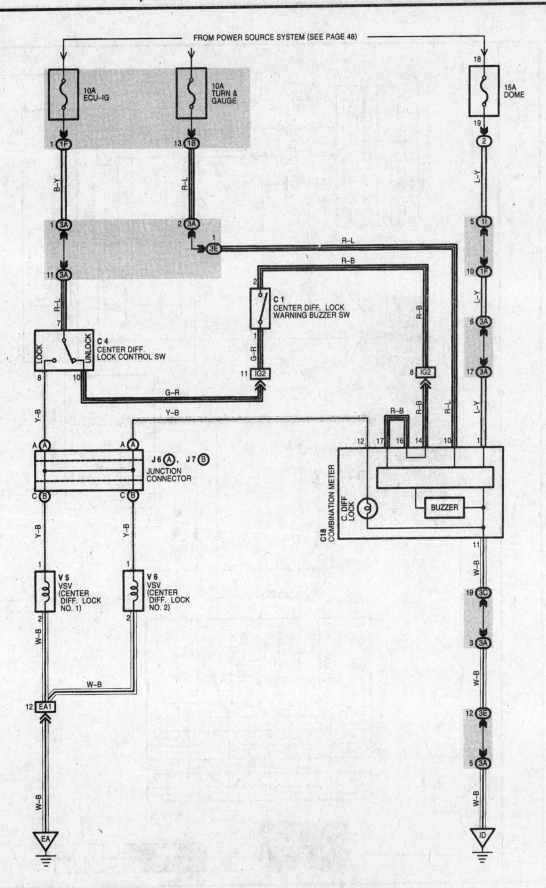

4WD center differential locking system (manual transaxle) - 1998 through 2000 models

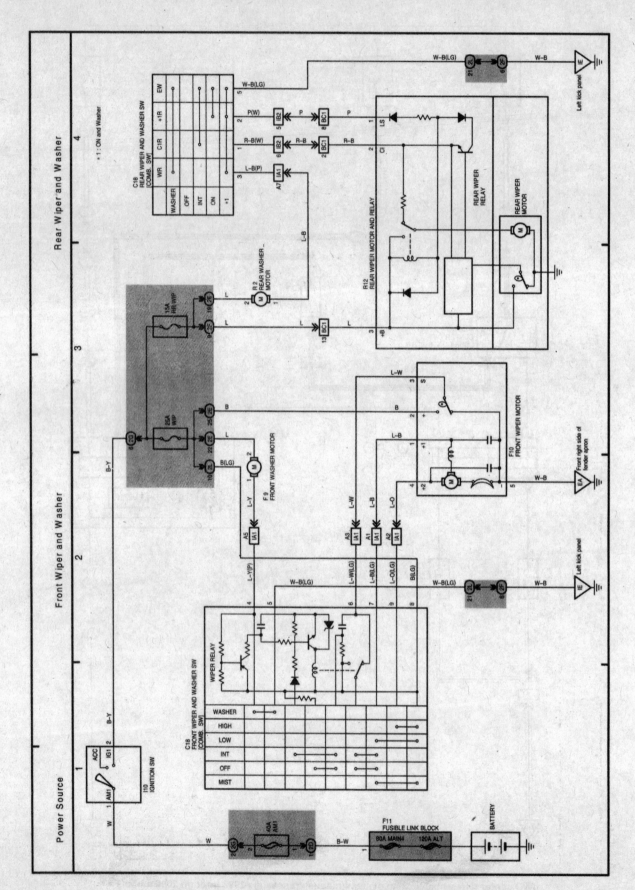

Front and rear wiper and washer system

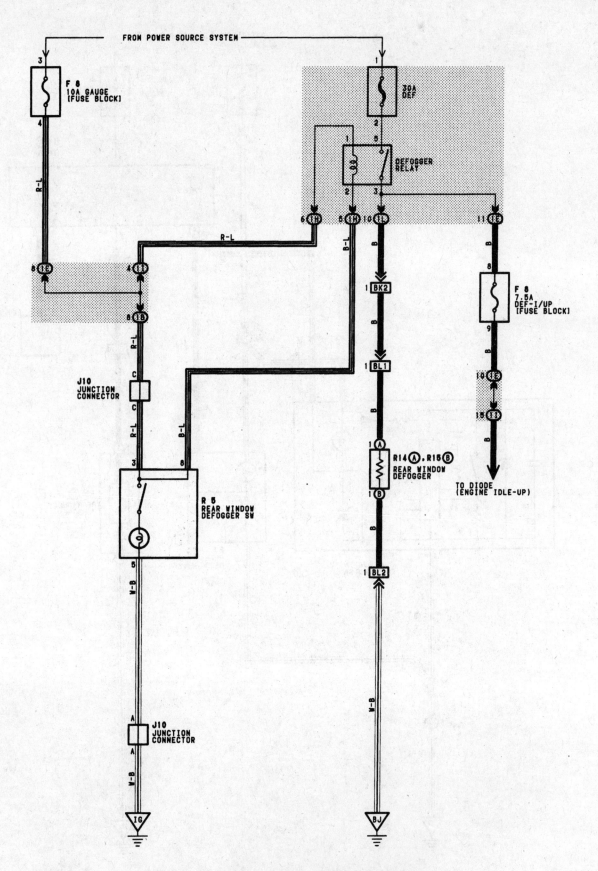

Rear window defogger system - 1996 and 1997 models

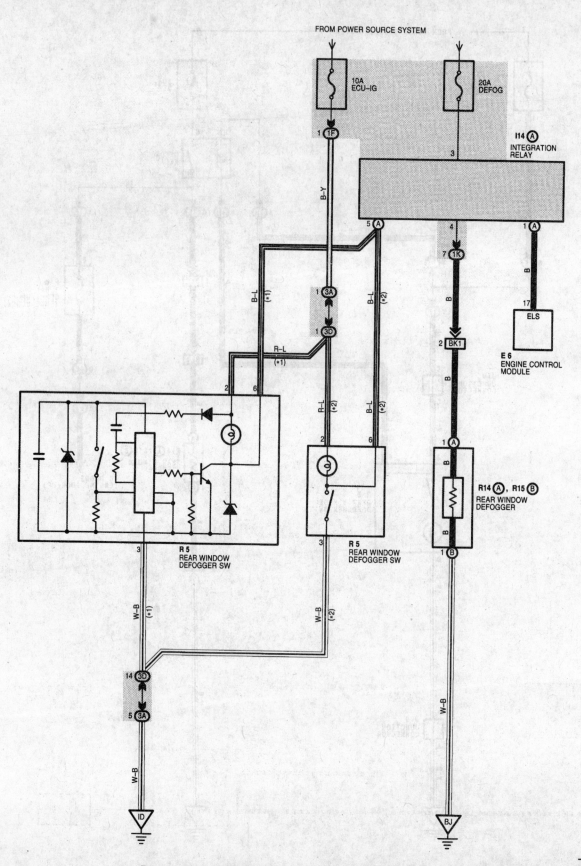

Rear window defogger system - 1998 through 2000 models

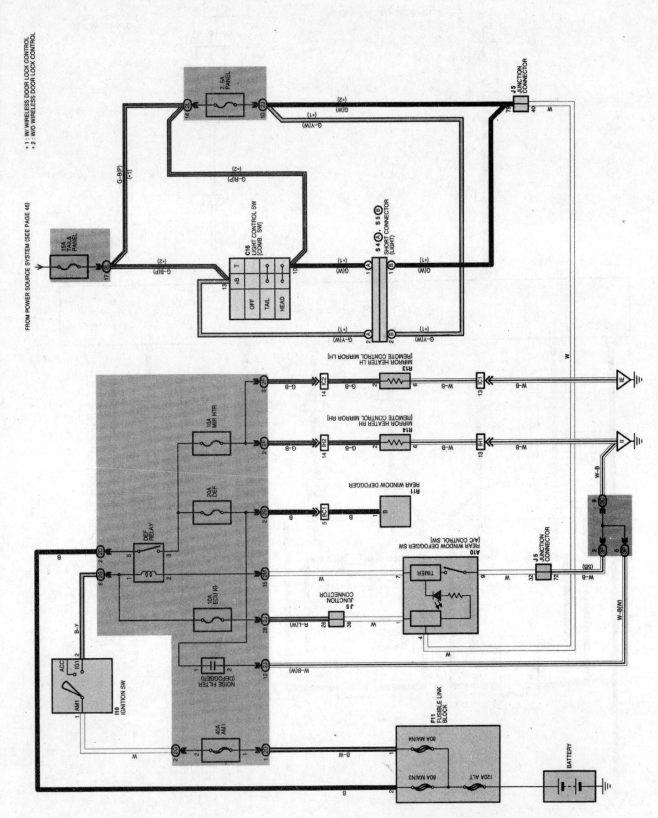

Rear window defogger system - 2001 and later models

Chapter 12 Chassis electrical system

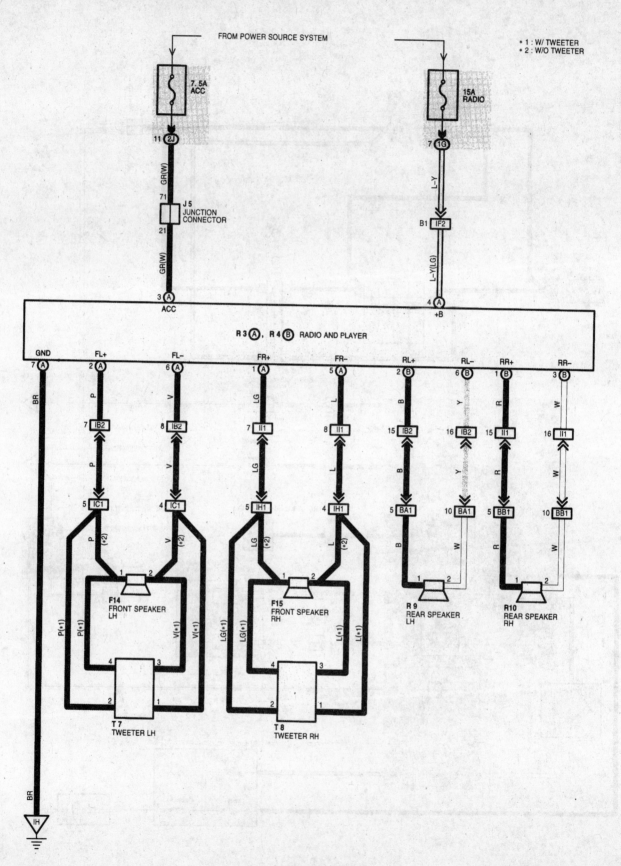

Typical radio system

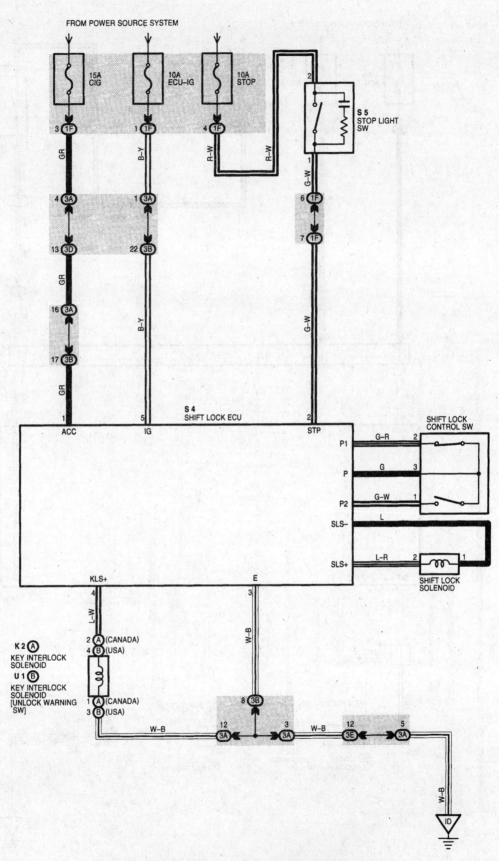

Shift lock control system - 2000 and earlier models

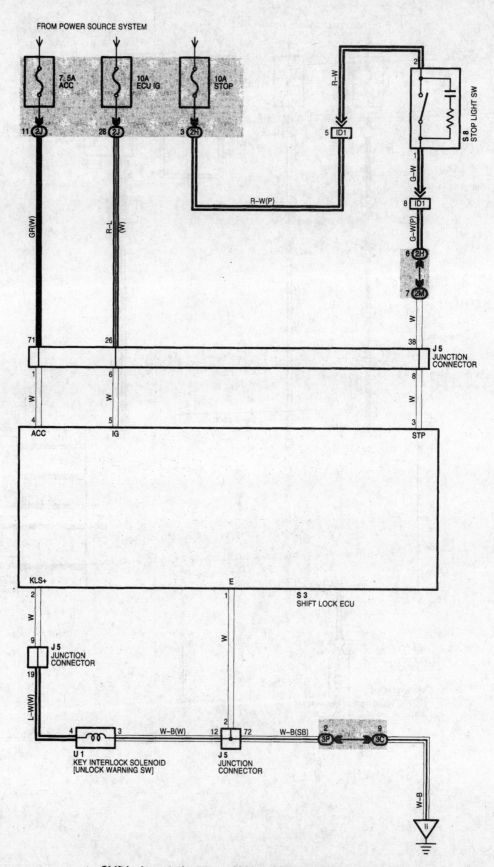

Shift lock control system - 2001 and later models

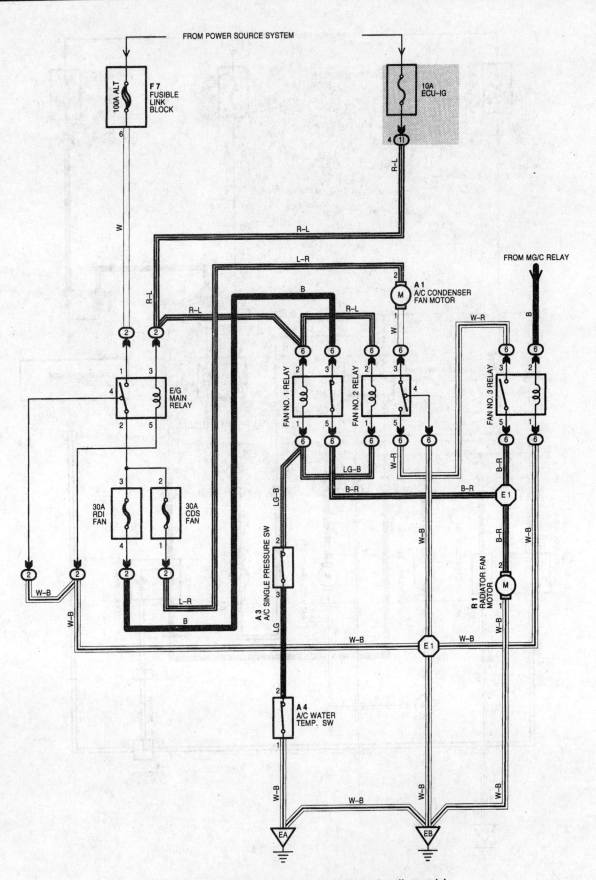

Radiator and condenser fan system - 2000 and earlier models

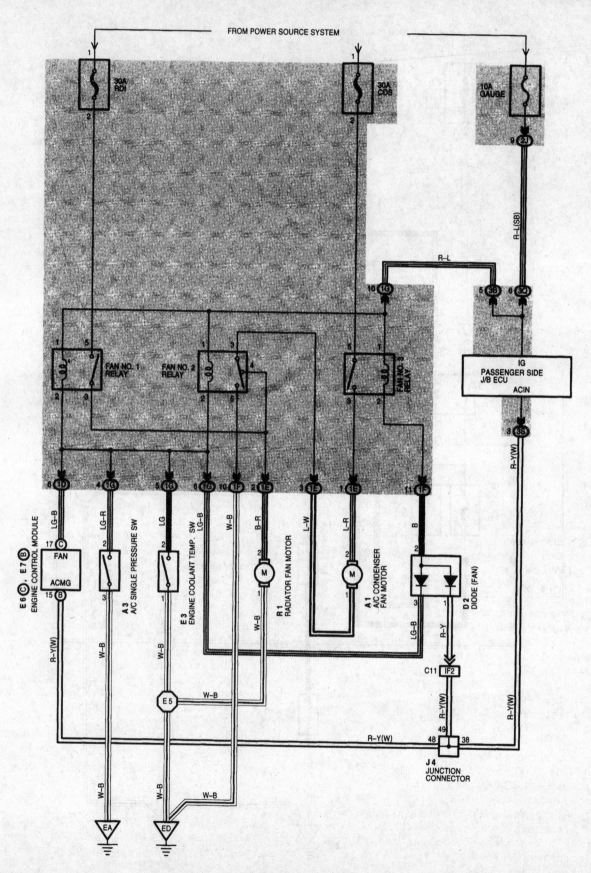

Radiator and condenser fan system - 2001 and later models

Index

A

About this manual, 0-2
Accelerator cable, removal, installation and adjustment, 4-12
Accelerator Pedal Position (APP) sensor, replacement, 6-20
Air conditioning
    and heating system, check and maintenance, 3-11
    compressor, removal and installation, 3-13
    condenser, removal and installation, 3-14
    control assembly, removal, installation and cable adjustment, 3-8
    receiver/drier, removal and installation, 3-13
Air filter housing, removal and installation, 4-10
Air filter replacement, 1-19
Air/fuel sensor and oxygen sensor, general information and replacement, 6-12
Airbag system, general information, 12-22
Alternator, removal and installation, 5-9
Antenna, replacement, 12-11
Antifreeze, general information, 3-3
Anti-lock Brake System (ABS), general information, trouble codes and component removal and installation, 9-3
Automatic transaxle, 7B-1 through 7B-10
    diagnosis, general, 7B-2
    fluid and filter change, 1-27
    fluid level check, 1-10
    oil seal replacement, 7B-2
    overhaul, general information, 7B-10
    Park/Neutral Position (PNP) switch, adjustment and replacement, 7B-6
    removal and installation, 7B-8
    shift cable, removal, installation and adjustment, 7B-5
    shift lock system, description and check, 7B-7
    Throttle Valve (TV) cable, check, adjustment and replacement, 7B-4
    torque specifications, 7B-1
Automotive chemicals and lubricants, 0-14

B

Back door
    latch, lock cylinder and handle, removal and installation, 11-17
    removal, installation and adjustment, 11-16
Back-up light switch, check and replacement, 7A-3
Balljoint, replacement, 10-8
Battery
    cables, replacement, 5-4
    check and replacement, 5-3
    check, maintenance and charging, 1-13
    disconnection, 5-2
    jump starting, 0-13
Blower motor, removal and installation, 3-8
Body repair
    major damage, 11-3
    minor damage, 11-2
Body, 11-1 through 11-24
Body, maintenance, 11-1
Booster battery (jump) starting, 0-13
Brake check, 1-18
Brake fluid change, 1-22
Brakes, 9-1 through 9-26
    Anti-lock Brake System (ABS), general information, trouble codes and component removal and installation, 9-3
    caliper, removal and installation, 9-10
    disc, inspection, removal and installation, 9-12
    hoses and lines, inspection and replacement, 9-19
    hydraulic system, bleeding, 9-19
    light switch, check and replacement, 9-22
    master cylinder, removal, installation and reservoir/grommet replacement, 9-18
    pad replacement, 9-8
    parking brake, adjustment, 9-21
    parking brake cables, replacement, 9-21
    parking brake shoes, inspection and replacement, 9-23
    pedal, check and adjustment, 9-22
    power brake booster, check, removal and installation, 9-20

shoes, drum brake, replacement, 9-13
torque specifications, 9-1
wheel cylinder, removal and installation, 9-17
Bulb replacement, 12-16
Bumpers, removal and installation, 11-7
Buying parts, 0-6

C

Cable replacement
accelerator, 4-10
battery, 5-4
parking brake, 9-19
Throttle Valve (TV), 7B-4
Caliper, disc brake, removal and installation, 9-10
Camshaft oil seal, replacement (2000 and earlier), 2A-10
Camshaft position sensor, replacement, 6-11
Camshafts and lifters, removal, inspection and installation
2000 and earlier, 2A-10
2001 and later, 2B-9
Capacities, lubricants and fluids, 1-2
Catalytic converter, 6-17
Center console, removal and installation, 11-18
Center support bearing, driveshaft, removal and installation, 8-10
Charging system
alternator, removal and installation, 5-9
check, 5-8
general information and precautions, 5-8
Chassis electrical system, 12-1 through 12-23
Chemicals and lubricants, 0-14
Circuit breakers, general information, 12-3
Clutch and driveline, 8-1 through 8-12
Clutch
components, removal, inspection and installation, 8-4
description and check, 8-2
hydraulic system, bleeding, 8-4
master cylinder, removal and installation, 8-3
pedal freeplay, check and adjustment, 1-13
release bearing and lever, removal, inspection and installation, 8-5
release cylinder, removal and installation, 8-3
start switch, replacement, 8-6
torque specifications, 8-2
Coil spring (rear), removal and installation, 10-11
Compressor, air conditioning, removal and installation, 3-13
Condenser, air conditioning, removal and installation, 3-14
Control arm, removal, inspection and installation, 10-7
Conversion factors, 0-15
Coolant temperature sending unit and radiator fan switch, replacement, 3-8
Coolant temperature sensor, replacement, 6-11
Cooling, heating and air conditioning systems, 3-1 through 3-14
Cooling system
antifreeze, general information, 3-3
check, 1-17
engine cooling fans, replacement, 3-4
radiator and coolant reservoir, removal and installation, 3-4

servicing (draining, flushing and refilling), 1-25
thermostat, check and replacement, 3-3
torque specifications, 3-1
water pump, check and replacement, 3-6
Cowl cover and vent tray, removal and installation, 11-11
Crankshaft front oil seal, replacement
2000 and earlier, 2A-10
2001 and later, 2B-15
Crankshaft Position (CKP) sensor, replacement, 6-11
Crankshaft pulley/vibration damper, removal and installation
2000 and earlier, 2A-7
2001 and later, 2B-15
Cruise control system, description, 12-18
Cylinder compression check, 2C-3
Cylinder head
removal and installation
2000 and earlier, 2A-13
2001 and later, 2B-13
torque specifications
2000 and earlier, 2A-2
2001 and later, 2B-2

D

Dashboard trim panels, 11-18
Daytime Running Lights (DRL), general information, 12-21
Defogger, rear window, check and repair, 12-12
Diagnosis, 0-18
Diagnostic trouble codes, 6-2
Differential (4WD models) removal and installation, 8-12
Differential oil seals (4WD models), replacement, 8-11
Disc (brake), inspection, removal and installation, 9-12
Disc brake
caliper, removal and installation, 9-10
pads, replacement, 9-8
Distributor
removal and installation, 5-7
cap and rotor, check and replacement, 1-24
Door (back)
latch, lock cylinder and handle, removal and installation, 11-17
removal, installation and adjustment, 11-16
Door
latch, lock cylinder and handles, removal and installation, 11-13
trim panels, removal and installation, 11-12
window glass regulator, removal and installation, 11-15
window glass, removal and installation, 11-15
removal, installation and adjustment, 11-13
Driveaxle
boot check, 1-22
boot replacement, 8-8
removal and installation, 8-6
Drivebelt check, adjustment and replacement, 1-15
Driveplate/flywheel, removal and installation
2000 and earlier, 2A-18
2001 and later, 2B-18
Driveshaft check, removal and installation, 8-9
Drum brake shoes, replacement, 9-11

E

Electric side view mirrors, description, 12-18
Electrical troubleshooting, general information, 12-1
Electronic fuel injection system
  check, 4-13
  general information, 4-13
Emissions and engine control systems, 6-1 through 6-20
Engine Coolant Temperature (ECT) sensor, replacement, 6-11
Engine cooling fans, replacement, 3-4
Engine electrical systems, 5-1 through 5-12
Engine oil and oil filter change, 1-11
Engine overhaul
  cylinder compression check, 2C-3
  external components, reassembly sequence, 2C-7
  external components, disassembly sequence, 2C-6
  general information, 2C-2
  initial start-up and break-in after installation, 2C-7
  oil pressure check, 2C-2
  rebuilding alternatives, 2C-4
  vacuum gauge diagnostic checks, 2C-3
Engine removal, methods and precautions, 2C-5
Engine, removal and installation, 2C-5
Engines, 2000 and earlier, 2A-1 through 2A-20
  camshaft oil seal, replacement, 2A-10
  camshafts and valve lifters, removal, inspection and installation, 2A-10
  crankshaft front oil seal, replacement, 2A-10
  cylinder head
    removal and installation, 2A-13
  exhaust manifold, removal and installation, 2A-5
  flywheel/driveplate, removal and installation, 2A-18
  intake manifold, removal and installation, 2A-4
  oil pan, removal and installation, 2A-15
  oil pump, removal, inspection and installation, 2A-16
  powertrain mounts, check and replacement, 2A-19
  rear main oil seal, replacement, 2A-18
  repair operations possible with the engine in the vehicle, 2A-3
  timing belt and sprockets, removal, inspection and installation, 2A-6
  Top Dead Center (TDC) for number one piston, locating, 2A-3
  torque specifications, 2A-2
  valve cover, removal and installation, 2A-4
Engines, 2001 and later, 2B-1 through 2B-18
  camshafts and lifters, removal, inspection and installation, 2B-9
  crankshaft front oil seal, replacement, 2B-15
  crankshaft pulley/vibration damper, removal and installation, 2B-15
  cylinder head, removal and installation, 2B-13
  exhaust manifold, removal and installation, 2B-13
  flywheel/driveplate, removal and installation, 2B-18
  intake manifold, removal and installation, 2B-12
  oil pan, removal and installation, 2B-16
  oil pump, removal and installation, 2B-16
  powertrain mounts, check and replacement, 2B-18
  rear main oil seal, replacement, 2B-18
  repair operations possible with the engine in the vehicle, 2B-3
  timing chain and sprockets, removal, inspection and installation, 2B-5
  Top Dead Center (TDC) for number one piston, locating, 2B-3
  torque specifications, 2B-2
  valve cover, removal and installation, 2B-3
  Variable Valve Timing (VVT) system, description, 2B-4
Evaporative emissions control (EVAP) system, 1-26, 6-17
Exhaust Gas Recirculation (EGR) system (2000 and earlier models), 6-16
Exhaust manifold, removal and installation
  2000 and earlier, 2A-5
  2001 and later, 2B-13
Exhaust system
  check, 1-27
  servicing, general information, 4-18

F

Fans, engine cooling, replacement, 3-4
Fault finding, 0-18
Filter replacement
  air, 1-19
  automatic transaxle, 1-27
  engine oil, 1-11
  fuel, 1-22
  interior ventilation, 1-22
Fluid level checks, 1-7
  automatic transaxle, 1-10
  battery electrolyte, 1-9
  brake and clutch fluid, 1-9
  engine coolant, 1-8
  engine oil, 1-7
  manual transaxle, 1-21
  power steering fluid, 1-9
  rear differential, 1-22
  transfer case, 1-21
  windshield washer fluid, 1-9
Fluids and lubricants
  capacities, 1-2
  recommended, 1-1
Flywheel/driveplate, removal and installation
  2000 and earlier, 2A-18
  2001 and later, 2B-18
Front fender, removal and installation, 11-9
Fuel and exhaust systems, 4-1 through 4-20
  filter replacement, 1-22
  fuel rail and injectors, removal and installation, 4-16
  injection system, check, 4-13
  injection system, general information, 4-13
  level sending unit, replacement, 4-8
  lines and fittings, general information, 4-4
  pressure regulator, removal and installation, 4-8
  pressure relief, 4-2
  pulsation damper, replacement, 4-16
  pump, removal and installation, 4-5
  pump/fuel pressure, check, 4-3
  system check, 1-20
  tank
    cleaning and repair, general information, 4-10
    removal and installation, 4-8

throttle body, check, removal and installation, 4-14
torque specifications, 4-1
Fuses and fusible links, general information, 12-3

G

General engine overhaul procedures, 2C-1 through 2C-12

H

**Hazard flasher and turn signal, check and
replacement, 12-5**
Headlight
adjustment, 12-14
bulb, replacement, 12-13
housing, replacement, 12-15
**Heater and air conditioning control assembly, removal,
installation and cable adjustment, 3-8**
Heater core, removal and installation, 3-9
**Heating and air conditioning system, check and
maintenance, 3-11**
Hinges and locks, maintenance, 11-3
**Hood latch and release cable, removal and
installation, 11-6**
Hood, removal, installation and adjustment, 11-6
Horn, check and replacement, 12-16
Hub and bearing assembly, removal and installation
front, 10-9
rear, 10-11

I

Idle Air Control (IAC) valve, replacement, 6-15
Ignition switch and key lock cylinder, replacement, 12-7
Ignition system
check, 5-6
coil(s), check and replacement, 5-6
distributor, removal and installation, 5-7
general information and precautions, 5-5
igniter (1996 and 1997 models), replacement, 5-7
Initial start-up and break-in after installation, 2C-7
Instrument cluster, removal and installation, 12-8
Instrument panel switches, replacement, 12-7
Instrument panel, removal and installation, 11-21
**Intake Air Temperature (IAT) sensor (2000 and earlier
models), replacement, 6-9**
Intake manifold, removal and installation
2000 and earlier, 2A-4
2001 and later, 2B-12
Interior ventilation filter replacement, 1-22
Introduction to the Toyota RAV4, 0-4

J

Jacking and towing, 0-12
Jump starting the vehicle, 0-13

K

Key lock cylinder and ignition switch, replacement, 12-7
Knock sensor, replacement, 6-14

L

Lubricants and chemicals, 0-14
Lubricants and fluids
capacities, 1-2
recommended, 1-1

M

Maintenance schedule, 1-6
Maintenance techniques, tools and working facilities, 0-6
**Manifold Absolute Pressure (MAP) sensor (2000 and
earlier models), replacement, 6-8**
Manifold, removal and installation
exhaust
2000 and earlier, 2A-5
2001 and later, 2B-13
intake
2000 and earlier, 2A-4
2001 and later, 2B-12
Manual transaxle, 7A-1 through 7A-6
back-up light switch, check and replacement, 7A-3
lubricant change, 1-28
lubricant level check, 1-21
oil cooler, removal and installation, 7A-6
overhaul, general information, 7A-5
removal and installation, 7A-3
shift cables, removal and installation, 7A-2
shift lever, removal and installation, 7A-3
torque specifications, 7A-1
**Mass Airflow (MAF) sensor (2001 and later models), check
and replacement, 6-8**
Master cylinder, removal and installation
brake, 9-18
clutch, 8-3
Mirrors
electric side view, description, 12-18
removal and installation, 11-16

O

**Oil cooler, manual transaxle, removal and
installation, 7A-6**
Oil pan, removal and installation
2000 and earlier, 2A-15
2001 and later, 2B-16
Oil pressure check, 2C-2
Oil pump, removal and installation
2000 and earlier, 2A-16
2001 and later, 2B-16
On Board Diagnostic (OBD) system and trouble codes, 6-2
**Oxygen sensor and air/fuel sensor, general information
and replacement, 6-12**

P

Pads, disc brake, replacement, 9-8
Park/Neutral Position (PNP) switch, adjustment and
    replacement, 7B-6
Parking brake
    adjustment, 9-21
    cables, replacement, 9-21
    shoes, inspection and replacement, 9-23
Positive Crankcase Ventilation (PCV) system, 6-16
Positive Crankcase Ventilation (PCV) valve and hose
    check and replacement, 1-29
Power brake booster, check, removal and installation, 9-20
Power door lock system, description, 12-19
Power steering
    pump, removal and installation, 10-17
    system, bleeding, 10-18
Power sunroof, description, 12-21
Power window system, description, 12-19
Powertrain Control Module (PCM), removal and
    installation, 6-6
Powertrain mounts, check and replacement
    2000 and earlier, 2A-19
    2001 and later, 2B-18

R

Radiator and coolant reservoir, removal and
    installation, 3-4
Radiator fan switch and coolant temperature sending unit,
    replacement, 3-8
Radiator grille, removal and installation, 11-10
Radio and speakers, removal and installation, 12-11
Rear differential (4WD models)
    lubricant change, 1-29
    lubricant level check, 1-22
    oil seals, replacement, 8-11
    removal and installation, 8-12
Rear main oil seal, replacement
    2000 and earlier, 2A-18
    2001 and later, 2B-18
Rear window defogger, check and repair, 12-12
Receiver/drier, removal and installation, 3-13
Recommended lubricants and fluids, 1-1
Relays, general information and testing, 12-4
Release cylinder, clutch, removal and installation, 8-3
Repair operations possible with the engine in the vehicle
    2000 and earlier, 2A-3
    2001 and later, 2B-3
Routine maintenance, 1-1 through 1-32

S

Safety first!, 0-17
Scheduled maintenance, 1-6
Seat belt check, 1-18
Seats, removal and installation, 11-22
Shift cable, removal and installation
    automatic transaxle, 7B-5
    manual transaxle, 7A-2

Shift lever, removal and installation, 7A-3
Shift lock system, automatic transaxle, description and
    check, 7B-7
Shock absorber (rear), removal, inspection and
    installation, 10-9
Shoes, drum brake, replacement, 9-13
Spare tire, installing, 0-12
Spark plug
    check and replacement, 1-23
    type and gap, 1-2
Spark plug wire, distributor cap and rotor, check and
    replacement, 1-24
Stabilizer bar and bushings, removal and installation
    front, 10-6
    rear, 10-9
Starting system
    general information and precautions, 5-10
    starter motor and circuit, check, 5-10
    starter motor, removal and installation, 5-11
Steering
    and suspension check, 1-21
    column covers, removal and installation, 11-20
    column switches, replacement, 12-6
    column, removal and installation, 10-13
    gear boots, replacement, 10-15
    gear, removal and installation, 10-16
    knuckle and hub, removal and installation, 10-9
    wheel, removal and installation, 10-12
Strut assembly (front), removal, inspection and
    installation, 10-4
Strut/spring assembly, replacement, 10-5
Sunroof, adjustment, 11-23
Suspension and steering systems, 10-1 through 10-20
    torque specifications, 10-1
Suspension arms (rear), removal and installation, 10-10

T

Thermostat, check and replacement, 3-3
Throttle body, check, removal and installation, 4-14
Throttle Position Sensor (TPS), replacement, 6-8
Tie-rod ends, removal and installation, 10-15
Timing belt and sprockets, removal, inspection and
    installation, 2A-6
Timing chain and sprockets, removal, inspection and
    installation, 2B-5
Tire and tire pressure checks, 1-10
Tire rotation, 1-18
Tire, spare, installing, 0-12
Top Dead Center (TDC) for number one piston, locating
    2000 and earlier, 2A-3
    2001 and later, 2B-3
Torque specifications
    *Torque specifications can be found in the chapter that deals
        with the particular component being serviced*
Towing the vehicle, 0-12
Transaxle, automatic , 7B-1 through 7B-10
    diagnosis, general, 7B-2
    fluid and filter change, 1-27
    fluid level check, 1-10
    oil seal replacement, 7B-2

overhaul, general information, 7B-10
Park/Neutral Position (PNP) switch, adjustment and
    replacement, 7B-6
removal and installation, 7B-8
shift cable, removal, installation and adjustment, 7B-5
shift lock system, description and check, 7B-7
Throttle Valve (TV) cable, check, adjustment and
    replacement, 7B-4
torque specifications, 7B-1
Transaxle, manual, 7A-1 through 7A-6
    back-up light switch, check and replacement, 7A-3
    lubricant change, 1-28
    lubricant level check, 1-21
    oil cooler, removal and installation, 7A-6
    overhaul, general information, 7A-5
    removal and installation, 7A-3
    shift cables, removal and installation, 7A-2
    shift lever, removal and installation, 7A-3
    torque specifications, 7A-1
Transfer case (4WD models with automatic transaxle)
    lubricant change, 1-28
    lubricant level check, 1-21
Trouble codes, 6-2
Troubleshooting, 0-18
Tune-up and routine maintenance, 1-1 through 1-32
Tune-up general information, 1-7
Turn signal and hazard flasher, check and
    replacement, 12-5

U

Underhood hoses, check and replacement, 1-17
Upholstery and carpets, maintenance, 11-2

V

Vacuum gauge diagnostic checks, 2C-3
Valve clearance, check and adjustment, 1-29
Valve cover, removal and installation
    2000 and earlier, 2A-4
    2001 and later, 2B-3
Variable Valve Timing (VVT) system, description, 2B-4
Vehicle identification numbers, 0-5
Vehicle Speed Sensor (VSS), replacement, 6-15
Vibration damper/crankshaft pulley, removal and
    installation, 2B-15
Vinyl trim, maintenance, 11-2

W

Water pump, check and replacement, 3-6
Wheel
    alignment, general information, 10-19
    cylinder, removal and installation, 9-17
    studs, replacement, 10-18
Wheels and tires, general information, 10-19
Window glass regulator, removal and installation, 11-15
Window glass, removal and installation, 11-15
Windshield and fixed glass, replacement, 11-3
Windshield wiper blade, inspection and replacement, 1-12
Wiper motor, check and replacement, 12-9
Wiring diagrams, general information, 12-23

Haynes Automotive Manuals

NOTE: If you do not see a listing for your vehicle, consult your local Haynes dealer for the latest product information.

HAYNES XTREME CUSTOMIZING
- **11101** Sport Compact Customizing
- **11102** Sport Compact Performance
- **11110** In-car Entertainment
- **11150** Sport Utility Vehicle Customizing
- **11213** Acura
- **11255** GM Full-size Pick-ups
- **11314** Ford Focus
- **11315** Full-size Ford Pick-ups
- **11373** Honda Civic

ACURA
- **12020** Integra '86 thru '89 & Legend '86 thru '90
- **12021** Integra '90 thru '93 & Legend '91 thru '95
- **12050** Acura TL all models '99 thru '08

AMC
- Jeep CJ - *see JEEP (50020)*
- **14020** Mid-size models '70 thru '83
- **14025** (Renault) Alliance & Encore '83 thru '87

AUDI
- **15020** 4000 all models '80 thru '87
- **15025** 5000 all models '77 thru '83
- **15026** 5000 all models '84 thru '88

AUSTIN-HEALEY
- Sprite - *see MG Midget (66015)*

BMW
- **18020** 3/5 Series '82 thru '92
- **18021** 3-Series incl. Z3 models '92 thru '98
- **18022** 3-Series, '99 thru '05, Z4 models
- **18025** 320i all 4 cyl models '75 thru '83
- **18050** 1500 thru 2002 except Turbo '59 thru '77

BUICK
- **19010** Buick Century '97 thru '05
- Century (front-wheel drive) - *see GM (38005)*
- **19020** Buick, Oldsmobile & Pontiac Full-size (Front-wheel drive) '85 thru '05
  Buick Electra, LeSabre and Park Avenue; Oldsmobile Delta 88 Royale, Ninety Eight and Regency; Pontiac Bonneville
- **19025** Buick Oldsmobile & Pontiac Full-size (Rear wheel drive) '70 thru '90
  Buick Estate, Electra, LeSabre, Limited, Oldsmobile Custom Cruiser, Delta 88, Ninety-eight, Pontiac Bonneville, Catalina, Grandville, Parisienne
- **19030** Mid-size Regal & Century all rear-drive models with V6, V8 and Turbo '74 thru '87
  Regal - *see GENERAL MOTORS (38010)*
  Riviera - *see GENERAL MOTORS (38030)*
  Roadmaster - *see CHEVROLET (24046)*
  Skyhawk - *see GENERAL MOTORS (38015)*
  Skylark - *see GM (38020, 38025)*
  Somerset - *see GENERAL MOTORS (38025)*

CADILLAC
- **21030** Cadillac Rear Wheel Drive all gasoline models '70 thru '93
  Cimarron - *see GENERAL MOTORS (38015)*
  DeVille - *see GM (38031 & 38032)*
  Eldorado - *see GM (38030 & 38031)*
  Fleetwood - *see GM (38031)*
  Seville - *see GM (38030, 38031 & 38032)*

CHEVROLET
- **24010** Astro & GMC Safari Mini-vans '85 thru '05
- **24015** Camaro V8 all models '70 thru '81
- **24016** Camaro all models '82 thru '92
- **24017** Camaro & Firebird '93 thru '02
  Cavalier - *see GENERAL MOTORS (38016)*
  Celebrity - *see GENERAL MOTORS (38005)*
- **24020** Chevelle, Malibu & El Camino '69 thru '87
- **24024** Chevette & Pontiac T1000 '76 thru '87
  Citation - *see GENERAL MOTORS (38020)*
- **24027** Colorado & GMC Canyon '04 thru '08
- **24032** Corsica/Beretta all models '87 thru '96
- **24040** Corvette all V8 models '68 thru '82
- **24041** Corvette all models '84 thru '96
- **10305** Chevrolet Engine Overhaul Manual
- **24045** Full-size Sedans Caprice, Impala, Biscayne, Bel Air & Wagons '69 thru '90
- **24046** Impala SS & Caprice and Buick Roadmaster '91 thru '96
  Impala - *see LUMINA (24048)*
  Lumina '90 thru '94 - *see GM (38010)*
- **24047** Impala & Monte Carlo all models '06 thru '08
- **24048** Lumina & Monte Carlo '95 thru '05
  Lumina APV - *see GM (38035)*

- **24050** Luv Pick-up all 2WD & 4WD '72 thru '82
  Malibu '97 thru '00 - *see GM (38026)*
- **24055** Monte Carlo all models '70 thru '88
  Monte Carlo '95 thru '01 - *see LUMINA (24048)*
- **24059** Nova all V8 models '69 thru '79
- **24060** Nova and Geo Prizm '85 thru '92
- **24064** Pick-ups '67 thru '87 - Chevrolet & GMC, all V8 & in-line 6 cyl, 2WD & 4WD '67 thru '87; Suburbans, Blazers & Jimmys '67 thru '91
- **24065** Pick-ups '88 thru '98 - Chevrolet & GMC, full-size pick-ups '88 thru '98, C/K Classic '99 & '00, Blazer & Jimmy '92 thru '94; Suburban '92 thru '99; Tahoe & Yukon '95 thru '99
- **24066** Pick-ups '99 thru '06 - Chevrolet Silverado & GMC Sierra '99 thru '06, Suburban/Tahoe/Yukon/Yukon XL/Avalanche '00 thru '06
- **24070** S-10 & S-15 Pick-ups '82 thru '93, Blazer & Jimmy '83 thru '94
- **24071** S-10 & Sonoma Pick-ups '94 thru '04, including Blazer, Jimmy & Hombre
- **24072** Chevrolet TrailBlazer & TrailBlazer EXT, GMC Envoy & Envoy XL, Oldsmobile Bravada '02 thru '07
- **24075** Sprint '85 thru '88 & Geo Metro '89 thru '01
- **24080** Vans - Chevrolet & GMC '68 thru '96
- **24081** Chevrolet Express & GMC Savana Full-size Vans '96 thru '07

CHRYSLER
- **25015** Chrysler Cirrus, Dodge Stratus, Plymouth Breeze '95 thru '00
- **10310** Chrysler Engine Overhaul Manual
- **25020** Full-size Front-Wheel Drive '88 thru '93
  K-Cars - *see DODGE Aries (30008)*
  Laser - *see DODGE Daytona (30030)*
- **25025** Chrysler LHS, Concorde, New Yorker, Dodge Intrepid, Eagle Vision, '93 thru '97
- **25026** Chrysler LHS, Concorde, 300M, Dodge Intrepid, '98 thru '04
- **25027** Chrysler 300, Dodge Charger & Magnum '05 thru '07
- **25030** Chrysler & Plymouth Mid-size front wheel drive '82 thru '95
  Rear-wheel Drive - *see Dodge (30050)*
- **25035** PT Cruiser all models '01 thru '03
- **25040** Chrysler Sebring, Dodge Avenger '95 thru '05
  Dodge Stratus '01 thru 05

DATSUN
- **28005** 200SX all models '80 thru '83
- **28007** B-210 all models '73 thru '78
- **28009** 210 all models '79 thru '82
- **28012** 240Z, 260Z & 280Z Coupe '70 thru '78
- **28014** 280ZX Coupe & 2+2 '79 thru '83
  300ZX - *see NISSAN (72010)*
- **28018** 510 & PL521 Pick-up '68 thru '73
- **28020** 510 all models '78 thru '81
- **28022** 620 Series Pick-up all models '73 thru '79
  720 Series Pick-up - *see NISSAN (72030)*
- **28025** 810/Maxima all gasoline models, '77 thru '84

DODGE
- 400 & 600 - *see CHRYSLER (25030)*
- **30008** Aries & Plymouth Reliant '81 thru '89
- **30010** Caravan & Plymouth Voyager '84 thru '95
- **30011** Caravan & Plymouth Voyager '96 thru '02
- **30012** Challenger/Plymouth Saporro '78 thru '83
- **30013** Caravan, Chrysler Voyager, Town & Country '03 thru '06
- **30016** Colt & Plymouth Champ '78 thru '87
- **30020** Dakota Pick-ups all models '87 thru '96
- **30021** Durango '98 & '99, Dakota '97 thru '99
- **30022** Dodge Durango models '00 thru '03
  Dodge Dakota models '00 thru '04
- **30023** Dodge Durango '04 thru '06, Dakota '05 and '06
- **30025** Dart, Demon, Plymouth Barracuda, Duster & Valiant 6 cyl models '67 thru '76
- **30030** Daytona & Chrysler Laser '84 thru '89
  Intrepid - *see CHRYSLER (25025, 25026)*
- **30034** Neon all models '95 thru '99
- **30035** Omni & Plymouth Horizon '78 thru '90
- **30036** Dodge and Plymouth Neon '00 thru '05
- **30040** Pick-ups all full-size models '74 thru '93
- **30041** Pick-ups all full-size models '94 thru '01
- **30042** Dodge Full-size Pick-ups '02 thru '08
- **30045** Ram 50/D50 Pick-ups & Raider and Plymouth Arrow Pick-ups '79 thru '93
- **30050** Dodge/Plymouth/Chrysler RWD '71 thru '89
- **30055** Shadow & Plymouth Sundance '87 thru '94
- **30060** Spirit & Plymouth Acclaim '89 thru '95
- **30065** Vans - Dodge & Plymouth '71 thru '03

EAGLE
- Talon - *see MITSUBISHI (68030, 68031)*
- Vision - *see CHRYSLER (25025)*

FIAT
- **34010** 124 Sport Coupe & Spider '68 thru '78
- **34025** X1/9 all models '74 thru '80

FORD
- **10355** Ford Automatic Transmission Overhaul
- **36004** Aerostar Mini-vans all models '86 thru '97
- **36006** Contour & Mercury Mystique '95 thru '00
- **36008** Courier Pick-up all models '72 thru '82
- **36012** Crown Victoria & Mercury Grand Marquis '88 thru '10
- **10320** Ford Engine Overhaul Manual
- **36016** Escort/Mercury Lynx all models '81 thru '90
- **36020** Escort/Mercury Tracer '91 thru '00
- **36022** Ford Escape & Mazda Tribute '01 thru '07
- **36024** Explorer & Mazda Navajo '91 thru '01
- **36025** Ford Explorer & Mercury Mountaineer '02 thru '07
- **36028** Fairmont & Mercury Zephyr '78 thru '83
- **36030** Festiva & Aspire '88 thru '97
- **36032** Fiesta all models '77 thru '80
- **36034** Focus all models '00 thru '07
- **36036** Ford & Mercury Full-size '75 thru '87
- **36044** Ford & Mercury Mid-size '75 thru '86
- **36048** Mustang V8 all models '64-1/2 thru '73
- **36049** Mustang II 4 cyl, V6 & V8 models '74 thru '78
- **36050** Mustang & Mercury Capri '79 thru '86
- **36051** Mustang all models '94 thru '04
- **36052** Mustang '05 thru '07
- **36054** Pick-ups & Bronco '73 thru '79
- **36058** Pick-ups & Bronco '80 thru '96
- **36059** F-150 & Expedition '97 thru '03, F-250 '97 thru '99 & Lincoln Navigator '98 thru '02
- **36060** Super Duty Pick-ups, Excursion '99 thru '06
- **36061** F-150 full-size '04 thru '06
- **36062** Pinto & Mercury Bobcat '75 thru '80
- **36066** Probe all models '89 thru '92
- **36070** Ranger/Bronco II gasoline models '83 thru '92
- **36071** Ranger '93 thru '08 & Mazda Pick-ups '94 thru '08
- **36074** Taurus & Mercury Sable '86 thru '95
- **36075** Taurus & Mercury Sable '96 thru '05
- **36078** Tempo & Mercury Topaz '84 thru '94
- **36082** Thunderbird/Mercury Cougar '83 thru '88
- **36086** Thunderbird/Mercury Cougar '89 and '97
- **36090** Vans all V8 Econoline models '69 thru '91
- **36094** Vans full size '92 thru '05
- **36097** Windstar Mini-van '95 thru '07

GENERAL MOTORS
- **10360** GM Automatic Transmission Overhaul
- **38005** Buick Century, Chevrolet Celebrity, Oldsmobile Cutlass Ciera & Pontiac 6000 all models '82 thru '96
- **38010** Buick Regal, Chevrolet Lumina, Oldsmobile Cutlass Supreme & Pontiac Grand Prix (FWD) '88 thru '07
- **38015** Buick Skyhawk, Cadillac Cimarron, Chevrolet Cavalier, Oldsmobile Firenza & Pontiac J-2000 & Sunbird '82 thru '94
- **38016** Chevrolet Cavalier & Pontiac Sunfire '95 thru '04
- **38017** Chevrolet Cobalt & Pontiac G5 '05 thru '09
- **38020** Buick Skylark, Chevrolet Citation, Olds Omega, Pontiac Phoenix '80 thru '85
- **38025** Buick Skylark & Somerset, Oldsmobile Achieva & Calais and Pontiac Grand Am all models '85 thru '98
- **38026** Chevrolet Malibu, Olds Alero & Cutlass, Pontiac Grand Am '97 thru '03
- **38027** Chevrolet Malibu '04 thru '07
- **38030** Cadillac Eldorado, Seville, Oldsmobile Toronado, Buick Riviera '71 thru '85
- **38031** Cadillac Eldorado & Seville, DeVille, Fleetwood & Olds Toronado, Buick Riviera '86 thru '93
- **38032** Cadillac DeVille '94 thru '05 & Seville '92 thru '04
- **38035** Chevrolet Lumina APV, Olds Silhouette & Pontiac Trans Sport all models '90 thru '96
- **38036** Chevrolet Venture, Olds Silhouette, Pontiac Trans Sport & Montana '97 thru '05
  General Motors Full-size Rear-wheel Drive - *see BUICK (19025)*

GEO
- Metro - *see CHEVROLET Sprint (24075)*
- Prizm - '85 thru '92 *see CHEVY (24060)*, '93 thru '02 *see TOYOTA Corolla (92036)*
- **40030** Storm all models '90 thru '93
  Tracker - *see SUZUKI Samurai (90010)*

(Continued on other side)

Haynes North America, Inc., 861 Lawrence Drive, Newbury Park, CA 91320-1514 • (805) 498-6703 • http://www.haynes.com

Haynes Automotive Manuals (continued)

NOTE: If you do not see a listing for your vehicle, consult your local Haynes dealer for the latest product information.

GMC
Vans & Pick-ups - *see CHEVROLET*

HONDA
42010 **Accord CVCC** all models '76 thru '83
42011 **Accord** all models '84 thru '89
42012 **Accord** all models '90 thru '93
42013 **Accord** all models '94 thru '97
42014 **Accord** all models '98 thru '02
42015 **Honda Accord** models '03 thru '07
42020 **Civic 1200** all models '73 thru '79
42021 **Civic 1300 & 1500 CVCC** '80 thru '83
42022 **Civic 1500 CVCC** all models '75 thru '79
42023 **Civic** all models '84 thru '91
42024 **Civic & del Sol** '92 thru '95
42025 **Civic** '96 thru '00, **CR-V** '97 thru '01, **Acura Integra** '94 thru '00
42026 **Civic** '01 thru '05, **CR-V** '02 thru '06
42035 **Honda Odyssey** all models '99 thru '04
42037 **Honda Pilot** '03 thru '07, **Acura MDX** '01 thru '07
42040 **Prelude CVCC** all models '79 thru '89

HYUNDAI
43010 **Elantra** all models '96 thru '06
43015 **Excel & Accent** all models '86 thru '98
43050 **Santa Fe** all models '01 thru '06
43055 **Sonata** all models '99 thru '08

ISUZU
Hombre - *see CHEVROLET S-10 (24071)*
47017 **Rodeo, Amigo & Honda Passport** '89 thru '02
47020 **Trooper & Pick-up** '81 thru '93

JAGUAR
49010 **XJ6** all 6 cyl models '68 thru '86
49011 **XJ6** all models '88 thru '94
49015 **XJ12 & XJS** all 12 cyl models '72 thru '85

JEEP
50010 **Cherokee, Comanche & Wagoneer Limited** all models '84 thru '01
50020 **CJ** all models '49 thru '86
50025 **Grand Cherokee** all models '93 thru '04
50029 **Grand Wagoneer & Pick-up** '72 thru '91 Grand Wagoneer '84 thru '91, Cherokee & Wagoneer '72 thru '83, Pick-up '72 thru '88
50030 **Wrangler** all models '87 thru '03
50035 **Liberty** '02 thru '04

KIA
54070 **Sephia** '94 thru '01, **Spectra** '00 thru '04

LEXUS
ES 300 - *see TOYOTA Camry (92007)*

LINCOLN
Navigator - *see FORD Pick-up (36059)*
59010 **Rear-Wheel Drive** all models '70 thru '05

MAZDA
61010 **GLC Hatchback (rear-wheel drive)** '77 thru '83
61011 **GLC (front-wheel drive)** '81 thru '85
61015 **323 & Protegé** '90 thru '00
61016 **MX-5 Miata** '90 thru '97
61020 **MPV** all models '89 thru '98
Navajo - *see Ford Explorer (36024)*
61030 **Pick-ups** '72 thru '93
Pick-ups '94 thru '00 - *see Ford Ranger (36071)*
61035 **RX-7** all models '79 thru '85
61036 **RX-7** all models '86 thru '91
61040 **626 (rear-wheel drive)** all models '79 thru '82
61041 **626/MX-6 (front-wheel drive)** '83 thru '92
61042 **626, MX-6/Ford Probe** '93 thru '01

MERCEDES-BENZ
63012 **123 Series Diesel** '76 thru '85
63015 **190 Series** four-cyl gas models, '84 thru '88
63020 **230/250/280** 6 cyl sohc models '68 thru '72
63025 **280 123 Series** gasoline models '77 thru '81
63030 **350 & 450** all models '71 thru '80
63040 **C-Class:** C230/C240/C280/C320/C350 '01 thru '07

MERCURY
64200 **Villager & Nissan Quest** '93 thru '01
All other titles, see FORD Listing.

MG
66010 **MGB** Roadster & GT Coupe '62 thru '80
66015 **MG Midget, Austin Healey Sprite** '58 thru '80

MITSUBISHI
68020 **Cordia, Tredia, Galant, Precis & Mirage** '83 thru '93
68030 **Eclipse, Eagle Talon & Ply. Laser** '90 thru '94

68031 **Eclipse** '95 thru '05, **Eagle Talon** '95 thru '98
68035 **Mitsubishi Galant** '94 thru '03
68040 **Pick-up** '83 thru '96 & **Montero** '83 thru '93

NISSAN
72010 **300ZX** all models including Turbo '84 thru '89
72011 **350Z & Infiniti G35** all models '03 thru '08
72015 **Altima** all models '93 thru '06
72020 **Maxima** all models '85 thru '92
72021 **Maxima** all models '93 thru '04
72030 **Pick-ups** '80 thru '97 **Pathfinder** '87 thru '95
72031 **Frontier Pick-up, Xterra, Pathfinder** '96 thru '04
72032 **Nissan Frontier & Xterra** '05 thru '08
72040 **Pulsar** all models '83 thru '86
Quest - *see MERCURY Villager (64200)*
72050 **Sentra** all models '82 thru '94
72051 **Sentra & 200SX** all models '95 thru '04
72060 **Stanza** all models '82 thru '90

OLDSMOBILE
73015 **Cutlass** V6 & V8 gas models '74 thru '88
For other OLDSMOBILE titles, see BUICK, CHEVROLET or GENERAL MOTORS listing.

PLYMOUTH
For PLYMOUTH titles, see DODGE listing.

PONTIAC
79008 **Fiero** all models '84 thru '88
79018 **Firebird** V8 models except Turbo '70 thru '81
79019 **Firebird** all models '82 thru '92
79040 **Mid-size Rear-wheel Drive** '70 thru '87
For other PONTIAC titles, see BUICK, CHEVROLET or GENERAL MOTORS listing.

PORSCHE
80020 **911** except Turbo & Carrera 4 '65 thru '89
80025 **914** all 4 cyl models '69 thru '76
80030 **924** all models including Turbo '76 thru '82
80035 **944** all models including Turbo '83 thru '89

RENAULT
Alliance & Encore - *see AMC (14020)*

SAAB
84010 **900** all models including Turbo '79 thru '88

SATURN
87010 **Saturn** all models '91 thru '02
87011 **Saturn Ion** '03 thru '07
87020 **Saturn** all L-series models '00 thru '04
87040 **Saturn VUE** '02 thru '07

SUBARU
89002 **1100, 1300, 1400 & 1600** '71 thru '79
89003 **1600 & 1800** 2WD & 4WD '80 thru '94
89100 **Legacy** all models '90 thru '99
89101 **Legacy & Forester** '00 thru '06

SUZUKI
90010 **Samurai/Sidekick & Geo Tracker** '86 thru '01

TOYOTA
92005 **Camry** all models '83 thru '91
92006 **Camry** all models '92 thru '96
92007 **Camry, Avalon, Solara, Lexus ES 300** '97 thru '01
92008 **Toyota Camry, Avalon and Solara and Lexus ES 300/330** all models '02 thru '06
92015 **Celica Rear Wheel Drive** '71 thru '85
92020 **Celica Front Wheel Drive** '86 thru '99
92025 **Celica Supra** all models '79 thru '92
92030 **Corolla** all models '75 thru '79
92032 **Corolla** all rear wheel drive models '80 thru '87
92035 **Corolla** all front wheel drive models '84 thru '92
92036 **Corolla & Geo Prizm** '93 thru '02
92037 **Corolla** models '03 thru '05
92040 **Corolla Tercel** all models '80 thru '82
92045 **Corona** all models '74 thru '82
92050 **Cressida** all models '78 thru '82
92055 **Land Cruiser FJ40, 43, 45, 55** '68 thru '82
92056 **Land Cruiser FJ60, 62, 80, FZJ80** '80 thru '96
92060 **Matrix & Pontiac Vibe** '03 thru '08
92065 **MR2** all models '85 thru '87
92070 **Pick-up** all models '69 thru '78
92075 **Pick-up** all models '79 thru '95
92076 **Tacoma, 4Runner, & T100** '93 thru '04
92077 **Tacoma** all models '05 thru '09
92078 **Tundra** '00 thru '06 & **Sequoia** '01 thru '06
92079 **4Runner** all models '03 thru '09
92080 **Previa** all models '91 thru '95
92081 **Prius** all models '01 thru '08
92082 **RAV4** all models '96 thru '05

92085 **Tercel** all models '87 thru '94
92090 **Toyota Sienna** all models '98 thru '06
92095 **Highlander & Lexus RX-330** '99 thru '06

TRIUMPH
94007 **Spitfire** all models '62 thru '81
94010 **TR7** all models '75 thru '81

VW
96008 **Beetle & Karmann Ghia** '54 thru '79
96009 **New Beetle** '98 thru '05
96016 **Rabbit, Jetta, Scirocco & Pick-up** gas models '75 thru '92 & Convertible '80 thru '92
96017 **Golf, GTI & Jetta** '93 thru '98 & **Cabrio** '95 thru '02
96018 **Golf, GTI, Jetta** '99 thru '05
96020 **Rabbit, Jetta & Pick-up** diesel '77 thru '84
96023 **Passat** '98 thru '05, **Audi A4** '96 thru '01
96030 **Transporter 1600** all models '68 thru '79
96035 **Transporter 1700, 1800 & 2000** '72 thru '79
96040 **Type 3 1500 & 1600** all models '63 thru '73
96045 **Vanagon** all air-cooled models '80 thru '83

VOLVO
97010 **120, 130 Series & 1800 Sports** '61 thru '73
97015 **140 Series** all models '66 thru '74
97020 **240 Series** all models '76 thru '93
97040 **740 & 760 Series** all models '82 thru '88
97050 **850 Series** all models '93 thru '97

TECHBOOK MANUALS
10205 **Automotive Computer Codes**
10206 **OBD-II & Electronic Engine Management**
10210 **Automotive Emissions Control Manual**
10215 **Fuel Injection Manual, 1978 thru 1985**
10220 **Fuel Injection Manual, 1986 thru 1999**
10225 **Holley Carburetor Manual**
10230 **Rochester Carburetor Manual**
10240 **Weber/Zenith/Stromberg/SU Carburetors**
10305 **Chevrolet Engine Overhaul Manual**
10310 **Chrysler Engine Overhaul Manual**
10320 **Ford Engine Overhaul Manual**
10330 **GM and Ford Diesel Engine Repair Manual**
10333 **Engine Performance Manual**
10340 **Small Engine Repair Manual, 5 HP & Less**
10341 **Small Engine Repair Manual, 5.5 - 20 HP**
10345 **Suspension, Steering & Driveline Manual**
10355 **Ford Automatic Transmission Overhaul**
10360 **GM Automatic Transmission Overhaul**
10405 **Automotive Body Repair & Painting**
10410 **Automotive Brake Manual**
10411 **Automotive Anti-lock Brake (ABS) Systems**
10415 **Automotive Detailing Manual**
10420 **Automotive Electrical Manual**
10425 **Automotive Heating & Air Conditioning**
10430 **Automotive Reference Manual & Dictionary**
10435 **Automotive Tools Manual**
10440 **Used Car Buying Guide**
10445 **Welding Manual**
10450 **ATV Basics**
10452 **Scooters, Automatic Transmission 50cc to 250cc**

SPANISH MANUALS
98903 **Reparación de Carrocería & Pintura**
98904 **Carburadores para los modelos Holley & Rochester**
98905 **Códigos Automotrices de la Computadora**
98910 **Frenos Automotriz**
98913 **Electricidad Automotriz**
98915 **Inyección de Combustible 1986 al 1999**
99040 **Chevrolet & GMC Camionetas** '67 al '87
99041 **Chevrolet & GMC Camionetas** '88 al '98
99042 **Chevrolet & GMC Camionetas Cerradas** '68 al '95
99055 **Dodge Caravan & Plymouth Voyager** '84 al '95
99075 **Ford Camionetas y Bronco** '80 al '94
99077 **Ford Camionetas Cerradas** '69 al '91
99088 **Ford Modelos de Tamaño Mediano** '75 al '86
99091 **Ford Taurus & Mercury Sable** '86 al '95
99095 **GM Modelos de Tamaño Grande** '70 al '90
99100 **GM Modelos de Tamaño Mediano** '70 al '88
99106 **Jeep Cherokee, Wagoneer & Comanche** '84 al '00
99110 **Nissan Camioneta** '80 al '96, **Pathfinder** '87 al '95
99118 **Nissan Sentra** '82 al '94
99125 **Toyota Camionetas y 4Runner** '79 al '95

Over 100 Haynes motorcycle manuals also available

6-09

Haynes North America, Inc., 861 Lawrence Drive, Newbury Park, CA 91320-1514 • (805) 498-6703 • http://www.haynes.com